Birth and Rebirth Through Genesis: A Timeless Theological Conversation

Genesis 1-3

Birth and Rebirth Through Genesis:
A Timeless Theological Conversation
Genesis 1-3

Birth and Rebirth Through Genesis: A Timeless Theological Conversation
Genesis 1-3

Michael L. Samuel

Foreword by Professor Marvin Wilson

ISBN: 1-4563-0171-3

Library of Congress Control Number: 2010915903

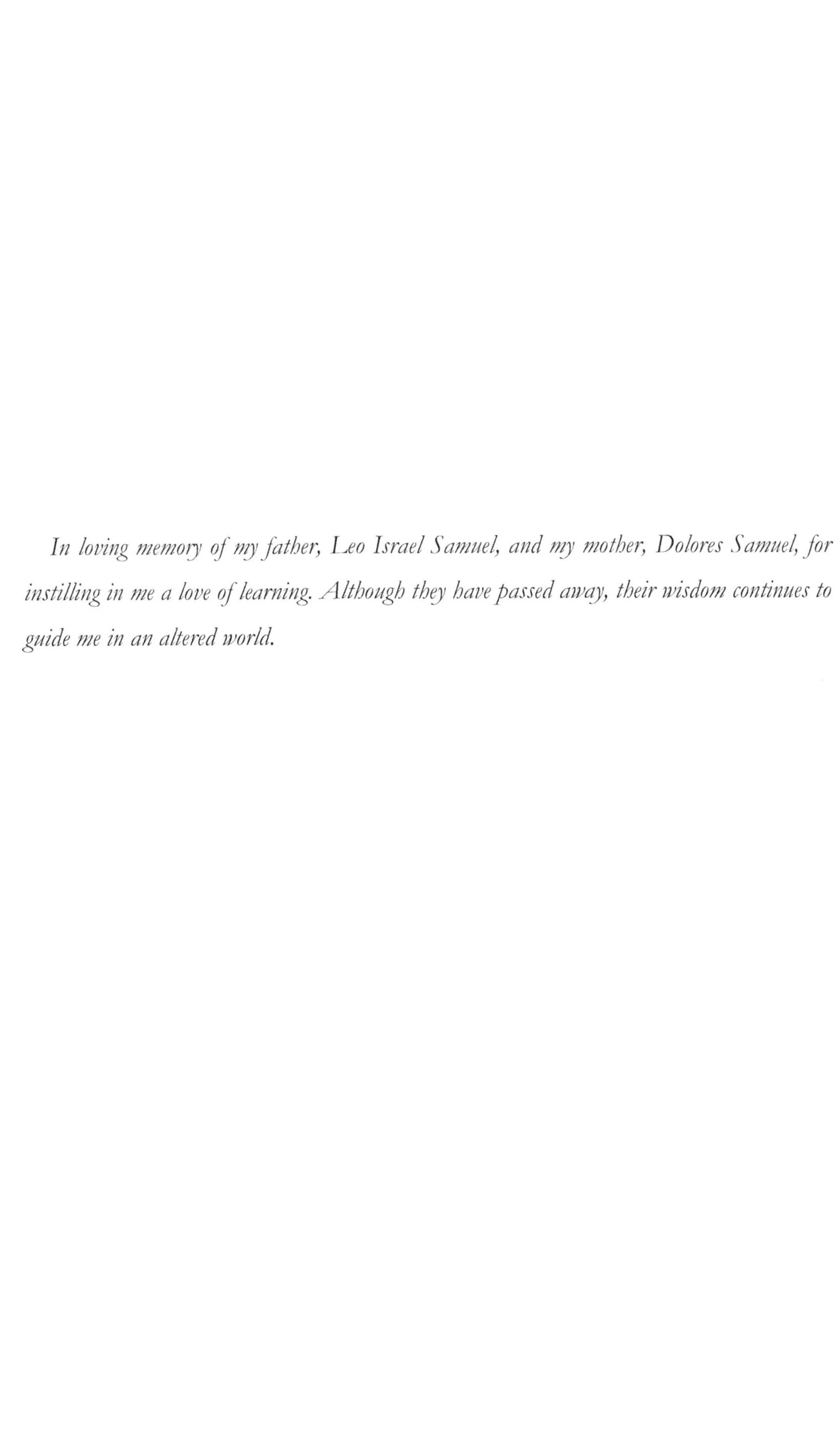

In loving memory of my father, Leo Israel Samuel, and my mother, Dolores Samuel, for instilling in me a love of learning. Although they have passed away, their wisdom continues to guide me in an altered world.

הפוך בה והפוך בה דכולך בה וכולה בה
תחזי וסיב ובלה בה ומינה לא תזוע שאין לך מדה טובה הימנה

"Turn it over and over because everything is in it, *and all of you is in it* and reflect upon it and grow old and worn in it and do not leave it, for you have no better lot than that."

Avot 5:22

Contents
Abbreviations

Another Account of the Creation Gen 2:4b-17 **153**

Alone in an Edenic Paradise (2:15-25) **181**

Abbreviations:

ABD	D. N. Freedman, et al., eds., *Anchor Bible Dictionary*. 6 vols. New York: Doubleday, 1992
ANEP	J. B. Pritchard, ed., *The Ancient Near East in Pictures. 2nd ed.* Princeton: Princeton University, 1969
ANET	J. B. Pritchard, ed., *Ancient Near Eastern Texts Relating to the Old Testament.* 3rd ed. Princeton: Princeton University, 1969
ARN	Avot de-Rabbi Nathan, versions I and 2, ed. S. Schechter (1887, reprinted 1967)
BA	Biblical Archaeologist
BAR	Biblical Archaeology Review
BASOR	Bulletin of the American Schools of Oriental Research
BDB	F. Brown, S. R. Driver, C. Briggs, Hebrew and English Lexicon of the Old Testament. Repr. Oxford: Clarendon, 1959
BHS	K. Elliger and W. Rudolph, eds., *Biblia Hebraica Stuttgartensia.* Stuttgart: Deutsche Bibelstiftung, 1967–77
BR	*Bible Review*
BSac	*Bibliotheca Sacra*
B.T.	Babylonian Talmud
CBQ	*Catholic Biblical Quarterly*
CHAL	W. Holladay, *A Concise Hebrew and Aramaic Lexicon of the Old Testament.* Grand Rapids: Eerdmans, 1971
EncJud	*C. Roth and G. Wigoder, eds., Encyclopaedia Judaica.* 16 vols. Jerusalem: Keter, 1971–1
HALOT	W. Baumgartner, et al. *The Hebrew and Aramaic Lexicon of the Old Testament.* Volumes 1-4 combined in one electronic edition. Leiden; New York: E.J. Brill, 1999, c1994-1996.
HUCA	*Hebrew Union College Annual*
J.T.	Jerusalem Talmud
IB	*The Interpreter's Bible,* I, 1952
IBD	*The Interpreter's Bible Dictionary,* 1962
ISBE	G. W. Bromiley, et al., eds., *International Standard Bible Encyclopedia,* 4 vols. Rev. ed. Grand Rapids: Eerdmans, 1979–88
JB	*Jerusalem Bible*
JBL	*Journal of Biblical Literature*
JETS	*Journal of the Evangelical Theological Society*
JJS	*Journal of Jewish Studies*
JNES	*Journal of Near Eastern Studies*
JNWSL	*Journal of Northwest Semitic Languages*
JPOS	*Journal of the Palestine Oriental Society*
JPT	*Journal of Psychology and Theology*
JQR	*Jewish Quarterly Review*
JRT	*Journal of Religious Thought*
JSOT	*Journal for the Study of the Old Testament*
L.	Latin
LXX	Septuagint
masc.	masculine
mg.	margin
ms(s).	manuscript(s)
MT	Masoretic Text
NAB	The New American Bible

NBD	*The New Bible Dictionary* edited by J. D. Douglas et al., 1962.
NEB	New English Bible
NICOT	*New International Commentary on the Old Testament*
NIV	New International Version
NJB	New Jerusalem Bible
NJPS	New Jewish Publication Society Version
NKJV	New King James Version
NT	*New Testament*
O. Fr.	Old French
REB	Revised English Bible
RSV	American Revised Standard Version, 1952.
SP	Samaritan Pentateuch
TDNT	G. Kittel and G. Friedrich, eds., *Theological Dictionary of the New Testament. 10* vols. Tr. G. W. Bromiley. Grand Rapids: Eerdmans, 1964–76
TDOT	G. Botterweck and H. Ringgren, eds., *Theological Dictionary of the Old Testament*. Vols. 1-. Tr. D. Green, et al. Grand Rapids: Eerdmans, 1974–
Tg.	Targum Onkelos
TLOT	E. Jenni and C. Westermann, *Theological Lexicon of the Old Testament*. Peabody, MA.: Hendrickson Publishers, 1997.
TWOT	R. L. Harris, et al., eds., *Theological Wordbook of the Old Testament*. 2 vols. Chicago: Moody, 1980
UT	Cyrus H. Gordon, *Ugaritic Textbook*. AnOr 38. Rome: Pontifical Biblical Institute, 1965
Vulg.	Vulgate
VT	*Vetus Testamentum*

Foreword

It is a personal delight to write this Foreword to *Birth and Rebirth through Genesis*. I have had the pleasure of knowing Rabbi Dr. Michael Samuel for more than a decade. During this time we have spent dozens of hours discussing Torah together. In particular, I have greatly enjoyed my many conversations with Rabbi Samuel over his manuscript as he was finalizing his commentary and completing his edits. These interactions were always respectful as each would listen to the point being raised by the other. For me, a Christian professor of Hebrew Bible for more than four decades, each discussion with Rabbi Samuel proved stimulating, enlightening and very enriching. Personally, I became invigorated through these discussions as we would exchange exegetical comments, examine parallel passages, and compare and contrast classic and contemporary perspectives on the Torah.

One of the strengths of this commentary is the way it handles difficult and theologically diffuse passages. On most controversial passages, Rabbi Samuel presents alternative ways of understanding the text, thus allowing the reader to evaluate options and choose. In our personal discussions over the manuscript, our mutual respect for each other as well as our joint high regard for the text of Scripture always made these discussions very worthwhile and enjoyable learning experiences to me, as "iron sharpens iron" (Proverbs 27:17).

I believe that all who carefully read this book are in for a deeply rewarding experience. A study of the text and commentary of *Birth and Rebirth through Genesis* will contribute greatly to an understanding of the rich and diverse fabric of biblical narrative and provide an appreciation for its creative application to the problems of the modern world. In making the above observation, however, I am reminded there is yet a deeper point to be made, one powerfully illustrated by the following Hasidic story. Once, a relatively young *talmid* (disciple), with a sense of satisfaction and accomplishment, came up to his Rebbe. The disciple excitingly exclaimed, "Rebbe, you will be pleased to know that I have gone through the Talmud three times!" Sitting back and stroking his white beard, the Rebbe replied, "My son, the question is not how many times you have gone through the Talmud, but how many times the Talmud has gone through you."

Rabbi Samuel's work, *Birth and Rebirth through Genesis,* provides a valuable tool for both Jew and Christian to help the student grasp and retain the meaning of the Torah. The commentary is lucidly written and its various indexes make it very "user friendly" as a tool for research. This work will enable any serious student, in the words of the Mishnah, to be more like "a sponge" type of learner so he "soaks up everything" rather than "the funnel" type who "takes in at this end and lets out at the other" (Avot 5:15). Any neophyte of biblical literature quickly knows the early chapters of Genesis are no place for "speed reading" the biblical text. Readers need all the assistance they can get to grasp what the text is saying and how it may be understood so that it will "stick."

Here Rabbi Samuel and his "educator's eye" provides for the reader a highly effective source of study by locating key themes and sub themes, and by breaking the text down and analyzing it so its meaning can be readily "soaked up."

In addition to our friendship, Rabbi Samuel and I share much in common. Professionally, each of us is trained in Hebraic and Semitic sources, and each of us has a high appreciation of the Torah as the Word of God. We have each been mutually enriched by our discussions of the Torah and Hebraic heritage. Yet, at the end of the day, on a personal level, each of us comes to the Book of Genesis through a slightly different set of lenses or theological grid. Rabbi Samuel approaches this material from his Jewish perspective and I from through my Christian orientation and world view. *Birth and Rebirth through Genesis* is a Jewish theological commentary, yet one which connects the Jewish world to the Christian world, and the Christian world to the Jewish world.

One of the things I like most about this work is the fact it is a work from which both Jews and Christians can read with much profit. Specifically, in this commentary, Christians will especially appreciate the sensitive, thoughtful and respectful manner in which Rabbi Samuel engages Christian scholarship. The verse by verse discussions in this manuscript on Genesis indicate a willingness to listen and weigh carefully what Jewish *and* Christian scholarship are saying, a tremendous service which helps to clarify and expand the discussion on this "Book of Beginnings" so that it might be of optimum value to both Jewish and Christian readership. An important underlying premise of this book—one which I greatly celebrate—is that Christians can learn from Jews and Jews from Christians.

Birth and Rebirth through Genesis is sure to have considerable appeal as an academic text in both colleges and seminaries for courses on the Jewish Scriptures, Pentateuch, science and the Bible, and comparative biblical theology. Rabbi Samuel's scholarly, exegetical treatment of the biblical text is enhanced on many pages by the addition of nuanced discussions of key theological expressions and by various word studies of important Hebrew and Greek terms. Much to the surprise of many Jews and Christians, Judaism is much more than the history of a civilization and the survival of a people; Judaism also possesses a venerable theology. In this volume, Rabbi Samuel goes into considerable detail to show why.

A useful and striking example of how the author demonstrates his scholarly acumen is in his treatment of the controversial and much debated third chapter of Genesis. While Genesis 3 and the "fall into sin" is one of the most theologically pivotal chapters in all of Scripture for Christians, this chapter is frequently not given adequate examination or extensive discussion in Jewish theological works. Rabbi Samuel, however, gives a rather lengthy and nuanced treatment of the topic of original sin, the nature of human nature, and the importance of the Augustinian and Pelagian debate. Rabbi Samuel's theological discussion clearly shows the points of convergence between Christianity and Judaism as well as the points of divergence. The rabbi concludes that at the end of the day, "mother and daughter" are close, but different religions. One of the important features of Rabbi's Samuel's work, however, is that he shows that neither Judaism nor Christianity is monolithic. Each tradition has theological diversity that must be acknowledged and clarified. One of the most important arguments for Christian-Jewish relations is that the encounter often exposes stereotypes, caricatures and half-truths concerning the other. For two thousand years Genesis 3 has largely remained a watershed of theological dissidence between Christians and Jews. In *Birth and Rebirth through Genesis*, however, Rabbi Samuel astutely points out that the differences of interpretation within Judaism and Christianity are much more variegated than most people of faith realize.

The Torah is the bedrock of Judaism and Christianity, and the Book of Genesis the port of entry into the Torah. Torah is teaching, guidance or direction for living. Genesis is a book of "firsts" in Scripture. Among the more notable "firsts" are the creation of the first human pair (Adam and Eve), the first commandment ("be fruitful and increase"), the first moral failure (the disobedience of the man and woman in the Garden of Eden), the break with pagan idolatry and beginnings of an elect covenantal family (Abraham). Furthermore, the opening chapters of Genesis connect Jew and Christian to many of the key questions related to human existence including the sanctity of life (man made in the divine image), sexuality, "earth keeping," good and evil, free will, capital punishment, linguistic diversity and more. Christians will especially appreciate the discussion of these and other topics in *Birth and Rebirth in Genesis* because Christians tend to spend more time in the Prophets and Psalms than they do in the Torah.

The genius of *Birth and Rebirth through Genesis* is the fact it combines lexical, exegetical, theological and ethical insights into a holistic medley. Rabbi Samuel assists his readers through many valuable excursuses interlarded throughout his discussion of the text of Genesis. These "mini essays" often apply, illustrate, or rationally interact with the findings of science, literature, philosophy, psychology, anthropology, world religion and other disciplines. This work is scholarly, yet accessible. The author is not simply interested in perpetuating the "scholarly consensus *du jour*" but is interested in exploring the meaning of the biblical text through interaction with ancient and modern writers. Christians will especially appreciate the numerous insights of medieval Jewish scholars not found in most Christian commentaries on Genesis. Jews, on the other hand, will come to appreciate much of the discussion found in classic and modern Christian commentators on Genesis.

In a masterful way, Rabbi Samuel shows how the text of Genesis is intended to create a dialogue with the reader that leads to action. In a profound sense, *Birth and Rebirth through Genesis* is an intergenerational theological conversation. Readers can interact with the biblical characters as they learn to "listen" to the biblical text. These characters such as Adam, Eve, Cain and Noah are lives to be continued, not simply names to be contemplated. The conversation continues with us, the readers and interpreters. Ancient Israel had a relationship with the Torah but that relationship remains alive and continues with each new generation with its own responsibility to creatively interact anew with the text.

The important starting point of a dynamic process of understanding is the intended meaning of the biblical author. The authors of Scripture indeed give us an inspired text. The text, however, must always point beyond itself. Treating a sacred text as though it is a fetish not only diminishes its true sanctity, it also lends itself to bibliolatry. When studying the work of a great commentator—whether past or present—it is important to keep in mind that no one single interpreter ever "controls" the text for all time. Rather there is a dynamic fluidity to the text necessitated and brought about by an unending conversation between the reader and text. Collectively, the community of faith has a major responsibility in seeing that the text does not be treated as static or as a sacred relic. Quite the contrary, the biblical text is a divinely charged living word capable of illuminating new generations of readers who actively engage its wisdom.

In this age of maturing Christian-Jewish dialogue, *Birth and Rebirth through Genesis* illustrates the necessity and vitality of the exchange of Jewish and Christian perspectives on the text. The biblical text is an ancient tapestry with many interwoven strands of thought. Each new generation, however, examines and reexamines that ancient word so that new light might break forth to further illumine the path stretching before us. Rabbi Samuel shows why, in this 21st century, serious biblical scholarship cannot be isolated or self-contained. Jews and Christians must understand and respect their own theological uniqueness and distinctiveness. Rabbi Samuel, however, also shows the necessity of Jews hearing serious Christian reflections and commentaries on Genesis, and Christians hearing those scholarly Jewish voices representative of the original "People of the Book."

Birth and Rebirth through Genesis is a book for Jews and Christians. Genesis is one of the many gifts of Jewish people to Christians. But the coin of interfaith has two sides. In his commentary, Rabbi Samuel is interested in pointing out the other side of that coin. Indeed, he skillfully shows how certain thoughtful Christian reflection over many centuries on the Hebrew text of Genesis is one of the potential—yet largely undiscovered—gifts of Christians to Jews.

May this significant work of Rabbi Samuel show the importance of the spirit of reciprocity for this generation of biblical scholarship. May it be a "listening generation" such as the creation of this theological commentary of Rabbi Samuel displays, namely by listening sincerely, sympathetically and appreciatively to the biblical text, by listening to the rich variety of commentators past and present on the text, and by listening to one's partner in interfaith dialogue about the text.

Marvin R. Wilson, Ph.D.
Professor of Biblical and Theological Studies
Gordon College
Wenham, MA
Author of: *Our Father Abraham: Jewish Roots of the Christian Faith*

Acknowledgements

I would like to take this opportunity to thank a number of people who assisted me with feedback and criticism, as well as time and patience throughout the process of this work.

To Professor Marvin Wilson—a special thank you for writing such a gracious foreword. The encouragement and hours that you have generously lavished on the project since its inception have proven to be invaluable.

To my friend Paul Pines, I want to thank you for inspiring me to write this work, and even more so, for showing me how the Book of Genesis can be read as a metaphor for the soulful journey in a world struggling to evolve.

To my good friend, Hakham Avraham Ben-Rahamiël Qanaï, I especially want to thank you for your unwavering support and criticism. Your fearlessness to debate the classical medieval rabbinic scholars and their modern counterparts has been an inspiration to me. Throughout my numerous interactions with you, I have learned that contemporary Judaism has much to gain from an honest encounter with Karaite biblical scholars and tradition.

To Fern Baker, you are the best friend any writer can ever have. Your editing skills have proven to be peerless and I want to thank you for the diligence and time you devoted to this labor intensive project.

To Professor Bob Haak, I want to thank you for your much appreciated input regarding some of the earlier drafts of the manuscript.

To my family: Moshe, Mendy, Naftali, Susan, Mark, Hali Yuda, Kaisha, Kama, Liam Shaul, Jeanie, Jeri, Ian, Mason, Leo, Chase, Melissa, Phillip, and Brian, I want to extend my deepest heartfelt thanks for your moral support; this work was written especially for your generation.

To Zoe, our newest granddaughter, and Judy.

Introduction to Genesis

1. The Mythos of Genesis

God loved stories so much that He created people.

—MARTIN BUBER, *Attributed*

The world in its entirety is but a book that God, the Holy Blessed One, has made, and the Torah is the commentary that He composed on that book.

—R. ZADOK KOHEN, *Machashavot Harutz*

The language of the Bible is not a scientific language of facts, but a metaphorical language of images.

—HANS KUNG, *Does God Exist?*

The necessity of commentary, like poetic necessity, is the very form of exiled speech. In the beginning is hermeneutics. But the shared necessity of exegesis, the interpretive imperative, is interpreted differently by the rabbi and the poet. . . . The original opening of interpretation essentially signifies that there will always be rabbis and poets. And two interpretations of interpretation [sic]. The Law then becomes question and the right to speech coincides with the duty to interrogate. The book of man is a book of question. "To every question, the Jew answers with a question"—Reb Lema.

—JACQUES DERRIDA, *Writing and Difference*

No other book in the history of civilization has gripped and shaped the world's imagination quite like the Bible. Its images, metaphors, and stories possess a unifying theme that speaks to the nature of the human condition in all of its guises. Unlike the other creatures of the earth that live by their primal instincts, humankind lives in a mythical universe. The Bible recognizes this truth; almost every narrative of the Bible, in one way or another, addresses the nature of our existential predicament. Certainly what is true of the Bible, in general, is especially true with respect to the book of Genesis—a book about our primal beginnings and longings. Merely reading the familiar stories of old without thoughtful or dialogical discourse misses the point of why they were originally told. If the Torah is, as its name suggests, "instruction" or "teaching," then it behooves us to think about the existential depth of this sacred text, which continues to consciously and unconsciously shape the world we live in. As a compendium of sacred wisdom, Genesis addresses nearly every human concern we have experienced since the beginning of recorded history.

How we understand our sacred texts matters. Genesis teaches us that our lives are part of a story that began long ago when human beings first wondered about their place in the cosmos. What is the purpose of human existence? How did the world come to be? How do all things interrelate? How should we interact? Genesis presents a symbolic story that addresses these primal questions—one that continues to guide and inspire. Genesis not only describes how all races of people relate to the Divine Presence that fills the universe, but also provides valuable insight as to how each of us are spiritually interconnected. Genesis reminds us that the Edenic peacefulness depicted in chapters 2-3 is not an illusion; the prophets teach us that this Edenic reality is attainable by living a purpose-laden life that is suffused with love and compassion toward God's Creation[1]. Genesis teaches life has a Source, and that this Source gives meaning to life. Its lessons are timeless. The existential message of Genesis transcends the problems of its canonic historicity.

The present work aims to examine the book of Genesis as generations of Jewish teachers have theologically and exegetically done for more than two millennia. It is an attempt to show what Genesis has meant in the past and how it relates to the present as a living and breathing presence in the lives of believers largely—but not at all exclusively—through the prism of rabbinic tradition.[2] In distilling the underlying theological themes that define the book of Genesis, I have not forced or molded the text into a predetermined model, philosophy, or school of biblical interpretation; nor have I glossed over its more problematical issues. This exposition is admittedly idiosyncratic, if not postcritical.[3]

---

[1] Throughout this commentary, the term *Creation* is capitalized when it occurs as a theological event or concept. When referring to creation generically, e.g., "creation myth"—the term will remain lower-cased.

[2] The precise origin of Rabbinic Judaism is shrouded in controversy and mystery. Rabbinic (or Pharisaic) Judaism can be traced back to Ezra and the beginnings of the scribal movement in the fifth century B.C.E. After Ezra restored the Temple, he assigned the interpretation of the Law to the priesthood and Levites (Neh. 8:7, 9; 2 Chr. 17:7–9), but later the scribes, consisting of lay members of the Jewish community who were educated in the laws of the Torah, interpreted these laws independently of the Temple. Concurrently, these scribes served as magistrates and administrators of the Law, and evidently were widely respected by the masses (*cf.* Sirach 38:24–39:11). The earliest mention of the Pharisees occurs at the time of the Maccabees under the leadership of the Hasmonean priest, John Hyrcanus I (*cf.* Josephus, *Ant.* 13.10.5–7 §§288–99), who was the nephew of Judas Maccabeus (ca. 135–105 B.C.E). According to Josephus, the Pharisees first appeared two reigns earlier, at the time of Jonathan (*Ant.* 13. 5, 9). At this time, a group re-ferred to as Hasidim ("the pious ones"), revolted against the excesses of the Maccabean rulers. Two important offshoots developed at this time: the Essenes and the Pharisees. The former lived a very ascetic life-style, while the latter, largely made up of ordinary people, tried to improve the observance of Jewish life. Like Sirach before him, Josephus mentions the influence and popularity the Pharisees enjoyed in his time (*Ant.* 13.10.6 §§297–98; 18.1.3–4 §§12–17). By the first century, they had almost completely supplanted the authority of the priesthood; in effect, the Sage had replaced both the High Priest and the Prophet as the spiritual leader of Israel. Rabbinic tradition continued to develop, first in the form of the Mishnah, Tosefta, Sifre, Mechilta, Midrash, and later in the form of the Jerusalem and Babylonian redactions of the Talmud—the latter of which was finally redacted by the 6th century C.E.

[3] Peter Ochs explains the strengths of the postcritical approach to biblical interpretation:

> In some ways, these postcritical rules appear postmodern: they emerge out of criticisms of the

Reading any ancient text as familiar as Genesis continues to expose the reader to an unfamiliar and unchartered world. How does the world of the Bible differ from life as we experience it? What are the issues and mega-themes that recur throughout the chapters of Genesis? How does the text speak to contemporary problems and concerns? Even a superficial reading of Genesis evokes an array of thoughtful questions raised by today's educated readers: Can a scientific view of the universe be reconciled with a biblical view of the universe? What role does "myth" play in the Genesis stories? Is the imperative to exert "dominion" over creation compatible with today's ecological ethics? Were human beings ever meant to live forever? Is sexism ordained as part of the creative order?

Theological questions are no less daunting for a modern reader: What are the images of God being portrayed in the narrative? How have conflicting perceptions of the Divine changed over the life of the biblical text? What are the possibilities of human freedom, as well as its limitations? How does the divine initiative interface with human responsibility? How do the images of the Divine challenge a contemporary understanding of faith in action and within the community? Interpreting Genesis theologically is not for the timid or for the faint-hearted. Commentators, theologians, and thoughtful readers throughout history have grappled with these questions and many more. There is a tendency among some commentators and theologians to present the appearance of unanimity, which can essentially diminish the dialectical tension of a text; subsequently, the reader is prevented from experiencing the exhilaration and energy that originally sparked these kinds of discussions. The pursuit and process of questioning for the sake of veracity and relevance is not only desirable, but necessary. Disputations, raucous debates, and the polyvalence of interpretation have animated Jewish and Christian discussions since the days of Late Antiquity.

Sadly, more often than not, these debates had a polemical edge to them that generated more heat than light. Historically, one of the main reasons why the early Jewish and Christian communities developed their exegetical traditions apart from one another was due to the efforts of the patristic theologians to delegitimize Judaism as a religion, and in doing so, denied the Jewish origins of Christianity. Yet, there were occasional times when Jewish scholars did readily discuss Christian theological or exegetical themes in the spirit of clarifying Judaism's own viewpoints on subjects pertaining to good and evil, or the nature of humankind, or when it pertained to the

---

modern search for sources of individual self-certainty, and they emphasize the communal, dialogic and textual contexts of knowledge and the contributions made by interpreters to the meaning of what they interpret. In other ways, however, the postcritical rules appear premodern: they describe themselves as rules of reasoning that serve the theological and moral purposes of particular traditions of scriptural interpretation. The postcritical rules belong, in other words, neither to postmodernity nor to premodernity, but rather to a dialogue that is now unfolding between a contemporary family of scholars and their scriptural traditions. . . . See Peter Och ed., *The Return to Scripture in Judaism and Christianity: Essays in Postcritical Scriptural Interpretation,* (New York: Paulist Press, 1993), 1-3.

moral behavior of a great leader such as King David. In fact, some medieval scholars, like Maimonides, paid an indirect compliment to Christianity, praising it as a faith that served to help spread ethical monotheism to the world.[4]

Despite an occasional backhanded tribute given by one faith to another, ideological ghettos separated Jewish and Christian scholars and prevented them from having direct and meaningful exchanges of opinions and insights; seldom did ideas find an open marketplace for such pointed discussions. Today, there is a sincere movement within academic and theological circles to better understand the Jewish roots of the Christian faith. By the same token, there is considerable effort within the Jewish community to understand Jesus—not as a savior—but as a first century Jewish figure, who might have exerted more of an influence on early rabbinic tradition and ethics than has been commonly professed by most rabbinic scholars. The willingness to engage and to respectfully listen to the "Other"[5] constitutes a welcome change that can only benefit diverse religious communities.

For the contemporary era, current issues such as: biblical prohibitions on homosexuality, the rise of feminism, eco-justice, bioethics, as well as other relevant issues, challenge the canons of tradition on every conceivable level. Within the book of Genesis, a sacred text to Jews, Christians and Muslims, there is much that each faith can learn from the other by sharing the fruits of diligent study in search of wisdom and truth—especially with regard to the complex issues of our times. Since each religion has its own "spin" on the text, it is important to acknowledge these differences. In addition, it is no less important to define the points of convergence as well. This approach proposes a new interpretive paradigm that has not been widely utilized since the Golden Age of Spain, when Jews, Christians and Muslims felt secure and comfortable enough to incorporate ideas from faiths other than their own in the spirit of freedom and mutual respect.[6]

---

[4] Maimonides, MT *Hilchot Melachim* 11:3.

[5] According to the French Judaic philosopher Emanuel Lévinas, the "Other" represents a different experiential reality that co-exists on some level with the self. The Other is autonomous—if not commanding—in terms of how I relate to this reality that stands before me. When the Other suffers, I have a duty to respond. I must act. Unlike the I/Thou relation that bases itself on a more personal relation with another, the Other does not necessarily presuppose such an intimate relation. A person can be a complete stranger and yet my moral and ethical obligation to that person remains unaffected. I am no less obligated to the stranger than I am to my friend.

[6] Maimonides' son, Rabbi Abraham, advocated a Jewish form of Sufism, a movement of mystical Islam that flourished in his time. According to Samuel Rosenblatt, there were dervish fraternities that R. Abraham reached out to in the spirit of fellowship and respect. R. Abraham writes that their organization resembled the kind of spiritual guilds that the ancient prophets of Israel once had, whom he considered to be the spiritual heirs of the biblical prophets. He further recommends that Jews adopt certain Sufi mystical practices, e.g., solitary contemplation and mantra-like repetitions of the divine names designed to facilitate spiritual awakening and gnosis. R. Abraham thus demonstrates that it is possible to be open-minded to other faith traditions which

❖ *Reading through the Eye of Imagination*

To fully appreciate Genesis and grasp its inner meaning, it helps to read its stories with the eye of imagination—and the passion of a searching heart. In doing so, we begin to contemplate a world where God's presence is encountered in every moment of existence. We cannot treat the content of this ancient spiritual text as if it is the fossilized archive of some long-extinct people. Nor can we discern its significance as if we were performing a postmortem on a cadaver. Of course, what applies to Genesis applies no less to the rest of the Pentateuch. The Torah has a pulse—it is a story based on the faith and ethical values of a people who have defied the vicissitudes of persecution for thousands of years.

While reductive methods of modern historical and critical methods have proven useful in the examination of the Torah and especially its canonic transmission, reductionistic approaches are limited in what they can disclose about a sacred text. To an academic or an agnostic, this statement obviously involves a teleological leap of faith that he or she may not be willing to make. Yet, even if one were to take the attitude that Genesis is, at the very least, a valuable part of Western literature, then reading it as such can still be stimulating and significant. Furthermore, its overall spiritual thrust evokes a response even from the ambivalent soul who is adrift in a sea of doubt.

Genesis offers a parabolic look at the human condition that is as noteworthy as any of the philosophical homilies offered by Plato and Greek philosophy. With this thought in mind, not everything that is recorded in the book of Genesis is meant for emulation. The biblical writers wished to teach that cursing one's children, as Noah did with Ham and Canaan, created generations of dysfunction. Practicing favoritism often results in family tragedies as we see in the stories of Isaac and Rebecca or with Jacob and his sons.

The family discord and ensuing struggles between the descendants of Isaac and Ishmael are grim reminders of how we still suffer for the sins of our parents. Perhaps one of the most important themes in the course of Genesis is the power of human forgiveness and its ability to heal shattered lives and broken hearts. For these reasons and more, the lessons of Genesis are legion. Finally, Genesis is so very important because it encourages us to ask ultimate questions that require ultimate responses. If the cosmos has a beginning that derives from the existence of a personal God, then it behooves each of us to reflect on our personal role in the grand scheme of Creation.

---

may then serve to enhance the Judaic faith. See Samuel Rosenblatt, *The High Ways to Perfection of Abraham Maimonides* (New York: AMS Press, 1927), 44-53.

❖ *Genesis as Myth*

Myth is the garment of mystery
—*THOMAS MANN*

The term *myth* is one of the most widely reviled and misunderstood words in the dictionary. Religious people especially take offense to the Bible referred to as μῦθος (*mythos* = "myth"). There is good reason for this common but unjustified perception. Since the time of the Sophists, *mythos* was contrasted with *logos* (reason); the latter is factual and observable while the former is unhistorical or pre-scientific. As a result, oftentimes myth is frequently substituted as a synonym for lies, falsehood, and half-truths. In reality, historians of myth and comparative religion regard this term very differently. Briefly defined, myth expresses something about the experience of the sacred through its narrative. Creation myths in particular, speak about the sacred origins of how the present world came to be as it is. As Mircea Eliade notes, "The myth relates a sacred history, that is, a primordial event that took place at the beginning of time, *ab initio*."[7]

Myth reveals the presence of the sacred in a manner that is transhistorical and this quality is what defines it as a *lived reality*. Eliade further argues that the sacred does not exist as a dimension that is apart from the profane[8], but indeed exists *within* it, and is capable of manifesting itself at any time or moment. This explains why the sacred participates in the fullness of being, unlike the profane that is circumscribed by the boundaries of ordinary time and space. Myth connects the present day reality with the seminal events of a prehistorical past. Accordingly, mythical consciousness thrives in the immediacy of the present rather than in the past; both the symbol and the symbolized co-exist on a single plane of existence. It is important to add, as the renowned psychologist C. G. Jung (1875-1961) explains: "The primitive mentality does not *invent* myths, it *experiences* them. Myths are original revelations of the preconscious psyche. Many of these unconscious processes may be indirectly occasioned by consciousness, but never by conscious choice. Others appear to arise spontaneously, that is to say, from no discernible or demonstrable conscious cause."[9]

From a different perspective, Eliade asserts that myth flourishes in the face of mystery and awesome incomprehension. Mythic stories invite people to let go of

---

[7] Mircea Eliade, *The Sacred and the Profane* (New York: Harcourt, Brace, and Jovanovich, 1959), 95.

[8] Originally, the term *profanum* referred to the area of secular space that bordered upon sacred space, e.g., a Temple or shrine that was called the *sanctum* because it was designated solely for holy purposes. However, in the *profanum*, this area of space was permitted for ordinary non-holy usages.

[9] Carl G. Jung, "The Psychology of the Child Archetype" in *The Archetypes and the Collective Unconscious*, Vol.9, pt. 1, 2nd ed., (Princeton, NJ. Princeton University Press, 1940), par. 261.

themselves to their immediacy and transcendence. One of the chief characteristics of creation stories in particular is that:

> [The myth is an] irruption of the sacred into the world . . . that *establishes* the world as reality. Every myth shows how a reality came into existence, whether it be the total reality, the cosmos, or only a fragment—an island, a species of plant, a human institution. To tell how things came into existence is to explain them and at the same time indirectly to answer another question: *Why* did they come into existence? The "why" is always implied in the "how"—for the simple reason that to tell *how* a thing was born is to reveal an eruption of the sacred into the world, and the sacred is the ultimate cause of all existence.[10]

In truth, myth has never been meant to explain empirical facts about the natural world, but rather aims to disclose the sacred meaning that is present within the natural observable universe. To a mythical imagination, reality is experienced as a living presence and process. Consequently, myth influences and molds contemporary reality; it shapes the destiny of individuals, religions, and nation-states. Psychologist Rollo May points out in one of his last but most provocative books, *The Cry for Myth,* that myths unite the contradictions and antinomies of life whether they be conscious or unconscious, historical or present, social or individual. "Whereas empirical language refers to objective facts, *myth refers to the quintessence of human experience, the meaning and significance of human life.* The whole person speaks to *us,* not just to our brain."[11] According to anthropologist Bronislaw Malinowski (1884-1942), myth is relevant and contemporaneous with the primordial events that originate in the psyche of primal man:

> Studied alive, myth, as we shall see is not symbolic, but a direct expression of its subject matter; it is not an explanation in satisfaction of a scientific interest, but a narrative resurrection of a primeval reality, told in satisfaction of deep religious wants, moral cravings, social submissions, assertions—even practical requirements. Myth fulfills in primitive culture an indispensible function: it expresses, enhances, and codifies belief; it safeguards and enforces morality; it vouches for the efficiency of ritual and contains practical rules for the guidance of man. Myth is thus a vital ingredient of human civilization; it is not an idle tale, but a hard-worked force; it is not an intellectual explanation or an artistic imagery, but a pragmatic charter of primitive faith and moral wisdom.[12]

If myth figures so prominently in the early Genesis stories, how is one to understand the host of human personalities that populate the "mythical" landscape? Did Adam, Eve, Noah and his children, Abraham, Isaac, Jacob and a host of other biblical personalities

---

[10] *The Sacred and the Profane, op. cit.*, 97-98.

[11] Rollo May, *The Cry for Myth* (New York: W.W. Norton, 1991), 26.

[12] Bronislaw Malinowski, *Magic, Science, and Religion and Other Essays* (Prospect Heights, IL: Waveland Press, 1948), 101.

in Genesis live in the world of *real time*? The Founding Fathers of Genesis may very well have been genuine historical figures, but that debate is almost totally irrelevant. Rollo May correctly observes, "It does not matter in the slightest whether a man named Adam and a woman named Eve ever existed or not; the myth about them in Genesis still presents a picture of the birth and development of human consciousness which is applicable to all people of all ages and religions."[13]

The biblical writer ultimately suspends *real time* and narrates the lives of its personalities in *mythic time*. A mythic character does not live in a temporal existence like ordinary people do, but lives in an almost virtual reality that never ends—so long as people identify with the story and its characters. Myths are, after all, archetypal patterns that are embedded within human consciousness. Their struggles and triumphs serve as parables and allegorical tales mirroring the human condition. From this vantage point, the Abraham, Isaac, and Jacob of Jewish tradition become more important than proving their historical existence.

Although a myth may strike the modern consciousness as something childlike, its simplicity and forcefulness make sense if one were to ponder life's journey and its adventure in terms that are creative and relevant. The absence of myth in modern life is not without serious consequences that will ultimately prevent the individual from discovering his spiritual center, thus denying him the possibility of experiencing meaning and personal renewal. Again, as C. G. Jung notes, "Not merely do they represent, they are the psychic life of the primitive tribe, which immediately falls to pieces and decay when it loses its mythological heritage, like a man who has lost his soul. A tribe's mythology is its living religion, whose loss is always and everywhere, even among the civilized, a moral catastrophe."[14] The rampant use of mind-altering substances in contemporary times for the purpose of achieving a nirvana-type experience, reflects an ontological hunger that many people throughout time have yearned for—one that is not accessible from within the discursive world of logic and academia. Even if the experience proves to be a dangerous one, tragically, sometimes the user prefers risking his life for a crescendo of sensation and exhilaration rather than feeling confined to a life of boredom and quiet desperation.

In the absence of myth, cults of all varieties continue to fill the contemporary psychological landscape. For example, one of the reasons for the resurgence of tattooing one's body is because it expresses a desire to symbolically distinguish oneself from the rest of humanity. The hunger for myth finds other forms of expression as well. Literary characters such as super-heroes borrowed from ancient myths and sagas—whether in

[13] Rollo May, *The Cry for Myth, op. cit.*, 27.

[14] Carl G. Jung, "The Archetypes and the Collective Unconscious", Second ed. *The Collected Works of C.G. Jung Vol. 9, Part I* (Princeton, NJ: Princeton University Press, 1950), 154.

print or film—continue to inspire, entertain, and thrill. Contemporary heroes of the imagination such as *Superman, Spider-man* or *Batman* serve as a source of identification for those who psychologically long for self-actualizing their inner strengths and abilities in an effort to connect with the great myths of the past.

❖ *Where Genesis and Homer Differ*

In his famous essay, *Odysseus's Scar,* Erich Auerbach stresses the philosophical contrast between the Bible's personalities with those of Homer.[15] Auerbach claims that Homer leaves little doubt in the reader's imagination. Every hero's thought is externalized for the benefit of his audience with complete clarity. The world of Homer is self-contained; his poems do not conceal anything, for the author provides all the background information needed to understand his story; "he can be analyzed, but he cannot be interpreted."[16] In contrast, the Bible seeks to create a μίμησις (*mimesis*), a Greek term that means "imitation," but the term really connotes "a portrayal of reality," which aims to transfix and transform the inner world of its reader, as a result of encountering the characters *within* its story. By such means, the biblical narrative makes an absolute claim regarding its truth—and it compels the reader to accept it. Nobody reading its story will walk away feeling quite the same as before. Auerbach contrasts these two narrative traditions:

> The world of the Scripture stories is not satisfied with claiming to be a historically true reality; it insists that it is only the real world, is destined for autocracy. All other scenes, issues, and ordinances have no right to appear independently of it. Far from seeking, like Homer, merely to make us forget our own reality for a few hours, it seeks to overcome our reality: we are to fit our own life into its world, feel ourselves to be elements in its structure of universal history. . . . We are to fit our own life into its world, feel ourselves to be elements in its structure of universal history. . . . Everything else that happens in the world can only be conceived as an element in this sequence; into it everything that is known about the world must be fitted as an ingredient of the divine plan.[17]

Auerbach's insight is brilliantly stated. The Hebraic world of the Scriptures unfolds a worldview where the reader becomes more than just an observer; he becomes in an almost mystical sense—a silent participant. The French anthropologist, René Girard, adds that the process of mimesis is not always a

---

[15] Erich Auerbach, *Mimesis: The Representation of Reality in Western Literature* (Princeton: Princeton University Press, 1953), 3-24.

[16] Ibid., 13.

[17] Ibid., 14-15, 22.

conscious psychological process—it functions unconsciously as well. The characters of the Bible (or other works of world literature), often become role models to imitate, thus reinforcing cultural and social behavior by defining what is and what is not acceptable.[18]

Biblical personalities possess teleological complexity and psychological depth that leave its readers wondering about the main character's inner thought processes. For example: What was the first conversation Adam and Eve had after their expulsion? How did Abel respond to his brother's rejection? How did the first parents react to their son Abel's death? How did Abraham psychologically respond to YHWH's demand that he sacrifice his beloved Isaac? What was Isaac's near-death experience psychologically like? The absence of detail always triangulates the reader directly into the narrative. Moral lessons gleaned from the stories of Genesis transcend the questions of historical factuality. Each biblical episode preserves not just the narrative's experiential quality more cogently than most other formats, but bursts with profound existential energy pulsating throughout the narrative—from the ancient past to the immediate present.

The lives of these human beings, more often than not, are controlled by their gods, who are intricately involved in mortal life. According to Homer, when Achilles confronts Agamemnon for the crime of stealing his wife, Agamemnon offers an ingenious defense: "I was not to blame. It was Zeus and Fate and the Fury who walks in the dark that blinded my judgment that day at the meeting when I took Achilles' prize . . ."[19] This concept was frequently enacted on the stages of ancient Greek theater, where the role of the powerful and intrusive god(s) was enhanced by means of a mechanical flying device known as *deus ex machina*. In reality, it was the gods who were the main actors here. In the Bible, one would never find the attitude that human beings are mere pawns of YHWH. When Cain kills Abel, he cannot blame YHWH for what he does to his brother. Although the hand of Providence is present in the sale of Joseph, nevertheless, it is the brothers who bear the moral responsibility for their brother's disappearance. Even Pharaoh, whose freedom is curtailed, is still ultimately responsible for the misery he causes the Israelites.

There is another important distinction separating the biblical protagonists from their Greek counterparts as revealed in Homer's Iliad. The mortal heroes of Greek mythology are not particularly noted for their self-reflectivity (except for Narcissus!). Psychologist Julian Jaynes adds an interpretation that complements Auerbach's thesis:

---

[18] René Girard, *Things Hidden Since the Foundation of the World* (New York: Continuum, 2003). This point will become even more important in the Cain and Abel story as Girard explores the cultic roots of mimesis as the driving mechanism that produces violence in society.

[19] *Iliad,* Book XIX: 270, translated by Walter A. Kaufmann, *Tragedy and Philosophy* (Princeton: Princeton University Press, 1992), 154.

> Characters of the Iliad do not sit down and think out what to do. They have no conscious minds such as, we say, we have, and certainly no introspections. It is impossible for us with our subjectivity to appreciate what it was like. When Agamemnon, king of men, robs Achilles of his mistress, it is a god that grasps Achilles by his yellow hair and warns him not to strike Agamemnon (I: 197ff.). It is a god who then rises out of the gray sea and consoles him in his tears of wrath on the beach by his black ships, a god who whispers low to Helen to sweep her heart with homesick longing. . . . The beginnings of action are not in conscious plans, reason, and motives; they are in the actions and speeches of gods. To another, a man seems to be the cause of his own behavior—but not to the man himself. When, toward the end of the war, Achilles reminds Agamemnon of how he robbed him of his mistress, the king of men declares, "Not I was the cause of this act, but Zeus, and my portion, and the Erinyes [furies] who walk in darkness: it was they in the assembly who put wildness upon me on that day when I arbitrarily took Achilles' prize from him, so what could I do? Gods always have their way (19:86-90). [20]

There can be little doubt that the myths and plays of ancient Greece also reveal a tragic dimension of human life. Plato's criticism of Greek tragedy and poetry is an important case in point. According to him, poets tend to imitate the most negative impulses of the soul, rather than its most noble features. For young people in particular, Plato believes that such mimetic behavior could only lead to developing bad habits, crude language, and inappropriate responses to crisis (395c-d). Young guardians would fare better by putting their attention to the dramatized positive role models who are portrayed as living by a principle of virtue. Secondly, by giving an outlet for such negative expression, the poet's words give license to an audience for expressing emotions that ought to remain repressed.[21]

For the most part—with the exception of some stories, e.g., Moses, Samson, King Saul and Job—the biblical writers adopted a different and more hopeful attitude. As Auerbach writes:

> Humiliation and elevation go far deeper and far higher than in Homer, and they basically belong together. The poor beggar Odysseys is only masquerading, but Adam is really cast down, Jacob made a refugee, Joseph really in the pit and then a slave to be bought and sold. But their greatness, rising out of humiliation, is almost superhuman and an image of God's greatness. The reader clearly feels how the extent of the pendulum's swing is connected with the intensity of the personal history—precisely the most extreme circumstances in which we are immeasurably forsaken and in despair, or immeasurably joyous and exalted . . . [22]

---

[20] Julian Jaynes, *The Origins of Consciousness in the Breakdown of the Bicameral Mind* (Boston, MA: Houghton Mifflin Company, 1976), 72-73.

[21] Plato, *The Republic* 603-606e.

[22] Erich Auerbach, *Mimesis: The Representation of Reality in Western Literature*, *op. cit.*, 18.

And so the pendulum swings in reverse, as portrayed in the difficult life of King David, who after his great triumphs, begins a path of self-indulgence that nearly destroys him and his kingdom—only to find his spiritual center anew. Rather than focusing on the tragic dimension of earthly existence, Genesis (as well as the other books of the Tanakh[23] is concerned with the theme of personal redemption. Like the characters of Greek myths, each character is portrayed in Genesis as struggling with certain personality flaws. But unlike the Greek protagonist, the biblical counterpart is never the victim of circumstances beyond his or her control. Adam and Eve's expulsion from Eden is the result of their decision to eat the forbidden fruit. Cain is not the victim of a capricious deity, but only of his own darker impulses and insecurities. The Jewish perspective is firmly rooted in the notion that every human being acts with complete freedom and is always morally accountable to God for one's actions.

Like the *Iliad* and the *Odyssey*, the book of Genesis is the product of an oral age when the patriarchal and matriarchal stories were recounted or may have even been acted out or sung. Whole families might have gathered around a fire, and listened intently to the beautiful old stories about the dawn of the world or the dangerous exploits of the patriarchs, which they had heard so often, yet never tired of hearing. As these same stories were repeated, the story-tellers often developed new interpretive perspectives while embellishing the tales anew. And so Midrash was born.

❖ *Who is the Protagonist of Genesis? God or Humanity?*

Abraham Joshua Heschel may have been correct in asserting that the entire Torah is in one sense, "a Midrash about God." However, one could just as easily reverse Heschel's comment and suggest that the Torah is *God's Midrash about humankind*—or more specifically—God's Midrash about the people of Israel. In Greek dramatic terms, the question might be phrased in this way: Is God the *protagonist* of Genesis, or is man? In other words, whose story is it? Behind every human narrative lurks an unpredictable Deity whose own "personality" is no less complex than His creation. Make no mistake about it: in the Torah's cast of characters, God is as much a principle player as are many of its main human actors. Theologically speaking, Creation invites individuation not just for humanity, but (paradoxically) for the Creator as well (e.g., God later decides in Genesis 8:21 that destroying the world may not have been the best solution for dealing with human waywardness, given the human propensity for committing evil). The ancient imagery appeals to the very young at heart, but also lends itself to deep and

[23] The Tanakh is the sacred book of Judaism that consists of the Pentateuch (i.e., the Five Books of Moses, commonly referred to as the Torah), the Prophets, and the Writings (Hagiographa). It is also known as the Hebrew Scriptures.

philosophical reflection. The unknown storytellers' approach is cleverly prescriptive and always profoundly entertaining. Genesis is as much drama as it is poetry for the soul.

❖ *Genesis as a Spiritual Journey*

In Greek philosophical thought, the term γένεσις (*genesis*) connotes more the idea of *origin* and *beginning*. Perhaps the Sages of Alexandria consciously named this book Genesis in order to stress the idea of *becoming*. In theological terms, Genesis points to a process of creation that is ongoing, flowing, and continuous—each of these nuances is conveyed in the Greek word *genesis*. Ancient teachers of Israel perceive the stories of Genesis as parabolic lessons that continue to unfold in the lives of future generations.[24] Genesis, as its Greek name implies, denotes an inner movement toward the highest possible degree of being that finds its decisive realization in God. The personalities of Genesis undergo radical transformation and ultimately evolve morally and spiritually—despite their initial reluctance. Genesis stresses the idea that God and humankind co-create human evolution and spiritual growth. An analogy from the book of Jeremiah best captures the imagery of how God partners with mortals, shaping them much like a potter who struggles with second-rate clay.

> The word that came to Jeremiah from the LORD: "Come, go down to the potter's house, and there I will let you hear my words." So I went down to the potter's house, and there he was working at his wheel. The vessel he was making of clay was spoiled in the potter's hand, and he reworked it into another vessel, as seemed good to him. Then the word of the LORD came to me: "Can I not do with you, O house of Israel, just as this potter has done?" says the LORD. "Just like the clay in the potter's hand, so are you in My hand, O house of Israel."
>
> Jeremiah 18:1-6

The potter metaphor is also reminiscent of the Genesis narratives (2:7) where God forms (וַיִּיצֶר = *wayyîṣer*) humankind out of the dried mud and clay of the earth. In a homiletical sense (in the spirit of Hassidic parables), this may suggest that the formation of Adam is never something that is ever truly "complete." In a manner of speaking, God's participation in Adam's spiritual development continues throughout his life. As is the case with Adam, it is no less the case with humanity. The brilliant Christian thinker, Irenaeus (*ca.* 180 C.E.), arrives at one of the most important intuitions of Western spirituality, capturing the essence of this point by distinguishing between the "image" and the "likeness" of God in the creation of humanity. The term "image" denotes the raw substance which has the spiritual potential that can enable each human being to transform him/herself into a "likeness" of the Divine. Hopefully, each of us embarks on a life journey where we will ideally develop from being mere "creatures of God" to becoming true "children of God."[25]

---

[24] Cf. Ibn Ezra on Gen. 9:18; Ramban on Gen. 12ff. and *Beth HaLevy* on Gen. 26:29; *Torah Temimah* Gen. 22, note 26. Zohar 1:82a; 3:52a.

[25] Irenaeus, *Against the Heresies* 5.6.1:

Jung refers to this moral evolutionary development leading to the wholeness of the psyche as "individuation."[26] Spiritual growth is a lifelong process that seeks to bring about a whole and integrated personality. At the core of self-realization is the religious paradox of struggle and surrender to the Spirit of God that shapes us from within. Our souls inevitably surrender to the darkness and ambiguity of God who is portrayed as prodding the process of human individuation. This theme is very visible in every story of Genesis. In fact, all of these figures ultimately become something radically different from what they were at the start of their personal narrative. When we first meet Rachel, her best feature described is her beauty, but as a result of the struggles with her sister Leah, Jacob, and ultimately with God, she comes to a spiritual realization about her own quest for love and acceptance. Throughout every story in Genesis, birth and rebirth occur time and time again as each protagonist undergoes radical character transformation.

❖ *Contrasting Shadow with Light*

The theme of birth and rebirth is not found only +throughout Genesis, but is present in the other books of the Tanakh as well (see the pericopes[27] of Moses and Jonah). No human being is born perfect. In this sense, every saint has a past—every sinner a future.

For if anyone takes away the substance of flesh, that is, of the handiwork [of God], and understands that which is purely spiritual, such then would not be a spiritual man but would be the spirit of a man, or the Spirit of God. But when the spirit here blended with the soul is united to [God's] handiwork, the man is rendered spiritual and perfect because of the outpouring of the Spirit, and this is he who was made in the image and likeness of God. But if the Spirit be wanting to the soul, he who is such is indeed of an animal nature, and being left carnal, shall be an imperfect being, possessing indeed the image [of God] in his formation *(in plasmate)*, but not receiving the similitude through the Spirit; and thus is this being imperfect. Thus also, if any one takes away the image and sets aside the handiwork, he cannot then understand this as being a man, but as either some part of a man, as I have already said, or as something else than a man. For that flesh which has been molded is not a perfect man in itself, but the body of a man, and part of a man. Neither is the soul itself, considered apart by itself, the man; but it is the soul of a man, and part of a man. Neither is the spirit a man, for it is called the spirit, and not a man; but the commingling and union of all these constitutes the perfect man.

[26] Jung uses the term *individuation* to denote "the process by which a person becomes a psychological 'in-dividual,' that is, a separate indivisible unity of 'whole'" (*Consciousness, Unconscious, and Individuation* [CW 9i. par. 489]). Individuation involves a lifelong process that seeks to bring about a whole, integrated human personality. The essence of this process is the establishment of a living relationship between the ego, as the center of the conscious personality, and the "Self," i.e., the God-centered presence (*Imago Dei*–the "Image of God") that is at the epicenter of the human personality. Jung states that God is responsible for prodding the "Self" to actualize one's own greatest potential in the quest for meaning and purpose, as each person meets and overcomes the various challenges that s/he faces in a lifetime. This new appreciation of the reality and wholeness of the psyche, which in turn makes possible a new paradigm of unity, can however, only be achieved by one individual at a time. This is the process, referred to by Jung as individuation. Development of the individual to maturity and fulfillment is marked by the progress of the ego when it becomes increasingly aware of its origin out of the larger, archetypal psyche (the Self) and the nature of its relationship to that phenomenon.

[27] The term *pericope* refers to an extract or selection from a book, especially a reading from Scripture.

Jewish folk-wisdom has always understood this great life-affirming spiritual intuition. Jungian psychology has much to say about the darker forces that lurk within the human soul yearning for conscious expression. As defined by Jung, the archetype of the "shadow" represents the hidden or unconscious aspects of oneself–both good and bad–which the ego either represses or never recognizes, as he notes: "The shadow is the thing a person has no wish to be."[28] The more unaware we are about this darker and amoral side, the less likely we will mindfully confront and change our inner nature.[29] To become self-aware, it is imperative that each of us find a way to integrate our "shadow" nature. This spiritual and psychological task is not without its challenges and difficulties, as Jung explains further:

> The shadow is a moral problem that challenges the whole ego-personality, for no one can become conscious of the shadow without considerable moral effort. To become conscious of it involves recognizing the darker aspects of the personality as present and real. This act is the real existential condition for any kind of self-knowledge, and therefore, as a rule, meets with considerable resistance.[30]

Awareness of these internal psychological forces can enable a person to be deliberate in thought, word, and deed, while unawareness of the shadow can often lead to the scapegoating of others. Shadow projections are among some of the most pernicious attitudes evident in many social and racial biases. Misogyny, for example, is due to a man's refusal to recognize his own inner feminine nature that yearns for a conscious expression. The same dynamic is present in any kind of social prejudice.

Conversely, it would be a mistake to identify the shadow with forces of evil; the shadow reflects the underdeveloped good that has yet to become fully realized and conscious. There is another element of the shadow that represents the repressed goodness each of us has which yearns to emerge into consciousness.[31] Jung refers to this

---

[28] Carl Gustav Jung, "Aion: Researches into the Phenomenology of the Self" *The Collective Works of C.G. Jung*, Vol. 9 Part II [Princeton, NJ: Bollingen, 1959), 14.

[29] An extreme example of shadow archetype can be seen in Robert Louis Stevenson's story of *Dr. Jekyll and Mr. Hyde.* In this classic narrative, Dr. Jekyll, considers himself to be a kind, loving, and accepting doctor; yet he remains dishonest in facing himself as he really is. Little does he realize that there are two men who inhabit the same body and personality. At first, he changes in order to indulge in all the forbidden pleasures that were off-limits to Dr. Jekyll, but as his evil side progressively grows stronger, it is Hyde who dominates, until he is totally transformed into the Hyde persona. Had Jekyll been aware of the contradictions in his inner self, he might have been more capable of domesticating his inner savage.

[30] Carl G. Jung, *Aion: Researches into the Phenomenology of the Self, op. cit.,* par.14.

[31] Talmudic wisdom teaches that sometimes a good person will dream of doing bad deeds, while a bad person will occasionally dream of doing good deeds—depending on the thoughts each one has in the course of a day (BT Berakhot 55b).

presence of the psyche as the "Golden Shadow." This manifestation of the psyche is always present in the heroes and heroines of the Genesis story. God refuses to give up on His chosen ones; Divine creativity turns inward, *the human spirit is a work in progress.* Jung explains further: "The shadow is not, however, only the dark underside of the personality. It also consists of instincts, abilities, and positive moral qualities that have either long been buried or have never been conscious. The shadow is merely somewhat inferior, primitive, unadapted, and awkward; not wholly bad. It even contains childish or primitive qualities which would in a way vitalize and embellish human existence, but—convention forbids!"[32]

Admitting that the shadow exists is a crucial step in breaking its compulsive hold on the individual. One of the best illustrations of this in the book of Genesis is the story of Jacob, a man who is in every sense a creature fashioned from the forces of Creation itself—light and darkness commingled as one. As a young man, Jacob feels spiritual yearnings within his heart, but acts ruthlessly in achieving his goals. Jacob's transformation occurs once he becomes consciously aware of what he has been, and chooses to become something altogether different. By developing an awareness of his spiritual center, Jacob finally learns to shed the fears that commandeer his soul and discovers an inner center of peace. He discovers that blessings can only be obtained through just and honest means—without fanfare or manipulation (see Excursus 26 for more detail of the shadow archetype and its relation to the Fall).

2. Conversing with Genesis

❖ *Finding One's Own Interpretive Voice*

One 16th century rabbinic scholar, Rabbi Eliezer Ashkenazi, exhibited integrity transcending the parochial world he inhabited, and called upon his readers to show independence of thought that challenged the theological correctness of his era. His prescription for honesty and intellectual truthfulness can certainly apply to our own generation as well:

> Neither should we be concerned about the logic of others—even if they preceded us—preventing our own individual investigation. Much to the contrary, just as [our forbearers] did not wish to indiscriminately accept the truth from those who preceded them, and that which they did not choose [to accept] they rejected, so it is fitting for us to do. Only on the basis of gathering many different opinions will the truth be tested. . . . Do not be dismayed by the names of the great personalities when you find them in disagreement with your beliefs;

---

32 C. G. Jung, "The Shadow," *The Collective Works of C.G. Jung,* 9 Vol. II, (Princeton, NJ: Bollingen, 1959), par.14.

> you must investigate and interpret, because for this purpose were you created, and wisdom was granted you from Above, and this will benefit you.[33]

From R. Ashkenazi's opinion, one may surmise that the truth can always stand up to scrutiny. All the various approaches concerning the origin and redaction of the Pentateuch have much value and wisdom to impart. Early rabbinic exegetes deserve considerable credit for pointing out many textual anomalies that require clarification. Granted, many of the Midrashic answers given may not be grounded in a realistic understanding of the text, but the questions they raise regarding the text's meaning are important. Conflicting interpretations—especially in a dialogical setting—frequently draw attention to nuances and ideas that one participant or interpreter may have overlooked or failed to take adequately into account. Conflicting interpretations also expand the text and force each participant to re-articulate earlier stated ideas that take into account the criticisms of the other side. In the midst of a discussion, one party may see truth in an oppositional point of view.

The need to occasionally acknowledge interpretive fallibility is an essential feature if one is to arrive at a truth. The absence of consensus is not a negative thing per se—in fact, quite the opposite. Contrary to Aristotle's law of non-contradiction;[34] namely, "a thing and its opposite cannot both be true,"[35] rabbinic wisdom believes that truth is best served when contrarian interpretations challenge one another.[36] Truth is frequently discovered through a process of adversity and contradiction. Regardless how a person interprets a classical text like the Bible—or for that matter any great work of literature—there will always be somebody else who will interpret it differently. Disagreement is

---

[33] Cited from Alan Dershowitz's *The Genesis of Justice* (New York: Time Warner, 2000), 18-19.

[34] See, e.g., Aristotle, *On Interpretation* c.12: "But since it is impossible that contradictory propositions should both be true of the same subject, it follows that 'it may not be' is not the contradictory of 'it may be.' For it is a logical consequence of what we have said, either that the same predicate can be both applicable and inapplicable to one and the same subject at the same time, or that it is not by the addition of the verbs 'be' and 'not be', respectively, that positive and negative propositions are formed . . ." (*The Basic Works of Aristotle,* Richard McKeon ed. [New York: Modern Library Philosophy, 2001], 55).

[35] Aristotle actually derives this idea in Plato's *Republic,* speaking through the character Socrates, who observes: "It's plain that the same thing won't be willing at the same time to do or suffer opposites with respect to the same part and in relation to the same thing" (*The Republic* 436b).

[36] R. Baruch Epstein makes this exact point in his *Torah Temimah Commentary* on Numbers 11:11:

> Many of wondered how the Sages could have said, "This point of view and that point of view are the words of the Living God! How is it possible for both to be right when one says something is permitted while the other argues that it is forbidden? As mentioned elsewhere (cf. *Torah Temimah* on Song of Songs 2, note 54) contrasting opinions serve to clarify the truth. Without contradiction, the truth would never truly be understood. Hence, each perspective constitutes the words of the Living God. The Divine will creates dialectical tension that is necessary whenever people attempt to clarify the truth.

something that is not only endemic—it is inevitable. Whenever a new idea or approach is introduced, attention is drawn to aspects of a text that one might have overlooked or failed to take adequately into account. Arguments—whether they happen to be contrarian or supportive—force a person to modify an earlier stance. By the same token, one person's ideas may have an equally powerful influence on someone else. While interpretation typically refines the next interpretation, controversy remains our constant companion.

How should one respond to this conundrum? If unanimity is really the goal, what incentive would there be for new interpretive ideas? Conversely, dissent is not necessarily indicative of a communications breakdown. Oftentimes a consensus of a people may be predicated upon an error (e.g., Ptolemy's geo-centric view of the universe is but one obvious example). The desire to create a stable consensus can threaten to immobilize a person(s) or a society in error.

Dissent can be beneficial, and often leads to new discoveries and ideas. Moreover, dissent ensures that there will be some sort of accountability on the part of the originator. This would explain why peer review is a necessary process whenever new articles on any subject are introduced. A community of readers and interpreters create a network that produces alternative viewpoints worthy of reflective consideration. Differences of insight do not necessarily mean disagreement on the core issues of a story or discussion. Throughout Jewish and Christian exegetical traditions, rarely has there been a stable consensus. If this was the case in ancient times, why should it be any different today? The focus of scholarly dissent may change over time, but the fact of disagreement does not go away; indeed it is a necessary part of the learning process.

Every biblical commentary (to a greater or lesser extent) offers varying responses, often to the same question; at times they pose different questions and may also argue as to which questions ought to serve as the focal point of a discussion. The purpose of their commentaries is not to create a *monologue* with the reader but to stimulate a living *dialogue* for both the reader and his community. In light of this, we can boldly say that questioning the great interpreters of the past need not undermine faith; on the contrary, it has the potential of strengthening it. Conversely, the fear of new ideas in many ways undermines faith in the Divine message of the Torah. Perhaps one of the greatest gifts of the Socratic and Talmudic milieu to the Western world is the need to question everything that is believed to be the "truth." The fluid nature of Judaic theology demonstrates a historical resiliency that has the innate ability to maintain its structural and spiritual integrity against any wave of modernity or textual criticism.

While *Birth and Rebirth through Genesis: A Timeless Theological Conversation* is primarily a theological exposition of biblical themes that are scattered throughout the chapters of Genesis, the title implies that it is also an exegetical work, intended to honor the nature of the *peshat* (the contextual meaning of the text)[37] with its rich history of intertexuality. The text is a nexus where ideas and thoughts of the past converge with the present and future. The exegetical component is extremely important, for good exegesis can provide a solid contextual basis for eisegetical insight and wisdom.

❖ *What exactly is a Conversation?*

What is the purpose of a conversation? The root "converse"[38] connotes an informal or intimate verbal interchange of thoughts, information, and feelings between two or more persons. When we converse, we are engaging in one of the quintessential features that define us as human beings. Participating in conversation involves listening, asking questions, responding, agreeing, and disagreeing—depending on the content and context of the discussion. The fluidity of conversation moves and expands, depending on the input of its participants.[39] Oftentimes, it involves disagreeing with the person who is conversing (often referred to throughout this work by the neologism, "con-versing"[40]).

[37] The term *peshat* is often translated as the "plain" or "literal" sense of a biblical passage. However, this definition is really quite misleading. In both Jewish and Christian exegetical history, seldom have commentators ever agreed on the literal meaning of verse, which Christian scholars refer to as *sensus literalis*. Since the time of the 19th century, the literal sense has often meant "the original meaning" in light of its historical development. The protean nature of *peshat* continues to challenge scholars and lay people alike, much as it has since the beginning of rabbinic and Christian interpretation and is directly related to the differences found between exegetical and eisegetical approaches. For the purposes of this commentary, *peshat* is referred to as the contextual meaning of the text, for context is not limited necessarily to grammatical, linguistic, and historical methods, but may also include literary, cultural, structural, and theological perspectives, which produce radically different interpretive views of a text depending upon the ideological position one starts from (see the section entitled: *PaRDeS: The Four Layers of Rabbinic Interpretation* for a further treatment of this important topic).

[38] According to *Etymology Online*, conversation dates back to 1340 and derives from O. Fr. *conversation,* from L. *conversationem*, nom. *Conversation*, "act of living with"; prp. of *conversari* "to live with"; "keep company with"; lit."turn about with," from L. *com-* intens. prefix + *vertare,* freq. of *vertere* (see versus. Originally "having dealings with others"; also "manner of conducting oneself in the world"; used in the specific sense of "talk."

[39] A similar approach can also be seen in the writings of Plato. Although he wrote 26 tracts of philosophy, Plato never appears as a participant in his own dialogues. This latter point makes him unique in the history of Western philosophy, but what is significant about this approach is the fact that Plato raises questions that are designed to involve the reader in the discussion. In the final analysis, Plato believes that the reading audience is smart enough to draw their own conclusions. The Talmud also makes use of this same method of discussion by drawing its students into an ongoing dialogue with the text, tradition, and each other.

[40] According to theologian David R. Blumenthal, *con-versing* aims to displace the conventional or orthodox understanding intimated by a sacred text and its generation of interpreters, with that which is seen and perceived by the psyche of the modern reader. Briefly described:

> "Converses" is an overturning of the literary, social, and ethical hierarchies of the text. It is a counter-reading, a deconstruction (though not in the contemporary technical sense of the term). . . . It is a pointing to the fissures and gaps between the text and the conscious-unconscious of the contemporary reader. It is an under-understanding, an inversion of the text-tradition . . . (*Facing the Abusing God: A Theology of Protest*

Common characteristics of a conversation typically include:

(1) An experiential understanding that each party brings from his or her own life.
(2) A personal narrative that often includes earlier conversations on a given topic.

(3) A combination of spoken and unspoken dialogue which may influence each participant's perspective.

(4) An agreement to disagree in order to keep the channels of dialogue flowing. Respect is essential in any kind of communicative setting.

In short, the essence of meaningful conversation involves an element of surprise; i.e., disclosure that defies predictability in the germination of creative thought. The absence of predictability along with the flow of asymmetrical ideas allow for a creative tension and a deepening of insight; when we converse, we sense a movement towards a *telos* (goal) which becomes illuminated by the contrasting hues of understanding. The trajectory of a conversation may even become chaotic as new and unanticipated directions unfold and become infused with different shades of meaning and significance. For honest dialogue to occur, participants ought to shed the ego's desire to monopolize or control the flow of thought. The beauty of conversation allows for each participant to expand his/her horizon of perspective, allowing for growth and transformation of all of the participants through meaningful dialogue.

❖ *A Timeless Theological Conversation*

Thus far we have explained the dynamics of conversation between actively engaged participants who show a willingness to share ideas when meeting one another face to face. However, is it possible to converse with the author of a sacred text, or a commentator who is not present? In light of the thoughts expressed by Russian philosopher and literary critic Mikhail M. Bakhtin (1895-1975), great works of literature create conversations with characters, narrators, and authors. According to Bakhtin, literary forms carry meaning that a writer may consciously or unconsciously imply but never fully articulates. The spoken and written word cannot be viewed as a *monologic* aspect of discourse which aims to subordinate the speech of others to a single controlling voice or consciousness. Regardless of whether one is the author or reader, no expressed word or text can ever be accused of having merely one dimension of meaning. The tyranny of a monological interpretive attitude is dangerous since it cuts off honest inquiry and the freedom to dissent. An absence of disagreement or controversy is not necessarily a mark of success. By the same token,

[Louisville, KY: Westminster/John Knox Press, 1993], 60).

disagreement is not a mark of failure; there are endless and worthy responses to any substantive question.

Indeed, the etymology of "dialogue" bears witness to the importance of this discussion. The Catholic theologian Raimondo Panikkar draws attention to this point:

> Dialogue seeks truth by trusting the other, just as dialectics pursues truth by trusting the order of things, the value of reason and weighty arguments. Dialectics is the optimism of reason; dialogue is the optimism of the heart. Dialectics believes it can approach truth by relying on the objective consistency of ideas. Dialogue believes it can advance along the way to truth by relying on the subjective consistency of the dialogical partners. Dialogue does not seek primarily to be *duo-logue*, a duet of two *logoi*, which would still be dialectical; but a δια-λόγος (*dia-logos*), a piercing of the logos to attain a truth that transcends it.[41]

A *dialogic* paradigm, therefore, opens up the language of the classic to interpretation and re-interpretation, while at the same time de-centers the hierarchies of power that seek to control the text. In contrast, monological discourse approaches ideas from a perspective that is static and exclusionary of other thought patterns, whereas dialogical approaches promote fluidity, the shifting of ideas, and the formation of new thought. For Bakhtin, every word anticipates a response from within the context of a dialogical union with the spokesperson or initiator. To receive the word is to be in a state of continuing dialogue, for the word is *a living presence.*[42]

The personal vantage point of a reader enables one to see beyond the periphery of what may have been the writer's purview. If we could imagine a reader and the writer of a text or with the interpreter sitting opposite one another, what would we see? Bakhtin answers:

> When I contemplate a whole human being who is situated outside and over against me, our concrete, actually experienced horizons (i.e., ranges of vision) do not coincide. For at each given moment, regardless of the position and the proximity of this other human being whom I am contemplating, I shall always see and know something that he, from his place outside and against me, cannot see himself: parts of his body that are inaccessible to his won gaze (his head, his face and its expression); the world behind his back, and a whole series of objects and relations, which in any of our mutual relations are accessible to me but not to him. As we gaze at each other, two different worlds are reflected in the pupils of our eyes . . . [43]

---

[41] Raimondo Panikkar, *Myth, Faith and Hermeneutics* (Philadelphia: Paulist Press, 1980), 6.

[42] Mikhail Bakhtin, *Problems of Dostoevsky's Poetics* (ed. and tr. Caryl Emerson [Theory and History of Literature 8; Minneapolis: University of Minnesota Press, 1984]), 300.

[43] Bakhtin's essay, "Author and Hero" published in *Aesthetic Activity, Art and Answerability: Early Philosophical Essays* (University of Texas Slavic Series, 9 Austin: University of Texas Press, 1990), 23.

This may explain the old adage, "Sometimes we can't see even the nose that is on our faces." According to Bakhtin, that statement is actually quite true. We can only see certain contours of our faces, but the other person who is looking at us, can see our face far better than we can (without the help of a mirror, of course!). The same principle applies to how we look at any interpretive text. For our purposes, any work on Genesis involves a dialogue with the great sages and teachers of the past who have thoughtfully expounded the sacred text with an eye for new insight and teachings. The exegetical and theological themes of Genesis deserve to be openly debated much in the same spirit advocated by Rabbi Ashkenazi and later by Mikhail Bakhtin, Martin Buber, Raimondo Panikkar, Jacques Derrida, Hans Georg Gadamer and numerous others. The dialogic paradigm should forever replace the monologic thinking of those who believe it is their destiny to control the ebb and flow of the text. Nothing less will do.

What is true of how we interact with literature in general, applies no less to how we engage the Book of Genesis in particular. Embedded in the biblical text are doubled-edged meanings and multiple nuances: wordplays abound. The Divine word is best heard through the polyphonic voice of its readers, interpreters, and author alike. With this task specifically at hand (when interpreting Genesis), it is vital that we, the readers, engage in an ongoing dialogic discourse that includes not just the written text–i.e., narrators and its characters, but also includes generations of scholars from both Judaic and other traditions in creating an *interpénétration* of discourses issuing from many different centers. Every participant has an honored place at the interpretive table where ideas are exchanged. Rather, a "plurality of consciousness" can occur only when numerous voices meet and expand their understanding in the free flow of ideas and perspectives. All of this creates what he describes as "polyphony"[44] or *heteroglossia*–the coexistence and interplay of several types of discourse covering the social milieu of various generations that have engaged the text throughout history.

❖ *The Playful Subtlety and Nuance of Language*

Israel's most famous poet, Nahum Hayim Bialik, expressed the thought, that reading the great works of the Jewish canon in any other language other than Hebrew is like kissing a bride through her veil. All biblical writers possess a penchant for subtlety that defies translation. One of the aspects of Biblical Hebrew that is often ignored by modern translations (such as the NJPS or the NRSV) is the subtle use of particles that add slight,

[44] Mikhail Bakhtin explains, "Dostoevsky . . . creates . . . free people, capable of standing alongside their creator, capable of not agreeing with him and even of rebelling against him. A plurality of independent and unmerged voices and consciousnesses, a genuine polyphony of fully valid voices is in fact the chief characteristic of Dostoevsky's novels" (*Problems of Dostoevsky's Poetics*, trans. Caryl Emerson [Theory and History of Literature 8; Minneapolis: University of Minnesota Press, 1984], 6. This same point may certainly be applied to the book of Genesis as well, whose variegated personalities and stories continue to challenge young and old alike.

but important emphasis and nuance to words, phrases, and sentences, much in the same way tonality affects ordinary conversation.[45] In addition, words frequently have more than just one meaning in a language, and Biblical Hebrew is no exception; the poetic style of the biblical writers determines words that yield a multiplicity of meanings to an educated reader who is sensitive to their nuances.

French psychologist and philosopher Jacques Lacan (1901-1981), argues that if we are to understand the language of the unconscious, or for that matter, discuss the unconscious, it is vital to keep in mind that it is a discourse that rests upon something that always points beyond itself. In other words, *nothing is as it seems* when it comes to human communication. There are multiple layers of meaning that always remain unarticulated and unexpressed. Based on the Freudian paradigm, Lacan insists that behind all meaning lies non-meaning, and behind all sense lies nonsense, i.e., the level of meaning that is not readily apparent to the reader's eye initially; it might seem unintelligible, but it becomes clearer upon deeper reflection. This method enabled Freud to look for puns, a *lapsus linguae*[46] ("slip of the tongue") or for the merging of two words; wordplays typically serve as a port of entry into the patient's unconscious. One little verbal miscue can intimate a whole chain of associations which the subject may not have intended, but through which his unconscious desire is given indirect expression.[47]

Anyone reading Genesis with an eye to fine detail will also probably detect a number of puns; some of them are playfully funny, some are quite serious in their tone. In any event, the pun serves as a literary device to convey ideas that are deeper than what the text might indicate on the surface. Sometimes, a pun can increase the understanding of a text without interrupting its flow. Unfortunately, without the help of a commentary, it is nearly impossible to pick up the subtleties of language and its gentle humor. The power

[45] The NRSV, the NJPS, and other translations render Genesis 22:2 as: "He said, 'Take your son, your only son Isaac, whom you love . . .'" However, these translations render קַח־נָא אֶת־בִּנְךָ (*qaḥ-nāʾ ʾet̲-bink̲ā*) as a direct imperative "Now take your son . . ." However, as Rashi observes, the particle נָא (*nāʾ*) really connotes a request, as if to say: "**Please** take [your son] . . ." or "[Pray,] take your son." The implication of this translation suggests that God never demands that Abraham comply, but merely requests his cooperation. Rashi's interpretation alters the reader's perception of the narrative by applying tonality to the story.

[46] From Latin *lapsus* (error) + *lingua* (tongue).

[47] It is well-known that Lacan was a brilliant punster who loved playing with language. Puns and other wordplays are an important part of human conversation preventing it from degenerating into monotonic communication. Puns allow us to play with the language and permit the text to become more intimate and enjoyable. On the other hand, sometimes the pun can cut deeper than the sword. This expository technique actually has antecedents in Ibn Ezra's Torah commentary where at times he makes a pun on a concept he is considering, and at other times when he takes issue with certain scholars he enjoys lampooning. See Irene Lancaster, *Deconstructing the Bible: Abraham Ibn Ezra's Introduction to the Torah* (London: Routledge Curzon, 2004), 105, 143-145; 148, 153, 155, 157, 166, 232.

of the pun functions as a literary device, revealing the unconscious side of language that keeps the text psychologically nuanced, polyvalent, and fluid. However, most subtle wordplays and puns literally get lost in translation.

Tools of psychoanalysis are not limited to merely revealing the unconscious mind of the biblical writers; the same methodology can apply no less to any subsequent rabbinic or literary text.[48] Furthermore, the entire Midrashic method of interpretation is based on these pre-modern psychological nuances that remain embedded in the text. There is a very good reason why Freud, who came from a strong Judaic background, became the father of psychoanalysis. A similar argument can also be made about Jacques Derrida's concept of deconstruction, which also has strong rabbinic antecedents. The act of interpretation never leads directly to an original truth, but instead leads to a text that is—and will always be—in need of further interpretation, as every student of the Talmud knows.

Just as words may possess more than one meaning, so it goes for sentences, paragraphs and even complete narratives, thus leading to a kaleidoscope of possibilities. Some medieval scholars have expressed that the absence of vowel signs in the Torah allow for dynamic expression. In fact, there can be no unequivocal interpretation that excludes all others[49]—even the cantillation marks have their interpretive significance.[50] Moreover, the vowels and consonants co-exist much like the body and the soul. Jewish mystics sometimes liken the consonants to the body, while the vowels are likened to the

---

[48] Lacan's writing style can be very cryptic at times. One expositor of Lacan explains his theory of language as follows:

> The symptom arises where the world failed, where the circuit of symbolic communication was broken: it is a kind of 'prolongation of communication by other means': the failed, repressed word articulates itself in a coded, ciphered form. The implication of this is that the symptom can not only be interpreted but is, so to speak, formed with an eye to its interpretation . . . in the psychoanalytic cure the symptom is always addressed to the analyst, it is an appeal to him to deliver its hidden message. . . . This is the basic point: in its very constitution, the symptom implies the field of the big Other as consistent, complete, because its very formation is an appeal to the Other which contains its meaning . . . [Slavoj Zizek, *The Sublime Object Of Ideology* (London: Verso, 1989), 73].

[49] In B. Barry Levy's *Fixing God's Torah* (Oxford: Oxford University Press, 2001), 179, the author provides a comprehensive survey of various medieval rabbinic views that underscore the maculate nature of the Torah text, i.e., there never was or will be a "perfect" Torah text. Cf. R. David Weiss Halivni's *Revelation Restored: Divine Writ and Critical Responses* (Boulder, CO: Westview Press, 1997), 15-18.

[50] See, for example, the verse in Genesis 39:8, וַיְמָאֵן ׀ וַיֹּאמֶר אֶל־אֵשֶׁת אֲדֹנָיו "But **he refused** and said to his master's wife" (NRSV). The Masoretic cantillation of the verb וַיְמָאֵן (*wayəmāʾēn*) indicates a staccato note that immediately demands the attention of those hearing the biblical story read in the synagogue. Joseph's resistance was buckling. This note appears only three times in the Book of Genesis (cf. 19:16, 24:12). The shrill sound of this note in all three places in Genesis conveys trepidation and uncertainty; it also provides an operatic form of entertainment to the listening audience.

soul in that they reflect various shades of meaning, "Letter is like matter, and the vowel is like the spirit that animates it."[51]

Perhaps one of the most colorful metaphors used by the medieval rabbis when depicting the nature of the Torah is, as Professor B. Barry Levy observes, "the notion that the original Torah, like other heavenly objects, consisted of fire, in this case black fire written on white. While this ethereal presentation does not imply textual uncertainty, it does suggest an elusive, flickering, constantly resonating text, and various medieval treatments reinforced this less than concrete image."[52] Levy's exposition also has subtle platonic nuances. The rabbinic imagery of the Torah having being written in "white and black fire," may in part offer an earlier Judaic parallel to Plato's concept of εἶδος *(eidos* = "ideas"*).*[53]

If this theory is correct, the rabbinic analogy becomes a most apt metaphor for the Torah. According to Plato, every object in the phenomenal universe is an imperfect replica of an archetypal counterpart that is its true source of origin. The rabbis may have been intimating that the Torah consists of two forms: the physical and the spiritual, the former deriving from the latter. Despite the certain orthographic problems associated with the Torah's physical transmission, believers in its sacred stories can argue that the Torah's essence, as a spiritual teaching, still remains intact; it is a cosmic wisdom that derives from God and for this reason the Torah will always remain relevant to those who re-interpret its wisdom anew. (For further discussion, see Excursus 2.*)*

❖ *Deconstructing the Torah's Message: Ben Bag-bag's Wisdom*

A 1st century sage named Ben Bag-bag, once described the purpose of Torah study:

הפוך בה והפוך בה דכולה בה ובה תחזי וסיב ובלה בה ומינה לא תזוע שאין לך מדה טובה הימנה

(hafok bah dekola bah . . .)

"Turn it over and over because everything is in it and reflect upon it and grow old and worn in it and do not leave it, for you have no better lot than that"[54] (Avot 5:22). Barry Levy further points out that there are other variant readings that have a direct

---

[51] Moshe Idel, *Language, Torah, and Hermeneutics in Abraham Abulafia* (Albany, NY: SUNY University Press, 1989), 8.

[52] Ibid., 5.

[53] For further treatment of the *eidos,* see Excursus 14.

[54] Jacob Neusner, *The Mishnah: A New Translation* (New Haven, CT: Yale University Press), 679.

bearing on Ben Bag-bag's statement: הפוך בה והפוך בה דכולה בה דכולך בה (*hafok̲ bah we-happek̲ bah de-k̲ola b̲ah wekolak̲ bah*), " . . . because everything is in it, *and all of you is in it* . . ." This reading suggests, every personal life experience and situation finds expression in the words of Scripture.[55] Should one fail to find the answer one is looking for in a certain passage, then one should keep turning the pages until the appropriate scriptural passage is found.[56] However, the most interesting variant reading of all is the Kaufmann manuscript that states: הפוך בה והפוך בה דכולך בה וכולה בה (*hafok̲ bah we-happek̲ bah de-k̲olah bak̲ we-k̲olak̲ bah* . . .), "because all of it is *in you*—and all of *you is in it* . . ." Levy continues to explain that this reading anticipates both mystical as well as postmodern readings of the Torah.[57] Far from suffering from textual rigidity, Ben Bag-bag insists that the Torah allows for ever-changing deconstructive readings.

Perhaps Ben Bag-bag's statement may be read in another way that is equally plausible. The phrase הפוך בה can also mean "invert it", which may imply an imperative to turn the biblical text inside out by subverting the text's more obvious contextual meaning. The Sages frequently employed this method of interpretation in the way they deduced new Halachic practices, e.g., *lex talionis* would be one of the most obvious examples. In this case, the Sages purposely interpreted the "eye for an eye" (Exod. 21:24) law in terms of compensatory damages that took into account pain, psychological suffering, medical bills, disfigurement, and time lost from work[58], rather than insist that the law be carried out with ruthless justice. For the ancients, the Word of God was dynamic, alive, and always communicative. While

[55] During Late Antiquity, the Greeks and Romans utilized a method of divination when opening a tome of Homer or Virgil to a random place in the text. The first passage that would strike the eye would be considered a sign coming directly from the gods. Ancient Jews also used this form of divination. According to the Apocrypha, when Jewish soldiers fought the Seleucid armies, they would open a Torah scroll to a random place, which would (hopefully) prognosticate how the battle would unfold and how they could avert defeat (1 Mac. 3:48 and 2 Mac. 8:23). This method came to be known as bibliomancy, and for centuries the rabbis would ask children to recite a scriptural verse that they had learned in school, because the chosen verse was considered to be a portend of events to come (Cf. BT Haggiah 15a-b; BT Gittin 68a BT Hullin 95b; Esther Rabbah 7:13 [Vilna Ed.]). Children in particular—because of their innocence and purity of soul—were considered to possess the gift of prophecy, which would be in keeping with R. Johanan's statement: "Since the Temple was destroyed, prophecy has been taken from prophets and given to fools and children" (BT Bava Bathra 12b). Although Maimonides opposed divination, he was sympathetic to this form of Scriptural meditation—especially since the Talmud points out that even the Sages periodically engaged in this practice. See Maimonides' *Teshuvot HaRambam,* ed. J.Blau, (Jerusalem, 1957), *Responsa* No. 173.

[56] Midrash Shemuel on Avot 5:22.

[57] B. Barry Levy, *Fixing God's Torah: The Accuracy of the Hebrew Bible Text in Jewish Law* (New York: Oxford University Press, 2001), 5.

[58] Mishnah Bava Kama 8:1.

rabbinic scholars frequently inverted biblical law in order to meet the needs of their era,[59] so too is contemporary society grappling with new and different perspectives on complex issues concerning gender, family, homosexuality, and bio-ethics—to name just a few. Textual interpretive rigidity can lamentably silence the Torah from addressing the challenging problems that confront the present time.

❖ *A Tapestry of History*

According to French philosopher and theologian Paul Ricoeur, a text is any kind of discourse that is fixed to writing, but its origins are frequently oral in nature, as in the art of storytelling and myth. Ricoeur explains, "Fixation by writing takes the very place of speech, occurring at the site where speech could have emerged."[60] The text however, is not a static entity that is hermeneutically fixed or reified—texts invite encounter, discovery, dialogue, and interaction. In most instances, the reader cannot question what the author had in mind when penning his words and neither can the writer respond to the queries of the reader. Ricoeur terms this formation as a "double eclipse"[61] for in a sense, both writer and reader escape the notice of the Other; this absence of presence also creates an interpretive tension between reader and text. On one level, a text presents a trace of the writer's imagination and experience of the world. Once this experience is transcribed, the writer loses complete control of how his work will be interpreted, as Ricoeur and M. Bakhtin so note.[62] Left to its own, the written word remains in a dormant state until a reader enlivens the text's capacity to challenge and transform his personal worldview. Each instance of engaging the text becomes an event where the minds of the past and present meld together and become one.

The etymological meaning of "text" bears this point out. The English word "text" comes from the Latin *textus* "woven material," which in turn derives from the root *texere* "to weave." It is still fairly common to speak about "spinning a tale" or

---

[59] Here are just a few examples: The majority of sages commenting in the Mishnah on the biblical law pertaining to *lex talionis* (Exod. 21:24-2) interpreted this law in terms of compensation—contrary to Rabbi Eliezer, who insisted on a more literal interpretation (Bava Kama 8:1; cf. T. B. Bava Kama 83b-85b). The Torah prescribed death to the wayward and rebellious son (Deut. 21:18-21), which the Sages effectively abolished, along with the biblical laws regarding the apostate city found in Deuteronomy 12:12-18 (BT Sanhedrin 71a). During the 1st century, in an effort to ensure that loans would be made to those in need prior to the Sabbatical Year, Hillel instituted the legal provision known as *Prozbul*, which enabled the courts to collect the debts and circumvent the prohibition of Deuteronomy 15:2 requiring all debts to be cancelled during the seventh year (See Mishnah Shevi'it 10.3–6, BT Gittin 36a).

[60] Paul Ricoeur, *Hermeneutics and the Human Sciences: Essays on Language, Action and Interpretation* (Cambridge, MA: Cambridge University Press, 1989), 146.

[61] Ibid., 147.

[62] See further the section beginning with: *A Timeless Theological Conversation—Mikhail M. Bakhtin's Important Insight.*

"spinning a yarn," or "weaving a tale,"[63] or "weaving a theme."[64] While a text may be described as a "literary composition," when it comes to its readers and interpreters it ought to be viewed perhaps more accurately as a "literary tapestry." The imagery of a literary tapestry is intriguing with respect to the Torah since each generation's interpretations and commentaries continue to add new strands of thought that keep the text pertinent and contemporaneous. As a divine tapestry, Jewish tradition has always understood that each new generation re-weaves the sacred tradition, and in doing so, contributes toward its beauty and deeper understanding. The threads of interpretation may be different in their texture, quality, and color; nevertheless, each strand of interpretive insight adds, enhances, and preserves the ancestral tradition for future generations. Theologian R. David R. Blumenthal also touches on the theme of text as a woven fabric that continues to be rewoven by each new generation:

> The text is a fabric, woven (Latin *texere/textus*) from many threads. One thread is the received text—signs scratched, erased, and re-inscribed in eternity by many hands. One thread is the tradition— many conflicting voices echoing in the same eternity. One thread is the interpreter—gathering in, *com-prehending*, the threads into one fabric; but differently at different times. And one thread is the reader—calling and called to. All text-fabrics are created from other text—fabrics. Every reading is a gathering-in of older threads into a new tissue; an interweaving of the particular life of the reader with the tissue of the tradition. *The text-fabric is never finished.*[65] (Emphasis added.)

---

[63] Literary scholar Christine de Lailhacar sees the relationship between story-telling and weaving from a different, but yet complimentary way to the explanation introduced above:

> Spinning and "passing the thread through the needle`s eye"(c) are universal metaphors for storytelling, for instance, "to spin a seaman`s yarn," as narration can be compared to a thread. In ancient Europe, village women gathered in a *"Spinnstube"* (spinning room), each in front of her spinning wheel, telling stories to pass the long winter evenings. They must have deployed so much imagination that *"spinnen"* was later expanded to mean telling crazy stories. These villagers had no mythical "Africa" to spin back to, only the same old thread. So they had to use it for imaginative "embroidery" (e). Stories, therefore, accompanied the making of a maiden`s dowry, matrimonial sheets, baby linen, and funeral shrouds from generation to generation (*Liquid Crystal Wrapped in Rainbow Mist: Cecilia Vicuna and the Weaving of Water*). Cited from: [http://www.respiro.org/Issue16/Non_fiction/non_fiction_christine.html]).

There seems to be some anthropological support for de Lailhacar's theory. Africans practicing the Dogon religion believe the art of weaving to be especially associated with the power of speech, where the organs of the mouth "weave" sounds. A similar thought is expressed elsewhere in the Hindu sacred text Rig-Veda (1.164.5), where the "concealed footprints of the gods" seem to be thought of as an analogue for the sacrificial laws that are "woven" whenever the gods, in their function as divine priests, perform the sacrifice by the "weaving of words"—all of which serve a cosmic purpose in keeping the physical universe woven and intact (*EOR*, *op. cit.*, s.v., *Webs and Nets*, Vol. 15, 367).

[64] In the field of political commentary, a "spin master" refers to someone who possesses the ability to weave aspects of a concept in such a way so as to persuade the public.

[65] David R. Blumenthal, *Facing the Abusing God: A Theology of Protest* (Louisville, KY: Westminster/John Knox

Briefly defined, the process of making an intelligible analysis of a given text is what scholars commonly refer to as "hermeneutics," a word deriving from the Greek ἑρμηνεύω (*hermēneuō)* to "interpret," or "translate." This method aims to make intelligible one's own thoughts or the thoughts of others, whether oral or written.[66] Hermeneutics is the critical reflection of the interpretive process, especially with respect to biblical texts, with a goal to understanding its deeper meaning. Aside from ascertaining the straightforward meaning of the text, the study of hermeneutics is also concerned with the various influences that impact a reader's subjectivity and interpretation, such as beliefs, personal history, traditions, and so on (see Excursus 1).

The polyvalence of scriptural interpretation was well known in ancient times. The Academy of Rabbi Ishmael (*ca.* 2nd century) taught, "My word is like a fire that purges dross! It is like a hammer that breaks a rock in pieces!" (Jer. 23:29), i.e., "Just as a hammer can produce many sparks when it hits a flint, so too every single word that goes forth from the Holy Blessed One, splits up into seventy languages."[67] Such interpretive diffusion creates the possibility of diverse and contrarian viewpoints—all of which have a degree of legitimacy.[68] To the religious imagination of the rabbis, the process of revelation continues to unfold in new and unpredictable ways whenever two people or more have a thoughtful exchange of wisdom and scripture. Just as God's Oneness is inclusive of the many, so too does the Torah embrace infinite facets of meaning.

3. The Living Text

❖ *The Intricate Web of Intertexuality*

One of the most important literary and structuralist concepts to emerge in the last four decades of the 20th century is intertextuality—the connections that exist between texts.[69] With respect to text, philosopher Roland Barthes (1915-1980) writes:

Press, 1993), 60-61.

66 Originally, the term hermeneutic was etymologically associated with the Greek deity Hermes, whose eloquence made him the messenger of the gods; Hermes was also the deity of boundaries. From this association, three principles emerge regarding the act of interpretation: (1) interpretation involves examining a sign, a message, or a text (2) interpretation cannot occur without a "hermeneut" (i.e., the interpreter) (3) interpreting any text requires an audience of one or more people.

67 BT Shabbat 88b.

68 In a later Midrashic work dating back to the 11th or 12th century, the rabbis are believed to have said, "Because they knew how to explain the Torah with forty-nine reasons for the ritual cleanness [of an object] and a corresponding number for its uncleanness" (Ecclesiastes Rabbah 8:33).

69 This term was originally coined by poststructuralist philosopher and literary critic Julia Kristeva (1941-). According to her, the notion of intertextuality is mediated through, or filtered, by "codes" imparted to the

> We know that a text is not a line of words releasing a single "theological" meaning (the "message" of the Author-God), but a multi-dimensional space in which a variety of writings, none of them original, blend and clash. The text is a tissue of quotations drawn from the innumerable centres of culture. . . . His only power is to mix writings, to counter the ones with the others, in such a way as never to rest on any one of them. Did he wish to express himself, he ought at least to know that the inner "thing" he thinks to "translate" is itself a ready-formed dictionary, its words only explainable through other words, and so on indefinitely . . . [70]

No text—however well-venerated or popular—ever reflects a singular point of view, but reflects a cultural formation and history of interactions. Oftentimes, what one document obscures, another reveals and expands. Intertextuality weaves a connection of disparate texts, various interpretive traditions, writers and readers, actors and audiences, who share an interactive experience with one another, blazing a trail where new ideas may be explored, reevaluated, and expanded upon. Conversational interactions—whether they be contrarian in nature, or supportive—serve to reweave both texts and traditions in the spirit of creativity, generating a newer and more fluid understanding.

❖ *The Original Biblical Exegetes: Intrabiblical Commentaries*

According to Professor Michael Fishbane, the ancients played a dynamic role in re-interpreting their texts and traditions in an effort to deal with the social realities of their age. Exegesis did not derive from something that was external to a text; originally, it flowed from *within the text* centuries before the biblical canon was ever closed. This approach has been called an intratextual commentary or "inner biblical" exegesis. Ancient scribes were not merely concerned with the physical record of the holy books, they also happened to be master story-tellers who functioned as co-authors of the sacred texts. This approach serves to make the tradition more lexically consistent, more accessible, more theologically relevant—and ultimately more comprehensible. "Even more paradoxically: in the end," writes Fishbane, "it is their interpretations that have become the received tradition; their oral traditions are the written text given to the community."[71] James Kugel (Harvard University) illustrates how this concept works:

---

writer and reader by other texts. Every text does not exist in isolation and cannot be fully understood in isolation. Rather, the text alludes to references and quotations from other texts, which in turn condition its meaning rather than to an external reality. For example, a newspaper article may depend upon other previous news stories; a political speech may depend upon other political speeches or statements made by other politicians and civic leaders. A book about baseball presupposes that a reader understands the rules of the game. Even a recipe may depend upon a reader's familiarity with other food recipes. A text must be seen within a broader cultural system. See Tori Mil (ed.), *Kristeva Reader,* (New York: Oxford University Press, 1986), 34-62.

[70] Roland Barthes, "The Death of the Author" printed in *Image-Music-Text* (New York: Hill and Wang, 1978), 146-147.

[71] Michael Fishbane, *The Garments of Torah: Essays in Biblical Hermeneutics* (Indiana Studies in Biblical Literature) (Bloomington, IN: Indiana University Press, 2000), 7.

> For, even before the Bible had attained its final form, its stories, songs, and prophecies had begun to be *interpreted*. From very early times, sages and scholars in ancient Israel had made a practice of looking deeply into the meaning of these sacred writings, and, with each new generation, their insights and interpretations were passed on alongside the texts themselves. As a result, as each new age inherited what was to become the Bible's various books from the previous age, it also inherited a body of traditions about what those texts meant.[72]

Numerous examples can be cited throughout the Tanakh. Thus, in the book of Chronicles, one already sees how the ancient chronicler retells the histories of some of the earlier books, e.g., Genesis, the books of Samuel, Kings, and the Psalms. In the centuries leading up to the Common Era, many new popular Apocryphal books introduce a new proto-midrashic course that reexamines the older and better known biblical books such as the *Book of Jubilees*, *The Genesis Apocryphon*, and Josephus's *Antiquities*. One of the most famous books of that era was Pseudo-Philo's retelling of the biblical story from Adam to David. As precursors to the Midrashic literature that would follow, these works creatively retold the ancient stories in a newer and more contemporary idiom for their age.

❖ *Philo of Alexandria as the Godfather of PaRDeS*

In his day, Philo was a widely-respected master teacher and philosopher who dedicated himself to explaining the deeper meaning of the Torah's precepts in light of Hellenistic thought. Philo is remembered as one of the most important expositors of Platonic philosophy, but in many other ways Philo was no less critical of other schools of Greek philosophical thought that followed in the footsteps of Aristotle, Epicurus, and the Stoics.

After a devastating pogrom in the year 38 C.E. that left the Jewish section of Alexandria in a shambles, Philo led a delegation to Rome where he met with the Roman Emperor, Gaius Caligula, which ended in failure due to the Emperor's animus toward the Jews. However, Philo's efforts were not without some impact, for the next Roman Emperor, Claudius, restored religious and judicial rights to the Jews when he became Emperor in 41 C.E., though still denying Jews equal status with that of Greek citizens. The popular 2nd century B.C.E. work, *The Wisdom of Ben Sirach* contains an important description of the sage that in every way personifies the kind of life Philo of Alexandria lived (ca. 20 B.C.E. - 50 C.E.):

> How different the man who devotes himself to the study of the law of the Most High! He explores the wisdom of the men of old and occupies himself with the prophecies. He treasures the discourses of famous men, and goes to the heart of involved sayings. He studies obscure parables, and is busied with the hidden meanings of the sages; he is in attendance on the great, and has entrance to the ruler. He travels among the peoples of foreign lands to learn what is good and evil

[72] James Kugel, *The Bible as It Was* (Cambridge, MA: The Belknap Press of Harvard University, 1997), xii.

among men. His care is to seek the LORD, his Maker, to petition the Most High, to open his lips in prayer, to ask pardon for his sins. Then, if it pleases the LORD Almighty, he will be filled with the spirit of understanding; He will pour forth his words of wisdom and in prayer give thanks to the LORD, Who will direct his knowledge and his counsel, as he meditates upon his mysteries. He will show the wisdom of what he has learned and glory in the law of the LORD'S covenant. Many will praise his understanding; his fame can never be effaced. Unfading will be his memory, through all generations his name will live . . .[73]

Harry A. Wolfson notes that Philo was the first Jewish thinker to compose a philosophical commentary on the Pentateuch.[74] According to him, every scriptural text possesses a two-fold meaning: (1) the *obvious* or *manifest* meaning (φανερὰ = *phenera)* (2) an *underlying* meaning (ὑπόνοια = *hyponoia)* that includes the *allegorical* (ἀλληγορία = *allegoria)* which perceives a text as a reflection of a higher truth. Anticipating a view expressed in the Zohar, Philo views the allegory as the "soul" of the text—in contrast to the text's more "bodily" feature.[75] Only those who have a more mature capacity can readily grasp the text's deeper meaning.[76] Philo adds that the allegory "loves to hide itself" to those who are philosophically "initiated" to its circle.[77] There is no doubt that Philo prefers the allegorical approach to the literal, but he does admit that the literal sense of the text has its rightful place when it comes to exegesis.[78]

Like the Alexandrian Jewish philosopher Aristobulus who preceded him,[79] and Maimonides who succeeded him a millennium later, Philo claimed that no

---

[73] *Sirach* 39:1-11.

[74] A good number of these comments found in this subsection are based on H. A. Wolfson's seminal study, *Philo* Vol. 1, (Cambridge, MA: Harvard University Press, 1947), 115-138.

[75] Philo, *Migration of Abraham*, 36, 200.

[76] Ibid., 41, 236.

[77] Philo, *On Flight and Finding* 32, 179.

[78] It is conceivable that Philo may have been influenced by the Stoic philosophers of his era who frequently utilized the allegorical method in expounding the literary ideas and ethical beliefs found in Homer's writings, which they regarded as a repository of hidden and transpersonal wisdom.This approach is profoundly different from the more traditional approach that critically analyzes the structure and syntax of a text.

[79] F.W. Farrar adds in his analysis of the allegorical method as it was employed by the Jewish thinkers prior to Philo, "In answer to a question of Ptolemy, Aristobulus told him that Scripture was not to be literally understood (Eusebius, *Praep. Ev.* viii. 10). The "hand" of God means His might; the "speech" of God implies only an influence on the soul of man. The "standing" of God means the organization and immovable stability of the world. The "coming down" of God has nothing to do with time or space. The "fire" and the "trumpet" of Sinai are pure metaphors corresponding to nothing external. The six days' creation merely implies continuous development. The seventh day indicates the cycle of hebdomads which prevails among all living things—whatever that piece of Pythagorean mysticism may chance to mean ..." *History of Interpretation* (London: Macmillan and Co, 1886), 128.

anthropomorphic description of God should be interpreted literally—only figuratively. As to the purpose of such expressions, Philo writes that "these metaphors were written for training and admonition, but not because God's nature is as such."[80] Philo also makes use of what would later be described as *remez* (interpretive allusions drawn from numerology, anagrams, etc.) and his interpretations of the various biblical numbers easily fit that model of interpretation taught during the medieval era. Wolfson points out that Philo's differentiation between the literal and the allegorical are not always consistent in his interpretive treatment of the Edenic narrative, suggesting that the variance in Philo depended upon the sophistication of his listening audience.

Yet, sometimes even Philo's literal method comes to inform the reader an object lesson in Jewish ethics and philosophy. This is especially the case with *Questions on Genesis and Exodus*, where his method of interpretation relies on the contextual meaning of the narrative or precept—comparable to the medieval *derash* approach found in rabbinic commentaries.[81] In one passage Philo confesses his preference for the allegorical method over the exegetical: "This is the reason that is generally and widely stated, but I have heard another from men of high character who regard the contents of the Law as visible symbols of an invisible reality, which expresses the inexpressible" (*Special Laws* III 32:177).

❖ *PaRDeS: The Four Layers of Rabbinic Interpretation*

The concept of re-interpreting biblical narratives and their application to intra-biblical commentaries, which to some extent also occur in the Greek and Aramaic translations of the Bible as well as in the writings of the Pseudepigrapha, gave rise to other models of interpretation—most notably—Midrash. One of the most important hermeneutical paradigms introduced by the early and medieval rabbis is a belief that the Scriptures contain more than one layer of exegetical meaning. This intertextual approach came to be known during the medieval era by the acronym פַּרְדֵּס "PaRDeS," standing for "Peshat," "Remaz," "Derash," and "Sod." Briefly defined, *peshat* is based on the literal and factual meaning of a verse[82] and roughly corresponds to the medieval

---

[80] Philo, *On the Unchangeableness of God.* 11, 54.

[81] Although Philo's exegetical style of writing at times is comparable to the medieval scholars who champion a contextual approach to the text, at other times he was also quite mystical and views various pericopes as containing mystical and philosophical insight of a transpersonal nature. In one passage, Philo confesses his preference for the allegorical method over the exegetical: "This is the reason that is generally and widely stated, but I have heard another from men of high character who regard the contents of the Law as visible symbols of an invisible reality, which expresses the inexpressible" (*Special Laws* III 32:177).

[82] Lexical nuances of this term פְּשָׁט will clarify this ubiquitous rabbinic word. In general, פְּשָׁט *"peshat"* derives from the biblical root פָּשַׁט (*pāšáṭ*), connoting the idea of stripping something off, e.g., וַיַּפְשִׁיטוּ אֶת־יוֹסֵף אֶת־כֻּתָּנְתּוֹ—thus Joseph was "stripped" of his coat by his brothers (Gen 37:23), or וַיִּתְפַּשֵּׁט יְהוֹנָתָן אֶת־הַמְּעִיל,

concept of *sensus literalis* as developed by Thomas Aquinas and Nicholas of Lyra: "that which the author intends."[83] It is also helpful to remember that the early rabbinic approach of *peshat* serves to define the practical character of a community.[84] *Remez* (allusions) refers to the subtle types of word games and puns that are embedded in the text (cf. Gen. 1:31; 2:23; 6:8). Sometimes this may take the form of *Gematria* (numerology) *Temurah* (anagrams) and *Notarikon* (acrostics).

The third method of exegesis, *derash,* provides more of a philosophical, theological, and moralistic examination of the biblical pericope. As a general rule, the rabbis resorted to *derash* only when the text posed a problem that could not be adequately explained through the method of *peshat*. *Derash* as its root word connotes, implies a search for truth and authenticity, while *Sod* concerns itself with the mystical nuances

---

when "Jonathan 'took off' the cloak he was wearing" (1 Sam. 18:4). The verb is sometimes also used with respect to "stripping the slain" after a battle for the purposes of plunder or revenge. Likewise, Aaron was to be "stripped" of his priestly vestments before he died (Num 20:26, 28). The same verb is used with regard to animal sacrifices and has the meaning of "flaying" as in וְהִפְשִׁיט אֶת־הָעֹלָה — "The burnt offering shall be flayed" (Lev. 1:6), for the skins of an animal were property given to the priests. In Mishnaic Hebrew the verb נִפְשַׁט may sometimes connote "straightening something out," "to unfold" or "make something flat"; this usage corresponds to the Latin *explanare* ("to make plain or clear, explain,") lit. "to make level," or "flatten," from *ex-* ("out") + *planus* ("flat"). This description is how the Sages envisioned the methodology of interpreting the text. Common usage of פָּשָׁט suggests something that is obvious, or a matter of course. Early Talmudic texts suggest that the rabbis concurred that "a text cannot be taken from the meaning of its peshat." In mystical texts, the term הַפְּשָׁטָה implies something that is inherently abstract, i.e., when a concept is stripped of its concrete aspects, leaving a distilled essence.

[83] Aquinas adds, "Since the literal sense is that which the author intends, and since the author of the Holy Writ is God, Who by one act comprehends all things by His intellect, it is not unfitting, as Augustine says (*Confess.,* xii), if, even according to the literal sense, one word in the Holy Writ should have several senses" (*Summa* 1: Q. 1. Art 10). Like the rabbinic commentators of his era, Aquinas believes that all other aspects of interpretation ought to be subordinated to what he calls, "the literal sense."

[84] The British scholar Raphael Loewe astutely notes that when the early rabbis used the term "peshat," it did not usually refer to the "plain meaning" of the text as we now understand it to mean, but to the "traditional, familiar, and hence the authoritative meaning of the text." More often than not, the פְּשָׁט was used as a polemical tool of invalidating other rabbinic interpretations ("The 'Plain' Meaning of Scripture in Early Jewish Exegesis," *Papers of the Institute of Jewish Studies London*, vol. 1, ed. J. G. Weiss [Jerusalem: Magnes Press, 1964], 141 and 181). Loewe's interpretation seems accurate since the nascent Church (ca. late 2nd–4th century C.E.) referred to its Aramaic translation of the Bible as the *Peshitta*, the "authoritative" or "official text" that was used throughout the Syriac-speaking Christian lands. Loewe further believes that the traditional, the familiar, and the authoritative within the scriptural text are more the product of communal sensibilities than they are the product of individual insight. However, one could just as easily argue that sometimes the Sages imposed their interpretation upon the community, which in turn lent credibility to their perspective by virtue of the community's acceptance. More directly stated, according to early rabbinic tradition, the literal sense is not inherent in Scripture per se but rather is defined by rabbinic leadership as it responds to the needs of their community. Lastly, the primacy of the *peshat* approach, as advocated by the Sages, prevented the kind of metaphysical speculation that often leads to false messiahs and other charismatic movements that threaten to undermine a faith community.

and mega-themes that see the passage in broader cosmic terms. This is the method of interpretation found throughout the Kabbalah and in the Chassidic writings, however, whose origin has strong antecedents in the writings of Philo. There is a charming passage from the Zohar which illustrates this point:

> Rabbi Shimon said: Woe to the person who says that Torah presents mere stories and ordinary words! . . . Ah, but all the words of Torah are sublime words, sublime secrets! . . . This story of Torah is the garment of Torah and whosoever thinks that the garment is the real Torah and not something else—may his spirit deflate! He will have no portion in the world that is coming. . . . That is why David says: "Open my eyes so I can see wonders out of Your Torah!" (Psalms 119:18) what [*sic*] is under the garment of Torah! Come and see: There is a garment visible to all. When those fools see someone in a good-looking garment they look no further. But the essence of the garment is the body; the essence of the body is the soul! So, it is with Torah. She has a body: the commandments of Torah called "the embodiment of Torah." This body is clothed in garments: the stories of this world. Fools of the world look only at the garment, the story of Torah; they know nothing more; they do not look at what is under the garment.
>
> Those who know more do not look at what is under the garment but rather at the body that is under that garment. The wise ones, servants of the King on high, those who stood at Mt. Sinai look only at the soul, root of all, real Torah! In the time to come they are destined to look at the soul of Torah! Come and see: So it is above. There is a garment and body and soul and the soul of the soul. The heavens and their host are the garment. The Communion of Israel is the body who receives the soul, the Beauty of Israel. So is She the body of the soul. The soul we mentioned is the Beauty of Israel who is real Torah. The soul of the soul is the Holy Ancient One. All is connected, this one to that one. Woe to the wicked who say that Torah is merely a story! They look at this garment and no further. Happy are the righteous that look at Torah properly! As wine must sit in a jar so Torah must sit in this garment. So look only at what is under the garment! So all those words and all those stories they are garments![85]

Regardless of what level of PaRDeS one wishes to pursue, any interpretation that is advanced must be grounded in the *peshat*. To use a common analogy, one can build the most beautiful structure, but if the foundation of the building is weak or non-existent, it will collapse with the first strong gust of wind. The key to understanding the *peshat* requires a firsthand knowledge of Hebrew syntax and philology, combined with a critical eye for examining the text. The Sages summed up this principle well when they said, "A Scriptural text must never be deprived of its straight-forward meaning."[86] Exegetical as well as eisegetical interpretations ought to be grounded in the *peshat*.

---

[85] Daniel Matt, *Zohar, the Book of Enlightenment* (Philadelphia: Paulist Press, 1983), 43-44.

[86] BT Shabbat 63a.

❖ *Archaeology as a Pathway to Peshat*

Modern studies drawn from a variety of secular disciplines also illuminate the subtext of a biblical narrative: archeology, comparative mythology, anthropology, linguistic studies, as well as Mesopotamian history. The Torah is not so much about ancient history—in many ways it *is* ancient history. With this thought in mind, the warning of the Zohar not to forget that other layers of interpretation co-exist deserves to be respected. To the mystic, the Torah reads as a cosmic text that speaks on several concurrent levels. Along with the *sensus literalis* is the *sensus spiritulis* ("spiritual sense") that stresses the importance of personal transformation. Each level of PaRDeS resonates with the individual's soul according to his or her place along the spiritual continuum.[87]

Many people who are critical of the Bible's authenticity often assume that biblical stories do not have a shred of historical reality, and yet who can deny the historical context about which they were written? Whether one believes in the words of the sacred text as having a historical basis or not, one cannot ignore that Genesis—a book of Israel's sacred beginnings—is firmly rooted in the literature of the ancient Near East.

This point does not mean that archaeologists will someday discover the physical remains of Adam and Eve, or necessarily uncover the wreckage of Noah's ark. There is a strong mythic and etiological function that is present in the first eleven chapters of Genesis. As to the historicity of Genesis, there seems to be a general consensus among scholars that the narratives recorded in this book contain centuries of oral transmissions that were passed down through the generations. This orality of Genesis is similar to the Iliad, which was also based on ancestral stories that were written down long after they were orally recanted. Indeed, numerous details of the book's cultural elements make greater sense to us today, now that archeology has provided us with many of the records that date back to the earliest period of Israel's history. As G. E. Mendenhall observes, there is a rich textual tradition that predates the writing of the Pentateuch:

> A seemingly endless stream of details has shown us that the cultural milieu of these narratives lies in the Bronze Age, especially the period from 2000 to 1400 B.C.[E.]. . . . No longer does the cultural and religious history of Israel begin with a *tabula rasa* in the time of

---

[87] It is interesting to note that sometime during the 11th-12th century, the Benedictine monastic order called this meditational method of encountering God through the Scriptures as the "*Lectio Divina*" ("Divine Reading"). As a spiritual exercise, the *Lectio Divina* focuses on the *sensus spiritulis* that was used in the early part of the first century by scholars like Philo, Origen and later on by the Kabbalists through their cultivation of the doctrine of *kavanah* (spiritual attentiveness). Through the *Lectio Divina*, a scriptural passage can become a pathway to release our deepest concerns to God. With this devotional approach, the words of the Tanakh can once again become a living source of strength and spiritual guidance. See Michael Samuel, *The Lord Is My Shepherd: The Theology of the Caring God* (Northvale, NJ: Jason Aronson Inc., 1996), 201-232.

Moses. The religion of ancient Israel did not necessarily begin from scratch, so to speak, but rather it had behind it traditions which show a continuity extending over at least half a millennium. Furthermore, the very beginnings of this cultural continuity took place in a region which we now know to have been in close contact with the high civilizations of Mesopotamia preceding the migrations which mark the beginnings of Israelite traditions, associated with the name of Abraham.[88]

Many new discoveries have challenged a number of earlier suppositions concerning the origins of the Pentateuch. There can be no doubt that had the rabbis of Late Antiquity and beyond been familiar with this new hermeneutical approach, they would have revised many of their ideas, and have cited numerous illustrations from this relatively new historical field of endeavor. It is important to note that when the early theories of the 18-19th centuries were being conceived, relatively little was known about the ANE.[89] Since that time there have been many exciting archeological discoveries. Many customs of the patriarchal age are now much better understood in light of how Israel's neighbors lived. Here are some of the texts that are relevant to the book of Genesis:

- **Gilgamesh Epic**—(Southern Mesopotamia, ca. 2700- 2600 B.C.E.). In Babylonian legend, Gilgamesh is the ruler of Uruk (believed to be the biblical city of Erech in Gen. 10:10), who experiences many exploits with his friend, Enkidu, who then dies unexpectedly. Gilgamesh visits his ancestor Utnapishtim, the lone survivor of a great deluge, who informs him of a plant that would grant immortality. After obtaining the plant, in an unguarded moment, a mysterious serpent steals the plant and disappears. This narrative, considered to be one of the greatest literary achievements of all time, has important implications for the biblical story of the Fall (Gen. 3ff.) as well as the Flood (cf. Gen. 6–9).[90]

- **Adapa**—another Babylonian myth explaining how humankind lost its immortality. The myth tells about the hero Adapa, to whom the deity Anu offers the "food of life" and the "water of life." Adapa is deceived by the deity Ea, who convinces him that the offerings are really the bread and water of death.[91]

---

[88] G. E. Mendenhall, "Biblical History in Transition," in *The Bible and the Ancient Near East*, edited by G. E. Wright (Garden City: Doubleday and Company, 1961), 36-37.

[89] "Ancient Near East."

[90] A. Heidel, *Gilgamesh Epic and Old Testament Parallels* (2d ed. 1949).

[91] *ANET Ancient Near Eastern Texts Relating to the Old Testament,* 3d ed. with suppl., ed. J. B. Pritchard, Princeton, 1969, 101–3.

- **Enuma Elish**–("When on high . . .") is the title of the Babylonian creation epic written on cuneiform tablets depicting how the god Marduk triumphed over the older gods of chaos led by Tiâmat (goddess of the salt water and chaos) and her consort Kingu. After his victory, Marduk is proclaimed the supreme king of the Babylonian gods and Babylon, the center of the world. It is believed to have been written between 1792-1750 B.C.E.

- **Dumuzi and Enkimdu**–a Sumerian myth describing a contest between Dumuzi, the shepherd-god and Enkimdu, the farmer-god. Each deity competes for the affections of the goddess Inanna. However, unlike the Cain and Abel story, it is the shepherd-god who is rejected by the goddess, and who chooses the farmer-god as a more suitable mate! Ultimately, Enkimdu and Dumuzi work out a compromise: Enkimdu agrees to let Dumuzi graze his flocks anywhere in his territory, and Dumuzi accepts and brings the farmer-god and his bride a wedding gift.[92]

- **Mari texts**—(18th century) of the ancient city, Mari (now identified with Tell Ḥarîrī located near Abu Kemal, Syria) were excavated by A. Parrot in 1933. Since that time, over 25,000 Akkadian documents have been found that provide detailed information concerning the customs, languages, place names (e.g., Nahor, Terah, and Serug) and personal names of people who lived at the time of the biblical patriarchs.[93]

- **Cappadocian texts**–dating back to the early second millennium B.C.E. reflect many Hittite customs explaining why Abraham had to acquire legal title for purchasing a field from Ephron the Hittite (Gen. 23:9). Along with the purchase of land, came feudal obligations that were due to the local ruler of the land.

❖ *How We Read a Text Matters: Exegesis vs. Eisegesis*

With all the literature that has been written on Genesis, this commentary was written utilizing two fundamental interpretive sets of guidelines: *exegesis and eisegesis.*[94] Exegesis involves a process by which one draws out a meaning or meanings from a text. In contrast to exegesis, the process of eisegesis is a way of reading or imposing a pre-existing interpretation *onto* the text, especially whenever it supports a

[92] ANET, 41-42.

[93] M. Lehmann, "Abraham's purchase of Machpelah and Hittite Law," *BASOR* 129 (1953), 15–18.

[94] The term *exegesis* comes from the Greek ἐξαγεσθαι *ex* ("from") and *hēgeisthai,* ("to lead out" or "to interpret") while the etymology of *eisegesis* derives from the Greek εἰσαγεσθαι (*ei*='in") and *geisthai* "to lead in").

predetermined position,[95] custom, or conclusion.[96] To borrow a famous analogy from R. Yaakob Kranz[97] (1741-1804), the process of eisegesis is analogous to a person shooting a bull's-eye. One way involves using skill to hit the center of the target. The other method involves shooting at a random target and then painting concentric circles around wherever the arrow lands. For this reason, eisegetes are often criticized because they sacrifice objectivity for the sake of subjectivity. One could argue that if there is such a thing as an "objective truth" and an objective standard of right and wrong given by the Tanakh, then eisegesis and subjectivism must be marginalized in favor of exegesis.

Although eisegesis may seem arbitrary because of its inherent subjectivity, it does permit readers to situate themselves within the text, allowing for certain moral and practical lessons to be deduced and applied. No sermon would ever have the power to inspire a faith community if it did not convey a strong eisegetic message. Eisegesis allows for the text to remain practical and relevant.[98] If the Torah is truly as its name implies—a book of spiritual "instruction"—then its message must transcend the original context of its historicity to reveal a pathway for readers of every generation to experience the Divine. Unlike an exegetical approach, eisegesis allows the text to speak to new situations, thus acknowledging that the sacred text is polyvalent. It behooves a modern interpreter to integrate both exegetic and eisegetic approaches. Any new conceptual

---

[95] The Sages referred to this process as אסמכתא (*asmachta* = "a Scriptural support") and utilized אסמכתא as a means of deriving meaning and support for any given rabbinic viewpoint. See R. Yosef Zevin's *Talmudic Encyclopedia* Vol. 2, s.v. אסמכתא, 105-107.

[96] As a result, exegesis tends to be objective when employed effectively, while eisegesis is regarded as highly subjective. One who practices eisegesis is known as an eisegete; someone who practices exegesis is known as n exegete. The term eisegete is often used in a derogative fashion by religious academics.

[97] R. Yaakob Kranz is better known as the "Dubna Maggid."

[98] Like the Bible and Talmud, the text of the American Constitution rivals these Judaic classics in terms of the sheer number of commentaries and interpretations that have been written on it. The debate among bible scholars concerning exegesis and eisegesis has an interesting parallel with respect to how modern scholars interpret constitutional law. Both these great works require methodical interpretation and re-interpretation. Painstaking detail is devoted to examining the phraseology and context of both texts: an awareness of past interpretations a prerequisite for deciding new cases of law. When reexamining the issues posed by the text, scholars of both disciplines must show a willingness to ask new questions of old codes. Religious scholars—Jewish, Catholic, Liberal Protestant, or Biblical fundamentalists—frequently debate the "original intent" of the biblical writers in much the same fashion. For an excellent study from a theological perspective on this important subject, see Jaroslav Pelikan's *Interpreting the Bible and the Constitution* (New Haven: Yale University Press, 2004). Legal scholar James A. Whitson writes, "According to O. Holmes, textual language does speak its own conventional meaning, which can and should be interpreted without any special regard for the author's subjective consciousness' For Holmes, it is *only* the autonomous meaning of textual language that can be objective, and it is to the appeal of authorial consciousness which leads to interpretive subjectivism" (*Constitution and Curriculum: Hermeneutical Semiotics of Cases and Controversies in Education, Law and Social Sciences* [London: Taylor and Francis, 1991], 145. (See Oliver Wendell Holmes, "The Theory of Legal Interpretation", *Harvard Law Review*, Vol. 12 (1899), 417-420.

applications ought to find its grounding in an exegetical way within the text, i.e., its historical context, language and cultural background, rabbinic models of interpretation, and so on. Albeit such a concept may not be explicitly expressed, nevertheless, its meaning is certainly intimated by the text's more subtle nuances.[99]

One might well argue that the distinction between these two categories is not as great as it may seem, since texts are inevitably read in the light of the reader's beliefs system. Indeed all exegesis involves a certain degree of eisegesis, then paradoxically—*exegesis is eisegesis.* All exegesis takes place within a community, a tradition, or a given philosophical mode of thought.[100]

As James Kugel points out, sometimes the ancient Judaic commentators—both rabbinic and non-rabbinic (i.e., the Pseudepigraphal writings)—grafted their interpretations to the Pentateuchal text; at other times, they purposely took away from the text. Thus, in the rabbinic portrayal of Jacob and Esau, it is Esau who appears as villainous and duplicitous, while Jacob is portrayed as just an "honest" homeboy. How a character is conceived by the biblical writer is oftentimes different from how the same character may be perceived by subsequent generations. Contemporary scholarship teaches that all Midrashic interpretation must be measured against the cultural world it is indirectly commenting on.[101] For example, Midrashic deconstruction of the Jacob-Esau narrative says more about the community of faith's values than it actually does about the biblical text. Practically speaking, rabbinic interpretation is every bit as eisegetical as it is exegetical.

[99] The distinction between exegesis and eisegesis is very similar to the difference between "diachronic" and "synchronic" techniques used in literary criticism. Modern exegesis focuses on an existing text's genesis and history and is called "diachronic." The synchronic approach involves examining a particular text without paying regard to its historical genesis; the synchronic method begins with the text as it already is in its final form. Literary biblical criticism is based on the synchronic technique. German biblical scholar Helmut Utzschneider sees both the synchronic and diachronic methodologies as mutually complementary, "It may first of all be said that neither of the two perspectives exists on its own. Diachronic exegesis is inconceivable without synchronic elements–that is to say, without taking into account the linguistic form of the presently existing text; conversely, synchronic exegesis cannot deny–and generally has no wish to deny–the complex history of the text's development. To this extent, most exegetes may be said to recognize the justification of both perspectives" Cited from "Text, Reader, and Author—Towards a Theory of Exegesis: Some European Viewpoints" *Journal of Hebrew Scripture*, Vol. 1, 1997, 1-22.

[100] See Maimonides' exposition in the *Guide* 2:25—Maimonides argues that if the eternity of the universe could be scientifically proven beyond a doubt, he would be forced to interpret the Scriptures in a manner that is in harmony with science and reason despite the fact that the Scriptures say the exact opposite! As radical as Maimonides' argument is, it suggests that in an age such as ours where we are more critical of the various sources that may have been used in the Torah's redaction, it is the light of reason that must ultimately prevail.

[101] See Geoffrey H. Hartman and Sanford Budick's *Midrash and Literature* (New Haven and London: Yale University Press, 1986) for an excellent synopsis of articles exploring the relevance of Midrash in contemporary literary thought. Another equally intriguing book that analyzes the texture of Midrashic thought is Robert Graves and Raphael Patai's classical study on *Hebrew Myths: The Book of Genesis* (New York: Doubleday & Company, Inc.; 1st edition, 1964).

Rabbinic analysis encourages the text to be dialogically reinterpreted. A devoted Jewish reader undoubtedly reads the Bible differently from someone who is a devoted Christian reader. A feministic reading of Genesis 3 will be very different from a Pelagian (see chapter 3) or an Augustinian interpretation of the Fall.[102] Each of us understands a narrative on the basis of our personal histories, religious philosophies, and (or) values. Thus, any given text can have several layers of signification. One of the great challenges of our time is to find a way that allows the spirit of Scripture to actively shape and transform the world of its readers and their communities in a manner that teaches respect for life and the maintenance of our social order.

❖ *Rediscovering and Recovering the Heavenly Dimension of Torah*

> *Authentic spiritual language about God does not confuse the map with the territory, the symbol with the thing. Literalism concentrates on the letter and misses the spirit; it gets the words but never the music, creates a spiritual tone-deafness. You can starve to death trying to eat a cookbook.*[103]
>
> —SAM KEEN, *Hymns to an Unknown God*

To adequately appreciate the text of Genesis, we need to have the curiosity of a Sherlock Holmes when it comes to sleuthing the hidden ideas that permeate the biblical text. Finding the hidden subtext requires looking to rabbinic tradition and modern critical studies. To its credit, biblical criticism provides an important glimpse into the cultural setting that forms the backdrop of a given narrative or law in the ancient world, while also enhancing our appreciation of the biblical story. Biblical writers also made use of mythical or literary motifs drawn from its neighbors, recasting elements of these stories to fit an ethically monotheistic and monistic belief.[104]

Yet despite our knowledge of the ancient world, it is presumptuous to claim what the ancient writer(s) had in mind; yet, some modern scholars make that assertion without

---

[102] Perhaps one of the best examples of how two rival religious traditions view a text can be seen in how each faith interprets the verse: In Jerome's translation Isaiah 7:14, "Therefore the Lord himself shall give you a sign. Behold a virgin shall conceive, and bear a son, and his name shall be called Emanuel." However, the Jewish translation reads, "Therefore the Lord Himself shall give you a sign: behold, the young woman shall conceive, and bear a son, and shall call his name Immanuel." Both translations reflect the theological underpinnings of their religious communities.

[103] Sam Keen, *Hymns to an Unknown God* (New York: Bantam, 1994), 54.

[104] A good example of deliberate cross-cultural borrowing is from the Book of Proverb's "The Words of the Wise Men" in Proverbs 22:17-24:22 and in 24:33-34 and appears to have been strongly influenced by the *Teachings of Amenemope*. Portions mentioning the Egyptian deities were expunged. Perhaps when King Solomon interacted with Egypt, he had learned about their wisdom tradition that influenced his thinking in the book of Proverbs.

experiencing even the least degree of uncertainty. While some of the newer reductive methods have proven useful in the examination of the Torah—especially with respect to its canonic transmission—reductionistic approaches are limited in what they can disclose about the nature of a sacred text and the values that inspired its writing. For those who believe in the relevancy of the Torah's message, the text has a pulse: a living story that resonates with meaning. Often more is conveyed by what is *not* explicitly said than by *what is.* Textual ambiguity is as divinely inspired as it is exegetically and eisegetically seductive. The Presence of the Sacred is discovered within the space of interpretation, transcending both the immediate context of the text and the person who is reading it. Early rabbinic texts of the Midrash, along with the medieval rabbinic and Karaite commentaries recognized this phenomenon and treated the Torah text much like the way a lover reads and re-reads a love letter from his beloved. For the faith community, the Torah is a love letter that never ceases to impart new meaningfulness and inspiration.

Abraham Joshua Heschel was well aware of this dilemma that confronts all serious students of rabbinic tradition. Orthodoxy's reticence to engage modern biblical criticism in a meaningful and non-polemical dialogue has been rare until recent times; biblical criticism—whether it be of the "higher" or "lower" variety—has been perceived as a dangerous innovation undermining the traditional view that God dictated the *entire* Torah to Moses at Sinai. According to Heschel, the historical-critical methods of our age pose no problem whatsoever to a more traditional understanding of "Torah from Heaven." Heschel posits that the heavenly dimension of the Torah does not depend upon a theory of divine dictation for validity; the Torah's transcription and redaction has long been rabbinically recognized as a human enterprise endowed with the spiritual Presence of the Divine—is present in every stage of its redaction.

> You cannot grasp the matter of the "Torah from Heaven" *unless you feel the heaven in the Torah.* All temporal questions are in the context of eternity. The scroll of the Torah is the wondrous become fixed, a great event become routine. But whoever denies the wondrous has no share in this world; how much more so can such a person have no dealing with heavenly matters. If this event is like an everyday occurrence, given to accurate apprehension and description, then it is no prophecy. And if the prophetic encounter is sublime and awesome, without parallel in the world, then it is clear that no description will do it justice, and silence becomes it (Emphasis added).[105]

Like the Bible itself, Heschel also insists that deciphering the metaphors of the Talmud with respect to the nature of revelation is a demanding task, since rabbinic language is nuanced and deep; there are layers of meaning that are subtle and full of metaphorical wisdom just waiting to be uncovered.

> Don't think the intellect grasps only the enduring, received, given text, but that it cannot understand the mystery of prophecy, and event that, having occurred, cannot repeat. For the

[105] Ibid., 668.

intellect itself, rises up in question about the genesis of the book: not concerning the nature of the quill and ink with which it was penned, nor on the material of its tablets or sheets, but rather concerning the mystery of its inspiration.

Even those of little faith will acknowledge that whatever hand wrote the Torah included the "finger of God." But of what use is such a formation if the meaning of "finger of God" is alien to one's understanding? One who has never seen the lights of heaven, one who has never looked and seen in the skies "the work of God's fingers" (Psalm 8:4), one who has not seen the heavenly in the Torah—how will such a person understand the meaning of the phrase "Torah from Heaven"? . . . The expression, "The Holy and Blessed One spoke and Moses wrote" is nothing but a way of giving voice to amazement in the face of the hidden and wondrous, and it should be treated as is any phrase, the role of which is to ease communication and to bring the mysterious into contact with common sense; that is, its value is dissipated as soon as it is taken literally. Literalism with respect to the divine mysteries is a stepping out of bounds, and it obscures more than it explicates. . . . The language "Torah from Heaven" is formulated for the human ear, but it is of no use if the ear is sealed off to its import.[106]

4. Theology & Authorship of Genesis

❖ *Why Begin the Torah with Genesis?*

One of the important questions raised by Rashi (1040–1105) in the beginning of his famous commentary is this: "Why did the Torah begin with the Book of Genesis and not with the first commandment found in the book of Exodus—the precept of sanctifying the New Moon?" For Rashi, who lived during the period of the Crusades, the creation story stresses how God is the Owner and Proprietor of the universe and, therefore, God alone has every right to give the Land of Canaan to whomever He pleases; in this case, He bequeaths it to the nation of Israel. As God's people, Israel has a bond with the land that is eternal and irrevocable.[107] Rashi's opening salvo was quite a remarkable comment to make at a time

[106] Abraham Joshua Heschel and Gordon Tucker (tr. and ed.), *Heavenly Torah: As refracted through the Generations* (New York: Continuum, 2006), 666-667.

[107] Rashi's subtle insight captures one of the most important themes of Genesis: the concept of land. In the Abraham pericope, God promises the Holy Land as a gift to Abraham and his descendants. "Land" has a rich and sacred dimension that is inextricably connected to Israel's possession of it. Israel's capacity to believe in the divine promise that God made to Abraham is the key that enables future generations to take physical possession of it; this same faith is also what defines Israel's stewardship of the Land. Although the patriarchs and their children (with the exception of Isaac) experienced life outside of God's Promised Land, their invisible and sacred bond remained eternally intact. The theme of land is what ties all the books of the Pentateuch together. The God who created the heavens and the earth is also the God who guided His people to their Promised Land through the prophet Moses and his successor, Joshua, thus fulfilling the biblical promise given to the patriarchs. From Rashi's comment, God's designation as "Creator" is historically and inextricably bound up with the success of Israel as His people. To achieve their ultimate purpose, Israel requires the Promised Land to fully realize their mission in the world. For this reason, the Creation narratives form an essential basis for the biblical legislation that follows in the other books of the Pentateuch as noted in Mizrahi's supra-commentary on Rashi.

when Christians and Muslims were fighting for control of the Holy Land. What began long ago as an ideological struggle during the age of the Crusades continues to haunt present-day reality in the Middle East.

Ramban[108] (1194–1270), as well other Judaic commentators, finds Rashi's answer to be inadequate.[109] The importance of Genesis goes beyond the primacy of the Land of Israel as Rashi envisages. In fact, the purpose of the creation narrative is to teach the importance of *creatio ex nihilo*—nothing would exist were it not for the creative power of God. Every creature and entity could not exist were it not due to the conscious act of the Divine bringing each being into existence at every moment.

Like Ramban, Rashbam[110] (ca. 1085-1158) also supports the doctrine of *creatio ex nihilo*, while adding, "Do not imagine that this world you now see and experience had existed forever, for everything in the universe had an absolute beginning—that is why the Torah states from the onset: "At the beginning of the creation of the heaven and the earth . . ." (1:1). Furthermore, reasons Rashbam, the purpose of the creation narrative is to explain why the Sabbath is the cornerstone of all the Jewish holidays—a point that is emphatically stressed in the Decalogue: "Remember to keep holy the Sabbath day. . . . In six days the LORD made the heavens and the earth, the sea and all that is in them; but on the seventh day he rested. That is why the LORD has blessed the Sabbath day and made it holy" (Exod. 20:8-10). By observing the Sabbath, Israel bears witness to the world that God is the sole Creator of the universe.

Among the patristic fathers, Theodoret of Cyprus (393-457) explains that after centuries of oppression and assimilation, the Israelites became religiously indistinguishable from their Egyptian masters who believed solely in a visible creation. Consequently, the Israelites had forgotten about the one and true God of their ancestors, who created the heavens and the earth. "The statement that heaven and earth and the other parts of the universe were created and the revelation that the God of the universe was their Creator provided a true doctrine of God sufficient for people of that time."[111] Theodoret's point is significant. From the very outset of their freedom, Moses begins re-educating his people by teaching them about the creation story. The purpose of the Sabbath thus serves to teach the people of Israel about the nature of true faith and belief in God. Maimonides later expresses a similar point. According to him, each biblical

---

[108] Ramban is an acronym for Rabbi Moshe ben Nachman.

[109] Saadia Gaon, Rashbam, Maimonides, Seforno, and Shadal are only a few such examples.

[110] Rashbam is a Hebrew acronym for Rabbi Shmuel, son of Meir. His father was Meir ben Shmuel and his mother was Yocheved, a daughter of Rashi.

[111] Theodoret of Cyprus, *The Questions on the Octateuch: On Genesis and Exodus,* tr. John F. Petruccione and Robert C. Hill, (Washington: Catholic University of America, 2007), 7.

precept—in one manner or another—aims to raise humankind, as theologian David Hartman notes, "from an anthropocentric to a theocentric concept of religious life."[112]

Karaite exegete and theologian Aharon ben Eliahu (1260-1320), sharing a somewhat similar opinion to that of Rashbam, points out that the principles of Providence and prophecy would be inconceivable were it not for the belief that God created the world. "Moses," argues Aharon, "wished to impress upon his people that they look only to God as the Ultimate Cause of their existence." Like Rashbam, Aharon explains that the purpose of the Creation narrative also serves to theologically reinforce the celebration of the Sabbath.

❖ *Genesis and the Origin of Ethical Monotheism*

R. Samuel David Luzzato (1800-1865) offers an altogether different interpretation. According to him, the opening salvo of Genesis teaches:

> Now God wanted to proclaim to humankind about the unity of the world and the unity of the human race, for in error in these two matters caused many evils in ancient times. Without knowledge of the world's unity, it followed that people believed in private gods with limitations and imperfections, and that people would do evil deeds in order to win their favor. . . . Without knowledge of the unity of the human race it followed that one people would hate and despise another and that physical force—not justice and righteousness—would rule among them. These two cardinal principles—the unity of the world and the unity of the human race—are the overall purpose in the story of Creation.[113]

S. D. Luzzato's position is reminiscent of the early rabbinic view of 2nd century sage, R. Simon Ben Azzai, who thought that the greatest single principle one may derive from the Genesis story—or for that matter, the entire Pentateuch—is the statement in Genesis affirming that God created humankind in His Divine image (Gen. 1:26; 5:1). According to Ben Azzai, the most supreme ethical principle in the Torah is the teaching of divine equality and equity. Moreover, this principle exceeds even the famous Levitical passage, "You shall love your neighbor as yourself" (Lev. 19:18). For Ben Azzai, respecting the divine image beginning first with oneself, and then with others ensures that society will be just and moral. To insult or harm the divine image in any of its forms is to deny the essential brotherhood and sisterhood of humankind. This is why Ben Azzai affirms that the verse affirming the Divine image is by far the most comprehensive principle of the entire Torah—the bedrock of all biblical morality.[114]

---

[112] David Hartman, *Maimonides: Torah and Philosophic Quest* (New York: JPS, 1976), 170.

[113] Daniel A. Klein (tr.), *The Book of Genesis: A Commentary by Samuel David Luzzato* (Northvale, NJ: Jason Aronson Inc., 1998), 2.

[114] Cf. Sifra to Kedoshim 4:12.

The opening chapters of Genesis thus provide the theological basis for ethical monotheism. Since all races of humankind are made in the image and likeness of God, anyone denying this principle will result in a world that is riddled with violence, tragedy, and needless suffering. One may further argue that this particular theme links together the books of Genesis and Exodus. People cannot mistreat one another with impunity, for in God's creative order there is accountability. Humankind's very survival depends upon mastering the forces of chaos that threaten its very survival. The same God Who creates the universal laws that govern the cosmos also creates the moral law by which humanity must abide. The Decalogue at Sinai is more than a mere ethical prescription—all ethics regarding how one treats one's fellow beings derive from the creation narrative.

More recently, Richard Elliot Friedman in his Torah commentary, also takes sharp aim at Rashi's exposition, arguing that the commandments *are not* the sole purpose of the Torah—a view that deserves to be exegetically and theologically examined. Friedman's perspective resonates neatly with the expositions thus far examined:

> The Torah's story is no less important than the commandments it contains. Law in the Bible is never given separately from history. The Ten Commandments do not begin with the first "Thou shalt" but with the historical fact that "I brought you out of the land of Egypt . . ."
>
> . . . Another lesson is that, in the Torah, the divine bond with Israel is ultimately tied to the divine relationship with all humanity. (Rashi does not refer to the first *commandment*: "Be fruitful and multiply," which is given to all humankind, but rather refers to the first commandment given to *Israel*, which is Passover.[115]) The first eleven chapters establish a connection between God and the entire universe. They depict the formation of a relationship between the creator and all the families of the earth. This relationship will remain as the crucial background to the story of Israel that will take up the rest of the Torah.[116]

❖ *More on the Theology of Genesis*

The early chapters of Genesis are also replete with several other theological motifs. At the root of Genesis's theology is the central belief that humans are not mere epiphenomena in the cosmos. Life on this world did not just happen to emerge by sheer chance. The human capacity to be self-reflective and self-aware of its place in the cosmos reflects a quality that derives from the Creator. Genesis emphasizes that there exists a

---

[115] In fact, the first commandment given to the Israelites was the precept to observe the New Moon (Exodus 12:1ff.). Passover can never be observed without first establishing when the New Moon holiday occurs.

[116] Richard Elliot Friedman, *Commentary on the Torah* (San Francisco: Harper Collins, 2001), 5.

great "chain of being" that permeates all layers of reality. Much like the waves of the ocean that continuously undulate, creation also surges with the harmonic energy that structures order and symmetry. Other aspects include:

- God's existence precedes Creation. All reality begins in the consciousness of God, which is mysteriously related to our consciousness and awareness of the Divine. This idea was once metaphysically intimated by the Chinese philosopher Chuang Tzu, who said, "I dreamed I was a butterfly, flitting around in the sky; then I awoke. Now I wonder: Am I a man who dreamt of being a butterfly, or am I a butterfly dreaming that I am a man?"

- At the root of what we perceive as the cosmic reality is the Divine Reality that makes the existence of the cosmos possible. Were it not for the will and desire of the Creator, everything in the universe would remain in a formless state of nonbeing. Genesis 1 describes how God creates the universe with complete and total freedom.

- Each entity in creation points to the presence of One Being who alone is the governing principle of all reality.

- God is a relational Being Who addresses each entity—great or small. This "cosmic personalism"[117] in which the Creator engages every particle of Creation in a mysterious but personal manner, summons from Creation an intimate and immediate response.

- Throughout the Tanakh, God is frequently called, בּוֹרֵא הַשָּׁמַיִם (*bôrë hašámayim*) "Creator of the Heavens" (Isa. 45:18), i.e., "the One who creates."[118] Creation is not a past event; it is continuous and perpetual and does not exist outside of God in either a spatial or temporal sense.

- Genesis stresses the importance of human stewardship of the earth (Gen 1:27; 2:15). Every entity serves a divine purpose in praising God and enriches human life. Creation is not only important in terms of the practical utility they offer to humankind; in God's sight, each entity expresses the aesthetic beauty of Creation and are valued for its own uniqueness (Job 38–39; Ps. 104).

---

[117] The term *cosmic personalism* comes from the British Anglican theologian Austin Farrer (1904-1968). See Charles Conti, *Metaphysical Personalism: An Analysis of Austin Farrer's Metaphysics of Theism* (New York: Oxford University Press, 1995), 22-59.

[118] *Cf.* Isa. 40:28, 42:5, 43:15, 45:18, 57:19, 65:17-18.

❖ *Creation and its Existential Implications*

If God is at the epicenter of reality, and human consciousness is not a mere by-product of matter, then the implications of our existence become inescapable. Individuals cannot live in a state of indifference to God's calling without experiencing the consequences of their self-induced alienation. Indeed, the sense of meaninglessness that pervades our present time is rooted in a collective inability to recognize the grandeur of God's Creation and its moral and spiritual implications for human existence. The Lutheran theologian, Dietrich Bonhoeffer, grappled with Nazism, penning these words just before he was killed, about the spiritual *dis-ease* that riddled Europe in his time:

> Critical philosophy is therefore in systematic despair of its own beginning and of every beginning. Whether critical philosophy proudly renounces that which is not in its power to obtain or whether its resignation leads to its complete destruction, it is always the same hatred of the beginning, of which we have no knowledge. Man no longer lives in the beginning—he has lost the beginning. Now he finds he is in the middle, knowing neither the end nor the beginning, and yet knowing that he is in the middle, coming from the beginning going towards the end. He sees that his life is determined by these two facets, of which he knows only that he does not know them. The animals do not know about the beginning and the end; therefore they know no hatred or pride. Man, aware of being totally deprived of his self-determination—because he comes from the beginning and is moving toward the end without knowing what this means—hates the beginning and rises up against it in pride. There can be nothing more disturbing or agitating for man than to hear someone speak of the beginning as though it were not totally ineffable, unutterably dark beyond of our blind existence.[119]

The notion of a purposeful creation, namely, a creation that has an ultimate *telos* (goal), implies that we, as God's entrusted creation, are responsible to the Creator for how we utilize our time, talent and treasure. Bonhoeffer's perceptive insights apply no less to the postmodern culture of our times. Fascination with creation ought to heighten our sensitivity to the specialness of our existence. Our ability to wonder, imagine, and be self-reflective is not a fortuitous development.

Other theological motifs emerge from the creation stories that are also important to consider: God's oneness is reflected throughout the diversity and wonder of Creation, perceived as the blending of binary oppositions: the One—and the many, nothingness—creation, heaven—earth, chaos—cosmos, day—night, sacred—profane, work—rest, male—female, good—evil, life—death, and so on. The Tanakh denies the doctrine of two separate eternal principles, the one good and the other evil; its view of God and the universe is essentially and wholly unified. All duality finds unification in the oneness of God, each

---

[119] Dietrich Bonhoeffer, *Creation, Fall and Temptation: Two Biblical Studies* (New York: Simon and Schuster, reprinted 1989), 12-13.

side serving its purpose in the greater scheme of how the universe, nature, and humanity function. Nothing in the universe operates merely by one set of principles; rather, everything is a balanced mixture and cooperative blending of these contrasting energies. Clearly, these binary distinctions have both profound ontological and moral implications for such concepts as *creatio ex nihilo* (creation from nothing) and theodicy (a vindication of divine justice in the face of the existence of evil).

❖ *The Power of One Family*

God's method of transforming and blessing the world is subtle but effective. Through Abraham and his chosen descendants, God designates a people who will infiltrate society as "insiders," serving as exemplars for how humanity must live. Abraham becomes in a new sense, the "new Adam." With Abraham, the reader of Genesis soon discovers a God who seeks a relationship with a particular man and his family through whom all the families of the earth shall receive blessings. Special emphasis on the family is also significant for it teaches that the ultimate transformation of society—and by extension the world—occurs through the nuclear family founded by Abraham, whose ultimate challenge was to spiritually alter humanity. Likewise, the concept of family stresses the importance of tradition. Each generation is, in a literal sense, the link that connects the past with the present and future. Essentially, one can only deduce that effective parenting holds the key to the kind of world in which human beings yearn to live.

Virtually all the narratives of Genesis reflect not only the strengths of the principal characters but also their weaknesses, fragility, and certainly their humanity. The notion of being "chosen" sometimes has its dark side, and the characters go to great lengths to see that God's blessings are hoarded rather than shared (Cain/Abel, Isaac/Ishmael, Jacob/Esau, and Joseph/brothers). At other times the "outsider" is viewed suspiciously and even dealt with violently (note the story of Dinah and Shechem).

On a positive note, the biblical narrator of Genesis stresses that family dysfunction can be consciously terminated either by changing one's destiny (symbolized by the changing of one's name) or through the power of forgiveness. Ultimately, the family of Abraham finds its most ideal expression in Joseph, whose love of humanity saves a world stricken by famine. In short, Genesis focuses on the spiritual formation of our personal identities. Each one of us is called upon to develop our inner selves with the help of God. The process is never easy for it involves wrestling with the Divine on many different levels.

If there is any one word that best describes the Book of Genesis (and the other books of the Tanakh), it is the concept of "homecoming." Genesis addresses the fundamental relationship between God and humanity with respect to an earthly journey which includes spiritual homelessness, suffering, despair, and profound desire for blessing. Adam and Eve's expulsion from Eden resonates with our own deep estrangement from God and our longing as a species to somehow find our way back to our spiritual home.[120] It is also a foreshadowing of the Israelites' experience in Egypt as well as their forty years of living in the wilderness. One could further argue that Israel's state of homelessness parallels the exile of the Shekhinah (the Divine Presence), which is boldly depicted in the Midrashic and mystical rabbinic literature as the "Exiled Being" Who escorts Israel throughout her wanderings in history, waiting for God to redeem her.[121]

Genesis emphasizes how the origin of the world and the origin of Israel are intertwined. The fate of God and Israel is, in a manner of speaking, inseparable. Israel represents God's stake in history to which every covenantal member must bear witness. A tangible expression of this reality occurs when Abraham enters into a covenantal bond with God. Once made, the covenant remains forever intact. Just like the vows of marriage, God and Israel have pledged their love and faithfulness to each other (cf. Hosea 2:21-22[122]). The bond existing between God and Israel is crucial: Israel serves as the locus through which God's Presence is realized within all Creation. As the bearer of the Abrahamic mission, Israel must come to terms with her spiritual destiny and purpose.

At the heart of the patriarchal stories is a God who is always present, guiding and protecting His people from those who would cause them harm. One could say that God is humanity's greatest fan and advocate—despite His people's myopia and stubbornness. For all the many foibles and failings of God's chosen ones, it is these very men and women and their descendants who are chosen to transform the world. Despite Israel's occasional reluctance to accept her special vocation, in the end, she regains her spiritual composure and centeredness; the blessings promised are eventually realized. In each of

---

[120]The other books of the Pentateuch express the same thought: "You shall not oppress a resident alien; you know the heart of an alien, for you were aliens in the land of Egypt" (Exod. 23:9 NRSV). Israel must show fairness toward all of its citizens, refraining from taking advantage of those who are weakest in their society: specifically the widow, orphan and resident alien (cf. Deut.10:17–18; 24:17; 27:19). In the Book of Exodus, Israel suffers because of their homeless status; in the Book of Numbers they are condemned to wander as homeless vagabonds, while in the Book of Deuteronomy, the Israelites finally return to their ancestral home that was promised by God to their ancestors.

[121] "Wherever Israel went into exile, the Shekhinah was also exiled with them; they were exiled to Egypt, the Shekhinah was with them. . . . When they were exiled to Babylon, the Shekhinah was with them. . . . When they were exiled to Elam, the Shekhinah also went with them, as it is said, 'My throne I will set up in Elam and destroy from there king and princes, says the LORD. . .'" (Jer. 49:38). *Mekhilta de-R. Ishmael, Massekhta de-Pisha*, xiv, 51–52; *Mekhilta de-R. Simeon b. Yohai*, 79.

[122] Cf. Exod.12:24; 22:16; Deut 20:7; 22:23, 25, 27, 28; 28:30; 2 Sam. 3:14; Isa. 45:23-25; 51:22; 54:5; 54:8-10; 54:14; 60:21; 62:3-5. Jer. 3:14-15; 4:2; 31:31-37; 32:38-41. Ezek. 37:25-28; 39:29; Pss. 36:5-7; 85:10; 130:8; et al.

the patriarchal narratives, the protagonists finally realize their inner spiritual potential and become worthy of the blessings promised to them. Indeed, the narratives of Genesis also tell the story of how the Israelite people were born and how they serve as witness to God in a spiritually confused world.

❖ *The Authorship of Genesis*

The name *Genesis* was given to the Septuagint (Greek) translation of the book. It comes from the Greek word Γένεσις (*genesis*) which can mean "birth" or "history of origin" and the original name of the book of Genesis derives from Genesis 5:1 as βίβλος γενέσεως (*biblios geneseos*). It is also sometimes referred to as Γένεσις κόσμος (*genesis kósmos* ="the origin of the universe"). In the fourth century, Jerome later refers to the first book of the Bible as "Liber Genesis" in his Vulgate. Genesis is the first of the Five Books of Moses, commonly referred to as the Pentateuch, a word which derives from the Greek πεντά (*penta* = "five") and τευχος (*tuchos* = "book"). Bible scholars are uncertain when the Pentateuch became divided into the five books.

One likely theory suggests that originally the Pentateuch and the historical texts were preserved together during the pre-exilic period. In the fifth century B.C.E., Ezra the Scribe, became the first person to separate the Pentateuch from the other books of the Bible, which were already widely considered to be sacred texts.[123] As the Redactor of the Torah, Ezra changed the old Hebrew script into the Aramaic block letters that are used today; in addition, he also standardized the spelling. The division of the Torah into five books was necessary because not everyone could afford to own a whole Torah scroll. Throughout rabbinic literature, Ezra had a stature in Jewish history that was second only to Moses, R. Yose who exclaimed: "Had the Torah not been revealed to Moses, it would have been revealed to Ezra!"[124]

❖ *The Pentateuch and the Documentary Hypothesis*

Biblical source criticism is usually associated with the name of Jean Astruc (1684-1766), a French Catholic physician, who published a book in 1753, where he sets forth a number of conjectures about the original documents that Moses had used to compose the Book of Genesis. Although Astruc does not deny the Mosaic authorship of the Pentateuch, he does observe that Genesis reflects two distinct sources. Astruc bases his theory on the fact that throughout Genesis 1, the Hebrew name for God—Elohim—appears, while in the

---

[123] Francis I. Anderson and Dean Forbes, "Spelling in the Hebrew Bible" (Rome: *BibOr,* 1986), 321-322.

[124] BT Sanhedrin 21b; for an excellent resource on the role of Ezra in the redaction of the Torah, see David Weiss Halivni's *Revelation Restored: Divine Writ and Critical Responses* (Boulder, CO: Westview Press, 1997), 15-18.

second chapter, Moses utilizes the name LORD, or YHWH. Moses copied these two accounts. Since the names of these two authors remain anonymous, the author of Genesis 1 became known as the Elohist, or "E," while the author of Genesis 2 was known as the Yahwist, or "J."

The portion of Genesis 1:1–2:4*a* describes the Priestly version (commonly referred to as "P"), while Genesis 2:4b-25 presents the Yahwist version of the Creation narrative. Although this approach by modern standards is both facile and quaint, over the next century and a quarter, scholars refined this theory and two men, K. H. Graf (1815-1869) and Julius Wellhausen (1844-1918), gave it its classic expression. Today, scholars commonly refer to Wellhausen and Graf's theories as the "Documentary Hypothesis." Accordingly, there are four sources behind the Pentateuch documents:

- J (Yahwist)—believed to have been written during the reign of Solomon, it is from the theology of the "J" tradition that the notion of a God of history and redemption was born.

- E (Elohist)—based on passages containing the name Elohim (*ca.* 750 B. C. E.), the Elohist is believed to have been written in the Northern Kingdom, where his work was merged with the "J" version by a redactor sometime toward the end of the seventh century B.C.E.

- D (Deuteronomist)—is believed to have been composed *ca.* 621 B. C. E. during the time of the reign of Josiah, who initiated a great religious reformation (2 Kgs. 22).

- P (Priestly Code)—includes all of Leviticus and other parts of the Pentateuch. This section is believed to have been produced not long after the fall of Jerusalem to the Babylonians (ca. 587 B.C.E). P refers to God as Elohim, since like the Elohist, the Divine name YHWH was not revealed until the time of the Exodus (Exod. 6:3). More than any segment of ancient Israelite society, the priestly tradition concerned itself with genealogies, cultic regulations regarding the Sanctuary, and utilized a stylistic form of narration. Documentary theorists since 1877 have dubbed this section as "H", claiming that Leviticus 17-26 is a later addition composed during the Babylonian exile (as alluded to in Lev. 26:34-35). Most likely, it contains information that pre-dates the monarchial period and may include some of Israel's oldest social, ethical and cultic laws, and traditions which were eventually incorporated into the "P" text.[125]

[125] For works pertaining to the Documentary Hypothesis, see Julius Wellhausen, "Prolegomena to the History of Israel", the first English edition, with William Robertson Smith's Preface, (Eugene, OR: Wipf & Stock

The various traditions of the Documentary Hypothesis are commonly referred to by a single, distinguishing letter serving as an easily recognizable form of shorthand: hence P refers to the priestly tradition, J to the Yahwist, and so forth, as noted above. However, it is important to remember that the Documentary Hypothesis is still based on theory, albeit a theory that can offer unique interpretations of the biblical text.

Moreover, this is a form of shorthand that is more easily recognizable to the reader. Many of the modern scholars of the critical school see the contrast of the divine names Elohim in chapter 1 and YHWH /Elohim as an indication that the Redactor of the Scriptures, a.k.a. "R" (which traditionalists affectionately refer to as "Rabbenu" our teacher") utilizes two different traditions for the two creation stories found in the first two chapters of Genesis. Based upon this theory we may say that the entire book of Genesis points to a single redactor who conflated all of the different oral histories that were passed down throughout the generations.

❖ *Reductionistic and Holistic Approaches to the Pentateuch*

It should be pointed out that with the beginning of the twentieth century, a new movement emerged that would soon challenge many of the most cherished beliefs of the Source Critics. Many of today's modern critics think that historical-critical methods are overly concerned with the origin of the biblical text rather than with understanding its overall content and meaning. In an effort to uncover what some scholars believe to be the original historical setting of the Bible, this methodology has resulted in the fragmentation of the biblical text; subsequently, often times it is dismissed as if it were the remains of some long extinct people. Jewish tradition regards its Torah as a *living covenant* that is directly related to the formative events that shaped its ancient past. For those who take the spiritual message of the Tanakh seriously, this *a priori* belief is essential for the person of faith.

Classical scholar and philosopher Walter Kaufmann takes aim at the reductionistic methods of Documentary Hypothesis, which he believes fails to explain the organicity and overall message of the Bible:

> Imagine a Higher Critic analyzing Goethe's Faust, which was written by a single human being in the course of sixty years. The scenes in which the heroine of Part One is called Gretchen would be relegated to one author; the conflicting conceptions of the role of Mephistopheles

---

Publishers, 2003); Umberto Cassuto, *The Documentary Hypothesis and the Composition of the Pentateuch* translated by Israel Abrahams. 1st English ed. Jerusalem: Magnes, 1961; Richard E. Friedman, *Who Wrote the Bible?* (New York: Harper and Row, 1987); John Van Seters, *Abraham in History and Tradition* (New Haven: Yale University Press, 1975); Yehezkel Kaufmann and Moshe Greenberg tr.), *The Religion of Israel, from Its Beginnings to the Babylonian Exile,* (Chicago: University of Chicago Press, 1960).

> would be taken to call for further divisions, and the Prologue in Heaven would be ascribed to a later editor, while the prelude on the stage would be referred to yet a different author. Our critic would have no doubt whatsoever that Part Two belongs to a different age and must be assigned to a great many writers with widely different ideas. The end of Act IV, for example, points to an anti-Catholic author who lampoons the church, while the end of Act V was written by a man, we should be told, who, though probably no orthodox Catholic, was deeply sympathetic to Catholicism. Where do we find more inconsistencies in style and thought and plan: in Goethe's Faust or in the Five Books of Moses?[126]

It is no coincidence that the historical-critical theory developed in a century which preferred reductionism as the scientific method of choice. As a philosophical and scientific doctrine, reductionism contends that a system can be fully understood in terms of its isolated parts. However, there is an opposing attitude that believes a system can best be understood in terms of its function as a living organism. The distinction being made here is sometimes referred to as "holism versus reductionism." Astrophysicist Paul Davies makes an observation that could just as easily be applied to how the 19th century Source Critics and their 21st century supporters regard the Bible:

> The main thrust of Western thinking over the last three centuries has been reductionist. Indeed the use of the word 'analysis' in the broadest context nicely illustrates the scientist's almost unquestioning habit of taking a problem apart to solve it. But of course some problems such as (jigsaws) are solved by putting them together—they are synthetic or 'holistic' in nature. The picture on a jigsaw, like the speckled newspaper image of a face, can only be perceived at a higher level of structure than the individual pieces—the whole is greater than the sum of its parts . . .
>
> . . . To say that an ant colony is nothing but a collection of ants is to overlook the reality of colonial behavior. It is as absurd as saying that the computer programs are not real—they are nothing but electrical pulses. Similarly, to say that a human being is nothing but a collection of cells, which are themselves nothing but bits of DNA and so forth, which in turn are nothing but strings of atoms and therefore conclude that life has no significance, is muddle-headed nonsense. Life is a holistic phenomenon.[127]

The difference between the holistic versus the reductionist approach, according to Davies, may be compared to the famous parable about the blind men in India who were examining an elephant. One person felt the leg and said, "It is a tree." Another felt the ear and said, "It is a fan." Another person felt the trunk and said, "It is a water pipe." The last blind man felt the tail and said, "It is a rope." One could say that the blind men's approach epitomizes how reductionism functions. Only by

---

[126] Walter Kaufmann, *Critique of Religion and Philosophy* (Princeton, NJ: Princeton University Press, 1978), 377-378.

[127]Paul Davies, *God and the New Physics* (New York: Schuster and Schuster, 1983), 63.

putting all the animal's parts together, can one conclude that it is indeed an elephant. The approach of holism teaches that the whole is always greater than the sum of its parts.

❖ *Newer Critical Approaches*

The term "criticism" frequently carries some negative connotations in the way it is used in contemporary society—especially when it is associated with the adjective "biblical." The critic is typically regarded as someone who makes or reserves judgment upon something or someone, who has failed to live up to certain expectations. "Criticism" is frequently synonymous with condemnation or judgment. Yet, there is another kind of criticism, which in particular connotes: the systematic activity of analyzing, verifying, classifying, interpreting, or evaluating literary or other artistic works. Such a working definition is especially apt here. Here are some new genres of biblical criticism that have developed in the last hundred or more years:

A. Form Criticism: At the turn of the 20th century, the German Bible scholar Hermann Gunkel began to ask whether the approach of the Brothers Grimm—concerning the origin of German folktales originating from oral traditions—might not also be applicable to understanding the biblical narratives as well. Gunkel believes that the diversity and the discrepancies of the Bible may have been more the result of different oral traditions which had evolved over the centuries, possibly containing an "historical echo" that was essentially embellished over time, thus preventing these stories from becoming a reliable source for determining a historical record.[128] Tales about Creation and the lives of the patriarchs were passed down from generation to generation, becoming the building blocks of an oral society before they finally crystallized into a literary form. Form criticism has become one of the most valuable tools for the reconstruction of the pre-literary tradition.

Gunkel is convinced that the narratives behind the Scriptures are more the result of a community's collective memory than they are by the skilled authors who penned them. In the final analysis, claims Gunkel, the transmissions of these tales depended upon the faith community to maintain and pass on. One way of understanding the Bible, is to break the text down into a series of pericopes, which are in turn analyzed and categorized by genres (e.g., prose, verse, letters, apodictic laws, laws, court records, warrior hymns, poems of lament, and so on). The form critic then theorizes on the pericope's cultural context in which the biblical text was composed.[129]

---

[128] Hermann Gunkel and Mark Biddle (tr.), *Genesis*, (1910; 3d ed. Macon, GA: Mercer University Pre, 1994), xiv-xvii.

[129] Hermann Gunkel and John J. Scullion (tr.), *The Stories of Genesis* (N. Richland Hills, TX: D and F Scott Publishing, 1998). Cf. *The Legends of Genesis* Hermann Gunkel and W. H. Carruth (tr.) (Chicago: Open Court Publishing Co., 1907).

B. Traditional Criticism: This methodology examines the oral and written traditions, as well as other integral forces that contribute to the Bible's present construction, and attempts to trace the various evolutionary stages through which these traditions were handed down—as well as the forms that resulted at these various stages—before reaching the people who committed them to writing. For example, the patriarchal stories may have been derived from a variety of different locations before they were finally collected, edited, and merged together.

C. Redactional Criticism: The early 20th century Judaic scholar, Franz Rosenzweig, once quipped that "R" ought to be rendered *Rabbenu* (in Hebrew, "our Master"), since it is to the credit of the Redactor to whom we owe the present form of Scriptures that we now possess. Orthodox Jews traditionally identify this role as belonging to Moshe (Moses) *Rabbenu*. Since the end of WWII, redactional criticism places considerable emphasis on how the final form of the Scriptures assumes shape; even more so than some of the other critical approaches, it also focuses on the nature of authorial intent. In addition, redactional criticism tries to understand the social and religious forces that may have given final assemblage to the sacred text. Sometimes strands of older traditions (written or oral) were collected in order to address new situations that had risen in the life of the nation. There is no unanimity as to whether the final redaction is the product of a long series of redactions, or whether it was the result of a single redaction. Talmudic tradition, as indicated earlier, sees the role of Ezra and his school as pivotal here (see Excursus 2b).

D. Literary Criticism: One of the condemnations often aimed at the heart of source criticism is the heavy-handed and reductionist manner in which the Bible is treated. Like redactional criticism, literary criticism primarily concerns itself with the text in its entirety; i.e., the text constitutes a "world" in its own right independent of what its authors may have originally intended. Subsequently, literary criticism attempts to analyze biblical texts in much the same ways other great works of literature are studied and interpreted. One of its best representatives is Erich Auerbach, who is among the first scholars to compare and contrast Homer's Odysseus with the biblical story of the Akedah—"The Binding of Isaac" (See the earlier section "Where Genesis and Homer differ"). Northrop Frye is another example of a literary scholar who interprets the Bible in terms of its cultural impact upon Western imagination as revealed in both art and literature. In his *Great Code,* for example, Frye demonstrates the liberating vision of how the Bible redeems the human condition, offering the possibility of hope and freedom for all humankind. Indeed, the casting off of tyranny and human exploitation is one of the Bible's lasting legacies to the modern era and is one of the theological cornerstones of American values.

Antecedents of literary criticism are indeed quite ancient. The Pseudepigraphal writings may have been among the first proto-Midrashic efforts to explain the Bible in a more popular idiom; R. Ishmael himself stresses repeatedly how "the Torah speaks in the language of humankind."[130] Early Christian writers occasionally compared the philosophical genres of Greek and Latin literature with the various biblical narratives (e.g., Origen's treatment of Lot and his daughters[131]). Oftentimes, literary criticism can also draw analogies between the Bible and the literary world of Mesopotamia and its neighbors. Several scholars use a literary approach when comparing the covenantal imagery and language of Deuteronomy with the language found in the ANE documents known as the suzerain treaties.[132] Umberto Cassuto, Peter Craigie, Cyrus Gordon, Michael Fishbane and others have demonstrated numerous similarities when comparing Ugaritic poetry and the Bible in terms of their expressions, metaphors, parallelisms and meter, the reflective way in which they were written, the expressive manner in which they might have been read, and so on.

E. Canonical Criticism: Canonical criticism, a method which is eisegetical in nature, aims to situate the world of the reader into the pages of the sacred text. This approach has been championed largely by Brevard Childs, and more than other earlier methodologies, attempts to examine the biblical text from a theological and conceptual perspective—specifically from within the context of the faith community that enshrines its words. In one well-known quote, Childs exclaims, "Israel defined itself in terms of a book! The canon formed the decisive *Sitz im Leben* (cultural context) for the Jewish community's life, thus blurring the sociological evidences most sought after by the modern historian."[133] Since its significance is contingent upon the faith community, the meaning attached to the sacred words has always been fluid. More to the point, the Tanakh is not just an historical recollection of the past—it contains a message for the present day social situation. Every generation has utilized the Tanakh to address the issues of its day. As always, the history of the community and its interaction with the biblical text mediate the meaning of the Tanakh today.

From this writer's perspective, canonical criticism enjoys a decisive advantage over source criticism, for the goal is to expound upon the Scriptures in ways that are truly valid and contemporary. However, Childs concedes that this interpretive technique does not claim to be a substitute for historical-critical methods; rather, the aim is to enhance our appreciation of the text, enabling us to relate to it within a modern theological and philosophical context.

---

[130] See BT Berakhot 31b; BT Sanhedrin 64b; *Sifre* Numbers 112.

[131] *Origen against Celus*, c. 45.

[132] ANET, 199–266, 529–541; Meredith G. Kline, *Treaty of the Great King* (Grand Rapids, MI: Eerdmans, 1963); G. E. Mendenhall, *Law and Covenant in Israel and the Ancient Near East* (Pittsburg: Biblical Colloquium, 1955).

[133] Brevard Childs, *Introduction to the Old Testament as Scripture* (Philadelphia: Fortress, 1979), 78.

F. Narrative Criticism: Unlike the reductionistic approaches of the source critics, narrative criticism is more concerned with how the text works—by interpreting them as stories. Plot and characterization are considered more important than whether the text is historically reliable or not. In this pre-critical method, the biblical personalities' life experiences become the locus through which the reader encounters the Divine. Biblical narratives are essentially rooted in the existential drama of human life. Special attention is given to the elements in the text which have to do with plot, characterization and point of view. This methodology claims that the biblical stories serve as a mirror of the "real" world; as such, the narrative world has the potential to transform the inner life of its readers. To its credit, narrative analysis refuses to allow the text to become theologically and historically sterile.

G. Structuralism: Swiss linguist Ferdinand de Saussure (1857-1913) argues that language echoes certain universal patterns or structures of thought that condition the way we perceive the world and its pre-existing organizational structures. Structuralism aims to discover the interrelationships existing between the elements within a text (e.g., rhetoric, poetic devices, phonemes[134], cultural and linguistic expression) and the anthropological realities and deep structures that circumscribe these universal elements (e.g., its mythic beliefs)—all of which define and govern societal consciousness.[135]

Claude Lévi-Strauss is recognized for establishing structuralism in his study of anthropology, theorizing that all languages share a mental structure, which organize the great spectrum of human experience in terms of binary oppositions (e.g., light—dark, good—evil, life—death, male—female, sacred—profane, and so on). Moreover, these "deep structures" of consciousness exist in all cultures around the world and determine perceptions of reality. One might note that Lévi-Strauss's exposition of structuralism bears a striking similarity to C. G. Jung's theory of the archetype (which could ultimately be traced back to Plato's doctrine of the eternal forms) that permeate human consciousness and are present in every place and every epoch of history.[136] The same may also be said of Mircea Eliade and Joseph Campbell's

---

[134] A phoneme is a speech sound that distinguishes one word from the other, for example the sounds "d" and "t" in the words "bad" and "bat." A phoneme thus represents the smallest phonetic unit in human communication. In classical structuralist terms, the linguistic sign consists of a signifier and the signified, which function together in transmitting a creative, definitive, and univocal meaning, and thus prevents a sign from being improperly understood. The purpose of the interpretation is to semantically establish with a degree of exactitude, the meaning which the text originally wished to convey. The one true meaning of the text is authoritatively determined by the unchanging rules that dictate how a text ought to be read. Psychoanalysis and deconstructionism have challenged these assumptions, and maintain that the relationship between the signifier and the signified may be less fixed than previously imagined.

[135] See Claude Levi-Strauss, "The Structural Study of Myth," in *Structural Anthropology* (Garden City, NY: ET, 1963). Edmund Leach, *Genesis as Myth and Other Essays* (London: Jonathan Cape, 1969), 7-24.

[136] For an interesting comparison between C.G. Jung and Claude Lévi-Strauss, see E.d'Aquili, "The Influence of Jung on the Work of Claude Lévi-Strauss", *Journal of the History of the Behavioral Sciences,* 1975, vol. 11, 41-8;

approaches. Each of these thinkers explores the archetypal motifs that are present in all religions, mythologies, legends, art forms, social institutions, dreams, and fairy tales; their language is always metaphorical in nature. In addition, these structures of primitive thought remain embedded and viable in our conscious minds. Jung recalls:

> For years I have been observing and investigating the products of the unconscious in the widest sense of the word, namely dreams, fantasies, visions, and delusions of the insane. I have not been able to avoid recognizing certain regularities, that is, types. There are types of situations and types of figures that repeat themselves frequently and have a corresponding meaning. I therefore employ the term "motif" to designate these repetitions. Thus there are not only typical dreams but typical motifs in dreams. . . . [These] can be arranged under a series of archetypes, the chief of them being . . . the shadow, the wise old man, the child (including the child hero), the mother ("Primordial Mother" and "Earth Mother") as a supraordinate personality ("daemonic" because supraordinate), and her counterpart the maiden, and lastly the *anima* in man and the *animus* in woman.[137]

Myths especially disclose these deep structures of thought existing within the human mind. Although such stories will vary from culture to culture, they all share a mutual purpose: mediating between different patterns of social organization and representing meaningful ways of interpreting the world. By examining and comparing these ancient mythical structures and their impact upon present-day society, the reader is better able to grasp and understand how the myth's deeper structures possess a quality transcending time and circumstances, thus expressing a symbolic and timeless meaning that reveals the paradoxes existing at the heart of human societies.

As an alternative to finding meaning inherent in words or thoughts per se, structuralists examine the ways human beings have traditionally shaped their thoughts and expressions. In terms of biblical studies, structuralism is concerned with the received text in its present form; authorial intention and historical context are not necessarily the determiner of meaning, rather, meaning is defined by codes that are derived from the unconscious limitations of linguistic convention. Jacques Lacan applies many of the principles of structuralism to the field of psychoanalysis, as one Jungian scholar notes:

M.J. Chang, "Jung and Lévi-Strauss: Whose Unconscious?", *Mankind Quarterly,* 1984, vol. 25, 101-14. It is important to add that while there are similarities in both their theories, there are also important distinctions. Lévi-Strauss regards the collective and unconscious basis of myths as being determined by society, whereas Jung considers the collective unconscious as being genetically determined. Lévi-Strauss also credits the Russian formalist, Vladimir Propp, (*The Morphology of the Folk Tale,* circa 1922) with anticipating many of his own formulations on the structural analysis of myth. Propp also anticipates Campbell's study on the "monomythic" structure of *The Hero's Journey* by even many more years.

[137]C. G. Jung, "The Psychological Aspects of the Kore," ibid., par. 309.

> Lacan went beyond the proposition that the unconscious is a structure that lies beneath the conscious world; the unconscious itself is structured, like a language. This alone would suggest parallels with Jung, and Lacan is said to have tried to meet him. Lacan divides the phenomena with which psychoanalysis deals into three "orders": (1) the Symbolic, which structures the unconscious by a fundamental and universal set of laws; (2) the Imaginary, which approximates to psychological reality, inner world processes (such as fantasy, projection, and introjection), attitudes and images derived from, but not the equivalent of, external life. This is considered by Lacan to be our means of coping with the pain of separation (or rupture, as he calls it), the rupture of birth, of weaning, of growing up; (3) the Real, corresponding not only to external reality but also to what might be called the mystery of reality . . .[138]

In an effort to define the common psychological thread that unites various biblical texts, as well as to compare these with similar archetypical motifs expressed in other cultures, several structural ideas are utilized throughout this work. This approach will prove quite useful in deciphering the mythic content of Genesis 1-3. However, as important as the structural approach is, in terms of interpreting the deeper structure of the text, it represents merely just one way of interpreting the Tanakh.

H. Psychological Criticism: This new school of interpretation attempts to understand the psychological thought processes behind the literature, in general, and particularly within the Bible. This approach attempts to examine the relationship between the author and characters' conscious and unconscious psyches. Various insights gleaned from the writings of Sigmund Freud, Carl G. Jung, Carl Rogers, Ernest Becker, Joseph Campbell, Abraham Maslow, Erick Fromm, Jacques Lacan, and numerous other psychoanalytical philosophers—when applied to the subtle nuances and textual word-play of the biblical narrative—enhance and aid the process of fleshing out the multi-layered meanings of the stories, and the characters' complex personalities.

I. Theological Criticism: This neologism best describes the primary methodology utilized in this commentary, the aim of which is to take into account the theological underpinnings of the text as understood by various biblical interpreters and commentators over a span of 2300 years. Such an approach brings into focus the diverse theological, structural, mythical, psychological and metaphysical disciplines that have contributed toward a unique understanding of the biblical text and its spiritual relevance. Both written and spoken words convey symbolic and structural concepts, distinctive meanings, and subtle nuances; thus, a foundational knowledge of the various biblical languages provides valuable insight regarding the thought-processes of ancient Israel.

---

[138] Andrew Samuels, *Jung and the Post-Jungians* (London: Routledge, 1990), 40.

Similarly, this method of scriptural interpretation and exegetical application draws thought-provoking ideas from such comparative studies as structural criticism, archetypal psychology, ancient history, Semitic mythology, source criticism, comparative linguistics, intratextual biblical thought, traditional theology, psychoanalysis, anthropology, sociology, and postmodern philosophy—most of which are capable of illuminating and enhancing any established time period's appreciation of a biblical text. In contrast to other critical methods used to examine the Tanakh, theological criticism will not shy away from asking the difficult questions that challenge a faith community to confront, re-examine, and apply new meaning to a continuously evolving theology. This interpretive approach also recognizes the synchronic and diachronic characteristics influencing theological perspectives that ultimately derive from a wider social and cultural context.

Conclusion: Although there are indeed many other critical approaches, this work is not intended to provide a complete digest of all methodologies, but only those that pertain to the main substance of this commentary. However, one point can be made with a reasonable degree of certainty: no one scientific approach—including the historical-critical method—can claim to be totally adequate in the process of comprehending the biblical text, with all of its richness and complexities. Therefore, it is not surprising that other methods and approaches serve to explore and expound more profoundly the various hermeneutical aspects and dimensions worthy of a reader's attention. When studying a text like Genesis—or for that matter any great work of literature—it is crucial to keep in mind our own natural prejudices and beliefs that influence our comprehension of a classical text like the Bible. Maintaining a degree of self-consciousness regarding one's predisposition toward the understanding of the text, as well as the ever-shifting horizons of its interpretations, open the doorway to a more honest and potentially rewarding spiritual experience.

Gen 1:1-25
The Birth of Creation

1 In the beginning when God created[a] the heavens and the earth, 2 the earth was a
formless void and darkness covered the face of the deep, while a wind from God[b] swept
over the face of the waters. 3 Then God said, "Let there be light"; and there was light. 4
And God saw that the light was good; and God separated the light from the darkness. 5
God called the light Day, and the darkness he called Night. And there was evening and
there was morning, the first day.

6 And God said, "Let there be a dome in the midst of the waters, and let it separate the
waters from the waters." 7 So God made the dome and separated the waters that were
under the dome from the waters that were above the dome. And it was so. 8 God called
the dome Sky. And there was evening and there was morning, the second day.

---

[a] **Or *when God began to create* or *In the beginning God created***
[b] **Or *while the spirit of God* or *while a mighty wind***

[9] And God said, "Let the waters under the sky be gathered together into one place, and
let the dry land appear." And it was so. [10] God called the dry land Earth, and the waters
that were gathered together he called Seas. And God saw that it was good. [11] Then God
said, "Let the earth put forth vegetation: plants yielding seed, and fruit trees of every
kind on earth that bear fruit with the seed in it." And it was so. [12] The earth brought
forth vegetation: plants yielding seed of every kind, and trees of every kind bearing fruit
with the seed in it. And God saw that it was good. [13] And there was evening and there
was morning, the third day.

[14] And God said, "Let there be lights in the dome of the sky to separate the day from the
night; and let them be for signs and for seasons and for days and years, [15] and let them
be lights in the dome of the sky to give light upon the earth." And it was so. [16] God
made the two great lights—the greater light to rule the day and the lesser light to rule
the night—and the stars. [17] God set them in the dome of the sky to give light upon the
earth, [18] to rule over the day and over the night, and to separate the light from the
darkness. And God saw that it was good. [19] And there was evening and there was
morning, the fourth day.

[20] And God said, "Let the waters bring forth swarms of living creatures, and let birds fly
above the earth across the dome of the sky." [21] So God created the great sea monsters
and every living creature that moves, of every kind, with which the waters swarm, and
every winged bird of every kind. And God saw that it was good. [22] God blessed them,
saying, "Be fruitful and multiply and fill the waters in the seas, and let birds multiply on
the earth." [23] And there was evening and there was morning, the fifth day.

[24] And God said, "Let the earth bring forth living creatures of every kind: cattle and
creeping things and wild animals of the earth of every kind." And it was so. [25] God made
the wild animals of the earth of every kind, and the cattle of every kind, and everything
that creeps upon the ground of every kind. And God saw that it was good.

❖ *Why Is There Something Rather Than Nothing?*

The huge concentric waves of universal life are shoreless.
The starry sky that we study is but a partial appearance.
We grasp but a few meshes of the vast network of existence.

—VICTOR HUGO, *Essay on William Shakespeare*

We shall not cease from exploration,
and the end of all our exploring
will be to arrive where we started
and know the place for the first time.
—*T. S. ELIOT, Poetry, Plays and Prose*

"Lift up your eyes on high and see: Who has created these?" (Isaiah 40:26).[139] When the ancient biblical writers beheld the awe-inspiring complexity of the universe, they probably wondered: Why is there something rather than nothing? Why is there an order manifested in the cosmos? How did it get there when it did not have to be there? Who gave it when it did not have to be given? Why am I even capable of conceptually expressing this immense mystery? More specifically, why do I even exist? Philosopher Martin Heidegger rightly observed that this is the most basic question of philosophy.[140]

Albert Einstein poetically expressed the mystery of the universe:

> The most beautiful experience we can have is the mysterious. It is the fundamental emotion which stands at the cradle of true art and true science. Whoever does not know it and can no longer wonder, no longer marvel, is as good as dead, and his eyes are dimmed. It was the experience of mystery–even if mixed with fear—that engendered religion. A knowledge of the existence of something we cannot penetrate, our perceptions of the profoundest reason and the most radiant beauty, which only in their most primitive forms are accessible to our minds—it is this knowledge and this emotion that constitute true religiosity; in this sense, and in this alone, I am a deeply religious man.[141]

Today's cosmologists are asking the same great questions once raised by the theologians and philosophers since antiquity: *Why is there something rather than nothing?* Are the laws of nature unique or necessary? Are life and consciousness inevitable? If nothingness or non-being is the natural state of the universe, as philosopher Gottfried Wilhelm Leibnitz (1646-1716) inquired: Why is there a universe at all? Surely nothingness is easier and simpler to grasp than something! The fact that a universe does exist forces us to give an explanation as to why that is so; if nothing existed, there would be no reason to account for its existence. Leibnitz could only conclude: If the state of nothingness is more natural than existence,[142] then the existence

[139] For similar verses in the Tanakh that accentuate the awe, mystery and wonder of the universe, see Deut. 4:19; Isa. 44:24; 45:7; 48:13; 51:6; Jer. 10:11, 1; Job 31:26-28; Pss. 8:3-4; 19:1; 33:6; 102:25; 148:3-6; *et al.*

[140] M. Heidegger, *Introduction to Metaphysics,* R. Manheim (tr.) (Garden City, NY: Doubleday, 1961), 1-42.

[141] Albert Einstein, *The World as I See It* (New York: Philosophical Library, 1934), 15.

[142] For Leibnitz, it does not suffice to say that the world is just "there" or "given." The philosopher further elaborates on his position:

of the universe in all of its splendor and wonderment must be due to the will of God who brought all things into being.[143] For the ancient biblical writers, God, alone, is the sole reason for the existence of the universe—regardless of how it came into being. Aharon ben Eliahu presents this theological principle succinctly:

> We know that the existence of this world, which we shall presently investigate and examine, has come into being *ex nihilo* as regards both its quality and its quantity; that it is not capable of maintaining itself, but requires a force external to itself that has brought it into being *ex nihilo* and has endowed it with existence, perfecting its form and sustaining its being.[144]

Paul Davies argues in his ground-breaking book, *God and the New Physics* that "it may seem bizarre, but in my opinion science offers a surer path to God than religion."[145] For the atheist, it is necessary to take a teleological leap of faith, for there is no logical explanation as to why the universe *is* rather than *is not*. When viewed from this simple perspective, it is clear that the biblical writers wished to explain why the world exists as it presently does. The book of Genesis was based upon this axiomatic belief; an explanation of the duo narratives that make up the first chapters of the Genesis story will be soon discussed.

❖ *The First of Two Creation Stories*

There are two distinctive accounts in the opening chapters of Genesis 1:1–2:4a and Genesis 2:4b–25 that tell of the creation of the physical world and the creation of humanity. The first account depicts God as full of majesty and transcendence,

---

> So far I have spoken only of what goes on in the natural world; now I must move up to the metaphysical level, by making use of a great though not very widely used principle, which says that nothing comes about without a sufficient reason; i.e., that for any true proposition P, it is possible for someone who understands things well enough to give a sufficient reason why it the case that P rather than not P. Given that principle, the first question we can fairly ask is: Why is there something rather than nothing? After all, nothing is simpler and easier than something. Also, given that things have to exist, we must be able to give a reason why they have to exist as they are and not otherwise (*The Principle of Love and Grace Grounded on Reason*, [tr. Jonathan Bennett] http://www.earlymoderntexts.com/pdf/leibpng.pdf).

[143] Leibnitz concludes why God must be regarded as the only logical explanation for the universe:

> Now this sufficient reason for the existence of the universe cannot be found in the procession of contingent things. . . . So the sufficient reason, which needs no further reason, must be outside the procession of contingent things, and is found in a substance which is the cause of that procession and which is a necessary being containing the reason for His existence in Himself . . . and this final reason we call "God" (Leibniz, *Philosophical Writings* [tr. M. Morris and G.H.R. Parkinson; London, 1973], §7–8).

[144] *Introduction to Etz Hayyim* (translator and date of publication unknown).

[145] Paul Davies, *God and the New Physics* (New York: Simon and Schuster, 1983), ix.

omnipotence, and benevolence—a Creator whose ontological identity is a given. It eloquently depicts God defining the limits of the cosmos, world, and the succession of the seasons, as well as the holiness of the Sabbath, which becomes the touchstone for all the other biblical holidays. God's creativity is portrayed throughout the seven days to signify completeness and perfection, thus establishing the weekly pattern of six days of work and one day of rest for Israel as a terrestrial imitation of the divine "week."[146]

God's final royal action is to establish His image in His kingdom, the created universe. Humanity becomes God's representative on earth, charged with the responsibility of acting as stewards over His Creation. The seven-part dramatic formation of the universe also shows the reader that everything in the cosmos would not exist, were it not for the power and gratuitous nature of the Creator. The biblical account of the creation stories found in Genesis invites comparisons with other creation stories drawn from ancient Near Eastern mythology. To appreciate the unique message of Genesis, it is imperative that we familiarize ourselves with the various literary forms, symbolism, and archetypal imagery that form the bedrock of the ancient Mesopotamian cultural environment. While there are many similarities to be discovered in such a study, it is also important to pay attention to the differences. (See Excursus 5 for more detail regarding some of the theological and critical distinctions between these two versions)

❖ *Day One of Creation (Gen. 1-5)*

1:1 בְּרֵאשִׁית בָּרָא אֱלֹהִים אֵת הַשָּׁמַיִם וְאֵת הָאָרֶץ — **In the beginning when God created the heavens and the earth** — The first verse of Genesis contains seven words that allude to the importance of the Sabbath—the crown of Creation. From its inception, the Sabbath was set apart from all the other days of Creation to eventually be observed by all humankind (cf. Isa. 56:2-7) through witnessing Israel's devotion to the Sabbath (Exod. 31:16-17). Patterns of seven, representing full circle or completion of a cycle, figure prominently in other scriptural passages, e.g., the seven years of the Sabbatical year cycle (Lev. 25:1-7), and the seven Sabbatical Years of a Jubilee cycle (Lev. 28:5-13). The common thread, in each of these numerological parallels, emphasizes God as Originator and Preserver of the created order. This same sacred numerological template appears later in the sacrificial system, where blood is sprinkled upon the altar seven times (Lev. 16:14, 19), as well as in the laws regarding cultic purification rites involving bodily discharges and the counting of seven days toward the individual's re-integration into the cultic community and sanctum (Lev. 15:1-18; 25-28). Finally, this pattern is evident in the ceremonial purification of one who is recovering from leprosy as described in Leviticus 14:1–32. Each of these cases symbolizes the

[146] *Cf.* Philo, *On the Creation*, 30:89.

completeness of purification and the individual's return to an original state of purity—analogous to the innocence and purity that existed at the dawn of creation.

❖ *Creation as Kenosis*

בְּרֵאשִׁית בָּרָא אֱלֹהִים — **In the beginning when God created** — From a purely human perspective, the act of creation ought to be seen as an act of self-giving on the part of the Creator; Creation exists solely because of God's unconditional love (ἀγάπη = *agápē*). This divine love makes a space (kένωσις = a kenosis or "self-emptying"[147]) so that there may be room for the Other—namely, Creation. At the deepest metaphysical level imaginable, we surprisingly discover that God is also a relational Being; by creating the universe, God reveals He has a personal stake in the existence of Creation.[148]

God merely contemplates Creation as a possibility, and effortlessly, it comes into being. Unlike the creator of Plato's universe, who struggles mightily with the recalcitrant chaotic matter as he attempts to model it in the image of the ethereal Forms[149], the God of Israel creates chaotic matter with ease and grace. Unlike the pagan gods of antiquity—who themselves were the by-products of the primal chaos—God's reality transcends the boundaries of the temporal and spatial universe. His ontology and existence are totally independent of Creation. God is, in the most literal sense, wholly Other than Creation.

Occasionally misunderstandings occur when foreign concepts and terminology are grafted onto the text from other ancient texts or mythologies that have no bearing whatsoever on a given verse (see notes on Gen. 1:2). For all of its elegant simplicity, the biblical writer does not appear to be concerned with such theological conjectures or speculations. Yet, in the opening verse the biblical narrator makes a straight-forward theological claim—God created *everything*[150] and this is why we find the use

---

[147] The TDNT (Vol. 3, 661) defines Kένωσις as "to make empty," or "to deprive of content or possession." This term is sometimes theologically used as the ancient Christian equivalent to the Lurianic concept of the *tsimtsum* (cf. Excursus 11). Curiously, the first aorist third person singular form ἐκένωσεν (Phil. 2:7) is the sole reference to kenosis in the NT. However, this term appears frequently in the early patristic literature (cf. G. W. H. Lampe, *A Patristic Greek Lexicon,* 744-46).

[148] For a more expansive treatment of this theme, see Excursuses 4, 6, 10.

[149] Plato, *Timaeus* 5. 27-30.

[150] The Targum Neofiti and certain rabbinic Midrashic texts support such a reading. Neofiti, for example, renders בָּרָא as שכלל "completed," signifying that God completed the creation of the heavens and the earth on the first day (cf. Gen. Rabbah 10:4 and 1:14).

of a merism[151] appearing in the opening passage.[152] Why begin the first book of the Torah with such a revolutionary introduction? Philosopher Susan Handelman explains:

> With the deceptively simple words "In the beginning God created the heavens and the earth," the Hebrew Bible begins. In fact, however, this statement was (long before Derrida) a supreme challenge to the entire classical tradition of Western metaphysics: to assert that matter was not eternal, that the world had a temporal origin, that substance came into being through divine fiat, indeed through divine speech ("And God said: 'Let there be . . . '") threatened the foundations of Greek ontology.[153]

The Judaic creation story certainly has other broad implications that are no less challenging to classical Greek thought. If creation has an ultimate purpose and direction a τέλος (*telos*="completion" or "consummation"), then we, as God's creation, cannot self-consciously live our lives as if we lack ultimate meaning and spiritual direction. In a God-centered existence, there is responsibility and accountability that each of us—by virtue of being made in the likeness of our Creator—must give. Briefly stated, the entire cosmic order is (1) grounded in the will of the Divine, (2) established since the beginning of time, (3) founded in the ethical order that governs human existence.

❖ *Wisdom's Role in Creation*

Sometime during the fifth or fourth century B.C.E., the Wisdom/Sophia tradition began to infiltrate Jewish religious sensibilities. At first it was introduced as a series of epigrams containing proverbial wisdom; however, in theological terms, the notion of Sophia came to personify God's own wisdom. Over the centuries, this new concept influenced generations of Jewish thinkers and mystics—especially during the medieval period when Jewish thought renewed its historic love affair with Greek wisdom. Abraham Ibn Ezra (c. 1089–1164) asserts that the creation of heaven and earth is preceded by the mystical appearance of Wisdom who is sometimes called רֵאשִׁית (*rēʾšîṯ* = "beginning") (See Prov. 3:19; Ps. 104:24).

The Kabbalists would later view Wisdom as the seminal seed and geometric point from which all creation emanates.[154] Their ideas were indirectly shaped by the early

---

[151] The term *merism* denotes a contrasting set of opposites that conveys the idea of totality.

[152] See the commentary on Genesis 1:1, *"Heaven and Earth" as Totality* later in this chapter concerning the function and purpose of merism.

[153] Susan Handelman, *Slayers of Moses* (Albany, NY: SUNY, 1982), 27.

[154] The difference between the Hellenistic and the Kabbalistic view of Wisdom is that the former views Wisdom as a feminine principle, whereas the latter views it as essentially a masculine principle.

Judaic and Hellenistic texts which conceived of Wisdom poetically as being the "firstborn daughter of God" and "Mother of Creation." According to the Jewish mystical imagination, wisdom truly personifies the "thought" of God that is ever-present in the universe. In light of this reason, Wisdom is plainly presented here as the first of God's creatures and as God's collaborator in the creation of all that was yet to be created, and it is Her presence that now suffuses the entire created order. In the book of Proverbs, "Lady Wisdom" is portrayed as saying:

> The LORD created me at the beginning of his work,
> the first of his acts of long ago.
> Ages ago I was set up,
> at the first, before the beginning of the earth ...
> When he established the heavens,
> I was there, when he drew a circle on the face of the deep.
> Prov. 8:22–27

A similar thought is also poetically expressed in the *Wisdom of Sirach* (Ecclesiasticus):

> Wisdom praises herself, and tells of her glory in the midst of her people:
> "Before the ages, in the beginning,
> He created me,
> and for all the ages I shall not cease to be."
> —Sir. 24:1–9

Both readings constitute an intrabiblical commentary on the original story of creation as depicted in Genesis. Wisdom acts as the foundation of the cosmos, and as the sole witness to God's Creation of the world. In the later Midrashim, the wisdom principle came to be redefined and personified as the Torah itself. "God looked into the Torah and created the world" (Gen. Rabbah 1:1).[155] Literary scholar Susan Handelman observes, "In the rabbinic imagination, the Torah is not an artifact of nature, a product of the universe; the universe, on the contrary, is the product of the Torah."[156]

[155] The Jerusalem Targum paraphrases בְּרֵאשִׁית as בחכמה "With [or 'In'] wisdom God created . . ." Compare this text with the Targum Neofiti's interpretive rendering (מלקדמין בחכמה ברא דיי), while the Targum of Onkelos translates the opening salvo as בְּקַדמִין בְּרָא יוי ("At first God created . . ."). Likewise the Midrash also alludes to this same theme: "God looked into the Torah and created the world" (Gen. Rabbah 1:1). Wisdom acts as the foundation of the cosmos, serving as the sole witness to God's Creation of the world.

[156] Susan Handelman, *Slayers of Moses, op. cit.* 37.

❖ *"From My Flesh, I Behold God"*
—Job 19:26

Another Interpretive View: In the beginning when God created – Some Jewish mystics and exegetes explain that רֵאשִׁית (*rē'šîṯ*), derives from ראשׁ (*ro'š*) signifying "head," i.e., the seat of conscious thought. However, Husserl and Lévinas argue that consciousness is always aware of *something* as opposed to *nothing*.[157] Creation, as it exists in the mind of God is always a divine and innate actuality.[158] It would seem that the biblical narrator intentionally uses this word to convey the notion that we all exist as a thought within the consciousness of the Divine. Therefore, Creation has no other existence outside of the Divine Consciousness, which gives Creation its form and sense of ontological being.[159] However, according to British theologian Keith Ward, here lies the supreme irony: "The cosmos not only springs from a Supreme Consciousness: it is destined to produce beings that will relate in knowledge and in cooperative action to that Consciousness. . . . The cosmos must be such that it will produce beings of awareness, intention, a sense of transcendence, and the possibility of conscious union with God."[160] Ward's interpretation adds new meaning to the passage, "From my flesh I see God" (Job 19:26). By contemplatively gazing into the inner processes of our souls, we may come to the novel recognition that we perceive only the outer manifestation and presence of a deeper hidden reality that we can not only sense—but can also personally relate to. Indeed, this innate sharing and

---

[157] Lévinas explains, "The world seems to be indispensible to a consciousness which is always a consciousness of something." *Theory of Intuition in Husserl's Phenomenology:* Second Edition (SPEP) (Evanston, IL: Northwestern University Press; 2 edition, 1995), 150.

[158] According Aristotle (who interestingly defers to Plato's doctrine of the ethereal forms in his *De Anima* 3:5), argues that just as the sun illuminates all physical world and makes awareness possible, so too, there is a supraphysical cause that is the source of all human consciousness that stimulates and engenders thought. Aristotle feels compelled to admit the source of human reason cannot be derived from human biology per se, but must stem from an external source of intellect (*nous thyrathen*) that produces this immortal consciousness existing within humankind, termed the *Active Intellect* by such theologians as Philo (in his doctrine of the Logos), Maimonides, and Gersonides.

[159] This idea finds ample expression in the writings of Lurianic Kabbalah as articulated by R. Sheneir Zalman of Liadi (*Tanya* Part II) and his chief disciple R. Aaron Horowitz of Starosseljie (1766-1828). Cf. Louis Jacobs, *The Seeker of Unity: The Life and Works of Aaron of Starosselje* [New York: Basic Books, 1966]. George Berkeley (1685–1753) also argues that what we define as "reality" is nothing more than a perception on the part of the perceiver. Thus, Berkeley's principle *esse est percipi* ("to be is to be perceived") boldly resolves that there is no existence of matter independent of perception. Berkeley denies that material substance exists apart from its perceptibility. It is the Divine consciousness that calls all sensible things into existence, which gives these ideas the ontological existence that they have for us. See George Berkeley, *Principles of Human Knowledge / Three Dialogues Between Hylas and Philonous,* ed. by Roger Woolhouse (New York: Penguin, 1988).

[160] Keith Ward, *The Big Questions in Science and Religion* (West Conshohocken, PA: Templeton Foundation Press, 2008), 247.

purposeful commingling of the human and Divine Consciousness constitute one of the greatest miracles of all Creation.

❖ *Creation as Novelty*

בָּרָא – **created** – The verb בָּרָא (*bārāʾ* = "created") connotes God's absolute effortless creativity. In the Tanakh, this term is used exclusively with respect to Divine creativity, for human creativity is limited by the materials it has access to—this is not so with God. This distinction may also explain why many medieval rabbinic thinkers like Saadia[161], Maimonides[162], Ramban[163], Abarbanel[164], Seforno[165] and others believe this verb alludes to the concept of *creatio ex nihilo* (creation from "nothing") since only God can create from the non-existent. Elsewhere in the Tanakh, בָּרָא introduces something surprisingly novel, wonderful, and awe-inspiring.[166] For a theological exposition on the importance of novelty, see Excursus 8a and 8e.

It appears that Ibn Ezra is less convinced and contends that the linguistic evidence does not support such an interpretation.[167] The verb בָּרָא may also mean to fashion something out of already existing materials (e.g., the creation of man, whose body came from the dust of the earth, and whose soul issued forth from God's breath).[168] Ibn

---

161 See *Emunot v De'ot* 1:1 and his Arabic translation of the Bible, where he takes Gen. 1:1 as an independent sentence.

162 Maimonides, *Guide* 2:30 and 3:10.

163 Ramban insists that בָּרָא indeed implies creation from nothing, "The Blessed Holy One created everything out of complete nothingness. There is no other word in the Hebraic language for bringing existence out of non-existence other than *bara*. And there is nothing under the sun or above it to generate a beginning out of nothingness. He alone brought the cosmos into being—out of complete and absolute non-being. At its nascent state of existence, this ethereal matter only possessed the potential to assume form, which the Greeks referred to as ὕλη (*hyle*). After creating *hylic* matter He did not create anything; God merely formed and arranged the rest of creation from out of this ethereal substance."

164 *Abarbanel's Commentary* on Genesis 1:1.

165 See *Seforno's Commentary* on Genesis 1:1.

166 Gen. 1:21; Exod. 34:10; Num. 16:30; Psa. 104:30; Isa. 48:7, et al.

167 See Excursus 8: *Further Reflections on Creatio ex Nihilo* for discussion.

168 Ibn Ezra's second interpretation is remarkably similar to the Septuagint's use of ἐποίησεν (*epoiesen*) a word that is reminiscent of Plato's description of God as ὁποιῶν, "the creator" (see Plato, *Timaeus*, 76 c). The term ποιέω (*poieo*) connotes aesthetic making, broadly designates all craftsmanship, and more narrowly refers to the making of poems, plays, pictures, or sculptures. This usage might seem to mitigate against the belief in a *creatio ex nihilo*; otherwise the Septuagint would have used κτίζω (*ktizō* = "create"), which implies "bringing into

Ezra's comments could also suggest the universe was constructed out of pre-existent matter. However, pre-existent matter need not imply a dualism; it may imply that this ethereal substance is "pre-eternal" only in relationship to the world but not in relationship to God. In conclusion, Ibn Ezra theorizes that the primary meaning of בָּרָא means "to cut down" or "set a boundary."[169] S.R. Driver supports Ibn Ezra's perspective and adds that the verb בָּרָא (*bārā'*) is related to the Arabic *barāy* "to fashion" or "shape by cutting." Nevertheless, Driver admits that "in its simple conjugation, it refers exclusively to God and denotes the production of something fundamentally new, by the exercise of a sovereign originative power, altogether transcending that possessed by man."[170]

Some modern Hebraists contend that בָּרָא is related to the South Arabic word "*br*" meaning "to build," or "to bring forth," or "give birth to" and is probably related to the Aramaic word בַּר (*bar*), "child"[171] (as in the modern "Bar Mitzvah" = "a son of a precept"), or "son" (e.g., Ezek. 28:13,15). Creativity is expressed in the way we give birth to something from the very depths of our innermost being.[172] Often, when the Scriptures speak about Creation, it involves "giving birth" to a new reality.[173]

In the end, there is no clear consensus as to the meaning or origin of this important term. The theological principle of *creatio ex nihilo* is not contingent upon the verb ברא. Light was created only when God spoke the words, "Let there be light" (v. 3); there is not even the slightest hint that God formed the light out of the primordial chaos and this theological approach has sometimes been called *creatio per verbum*—"creation from the word." Such a concept reflects a more precise mythopoetic understanding concerning the nature of reality as a creative expression of the Divine (see notes on Genesis 1:3; 1:27 and Excursus 8).

---

being." On the other hand, the Septuagint often uses both expressions synonymously. See H. R. Balz and G. Schneider's *Exegetical Dictionary of the New Testament* (Grand Rapids, MI: Eerdmans, 1990), Vol. 2:325.

[169] Josh. 17:15; Ezek. 23:17.

[170] BDB 135:1; S. R. Driver, *The Book of Genesis*, 3.

[171] HALOT: 153.

[172] In one of the most audacious metaphors found anywhere in the Tanakh, the prophet Isaiah likens the Divine pathos to a woman struggling to give birth: "For a long time I have held my peace, I have kept still and restrained myself; now I will cry out like a woman in labor, I will gasp and pant" (Isaiah 42:14).

[173] This idea can also be seen in the prophetic writings of Isaiah (Isa. 65:17–18). See HALOT: 153.

❖ *The Meaning of "Elohim"*

אֱלֹהִים – God – Why is God's name in Genesis 1:1 אֱלֹהִים (*ʾĕlōhîm*) written in the plural? Many Christian readers presume there are intimations of the Trinity, but this view has been rejected not only by rabbinic scholars, but by Christian exegetes as well[174] as having no linguistic basis whatsoever in the Scriptures. In Biblical Hebrew, as in other Semitic languages, an inferior speaks to a superior in the plural. Such a form of address is commonly referred to as "plural of majesty" (*a pluralis excellentis*). This custom still persists even in modern countries like Britain, where the "royal we" is still commonly used. The significance of the plural form in the Hebrew usage suggests a plentitude of power and majesty or of intensification, i.e., the superlative "God of gods," "the absolute highest God," "the quintessence of all divine powers," and the "fullness of being." Put in different terms, Biblical Hebrew often uses the plural form of a word when expressing an abstract noun.[175] As such, they tend to be more often masculine, but feminine nouns can also be expressed in the plural.[176] Biblical Hebrew does, however, have a singular form for God אֱלוֹהַ (*ʾĕlôah*) that is employed in the poetical passages of the Tanakh (appearing 59 times)[177], albeit the plural of majesty is more often generally used.

Another Interpretive View: אֱלֹהִים – God – The etymology of אֱלֹהִים (*ʾĕlōhîm*) most likely derives from אֵל (*ʾēl*), meaning "strength," or "power"[178] as in יֶשׁ־לְאֵל יָדִי (*yeš-ləʾēl*

---

[174] John Calvin observes: "Moses has it *Elohim*, a noun of the plural number. Whence the inference is drawn, that the three Persons of the Godhead are here noted; but since, as a proof of so great a matter, it appears to me to have little solidity, I will not insist upon the word; but rather caution readers to beware of violent glosses of this kind . . . (*Commentaries on the First Book of Moses, Called Genesis*, trans. John King [Grand Rapids, MI: Eerdmans, 1948], 70–71).

[175] Examples include: בְּתוּלִים (*bĕtûlîm*) denotes "virginity," as opposed to the singular word for בְּתוּלָה (*bĕtûlā* ="virgin"); דּוֹדִים (*dôdîm* = "erotic love") as opposed to דּוֹד (*dôd* = "beloved"); מַיִם (*mayîm*= water [Biblical Hebrew has no singular form for "water"]); זָקֵן (*zāqēn* = "an elder"), as opposed to זְקֻנִים (*zĕqunim* = "old age"); נַעַר (*naʿar* ="a youth") as opposed to נְעוּרִים (*nĕûrîm*), and so on. Rashi and Kimchi note that verbs denoting God's actions are always written in the singular and never in the plural.

[176] Feminine abstract nouns are more commonly expressed in the singular, e.g., אֱמוּנָה ("faithfulness"); גְּבוּרָה ("strength"); אֱמֶת ("truth"); but can be expressed in the plural as well, e.g., תַּהְפֻּכוֹת ("perversity"); בִּינוֹת ("understanding"); חָכְמוֹת ("wisdom"); and so on.

[177] Deut. 32:15; 2 Chr. 32:15; Neh. 9:17; Job 3:4, 23; 4:9, 17; 5:17; 6:4, 8f; 9:13; 10:2; 11:5ff; 12:4, 6; 15:8; 16:20f; 19:6, 21, 26; 21:9, 19; 22:12, 26; 24:12; 27:3, 8, 10; 29:2, 4; 31:2, 6; 33:12, 26; 35:10; 36:2; 37:15, 22; 39:17; 40:2; Pss. 18:32; 50:22; 114:7; 139:19; Prov. 30:5; Isa. 44:8; Dan. 11:37ff; Hab. 3:3.

[178] As noted by the Moroccan Karaite philologist David ben Avraham al-Fisi (*ca.* mid 10th century) in *Kitab*

yāḏî laʿăśôṯ) "it is within my power" (Gen. 31:29)[179] and is a common Semitic word. A derived meaning from אֵל is אֵלוֹן (*ʾēlôn* = "oak tree"), since its wood is extremely strong; and the אֵלָה (*āʾēlāh* = "pastachio tree") which is also known for its hard wood.

It is no linguistic accident that one Hebrew name for God, אֱלֹהִים, also means "Judge." The connection between these two meanings is obvious: the judges of primitive and early societies were their most powerful warriors; at their command, their foot-soldiers carried out their will. The Creator of natural law is also the Giver of the moral law. God defines the moral order that serves as the basis for ethical values and for self-discipline. Indeed it is God to whom all inhabitants of the world are ultimately accountable.[180]

Paul Tillich's theological insights are especially relevant here. Tillich considers God the creative "ground of all being" that underlies all of nature and beyond. "He stands against the world, in so far as the world stands against him, and He stands for the world, thereby causing it to stand *for* Him. This mutual freedom from each other and for each other is the only meaningful sense in which 'supra' in supra-naturalism can be used. Only in this sense can we speak of 'transcendent' with respect to the relation of God and world. To call God transcendent in this sense does not mean that one must establish a 'superworld' of divine objects. It does mean that, within itself, the finite world points beyond itself."[181]

❖ *"Heaven and Earth" as Totality*

אֵת הַשָּׁמַיִם וְאֵת הָאָרֶץ – **the heavens and the earth** – The expression "the heavens and the earth" constitute a pair of contrasting opposites, which include everything in between; i.e., the entire cosmos.[182] This literary device, better known to biblical scholars as *merism* (from the Greek μέρος (*meros* = "part")[183] is used whenever a writer or a speaker wishes to describe a contrasting set of opposites conveying the idea

---

Jami' Al-Alfaz Solomon Skoss ed. Vol. 1 (New Haven, CN: Vol. 20 Yale Oriental Researches, 1936), 97. Ramban arrived at a similar conclusion in his commentary on Genesis 1:1.

179 Cf. Exod. 15:15; Deut. 28:32; 2 Kgs. 24:15; Eze. 17:13; 32:21; Mic. 2:1 Prov. 3:27 Job 41:17; Neh. 9:17; et. al.

180 Cf. Rabbi N. T. Berlin's commentary *HaEmek Davar* on Gen. 1:1.

181 Paul Tillich, *Systematic Theology*, Vol. II (Chicago: University of Chicago, 1957), 7.

182 The expression "heaven and earth" connotes the entire universe not just in Biblical Hebrew, but also in Egyptian, Akkadian, and Ugaritic texts as well (see M. Ottosson's article in the *TDOT* 1:389–91).

183 Since ancient times, the philosophical relationship between a "part versus the whole," or "the many and the one" fascinated and stimulated the growth of Western thought.

of totality—covering everything that is subsumed by its two constituent parts.[184] Some Jewish exegetes and mystics sometimes homiletically interpret "heaven" as meaning the spiritual universe, while "earth" connotes everything that exists in the physical universe.[185] By stating that God created *everything,* the biblical narrator can begin to delineate *how* the creation of this world took place.[186]

It has often been asked by commentators throughout history: Why does the Torah not mention that God created the waters? Rashi answers this question by pointing out that the Torah is not written in chronological order[187] and such a view is consistent with how he translates the first verse of Genesis 1:1 (see Excursus 5).[188] In light of the above, there is considerable merit to Rashi's position. On the other hand, Jon D. Levenson (Harvard University) deduces from this verse a different interpretation. Like Gersonides[189] (1288-

---

[184] A well known English merism is the phrase, "lock, stock, and barrel," which is a common way of expressing "everything."

[185] See Genesis Rabbah 1:10; Zohar 1:29-b30a; Torah Temimah on Gen. 1:1, note 16; R. Sheneir Zalman's *Tanya*, Part 3:5; 4:7.

[186] This point is also stressed in both Rashbam and in Aharon ben Eliahu's *Keter Torah* commentary to 1:1. For other Karaite parallels, see Hacham Ali ben Suleiman's *Judeao-Arabic Commentary on the Pentateuch*, who cites the views of Hacham Yosef ben Noach (ca. 780 C.E.), and Hacham Aharon ben Yehoshua (ca. 9th century).

[187] For other scriptural illustrations, see Rashi's commentary on: Exod. 4:20; 18:13; 31:18; Lev. 8:2; Num. 9:1; 1 Kgs. 3:3; Isa. 1:1; Eze. 1:3; 29:17; Psa. 72:20; Neh. 1:1. From Rashi's words, one would have expected to see this principle mentioned several times in the Talmud, and yet, it is recorded only once in BT Pesachim 6b, "R. Menasia b. Tahlifa said in Rab's name: 'This proves that there is no chronological order in the Torah.'"

[188] Various other scriptural passages provide a variance of possibilities as to the sequence of events delineated in the creation story. For example, Job 38:1–11 contains the following order of Creation: the earth, its cornerstone, the morning stars, the sons of God, the doors of the sea, clouds, and darkness. Proverbs 5:22–28 presents another order: wisdom, the beginning of the earth, depths, wells, water, mountains, hills, land, fields, dust, heaven, skies, fountains, and the sea. These two additional biblical readings could constitute intrabiblical commentary on the original story, although Pentateuchal source criticism suggests that they originate in entirely different traditions concerning the Creation. Either way, they show that the precise order of Creation was not a cause for great alarm in the rabbinic community, and did not suffer from the kind of dogmatic rigidity seen in the days of the early Church.

[189] Seymour Feldman explains why Gersonides regards the chaotic waters of the universe as the pre-eternal substratum from which the world was gradually formed:

> The heavenly bodies are described as being created "in the waters", and once created these bodies separate the "upper waters" from the "lower waters" (Gen. 1:6-8). Now what are these waters within or from which the heavenly bodies were created? This is nothing other than "the matter that doesn't keep its shape," the primordial formless stuff out of which the physical world was made, the astronomical importance of which was discussed by Gersonides in Book 5, part 2, chapter 2. Unlike the heavenly bodies this watery stuff has no intrinsic shape or form. In creating the universe God literally *in-formed* parts of this matter, thus producing the heavenly and earthly bodies, the former causally prior and superior in substance to the latter. As if unconsciously sensing the novelty of these ideas, Gersonides cites a number of biblical and rabbinic texts to support this reading of the story of

1344), Levenson assumes that the waters of creation are primordial, and therefore, were *not* created by God.[190]

However, with regard to the biblical writer's use of merism, both Gersonides and Levenson neglect to consider that the term אֶרֶץ does not necessarily refer exclusively to "dry land," but to the earth as a whole; i.e., the land together with all its watery regions.[191] When the Torah speaks of אֶרֶץ יִשְׂרָאֵל (*ʾéreṣ yiśrāʾēl* = "Land of Israel"), this expression includes not just the dry land of the country but also its rivers, lakes, seas and various waterways. When the Torah wishes to contrast land with water, it will use either the term אֲדָמָה or (*ʾădāmāʰ* = "earth" or "ground") or יַבָּשָׁה (*yāḇšāʰ* = "dry land"). The noun יַבָּשָׁה is specifically used in contrast to water, e.g., water bodies that become dry (as seen in the splitting of the Sea of Reeds). Likewise, אֲדָמָה is land that is cultivated by water and farming. In addition, when the biblical author writes "the Spirit [or "mighty wind"] of God swept over the face of the waters," it is obvious that he was speaking only of the earthly waters and not the heavenly waters—as subscribed to by many ancient mythologies.

Finally, the theological implications of Gersonides and Levenson's position are significant; if God's power is ontologically limited by the existence of chaos, then God's power is also ontologically limited by a reality—besides God—that He cannot completely control, resulting in dualism. A remark by the Russian theologian Nicolai Berdyaev (1874-1948) cuts to the heart of the problem; the real issue at stake is the matter of Divine freedom, which in turn becomes the template for human freedom. Berdyaev adds that "Creation means transition from *non-being* to *being* through a free act. . . . *Creation presupposes freedom and arises out of freedom*"[192] (see Excursus 8).

---

the creation of the *raqi'a* (Levi ben Gershom and Seymour Feldman, *The Wars of the Lord,* Vol. 3 [Philadelphia: JPS, 1984], 210).

[190] Jon D. Levenson, *Creation and the Persistence of Evil: The Jewish Drama of Divine Omnipotence* (San Francisco: Harper & Row, 1988), 5.

[191] The TWOT writes: "The first two meanings listed above are far and away the most crucial. That is, *ʾéreṣ* designates either (a)"earth" in a cosmological sense or (b)"land" in the sense of a specific territorial designation, primarily the land of Israel" (TWOT: 167). See also TDOT Vol. 1, 388-405.

[192] Charles Hartshorne and William L. Reese (ed.), *Philosophers Speak of God* (Chicago: University of Chicago Press, 1953), 291. The 18th century Jewish philosopher S. L. Steinheim seems to have anticipated Berdyaev's penetrating insight: "There is a concentric connection between the ethical and the physical in *the doctrine of the world's creation.* In God is freedom to act or let happen; the creation or noncreation is the act that impresses and expresses itself similarly in man (in the image of God) and, in addition, on account of his egotistical nature, can shape itself with respect to his fellow creatures for good or evil. The verdict on whether there is or is not freedom depends on the revealed doctrine of creation. And this doctrine impressed the seal of truth upon our deeply felt, inextinguishable consciousness of freedom through the incomparable promise, even as God imprinted on the works of His hand the sign of authenticity" Joshua O. Haberman, *Philosopher of Revelation: The Life and Thought of S. L. Steinheim* (Philadelphia: JPS, 1990), 223.

❖ *The Real Meaning of T̲ōhû and B̲ōhû*

1:2 וְהָאָרֶץ הָיְתָה תֹהוּ וָבֹהוּ – the earth was a formless void – the 10th century Jewish grammarian and theologian, Saadia Gaon, astutely observes that neither the existence of wind or water precede the creation of the heavens and the earth; rather, both these forces are only subsequent to the earth's creation, which consists of the elements earth, water, and wind.[193] He further contends that intratextual passages from the Tanakh also bear this point out: "For lo, the one who forms the mountains, creates the wind. . ." (Amos 4:13); and "The sea is his, for he made it, and the dry land, which his hands have formed" (Psa. 95:5); and finally, "Praise him, you highest heavens, and you waters above the heavens! Let them praise the name of the LORD, for he commanded and they were created" (Ps. 148:4-5).[194] Saadia's point supports what we just mentioned in our notes on Genesis 1:1.

Scholars often assume the biblical idea of תֹהוּ וָבֹהוּ is the Hebraic equivalent of the Greek notion of "chaos" (from the Greek Χάος). However, this translation only begs the issue: What exactly is meant by the Greek term "chaos"? How was chaos originally used in the ancient Greek texts? Did its definition change over time, and if it did, how? Historically, chaos first appears in Hesiod's *Theogony* (ca. 850 B.C.E.); its original meaning simply meant "chasm" or "gaping void."[195] For Hesiod, Chaos is the progenitor of the primeval deities: *Gaia* (Earth), *Tartarus*, *Erebus* (Darkness), and *Nyx* (Night). From Chaos emerged the worlds of the gods, the earth, and humankind.[196] When Hesiod wrote his work, he drew upon earlier mythical sources; his essential view of Chaos was unquestionably critical, for the Titans personified the surging and undisciplined passion of the earth's primordial condition, which ultimately had to be violently defeated by Zeus, the god responsible for establishing the stability and universality of the Olympian order.

---

[193] Rashbam arrives at a similar conclusion on Genesis 1:1.

[194] Saadia, *Emunot VeDeot* 1:1.

[195] For a similar usage in other classical texts, see Aristophanes, *Aves* 1218; *Bacchylides* 5, 27.

[196] First came the Chasm; and then broad-breasted Earth, secure seat for ever
of all immortals who occupy the peak of snowy Olympus;
the misty Tartara in a remote recess of the broad-pathed
earth; and Eros, the most handsome among the immortal gods,
dissolver of flesh, who overcomes the reason and purpose
in the breasts of all gods and men . . .

Hesiod's Theogony, trans. M. L. West (New York: Oxford, 1988), 6.

For the Roman poet Ovid, chaos is a confused and formless mass from which the Maker of the Cosmos fabricated the ordered universe.[197] As later Hellenistic thought developed, chaos eventually became specifically associated with the notion of primordial matter, e.g., either with water[198], or with primordial time[199] and the netherworld.[200] In the Gnostic[201] literature, chaos takes on a more philosophical meaning, and is bound up with darkness, shadow, and non-being.[202] The presence of chaos is dispelled only by the power of "Pistis Sophia," who is the "Spirit of Wisdom."[203]

---

[197] In Ovid's poetic compendium of mythology known as the *Metamorphosis*, the poet describes the state of chaos that existed before the earth assumed its present form:

> Before the ocean and the earth appeared—
> before the skies had overspread them all—
> the face of Nature in a vast expanse
> was naught but Chaos uniformly waste.
> It was a rude and undeveloped mass,
> that nothing made except a ponderous weight;
> and all discordant elements confused,
> were there congested in a shapeless heap.
>
> P. Ovidius Naso, *Metamorphoses,* Book 1, line 5

[198] The Stoics, deriving the word from *χὲω,* defined Chaos as the elemental Water (school on Apoll. Rhod. i. 498).

[199] Cf. *Papyri Graecae Magicae*, ed. K. Preisendanz IV 2535f.) viewed chaos as the air between heaven and earth (e.g. Aristophanes, Aves 1218; Bacchylides 5, 27), and the (whole or part of the) netherworld (e.g., Ps-Plato, Axiochus 371e).

[200] *Pseudo-Plato Axiochus* 371e.

[201] The term γνῶσις (*gnosis* = "knowledge") refers to an intuitive apprehension of esoteric and spiritual truths pertaining to divine mysteries. Many of these doctrines derive from Hellenistic, pagan, Jewish, and early Christian sects; their doctrines stress the importance of a firsthand knowledge and experience of God. The salvation of the human race depends upon awakening this spiritual capacity within the human soul.

[202] According to *The Nag Hammadi* writings, chaos is a pre-eternal force to the world:

> Seeing that everybody, gods of the world and mankind, says that nothing existed prior to chaos, I in distinction to them shall demonstrate that they are all mistaken, because they are not acquainted with the origin of chaos, nor with its root. Here is the demonstration. How well it suits all men, on the subject of chaos, to say that it is a kind of darkness! But in fact it comes from a shadow, which has been called by the name darkness. And the shadow comes from a product that has existed since the beginning. It is, moreover, clear that it (viz., the product) existed before chaos came into being, and that the latter is posterior to the first product (J. M. Robinson and R. Smith, *The Nag Hammadi Library in English,* 4th rev. ed. [Leiden; New York: E.J. Brill, 1996], 172).

[203] In Gnostic thought "to be in exile" is to be unredeemed; such a state of ignorance keeps the soul apart from its true Source—the Creator. In these and other texts, knowledge thus becomes the necessary key to

The mythical association of Greek mythology does not fit with the biblical cosmogony of the universe. The תֹהוּ וָבֹהוּ of Genesis 1:2 hardly resembles the Greek idea of "chaos," or for that matter, the Latin "Nihil." Cultural and mythical concepts do not always translate from one language to the other, nor do they always have an equivalent parallel. The biblical writer does not say the world was a disorderly chaos and confused mass, but simply that it was not yet ready to be inhabited by humankind. At the beginning of creation, the earth was nothing more than a barren wasteland—a world desolate of life.[204]

According to the biblical imagination, YHWH is Creator and Author of good and evil, יוֹצֵר אוֹר וּבוֹרֵא חֹשֶׁךְ עֹשֶׂה שָׁלוֹם וּבוֹרֵא רָע אֲנִי יְהוָה עֹשֶׂה כָל־אֵלֶּה "I form the light, and create the darkness, I make well-being and create woe; I, the LORD, do all these things" (Isa. 45:7). This verse is a complete rejection of the Zoroastrian belief that the universe is governed by two opposing principles, the power of light and the power of darkness.[205] In Isaiah's monistic vision, there is no duality whatsoever. YHWH is the sole Creator of opposites—there is no ontological state that exists apart from God's sovereignty—even evil and chaos serve God's creative purpose. Lastly, the Book of Job also echoes this same sentiment, גַּם אֶת־הַטּוֹב נְקַבֵּל מֵאֵת הָאֱלֹהִים וְאֶת־הָרָע לֹא נְקַבֵּל "Shall we accept good from God, and not trouble?" (Job 2:10). The destructive forces alluded to in Isaiah 45:7 all fulfill an important purpose in the overall grand scheme of history and nature.

In Arabic *tīh* can mean "wilderness" and "empty place." The semantic fields of other Semitic languages seem to bear this out as well. In Ugaritic *thw* denotes a

---

personal salvation and liberation from the earthly shackles that binds its consciousness.

[204] Onkelos's definition is more precise than Rashi and translates תֹהוּ (*tōhû*) as צַדְיָא (*ṣādyâ* = "desolation"); this reading better describes the original condition of the earth. The term בֹהוּ may be related to the Arabic cognate *bahiya* "was empty." This noun בֹהוּ appears only in Isaiah 34:11 and Jeremiah 4:23, where it implies a world that is a formless wasteland bereft of light and life itself. In each instance בֹהוּappears, it is in context with תֹהוּ and both expressions signifies "empty wilderness." See Gur Aryeh's exposition of Rashi, who understands Rashi's explanation as "bewilderment and void" while R. E. Mizrachi (*ca*, 16th century) thinks תֹהוּ וָבֹהוּ should be read as an adverbial phrase, i.e., "astonishingly empty." Both these rabbinic explanations are questionable for the reasons mentioned above.

[205] Cf. F. Cumont, *Mysteries of Mithra* (Whitefish, MT: Kessinger Publishing, Facsimile of 1910 Ed. edition repr.1997); J. Hinnells, ed., Mithraic Studies: Proceedings of the First International Congress of Mithraic Studies, Volumes One and Two (Manchester, Manchester University Press, 1975); M. J Vermaseren, *Mithras, the Secret God* (New York: Barnes and Nobles, 1963).

"wasteland," or "wilderness." This pattern occurs elsewhere in the Tanakh; every instance where either תֹהוּ (*tōhû*) or בֹהוּ (*ḇōhû*) appears it almost always refers to a barren tract of land.[206] This land may have been barren to begin with (as seen here in the creation story), or else it might have become a wasteland as a result of war, natural disaster, or as an act of divine retribution (Isa. 34:11). A biblical text must first be properly understood in terms of its language and context before advancing any kind of theological or metaphysical speculative interpretation. When exegesis fails to adhere to this simple principle, the speculative reading being advanced lacks a solid foundation.

Among the medieval Christian exegetes, Martin Luther appears to have a far better grasp of the nature of תֹהוּ וָבֹהוּ than did many of his postmodern counterparts:

> A wider significance attaches to the Hebrew words תֹהוּ (*tōhû*) and בֹהוּ than can be reproduced in translation. Yet they are used frequently in the Holy Scripture. תֹהוּ is employed in the sense of "nothing," so that the earth is a בֹהוּ, which so far as it itself is concerned, is empty, where there are no roads, no separate localities, no hills, no valleys, no grass, no herbs, no animals, and no men. Such indeed was the first appearance of the unfinished earth; for since mire was mixed with the water, it was not possible to observe the distinctive marks which are observable now, after it has been finished.
>
> Thus Isaiah, in the chapter where he threatens the earth with desolation, says (34:11): "There will be stretched over it the line תֹהוּ and the plummet בֹהוּ," i.e., the earth will be laid waste to such an extent that neither human beings nor beasts of burden will remain, and the houses will be laid waste and everything thrown into confusion and disorder. This is how Jerusalem was later laid waste by the Romans, and Rome by the Goths, to such an extent that the traces of the very famous ancient city cannot be pointed out. You now see the earth standing out above the waters, the heaven adorned with stars, the fields with trees, the cities with houses, etc.; but when all these are removed and thrown together into a shapeless mass—what then results Moses calls תֹהוּ and בֹהוּ.[207]

One last thought: תֹהוּ וָבֹהוּ is the Torah's first example of how the biblical writer(s) takes pleasure in expressing alliteration[208] and rhyming. Later in this chapter we find

---

[206] Cf. Isa. 24:10; 34:11; 45:18; 45:19; Jer. 4:23.

[207] M. Luther *Luther's works, Vol. 1*: "*Lectures on Genesis: Chapters 1-5*" Trans. J. J. Pelikan, H. C. Oswald & H. T. Lehmann (St. Louis: Concordia Publishing House 1999, c1958), 6-8. The last portion of Luther's comment "the heaven adorned with stars" does not apply here, since the verse is speaking solely of the earth being a "barren wasteland."

[208] An alliterative is the repetition of the same sounds or of the same kinds of sounds at the beginning of

another similar type of alliteration: פְּרוּ וּרְבוּ וּמִלְאוּ (*pɔrû ûrɔḇû ûmilʾû*), "Be fruitful, and multiply, and fill . . ." (Gen. 1:22).[209] Indeed, there are many other examples of this type of rhythmic pattern scattered throughout the Pentateuch and the Tanakh.[210]

❖ *The Obsession with Chaos*

The biblical narrator illustrates God's total mastery over all the polarities that are present within the universe. Cosmos and chaos, order and confusion, life and death, good and evil, the sacred and the profane, are all harmoniously subsumed under the majestic power of אֱלֹהִים (*ʾĕlōhîm* = "God"), Who establishes the balance. The role of humanity is to protect the harmony of the universe from the forces of chaos that are ever present within us. Remarkably, ever since the dawn of human existence, humanity has always had a keen intuition that beneath the orderly structure of the world is "an abyss of formlessness"[211] which could engulf all of Creation at any given moment.

Primal peoples since the beginning of recorded history were always aware of the distinct possibility that the world—and everything in it—could dissolve into the great void of chaos. Although God created chaos and structured it into a cosmos, humanity has the power to unravel creation. For the first time in history, we now live in an era where a return to the formless is a very real ontological possibility. The United States and Russia have the capability of destroying the world eighteen times over. Many other nations are now involved in a nuclear arms race that will eventually threaten

words or in stressed syllables that are typical of tongue-twisters. Famous examples include, "How much wood would the woodchuck chuck if the woodchuck could chuck wood?" or "She sells seashells by the seashore . . ." and "Peter Piper picked a peck of pickled peppers . . ."

[209] Marvin Wilson calls attention to an insight by historian of Near Eastern cultures and languages, Cyrus Herzl Gordon (1908-2001), who fondly refers to this particular type of alliteration as possessing a "boogie-woogie" construction. The reader will recall that boogie-woogie is a style of blues music characterized by an up-tempo rhythm, a repeated melodic pattern in the bass, and a series of improvised variations in the treble.

[210] Other examples include: נָע וָנָד (*nāʿ wānāḏ*) "a fugitive and a stranger" (Gen. 4:12); בֶּרַע מֶלֶךְ סְדֹם וְאֶת־בִּרְשַׁע מֶלֶךְ (*eṯ-béraʿ mélek̲ sɔḏōm wɔʾeṯ-biršaʿ*) "made war on King Bera of Sodom, King Birsha of Gomorrah" (Gen. 14:2); later on in Genesis we find a more complex alliteration: גָּד גְּדוּד יְגוּדֶנּוּ וְהוּא יָגֻד עָקֵב (*gāḏ gɔḏûḏ yɔḡûḏénnû wɔhûʾ yāḡūḏ ʿāqēḇ*) "As for Gad, raiders shall raid him, But he shall raid *at* their heels" (Gen. 49:19); מֵי הַמָּרִים הַמְאָרְרִים (mê hammārîm hamɔʾārărîm) "the water of bitterness that brings a curse" (Numb. 5:18); וַנֵּפֶן וַנִּסַּע (*wannēpen wannissaʿ*) "Then we turned, and took our journey" Deut. 2:1); אֲרַמִּי אֹבֵד אָבִי (*ʾărammî ʾōḇēḏ ʾāḇî*) "My father was a fugitive Aramean" (Deut. 26:5).

[211] Gerhard Von Rad, *Genesis, A Commentary* (Philadelphia: Westminster Press, 1972), 51.

human existence and civilization as we now know it. There exists a fragile line separating life from death that must not be violated. Humanity's dangerous fascination with death and nonbeing must not bring the world to an untimely demise.

וְחֹשֶׁךְ עַל־פְּנֵי תְהוֹם – **and darkness covered the face of the deep** – There is an old theological debate as to whether darkness is simply the absence of light, as taught in Platonic philosophy, or whether it is a new creation.[212] Darkness and light are relative terms to humans who see through the eye, but from the perspective of the Divine, darkness is as transparent to God as light (Ps. 139:12). Modern physicists consider darkness as the total absence of energy—*not so for God.*

The Septuagint translates the term תְהוֹם (*tĕhôm* = "the deep") as ἀβύσσου (*abyssos* = "abyss"). According to the ancient Semitic cosmogony, the abyss is the primordial ocean. Many modern bible scholars see in the verse a vague allusion to the Babylonian creation epic, *Enuma elish,* where Tiâmat, the fearsome goddess of the primeval oceans and the mother of the gods, is killed by the young storm god, Marduk. After defeating Tiâmat, Marduk cleaves her body into two halves; the upper portion he uses to fashion the sky, and the lower half he sets in place as the earth. In dramatic contrast, the Torah makes it clear that God did not have to contend with "rival deities" in order to create an orderly world.[213] By the time this story was finally written down, the biblical narrator utilized many Semitic loanwords which found their way into the Hebrew lexicon deriving from common Semitic usage.[214] Hebrew words are more often characterized by their use and context and not by their etymology.[215] In every place where תְהוֹם appears in the Tanakh, it never denotes anything else but waters—whether they be primeval, subterranean, oceanic, or rivers.

וְרוּחַ אֱלֹהִים – **while a wind from God** — Older bible translations[216] defined רוּחַ אֱלֹהִים

---

[212] See, for example, the verse in Isaiah: "I form light and create darkness" (Isa. 45:7).

[213] Evidence of a great cosmic conflict between YHWH and the forces of chaos, as represented by the sea, can be discerned in Job 26:12-13. Intimations within the Torah can be read in between the lines at the splitting of the Sea of Reeds, where Pharaoh and his army met defeat. For further literature on this topic, see W. White's "Tiamat," in *ZEPB*, V, 744-45. For the critical view, cf. H. G. May, "Some Cosmic Connotations of *Mayim Rabbim* 'Many Waters'," *JBL* 74:9-21.

[214] HALOT: 1690.

[215] As noted by J. Barr, *The Semantics of Biblical Language* (Oxford: Oxford University Press, 1961), ch. 6.

[216] The NRSV translation has its antecedents in Targum Onkelos, BT Hagigah 12a, Rashbam, Bechor Shor, Saadia and Ibn Ezra's commentary.

(*rûaḥ ʾĕlōhîm*) as "the spirit of God." Both these readings are plausible.[217] The term רוּחַ (*rûaḥ*) connotes a moving power that is both mysteriously intangible and unseen; hence, "mighty wind" is an apt metaphor. When read in this context, *ʾĕlōhîm* is used not as a noun but rather as a descriptive adjective connoting a sense of that which is "powerful" and "awesome,"[218] or suggesting a quality akin to that of a mighty tempest. This may also be the meaning of Genesis 2:4, where the Divine Name יְהוָה אֱלֹהִים (YHWH [*ʾăḏōnāy*] *ʾĕlōhîm*) are linked so as to suggest the meaning, "Almighty God", for only an Almighty God can create a world (see notes to 2:4).

One might further add that רוּחַ is the life-breath and life-principle that transforms the chaos of creation into a cosmos. In theological terms, רוּחַ alludes to the most profound dimension that converts, liberates, and sublimates human existence. Johann Peter Lange (1802-1884) is partial to the older translation, "The breath is the life-unity and life-motion of the physical creature; the wind is the unity and life-motion of the earth; the spirit is the unity and life-motion of the life proper to which it belongs; 'the spirit of God' is the unity and life-motion of the creative divine activity. It is not a 'wind of God' to which the language here primarily relates."[219] However, it seems that both translations are equally worthy of consideration.

❖ *A Hellenistic Reading of the Text*

Another Interpretive View: And the Spirit of God – Older bible translations like the KJV follow the Septuagint's rendering πνεῦμα θεοῦ *(pneuma Theo* = "Spirit of God")—an opinion that most modern bible scholars reject on the basis of the text's contextual meaning. Obviously this translation differs considerably from the more recent rendering which prefers "a mighty wind." However, one 19th century scholar gives nothing less than a "spirited" defense of the older translation.

> *Ruach Elohim* is not a breath of wind caused by God (*Theodoret*, etc), for the verb does not suit this meaning, but the creative Spirit of God, the principle of all life (Ps. xxxiii. 6, civ. 30), which worked upon the formless, lifeless mass, separating, quickening, and

[217] As noted in the Vulgate and Rashi. However, the Targum Neofiti prefers: ורוח דרחמין "the Spirit of Mercy." For other Christian interpretations, cf. Augustine, *Confessions* 13:4; Ambrose *FC* 42:32-33; Jerome, *Homilies* 10; Ephrem the Syrian, *Commentary on Genesis ESOO* 1:117.

[218] Other examples of this kind of usage in the Tanakh include the Hittites speaking of Abraham as a נְשִׂיא אֱלֹהִים "mighty prince" (Gen. 23:6), Leah's description of her struggle as נַפְתּוּלֵי אֱלֹהִים: "mighty wrestlings" (Gen. 30:8), or קֹלֹת אֱלֹהִים "the mighty thunderings" of the Sinai theophany (Exod. 9:28).

[219] J. P. Lange, P. Schaff, T. Lewis and A. Gosman, *Genesis, or, the First Book of Moses—Together with a General Theological and Homiletical Introduction to the Old Testament*, 5th rev. ed. (New York: Charles Scribner, 1884), 164.

preparing the living forms, which were called into being by the creative words that followed.[220]

Several feminist theologians also prefer the older translation—albeit for different reasons. An assertion can be made that despite the seemingly ubiquitous amount of masculine metaphors that exist within the world of the Tanakh, there is much activity that is ascribed to God that is admittedly maternal: giving birth to and nurturing children.[221] Yet it is important to keep in mind that God is never directly addressed as "mother," or in feminine terms. According to some thinkers, רוּחַ is a feminine noun and this would imply that the "Spirit" of God ought to be viewed not in masculine terminology, i.e., not as "He," but as "She."[222] While it is true that רוּחַ is usually used as a feminine noun, sometimes it can connote the male gender as well. For instance, in Numbers 11:31, רוּחַ is masculine, as well as in Isaiah 57:16.

But more importantly, it is specious to exegetically assume that the gender of a word invariably indicates something about the sexual identity of the object being named. They are not one and the same. For example: the Hebrew word for "foot" רֶגֶל (*rā̆gel*) is feminine; יָד (*yad*) "hand" is also feminine; עַיִן (*áyin*) "eye" is feminine, אֹזֶן (*ʾózen*) "ear" is also feminine. Curiously, "penis" שָׁפְכָה (*šāp̄kāh*) is feminine while the name for "womb" רֶחֶם (*réḥem*) is masculine; the word for "breasts" שָׁדַיִם (*šāḏáyim*) is also a masculine noun. In the Hebrew language, gender is relevant only to grammar and not to sexuality; no logical reason is given as to why inanimate objects are engendered. On the semantic level, a distinction is made between masculine and feminine. Indeed, there are many more examples that can be cited, but the point of these illustrations is to show that one cannot theologically extrapolate the sexual ideation of the Divine on the basis of the gendered word. More important than linguistic shades of meaning—*God is not bound by gender.*

---

[220] C. F. Keil & F. Delitzsch, *Commentary on the Old Testament,* Vol. 1, 16 (Peabody, MA: reprinted by Hendrickson, 2001).

[221] Isa. 42:14; 49:15; 54:10; Hos. 11:3-4, et al.

[222] Jerome writes in his commentary to Isaiah that the Holy Spirit is the designated representation of the feminine principle and is further supported by the Hebrew word for "spirit." To quote Jerome, the author of the Latin Vulgate: "In the Gospel of the Hebrews that the Nazarenes read it says, 'Just now my mother, the Holy Spirit, took me.' Now no one should be offended by this, because 'spirit' in Hebrew is feminine, while in our language [Latin] it is masculine and in Greek it is neuter. In divinity, however, there is no gender" (*Jerome's Commentary on Isaiah 11*). Feminist theologians may note Jerome's last point. Among modern thinkers, the tendency to equate *ruach* with the feminine continues to attract new adherents. Lutheran theologian Jürgen Moltmann stresses this point in *God in Creation: A New Theology of Creation and the Spirit of God*, "And because, to the Hebrew mind, the Spirit (*ruach*) is feminine, this divine life of creation must be apprehended through feminine metaphors" (New York: Harper Collins, 1993), 10; cf. *The Spirit of Life: A Universal Affirmation* (Minneapolis: Augsburg Fortress Publishers, 1992), 42; See Barbara Newman, *Sister of Wisdom: St. Hildegard's Theology of the Feminine* (Berkeley: University of California Press University, 1987), 190.

❖ *An Existential Interpretation of Genesis 1:2*

Another Interpretive View: And the Spirit of God (KJV) – One of the most interesting, existential insights on this passage comes from the 18th century American philosopher and theologian, Jonathan Edwards, whose interpretation captures a seminal thought that resonates throughout the Tanakh; namely, human beings cannot live in an impersonal universe, without yielding to the forces of despair and meaninglessness. This concept is reminiscent of the famous passage from Macbeth (V.v):

> To the last syllable of recorded time,
> And all our yesterdays have lighted fools
> The way to dusty death. Out, out, brief candle!
> Life's but a walking shadow, a poor player
> That struts and frets his hour upon the stage
> And then is heard no more: it is a tale
> Told by an idiot, full of sound and fury,
> Signifying nothing.

Each human being depends on the Spirit of the Divine for the capacity to live with a sense of transcendence, purpose and fulfillment. Presbyterian theologian Walter Brueggemann adds, "The lives of many people are chaotic. . . . In such a context, the text claims that even the chaos of our historical life can be claimed by God for his grand purposes."[223] However, Edwards warns that an abyss of non-being threatens to consume our souls once we become forgetful or detached from the Source of our life and vitality, which recreates us a new:

> "And the earth was without form and void." *Tohu, Bohu,* which last are words signifying vanity and emptiness. Thus God was pleased in the first state of the creation to show what the creature is in itself; that in itself it is wholly empty and vain, that its fullness or goodness is not in itself, but in him, and in the communications of his Spirit, animating, quickening, adorning, replenishing, and blessing all things. The emptiness and vanity here spoken of, is set in opposition to that goodness spoken of afterwards. Through the incubation of the Spirit of God, (as the word translated "moved" signifies) the Spirit of God is here represented as giving form, and life, and perfection to this empty, void, and unformed mass, as a dove that sits infuses life, and brings to form and perfection the unformed mass of the egg. Thus the fullness of the creature is from God's Spirit. If God withdraws from the creature, it immediately becomes empty and void of all good. The creature as it is in itself is a vessel, and has a capacity, but is empty; but that which fills that emptiness is the Spirit of God.[224]

---

[223] Water Brueggemann, *Genesis* (Atlanta: John Knox Press, 1982), 29.

[224] Tyron Edwards ed., *The Works of Jonathan Edwards,* Volume Two, *Notes on the Bible* (repr. Carlisle, PA: Banner of Truth, 1984), 1636-1637.

❖ *Intimations of the Cosmic Egg?*

מְרַחֶפֶת עַל־פְּנֵי הַמָּיִם – swept over the face of the waters – The "mighty wind of God" swept over the deep waters of the unformed and surging oceans. What distinguishes the biblical depiction from the Babylonian creation myth, *Enuma elish*, is the total absence of conflict. In the biblical creation story, both the untamed forces of darkness and the watery abyss obediently yield to the power of God's wind. The archetype of water is inextricably related to the formation of human life; ancient cultures across the world have long recognized that water is related to the processes that create and sustain life, e.g., dew, rain, and storms.

The verb "swept" (מְרַחֶפֶת = *mərahépet*) from the root רָחַף (*rāḥap*) implies dynamic and energetic movement, just as a mother bird actively warms her young so as to facilitate their growth.[225] God's wind is sometimes likened to a mother bird that lovingly hovers over her nest seeking to create and nurture life from the depths of the dark, shadowy chaos beneath.[226] On a deeper interpretive level, the imagery of a mother bird incubating her young suggests the world may have been generated from what was mythically regarded as the "cosmic egg." The cosmic egg symbolizes a state of primordial perfection from which proceeds the created order and without which the world could never develop. The "wind" or "Spirit" of God is what will transform this cosmic egg into the multiplicity of the phenomenal world through a process of separation and differentiation. The mother-hen/egg relationship also points to an essential organic unity and cosmogonistic relationship between God and creation. This belief has its roots in nearly all cultures across the world.[227]

---

[225] The verb מְרַחֶפֶת (*mərahépet*) is in its *piel* construction (connoting intense activity) and may be translated here as "brooded." "In place of what is written in our codices as *moved*, the Hebrew has *mĕraḥepet*, which we can render as 'was brooding over' or 'was keeping warm', in the likeness of a bird giving life to its eggs with warmth" (*Jerome's Hebrew Questions on Genesis* [Robert Hayward; Clarendon Press, 1995], 30). E.A. Speiser notes that the same root occurs in Ugaritic, meaning "to be in movement." If we apply that idea to our passage, what emerges is a picture of God's spirit, or a wind from God, "sweeping," "flying," "moving" over the waters, giving the universe the shape it would eventually have. Gerhard Von Rad explains that מְרַחֶפֶת is not to be translated as "brood," but, according to Deut. 32:11 and Jer. 23:9, the verb appears to have the meaning of "vibrate," "tremble," "move," and "stir" (E. Speiser, *op. cit.*, 49).

[226] As in Deut. 32:11; Isa. 31:5.

[227] The symbolism of the cosmic egg may be found in various cultures around the world, including ancient Greece (which subscribed to the Orphic tradition), and from South Africa to China. In India, this concept, known as the *brahmanda* ("egg of Brahma"), the Absolute (Brahman) becomes increasingly more personal and oriented to the world with each subsequent creation.

❖ *From Primal Speech to Revelation*

1:3 וַיֹּאמֶר אֱלֹהִים – Then God said – The Semitic root *ʾāmar* in Old Southern Arabic means "to order" (the Modern Arabic word "Emir" – a prince, chieftain, or governor is derived from this ancient Semitic usage); in Akkadian and Ugaritic, it means "to see" or "make visible," or "be visible"; in Tigre, the root *ʾāmar* means "make known" or "recognize." Thus, the semantic evolution of this word gave rise to "speak"; i.e., to manifest a thought in a manner that is plain and clear.[228] Each of these semantic fields of meanings is also present in the verb וַיֹּאמֶר (*wayyṓʾmer*). The verb אָמַר (*ʾāmar* "say") could mean that God may have "spoken" or "communicated" or "made known" His Presence to the world. [229] Regardless how we translate the verb, Creation becomes known and visible for the first time. Hebraic verbs are action oriented and are full of dynamic movement. God is never described as a static entity; therefore, God's Presence is typically evocative in the Tanakh—in sharp contrast with the Greek notion of οὐσία (*ousia* = "eternal being")—articulated by Aristotle and Plotinus, which is passive and in a state of constant repose. The time factor is irrelevant here to speculate over. When God "communicated" or "spoke" is impossible to say; indeed, this process of creative manifestation may have taken aeons to accomplish.

Since the earliest of times when the Bible was first translated into Greek and later into Aramaic, intellectual Jews wondered about the biblical use of metaphors that describe God as possessing anthropomorphic qualities. Early rabbinic exegetes wondered: Did God, indeed "speak"? Undoubtedly, nearly all the early translators of the Septuagint and Targum were sensitive to this particular problem—along with its sundry theological implications.[230] Jewish thinkers like Philo of Alexandria, Maimonides and

---

[228] HALOT: 68; TDOT: 1:328.

[229] One might wonder what is the distinction between אָמַר (*ʾāmar* = "say") and the root דִּבֵּר (*dibber* = "speak"), especially since in English the terms are sometimes used synonymously. The verb אָמַר simply means to convey a message; how that message is conveyed will vary depending upon the medium of communication. It might be through a letter or action (e.g., "John is hitting Peter in the face, what does this action say or speak about John"?); written words, or hand signs; or it might include verbal communication. When דִּבֵּר is used, it always conveys verbal communication; this may take the form of two parties exchanging words to one another in a conversation; it may also refer to anything that is heard in person or in a dream or in a visionary experience.

[230] Many scholars argue that a Gnostic influence is evident in much of the Targumic literature. Targum Neofiti's rendering of the verse here reveals this influence: ואמר ממרא דיי – it is the *Memra* (the "Divine Word") that creates the world—and *not God*. The *Memra* functions as an intermediary between God and humankind. Thus, it is the *Memra* that creates the world, appears to Adam, Abraham, and Moses. The *Memra* wrestles with Jacob, and later redeems Israel from Egypt, and works miracles (for a complete list of references where this pattern occurs in Targum Onkelos, see Onkelos's translation of Gen. 3:8ff; 9:16; 21:20, 22; 26:28; 28:20f; 31:49f; 39:2f, 21; 48:21; Exod. 10:10; 16:3, 8; 17:1; 18:19; 19:17; 24:2; Lev. 8:35; 24:12; Num. 3:16, 39, 51; 4:37, 41, 45, 49; 9:8, 18ff, 23; 10:13; 11:20; 13:3; 14:41, 43; 22:18; 23:21; 24:13; 33:2, 38; 36:5; Deut. 1:26, 43;

Gersonides (as well as Augustine, Pseudo-Dionysus, and Aquinas among the Christian thinkers of the medieval era) tried to soften and redefine the nuances of such colorful language when describing God. It is essential to keep in mind that the biblical writers never had a problem using such human-esque imagery. Indeed, quite the opposite! The more tangible the theophany or spiritual experience of the patriarchs and the Israelites was to the Hebraic mind, the more daring became the metaphors. As the Sages claim, "The Torah speaks in the language of people." [231]

Some patristic and rabbinic scholars understood this verb as a figure of speech, which simply meant that God "willed,"[232] i.e., this act of Creation was expressed ineffably.[233] Theodoret explains the text somewhat differently: "He was not commanding anyone to create but summoning things not in existence, His will constituting a command. Scripture says, 'God made everything He wished' (Psa. 115:3). If however, He also used speech in creation, it was clearly not for the benefit of the lifeless elements but for the invisible powers, so that they might learn that, at His bidding, the non-existent came into existence."[234]

Alternatively, Ibn Ezra insists that the wording of this verse is meant to be read analogically. The notion of God "speaking" is meant to convey that creation required no exertion on God's part. Using the word *speaking,* the biblical narrator likens God's word to a monarch whose orders are immediately carried out by his eager servants—as opposed to a dictatorial power who forces his will upon his reluctant subjects. The absence of tension, as indicated by the ancient narrator, is a striking contrast to the Babylonian *Chaoskampf*[235] motif championed by Gunkel and his modern-day supporters. The peacefulness and grace, when contrasted to the violent struggle of

---

2:7; 4:33; 5:5, 25f; 9:23; 18:16; 34:5. With respect to the Targum Neofiti's use of the *Memra*, see Neofiti's translation on Gen. 1:3ff, 8, 10f, 16, 20, 22; 15:6; Lev. 9:4; Deut. 11:21; 12:14; 18:21. However, the notion of the Divine Word creating the heavens is not completely without antecedent in the Psalms, "By the LORD'S word the heavens were made; and all their hosts by the breath of His mouth" (Psa. 33:6).

[231] BT Berakhot 31b; *Sifre* Numbers 112.

[232] Augustine (*On the Literal Interpretation of Genesis* 5:19); Saadia Gaon (cited by Ibn Ezra), Maimonides (*Guide* 1:65), Ramban, Hizkuni, and R. Elijah ben Solomon Zalman (1720-1797), who is better known as the famous "Vilna Gaon" ("Genius of Vilna").

[233] Cf. Genesis 8:21; 17:17; 27:41; 1 Sam. 1:13; 27:1, Est. 4:6; Jer. 5:24; Hos. 7:2. Even without the word לִבּוֹ (*libbô*) it can mean "to think" or "deliberate" (Gen. 26:9; 44:28).

[234] *The Questions on the Octateuch: On Genesis and Exodus, op. cit.*, 27.

[235] By the term *Chaoskampf*, I am referring to a battle between the creator-god and the powers of the primordial chaos that is commonly found in many of the Semitic creation myths. H. Gunkel believed that the biblical writers also subscribed to this mythic motif.

warring deities, evokes a harmonious image of creation that can serve as a paradigm for our age.

Before Creation, there was silence. The words, "Let there be . . ." introduce a novel communication perforating the silence that precedes all creative existence. Ancient civilizations believed their gods were endowed with absolute power. The word of an Oriental or Mesopotamian ruler was absolute; his word could mean life and death to his subjects (see Excursus 8d). Ancient man naturally projected these same qualities to the Creator. Eliade points out creation myths always stress how the Sacred creates through an abundance of power and ability.

> Every creation is a divine work and hence an eruption of the sacred, it, at the same time represents an eruption of creative energy into the world. Every creation springs from abundance. The gods create out of an excess of power, an overflow of energy. Creation is accomplished by a surplus of ontological substance. This is why the myth, which narrates this sacred ontophany, this victorious manifestation of a plentitude of being, becomes the paradigmatic model for all human activities. For it alone reveals the *real*, the superabundant, and the effectual.[236]

The concept of *creatio per verbum* (creation from speech) is one of the most important teachings found in early and subsequent Kabbalistic writings: a theological perspective that seems to be experiencing a revival among contemporary Christian theologians and biblical scholars (see also Excurses 9). Some Jewish mystics point out that the spoken word is but an externalized expression of thought; the word actualizes a concept that until now has remained only a potentiality. The analogy of the universe existing as "God's Word" suggests that the entire created order originates as but one expression of the Divine Mind. Just as one word or sentence or conversation cannot exhaust the human capacity for self-expression, neither does the Divine Word exhaust God's creative ability to express Creation in a plenitude of ways. In one of the earliest Kabbalistic texts known as the *Sefer Yetsira (The Book of Creation)*, the ancient author envisions the universe as the "speech of God." Every minutiae, every particle of existence becomes likened to the letters of the alphabet coming together to form ideas and syntax—a virtual story about Creation. Centuries before Heraclitus introduced his doctrine of the Logos, ancient Israelite poets believed that the song of Creation could be discerned when we *listen* with spiritual attentiveness and mindfulness, as the Psalmist relates:

> The heavens are telling the glory of God;
> and the firmament proclaims his handiwork.
> Day to day pours forth speech,
> and night to night declares knowledge.
> There is no speech, nor are there words;

---

[236] Mircea Eliade, *The Sacred and the Profane, op. cit.*, 98.

their voice is not heard;
yet their voice goes out through all the earth,
and their words to the end of the world.

—Psalm 19:1-4

One of the oldest rabbinical prayers dating back to the early medieval era is the *Perek Shira* (*The Song of Creation*). This little book recounts how every one of God's creative works—from the macro to the micro—extols God as Creator. Creation's song derives from each entity's awareness of how God animates Creation every moment of its existence. This work was obviously inspired from the Psalm 19:1-6; 136:7-9; 148, *et al.* The Navajo Indians appear to have a similar understanding of the universe which they regard as an expression of thought and speech; the creation of the world is chanted into existence (this view is remarkably similar to the Vedas in the Hindu tradition). Philosopher Ben-Ami Scharfstein cites the Navajo scholar Gary Witherspoon (*Language and Art in the Navajo Universe)*:

> In the Navajo view, thought and speech cannot be separated, for speech is no more than the outer form of thought, which it extends and reinforces. 'This reinforcement reaches its peak after four repetitions, and therefore a request made four times cannot be easily denied.' Ritual comprises the ways in which speech imposes the form of thought on whatever needs to be created or restored.
>
> In the Navajo metaphysical order, knowledge always comes first. The essential reality or inner form of thought—knowledge—is listed as a primordial element of the universe. And as knowledge is the inner form of thought, thought is the inner form or reality of speech. Therefore, the hierarchy of reality is: knowledge, thought, speech, inner forms, and natural phenomena of all kinds, that is, all processes and beings. In contrast to Buddhists and others, the Navajo do not assume that language falsifies reality. "The idea that it might do so goes directly contrary to the Navajo scheme of things. This world, they believe, was transformed from knowledge, organized in thought, patterned in language, and realized in speech (symbolic action). The symbol was not created as a means of representing reality; on the contrary, reality was created or transformed as a manifestation of symbolic form. In the Navajo view of the world, language is not a mirror of reality; reality is a mirror of language." [237]

❖ *A Mystical Intimation Concerning Light*

יְהִי אוֹר וַיְהִי־אוֹר – **"Let there be light" and there was light** — In Psalm 104, God is depicted as being עֹטֶה־אוֹר כַּשַּׂלְמָה "robed in light as with a cloak." The imagery is

---

[237]Ben-Ami Scharfstein, *Ineffability: The Failure of Words in Philosophy and Religion* (Albany, NY: State University of New York Press 1993), 62.

rich with mystical symbolism.[238] Just as clothes reveal the role one plays in life, so too does God's light reveal His role as Creator. With respect to a person's clothing, some clothes are representational (e.g., the attire of a king or dignitary), while others are performance-related (e.g., actors, athletes), symbolic (e.g., the garments worn at a wedding or by the clergy), ornamental (e.g., fashion), and task-oriented (e.g., the uniform of the fireman or policeman). Although clothes are said to "make the man" in defining his outer relation to the world around him, clearly, clothes are never synonymous with the actual person, since they can be changed or discarded at will. By the same token, neither is the Creator synonymous with His garment of light—despite light's ethereal and luminescent nature, it is merely one way God manifests Himself to Creation. Mystics of the Kabbalah frequently refer to God as the "Divine Nothing"; by using this abstract term, they mean to say that God is indeed not an object or thing, transcending all metaphor, predicate, and thought—even the metaphor of light (see Excursus 11).

❖ *Creation as Seen Through the Eyes of Science*

Another Interpretive View: "Let there be light" and there was light – Some scholars think that from the very beginning, the Torah informs the reader that the existence of light does not derive from its own being, but derives directly from God. Light ought to justly be viewed as the first-born of creation.[239] German Jewish scholar Benno Jacob (1862-1945) writes: "Light is most congruous with God's own nature, a simile for absolute clarity and purity."[240] Generally speaking, light serves as a metaphor for life, blessing, renewal, salvation, gladness, success,[241] and in a broader sense, light conveys the concept of perfect being. In contrast, darkness is often associated with confusion (Job 5:14), terror (cf. Job 18:6, 18; Ps. 88:12), the exploitation of the innocent (Ps. 11:2), and gloom (Isa. 58:10). Jewish mystics add that as a metaphor, light reflects the source of all phenomenal reality; it is also the wellspring of spiritual illumination. Even a miniscule of light can dispel darkness, presenting the truth as things really are.

It has often been asked, "How could light be produced on the first day, as the sun was not created until the fourth day?" Some modern biblical scholars suggest that

---

[238] According to the Midrash, God originally wrapped Himself in a *tallit* (prayer shawl) of ethereal light (Gen Rabbah 3:4; cf. Zohar I 16b and *Midrash Soher Tov* on Psalm 104:4), but later retracted this light so that this light would later be reserved solely for the righteous in the Hereafter (Gen. Rabbah 3:6). *Ba'ale Turim* also briefly alludes to this interpretation in his commentary on Genesis 1:2.

[239] This viewpoint was also expressed long ago by Rashi in his commentary and later by 19th century scholars A. Dillman and Taylor Lewis.

[240] Benno Jacob, *The First Book of the Bible: Genesis* (Jersey City, NJ: Ktav, 1974), 3.

[241] Ps 4:7, 36; 19:1-6; 97:11; 104:19-20; Isa 60:19-20; Job 38:19-20.

the Torah talks about Creation from the vantage point of ancient Hebrews who may not have automatically associated the presence of light with the sun, just as dawn and dusk also appear to have light without the sun.[242] Others suggest that the stars and the sun were created on the first day, but did not become visible until the fourth day of Creation (BT Haggiah 12a).[243] Modern science interprets the creation of light in much more precise terms. Renowned astronomer Edmund Halley (1656–1742) argues: "These nebulae reply fully to the difficulty which has been raised against the Mosaic description of Creation, in asserting that light could not be generated without the sun."[244] Physicist Gerald Schroeder reconciles the contradiction by pointing out that originally, primitive earth was surrounded by clouds and a dense fog; the first rays of light may have needed more time for all clouds and mist to dissipate from the earth's atmosphere. This development took approximately one billion years for the earth's atmosphere to become clear enough to see the sun, the moon, and the stars. What was originally translucent then became transparent.[245] Today we know that stars and planets begin in a gaseous stage and then evolve into a solid state of mass and gas.

Recent discoveries in cosmology offer fresh perspectives that add immeasurably new understanding and appreciation of the biblical text, in ways the original faith community who heard this story could scarcely have imagined possible. The initial light of Creation may have been spawned from the original "Big Bang" that filled the universe with the presence of the light. At the birth of the universe, all matter and energy were compressed into a fiery mass of unimaginable density, which blew up (hence the name "Big Bang"). Out of this resulting inferno, and all within one billionth of a second, all the particles and forces we know today were created. When this explosion took place, the entire universe was filled with a bright light as order began to appear and replace dark chaos. It took three minutes for this kaleidoscope of ephemeral particles to give way to stable atomic nuclei. Physicist Steven Weinberg describes the physical state of the cosmos some 20 billion years ago, in the following terms:

---

[242] In terms of modern physics, light can include the electromagnetic spectrum of frequencies or wavelengths of electromagnetic waves. Light traditionally includes the range of frequencies that can be seen by human beings. Each different frequency or wavelength of light causes the eye to see a slightly different color. The waves associated with light are called electromagnetic waves because there are changes in electric and magnetic fields. Electromagnetic waves are transverse waves, moving like waves down a rope or waves on the surface of water. Unlike those waves, however, light does not need a substance through which to travel, for light has the ability to travel in a vacuum.

[243]Indeed, all the productions of heaven and earth were created *in potentia* on the first day, but each of them was put in its place on that day when it was so commanded (Rashi on Gen. 1:14).

[244] Cited from the R. Joseph Hertz's *The Pentateuch and Haftorahs Second edition* (London: Soncino Press, 1980), 2, which in turn was borrowed from M. Kalisch's *Commentary on Genesis*.

[245] Gerald Schroeder, *The Science of God* (New York: Free Press, 1997), 50.

> In the beginning there was an explosion . . . with every particle of matter rushing apart from every other particle; the heat of the universe, about a hundred thousand million degrees centigrade, was of such intensity that none of the components of ordinary matter, molecules or atoms, or even the nuclei of atoms, could have held together. The "matter" of the original explosion consisted, essentially, of electrons, positrons, photons, and neutrinos, and these particles were continually being created out of pure energy, and then after short lives being annihilated again.[246]

As mentioned earlier in the Introduction, such modernized interpretations of a text often say and reflect more about the perspective and world-view of the interpreter than it does about the original author, whose own viewpoint is somewhat shrouded in mystery.[247]

Astrophysicist Robert Jastrow, director of NASA's Goddard Institute for Space Studies, tells us that the Big Bang theory includes no explanation for the "seemingly fortuitous fact that the density of matter has just the right value for the evolution of a life-supporting universe."[248] Indeed, if one second after the Big Bang, the density of the universe had been one-millionth degree less, all the particles would have receded too rapidly for galaxies and stars to be formed. If the universe had been one-millionth degree denser, it would have collapsed in the early stage of development. In either case, we would likely not exist. Jastrow holds that the emergence of life has profound religious implications. In an often cited passage, he writes:

> Now we see how the astronomical evidence leads to a biblical view of the origin of the world (the word the Bible used to describe the universe). The details differ, but the essential elements in the astronomical and biblical accounts of Genesis are the same. The chain of events leading to man commenced suddenly and sharply at a definite moment in time, in a flash of light and energy . . .
>
> . . . Science has proven that the universe exploded into being at a certain moment. It asks, what produced the effect? Who or what put the matter and energy into the universe? . . . Science cannot answer these questions, because, according to the astronomers, in the first moments of its existence the universe was compressed to an extraordinary degree and consumed by the heat of a fire beyond human imagination. The shock of that instant must have destroyed every particle of evidence that could have yielded a clue to the cause of that great explosion. A sound explanation may exist for the explosive birth of our

---

[246] *The First Three Minutes* (New York: Basic Books, 1977), 5-6.

[247] For this reason, the artist and scientist will view a sacred text very differently from the anthropologist or theologian. Like beauty, the interpretation is all in the eye of the beholder and in many ways the reader's personal theology of the Bible (or for that matter, any great work of literature) will assume an almost neo-Midrashic-like quality to the text one studies (much like Derrida and Gadamer point out).

[248] Robert Jastrow, *God and the Astronomers* (New York: Warner Books, 1992), 93.

universe, but if it does science cannot find it. The scientist's pursuit of the past ends in the moment of creation . . .

. . . At this moment it seems that science will never be able to raise the curtain on the origin of creation. For the scientist who lived by his faith in the power of reason, the story ends like a bad dream. He has scaled the mountains of ignorance; he is about to conquer the highest peak; as he pulls himself over the final rock, he is greeted by a band of theologians who have been sitting there for centuries.[249]

1:4 וַיַּרְא אֱלֹהִים אֶת־הָאוֹר כִּי־טוֹב – And God saw that the light was good – The biblical narrator in this chapter writes about the creation of light before describing the creation of darkness (Rashbam). As mentioned earlier, the term *good* appears seven times in the creation narrative (cf. Gen. 1:10, 12, 18, 21, 25, 31), emphasizing the inherent goodness of God's Creation. The syntax is emphatic; others use the phrase, "God saw how good it was." The phrase is reminiscent of ancient Near Eastern descriptions of a craftsman being pleased with his work."[250] In the Tanakh, there is no evil principle within the created order opposing God, as is commonly portrayed in many myths of the ancient world. There is something profound about the metaphor of light that expresses the mystery of the Divine Presence and how this Supreme Reality unfolds within the human soul. In the mystical sense, light represents clarity and oneness with God.

Targum Neofiti usually translates the phrase כִּי־טוֹב as וְתָקֵן שְׁפַר (*wətāqqēn šəpar* = "He made pleasing and complete") but in this verse, he simply refers to it by the more generic Aramaic expression טַב "good." According to some scholars, this is because the creation of light remains in an incomplete state until the separation between light and darkness occurs (end of v. 4), and when there is a clear differentiation between day and night (v.5).[251] Gersonides adds that each stage of the creative process had conformed perfectly according to God's archetypal design. Thus, the biblical narrator expresses this harmony by the phrase, "and it was good."

Another Interpretative View: And God saw that the light was good – Rashbam explains that וַיַּרְא אֱלֹהִים (*wayyar' 'ĕlōhîm* = "And God saw") implies that God inspected the light much like Moses and Samuel's mothers inspected their children to see that they were healthy. This exposition raises a theological question: Why would God

---

[249] Ibid., 105.

[250] E. Fox, *The Five Books of Moses: Genesis, Exodus, Leviticus, Numbers, Deuteronomy: A New Translation with Introductions, Commentary, and Notes* (New York: Schocken Books, 1995), Vol. 1.

[251] See Bernard Grossfeld and Lawrence F. Schiffman, *Targum Neofiti 1: An Exegetical Commentary to Genesis Including Full Rabbinical Parallels* (New York: Sepher Hermon Press, 2000), 60.

need to "inspect" the light to see whether the light was good or not? Surely the Creator knew from the very beginning that the light was indeed good! Thinkers since the time of Augustine admit that the Scriptures are merely speaking from the human perspective.[252] However, the biblical narrator may have wished to stress the inherent goodness that pervades all of Creation. Just as God "inspects" Creation, so too human beings ought to pay more attention to the goodness of God that pervades all Creation. Nahum Sarna likewise makes a similar point: "Reality is imbued with God's goodness. The pagan notion of inherent, primordial evil is banished. Henceforth, evil is to be apprehended on the moral and not the mythological plane."[253]

❖ *The Union of Opposites*

וַיַּבְדֵּל אֱלֹהִים בֵּין הָאוֹר וּבֵין הַחֹשֶׁךְ – **and God separated the light from the darkness** —As mentioned in the Introduction, the oneness of God is reflected through the diversity and blending of various twofold oppositions: nothingness–creation, heaven–earth, chaos–cosmos, day–night, sacred–profane, work—rest, male–female, good–evil, and so on. These dualities find unification in God's oneness, each serving its purpose in the greater scheme of how the universe, the world, and nature function. There are important ethical and ontological implications to the process of separation as evidenced in the biblical precepts governing the permitted and the forbidden, the pure and the impure, the holy and the not yet holy.

The concept of הבדלה (*habdālāh* = "separation") delineates the boundaries separating the sacred and profane. The key to humanity's ability to grow and individuate lies in the spiritual capacity to grasp the opposites that define the world and one's own inner being. It stands to reason, the physical preservation and growth of the species depend on our collective ability to recognize and differentiate between these binary polarities of being. As one 19th century commentator observes, "The creation of light, however, was no annihilation of darkness, no transformation of the dark material of the world into pure light, but a separation of the light from the primary matter, a separation which established and determined that interchange of light and darkness, which produces the distinction between day and night."[254]

[252] Augustine, *The Literal Interpretation of Genesis an Unfinished Book*. (Washington, DC: Catholic University of America Press, 1991), 5:22.

[254] C. F., F. Keil& Delitzsch, *Commentary on the Old Testament*. (Peabody, MA: Hendrickson, 2001), Vol. 1, xii-31

❖ *"Day" as a Segment of Time*

1:5 וַיִּקְרָא אֱלֹהִים לָאוֹר יוֹם – God called the light Day – The Hebrew word for "day," יוֹם (*yōm*), is used in five different ways in the first two chapters of Genesis. Simply defined, יוֹם denotes a measurement of time; i.e., an indefinite time period, ranging from relatively short to very long years and beyond (Exod. 2:23); יוֹם יוֹם (*yōm yōm*) "day after day," or "daily,"; i.e., a relatively long period of time (Gen. 39:10). Its usual meaning is a time of daylight as distinct from a period of darkness; namely, night, as is the case here."[255] In v. 14, יוֹם stands for what we know as 24 hours; in v. 16, יוֹם means the illuminated part of the day; while in 2:4, יוֹם connotes the entire period during which the heaven and the earth were created. There are numerous examples of how the term יוֹם by itself, refers to a general time period or era[256] unless it is otherwise specified.[257]

It is important to note that there was nobody in existence to measure this span of time. With the absence of other planetary bodies, it is impossible to say that the verse denotes a 12 or 24 hour period. The ancient exegetes were well aware of the problem posed by the text and proposed a novel interpretation. Philo of Alexandria, Origen, Augustine, and others maintained that the "day" ought not to be interpreted literally. Augustine's condemnation of biblical literalists of his time applies no less to those living today who insist upon a literal reading of Genesis. When reason and science contradict a literal reading of Scripture, the text begs to be re-interpreted in such a way that harmonizes reason and science, as Augustine states:

> It is too disgraceful and ruinous, though, and greatly to be avoided, that he [the non-Christian] should hear a Christian speaking so idiotically on these matters, and as if in accord with Christian writings, that he might say that he could scarcely keep from laughing when he saw how totally in error they are. In view of this and in keeping it in mind constantly while dealing with the book of Genesis, I have, insofar as I was able, explained in detail and set

---

[255] Cf. Gen. 7:4; 8:22; 29:7; Exod. 24:18; Ps. 139:12, etc.

[256] Isa 2:12; 13:6 13:9; 22:5; 34:8; 37:3; 58:4; 63:4; Joel 2:1; 2:11; 3:4, et al.

[257] The HALOT: 399 gives numerous examples: יוֹם תָּמִים = "a full day" (Josh 10:13); שְׁלֹשֶׁת יָמִים = "for three days" (Est. 4:16); יוֹם יוֹם (Ug.) = "day by day," "every day" or "daily"(Gen. 39:10; Exod. 16:5; Ps. 61:9; Prov. 8:30); יוֹם וָיוֹם = "every day" (Est. 3:4); יוֹם בְּיוֹם = "day by day" (Neh. 8:18; 2 Chr. 30:21); לְעֶת־יוֹם בְּיוֹם = "day after day" (1 Chr. 12:23); לְיוֹם בְּיוֹם = "day by day" (2 Chr. 24:11); כְּיוֹם בְּיוֹם = "as on each day" (1Sam. 18:10); שְׁנַיִם לַיּוֹם = "two every day" (Exod. 29:38); לִשְׁלֹשֶׁת יָמִים = "on the third day" (Amos 4:4); דְּבַר יוֹם בְּיוֹמוֹ = "the daily portion" (Exod.5:13, 19, 16:4 Lev 23:37 1 Kgs. 8:59 2 Kgs. 25:30 Jer. 52:34 Dan. 1:5; בִּדְבַר יוֹם = "as every day requires" (2 Chr. 8:13); לִדְבַר־יוֹם בְּיוֹמוֹ = (1 Chr. 8:14); כָּל־ הַיּוֹם = "all the day" (Isa. 62:6; 28:24): כָּל־יוֹם = "every day" (Ps. 14:03); בְּכָל־יוֹם = "every day" (Ps. 7:12).

forth for consideration the meanings of obscure passages, taking care not to affirm rashly one meaning to the prejudice of another and perhaps a better explanation.[258]

Although the Psalmist expresses the thought that a thousand years must seem to God like a passing day, or even a lesser period of time like a night-watch (Ps. 90:4), consisting of only three or four hours a night (Judg. 7:19), this passage must be read within a historical and cultural context. There can be no doubt that if the Psalmist would have known that the universe was actually billions of years old, he would have used an even more graphic metaphor in depicting what the passage of time was like in relation to God. This is another example of how the Torah speaks in the language of humankind, and as humankind evolves in its understanding of God and the universe, likewise, so do the metaphors one uses in describing God's relationship to the created order.[259] The beginning of the creation story must be seen and deciphered through the prism of mythopoetic imagery; overlooking the text's poetic qualities is to misinterpret the mythopoetic imagination that originally expressed this story.

❖ *A Literal Reading of "One Day"*

It is true some modern biblical scholars think that the Torah means exactly what it says; namely, the days consisted of only a 24 hour period.[260] While this approach is

---

[258] Augustine, *The Literal Interpretation of Genesis, op. cit.,* c. 19, vv. 1:19–20.

[259] Thomas Aquinas' attitude about the biblical use of metaphor is worthy of special mention. In Part 1 of the *Summa*, Article 9, he discusses the propriety of metaphorical language in the Scriptures: Should Holy Scripture use metaphors? Aquinas explains in lucid terms:

> I answer that, it is befitting Holy Writ to put forward divine and spiritual truths by means of comparisons with material things. For God provides for everything according to the capacity of its nature. Now it is natural for man to attain to intellectual truths through sensible objects, because all our knowledge originates from sense. Hence in Holy Writ, spiritual truths are fittingly taught under the likeness of material things. This is what Dionysius says (*Coel. Hier.* i): "We cannot be enlightened by the divine rays except they be hidden within the covering of many sacred veils." It is also befitting Holy Writ, which is proposed to all without distinction of persons — "To the wise and to the unwise I am a debtor" (Rom. 1:14) — that spiritual truths be expounded by means of figures taken from corporeal things, in order that thereby even the simple who are unable by themselves to grasp intellectual things may be able to understand it . . .
>
> . . . The ray of divine revelation is not extinguished by the sensible imagery wherewith it is veiled . . . and its truth so far remains that it does not allow the minds of those to whom the revelation has been made, to rest in the metaphors, but raises them to the knowledge of truths; and through those to whom the revelation has been made others also may receive instruction in these matters. Hence those things that are taught metaphorically in one part of Scripture, in other parts are taught more openly. The very hiding of truth in figures is useful for the exercise of thoughtful minds and as a defense against the ridicule of the impious, according to the words "Give not that which is holy to dogs" (Matt 7:6).

[260] Many advocates of this viewpoint include: Hermann Gunkel, who argues that "[t]he 'days' are of course

a plausible way of reading the text—certainly, it is not the only way of interpreting it. Nevertheless, when utilizing the principle, "The Torah speaks in the language of humankind," one could say that the biblical writer simply told the story of creation in a non-scientific way so that any person, regardless of background or education, could understand the biblical story based on a common experience.

Assuming that this literal interpretation of the text is correct, how does one reconcile the formation of the first 24 hour day without the existence of a sun, moon, or stars? One modern scholar offers a novel solution to the dilemma by ascertaining that the biblical author's understanding of the day (24 hours) did not depend upon the existence of the sun and the moon, even though the position of these heavenly bodies in the sky could serve for measuring this unit of time and for differentiating between the presence and absence of daylight (as per Gen. 1:14-18). Rather, the sun and the moon would not serve as sources of light on their own but as reflectors for transmitting the light to the earth[261], while the source of that light (created on the first day) would remain independent. This peculiar way of viewing the universe was not uncommon in the days of antiquity and figured in some cosmological theories in the ancient world, e.g., the cosmology of Anaximander, the famous Greek philosopher, mathematician, and astronomer of the 6th century B.C.E.[262]

וְלַחֹשֶׁךְ קָרָא לָיְלָה – **and the darkness He called Night** – Unlike Zoroastrianism and its Gnostic successor, Manichaeism[263], in which the Ahurimazda, the good god of light, is engaged in an eternal battle with Ahriman, the evil god of darkness, the

---

days and nothing else." S. R. Driver also explains the text in the same exact manner (*The Book of Genesis,* 6). Gerhard von Rad holds a similar view, "The seven days are unquestionably to be understood as actual days and as a unique, unrepeatable lapse of time in the world." G. Wenham writes, "There can be little doubt that here 'day' has its basic sense of a 24-hour period" (*Genesis,* 18). For an excellent article presenting the various viewpoints going back to ancient times, see Gerhard F. Hasel, "The Days of Creation in Genesis 1: Literal 'Days' or Figurative 'Periods/Epochs'" *Origins* 21(1):5-38 (1994). Among the other lexicons, the HALOT: 399, reads "day (of 24 hours)" for the creation day (Leiden: E. J. Brill, 1999, c1994-1996). William H. Holladay, *A Concise Hebrew and Aramaic Lexicon of the Old Testament* (Grand Rapids, MI: Wm. B. Eerdmans Publishing Co., 1971), 130, BDB: 398. Lastly, both the TDOT (6:25) and the TLOT (2:536) concur that "day" means in this instance, a 24 hour period.

[261] Ramban's commentary on Genesis 1:14 explicitly accepted Anaximander's theory.

[262] Baruch Halpern, "The Assyrian Astronomy of Genesis 1 and the Birth of Milesian Philosophy" (*Eretz- Israel* 27 2003), 76-77.

[263] Manichaeism was an ancient dualist belief system: a religious doctrine based on the separation of matter and spirit, and of good and evil that originated in the 3rd century by the Persian prophet Manes. Evil is associated with matter, while good is associated with mind. Its syncretic philosophy combined elements of Zoroastrianism, Buddhism, Christianity, and Gnosticism. Historically, the Roman government opposed Manichaeism and persecuted its followers.

Creator in Genesis masters both light and darkness; even darkness serves its purpose in the divine scheme of things. In calling forth light, God does not abolish the darkness that envelopes the earth. Night also serves God's purpose. The fact that God names the darkness is also significant. In times of antiquity, to name something or someone implied having dominion or ownership.[264] Naming requires a recognition and understanding of the entity's inner nature and being. Designating a name also bestows an identity or vocation upon that person or object. Whenever God "calls," there can be only one response: to fulfill the task to which one is enjoined.

וַיְהִי־עֶרֶב וַיְהִי־בֹקֶר - **And there was evening, and there was morning** – The term עֶרֶב (*ʿéreḇ*) refers to the time between sunset and nightfall. [265] Ibn Ezra thought עֶרֶב might be related to the word עֵרֶב (*ʿēreḇ*) "mixture" possibly because of the commingling between day and night, but this is more of a Midrashic reading.[266] Modern Hebraic scholars observe that עֶרֶב derives from the root עָרַב *(aʿraḇ)* "to set" and is related to the Akkadian *erēbu*, a common verb of wide usage which includes "entering" or "going down"—both these terms are used in reference to the sun's descent. Thus, *ereb ᵈšamši* means "sunset."[267] In contrast, the term בֹּקֶר (*bṓqer*) might be derived from the Arabic *bakara* (= "to split open"). Thus, בֹּקֶר connotes the "break of day," hence, "first light." [268]

Jewish tradition teaches that a day begins at nightfall, not at dawn (*cf.* Exod. 12:18 and Lev. 23:32).[269] However, Rashbam (1085–1174) notes that the biblical day of

[264] See Genesis 17:5, 15; 41:45; 2 Kgs. 23:34, 24:17; Dan. 1:7.

[265] Exod. 12:6; 16:12; 29:39, 41; 30:8; Lev. 23:5; Num. 9:3, 5, 11; 28:4.

[266] According to the entry found in the BDB, עֵרֶב (*'ēreb* = mixture) derives from an entirely different root. The BDB lists six different roots involving the letters ערב and their meanings are not the same.

[267] Specific references can be found in the HALOT: 877. Some scholars compare עֶרֶב to the Arabic, غَرَبَ (*ğaraba*) connotes "to *set*" and its parting from view is called غَرَبَ (*ğaraba*) "depart." Thus, in Arabic, the verb *ğarifa* means "the setting of the sun." Note that the Arabic letter *ğ* is pronounced like the French "r.".

[268] See C. Barth's article on *bṓqer* (TDOT: 2:210-228).

[269] The Jews were not the only people to reckon the new day from dusk; other ancient peoples of the Near East were believed to have followed the same custom. The Roman historian Tacitus writes: "The ancient Germans compute not the number of days, but of nights; the night appears to draw on the day" (*Tacitus*, ch. xi). And Caesar says of the Gauls, "They measure time not by the number of days, but of nights; and accordingly observe their birthdays, and the beginning, of months and years, so as to make the day follow the night" (*Bell. Gal.* 6:18).

Creation began with the dawn and not at twilight[270]—a view which his contemporary, Ibn Ezra, found unacceptable and even heretical.[271] Abraham Ibn Ezra most likely had Rashbam in mind when he wrote his *Letter of the Sabbath*:

> And the messenger of the Sabbath answered and spoke to me, "She has been told what thy pupils brought yesterday to thy house, books of commentaries on the Law, and there is it written to profane Sabbath eve; do thou gird up thy lions for the honor of Sabbath to wage the battle of the Law with the enemies of the Sabbath, and do not treat any man with partiality," And I awoke and my anger kindled within me and my spirit was very heavy; and I arose and warmed the fire in me and put on my garments and I washed my hands and there was written an explanation of Genesis 1:5. "And the evening and the morning," namely, that when the morning of the second day came, then one whole day had passed, for the night is reckoned as part of the preceding day. Then I almost rent my garments and the explanation too, for I said "it is better to profane a single Sabbath than allow Israel to profane many Sabbaths with fire if they saw the wrong interpretation, and we should all be exposed to ridicule and scorn in the eyes of the Gentiles." [272]

For Rashbam, the biblical writer is not interested in *when* a day ought to begin, but merely narrates *how* the creation actually took place.[273] Umberto Cassuto (1885–1951) concurs with Rashbam,[274] but then advances a novel explanation. According to him,

---

[270] "The verse does not say וַיְהִי לַיְלָה 'It was night time and it was day time which made one day', but rather, וַיְהִי־עֶרֶב 'it was twilight,' that is to say, this was the period of the day time that concluded once the last rays of light completely disappeared. And when the verse says וַיְהִי־בֹקֶר 'it was morning,' it means that the period of night time came to an end as the rays of dawn appeared. Then one whole day was completed."

[271] On the matter of heresy, Ibn Ezra's sharp criticism of Rashbam's view is undeserved. Rashbam merely feels that the contextual meaning of the text does not warrant a Halachic interpretation. Occasionally, Ibn Ezra sometimes offers an interpretation differing from the Talmudic exegetical tradition; e.g., his attitude about not seeking medical cures for natural illnesses (Exod. 29:28). However, as a general rule Ibn Ezra follows rabbinic interpretations when they do not contradict the plain meaning of the verse (cf. Lev. 22:22; Deut. 5:25). Ibn Ezra also hints that numerous passages in the Pentateuch could not have been of Mosaic origin (e.g., Gen.12:6; 22:24; Deut. 3:11; 31:22), as observed by Baruch Spinoza (*Tractatus Theologico Politicus*, c.7). Sometimes, the medieval exegetes went against rabbinic tradition when expounding upon the contextual meaning of a verse. A well-known example of this kind of non-rabbinic interpretation can also be seen in Rashi's commentary: "You shall not follow a multitude to do evil" (Exod. 23:2). Rashi notes: "There are Halachic interpretations for this verse given by the Sages of Israel, but the language of the verse does not fit its context according to them."

[272] See M. Friedlander, *Ibn Ezra in England: Transactions of the Jewish Historical Society of England, Vol. II* (London, 1894/5, 61-75) and reprinted in Cecil Roth's *Anglo-Jewish Letters* (Soncino Press, London, 1938), 5-6.

[273] As noted by M. Lookshin in his notes to Rashbam.

[274] Umberto Cassuto, *A Commentary on the Book of Genesis.* [1st English edition.] ed. (Jerusalem: Magnes Press Hebrew University, 1961), 28.

originally, the Israelites counted the day from the morning[275], not from the evening.[276] In each of these passages, when the Tanakh refers to the "next day," the time reference is specifically the morning.[277] "It will thus be seen that throughout the Bible there obtains only one system of computing time: the day is considered to begin in the morning, but with regard to festivals and appointed times, the Torah ordains that they shall be observed also on the night of the preceding day."[278]

Both Rashbam and Cassuto's expositions are problematic. If the Sabbath of Genesis 2:1 is directly connected to the Sabbath found in the Decalogue, one must seriously wonder why the Israelites never observed the Sabbath starting with the Saturday morning sunrise as one might expect based on Rashbam's own exposition of the present verse. Alternatively, Cassuto's interpretation still remains problematical for the same reason. It seems more likely that the Israelites often spoke of the "next day" much like modern people do today in Western countries. Simply put, people are not always precise in the way they speak of "today," knowing that technically, the new day does not actually begin until midnight. Ibn Ezra may have been a little harsh in his criticism of Rashbam, but the substance of his argument is justified.

יוֹם אֶחָד – one day – The Torah utilizes a cardinal rather than an ordinal number יוֹם רִאשׁוֹן *(yōm ri´šôn)* as it did with the other days of Creation. Ramban explains, "*First* implies precedence over another in number or grading, when both are in existence but in our case there was only *one day.*" Physicist Gerald Schroder explains, "Genesis used the absolute cardinal form for day one because it was viewing time from the beginning of time, a perspective from which there was no other time for comparison."[279] One of Gesenius's definitions of אֶחָד is the *one only* of its kind—an apt metaphor for God—and

---

275 The Reform Jewish scholar Jacob Lauterbach writes: "Benjamin of Toledo (second half of the twelfth century) reports a certain Jewish sect on the island of Cyprus whose members observed the Sabbath from Saturday morning to Sunday morning, or as he puts it, who desecrated the night preceding but kept holy the night following the Sabbath day" ("When Does the Sabbath Begin?" Jacob Z. Lauterbach, *Rabbinical Essays* (Cincinnati: HUC, 1951), 451.

276 Cf. Gen. 19:33–34; Judg. 6:38, 21:4; 1 Sam. 19:11.

277 For instance: "So they made their father drink wine that night. . . . On the *next day*, the firstborn said to the younger . . ." (Gen. 19:33–34); "*On the next day*, the people got up early, and built an altar there, and offered burnt offerings and sacrifices of well-being" (Judges 6:38); "David's wife, Michal, told him, 'If you do not save your life *tonight*, *tomorrow* you will be killed" (1 Sam. 19:11); "Moreover the LORD will give Israel along with you into the hands of the Philistines; *and tomorrow* you and your sons shall be with me; the LORD will also give the army of Israel into the hands of the Philistines" (1 Sam. 28:19).

278 Cassuto, *Genesis* I, 29–30.

279 Gerald Schroder, *The Science of God* (New York: Broadway Books, 1997), 65.

the Midrash utilized this reading to suggest that יוֹם אֶחָד ought to be rendered as "day of the One" – a view endorsed by Rashi, and more recently by C. H. Gordon.[280]

Another Interpretive View: And there was evening, and there was morning one day. – Based on the concept that יוֹם (*yōm*) connotes a unit of time, the verse also has a poetic meaning that is analogous to "It was the evening and morning of an age." Similar expressions are used in English, e.g., "the dawn of an age, it was the evening of an age." The latter expression is based on the Roman division of the day, which charts its beginning with sunrise. In contrast, Semitic peoples begin their day at sunset, while sunrise is the middle of the day.[281]

❖ *In Praise of Darkness*

Another Interpretive View: And there was evening, and there was morning one day. – There are a number of important questions relevant to the immediate biblical text: Why does God create darkness and light as opposites? What affirmative role does darkness play in the scheme of creation? Wouldn't the creation of light be sufficient by itself? According to Theodoret, both day and night are essential for the harmonious well-being of the world. Daylight affords human beings with the time to be creative and industrious. The light of day also brings to mind certain visible things requiring attention. Night, in contrast, provides the time for rest and renewal; it also provides a time when families come together, while providing the animal world a time for foraging (Psa. 104:20-24).

Theodoret further explains that darkness is not a substance per se, "but only an accident being a shadow cast by heaven and earth. That is why it vanishes when the light appears. Light, on the other hand, is and subsists as a substance; after setting, it rises, and after departing, it returns. . . . A house with no windows is full of darkness, but when a lamp is brought in, it lights up—not that darkness has moved off elsewhere, for, being insubstantial, it does not subsist. Rather, it is completely dissolved with the coming of light. After all, a shadow is caused by the roof, the floor, and the walls, and is dissipated by the beams of light . . . Darkness then, is neither an uncreated nor a created substance. Caused by created things, it is necessary and useful and proclaims God's wisdom." [282]

---

[280] C. H. Gordon, "His Name is 'One'" *JNES*, 29 [1970], 198-199.

[281] In Roman times, this distinction had some practical implications. At first, the Romans imposed a tax on the crops at the end of the day's harvesting, counting the beginning of the day from sunrise. Some enterprising farmers used to get up before sunrise, harvesting whatever they could to avoid the taxes, which were paid the day before. After the Roman government realized what was happening, they established the beginning of the day at midnight, thwarting the efforts of the farmers to avoid taxation.

[282] *The Questions on the Octateuch: On Genesis and Exodus, op. cit.,* 21-23.

❖ *Day Two of Creation (Gen. 1:6-8)*

1:6 וַיֹּאמֶר אֱלֹהִים יְהִי רָקִיעַ בְּתוֹךְ הַמָּיִם וִיהִי מַבְדִּיל בֵּין מַיִם לָמָיִם – And God said, "Let there be a dome in the midst of the waters, and let it separate the waters from the waters – The noun רָקִיעַ (*rāqîaᶜ*) derives from the root רָקַע *to overlay* with a thin plate (Isa. 40:19). Ancient Hebrews believed that the heavenly firmament was actually a firm and solid vault, perhaps resembling sapphire stone (Exod. 24:10), to which the stars were fastened. Beyond the vault existed a vast and heavenly ocean, whose dome arched above the earthly globe (HALOT: 1290). In Job 37:18, heaven is depicted as a shiny molten mirror. The biblical imagery of a solid firmament (or "dome") bears similarity to other ancient Near Eastern concepts of the universe. The Septuagint renders this term as στερέωμα (*stereōma*), something that is made up of solid matter. Nations of antiquity believed that the universe consisted of three kinds of space: (1) heaven, the residence of God and co-habited by pious and pure spirits; (2) earth, the dwelling place for humankind; (3) the netherworld, the abode of the departed—all of which the Greeks identified as Elysium, Earth, and Hades. In short, the Sumerians, Egyptians, and early Greeks shared a tripartite view of the universe consisting of the heavens, the earth, and the underworld. It is argued that various biblical texts—especially the poetic books of the Tanakh—indicate that the Israelites probably shared a similar concept of the world.[283] Other biblical texts present a picture of a four-storied universe[284] but more texts concur with the three-storied universe found in these other ancient traditions.[285]

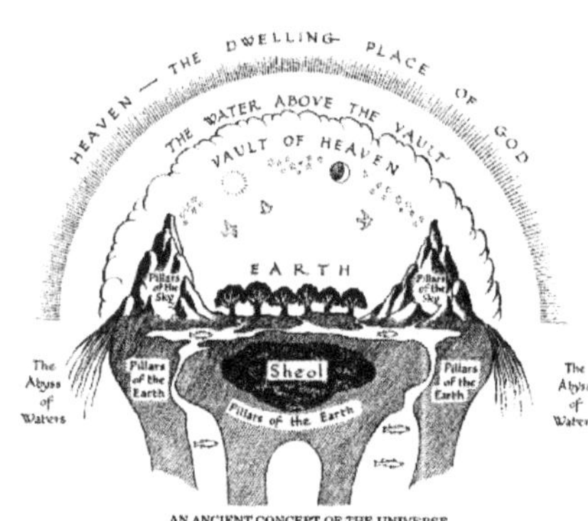

AN ANCIENT CONCEPT OF THE UNIVERSE

The ancient Israelite's scientific grasp of the universe was certainly—by contemporary standards—simple and unsophisticated. However, there are two ways of dealing with this problem: one possibility is that the biblical narrator may be merely describing how things *appear* to the human eye, hence the imagery described is meant only metaphorically—much like the way we still

[283] Cf. Exod. 20:4; Psa. 24:2.

[284] Job 11:8–9; Ps. 139:8-9.

[285] Cf. Gen. 49:25; Deut. 33:13; Ps 135:6.

speak of the sun "rising" or "setting" even though the sun remains relatively stationary in the heavens. Alternatively, "the Torah speaks in the language of humanity,"[286] i.e., the use of these terms reflects how the ancients experienced and understood their world within the universe. Therefore, it is not surprising to see the biblical narrator employ the familiar phraseology of its age.[287] Had the Torah been written in a more scientific era, the biblical narrator may have used the kind of phraseology that would reflect a very different understanding of the cosmos. In all probability, our current scientific knowledge of the universe will most likely seem "primitive" to those living 2000 years from now, as well.

1:7 וַיַּעַשׂ אֱלֹהִים אֶת־הָרָקִיעַ וַיַּבְדֵּל בֵּין הַמַּיִם אֲשֶׁר מִתַּחַת לָרָקִיעַ וּבֵין הַמַּיִם אֲשֶׁר מֵעַל לָרָקִיעַ – **So God made the dome and separated the waters that were under the dome from the waters that were above the dome.** – Why didn't the Torah say at the conclusion of the second day, "and God saw that it was good?" Rashi answers, "Since the work of the second day was not completed until the third day . . . and for this reason, anything that is incomplete cannot be termed as 'good.'"[288]

It is interesting to note that the Septuagint reads: καὶ εἶδεν ὁ θεὸς τὰ πάντα, ὅσα ἐποίησεν, καὶ ἰδοὺ καλὰ λίαν. καὶ ἐγένετο ἑσπέρα καὶ ἐγένετο πρωί, ἡμέρα ἕκτη. "And

---

[286] BT Berakhot 31b; cf. *Sifra*, Numbers 112.

[287] Cassuto writes similarly: "The Torah was not intended specifically for intellectuals but for the entire people, which is not concerned with philosophic or theological [or, for that matter, scientific—*MS*] speculation. It uses ordinary language plainly and without sophistication and pays no heed to inferences that later readers who are accustomed to ways of thinking wholly alien to the Bible may draw from its works" (*op. cit.,* 304). S. D. Luzzato likewise stressed this same point in the beginning of his Genesis commentary:

> Therefore it is not proper for the Torah scholar to force Scriptures from their literal meaning to make them conform according to the natural sciences, nor is it proper for the critic to deny the Divine origin of the Torah if he finds things in its stories that do not conform to the latest scientific research. Both scholar and critic ought instead to examine the inner nature of the human mind, and the different learning approaches nature takes when it speaks to each mind: to a child in its way, to a youth in another way, to an aged man in another. . . . So with all groups of human beings, nature speaks to their minds in a way particuarily befitting them for nature never reveals to any of them the naked truth without some veil or garb. And so the blessed Giver of the Torah (for the God Who created nature and the God Who gave us the Torah is one God), when He speaks to human beings, He must speak according to their level of understanding and not according to His (*The Book of Genesis, op. cit.,* 1-2).

[288] "After God finished the work associated with water and another work was commenced and finished, the words כִּי־טוֹב (*kî tôb*) are repeated, once in reference to the completion of the work of the second day — and again in reference to the completion of the work of that [the third] day."

God called the firmament Heaven, and God saw that it was good, and there was evening and there was morning, the second day." Could this be a more accurate reading than the Masoretic Text? One might argue that this possibility should not be ignored. However, whoever introduced this editorial gloss in the Septuagint, failed to take into consideration that the divisions of waters were not completed until the separation of the dry land from the water had occurred—all of which took place on the third day—as Rashi correctly concludes. Therefore, the most appropriate place to conclude with this refrain is at the end of the third day.

וַיְהִי־כֵן – **And it was so** – The word כֵּן often appears in particle phrases[289] indicates "prepare," "make ready," e.g., "Has he not made you and established you?" (Deut. 32:6).

❖ *"Heaven" as Metaphor*

1:8 וַיִּקְרָא אֱלֹהִים לָרָקִיעַ שָׁמָיִם – **God called the dome Sky** – Ramban argues the verse intimates a deeper meaning sensed than what is obvious[290], and his insight seems to be well justified. However, in his erudition, Ramban omitted an explanation to a more obvious question: Why is it that the Hebrew word for "sky" or "heaven" [שָׁמָיִם = *šāmáyim*] often symbolizes the dwelling place of the Divine?[291]

Mircea Eliade tackles this question head-on arguing that the heavens above represent a power, a presence, a piercing transcendence, and a holiness that leaves one awed with wonder. Standing beneath heavenly night skies, primal man realizes how petty and insignificant he really is, and whose very existence is transitory when compared to the heavens. As the Psalmist depicts, "As for mortals, their days are like grass; they flourish like a flower of the field" (Ps. 103:15).[292] By gazing contemplatively at the heavens, primal man's being became filled with an awe and mystery of God's infinite

---

[289] For examples of particle phrases, see Gen. 1:9, 1:11, and 2 Kgs. 2:10, *et al.*

[290] The *Stone Chumash* adds its own unique spin to Ramban's words: "Do not expect me to write anything about [the creation of the second day] since Scripture itself did not elaborate upon it. . . . The verses in their literal sense do not require such an explanation. Those who understand the explanation are forbidden to reveal it. For those of us who do not understand, [it is forbidden to speculate about the unknown]. Ramban's implication is clear: The 'firmament' and the 'upper and lower waters.' are among the mysteries of Creation that are either unknowable to Man or must be limited to those qualified to know them" Rabbi Nosson Scherman, *The Chumash: The Stone Edition* (Brooklyn, New York: Mesorah Publications, 1993), 4. See Charles Chavel's notes on Ramban, 37.

[291] Gen. 24:7; 28:13; 2 Chron. 36:23; Psa. 148:1-2; Ezek 1:26–28; Neh. 2:4; Isa. 63:15.

[292] Cf. Job 14:2; Isa. 40:6–7.

power and majesty as Eliade explains:

> The symbolism of transcendence derives from the simple realization of its infinite height. "Most High" becomes quite naturally an attribute of divinity. The regions above man's reach, the starry places, are invested with the divine majesty of the transcendent, of absolute reality, of everlastingness. . . . The "high" is something inaccessible to man as such. . . . The sky "symbolizes" transcendence, power, changelessness simply by being there. It exists because it is high, infinite, immovable, powerful. . . . The contemplation of the sky by its very nature enabled man to know not only his precariousness and the transcendence of the divinity, but also the sacred value of knowledge, of spiritual "force." Gazing into the clear blue sky by day or the multitude of stars by night, nowhere could one discern more completely the divine origin and sacred value of knowledge, the omnipotence of him who sees and understands, of him who "knows" all because he is everywhere, sees everything, and makes and governs all things. . . . He who sees and knows all, is and can do all.[293]

Therefore, when the Tanakh speaks about God "dwelling in Heaven," it is meant to be understood only metaphorically. Even the heavens cannot hope to contain the uncontainable God. Young King Solomon correctly intuited, "But will God indeed dwell on the earth? Even heaven and the highest heaven cannot contain you, much less this house that I have built!" (1 Kgs. 8:27).

Thus it is clear why heaven became a suitable metaphor for the Divine. Heaven represents a transcendental realm that stands ontologically apart from ordinary human experience and what we perceive as physical reality. Put in different terms, the heavenly and spiritual realms Ramban allude to are not about a spatial reality, but essentially about a non-spatial reality that defies the boundaries of Euclidean space. In an analogical sense, heaven is not unlike consciousness: It too, cannot be completely localized or confined to specific points in space or time. Quantum physicists refer to such a concept as "non-locality," which is an apt metaphor for heaven and the realm of eternity.

1:9 וַיֹּאמֶר אֱלֹהִים יִקָּווּ הַמַּיִם מִתַּחַת הַשָּׁמַיִם אֶל־מָקוֹם אֶחָד – **Let the waters under the sky be gathered together into one place** — This process occurred through the mighty wind mentioned in 1:2 (Rashbam). The *peshat* also suggests that the world was originally covered with nothing but water. It is interesting to compare the biblical position that the entire earth was covered with water to the view held by the Greek philosopher, Thales, who maintained that water is the principle, ἀρχῇ (*arche*), of all things and that the earth floats on water.[294]

[293] Mircea Eliade, *Patterns in Comparative Religion* (New York: Meridian, 1958), 59–60.

[294] See Aristotle, *Metaphysics*, I, 3, 983b 20-984a2.

וְתֵרָאֶה הַיַּבָּשָׁה – **and let the dry land appear** — This verse refers to the earth that was created on the first day, but the land remained hidden until the waters began to recede. The Torah does not disclose exactly how the dry land appeared. It might have been due either to unusually powerful volcanic activity resulting in an elevating of the earth, or perhaps to the deepening of the ocean floors creating large continental basins, or both.

וַיְהִי־כֵן – **And it was so** — Obediently, the chaotic waters of creation separate to allow the formation of dry land in accordance with God's will. The formation of the dry land contains important theological implications that pertain to Israel's future (Exod. 14–15; Isa. 46:26–28). When Israel experiences the parting of the Sea of Reeds, she will see how the forces of nature yield to the divine will, just as they did during the days of Noah. Like the ebb and flow of the seas, everything in Creation follows an ordained pattern. However, even natural law has its occasional fluctuation whether it is a tsunami, or an earthquake, or some other natural catastrophe. God's creation also allows for unpredictability and chaotic manifestations—*chaos too, is part of the creative order.*

1:10 וַיִּקְרָא אֱלֹהִים לַיַּבָּשָׁה אֶרֶץ וּלְמִקְוֵה הַמַּיִם קָרָא יַמִּים וַיַּרְא אֱלֹהִים כִּי־טוֹב – **God called the dry land Earth, and the waters that were gathered together he called Seas. And God saw that it was good.** — The term יַמִּים generally refers to any large body of water and is not limited to oceans. According to Jerome: "It is to be observed that every gathering together of waters, be they salt or sweet, is named "seas" according to the idiom of Hebrew."[295] Sometimes יָם may even refer to a large basin of water where water collects, e.g., יָם הַנְּחֹשֶׁת (*yām hannəḥ́ōšet*) the "molten sea" that formed an important part of Solomon's Temple. This large basin was used for the priests' washing; it stood about 7.5 ft. deep and 15 ft. from rim to rim. It is believed to have held approximately 11,000 gallons—enough water to provide 2,000 (1 Kgs. 7:26) or 3,000 baths (2 Chr. 4:5).

Another Interpretive view: God called the dry land Earth, and the waters that were gathered together he called Seas. – Note that the singular form of יָם (*yām*) is purposely avoided, since according to Ugaritic mythology, Yām is a son of El, who does battle with the storm deity, Baal. The deities of the Canaanite pantheon are not mentioned in the creation story.

---

[295] Jerome, *Questions on Genesis* on Gen. 1:10.

❖ *Day Three of Creation (Gen. 1:11-13)*

1:11 וַיֹּאמֶר אֱלֹהִים תַּדְשֵׁא הָאָרֶץ דֶּשֶׁא עֵשֶׂב מַזְרִיעַ זֶרַע – **Then God said, "Let the earth put forth vegetation: plants yielding seed** – The term דֶּשֶׁא (*déše*ʾ) is a general term for young fresh grass, green plants, vegetation, and various herbs in their earliest stages of growth, e.g., grasses and seed-bearing vegetation for human or animal consumption. Examples of grass are wild rice, millet, or any types of grains subsumed under the heading "grass."[296] Note that all grains are grasses, but not all grasses are considered grains; e.g., bluegrass, a common type of grass used for seeding lawns.

❖ *The Art of Wonderment: Is Life a Miracle?*

Another Interpretive View: **Then God said, "Let the earth put forth vegetation: plants yielding seed** – What exactly are the biological characteristics of life? The hallmark of life consists of the ability to: (1) draw nutrients from the environment; (2) convert nutrients into energy; (3) excrete waste products; (4) reproduce. These principles ecologically apply to all the known creatures that science has thus far observed in this world. The well-known evolutionary biologist and outspoken atheist, Richard Dawkins, states that each cell of life contains a digitally-coded database containing more informational content than all 30 volumes of the Encyclopedia Britannica put together, also stressing that this figure is for *each* cell, and not all the cells of a body put together.[297]

An alternative approach to Dawkins has been argued by biophysical chemist B.O. Küppers. In his study on the origin of life, Küppers asserts that a profound relationship exists between the law and chance when it comes to the early evolution of life. All forms of life phenomena are steered by information and that this information is already defined materially in a universal form at the level of the biological macromolecule. The question of the origin of life really ought to focus more on the origin of biological information.

> Even in the simple case of a bacterium, the genome consists of some 4×10^6 nucleotides, and the number of combinatoryially possible sequences is $4^{4 \text{ million}} = 10^{2.4 \text{ million}}$. The expectation probability for the nucleotide sequence of a bacterium is thus so slight that not even the entire space of the universe would be enough to make the random synthesis of a bacterial genome probable. For example, the entire mass of the universe, expressed as a multiple of the mass of the hydrogen atom, amounts to about 10^{80} units. Even if all the matter in space

---

296 There are many grass-like members of other flowering plant families, but only approximately 8,000 to 10,000 species in the family Poaceae, which belong to the order Cyperales, are true grasses. Some say that דֶּשֶׁא (*deše*ʾ) refers only to the vegetation, of which we see only the upper part, grass, moss (HALOT: 233).

297 Richard Dawkins, *The Blind Watchmaker* (New York: W.W. Norton & Co., 1986, 1996 ed.), 18.

> consisted of DNA molecules of the structural complexity of the bacterial genome, with random sequences, then the chances of finding among them a bacterial genome or something resembling one would still be completely negligible. It can naturally be objected that our statistical arguments are based upon the assumption of an entity with the complexity of a bacterial genome, while the historical process of the origin of life possibly took place by way of simpler forms of life. However, an appropriate analysis, based on probability theory, shows that not even an optimized enzyme molecule can arise in a random synthesis. Even the smallest catalytically active protein molecules of the living cell consist of at least a hundred amino acid residues, and they thus already possess more than 10^{130} sequence alternatives. . . . These striking numerical examples allow us to conclude with Monod that the design of a primitive organism has about the same chance of arising by pure chance, in a molecular roulette, as a general textbook of biochemistry has of arising by the random mixing of a sufficient number of letters.[298]

Paul Davies notes: "Genetic instructions are not merely information per se (as arises in, for example, thermodynamics and statistical mechanics), but represent a form of semantic information; i.e., they have to mean something. For a genetic instruction to be successful there has to be a molecular milieu capable of interpreting the message in the genetic code. The problem of how meaningful semantic information can emerge spontaneously from a collection of mindless molecules subject to blind and purposeless forces, presents a deep conceptual challenge." [299]

From the religious perspective, the complexity of life may not just be a matter of genetics, for the emergence of self-reflective life evokes a sense of awe that points to a Creator Who is the Source of all wonder.

The Hindu sacred text, *Chandogya Upanishad,* illustrates this truth with a well-known story about Svetaketu's conversation with his father Uddalaka. On one occasion, his father asks him to take a seed from a tree and to break it in order to find the hidden essence of the Nyagrodha tree. The father asks him: "What do you see there?" He replies, "The seeds are almost infinitesimal." His father wisely responds, "My son, that subtle essence which you do not perceive there, of that very essence this great Nyagrodha tree exists."

The biblical writers also sensed that the great hidden power of nature is not the product of blind natural forces that are at work, but rather reflect the creative energy with which God infused all living things—the miraculous creation of life. Abraham Joshua Heschel warns us about the inadequacy of words and restricted thought that

[298] B. O. Küpper, "Information and the Origin of Life," (Cambridge, MA: MIT Press, 1990, reprint,) 60, cited from Stephen C. Meyer's article, "The Origin of Life and the Death of Materialism" reprinted from *The Intercollegiate Review* 31, no. 2 (spring 1996).

[299] Paul Davies, "The Origin of Life II: How did it begin?"*Science Progress* (2001), 8, 17.

prevent us from experiencing the Ineffable: "The greatest hindrance to knowledge is our adjustment to conventional notions, to mental clichés. Wonder or radical amazement, the state of maladjustment to words and notions, is, therefore, a prerequisite for an authentic awareness of that which is. . . . Wonder rather than doubt is the root of knowledge."[300]

Another Interpretive View: Then God said, "Let the earth put forth vegetation: plants yielding seed – Gerald Schroder adds, "Contrary to scientific opinion held until recently, fossil data have demonstrated that the first simple plant life appeared immediately after liquid water and not billions of years later."[301] This development occurred some 3.8 billion years ago. Some cosmologists believe life on this world may originally have been seeded from asteroids that hit the earth in its infancy. Another theory, along the same line, suggests that when a large asteroid hit the earth, its impact caused rocks to be ejected from the earth (or some other life-bearing planet) into the universe, producing seeds that were necessary for life in this world. In effect, these microbes may have colonized other planets in the universe with life.

עֵץ פְּרִי עֹשֶׂה פְּרִי לְמִינוֹ אֲשֶׁר זַרְעוֹ־בוֹ עַל־הָאָרֶץ – **and fruit trees of every kind on earth that bear fruit with the seed in it** —"Fruit tree" is not to be understood here as that which would normally be identified as a fruit tree; it signifies all trees, not only those that bear fruit, but also those that have the power of propagating themselves by seeds. The word פְּרִי (*pĕrî*) is not limited *only* to fruit. All fruit can be considered פְּרִי but not all פְּרִי is necessarily fruit. For instance: spores, bacteria, fungi, algae, and non-flowering plants are examples of פְּרִי that are not fruit. When translating terminology from one language to another, it is important to keep in mind that words do not always have equivalent meanings; they may approximate in meaning, but they are not necessarily identical.

וַיְהִי־כֵן – **And it was so** — The original plants and trees were given the power to reproduce themselves with perfect similitude. To the discerning eye, this too is nothing less than wondrous. Not only is God's power visibly present in the giant sequoias of California that reach 300 feet or more in height, but the markings of Divine wisdom are no less evident in the formation of a single cell. The cell's ability to transform light energy into chemical energy, as well as its ability to cohere cooperatively in forming a complex multi-cellular aggregate, shows how God endowed life with a quality that operates even on the most microscopic level.

---

[300] Abraham Joshua Heschel, *Man Is Not Alone,* (New York: Harper and Row, 1951), 11.

[301] Gerald Schroder, *Science of God,* (New York: Free Press, 1997), 68.

1:12 וַתּוֹצֵא הָאָרֶץ דֶּשֶׁא עֵשֶׂב מַזְרִיעַ זֶרַע לְמִינֵהוּ – **The earth brought forth vegetation: plants yielding seed of every kind** – Older translations read "herbs yielding seed according to its kind" (ASV, KJV). The phrase "according to its kind" (or its equivalent) occurs ten times in this chapter, referring to vegetation and all living creatures. According to one well-known medieval mystical text, the harmony of the world—both physically and spiritually—depends upon human stewardship in ensuring that each species respect the boundaries God ordained since the beginning of Creation. Consequently, each species must commingle with only its own kind. [302] This concept will have later importance when the Torah prohibits mixing diverse seeds (Lev. 19:19, Deut. 22:9), as well as yoking together different species of animals (Deut. 22:10), or combining linen and wool (Deut. 22:11)—all of which are subsumed under the heading of "forbidden mixtures" known as כִּלְאַיִם (*kil'áyim*). Several medieval commentators view the purpose of these laws as being ecologically based, as humanity must respect the original pattern of creation.[303] This passage also contains important ethical implications for the present. As scientists begin to uncover the secrets of the human genome and cloning technology, such knowledge must be utilized wisely and reverently for the betterment of humankind.

וְעֵץ עֹשֶׂה־פְּרִי אֲשֶׁר זַרְעוֹ־בוֹ לְמִינֵהוּ – **and trees of every kind bearing fruit with the seed in it** – The Creator endowed each cell with a genetic memory of what preceded it, thus giving it the capacity to replicate its species in numbers only an advanced computer can calculate.[304] In addition to providing the world with ample

---

[302] "Therefore it is forbidden to confound species and mate them one with another, because this dislodges the heavenly power from its place and is a defiance of the celestial household. The word *kilaim* ("diverse kinds") may be connected with *kele* ("prison"), and it also bears the meaning of preventing, indicating that one who does this prevents the celestial powers from carrying out their function, and throws them into confusion" (Zohar III 86b, Soncino Translation). A similar point is stressed in *Sefer HaHinuch* a work that is commonly attributed to Rabbi Aharon HaLevi of Barcelona (1235-c. 1290). He writes, "From the outset of creation, God endowed each and every entity with a special nature to fulfill its purpose for the good of humankind. For that reason, He ordered each entity to fulfill its function according to each species, as it is written, *according to its kind* (Gen. 1:12, KJV). Cited from *Sefer HaHinuch, Mitzva* 62, (cf. *Mitzvah* 92, 244-245, 548-551).

[303] Cf. Ramban, Ibn Ezra, *Keter Torah*, and others on this verse.

[304] "At first one seed is deposited in the earth; from this one a tree springs, which in the course of its vegetative life produces one thousand five hundred and eighty-four millions of seeds. This is the first generation. The second generation will amount to two trillions, five hundred and nine thousand and fifty-six billions. The third generation will amount to three thousand nine hundred and seventy-four quadrillions, three hundred and forty-four thousand seven hundred and four trillions! And the fourth generation from these would amount to six sextillions two hundred and ninety-five thousand three hundred and sixty-two quintillions, eleven thousand one hundred and thirty-six quadrillions! Sums too immense for the human mind to conceive; and, when we allow the most confined space in which a tree can grow, it appears that the seeds of the third generation from one elm would be many myriads of times more than sufficient to stock the whole superficies of all the planets in the solar system" (Adam Clarke, *Commentary on the Old Testament* Vol. 1, *Genesis through Deuteronomy*, New

supplies of food, all living organisms depend on the complex process of photosynthesis, which is carried out by green plants.

וַיַּרְא אֱלֹהִים כִּי־טוֹב - **And God saw that it was good** — Among traditional Jews, Tuesday has been regarded as a most fitting day of the week to get married; the reason for this custom is because of the repetition of the sentence "And God saw that it was good" in the biblical account of the creation on that day (Gen. 1:10, 12).[305]

❖ *The Fourth Day (Gen. 1:14–19)*

1:14 וַיֹּאמֶר אֱלֹהִים יְהִי מְאֹרֹת – **Let there be lights**—The plural noun מְאֹרֹת (*me 'ōrōt*) comes from מָאוֹר (*mā 'ôr*) signifying "luminary," a body of light, light-bearer, and lamp.[306]

בִּרְקִיעַ הַשָּׁמַיִם לְהַבְדִּיל בֵּין הַיּוֹם וּבֵין הַלָּיְלָה - **in the dome of the sky to separate the day from the night** — Rashi writes in his commentary, based on the Talmudic passage in T.B. Hagigah 12a, that God created these celestial bodies on the first day, but on the fourth He commanded them to be suspended in the firmament (see notes to Gen. 1:3). According to this explanation, the old question of "How could plants grow on the third day without the sun?" can be answered. The sun was made on the first day of Creation, but it did not become visible until the fourth day.

וְהָיוּ לְאֹתֹת - **and let them be for signs** — To primal man, the stars functioned as lamps upon the earth. In ancient times, watching the movement of the stars and other celestial bodies enabled sailors to calculate their ship's position. Certain early Midrashim suggest that these signs also included heavenly portents, e.g., a solar or lunar eclipse was often a time of anxiety and dread. The rainbow was also considered an omen (see notes on Gen. 9:12).

וּלְמוֹעֲדִים - **and for seasons** - The word מוֹעֵד (*mô'ēd*) means temporal divisions

---

York: 1810, reprinted by Baker, Grand Rapids, MI:, 1983), 22.

[305] The Mishnah, in BT Ketuboth 2a states that virgins used to get married on Wednesdays so that, in the event she was found not to be a virgin, the aggrieved bridegroom could seek some financial remuneration by petitioning the *bet din* (Jewish court), which sat regularly on Thursdays. However, the custom arose to have it take place on Tuesdays in order to foil the custom of *jus primae noctis* (Latin for "right of the first night,"); i.e., the lord's purported legal right to deflower its virgins. For a reference to Tuesday being suitable for marriage in the New Testament, see John 2:1.

[306] Cf. Exod. 25:6, 27:20, 35:8, 14, 28, 39:37; Lev. 24:2; Num 4:9, 16; Pss. 74:16, 90:8; Prov. 15:30.

within the natural year, which are essential for preparing agricultural activities; it may also connote sacred holidays when the faith community renews itself spiritually along with the rest of Creation.

וּלְיָמִים וְשָׁנִים – **and for days and years** — The measuring of time, whether sacred or secular, helps people realize how the universe operates in an orderly manner. Without a conscious awareness of time, people are apt to lose their daily rhythm, and risk becoming spiritually disoriented, displaced, and crushed by the incessant movements of the world and the cosmos surrounding them. Through the measurement of time, daily life becomes much more organized, predictable, and meaningful. For religious people, the use of a calendar enables them to re-actualize the sacred moments of a festival or feast that gave birth to their religious and spiritual consciousness.

1:15 וְהָיוּ לִמְאוֹרֹת בִּרְקִיעַ הַשָּׁמַיִם לְהָאִיר עַל־הָאָרֶץ וַיְהִי־כֵן – **and let them be lights in the dome of the sky to give light upon the earth." And it was so.** — From the time God implemented this creative work onward, all light received by the earth is mediated through these luminaries.

1:16 וַיַּעַשׂ אֱלֹהִים אֶת־שְׁנֵי הַמְּאֹרֹת הַגְּדֹלִים אֶת־הַמָּאוֹר הַגָּדֹל לְמֶמְשֶׁלֶת הַיּוֹם – **God made the two great lights—the greater light to rule the day** — The sun and moon may be called "great," not necessarily because of their size per se, but also because of their function. Modern astronomy teaches us that even our sun is a relatively small and insignificant star when compared to the larger celestial bodies located in distant parts of the universe.

וְאֶת־הַמָּאוֹר הַקָּטֹן לְמֶמְשֶׁלֶת הַלַּיְלָה וְאֵת הַכּוֹכָבִים – **and the lesser light to rule the night and the stars** — The moon controls the ebb and flow of the oceans and influences wells and fountains. Over time, the observation of the moon's phases led to the development of the month, while the cycle of seasons led to the concept of the year. Knowing the exact positions of these celestial bodies was a vital and most practical necessity in terms of defining the time of day and the time of the year.

For the ancient shepherds of Judea, the moon provided much needed light when they would take their flock for a nocturnal grazing, to avoid the sun's rays during days when the temperature reached a blistering 115° Fahrenheit or 35° Celsius. In tropical climates, the moon's soft light was especially beloved by nomads and travelers. For those people with their pastoral roots in antiquity, the return of the moon to the nocturnal heavens became an occasion for rejoicing in the spirit of thanksgiving to God, and for bringing light back into the night. The ancient Israelites celebrated this occasion with special offerings on the Day of the New Moon ראש חדש (*rōʾš ḥōḏeš*) especially when the new moon occurred on a Sabbath.

The observant reader will notice something peculiar about this verse. Unlike the previous days of Creation, where the sky, heavens, earth, seas, and dry lands each are appropriately named, the sun and the moon do not receive any special names from God. Why the inconspicuousness of these majestic bodies? The biblical text may contain a hidden polemic directed against the various Near Eastern cults that worshiped the sun and the moon as spiritual deities.[307] Note that the names of the popular deities such as Shamash, the Mesopotamian sun god, and the lesser-known Ugaritic moon god, Yarih,[308] are also not mentioned. Both these deities commanded a popular following in ancient Israel.[309] Yet, in the eyes of the Torah, these celestial bodies were considered unworthy of worship. Nor do they astrologically control the lives and destinies of nations—and especially the people of Israel. God intended for these luminaries to serve humankind—quite the opposite of what was once believed. This account of Creation makes clear that these celestial bodies are not divine but are mere servants who obey the Creator.

1:17-18 וַיִּתֵּן אֹתָם אֱלֹהִים בִּרְקִיעַ הַשָּׁמָיִם לְהָאִיר עַל־הָאָרֶץ — **God set them in the dome of the sky to give light upon the earth.** וְלִמְשֹׁל בַּיּוֹם וּבַלַּיְלָה וּלֲהַבְדִּיל בֵּין הָאוֹר וּבֵין הַחֹשֶׁךְ – **to rule over the day and over the night and to separate the light from the darkness** The Torah emphasizes that these celestial bodies are intended to rule only over the day and the night, but that they do not exert any control over the human will. Humankind is not subservient to these astral entities.

❖ *The "Goldilocks Effect"*

וַיַּרְא אֱלֹהִים כִּי־טוֹב - **And God saw that it was good** – God carefully preordained the movement of the heavenly bodies in the cosmos. Had the Earth been

[307] The Babylonians were not the only ones to believe that the celestial bodies were animated beings. Plato and Aristotle also believed that the universe is alive, sentient, and endowed with purpose—a view that Maimonides also endorsed (cf. *Guide*, 2:4). Many passages of the Tanakh might seem to point to this belief, e.g., even every rock and tree and creature can be said to testify of God, while the heavens are said to declare his glory and show forth his handiwork (Ps. 8:1, 19:1, 104ff., 148ff; Ps. 104:3–4). The rabbis conceived of all of nature participating together in one grand divine song (cf. *Perek HaShirah*).

[308] This term is sometimes pronounced as *Yareʾaḥ*. For other possible pronunciations, see R.E. Clements's article in the TDOT, Vol. 6, (1990): 355–362. Many modern commentators are of the opinion that the names Terah and Jericho come from the same derivation.

[309] Cf. 2 Kgs. 17:16, 23:11; Isa. 47:13; Jer. 27:9; and Amos 5:26.

closer to the sun or larger than it presently became, the sun's rays would have incinerated the earth. Had the earth been just slightly farther away from the sun than its present orbit, life on our planet would have frozen. Had the earth's circular orbit (with a 3% variance) been like the elliptical orbit of the planet Mars, which varies by 42 million kilometers in its distance from the sun, the earth would incinerate annually once it came closest to the sun. Nothing is fortuitous about the Earth's orbit. Bar-Ilan University physicist Nathan Aviezer observes how fortunate this planet was in the cosmological scheme of the universe:

> Our planet Earth is very hospitable to life, abundant with air and water essential to life. Our neighbors Mars and Venus, however, have no water or air. Yet shortly after they were formed about 4.6 billion years ago, all three planets (Earth, Mars, and Venus) had comparable amounts of surface water. In fact, the deep channels that are observed today on the surface of Mars were carved out long ago by the copious, fast-flowing Martian primordial surface waters. Venus was once covered by deep oceans which contained the equivalent of a layer of water 3 kilometers deep over the entire surface of the planet. Why, then, are the two planets so completely different today?
>
> The difference in the subsequent development of Mars and Venus was due to their proximity to the Sun. Mars is somewhat more distant from the Sun than the Earth.This caused the temperature of Mars to drop in the course of time. Eventually, Mars became so cold that all its surface water froze, and as a result, the planet Mars has become completely devoid of all liquid water, thus preventing the existence of life as we know it on that planet. Venus, on the other hand, is somewhat closer to the Sun than the Earth, which caused it to gradually become hotter. As a result, Venus became so intensely hot, all its oceans and seas completely evaporated and then decomposed into hydrogen gas and oxygen gas, both of which later dissipated. Why did the Earth escape these catastrophes?
>
> The answer is that the Earth escaped these catastrophes by sheer accident! The Earth just happened to be sufficiently distant from the Sun that the runaway greenhouse effect did not occur and therefore all our surface water neither evaporated nor decomposed. Moreover, the Earth just happened to be sufficiently near the Sun that it remained warm enough to prevent all the oceans from freezing permanently into ice caps. Therefore, the Earth alone, of all the planets of the solar system, is capable of supporting life. This balance in the carbonate-silicate geochemical cycle is so delicate that if the Earth were only a few percent closer to or further from the Sun, the possibility for life could not exist. This enigmatic situation has become known among scientists as the "Goldilocks problem of climatology."[310]

The recent discovery of extrasolar planets orbiting other nearby stars, has given us a new appreciation as to the perfect conditions that exist on this planet, which produce life. One interesting planet, classified as Upsilon Andromeda b, orbits a star that is approximately 40 light-years away in the constellation Andromeda. It is a Jupiter-sized

---

[310] Nathan Aviezer, *In The Beginning: Biblical Creation and Science* (Hoboken, NJ: Ktav, 1990), 37.

planet that circles closely around its scorching star every 4.6 days—literally a world composed of fire and ice. Some planets float eerily through space with heat sources that someday may produce a new solar system, while others orbit pulsar stars, which emit such powerful bursts of energy—life as we know it would prove impossible. Paul Davies refers to our world as hitting the "cosmic jack-pot," and argues that the "cosmos" appears to have played a "conscious" role in the formation of life, and continues to play a pivotal role in the evolution of the cosmos (see Excursus 13).

❖ *Day Five of Creation (Gen. 1:20–23)*

1:20 וַיֹּאמֶר אֱלֹהִים יִשְׁרְצוּ הַמַּיִם שֶׁרֶץ נֶפֶשׁ חַיָּה – **Let the waters bring forth swarms of living creatures** — Not only was the earth endowed with the power to produce life, but so too were the waters.

וְעוֹף יְעוֹפֵף עַל־הָאָרֶץ עַל־פְּנֵי רְקִיעַ הַשָּׁמָיִם – **and let birds fly above the earth across the dome of the sky** — As G. Wenham notes: "From the ground, birds appear to fly against the background of the sky. This is one of the indications in the narrative that it is written from the perspective of a human observer."[311] (See notes to Genesis 2:4).

❖ *Animals Have Sentience and Soul*

1:21 וַיִּבְרָא אֱלֹהִים – **So God created** — Why is בָּרָא (*bārāʾ* = "created") used with reference to the "great creatures of the sea"? Are these "great creatures" singled out by the use of a special term? One suggestion is that the use of the verb בָּרָא at just this point in the narrative is intended to introduce something unprecedented; namely, the creation of the animals—a group of living beings—clearly distinguishable from the vegetation and physical world of the previous days.[312]

אֶת־הַתַּנִּינִם הַגְּדֹלִים – **the great sea monsters** — The noun תַּנִּינִם (*tannînim*) has been translated in a number of different ways. Older translations rendered it as "whales," "sea-creatures," "dragons," and other marine animals. In certain biblical passages, the תַּנִּין *(tannin)* may mean "a great serpent" or "crocodile"[313]; sometimes

[311] Gordon Wenham, *Genesis 1-15*, WBC (Dallas: Word, 2002), 24.

[312] Cf. *Abarbanel's Commentary*, G. von Rad, *(Genesis, op. cit.,* 56-57); C. Westermann (*Genesis 1-11*, *op.cit.*, 126).

[313] Cf. Exod. 7:9-12; Deut. 32:33; Ps. 91:13 *et al.*

symbolizing Egypt, Israel's nemesis (Ezek. 29:3, 32:2), or Babylon (cf. Jer. 51:34). Much of the biblical imagery here follows the descriptions familiar from the Ugaritic myth; e.g., the seven-headed serpent known as *tnn* who was also known as *Yamm* (Sea), Baal's fierce and dangerous enemy.[314]

The Torah makes specific mention of these creatures in order to stress that they are not rivals to the Divine. God alone reigns sovereign over all His creatures just as He reigns supreme over all forces of nature. Moreover, every creature obediently serves its purpose and is good in God's eyes. Their placement in the Genesis creation story indicates that their existence is totally benign. In fact, one of the most famous mythical creatures of the sea, the Leviathan, is described in the Psalms as a harmless and playful creature (Ps. 104:26)[315] and is frequently identified with the whale or dolphin.[316]

וְאֵת כָּל־נֶפֶשׁ הַחַיָּה הָרֹמֶשֶׂת – **and every living creature that moves** – The expression נֶפֶשׁ הַחַיָּה (*népeš haḥayyāh*) means "living soul."[317] Simply stated, humankind and the animal world share a mutual passion for life. Both animals and human beings share the qualities of breath, mind, *and personality*—as any pet-owner or zoologist will readily attest to! By the term "soul" we mean any entity that experiences feelings, perceptions and a capacity to act. These qualities form the basis of sentient life. The German Bible scholar Claus Westermann explains the expression נֶפֶשׁ הַחַיָּה "can describe the animals in general, animals and humans living together as living beings, and finally that which makes animals and humans 'living beings,' namely, the breath of life."[318] The

---

314 See James Pritchard, *The Ancient Near East: An Anthology of Text and Pictures* (ANET) (Princeton: Princeton University Press, 1958), 137–138b; Karel Van der Toorn, Bob Becking, and Pieter Willem Van Der Horst, *Dictionary of Deities and Demons in the Bible* (Leiden; Boston; Grand Rapids, Brill: Eerdmans, 1999), 511-514.

315 In Job 41:5, God joyfully plays with it, a creature of minor importance in the biblical imagination—contrary to the great significance it plays in Ugaritic mythology. See Karel Van der Toorn, Bob Becking, and Pieter Willem Van Der Horst, *Dictionary of Deities and Demons in the Bible, op. cit.,* 511-514. In addition, the Talmud cites an Aggadic tradition that says God plays with the Leviathan during the last three hours of the day (T. B. Avodah Zara 3b).

316 D. R. W Wood ed., *New Bible Dictionary* (Downers Grove, IL. InterVarsity Press 1996, c1982, c1962), 729.

317 By itself, the term נֶפֶשׁ (*nepeš*) has a broad range of semantic meanings throughout the Tanakh. The basic meaning of נֶפֶשׁ is associated with: (1)" throat" (cf. Isa. 5:14), (2) "desire," "appetite," and "hunger" (cf. Gen. 34:8; Hos. 9:4; Song. 1:7; 3:14), (3) "breath" as in "refreshing" (cf. Exod. 23:12; 31:17), for it is inhalation that makes a person or an animal a "living being" (Gen. 35:18; 1 Kgs. 17:2; Jer. 4:31).

318 Claus Westermann, *Genesis 1-11: A Continental Commentary* (Minneapolis: Augsburg Publishing House, 1984), 136.

ethical implications of נֶפֶשׁ are important for the way human beings relate both to each other as well as to the animal world, as it is written "The righteous know the needs of their animals, but the heart of the wicked is merciless" (Prov. 12:10). The English word for animal, derived from the Latin root *anima*, also means "soul." As stewards of God's creation, human beings must not treat any of God's sentient creatures with callous indifference.

וַיַּרְא אֱלֹהִים כִּי־טוֹב – **And God saw that it was good** – The recurring phrase "it was good" emphasizes that the world was suffused with original goodness, making it worthy of receiving God's blessing. There is no insufficiency or want, for God provides for all His creatures with all their unique needs. Even the lowly mosquito, which subsists on the blood of other creatures, fulfills a positive purpose in the scheme of creation, as do other noxious creatures. Even the dangerous creatures which co-inhabit this world are all God's creatures (vv. 2, 21).

Another Interpretive View: And God saw that it was good – Evil is not woven into the fabric of creation. Although creation is not considered to be complete without humankind, the rest of creation still has value and importance to God, who cherishes the work of His creativity; the world and all of its varieties of creatures are perceived as being inherently good. The Torah's optimism stands in stark contrast with pagan accounts that portray the world as a place of scarcity, an arena for power-driven deities competing with one another to expand their control and power over the universe. God created the world with a great deal of diversity and wonder. The whole earth is full of His glory and presence. Theodoret expresses a similar thought and argues that this passage may also serve as a refutation of the Gnostic opinion, which regards the world as an evil place. For this reason, argues Theodoret, the biblical narrator stresses the goodness of creation so that people will not find fault with what God esteems as good![319]

1:22 וַיְבָרֶךְ אֹתָם אֱלֹהִים לֵאמֹר פְּרוּ וּרְבוּ וּמִלְאוּ אֶת־הַמַּיִם בַּיַּמִּים וְהָעוֹף יִרֶב בָּאָרֶץ – **God blessed them, saying, "Be fruitful and multiply and fill the waters in the seas, and let birds multiply on the earth"** – The verse seems to imply that only the sea creatures and birds received this blessing, but not the land animals! Rashi felt perplexed as to why the land animals were not also included, and suggests that God refrained from doing so, in order to exclude the serpent, which was destined to be cursed.[320] Rashi's penchant for citing a Midrashic explanation hardly seems contextually fitting since reptiles are no less blessed than any other creature—land or sea. Aharon ben

---

319 *The Questions on the Octateuch: On Genesis and Exodus, op. cit.*, 27.

320 Gen. Rabbah 11:3, *Midrash Tadshe* 1.

Eliahu suggests a simpler explanation.[321] The primal couple's blessing is not limited to just them (v. 28); it pertains to everything else God made and blessed on that day, which includes the land animals and reptilian creatures.[322]

Nahum Sarna argues that God purposely avoided blessing the land animals, lest they multiply and compete with people, thus endangering human survival (Exod. 23:29; Lev. 26:22).[323] However, this explanation also seems unlikely. When God originally created the world, there was an abundance of food for every creature. Animals did not become competitive with humankind until after the Flood. Once humans chose to become carnivorous, their bond with the animal world changed; since humans were now allowed to hunt animals for food, what was good for the hunter was now equally good for the hunted—each becoming interchangeable. Thus, humankind became fair game to predatory animals and vice versa—this alone explains the enmity between them.

From the view of the biblical writers, the violence that is seen in the animal kingdom is but a symptom of a post-Edenic existence. God intended for humankind to live in peace and harmony with these creatures of the earth. The prophet Hosea envisions an era when Israel would live in a state of peace with all the wild animals of the field, birds, and creeping things (Hosea 2:20). Likewise, in the Messianic visions of Isaiah, the prophet foresaw a time when "The wolf will live with the lamb, the leopard will lie down with the goat, the calf and the lion and the yearling together; and a little child will lead them" (Isaiah 11:6). Subsequently, while exegetes like Maimonides and others have often interpreted this famous passage metaphorically, the literal meaning of the text should not be overlooked.

Another Interpretive View: וַיְבָרֶךְ אֹתָם אֱלֹהִים לֵאמֹר -- **God blessed them** – The biblical concept of blessing involves more than just wishing for benevolence. When used in the Tanakh, the term בָּרַךְ (*bērak̲* = "bless") includes anything that produces a sense of well-being and harmony with God and Creation. Typically, a blessing conveys the presence of a power to the object being blessed. God's blessings have diverse manifestations in the phenomenal world, which include: health, vitality, longevity, fertility, land, prosperity, and power.[324] With respect to this particular verse, God endows the animal kingdom with a capacity to replicate itself as often as necessary. Note

---

[321] Aharon ben Eliahu, *Keter Torah* (Eupatoria, 1867), 29.

[322] Elsewhere Rashi wrote that when God blessed the primal couple in verse 28, all the animals were also included in the first part of the verse "Be fruitful and multiply and fill the waters in the seas" (*Teshuvot L'Rashi* [*Responsa of Rashi*] #196).

[323] Nahum Sarna, *Genesis* JPSTC, 47

[324] Cf. Gen. 17:16; 20; 22:17; 48:4; Exod. 23:25; Deut. 7:3, 13; 7:12-14; 26:15; 28:4, 8, passim.

that although God gave the capacity to the plant world to multiply (see notes on 1:11), here God personally blesses the animal world because they are sentient creatures like humankind and have some degree of moral standing in the hierarchy of Creation.

1:24 וַיֹּאמֶר אֱלֹהִים תּוֹצֵא הָאָרֶץ נֶפֶשׁ חַיָּה לְמִינָהּ בְּהֵמָה וָרֶמֶשׂ – And God said, "Let the earth bring forth living creatures of every kind, cattle and creeping things — The word נֶפֶשׁ (*nepeš*) implies a soul, as distinguished from plants, which have unconscious life. See the notes to Genesis 1:21.

וְחַיְתוֹ־אֶרֶץ לְמִינָהּ וַיְהִי־כֵן – and wild animals of the earth of every kind. And it was so — The Torah classifies the animal kingdom in a threefold manner: (1) domestic animals, which are herbivorous by nature, and capable of being tamed and utilized for human purposes, such as cattle; (2) creeping things—reptiles, insects, and very small quadrupeds; (3) wild beasts, such as lions, tigers, or any animal that lives off the flesh of another.[325] The animals, like the plants (cf. v. 11; also, as regards the production of fishes by the waters, v. 20), are represented as having been produced by the earth.

The Emergence of Humankind
Gen.1:26-30

26 Then God said, "Let us make humankind in our image, according to our likeness; and let them have dominion over the fish of the sea, and over the birds of the air, and over the cattle, and over all the wild animals of the earth, and over every creeping thing that creeps upon the earth."
27 So God created humankind in his image, in the image of God he created them; male and female he created them.
28 God blessed them, and God said to them, "Be fruitful and multiply, and fill the earth and subdue it; and have dominion over the fish of the sea and over the birds of the air and over every living thing that moves upon the earth."
29 God said, "See, I have given you every plant yielding seed that is upon the face of all the earth, and every tree with seed in its fruit; you shall have them for food.
30 And to every beast of the earth, and to every bird of the air, and to everything that creeps on the earth, everything that has the breath of life, I have given every green plant for food." And it was so.
31 God saw everything that he had made, and indeed, it was very good. And there was evening and there was morning, the sixth day.

When the Holy One created man He set in him all the images of the supernal mysteries of the world above, and all the images of the lower mysteries of the world below, and all are designed in man, who stands in the image of God. . . . What, then, is man? Does he consist solely of skin, flesh,

[325] With respect to the latter, וְחַיְתוֹ־אֶרֶץ (*weḥayĕtô ereṣ*) signifies any "beast of prey" especially and only when it is accompanied by the qualifying term "land" or "field," as in חַיַּת הָאָרֶץ (Gen. 9:2) or חַיַּת הַשָּׂדֶה (Gen. 2:20).

bones and sinews? Nay, the essence of man is his soul; the skin, flesh, bones and sinews are but an outward covering, the mere garments, but they are not the man. When man departs (from this world) he divests himself of all these garments. The skin with which he covers himself, and all these bones and sinews, all have a symbolism in the mystery of the Supernal Wisdom . . .

—ZOHAR 2:75b-76a

Why have I two eyes if not to behold Thy glorious vision?
Why have I two ears if not to hear Thy gentle whisper?
Why have I the sense of smell if not to breathe the essence of Thy spirit?
Why have I two lips, Beloved, if not to kiss Thy beautiful countenance?
Why have I two hands if not to work in Thy divine cause?
Why have I two legs if not to walk in Thy spiritual path?
Why have I a voice if not to sing Thy celestial song?
Why have I a heart, Beloved, if not to make it Thy sacred dwelling?

—HAZARAT INAYAT KHAN, *Bowl of Saki*

❖ *Day Six of Creation (Gen. 1:26–31)*

The Midrash compares the appearance of man at this juncture of Creation to that of a king who prepares a lavish banquet, all for the guest of honor. The fowl of the air and the fish of the sea, what were they created for? Of what avail is a tower full of appetizing dainties, with no guest to enjoy them? Saadia Gaon (882–942 C. E.) likened the first six days of Creation to a builder who constructs a palace, and after decorating and furnishing it with all its needs, finally brings the owner who will live inside it.[326] Everything in creation was thus prepared for humankind—the crown of God's earthly creation.[327] In contrast with the rest of creation, humanity occupies a different position in the world (Psa. 8:1; Ezek. 28:12) in that God made humanity "a little lower than the angels" (Psa. 8:5). Humankind has been empowered to rule over the living things on earth but must in turn submit to being ruled over by God.

Despite humanity's special and privileged position in the scheme of creation, rabbinic wisdom teaches that humanity should remember its place with an attitude of humility, so "if a man's mind becomes too proud, he may be reminded that even the gnats preceded him in the order of creation."[328] In other words, humanity was a

[326] Saadia Gaon, *Emunot V'Deot,* Introduction to Part IV.

[327] Gen. Rabbah 8:6; Tosefta Sanhedrin 8:7–8.

[328] BT Sanhedrin 38a.

latecomer to a world that was already complete with a multiplicity of life-forms. Therefore, it is only apropos that human beings respect every creature—great and small—for everything in the created order preceded us.

❖ *Verbal Archaeology: "Image" and "Likeness"*

1:26 וַיֹּאמֶר אֱלֹהִים – Then God said – To His Heavenly retinue or to all of Creation (Kimchi).

נַעֲשֶׂה אָדָם – Let us make humankind – The plural נַעֲשֶׂה (*na'ăśeh*) "Let us make" has been interpreted in a number of ways and may convey: (1) "plural of majesty" (2) the plural of self-deliberation (3) the fullness of attributes and powers. As previously noted, there is no linguistic basis for those who argue for a Trinitarian view of the Deity, for the plural of majesty is never indicated with verbs or pronouns, but only with nouns. The German scholar Gerhard Von Rad explains, "The creation of man is introduced more impressively than any preceding work by the announcement of a divine resolution: 'Let us make man.' God participates more intimately and intensively in this than in the earlier works of creation."[329]

בְּצַלְמֵנוּ כִּדְמוּתֵנוּ – according to our likeness, in our image" – The expression בְּצַלְמֵנוּ (*bəṣalménû* ="In our image") refers to the image of the angels (Rashbam), or alternatively, to the image that God and His heavenly retinue designed (Rashi), while כִּדְמוּתֵנוּ (*kiḏmûṯénû* = according to our likeness") implies, "according to our wisdom," for when a human being fails to live in accordance with God's wisdom, he is more comparable to the beasts of the field who perish forever (Psa. 49:13).[330] Rashbam suggests that creation of the angels is only hinted at; the biblical narrator focuses primarily upon the earthly creations that are mentioned in Exodus 20:11 (Rashbam). Some rabbinic commentaries see the "divine image" in terms of the human capacity to consciously exercise moral decisions.[331]

---

[329] Gerhard von Rad, *Genesis: A Commentary* (Philadelphia, Westminster Press. 1972), 57.

[330] Rashbam's interpretation is similar to Irenaeus's exposition of "likeness," as we shall soon see in the next two sections ahead.

[331] Rabbi Meir Simcha HaKohen of Dvinsk writes, "Human freedom derives from the 'space' God vacates for humankind to make ethical choices, thus repudiating the philosophical doctrine of determinism. . . . When the Torah says, 'Let us make humankind in our likeness and in our image,' the Torah is 'merely speaking in the manner of people,'

רק זאת אנו יודעים, שלהבחירה החפשית הוא מצמצום האלקות, שהשם יתברך מניח מקום לברואיו לעשות כפי מה שיבחרו ושלל ממפעליהם הגזירה וההחלטה בפרטיות. ולכן אמר "אל לבו, נעשה אדם בצלמנו", פירוש, שהתורה מדברת בלשון בני אדם, שאמר

One could argue that דְמוּת (*dĕmût* = "likeness") connotes "a model" or "template" or "copy" (cf. 2 Kgs. 16:10; Isa. 40:18; Ezek. 23:15).[332] This particular abstract noun appears most frequently in Ezekiel's vision of the divine chariot.[333] C. Westermann notes that דְמוּת "fluctuates between 'representation' and 'something which is like.'"[334] Thus דְמוּת serves to soften the idea that humankind is made in the actual image of God.[335] By way of analogy, one could also say that a beast may share some external attributes with human beings; yet, one would not say that it bears the *image* of a human being. In the same manner, a human bears only a likeness to God, but he is not synonymous with God.

The noun צֶלֶם (*ṣélem*) frequently refers to a tangible model or figurine; i.e., a sculptured representation. צֶלֶם is related to the Arabic verb *ṣalama* "to hew, chop off, or cut." In Akkadian *ṣalmu* is a "statue, figure or image." Although צֶלֶם primarily pertains to "image" or "figurine," it may also be distantly related to the root צלם connoting "darkness," as in "little black one, little dark one"[336] Some ancient texts speak about man as being *ḵi miśulu śi illi* ("the shadow of God is man").[337] Just as the shadow is a faint

---

נניח מקום לבחירת האדם שלא יהא מוכרח במפעליו ומחויב במחשבותיו

[332] See TDOT: 3:257 and the TLOT: 1:340. This view is similar to Rashi's.

[333] Cf. Ezek 1:5, 10, 13, 16, 22, 26, 28.

[334] *Genesis 1-11*, 147.

[335] Some modern biblical scholars like Jeffrey Tigay contend that the ancient biblical writers understood the concept of "image" in physical terms! Just as the Aramaic word *demuta*, "likeness," appears in line 1 of the Tell Fekheriyeh inscription in the meaning "statue," so does the word *salma* "image" appears in line 22 with the same meaning. There we read, "The statue, which represents Hadad-Ishi, King of Guzana and of Sikan and of Zaran." Line 26 of the inscription again employs the word *demuta* to mean statue when it states, "He [Hadad-Ishi] made this statue better than (the statue) that preceded this (one)." Tigay, "The Image," p. 170; regarding the inscription, see Ali Abu-Assaf, Pierre Bordreuil, and Alan R. Millard, *La Statue de Tell Fekherye et son Inscription bilingue assyro-araméenne* (Paris, 1982); Jonas Greenfield and Aaron Shaffer, "Notes on the Akkadian-Aramaic Bilingual Statue from Tell Fekheryeh," in *Iraq* 45 (1983), 109–116; Frank Moore Cross, Jr., "Paleography and the Date of the Tell Fahariyeh Bilingual Inscription," in Z. Zevit, S. Gitin and M. Sokoloff, eds., *Solving Riddles and Untying Knots: Biblical, Epigraphic and Semitic Studies in Honor of Jonas C. Greenfield* (Winona Lake, 1995), 393–409.

[336] HALOT: 1029.

[337] Ivan Engnell, *Studies in Divine Kingship in the Ancient Near East* (New York: Blackwell, 1967,) vi. See Marten Stol, F. A. M. Wiggermann, *Birth In Babylonia & The Bible (Cuneiform Monographs, 14) (Cuneiform Monographs, 14)* (Boston: Brill, 2000), 148. Cf. *The Assyrian and Babylonian Letters Belonging to the Kouyunjik Collection(s) of the British Museum*, by R. F. Harper (Chicago, 1892–1914), the ancient scribe proclaims: "Man is the shadow of a god and

reflection of the individual beneath the sun, so too is the "image of God" only a faint reflection of the Divine. Differing from the attitudes of Egyptian and Mesopotamian society, the Torah declares that it is not just the king who bears within him the divine image; rather, every human being reflects the likeness of God and serves as His representative on earth. King and commoner alike share this Divine image and likeness.

❖ *The Participation Mystique of the Image*

To the archaic consciousness, an image shares in the reality of what it represents. However, the image means more than a simple representation—the idols contain the deities' "life-force" or *élan vital* much like the body "houses" the soul. Throughout the ANE, images and statues represented deities and kings. Roman emperors, for example, especially loved having their bust appear in all the countries of their Empire as a reminder of their political or military power and presence. If an ancient Celtic or Judean disrespected a Roman Emperor's statue, he would risk being executed, for an assault on the image was considered as though one assaulted the Emperor himself! Peoples of antiquity believed that the essence of a being "lives" within its image. Thus, a god is himself present and operative in his or her image. An Egyptian sculptor would symbolically animate the image by breathing into the mouth of the vessel, thereby infusing it with the deity's life force and being.[338] Once this rite occurred, the idol is believed to have magically participated in the divinity's existence and reality.[339]

By the same token, the "image of God" could also refer to the human body that houses the Presence and Reality of the Divine. Once God "breathes" into Adam's body, instantly it becomes a vessel for harboring the Divine. Therefore, the "image of God" represents the manifestation of an invisible and heavenly reality, form, and substance. More than any other entity on the planet, humans contain within their nature the "life force," the *élan vital* of the Creator who transcends Creation. Ibn Ezra adds that a

---

a slave is the shadow of a man; but-the king is the mirror of a god" (*ANET* 594). According to Philo, when speaking about the "image of God," he notes that the Logos is also "the shadow of God" since "He represents the world before God as High Priest, Intercessor, Paraclete. He is the Shekhinah, or glory of God; but also the darkness or shadow of God since the creature half conceals and half reveals the Creator" (*On Dreams* 1, 75).

[338] A passage from the Memphite Theology reveals, "He placed the gods in their shrines, He settled their offerings, He established their shrines, He made their bodies according to their wishes. Thus the gods entered into their bodies, Of every wood, every stone, every clay." See M. Lichtheim, *Ancient Egyptian Literature,* 3 vols. (Berkeley, CA: 1971), Vol. 1, 55.

[339] In some of the Eastern religions the masses regard the graven image as an embodiment of the deity. In the Hindu tradition, there is a ceremony called *pratishta* (a term used for dedicating a newly made idol for the deity it represents) where the maker or the owner of the idol consecrates the image by inviting the deity to take up residence. This idol then serves the worshiper as a locus of the deity, the focal point of his or her devotion.

person can understand the mystery of God's Presence by observing the mystery of the human soul, "Just as the soul is incorporeal and fills the body, which is a microcosm, in the same way, God fills the universe, for the Scriptures state, "in our image, according to our likeness." [340] Job expresses this same idea in poetic terms: "And from my flesh I shall behold God" (Job 19:26).

❖ *The Principle and Ideal of "Image" and "Likeness"*

Every generation has the task to re-weave its understanding of sacred text. What was true for the earliest generations of interpreters is no less true today. For the early Christian thinker, Irenaeus (*ca.* 180 C.E.), there is an important theological distinction between the terms "image" and the "likeness" of God. The concept of image denotes the raw substance which has the spiritual potential that can enable each human being to transform into a Divine "likeness" of God. Each of us embarks on a life journey where we will ideally evolve from being a mere "creature of God" to becoming a true "child of God."[341] This theological theme finds at least partial expression in the teachings of R. Hama bar Hanina (3rd c.), who explains that when it comes to imitating God, the best mortals can aspire to, is to be God-like by emulating God's ways in their behavior.[342]
The Divine image and likeness give humanity the capacity to choose to become an ethical being (cf. Exod. 35:21–22, 29).[343] Humanity's uniqueness is its ability to exercise free will, and to be self-reflective.[344] The concept of the *imago Dei* has especially great importance with respect to people who are physically incapacitated and struggle for the right to survive. The value of an individual does not end once that person ceases to offer society any further utility. Ultimately, it is God—and not society—who determines the

---

[340] Antecedents of this concept can be read in Philo, *On the Creation.*, 23; BT Berakhot 10a; Tanhuma Hayye Sarah 3; Zohar I, 125a. It is easy to detect a strong Stoic influence in the early rabbinic traditions that compare the relation of God and soul, which gives life to the body, as God fills the world and sees it without being seen (cf. Seneca, *Epistulea* 7, 65, 23). L. Ginzburg points out other Stoic ideas that influenced rabbinic thought (BT Sanhedrin 91b), e.g., according to which the soul enters the body at the time of conception (*Legends of the Jews,* 57; see Excursus 20).

[341] Irenaeus, *Against the Heresies* 5.6.1.

[342] See BT Sotah 14a.

[343] Maimonides observes that humanity's likeness to God must go beyond just cultivating the intellect. The expansion of human consciousness cannot afford to ignore the ethical. At the end of his *Guide* (3:34), Maimonides concludes that the philosophical knowledge of God means little, if anything, if it does not inspire humaneness, justice, and compassion for God's creatures (MT. *Hilchot De'ot* 1:5-7).

[344] Biblical ethics are founded in the belief that humanity was created in the image of God; the realization of this concept becomes a legal imperative. God enjoins His people to be like him (Lev. 19:2) and to walk in His ways (Deut. 10:12, 26:17). This concept is the consistent motivation for the commandments to love the stranger and treat the widow and orphan justly (Deut. 10:18-19), to be gracious to the poor (Exod. 22:26), and to judge righteously (Deut. 1:17).

worth of an individual. Although the body may be weak, a trace of the soul always remains and that vestige never ceases to exist until the time of death. Arguably, the same principle is no less present in the early formation of a human being while it is in its mother's womb. Questions concerning the beginning of life and the end of life must, therefore, be approached with the utmost reverence and respect.

❖ *The Meaning of "Dominion"*

וְיִרְדּוּ בִדְגַת הַיָּם וּבְעוֹף הַשָּׁמַיִם וּבַבְּהֵמָה וּבְכָל־הָאָרֶץ וּבְכָל־הָרֶמֶשׂ הָרֹמֵשׂ עַל־הָאָרֶץ —
And let them have dominion over the fish of the sea, and over the birds of the air, and over the cattle, and over all the wild animals of the earth, and over every creeping thing that creeps upon the earth – What does the Hebrew term for "dominion" imply? Does it connote exploitation and coercion? Some modern theologians believe that this passage in particular is responsible for Western exploitation of nature, and is directly culpable for the ecological woes of the world. But is such a view necessarily warranted? Without a clear knowledge of the Hebraic expression, it is difficult to ascertain its theological and ethical meaning. Significantly, the biblical term for "dominion" is referred to as רָדָה (*raḏā^h^*). Its precise etymology is complex. In some of the Semitic languages רְדָא means "plough," "rule," or "drive" as in forcing someone or something to follow a specific course and direction." It could also mean to "chastise," "domineer" or "compel." In Tigre *rädäya* means "to be ruled" and "to be tamed." In Arabic *radā* (*rdy*) means "tread," or "trample" (HALOT: 1190). Some scholars note that in Akkadian *rädadu* means "pursue" while in Assyrian, *radû* means "go" or "flow" and is similar to the common Hebrew verb יָרַד (*yarad*) " go downward."

However, Claus Westermann has persuasively argued that the basic meaning of the verb does not so much mean to rule but rather depicts how the shepherd travels with his flock.[345] In his commentary, Westermann offers one of the clearest theological explanations pertaining to this challenging biblical passage:

> Dominion over animals certainly does not mean their exploitation by humans. People would forfeit their kingly role among the living (that is what רָדָה is referring to) were the animals to become the object of their whim. The establishment of a hierarchal order between humans and the animals means that the animals are not there just "to vegetate"; the relationship between them is to be understood in a positive sense. . . . It is the attitude of humans towards other living beings that should characterize the human attitude to world about them; and this means a markedly personal attitude. People can remain human in their dominance over the animals: the shepherd speaks with a human voice which communicates to his fellow creatures (John 10:3). Something of this too

---

[345] Ibid., 355.

belongs to the rider, the horse trainer and even the hunter.[346] [347]

Norbert Lohfink also arrives at a similar conclusion. Lohfink argues that the noun רָדָה (*radāh*), which is usually translated as "to have dominion over" connotes the basic sense of "wandering about." Its semantic field includes "accompany," "guide," "pasture," "lead," "rule," and "command." The pastoral imagery of these word associations is striking. That is to say, the purpose of humankind is to shepherd God's creation. According to Lolfink, Genesis 1 ought to be viewed as a prophetic text, which presents a utopian vision of how humankind is meant to relate toward the rest of Creation. In such an ideal society, there is no war; neither is there exploitation of the created order. Humanity's role is to look after the welfare of Creation—much like the shepherd looks after the well-being of the flock he is entrusted to guard.[348]

Both Westermann and Lohfink's interpretation conceive of "dominion" in pastoral terms. In the ancient world, the king epitomized pastoral power; more than any other individual, the king was entrusted to uphold the cosmic order. The king's task was not only to provide order and promote life for the kingdom, but also had to defend the kingdom against the forces of chaos and death that could engulf it from time to time. Majestic power had to be used ethically and justly, publicly and privately. When the kings of Israel exploited those who were vulnerable, the prophets confronted their injustice and cruelty (2 Sam. 11-12; 1 Kgs. 21ff.). In Ezekiel 34ff. the prophet contrasts the wicked shepherd exploiting the flock with the righteous shepherd who acts compassionately toward his flock. The Hebraic concept of "dominion" suggests terms of graciousness, support, tenderness, attentiveness, and justice as defined in Psalm 23. The Torah advises that human beings would be wise to relate to all sentient creatures—great and small—as God, Himself relates to them. Humanity's "dominion" does not entitle us to cruelly exploit the animal world or nature. Hence "dominion" epitomizes the combined qualities that are involved in the wise stewardship and management of all God's creatures. Such stewardship recognizes the interconnectedness and interdependence of all entities that co-habit the earth with humanity.

1:27 וַיִּבְרָא אֱלֹהִים אֶת־הָאָדָם – So God created humankind in his image, –
Gerhard Von Rad's comments are especially insightful: "The use of the verb בָּרָא (*bārā)* in v. 27 receives its fullest significance for that divine creativity which is absolutely

346 Westermann, *Genesis 1-11*, *op. cit.*, 159-60.

347 In primal societies it is not uncommon for hunters to ask forgiveness from the animal prior to the act of slaying them for food.

348 N. Lohfink, *Great Themes of the Old Testament* (Edinburg: T&T Clark, 1982), 178-179. See M. Samuel, *The Lord is My Shepherd: The Theology of the Caring God* (Northvale, NJ: Jason Aronson Inc. 1996).

without analogy."[349]

בְּצַלְמוֹ בְּצֶלֶם אֱלֹהִים בָּרָא אֹתוֹ – **in the image of God he created them** – Many rabbinic commentators interpret בְּצֶלֶם אֱלֹהִים to mean "in the image of the angels"[350] (this interpretation would explain why the verse says, "Let us make . . . ") since אֱלֹהִים (*ʾĕlōhîm*) frequently refers to angelic beings.[351] This image is the source of our spiritual uniqueness and potential, and it is also the source of our existential angst in the Post-Edenic world, an important theme that will be discussed in a later chapter.

זָכָר וּנְקֵבָה בָּרָא אֹתָם – **male and female he created them** – The term אָדָם (*ʾāḏām*) is used as a collective noun and simply denotes "humankind." This understanding is also reflected in the Targum Neofiti translation, which invariably renders אָדָם as בַּר־נָשָׁא (*ḇar-nāšā* ="son of man," i.e., "the human race"). To the ancient Hebraic imagination, אָדָם refers to both the male and the female, for each gender possesses and partakes in the image of God equally.[352] According to one medieval

---

[349] Gerhard Von Rad, *Genesis: A Commentary*, *op. cit.,* 57.

[350] Cf. the commentaries of Pseudo Targum-Jonathan; Midrash Tanchuma Shemoth 18; Gen. Rabbah 8:11, 14:13; Rashi, Seforno, Rashbam and Ibn Ezra.

[351] Abarbanel disagrees with this interpretation and insist that אֱלֹהִים consistently refers to God throughout the creation story and not to the angels. This line of reasoning on the surface seems correct for nowhere does the creation story even mention anything about the creation of angels.

[352] Although the Genesis 1 story defines both male and female equally as possessing the image of God, classical Christian theologians regard the male as the normative image of God in such a way as to make woman the lower or the "fallen" part of the self. While it is never denied that women possess some relationship to the image of God, that image for the most part, is defined by their relationship to men. As mentioned earlier, Aquinas observes: "The image of God, in its principle signification, namely the intellectual nature, is found both in man and in woman. But in a secondary sense the image of God is found in man, and not in woman; for man is the beginning and end of woman, as God is the beginning and end of every creature" *Summa Theologica* (New York: Benziger, 1947), 1. Q. 93. A. 4; See also Q. 96, A. 3 and *Summa* 1 Q. 92]. See Calvin's commentary in the beginning of Leviticus 12, who unabashedly writes about women, ". . . there is more vice in this sex!" Among the medieval Judaic scholars, Don Isaac Abarbanel shared many of Aquinas' attitudes regarding the lowly nature of women (see B. Netanyahu's *Don Isaac Abarbanel - Statesman and Philosopher* [New York: JPS, 1953], 136-138. See Ba'ale Turim's exposition on Genesis 1:27. Regarding the blessing: שֶׁלֹּא עָשַׂנִי אִשָּׁה *cf. Tikiunei Zohar* 133a; *Doveri Sofrim* c. 12; *Dover Shabbat* [Parshat Achrei Mot c. 4]; *Hanhagat HaTsadikim—Minhagat Avraham HaLevy. Cf.* Ramban's exposition of Leviticus 1:3 and 3:4); Y.T. Langermann, Yemenite *Midrash: Philosophical Commentaries on the Torah* (New York: Harper Collins, 1996), 70. R. Eliezer Berkowitz, who was one of the most important Orthodox rabbinic scholars of the 20th century, candidly admits, "It is surprising that such negative opinions could find their place beside the most positive expressions of appreciation of the function of a woman in the life of the people" *Crisis and Faith* (New York: Sanhedrin Press, 1976), 100.

mystical text, each gender possesses aspects of the other sex; no one person possesses only masculine or feminine traits, "High mysteries are revealed in these two verses 'Male and Female He created them' to make known the Glory on high, the mystery of faith, out of this mystery, Adam was created. . . . Any image that does not embrace male and female is not a high and true image."[353]

In terms of human biology, every human being produces both male and female hormones such as: testosterone, estrogen, and others. Sex is determined by the presence or absence of the Y chromosome in the sperm that fertilizes the ovum to form an embryo. As well, gender is manifested by the relative amounts of male and female sex hormones infusing the fetus during development *in utero*. Rarely are babies born with indeterminate sexual characteristics and sometimes may be assigned a gender based on their appearance. Alternatively, they may undergo surgical procedures to align their external sexual characteristics with their hormonal or Y-chromosome status. Gender and sexual orientation are further characterized by the ratio of male and female hormones produced by the body before and during secondary sexual development from puberty to adulthood. Therefore, gender is not about duality but rather based on a number of biological occurrences which include a varying spectrum of female and male hormones ranging from the extremely masculine to the extremely feminine. Gender and sexual orientation are not conscious choices but are based on biological phenomena.[354]

Another Interpretive View: So God created humankind in his image, in the image of God he created them; male and female he created them – According to Tikva Frymer-Kensky, "The Bible's view of the essential sameness of men and women is most appropriate to monotheism. There are no goddesses to represent "womanhood" or a female principle in the cosmos; there is no conscious sense that there even exists a "feminine." Whenever radical monotheism came to biblical Israel, the consideration of one God influenced and underscored the biblical image of women."[355]

1:28 וַיְבָרֶךְ אֹתָם אֱלֹהִים וַיֹּאמֶר לָהֶם אֱלֹהִים – God blessed them, and God said to them – This is the very first time God directly addresses an entity who is capable of

---

[353] Daniel Matt, *Zohar, The Book of Enlightenment* (Philadelphia: Paulist Press, 1983), 55.

[354] The recent discovery of the "homosexual gene" a.k.a. Chromosome Xq28 suggests that homosexuality is a hereditary characteristic. The controversial article was authored by Dean H. Hamer, S.Hu, Victoria L. Magnuson, Nan Hu, and Angela M.L Pattatucci: "A Linkage Between DNA Markers on the X Chromosome and Male Sexual Orientation" *Science* 261, 321. However, this study only pertains to the area that influences individual variations in sexual orientation in men and not in women. Nevertheless, new scientific findings may impact how we view and interpret Leviticus 18:22 and 20:13.

[355] Tikva Frymer-Kensky, *In the Wake of the Goddesses: Women, Culture, and the Biblical Transformation of Pagan Myth* (New York: Free Press, 1992), 142-143.

not only listening to the Creator, but who can consciously respond! The dialogical relationship between God and humankind is predicated on the belief that the Creator formed humankind to enter into a dialogical and covenantal relationship based on mutuality. Note that there is no hierarchy with respect to the primal couple's status. Each is capable of entering into an "I and Thou" relationship with God.

פְּרוּ וּרְבוּ וּמִלְאוּ אֶת־הָאָרֶץ וְכִבְשֻׁהָ – **"Be fruitful and multiply, and fill the earth and subdue it"** — This refers to the entire inhabited world without any geographic or territorial limitation. Humans may dwell wherever they desire. God's blessing is evidential in the manifestation creating fertility, progeny, abundance, peace, happiness, vitality, health, and longevity. In short, blessing includes anything that produces a sense of well-being and harmony with God and Creation.

The verb וְכִבְשֻׁהָ (*wəḵiḇšúhā*) is usually translated as "subdue" and while the verb does connote coercion (either in an economic, sexual, or socio-political sense)[356] and conquest,[357] the context of the present verse must be viewed in terms of Adam's stewardship of the Garden (2:15). God never intended Edenic existence to be without work and toil. Not even Adam could afford to stand idly in a field and expect it to produce its fruits, vegetables, and grain. Creativity, industriousness, strength, and energy must be expended in order to enjoy the earth's produce and blessings.

וְכִבְשֻׁהָ וּרְדוּ בִּדְגַת הַיָּם וּבְעוֹף הַשָּׁמַיִם וּבְכָל־חַיָּה הָרֹמֶשֶׂת עַל־הָאָרֶץ – **and have dominion over the fish of the sea and over the birds of the air and over every living thing that moves upon the earth** — See Excursus 17.

❖ *The Biblical Roots of Vegetarianism*

1:29 וַיֹּאמֶר אֱלֹהִים הִנֵּה נָתַתִּי לָכֶם אֶת־כָּל־עֵשֶׂב זֹרֵעַ זֶרַע אֲשֶׁר עַל־פְּנֵי כָל־הָאָרֶץ וְאֶת־כָּל־הָעֵץ אֲשֶׁר־בּוֹ פְרִי־עֵץ זֹרֵעַ זָרַע לָכֶם יִהְיֶה לְאָכְלָה — **God said, "See, I have given you every plant yielding seed that is upon the face of all the earth, and every tree with seed in its fruit; you shall have them for food."** — In sharp contrast to the Mesopotamian myths, where the gods created humankind for the express purpose of providing food for them, here it is God who provides humankind with ample food. Adam is allowed to consume only plants and God does not permit him to slaughter a living creature for its flesh. Here, both humankind and the animal kingdom share a basic equality with respect to the consumption of food. It is only after the Flood that God

---

[356] *Cf.* 2 Chr. 28:10; Jer. 34:11, 16; Neh. 5:5.

[357] *Cf.* Num 32:22, 29; Josh. 18:1; 2 Sam. 8:11; 1 Chr. 22:18; Micah 7:19, and Zech 9:13.

permits humankind to partake of animal flesh for consumption.[358] Marcus Kalisch, British rabbinic scholar (1825-1888), writes about the vegetarian diet of Adam:

> The lifeless creation was produced for the living beings; vegetation was destined for men and animals; no being "with a living soul" was originally intended as the food for another living creature; man was assigned to eat the seed-giving plants, and grain, and the fruit of trees; to the animals were left the grass and the herbs (vv. 29-30). Although man was permitted the dominion over the beasts of the field, the fishes of the water, and the birds of the air, he was not allowed to extend that dominion to the destruction of life; he was the master, not the tyrant, of the animal kingdom — he might use, but not annihilate it. . . .
>
> . . . Every living being has a right to exist, and to enjoy its existence; God had blessed the animals with fruitfulness; man was not allowed to counteract that blessing by killing them for his sport or his appetite. God created' the world for peace and concord, no being should rage against another; the sin of man brought warfare among the living creatures; the cries of agony rent the air; man and beast raged among themselves, and against each other; the state of innocence was succeeded by the age of passion and violence; and it was only after the fall of man that animal food was permitted to him (9:3).[359]

Less than a century later, R. Abraham Isaac Kook (1864-1935) expressed a similar perspective, envisioning a time when human beings will once again live in a state of peace with the animal world, and will not need to subsist on them for sustenance:

> The thrust of the idealism that continues to develop will not remain forever in its confinement. Just as the democratic aspiration will emerge into the world through the general intellectual and moral perfection, "when man will no longer teach his brother to know the Lord, for they will all know Me, small and great alike" (Jer. 31:34), so will the hidden yearning to act justly toward animals emerge at the proper time.[360]

1:30 וּלְכָל־חַיַּת הָאָרֶץ וּלְכָל־עוֹף הַשָּׁמַיִם וּלְכֹל רוֹמֵשׂ עַל־הָאָרֶץ אֲשֶׁר־בּוֹ נֶפֶשׁ חַיָּה - And to every beast of the earth, and to every bird of the air, and to everything that creeps on the earth — This verse is inclusive of all animals, regardless of their individual species.

---

[358] "Like the green herbs, which I permitted to the first man, I have given you everything." See Rashi's comments on BT Sanhedrin 59b.

[359] Marcus M. Kalisch, *A Historical and Critical Commentary on the Old Testament* (London: Longmans, Brown, Green and Dyer, 1858), 78.

[360] "Talele Orot", *Tahkemoni*, Vol. I, (Bern, 1910, 21), cited from Ben Zion Bokser's, *Abraham Isaac Kook: The Lights of Penitence, the Moral Principles, Lights of Holiness, Essays, Letters, and Poems* (New York: Paulist Press, 1978), 23.

אֶת־כָּל־יֶרֶק עֵשֶׂב לְאָכְלָה וַיְהִי־כֵן – **everything that has the breath of life, I have given every green plant for food." And it was so.** – The verse implies that there was a time when the animals did not prey upon each other. Humankind and the animal world lived in equanimity and harmony. The prophet Isaiah envisions a return to the peacefulness of Eden where his prophecy "the lion shall eat straw like the ox" (Isa. 65:25) is realized. Such a time is characterized by peace and abundance, with nature spontaneously producing food and humans are living in close relationship with each other and with God (see notes to Gen. 9:3).

1:31 וַיַּרְא אֱלֹהִים אֶת־כָּל־אֲשֶׁר עָשָׂה – **God saw everything that he had made** – Rabbinic scholars suggest a novel and homiletical interpretation worth considering. The word "everything" includes death itself, for if death did not exist, the world would not be able to contain and sustain all its life-forms. Through the Midrashic use of the word "everything," the rabbis teach that death is not necessarily evil; rather, it is an indispensible component of the creative order. Perhaps, without death, human beings would never aspire toward ultimate perfection, nor would they ever feel the incentive to improve (see notes to Gen. 2:17) [361] Some Midrashic texts add that the verse also alludes to this libidinous energy, termed as the "evil inclination."[362] The Rabbis state: "Were it not for the evil inclination, nobody would build a house, marry and beget children."[363] Libido, ambition, desire, and everything else that makes us "human," has a potential of serving a divine purpose in God's plan for creation. The Talmud also likens the evil inclination to the "yeast that is in the dough that gives

[361] *Cf.* Gen. Rabbah 9:3; 9:7; 9:10; 9:30; (Vilna edition); Ramban on Gen. 1:31; Zohar 1:47a; 144b; 2:68b; 103a; 149b; 163a; 249a; *Yalkut Shimoni 16*; Tehilim 643; *Otzar Midrashim* (Einsenstein), 125; *Duties of the Heart* 2:3; *Shaare Teshuvah, Sh'ar 2*; *Torah Temimah* on Gen. 1:31.

[362] According to the early Halachic commentary know as the Sifre "all entities created from heaven derive both soul and body from heaven, and all entities created from earth derive both soul and body from earth. Man is an exception: his soul derives from heaven and his body from earth. When a person keeps the law and will of his Father in Heaven, then s/he is considered as one of the higher life-forms of Creation. But, should he fail to observe the Law and will of his Father in heaven, then behold! He exists as one of its lower life-forms" (*Sifre Deut.*, 305 on 33:2). One might wonder that if this libidinous force is so natural in a person, why would the Sages knowingly refer to it as something "evil"? The reason seems to be more rooted in the concept of the "natural soul" that has the ability to thwart and subvert a person's inclination to worship God. To use a well-known Hassidic analogy: When a man prays, often he becomes disturbed by foreign thoughts or distractions (e.g., money, family matters, sex, food, and so on); however, when a person is engaged in eating, or for that matter, any physical activity, that person is hardly distracted by thoughts of God! Thus, the inclination is sometimes called "evil" only on account of its raw undisciplined power, which often serves a human being's darker and less refined impulses. For a Christian treatment of the "natural soul" see Tertullian's *Treatise on the Soul* 11:2.

[363] Genesis Rabbah 9:7; Ecclesiastes Rabbah 3:15; *Midrash Tehillim* (S. Buber ed.) 9*; Yalkut Shimoni Parshat Bereshit* 16.

bread its appealing appearance (T.B. Berakhot 17a).[364]

❖ *The Experience of Divine Exuberance*

וְהִנֵּה־טוֹב מְאֹד – and indeed, it was very good – The NRSV (as well as the NJPS) translation fails to convey the cadence of this verse. Whenever the particle interjection הִנֵּה (*wəhinnēh* = "behold") appears in biblical narratives, it introduces something that is surprising and unexpected for the subject,[365] which in this case happens to be God. Writing, much like good art, is meant to convey the element of surprise to its audience, which serves to attract people's attention. On the surface the verse sounds like, "Wow! Look at what I have just done!" God seems pleasantly surprised by His own handiwork. Of course the biblical writer is getting somewhat carried away with himself in projecting a very human-esque reaction onto the Creator! Imagining God having "feelings" is another excellent example of how the Torah speaks in the language of humankind. In actuality, the writer imposes his own feelings into the text.[366] G. Wenham also explains that וְהִנֵּה implies "God's enthusiasm, as He contemplated his handiwork."[367] See notes to Genesis 6:21. More importantly, in contrast to the Gnostic view that the universe is tainted with evil, the verse indicates that all of creation is truly "very good"—even the chaos exists for good.

❖ *Perfecting Creation*

Another Interpretive View: and indeed, it was very good – Every aspect of Creation, from the most majestic galaxies to the most infinitesimal particle, functions as God intended it to.[368] Although the term *good* טוֹב (*ṭôb*) appears six times earlier[369] in

---

[364] R. Joshua ibn Shaib (*ca.* 1280-1340) interprets this Talmudic passage to mean (and the reason for this analogy is clear) a little bit of yeast helps the dough rise, but too much yeast, spoils the dough (*Derashot* on *Parshat Chukat*). Ibn Shaib's explanation is not completely accurate. While it is true the dough that has too much yeast will produce dough that is not especially flavorsome, it is frequently used for starting another batch of dough.

[365] S. R. Driver writes, "[T]he manner of their introduction by the particle הנה, and their occurrence usually after some verb of *seeing, ascertaining, perceiving,* shows that the stress lies not so much on the mere circumstance as such, but on *the impression it produces* upon the principal subject" (*A Treatise on the Use of the Tenses in Hebrew and Some other Syntactical Questions* [Oxford: Clarendon Press, 1881], 202).

[366] For a more serious illustration of this principle of the biblical writer's retrojecting into the "psyche" of God see the notes to Genesis 8:21.

[367] G. Wenham, *Vol. 1: Word Biblical Commentary: Genesis 1-15*, *op. cit.,* 34.

[368] See Ramban's commentary.

[369] Cf. Genesis 1:4, 10, 12, 18, 21, 25, 31.

the creation narrative, here it appears for the seventh time to symbolize completeness. The *peshat* reveals that it is only after God has created humankind—after His image and likeness—that Creation graduates from being merely "good" to becoming "very good." Some Jewish mystics observed that the letters of the word מְאֹד (*mĕʾōd* = "very") may also be read as an anagram for אָדָם (*ādām* = "human being").[370] A different perspective is offered in Ecclesiastes 7:29, "Behold, this only have I found, that God made humankind upright; but they have sought out many contrivances." Simply, people can choose to be upright and honest; the fact that they are not can only be attributed to the willful misuse of their God-given freedom. The text raises an important theological question: Can the existence of natural evil: tsunamis, cyclones, earthquakes, disease, and the like, be considered "good"? Human intervention in the places where these catastrophes occur reveal how humankind possesses the capacity to act upon nature's defects and transform Creation from being merely "good," to becoming that which is "very good." While evil is a pervasive part of the human experience, the upshot is that evil does not exist as an ultimate principle of reality. Although nature is far from perfect, humankind's ability and willingness to correct its flaws brings an added excellence and a completion to the Creator's handiwork.

Another Interpretative View — וְהִנֵּה־טוֹב מְאֹד וַיְהִי־עֶרֶב וַיְהִי־בֹקֶר יוֹם הַשִּׁשִּׁי — **and indeed, it was very good. And there was evening and there was morning, the sixth day** — Claus Westermann notes, "Most probably this is an aesthetic judgment and response to a brilliant act of creation."[371] It is worth adding that according to Plato, *eros* represents the craving for the beautiful that is capable of leading the soul upward to a philosophical appreciation of ideal beauty.[372] Eros is both the energy that actualizes all forms of life and the urge towards creative existence that surges through all living things. Maimonides explains this concept in familiar Judaic terms:

> What is the pathway that leads to the love and awe of God? Whenever contemplating God's great, wondrous deeds and creations, you will discover His boundless and infinite wisdom. Through this meditation, you will eventually come to love and praise everything that is associated with God's great Name. That is what King David meant when he said, 'My soul thirsts for God, for the living God' (Psalms 42:2). Whenever contemplating these things, you

---

[370] Gen. Rabbah 9:12; *Meshekh Hokhmah* notes in a homiletical vein, the word טוֹב (*ṭôḇ* = "good") is purposely missing from the creation of humankind, for humankind's goodness involves a moral choice that must be consciously and freely made (see notes on Gen. 1:26 regarding Pelagius's attack on Augustine regarding this particular point).

[371] *Genesis 1–11*, 167.

[372] Plato, *Symposium*, 180-181.

will experience awe and humility. You will come to realize that you are but an infinitesimal creature, lowly and unenlightened, standing with your puny little intellect as you attempt to understand the Perfect Mind. This is why King David said, "When I behold your heavens, the work of your fingers, the moon and the stars that you have established; what is man that you should consider him?'" (Ps. 8:3-5).[373]

❖ *A Structuralist Summary of Genesis 1:1-2:1*

Another Interpretative View: and indeed, it was very good. And there was evening and there was morning, the sixth day – In his brief exposition of French theologian Paul Beauchamp's structuralist interpretation of Genesis 1-2[374], John Barton points out that there are ten words for creation; i.e., where the text states "And God said . . ."[375] Beauchamp asserts that this set of ten utterances may be divided into two basic groups: 1:1-19 and 1:20-21; the first section pertains to the creation of heavens, while the second group pertains to the creation of the earth and its creatures. By the same token, each section contains five words signifying creative activity; the first containing 207 words, while the second contains 206 words. The first section of the creative narrative concludes with the sun, moon, and stars' dominion over the heavenly skies, while the second section concludes with humankind's dominion over the sundry life-forms of the earth. As is the case with all binary oppositions, each portion compliments the other. From Beauchamp's observation, one may deduce that the inanimate order of creation finds its most profound creative expression in the heavenly constellations, while the earthly order finds its most evolved creative expression in humankind—both the heavenly realm and the earthy realm serve to honor God as their Creator.[376] With respect to the Sabbath another pattern emerges. Whereas Genesis 1:1 speaks of how God created the heavens and the earth, Genesis 2:1 refers to its completion.

---

[373] MT *Hilchot Yesodei HaTorah* 2:2 (my translation). The eleventh century Spanish Judean philosopher, Bahya ibn Pakuda, explains that one of the ways an average person can come to discover God's Presence in the world is by a thoughtful meditation of creation and refers to this meditational pathway as the gate of "self-reckoning." The first principle we must realize is the unity of God that is visible in the multiplicity of creation. By observing the active workings of the Divine in creation, a person will come to understand the divine design that is manifest in all of nature (*Duties of the Heart,* Part 2).

[374] See Paul Beauchamp, *Creation et séparation: Etude exégétique du chapitre premier de la Genèse* (Paris: Aubier-Montaigne, 1969). It is interesting to note that this kind of structural arrangement has traditionally been the trademark of the Priestly tradition. Theologian W. Eichrodt explains that the priestly outlook is "strongly controlled by acceptance of the present world order as something fixed by divine law, where rights and duties are already apportioned, and everyone has his place to keep" (*Theology of the Old Testament* [London: SCM Press, 1961], Vol. I, 414).

[375] Cf. Gen. 1:3, 6, 9, 11, 14, 20, 24, 26, and 28f.

[376] John Barton, *Reading the Old Testament: Method in Biblical Study* (Philadelphia: Westminster Press, 1984), 124.

The Sabbath (2:1-4a)

2 Thus the heavens and the earth were finished and their entire multitude. [2]And on the seventh day God finished the work that he had done, and he rested on the seventh day from all the work that he had done. [3]So God blessed the seventh day and hallowed it, because on it God rested from all the work that he had done in creation.

A king once built a bridal chamber, which he plastered, painted, and adorned; now what did the bridal chamber lack? A bride to enter it! Similarly, what did the world still lack? The Sabbath!

—GENIBAH, *GenesisRabbah 10:9*

The Sabbath is a world revolution

—FRANZ ROSENZWEIG

The Sabbath is the anticipation of the Messianic time, just as the Messianic period is called the time of "continuous Sabbath."

—ERICH FROMM, *Forgotten Language.*

The Blessed Holy One lends a person an "extra soul" on the eve of Sabbath, and withdraws it at the close of Sabbath.

—RESH LEKISH, *T.B. Betza 16a*

It might seem somewhat strange that verse 2:1 marks the beginning of the second chapter since it disturbs the flow of the creation narrative and hardly seems to fit with what follows in Genesis 2:4. The NJPS and Fox's *Five Books of Moses* follow the Christian division of the chapters, which originated in the 16th century (after the invention of movable type) to accommodate what had become standard format.

❖ *The Ambiguity of Rest and Time*

2:1 וַיְכֻלּוּ הַשָּׁמַיִם וְהָאָרֶץ וְכָל־צְבָאָם – Thus the heavens and the earth were finished– and their entire multitude – It has been suggested that the word צָבָא

(*ṣəḇāʾ* = "multitude"), usually translated as "army" or "host," also means "member of a work gang," "laborer," "soldier," "multitude," or "vast array" in Akkadian. In some biblical passages, צָבָא may refer to the heavenly retinue as well.[377] Among ancient texts, the Septuagint translates צָבָא as κόσμος (*cosmos*). Cosmos is derived from the verb κοσμέω *(kosméō)* meaning "ordering," or "commanding" but it may also connote "adorning," "furnishing," and "bringing honor to."[378] It would seem that the Sages who wrote the Septuagint purposely chose this term to convey how the heavenly array of the stars remains forever obedient to the Divine Will. The pre-Socratic philosopher, Heraclitus deduced from the concept of the cosmos, that there exists a cosmic unity and great "chain of being" which is governed by a λόγος (= *logos*).

This principle is present in every particle of what is perceived as reality. Moreover, it is through the power of reason humankind understands this profound nexus that is wholly immanent law in the universe and the world.[379] In biblical terms, the Tanakh refers to this cosmic order as a "heavenly army" because all of Creation carries out the Divine Will of the Creator; much like an army carries out the will of its generals.[380] This expression is not limited to just the celestial constellations[381], but may also include the angelic order of existence as well.[382] The epithet "LORD of hosts" designates how God

---

[377] Cf. 1Kgs. 22:19; 2: Chr. 18:18; Psa. 103:21.

[378] According to the (TDNT 3:867), the term κοσμέω (*kosméō*)"to order" is used primarily as a technical military term for the placing of a host or the ordering of combatants, Homer *Iliad.* 2, 554; 3, 1; 12, 87; 14, 379; cf. *Odyssey*, 9, 157 (of hunters)

[379] The Catholic Encyclopedia of 1917 adds that the Stoic philosophers redefined Logos differently from Heraclitus:

> It reappears in the writings of the Stoics, and it is especially by them that this theory is developed. God, according to them, "did not make the world as an artisan does his work, but it is by wholly penetrating all matter that He is the demiurge of the universe" (Galen, "De qual. incorp." in "Fr. Stoic", ed. von Arnim, II, 6); He penetrates the world "as honey does the honeycomb" (Tertullian, "Adv. Hermogenem," 44), this God so intimately mingled with the world is fire or ignited air; inasmuch as He is the principle controlling the universe, He is called Logos; and inasmuch as He IS the germ from which all else develops, He is called the seminal Logos (*logos spermatikos*). This Logos is at the same time a force and a law, an irresistible force which bears along the entire world and all creatures to a common end, an inevitable and holy law from which nothing can withdraw itself, and which every reasonable man should follow willingly (Cleanthus,"Hymn to Zeus" in "Fr. Stoic" I, 527-cf. 537).

[380] Abraham Ibn Rambam, *Commentary on the Torah.*

[381] See for example: Deut. 4:19; 17:3; 2 Kgs. 17:16; 21:3-5; Ps. 33:6, 9; Isa. 24:21; 34:4; 40:26-28; 45:12; Jer. 8:2; Neh. 9:6, *et al.*

[382] 2 Kgs. 22:19; Neh. 9:6; Psa. 148:2.

acts as the Supreme Commander over all the innumerable hosts of spiritual and earthly agencies under His authority that form the heavenly retinue—"the armies of heaven"—by "He who spoke and the universe came into being."[383] Philosopher Ken Wilber writes that all of Creation inspires and evokes a sense of wonderment and unity—from the macro to the micro. Human beings cannot begin to appreciate its purpose in the world without adopting a holistic view of the universe that presents a unitive perspective of the cosmos.

> To understand the whole it is necessary to understand the parts. To understand the parts, it is necessary to understand the whole. Such is the circle of understanding. We move from part to whole and back again, and in that dance of comprehension, in that amazing circle of understanding we come alive to meaning, to value, and to vision: the very circle of understanding guides our way, weaving together the pieces, healing the fractures, mending the torn and fractured fragments, lighting the way ahead—this extraordinary movement from part to whole and back again, with healing the hallmark of every step, and grace the tender reward.[384]

❖ *The Sabbath and Cosmic Harmony*

The harmony of the universe in its entire splendor is precisely what humankind can potentially experience during the Sabbath. By celebrating the Sabbath, human effort brings completion to God's Creation, not through conquest or by means of technology, but through eloquent restraint. The universe and the tiny space which humankind occupies will continue to exist without human effort to tame and domesticate the forces of Creation. God intended for the Sabbath to be an island of solitude and reflection, where human beings delight in discovering the endless and never exhausting Mystery of all Being.

The realization of this basic spiritual truth may explain why the Sabbath becomes the locus through which Creation finds its joyful ascent in God. Among the modern theological thinkers of the 20th century, the celebrated scientist and mystic, Teilhard de Chardin, describes the rhapsody in celebrating God's gifts with a joy that is intense and life-affirming. Although he was not writing about the Sabbath, his sentiments capture the kind of contemplative experience and fullness of being that the Sabbath is meant to evoke each week:

> The aspect of life which most stirs my soul is the ability to share in an undertaking, in a reality, more enduring than myself: it is in this spirit and with this purpose in view that I try to perfect myself and to master things a little more. When death lays its hand upon me it will

---

383 *The Daily Siddur* (Hebrew).

384 Ken Wilber, *The Eye of Spirit: An Integral Vision for a World Gone Slightly Mad* (Boston, MA: Shambhala Publications, 2001), 1.

leave intact these things, these ideas, these realities which are more solid and more precious than I; moreover, my faith in Providence makes me believe that death comes at its own fixed moment, a moment of mysterious and special fruitfulness not only for the supernatural destiny of the soul but also for the further progress of the earth. . . . Thus to our peace is added the exaltation of creating, perilously, an eternal work which will not exist without us. Our trust in God is quickened and made firmer by the passionate eagerness of man [sic] to conquer the earth.[385]

❖ *"Be Still and Know that I am God"*

—Psalm 46:10

וַיְכַל אֱלֹהִים בַּיּוֹם הַשְּׁבִיעִי מְלַאכְתּוֹ אֲשֶׁר עָשָׂה - and He rested on the seventh day from all the work that He had done — In terms of the contextual meaning of the text, it is quite possible that the entire first chapter of Genesis was written to explain to a new reader why the Sabbath is so important to the Jewish people and ultimately for all humankind as envisioned in the prophetical writings (see Isa. 56:3-7).

Modern scholars like G. Robinson[386] and M. Tsevat argue that nowhere in the Tanakh does God demand that Israel rest on the Sabbath, and that resting is reserved only for God (Exod. 31:17), for animals, slaves, and foreigners (Exod. 23:12).[387] In fact, Robinson further contends that there is no evidence in the Hebrew Scriptures for any preoccupation with time or rest that would compare with the notion we have today. Moreover, he also conjectures that the two places where rest does appears in relation to the Sabbath (Exod. 23:12; 31:17) are actually the product of a post-exilic era—the essential character of the Sabbath having nothing to do with rest.

Such an idiosyncratic interpretation does not seem warranted for a number of reasons: (1) the sabbatical year of Leviticus 25:2ff and Exodus 23:10 plainly demonstrate how the earth's rest is patterned after the rest that is enjoyed by human beings on the Sabbath. (2) Sabbath rest is God's gift to a people who labored heavily under the yoke of Egyptian slavery (Deut. 5:15). The wording of this verse explicitly states that the servants are commanded to rest just as their masters are commanded to rest. The universality of the Sabbath extends to everyone; even the resident alien and the animals are commanded to rest just like the Israelites. Hence, since the Sabbath was meant to provide rest for the family members, servants, resident aliens, and animals in Exodus

---

[385] Teilhard de Chardin, *The Meaning of Human Endeavor* (New York: Harper & Row, 1965), 113-14.

[386] Gnana Robinson, *The Origin and Development of the Old Testament Sabbath: A Comprehensive Exegetical Approach*, Frankfurt am Main: Peter Lang, 1988.

[387] "The Basic Meaning of the Biblical Sabbath," *ZAW* 84 (1973), 447–457.

23:12, should it not apply to those whose custodial trust the latter was given to? (3) According to 31:17, the biblical text emphatically states Israel's observance of the Sabbath is meant to mirror God's own observance of this day. (4) Maimonides stresses that when Israel observes the Sabbath by resting, the act of resting serves to attest to the world that God alone is the Creator. Moreover, through Israel's witnessing, the whole world will come to observe the Sabbath day.[388]

The Sabbath remains one of Israel's greatest gifts to Western Civilization. In theological terms, God's resting is meant to teach the following lesson: God did not rest because of fatigue, but to teach humankind the importance of taking a rest day after a long week of productivity and creative activity. As theologian John Shea points out: "To tell a story of God is to create a world, adopt an attitude, to suggest a behavior. . . . In interpreting our traditional stories of God we find out who we are and what we must do. In telling stories about God, our own spiritual and life stories are told."[389] The Torah's depiction of God resting offers us a paradigm to model in our lives. R. Eliahu Dessler (1892-1953) similarly writes:

> By "rest" we do not mean the dead state of inaction and laziness, for this would be the antithesis of authentic being. By the term "rest" we mean: rest from the perpetual turmoil of material demands. This still center within the hurricane of life constitutes the true essence of the spirit. Here, at this epicenter, we make our contact with God's revealed Presence in the world. This is indeed the goal and perfection of creation.[390]

In summary, the Sabbath narratives and its legislation (see the notes on Gen. 2:3) unmistakably stress the importance of refraining from creative work so as to emulate the Creator, Who likewise refrains from initiating new creations in the seven days of creation. Rabbinic tradition has long recognized the essential character of the Sabbath: "What did God create on the seventh day? He created: tranquility, ease, peace, and quiet."[391] The Sabbath thus offers each individual the opportunity to remake and renew one's soul; it is the bridge that links nature and the social order together. In the end, rest is an obvious side-benefit when one ceases from work. See Excursus 18 for further studies regarding this important passage.

---

[388] Maimonides does not appear to have theologically endorsed the rabbinic notion that Gentiles are forbidden to observe the Sabbath. On the contrary, the observance of the Sabbath will "confirm thereby the principle of Creation which will spread in the world, when all peoples keep Sabbath on the same day" (*Guide* 2:31). The biblical passage in Isaiah 56:2-7 substantiates Maimonides' contrarian view.

[389] John Shea, *Stories of God—An Unauthorized Biography* (Chicago: Thomas Moore Association, 1978), 9.

[390] R. Eliahu Dessler, *Michtav M'Eliahu*, translated by Aryeh Carmel as *Strive For Truth* (Vol. 4), *Sanctuaries in Time: The Scriptural Aspects of the Festivals, Fasts, and Holy Days in the Jewish Year* (Jerusalem: Feldheim, 2002), 4.

[391] Genesis Rabba 10:9.

❖ *Why is the Sabbath Not Mentioned by Name?*

2:3 וַיְבָרֶךְ אֱלֹהִים אֶת־יוֹם הַשְּׁבִיעִי – So God blessed the seventh day — It is striking that the Torah does not refer to the seventh day as the Sabbath as one might expect. Instead, it is simply acknowledged as "the seventh day." Several modern exegetes[392] argue that this may have been due to the possibility that a reader might confuse the Sabbath with the Babylonian holiday of *šapattu*—an Akkadian word which phonetically sounds like שַׁבָּת (*šabbāth*). Indeed, there were other unlucky days in the Babylonian calendar such as the 7th, 14th (19th), 21st and 28th days of the months Elul and Marcheshwan.[393] Scholars, since the early 20th century, have even speculated on whether the biblical writers borrowed the Sabbath from the Babylonian culture.[394] In some ways, the prohibitions and taboos associated with these days parallel some of the Sabbatical restrictions:

> The shepherd of the great peoples shall not eat flesh cooked on coals or baked bread. He shall not put on clean (clothes). He shall not bring an offering. The king shall not travel by chariot. He shall not speak as ruler. At the place of the mystery the one who views the sacrifices shall not utter a word. The physician shall not lay his hands on a patient. (The day) is not suitable for carrying out plans. At night the king shall bring his gift to the great gods; he shall offer a sacrifice; the lifting up of his hands is then acceptable to the god.[395]

Michael Fishbane suggests a plausible relationship to the Akkadian *šapattu*. He proposes that "the term and status of the day as one of special character were retained, but the astrological associations were truncated and given new religious significance within the week."[396] According to this approach, it is important to see the biblical laws within the broader cultural context of its Mesopotamian environment. At the very least, such a comparative analysis can better help the modern reader differentiate between Israel's ancient theology and that of its neighbors.

וַיְקַדֵּשׁ אֹתוֹ – and hallowed it — The basic meaning of וַיְקַדֵּשׁ (*wayĕqadēš*) is "to

---

[392] S. R. Driver (*Genesis*, pp. 34-35); U. Cassuto (*Genesis*, Vol. 1, 65–68); V. Hamilton (*Genesis 1–17*, 142–143); G. Wenham (*Genesis*, *op. cit.*, Vol. 1, 35), to name a few.

[393] In the old Babylonian Epic of Atrahasis, the myth mentions *arḫu sebûtu u šapattu* "the first, seventh and fifteenth days" of the month as being auspicious times in the gods' plan to create humankind.

[394] T. G. Pinches, "Sapattu, the Babylonian Sabbath," *Proceedings of the Society of Biblical Archaeology*, 26 (1904), 5–56; Zimmern, 199–202, 458–460.

[395] Cited from the *TDNT*, Vol. 7, 2.

[396] Michael Fishbane, *Biblical Interpretation in Ancient Israel* (Oxford: Clarendon, 1985), 149.

make something holy, to set something apart, to distinguish it." Historically, sanctifying the Sabbath took two different forms: (1) cessation from all ordinary work that would diminish the sacred character of the day; (2) the consecration of the day, through prayer, blessing, meditation, study, food, drink, song, sexual intimacy, and celebration. Rabbinic tradition enhanced these characteristics by creating a beautiful mosaic of Sabbath traditions, some of which are purchasing special foods and dainties, welcoming the Sabbath with the kindling of candles at sunset, the wearing of beautiful clothes, eating three festive meals, and making the Kiddush prayer over wine. The Sabbath teaches the community of faith that the entire created order depends on God for its existence; we are to rest in imitation of God and in recognition that life is a gift. In tribute to God's graciousness, a day is set apart so that people might realize that it is God who ultimately provides for His creation.[397]

כִּי בוֹ שָׁבַת מִכָּל־מְלַאכְתּוֹ אֲשֶׁר־בָּרָא אֱלֹהִים לַעֲשׂוֹת – **because on it God rested from all the work that he had done in creation** — The NRSV translation assumes (much like M. Tsevat) that שָׁבַת (*šāḇaṯ*) means rested, but in this instance, "ceased" is preferable since this translation does not lend itself to the usual mistaken notion that God rested because He was tired (cf. Isa. 40:28). E. Speiser concurs with this point, translating the text, "for on it He ceased from all the work He had undertaken."[398] By saying that God "ceased from all the work He had done," the Torah intimates that God did not introduce any new creations into the world. However, God never stopped preserving Creation, recreating every fiber of existence as He continues to do, moment by moment.[399]

---

[397] This theological message would have practical implications for Israel. Prior to the Sabbath God blessed the day with a double portion of manna, but it would not descend at all on the Sabbath. (Gen. Rabbah 11:2).

[398] Among some of the other translations, the NEB reads "because that day He ceased from all the work He had set himself to do."

[399] Among the Judaic thinkers of antiquity, Philo explains creation could never endure were it not for the power of the Divine creating it anew each moment of its existence: "For God never leaves off making, but even as it is the property of fire to burn and of snow to chill, so it is the property of God to make: nay more so by far, inasmuch as He is to all besides the source of action"(*Allegorical Interpretations* 1:3). With respect to God "resting" on the Sabbath, Philo further explains that the operative term here is ἀνάπαυσις (*anapausis* "a ceasing"). Philo qualifies his remark: "And by 'rest' I do not mean 'inaction' (since that which is by its nature energetic, that which is the cause of all things, can never desist from doing what is most excellent), but I mean an energy completely free from labor, without any feeling of suffering, and with the most perfect ease" (*The Cherubim* 2:90). In Philo's theology, God can be said to be immutable, Whose vitality remains undiminished by activity. Yet, paradoxically, God's being remains free from weakness "even though he makes all things, he will not cease to be for all eternity at rest" (Ibid.). Thus, according to Philo, God's creativity does not at all conflict with the notion of Sabbath rest, for God's being remains unaltered by creation. The significance of the Sabbath thus serves as a necessity for humankind who requires a day of rest from work.

❖ *Is the Biblical Concept of Time Linear?*

Mircea Eliade claims that mythical thinking constructs time as circular, experiencing all events as the reoccurrence of primordial patterns. However, the biblical writers conceived of time as possessing a linear direction, much like the path of an arrow; hence, all events experienced in the world involve a breach with the past, and always introduce innovation and change.[400]

This writer takes issue with Eliade's perspective and would argue that the biblical notion of time incorporates both a linear and a cyclical quality. Such a concept is liturgically intimated in the Psalms, and also present in rabbinic literature; the person who observes the Sabbath is, in a mythic sense, a *living* witness to God's creation of the universe. By the same token, the observance of the Passover is more than just a historical recollection of what God once upon a time *did*; the Exodus continues to be relived through ritual, song, and story-telling, resonating in the contemporary consciousness of its participants who re-enact the mythic drama. In the Jewish liturgy, the Splitting of the Sea of Reeds is read faithfully each day, not only to dramatize an event that occurred shortly after Israel left Egypt, but also to intimate that the providential hand of God continues to unfold in miraculous and wonderful ways in the perseverance of His people. Indeed, Israel's redemption will be a re-dramatization of the Exodus experience.

Jacob Neusner also takes issue with Eliade and argues that in the rabbinical imagination, time and change have no significance by itself. Rabbinic thought conceived of biblical time in earthy and *paradigmatic* terms.

> Time is neither linear nor cyclical; it simply is not a consideration in thinking about what happens and what counts. Instead, paradigms for the formation of the social order of transcendence and permanence govern, so that what was now is, and what will be is what was and is. . . . Rabbinic thought formulates its conception of the world order—of the life of its "Israel" and the meaning of that life through time and change—in enduring paradigms that admit no distinction between past, present, and future. All things take form in a single plane of being; Israel lives not in historical time, moving from a beginning, to a middle, to an end, in a linear plan. Nor does it form its existence in cyclical time, repeating time and again familiar cycles of events. Those familiar modes of making sense out of the chaos of change and the passage of time serve not at all. . . . Rather, Israel lives in accord with an enduring paradigm that knows neither past, present, nor future. Appealing to the world of timeless myth, that Judaism accounts for how things are not by appeal to what was and what will be, but by invoking the criterion of what characterizes the authentic and true being of Israel, an idea or ideal defined by the written Torah and imposed upon the chaos of time and change. The pattern that controls recapitulates without regard to time or change, the paradigmatic lives of

---

[400] *Mircea Eliade, The Sacred and the Profane* (New York: Harcourt, Brace, and Jovanovich, 1959), 110.

the patriarchs and matriarchs, so that a single set of patterns governs. *Here history gives way to not eternity but permanence, the rules of what was or how to predict what will be, but only what it is that counts.*[401] (Emphasis added.)

❖ *Defining Work*

Another Interpretive View: because on it God rested from all the work that he had done in creation – Kugel observes that the term מְלָאכָה (*məlāʾkāh*) "work" appears in numerous priestly texts and is indicative of a kind of priestly "signature."[402] The absence of detail as to what constitutes the term *work* will certainly be discussed elsewhere in the Tanakh, but for the present, the biblical writer is merely speaking of work as creative activity, as described in the six days of creation. Numerous Semitic linguists think that the term מְלָאכָה derives from the Semitic root לְאַךְ (*laʾk*), "to send" or "depute."[403] A messenger (or an envoy) is thus called a מַלְאָךְ (*malʾak*) and this term is specifically used in conjunction with work in the sanctuary or work involving sacred objects.[404]

Perhaps there is a deeper reason explaining how these two seemingly variant words are interrelated. S. R. Hirsch proposes that מְלָאכָה ("work") in Biblical Hebrew always reflect the power of the creative mind, whose task is to reveal innovative thought and purpose. The same principle is true with respect to the מַלְאָךְ, whose sole task is dedicated to *expressing the will* of the party who sent him.[405] When contrasted with other similar terms like עָמָל (*ʿāmāl* ="toil" or "tedious" and "drudgery") or עֲבֹדָה (*ʿăbōdāh*), which is a

---

[401] Jacob Neusner, *The Idea of History in Rabbinic Judaism* (Boston: Brill, 2004), 4.

[402] James Kugel, *How To Read The Bible* (New York: Free Press, 2007), 54.

[403] According to the BDB 521 the same root appears also in Arabic *laaka,* "send" Ethiopic *laaka,* "send a messenger."

[404] See TDOT Vol. 8 (Grand Rapids, MI: Eerdmans 1997), 326.

[405] Hirsch writes, "Just as a מַלְאָךְ (*mal'ak*), a messenger, is the bearer and executor of the thought and intention of another, so too is מְלָאכָה a thing which has become the bearer and executor of the thought and the mind. Every material to which a directing mind has given a form conforming to a specific purpose, by being given that form, becomes the מְלָאכָה of that mind, its actual messenger; it serves as the bearer of the thought and intention of that mind. Hirsch erroneously thought מְלָאכָה is derived from מַלְאָךְ. In truth, they both derive from the same root לאך. To use a comparable illustration, the verb יָרָה (*y'rā*) means "to throw," "cast," or "shoot," which is another way of saying directing an object toward another object (Qal); however, in its Hiphil form לירות (*lîrôt*) can mean "to shoot" or "to teach" (Hiphil), one would not say that "teaching" is derived from "shooting," but rather both words come from a common root. The same principle holds true also with מְלָאכָה and מַלְאָךְ.

generic description of work, מְלָאכָה denotes more the idea of creative activity involving technical skill and craftsmanship.[406]

Although the Tanakh does not mention all the types of work that are forbidden, there are ample scriptural passages that provide a clear composite sketch as to what constitutes working on the Sabbath: ploughing and reaping (Exod. 34:21), pressing wine and carrying goods (Neh. 13:15), bearing burdens (Jer. 17:21), carrying on trade (Amos 8:5), and holding markets (Neh. 13:15ff.), collecting manna (Exod. 16:26ff.), gathering wood (Num 15:32ff.), and kindling fire for the purpose of boiling or baking (Exod. 35:3). The Mishnah in tractate Shabbat lists thirty-nine categories of forbidden work based on the tradition that these types of work were used in the construction of the Tabernacle.[407]

The Mishnah reads:

> The generative categories of acts of labor prohibited on the Sabbath are forty less one: He who (1) sows, (2) ploughs, (3) reaps, (4) binds sheaves, (5) threshes, (6) winnows, (7) selects [fit from unfit produce or crops], (8) grinds, (9) sifts, (10) kneads, (11) bakes, (12) shears wool, (13) washes it, (14) beats it, (15) dyes it, (16) spins, (17) weaves, (18) makes two loops, (19) weaves two threads, (20) separates two threads, (21) ties, (22) unties, (23) sews two stitches, (24) tears in order to sew two stitches, (25) traps a deer, (26) slaughters it, (27) flays it, (28) salts it, (29) cures its hide, (30) scrapes it, (31) cuts it up, (32) writes two letters, (33) erases two letters in order to write two letters, (34) builds, (35) tears down, (36) puts out a fire, (37) kindles a fire, (38) hits with a hammer, (39) transports an object from one domain to another.[408]

Jacob Neusner explains that the rabbinic understanding of work derives from God's creative activity as defined in the creation narrative. Any action must meet five basic conditions to constitute work on the Sabbath:

> First, a culpable act of labor on the Sabbath is one that in itself is whole and complete. It must not be partial or require further activity. Second, it is one in which one actor is responsible for the entire action. It is not an act begun by one party and completed by another. Third, it is one that produces permanent results. An act of labor that yields destruction is not culpable, only

---

[406] Cf. Exod. 33ff. where מְלָאכָה appears 33 times, or 13 times in Leviticus 23ff. and 7 times in Numbers 8ff.

[407] Rabbinic tradition teaches that the juxtaposition of the laws pertaining to the Sabbath and the activities involved in the construction of the Tabernacle are significant, as Rashi notes in his commentary on Exodus 35:1-3 "He prefaced the commands concerning the building of the Tabernacle with a warning to observe the Sabbath, to indicate that it does not override the Sabbath."

[408] J. Neusner, *The Mishnah: A New Translation* (New Haven, CT: Yale University Press, 1988), 187.

that produces enduring consequences. Fourth, the act of labor must be done in the ordinary manner. Fifth, the act of labor must carry out the plan, the intention of the actor. The actor must act willfully and produce the result he wished to bring about.

God's activities in Creation form the generative model. The acts of creation were whole and complete. God Himself, on His own, carried out each of them. The results of Creation were enduring. They were done in an ordinary way. And they all carried out God's intention in creating the world. These are matters deemed self-evident in the Creation-narrative.[409]

❖ *A Sanctuary of Holy Time*

Another Interpretive View: because on it God rested from all the work that he had done in creation – Abraham Joshua Heschel (1907–1972) posits that the Sabbath is an "architecture of sacred time,"[410] and suggests that the Torah's introduction of the Sabbath may be read as a polemic aimed against Babylonian mythology. The Babylonian epic story of Creation, *Enuma elish* culminates with the founding of the city and a temple—a virtual glorification of sacred space.

Heschel poignantly argues that while it is true that all peoples of antiquity venerated certain places as holy, the Torah places a far greater emphasis on the sanctification of *time* versus the sanctification of *space*. It is no coincidence that the word for sanctity is first associated with the Sabbath. When God blesses the Sabbath day (Gen. 2:3), it literally becomes, "a sanctuary of holy time." Sabbath rituals exemplify Judaism's quest to sanctify time. To the pagan, the notion of holiness is inextricably related to sacred space; as a result, there is a tendency for the primal psyche to project its concept of the divine into an object that is found in the phenomenal world. But the Sabbath is radically different. With the Sabbath, as Heschel notes, human beings leave the realm of holy space and enter into the realm of holy time.[411]

> Judaism teaches us to be attached to holiness in time, to be attached to sacred events, to learn how to consecrate sanctuaries that emerge from the magnificent stream of a year. The Sabbaths are our great cathedrals; and our Holy of Holies is a shrine that neither the Romans nor the Germans were able to burn; a shrine that even apostasy cannot easily obliterate.[412]

---

[409] Jacob Neusner, *Judaism's Story of Creation: Scripture, Halakhah, Aggadah* (Boston: Brill, 2000), 59.

[410] Abraham Joshua Heschel, *The Sabbath: Its Meaning for Modern Man* (New York: Farrar Straus and Young, 1951), xvi. It is ironic that Heschel utilized a spatial metaphor to describe the sacredness of time.

[411] The Zoroastrians also conceived of history as moving toward a *telos;* after the final rehabilitation of the earth implies its purification and its joining, with a purified hell, to the extension of heaven.

[412] *The Sabbath*, *op. cit.,* xvi.

The Sabbath also exerts a profound economic impact upon a society. As a symbol of sanctified time, the Sabbath releases men and women from the tyranny of a consumer-driven market economy. Keeping the Sabbath must be more than just a mere activity—it must foster a renewal of the soul. The Sabbath symbolizes the ideal state of creation where every creature great and small, stands in cosmic unity together in honor of the Creator. As a symbol of rest and renewal, the Sabbath signifies an inner serenity that permeates the spirit. The Sabbath also provides the context for appreciating the Eternal within the boundaries of sacred time. As a "cathedral of sacred time," the Sabbath stands apart from other precepts of the Torah that have more of a spatial dimension to its holiness. This may be illustrated with the following Hassidic anecdote: Two rebbes—the Vorker Rebbe and the Kotzker Rebbe—were discussing the relative importance of certain biblical *mitzvoth* (precepts). The Vorker Rebbe commented upon the holiness of the "four species"[413] that are held together and waved in honor of God. Once the precept has been performed, they are laid aside, for the precept has been properly carried out.

The Vorker Rebbe continued, "Such is the way with most *mitzvot*-as long as we hold them dear, we experience the holy; however, once we let go of the precept, the holiness departs. However during the holiday of *Sukkot* [Tabernacles], the holiness of the *sukkah* pervades every part of the person who is inside and the *sukkah's* holiness is even more pervasive." The Kotzker Rebbe replied, "There is one mitzvah whose holiness was even greater than that of the *sukkah*—the Sabbath, for once a Jew walks out of the *sukkah*, he is no longer surrounded by the aura of the *sukkah's* holiness, but that is not the case with the Sabbath, for no matter where a Jew goes during the Sabbath the quality of the Sabbath always remains with him." The holiness of time is something that remains, even in the absence of the holy Temple. Some Hasidic thinkers also see in the Sabbath a rich eschatological dimension, a quality that will not be fully realized until the Messianic Era, when every day will have the holy quality of the Sabbath.[414] For a more detailed critique of Heschel's exposition, see Excursus 19.

---

[413] The "Four Species" (Hebrew: ארבעת המינים = Arba'at Ha-Minim) refer to the: *lulav* (לולב) – a ripe, green, closed frond from a date palm tree, *hadass* (הדס) – boughs with leaves from the myrtle tree, *aravah* (ערבה) – branches with leaves from the willow tree, and the Etrog (אתרוג) – the fruit of a citron tree. During the holiday of *Sukkoth*, these four species are waved together by the worshiper in a special ceremony of thanksgiving to God. For a biblical description of the rite, see Leviticus 23:40.

[414] Rabbi Shlomo Riskin, *The Passover Haggadah* (New York: Ktav, 1983), 22-23.

Another Account of the Creation
Gen 2:4b-17

In the day that the LORD God made the earth and the heavens, 5 when no plant of the
field was yet in the earth and no herb of the field had yet sprung up—for the LORD God
had not caused it to rain upon the earth, and there was no one to till the ground; 6 but a
stream would rise from the earth, and water the whole face of the ground— 7 then the
LORD God formed man from the dust of the ground,[a] and breathed into his nostrils the
breath of life; and the man became a living being. 8 And the LORD God planted a garden
in Eden, in the east; and there he put the man whom he had formed. 9 Out of the
ground the LORD God made to grow every tree that is pleasant to the sight and good
for food, the tree of life also in the midst of the garden, and the tree of the knowledge
of good and evil.

10 A river flows out of Eden to water the garden, and from there it divides and becomes
four branches. 11 The name of the first is Pishon; it is the one that flows around the
whole land of Havilah, where there is gold; 12 and the gold of that land is good; bdellium
and onyx stone are there. 13 The name of the second river is Gihon; it is the one that
flows around the whole land of Cush. 14 The name of the third river is Tigris, which
flows east of Assyria. And the fourth river is the Euphrates.

15 The LORD God took the man and put him in the garden of Eden to till it and keep it.
16 And the LORD God commanded the man, "You may freely eat of every tree of the
garden; 17 but of the tree of the knowledge of good and evil you shall not eat, for in the
day that you eat of it you shall die."

'And he breathed into his nostrils the breath of life' (Gen. 2:7). Adam then arose and realized that he was a synthesis of Heaven and of earth, and so he cleaved with the Divine and was thus endowed with mystic Wisdom. And so it is with each human being who is made after the same model, a composite of the heavenly and the earthly; and all those who know how to sanctify themselves in the right manner in this world, when they beget a child cause the holy spirit to be drawn upon him from the region whence all sanctities emerge.

—ZOHAR I 130b

Rabbi Eliezer b. Rabbi Yose the Galilean observed, "The listener may think that is another narrative, whereas it is only the elaboration of the first."

—RASHI on Genesis 2:8

[a] Or *formed a man* (Heb *adam*) *of dust from the ground* (Heb *adamah*)

Contrary to the literary style of European writers, Semitic storytellers seldom ever tell the same story quite in the same way. With this thought in mind, one should not be too surprised to see a second creation account that expands in some ways details that were left out of the original creation story. Thus, chapter 1 provides a general framework of what God did in the beginning, while this chapter narrates a more detailed accounting of the story. Each version accentuates something the other doesn't. Genesis 1 focuses on the harmony and chronological order of creation, while Genesis 2 deals more with themes such as the problem of human loneliness and the need for human companionship. Genesis 2 presupposes chapter 1 and does not duplicate all the creation events, but sets the stage for what will follow in Genesis 3. (See Excursus 20a for a more comprehensive summary of this discussion and its relationship to the Documentary Hypothesis.)

2:4 אֵלֶּה תוֹלְדוֹת הַשָּׁמַיִם וְהָאָרֶץ – These are the generations of the heavens and of the earth – This section is the first of ten chapter headings (Gen. 2:4, 11–27; 5:1; 10:1; 11:10; 25:12, 19; 36:1, 9) that begin with "this is the story" or "this is the account of" introducing narratives. According to the author of *Keter Torah*, all of Genesis 1:2–2:4*a* to 2:4b is nothing more than a long parenthetical statement, thus Genesis 2:4 really continues the creation narrative that began with 1:1.

It is also important to remember that the notion of chapter divisions was not introduced until much later during the medieval period. The NRSV translation, "generations of the heavens and of the earth" is misleading; the text ought to be more accurately rendered, "This is the chronology of the heavens and the earth," since the biblical narrator is presenting the historical record of what happened after the first couple were made.

❖ *Differentiating between YHWH and 'Elohim*

Another Interpretative View: בְּהִבָּרְאָם בְּיוֹם עֲשׂוֹת יְהוָה אֱלֹהִים אֶרֶץ וְשָׁמָיִם – the day that the LORD God made the earth and the heavens – The expression בְּיוֹם (*bĕyôm*) is simply an idiomatic way of saying "at the time when." This phrase introduces the rest of the verse as a dependent clause. As already explained earlier, the term יוֹם (*yôm*), in its broadest definition, denotes a segment of time and is not limited specifically to a twenty-four hour period.

For the first time, the combination of Divine Names יְהוָה אֱלֹהִים (YHWH [*ʾădōnāy*] *ʾĕlōhîm*) appears. The biblical narrator (or redactor) wishes to intimate that YHWH and Elohim are one and the same; the same transcendent God who created the cosmos and all its beauty also enters into a personal relationship with humankind. For the community of Israel, these names are especially significant. According to Cassuto, by entering into a covenantal relationship with YHWH, Israel affirms that its national God is also the God of the entire created order.[415] Beyond that, the Creator God is also the Originator of the moral order.[416]

Cassuto makes a number of important points that differentiate the characteristics of these two Divine Names which one ought to keep in mind when interpreting this passage. The Divine Name אֱלֹהִים (*'Elohim)* appears whenever the Tanakh wishes to portray an abstract conception of God as perceived by the world of ancient Israel. It is the "idea of God conceived in a general sense as the Creator of the *material* world, as the Ruler of nature, and as the Source of life." However, whenever the Tanakh uses the Divine Name יְהוָה it connotes (1) an ethical aspect that is specifically associated with the people of Israel, (2) YHWH connotes a direct and intuitive notion of the Divine that is characteristic of the simple faith of the masses, whereas *'Elohim* expresses a more philosophical concept of the Divine as it pertains to the world and humanity, (3) YHWH is used when the Tanakh wishes to present an image of the Divine that is personal; as He relates to the welfare of human beings, whereas *'Elohim* occurs when Holy Writ speaks of God as a Transcendental Being, who stands entirely outside nature, and above it." I would only add that this particular Divine Name also occurs whenever depicting how God acts in the realm of history.

❖ *Canonizing Scribal Errors*

Another Interpretative View: בְּהִבָּרְאָם בְּיוֹם עֲשׂוֹת יְהוָה אֱלֹהִים אֶרֶץ וְשָׁמָיִם — **In the day that the LORD God made the earth and the heavens** – The orthography of בְּהִבָּרְאָם (*bəhibbār'ām*) appears odd. The Rabbis in the Talmud and Midrash offer

[415] *Genesis*, 87, cf. 246.

[416] Cassuto elaborates on this theme in his commentary:

> In the narrative of the garden of Eden, on the other hand, God appears as the ruler of the *moral* world, for He enjoins a given precept on man, and demands an account of his actions; that apart, stress is laid here on His personal aspect, manifested in His direct relationship with man and the other creatures. For these reasons the name *YHWH* was required in this section, and this is the name that we actually find. Its association, however, with the appellation *'Elohim,* which is restricted to this one section of the entire book, is easily explained by Scripture's desire to teach us that *YHWH,* which occurs here for the *first time,* is to be wholly identified with *'Elohim* mentioned in the preceding section; in other words, that the God of the moral world is none other than the God of the material world, that the God of Israel is in fact the God of the entire universe, and that the names *YHWH* and *'Elohim* merely indicate two different facets of His activity or two different ways in which He reveals Himself to mankind. Once this truth has been inculcated here, there is no need to repeat it later . . . (*Genesis* Vol 1, 87-88).

different answers[417], but their explanations fail to adequately explain the *peshat* of this anomaly. Once the Masoretic Text[418] (MT) was completed, some scribe accidentally misspelled the word בְּהִבָּרְאָם and later inserted a smaller letter ה (בְּ֫הִבָּרְאָם) into the misspelled word, much like the way we insert a carrot symbol over a misspelled English word. This practice harkens back to the era when the scribe did not compare a Torah scroll text to another, but wrote each word as it was dictated. Over time, even the mistakes become canonized by well-meaning scribes who believed the text had a deeper and more esoteric meaning.[419]

❖ *A Matter of Perspective: Last in Deed, First Conceived!*

In this version of creation, the biblical writer mentions the earth prior to the heavens. Why the discrepancy? It is possible that the precise chronological order did not concern the biblical writer like it would a modern person reading the text for the first time. Perhaps he felt that in all likelihood, God created the earth and the heavens at about the same period of time. The text is merely speaking from the vantage point of the human observer. Richard Elliot Friedman similarly proposes that the Priestly creation story is more heaven-centered; i.e., from God's perspective, which is essentially

---

[417] Rashi writes in his Torah commentary: "He created them with the letter ה (*hei*) as it is written בִּטְחוּ בַיהוָה עֲדֵי־עַד כִּי בְּיָהּ יְהוָה צוּר עוֹלָמִים 'for in [יָהּ] *Yah* the LORD is the Rock of eternity' (Isa. 26:4). With these two letters ה and י [*hei* and *yud*] of the Divine Name, He fashioned two worlds, and it teaches you here that this world was created with a ה (BT Menachot 29b)." A variant of Rashi reads: "Just as the ה is open at the bottom the world, so too, is the world open to those who repent. The World to Come was created with the letter י to inform the reader that at some future time, the righteous shall be exceptionally few in number, much like the letter י, the smallest of the letters. This verse also alludes to the fate of the wicked, who are destined to descend and see the abyss of Hell, which resembles the letter ה that is closed on all sides and open at its bottom, for them to descend there" (derived from Gen. Rabbah 12:10].

[418] The traditional Hebrew text is called the Masoretic Text (from *Masora* = "tradition"). The MT achieved its standard form early in the second century C.E. It was based on and substantially agreed with a much earlier textual tradition, as the Dead Sea Scrolls demonstrate. Historically, the text was only consonantal and had no vowels or accent marks. Among the different vocalization systems that developed, the Tiberian system (which places most of the vowel points below the consonants) eventually became the accepted practice and was established in the first half of the tenth century by the Karaite savants, Aaron ben Moshe ben Asher and Moshe ben Naphtali. It is most unfortunate that virtually all denominations of Judaism fail to acknowledge this great debt to Karaite scholarship. No Torah scroll would be properly written were it not for the Karaites' scrupulous maintenance of these ancestral scrolls.

[419] To use a well-known Jewish homily, the process is akin to the old story about a woman who used to cut the ends of the brisket off whenever she baked a brisket. Somebody asked her "Why?" She shrugged her shoulders and replied "I'll ask my mother." The woman went and asked her mother, but she too didn't know the answer. Together they asked the old matriarch who was living in a nursing home. She smiled and replied, "I cut the ends of the brisket so that it would fit into the pot!" The moral of the story is that sometimes traditions are often passed from generation to generation for no rational reason. The verb בְּהִבָּרְאָם is an example of how even scribal errors sometimes became canonized.

downwardly vertical, whereas the Yahwist sees creation from the human perspective, from the earth below gazing up toward the heavens. This interpretation also fits well with the contextual meaning of the *peshat*.[420]

Jewish mystics homiletically regard this verse as an allusion to the idea that humankind is the offspring of both the heavenly and the earthly realms, thus forming a unique blend of the spiritual and the physical.[421] Others have similarly suggested that in terms of the sequence of creation, heaven preceded earth, but in spiritual terms of importance, the earth preceded the heaven. This thought is conveyed in the Sabbath prayer: "From the beginning, from ancient times was she honored, what was last in deed, arisen first in thought."

2:5 וְכֹל שִׂיחַ הַשָּׂדֶה טֶרֶם יִהְיֶה בָאָרֶץ וְכָל־עֵשֶׂב הַשָּׂדֶה טֶרֶם יִצְמָח – **when no plant of the field was yet in the earth and no herb of the field had yet sprung up** — There was no wild vegetation because there was no rain. Such arid conditions still exist in much of the Middle East today. The fertility of the earth was made possible by water from streams rather than by falling rain. The narrative begins with the formation of plant life, leading to the roles that the Tree of Life and Tree of Knowledge play later in the narrative.

כִּי לֹא הִמְטִיר יְהוָה אֱלֹהִים עַל־הָאָרֶץ – **For the LORD God had not caused it to rain upon the earth** — This is the first verse that intimates that it is God Who opens and shuts the windows of the heavens, on which the earth's fertility depends.

וְאָדָם אַיִן לַעֲבֹד אֶת־הָאֲדָמָה – **And there was no one to till the ground** — This part of the verse explains why there is no cultivated grain, because there is no one to cultivate the earth. Therefore, God causes the mist to arise from the land, which produces moss and fungi; later, grass and other herbage appear and then the shrubs, and the trees.

2:6 וְאֵד יַעֲלֶה מִן־הָאָרֶץ וְהִשְׁקָה אֶת־כָּל־פְּנֵי־הָאֲדָמָה – **but a stream would rise from the earth, and water the whole face of the ground**— The NRSV translates אֵד (*'ēd*) as "stream," while the NJPS prefers "flow" and others render it as "surge," i.e., a breaking forth of water in some way from under the ground, possibly a subterranean

---

[420] Richard Elliot Friedman, *The Bible with Sources Revealed: A New View into the Five Books of Moses, op. cit.*, 35.

[421] Some Hasidic commentaries homiletically explain that within the depths of humankind's innermost being are aspects of existence of the material world *(olam)*, the spiritual *(nefesh)*, and the temporal *(shana)*. All three of these dimensions of creation converge as one within the being of humankind, corresponding to the very likeness of all that is.

stream of fresh water, possibly a river overflowing its banks.[422] One of the foremost biblical scholars of 20th century, William Foxwell Albright, thought its etymology may be related to the Akkadian *ʽēd* meaning "river" or "river god," from the Sumerian *id*, or "river" (see HALOT: 11). A subterranean spring's upward movement would certainly explain how the water "rises from the earth" and waters the ground.

Westermann notes that based on Job 36:27, it would seem that אֵד indicates a stream of water descending from the skies, however the wording, וְאֵד יַעֲלֶה מִן־הָאָרֶץ makes this rendering impossible. The traditional translation of "mist" (Delitzsch) or "vapor" (Gesenius) or "cloud" (Neofiti, Onkelos[423]) cannot be ruled out as a plausible possibility—especially since it fits the context of the passage in a manner that does no harm to the text. In meteorological terms, mist consists of fine droplets of water in the atmosphere near or in contact with the earth. Support for this reading is indicated by the verb יַעֲלֶה (*yaʿăleh* = "would rise") that immediately follows the noun אֵד, suggesting a process of evaporation, which eventually forms into clouds. Marcus Kalisch points out an interesting parallel to the biblical story from the Buddhist tradition, which purports that "golden clouds sent down, in primeval time, an immense quantity of water, which increased to a mighty sea; foam appeared on it in the course of centuries, and from this foam man and all living creatures came forth" (*Pallas, Reise* ii. 237)."[424]

❖ *A Divine Aesthetic in Motion*

2:7 וַיִּיצֶר יְהוָה אֱלֹהִים אֶת־הָאָדָם – **then the LORD God formed man** – The verb יָצַר (*yāṣar* = "mold") occurs most frequently in the nominative form, meaning "potter"; namely, the one who creates vessels out of clay. Theologically, this metaphor of God as a potter and artist is used to express three basic meanings: (1) creativity, (2) God's mastery over all creation, (3) the fragility of earthly existence.

- **Creativity:** The root word יָצַר may be used in relation to human and divine creativity. Indeed, the human body with its wondrous complexity, is no less a marvel today—even as scientists decipher the genetic secrets of DNA molecules

[422] See E. A. Speiser, *Genesis* (Anchor Bible Commentary Vol. 1; Garden City, NY: Doubleday, 1964), 16.

[423] The Targum of Pseudo Jonathan adds a midrashic flourish to Onkelos's reading, "But a cloud of glory descended from the throne of glory, and was filled with waters from the ocean, and afterward went up from the earth, and caused the rain to come down and water all the face of the ground." For other Talmudic views, see BT Ta'anit 9b and Gen. Rabbah 13:12 which list all the terms for clouds found in the Tanakh.

[424] Marcus M. Kalisch, *A Historical and Critical Commentary on the Old Testament, op. cit.*, 103

and living cells—than it was to the ancients who were perplexed about the body's astounding functions. The mysteries of the human body made the rabbis think of God as an artist. However, unlike a human artist who can portray beauty in only the most limited manner, God creates the human body with artistic wonder, internally and externally, as manifested in the common but miraculous creation of a child.[425] So impressed were the ancients with the functioning of the body, that the rabbis formulated a special blessing depicting its astonishing functions. Upon leaving a bathroom, a person washes the hands and recites:

> Blessed are You God, who rules the universe, fashioning the human body with wisdom; creating openings, arteries, glands, and organs; marvelous in structure; intricate in design. Should but one of them fail to function by being blocked or opened—it would be impossible to exist. Blessed are You God, Healer of all flesh; sustaining our bodies in wondrous ways.[426]

- **God's mastery over all creation:** In the Tanakh, clay's malleability illustrates how it is subject to the creative imagination of the artisan. [427] In one famous story (Jer. 18:6), the prophet Jeremiah depicts God as a determined potter who works to give creative expression to a difficult piece of clay that refuses to yield to the will of its maker. Despite the problems posed by the resulting handiwork, the imagery of the potter conveys God's determination to refashion and shape His people's destiny as He sees fit (Isa. 29:15; 41:25; 45:9). In each instance, human beings are not simply passive—their behavior actualizes the Divine intent for the better.

---

[425] We often marvel whenever we gaze at the great artistic masterpieces of history. Yet, even the greatest of human artists realize that their work is but a pale reflection of God's Creation. The painter Michelangelo knew this very well. Over the plaster vault of the Sistine Chapel arose the immense dome of God's sky, breathtaking in its simple beauty. Mountains, seas, the continents—all these, and much more, are the creative work of God, the Master Artist. God's world is so much grander and more awe-inspiring than Michelangelo's masterpiece; God's creation is art in continuous motion. Talmudic wisdom bears this out: "It is in the capacity of a human being to draw a figure on a wall, but he cannot invest it with breath and spirit, bowels and intestines. But the Holy One, blessed be He, is not so; He shapes one form in the midst of another, and invests it with breath and spirit, bowels and intestines. And that is what Hannah said: 'There is none holy as the Lord, for there is none beside You, neither is there any *tzur* [rock] like our God' (1 Sam. 2:2). What means, 'neither is there any *tzur* like our God'? There is no *tzayyar* [artist] like our God" (BT Berakhot 10a).

[426] This prayer derives from BT Berakhot 60b. The marvels of the human body always fascinated the rabbis. According to Rashi, the body is somewhat analogous to a water bottle; if there is a hole in the bottle, it loses its contents, but with the human body, there are many cavities and yet every human being has ample air to last a lifetime! Abudaraham notes that the human body has the wisdom to know when to utilize what is essential in food and when to extract its waste products. Some see the synthesis of the body and the soul as constituting the real miracle.

[427] Cf. Isa. 64:8; Jer. 18:6; Job 10:9; 33:6.

- **The fragility of earthly existence:** In the Psalms and in parts of Isaiah, the pottery imagery denotes the fragility of human existence (Ps. 31:12; Job 32:10). This thought later resonates in the Yom Kippur liturgy:

> Like the clay in the hand of the potter,
> He expands it at will and contracts it at will,
> So are we in Your hand, O Preserver of kindness . . . .

עָפָר מִן־הָאֲדָמָה – **from the dust of the ground** – The NRSV translation as it reads poses an interesting question. Ordinarily, the term עָפָר (*ʿāp̄ār*) is used to describe dry, pulverized earth or dried mud.[428] Thus, in the case of the wife who is accused of adultery, the priest must take the dust from the Tabernacle floor and use it in making a special potion (Num. 5:17). It appears that the reason why the NRSV translates עָפָר (*ʿāp̄ār*) is because Adam's fate is ultimately destined to return to the "dust" from whence he was humbly made; this theological usage occurring throughout the Tanakh[429] will be noted in more detail in a subsequent chapter. Nevertheless, it seems that a plausible translation of עָפָר in this instance is "clay"—especially because the earth was already watered before God removed the earthly substance for making Adam's body. This reading is also found in the NAB which reads: "The LORD God formed man *out of the clay* of the ground and blew into his nostrils the breath of life, and so man became a living being." Several Semitic and non-Semitic myths also speak of humanity being formed out of clay.[430]

❖ *The Origin and Meaning of "Adam"*

Another Interpretive View: from the dust of the ground – Note the assonance that appears between הָאָדָם (*hā̍ʾāḏām*) and הָאֲדָמָה (*hā̍ʾăḏāmā*^{h} = "ground"). This would be

---

[428] Deut. 9:21; see also 2 Sam. 16:13; Josh. 7:16; Eze. 27:30 *et al.*

[429] Eccl. 3:20; 12:7; Job 4:19; 8:19; 10:9; 34:15; Pss. 104:29.

[430] Several Babylonian myths, e.g., *The Epic of Gilgamesh*, *The Epic of Atrahasis,* and *The Poem of the Righteous Sufferer*—all describe how the gods formed man from clay. In *The Epic of Atrahasis* we find, "Let Nintu mix clay with his flesh and blood. Let that same god and man be thoroughly mixed in the clay," cited from W. Hallo, & K. L. Younger's *The Context of Scripture* (Leiden; New York: Brill, 1997), 451. For more illustrations see also ANET, 74. Sir James Frazer cites parallels of this story across the world. For example: Berosus, the Babylonian priest recount, "The god Bel cut off his own head, and the other gods caught the flowing blood, mixed it with earth, and fashioned men out of the bloody paste; and that, they said, is why men are so wise, because their mortal clay is tempered with blood divine. In Egyptian mythology, Khnoumou, the Father of the Gods, is said to have molded men out of clay on his potter's wheel. So too, in Greek legend the sage Prometheus is said to have molded the first men out of clay at Panopeus in Phocis. When he had done his work, some of the clay was left over, and might be seen on the spot long afterwards in the shape of two large boulders lying at the edge of a ravine . . ." (*Folklore of the Old Testament,* Vol. 1, [New York: Tudor Publishing, 1923], 5-7).

the equivalent in English of, "then God formed *the earthling* from the dust of the earth." The verse also indicates that human existence is bound up with the earth. God created Adam from the earth so that he would always be mindful of his humble beginnings and not assume that he is a god or a demigod. The connection between הָאָדָם and הָאֲדָמָה further suggests that being an earth-born creature, he shares the frailty of mortality—a quality that occurs no less in the animal world. M. Kalisch observes that this etymological connection is comparable to the Latin *homo* and *humus*—the dark brown organic component of soil that is derived from the remains of decomposed plant and animal life. As Kalisch further claims, "It hardly implies that man is a *ruler* of the earth, and much less, that he combines the nature of all the other terrestrial creatures."[431]

There is another nuance that is especially intriguing. The meaning of הָאֲדָמָה (*hā́ʾăḏāmāʰ*) probably refers specifically to "dark red earth." Support for this idea comes from the cognate languages of the ANE as well as the mythic parallels as previously discussed. For example, in Akkadian *ăḏāmṯu* means "dark red earth," while in Syriac an identical term is referred to as *ʾăḏāmṯ*; in Arabic, red tilled soil is called *ˌadamat*. Later on in Genesis 4:10, God confronts Cain with having shed his brother's blood:

> קוֹל דְּמֵי אָחִיךָ צֹעֲקִים אֵלַי מִן־הָאֲדָמָה *(qôl* ***dəmê*** *ʾāḥîḵā ṣōʿăqîm ʾēlay min-****hā̦ʾăḏāmāʰ****)*
> *What have you done? The voice of your brother's blood is crying out to Me from the blood- colored earth.*

Note the not-so obvious wordplay on the words "blood" (*dəmê*) and *ădāmā*—"the blood-soaked (and colored) earth" where he had been buried.

Another Interpretive View: from the dust of the ground – Some Hassidic scholars suggest that אָדָם derives from the word דְּמוּת (*dəmûṯ*) "likeness," or "pattern" (cf. Eze. 1:26, 19:10; Isa. 40:18), since humankind derives its spiritual likeness from the Divine. However, while there may be some midrashic value to such an interpretation, it lacks clear etymological support.

❖ *The Genetics of Mice and Men*

Some years ago, one of the popular American news magazines featured an article entitled "What is Man?" The average man was roughly 5 feet 10 inches tall, and weighed about 150 pounds. To the writer's surprise, he discovered that if we were to examine man's body chemistry, we would find:

---

[431] Marcus M. Kalisch, *A Historical and Critical Commentary on the Old Testament, op. cit.*, 106.

- Fat to make seven bars of soap.
- Iron to make a medium-sized nail.
- Sugar to fill a shaker.
- Lime to whitewash a chicken coop.
- Phosphorus to make 2,200 match tips.
- Magnesium for a dose of magnesia.
- Potassium to explode a toy cannon.

If one were to add up the cost of these substances, they would add up to a very insignificant amount—well under twenty American dollars. Such is the extent of our bodily worth as we were made out of the dust of the ground.

Science still continues probing the old scientific question: "What is man?" According to modern genetics, the human genome may encode about 30,000 (+/- another 10–20,000) genes in humans and mice, yet only 300 are unique to either organism. Both species have genes for a tail, even though in the case of humans the gene is not "switched on." About 99% percent of genes in humans have counterparts in the mouse genome and vice versa, which would explain why lab mice are considered to be model organisms for experimental studies. Another study conducted by an international team of 170 researchers, has shown there is about 93% of the common DNA between humans and the rhesus macaques; in the case of humans and chimpanzees, they share about 98-99% value. It is amazing that only a few percentage points separate human beings from those species that resemble them.[432]

Assuming that there are only 30,000 genes, that would be only 1/3 more than the 20,000 genes of the lowly worm, which goes to prove that it is not our genes that determine our immense complexity as a species—but something else—namely, our capacity to be self-aware, ethical, rational, and responsible beings (and that's being optimistic!). This would certainly add new meaning to the biblical verse, "How much less man, who is but a maggot, the son of man, who is only a worm?" (Job 25:6). Physically, we have much more in common with the worm than the biblical writer could have dared to imagine possible. Yet, despite our humble origins, humankind is much more than just a synthesis of chemical compounds held together with electrical charges, and brought about through a blind evolutionary process. There is something irreducible about the nature of human consciousness that evokes within us an Einsteinian sense of cosmic awe and wonderment; in synergistic terms, we will always be greater than the sum of our genetic parts. Theologically speaking, our capacity to be self-reflective exists because human consciousness derives from the innermost being of God.

---

[432] See D. J. Kevles, *The Code of Codes: Scientific and Social Issues in the Human Genome Project* (Cambridge, MA: Harvard University Press, 1992) and T. Wilkie, *Perilous Knowledge: The Human Genome Project and Its Implications* (Berkeley: University of California Press, c1993).

❖ *The Soul as Divine Breath*

וַיִּפַּח בְּאַפָּיו – **and breathed in his nostrils** – The imagery of God breathing life into man has its parallels in the rituals of ancient Egypt. In Egyptian ceremonies, a sculptor would symbolically animate the sacred images he had made by breathing into the mouth of the image. The inert stone was infused with the divinity's life force *(ba)*. Craftsmen in Egypt still maintain this custom before making a vessel, to symbolize giving creative life to their work.

נִשְׁמַת חַיִּים – **the breath of life** – Why was the metaphor of God "breathing into his nostrils" used to describe the creation of humankind, but not the animal realm? Ramban suggests that he who breathes into the nostrils of another imparts something of his own soul. Many Hasidic thinkers paraphrased Ramban's thought as "One who exhales, exhales from the very depths of one's innermost being."[433] The soul is, in a sense, a manifestation of the divine indwelling; i.e., a part of God's own innermost being is present in every human being. By breathing directly into Adam's nostrils, God infuses him with a part of His own personality, a creative commingling of the Divine and man. God's "inspiration" makes humankind unique among all God's creatures. This Divine breath instills us with the sacred and the transcendental; it forms the mysterious point of identity between humankind and God. Mystics and poets sometimes liken God's gift of breath to a divine kiss, which the poet Kahil Gibran describes as "a kiss as the beginning of a joint sigh knitting the breathing God had breathed into the clay which then became man . . ."[434] This "kiss of life" suggests that humankind is the gratuitous object of God's love.[435]

On a more sublime level, were it not for the power of the divine breath, human beings could never hope to experience transcendence. It is *because* of the depth and divinity of the spiritual breath within us that we can aspire to be ethically God-like. Theologically, the concept of breath figures prominently in the development of thought of many religious

---

[433] In the *Tanya* 1:2, R. Sheneir Zalman incorrectly attributes this statement to the Zohar, but no such passage exists. However, a slightly similar interpretation can be found in Ramban's commentary on this verse.

[434] Gert Borg, Ed de Moor, *Representations of the Divine in Arabic Poetry* (Amsterdam: Rodopi, 2001), 171.

[435] The "divine kiss" theme plays a significant role in Sufi mystical texts; more than being a routine expression of sexual desire, the kiss transmits sacred power. The "divine kiss" theme has parallels in rabbinical literature, see Shir HaShirim Rabah 1:12-13; 15-16; 18. The Zohar also discusses the nature of the divine kiss: Commenting on the verse "Let him kiss me with the kisses of his mouth" (Song of Songs 1: 2), the Zohar explains, "The act of kissing expresses the cleaving of spirit to spirit; therefore the mouth is the medium of kissing, for it is the organ of the spirit (breath). Hence, he who dies by the 'kiss of God' becomes so united with the Divine Spirit, which never separates from him" (Zohar II:124b; cf. Zohar II:146b).

and philosophical traditions.[436] The Egyptian *ka*, the Greek ψυχή *(psyche)* and πνεῦμα *(pneuma)*, the Latin *anima* and spiritus, and the Sanskrit *prana* all emphasize that breath plays an important role in the discovery of the authentic religious self and enlightenment. Breath is often viewed as a means to raising self-knowledge and mystical experience. By understanding the meaning of breath, one may discover the purpose of creation.

וַיְהִי הָאָדָם לְנֶפֶשׁ חַיָּה – and the man became a living being – Man became a "living being" נֶפֶשׁ חַיָּה (*népeš ḥayyāh*) because he was able to walk immediately, unlike the children born after him (Ibn Ezra). While it is true that all living beings—humans, animals, flying, swarming, and swimming creatures alike—have the breath of life in them (cf. Gen. 1:20, 30; Job 33:4), only man is said to be a *living being* by virtue of the Divine breath with which God personally endows him. The Torah reminds us that while we share a physical and biological similarity with the rest of the animal world, we differ in being created by בְּצֶלֶם אֱלֹהִים (*bəṣélem ʾĕlōhîm*) "in the image of God" (1:27).

Existentially, humanity stands higher than the animal world, which subsists on instinct alone to survive, whereas humankind requires a sense of meaning and purpose for its existence in the world and cannot find fulfillment living a purely animal-like existence. Psychologist and philosopher Viktor Frankl (1905–57) discovered, while in a concentration camp, that the most important drive is not the will to pleasure, nor is it even the will to power, but the *will to meaning*.[437]

2:8 וַיִּטַּע יְהוָה אֱלֹהִים גַּן־בְּעֵדֶן – And the LORD God planted a garden in Eden – The biblical narrator does not describe the general layout of the Garden of Eden, but a

---

[436] Depending upon its specific context, the term πνεῦμα (*pneuma*) can mean "breath," "breeze," "wind," and "spirit." The Greek philosophers used πνεῦμα in a variety of different ways to connote: (1) the agent of life; (2) the immaterial part of the human personality, in contrast to the outward and visible aspects; (3) the seat of the inner spiritual life of man that enables one to know God. In Stoic thought, *pneuma* is the elemental principle that (along with earth, water and fire) gives coherence to the human body and the earth's various entities, while at the same time differentiating one entity from the other. In its purest form, *pneuma* is ethereal and fire-like, epitomizing the Logos principle. As spiritual fire, it is the soul of man; on the vegetative level it is the spirit that animates and creates plants; on the inanimate level, *pneuma* gives coherence to the physical realm. *Pneuma* is sometimes referred to as the *quinta essentia*—the fifth element (or "quintessence") representing the highest essence thought to be the substance of the heavenly bodies and latent in all things. Upon death, the breath returns to the ethereal region where it fulfills its highest destiny when it becomes one with the cosmos. See Epictetus (50–130 C.E.), *Discourses*, III, 13, 14. According to Philo of Alexandria, *pneuma* represents the rational soul that is a personification of divine power; but the *pneuma* which a human being receives defines him as a morally rational being–a reflection of the soul's divine nature (*Who is the Heir of Divine Things?* Ch. 57).

[437] Many prisoners whose lives rested on a higher meaning, (whether they were involved in working out a mathematical thesis, or had dedicated themselves to preserving and copying segments from the Torah), seemed to have managed to survive Auschwitz as opposed to those who had no higher motivation, apart from survival. See Victor Frankl's *Man's Search for Meaning* (New York: Washington Square, 1963).

simple examination of the wording will reveal some details. The noun גַּן (*gan*) generally refers to a garden that is planted with trees, or a place that is guarded by a fence and is related to the root גָּנַן (*gāʾnan*) "to protect" 438 as well as to the Arabic verb *janna* "to cover," or "to protect." A derivative nuance of the noun, גנו means "to enclose," or "put a shield about," "fence," and "protect" (HALOT: 199). A "shield" is thus called מָגֵן (*māgēn*).

The Septuagint translates "garden" as παράδεισος (*paradeisos* = "paradise"), deriving from the Old Persian (Avestan) loanword *pairi-daēza,* meaning "walled enclosure," "pleasure park," or "garden" that was commonly used among Persian kings and aristocrats. The concept of a heavenly paradise developed during the Intertestamental period (1 Enoch 32:3–6; 77:3). At first it was believed to be somewhere on the earth,[439] but the ancients arrived at the belief that Paradise was a special place where one receives heavenly rewards for living a good and pious life here on earth.[440] It has also been suggested that the Hebrew root may be possibly derived from the Sumerian-Akkadian *edinu,* meaning plain or steppe. The HALOT finds the latter definition less likely and argues that "land of bliss" or "happy lands" are better definitions of עֵדֶן (*ʿēden).*

מִקֶּדֶם – in the east – The wording "in the east" (מִקֶּדֶם = *mîqqedem*) indicates that the events of Chapter 2 occurred "far away in an unknown land." However, in addition to the geographical meaning of "east," there is a mythical meaning as well. This thought finds expression in both Targum Onkelos and Jerome's Vulgate. The former renders מִקֶּדֶם as "long ago" as opposed to "in the east" and the latter renders it as *a principio*—from the beginning. If this reading is correct, מִקֶּדֶם implies the temporal notion of "ancient time," "a time before time." Mircea Eliade refers to this concept in many places in his works as *illo tempore* ("at this time"). That is to say, the events occurred at the beginning of mythical time and at a nonphysical level of reality. For primal peoples, this concept of time represents a reality higher and greater than any kind of historical reality known to them. With this one word we are immediately alerted to the symbolic meaning of the story.

❖ *Ibn Ezra's Secret*

וַיָּשֶׂם שָׁם אֶת־הָאָדָם אֲשֶׁר יָצָר – and there he put the man whom he had formed —When הָאָדָם (*hāʾādām*) occurs with the definite article, it means "the man,"

---

438 See *Gesenius's Hebrew and Chaldee Lexicon to the Old Testament Scriptures*, 175.

439 1 Enoch 32:3–6; 77:3.

440 See for example: 1 Enoch 60:8; 61:12; 2 Enoch 8–9; 2 Bar. 51:3; T. Levi 18:10–11; cf. also 2 Apoc. Bar. 4:3–7; 4 Ezra 7:36–38.

but when the definite article is missing, it is a personal name.[441] In one of his more controversial but cryptic statements, Ibn Ezra observes that the definite article found in front of Adam may contain a "secret."[442] What this secret might be has puzzled numerous commentators. Abarbanel conjectures that Ibn Ezra might have been of the opinion that the word הָאָדָם refers to the human species rather than to Adam, the individual.[443] It would seem that Ibn Ezra believes—in a mythical and potential sense—that all future generations of humanity were present together with Adam in the Garden.[444] Augustine expresses a similar perspective; namely, that Adam is a collective representative for all humanity.[445]

If this was Ibn Ezra's intention, we must wonder why he considered this to be a secret. It seems most likely that Ibn Ezra wanted to avoid any possible Augustinian allusions to the doctrine of Original Sin. Ibn Ezra appears to have felt that the story of Adam and Eve is a parable about the human condition as we now understand and experience it. If we listen carefully, if we allow ourselves to be caught up into the story, we begin to see ourselves standing before the forbidden tree, conflicted between obedience to God and our freedom to act autonomously and apart from God.[446] Human

---

[441] Unlike Targum Neofiti, Onkelos translates the הָאָדָם as the personal name אָדָם rather than the species.

[442] Ordinarily, a proper noun does not require a definite article placed in front of it.

[443]Abarbanel says, "Ibn Ezra stirred the world by saying that the definite article which precedes the word *'ādām* contains a secret. By this he means that if *'ādām* were a proper noun, the definite article could not be prefixed, and therefore *'ādām* should be understood as a noun designating the genus of mankind, rather than an individual. To this I answer that *'ādām* represents a single man and at the same time mankind as a whole, since there was no one else" (cited from Norman Strickman and Arthur Silver's translation of *Ibn Ezra's Genesis Commentary*). See R. Joseph Albo's *Sefer haIkarim* 1:11.

[444] This does not mean, as the early Christian theologian Augustine thought, that all human beings born after Adam are tainted with his sin. Judaism has long taught that every human being is born sinless, and is, therefore, inherently capable of living a sinless life. What it does mean is that Adam's choice had a profound impact on all generations that followed him, but like Pelagius before him, each human being is responsible for the choices he or she makes.

[445]Augustine was famous for saying *Omnes enim fuimus in ilio quando omnes fuimos ille unus* ("For we all were in that one [man], while we all were that one [man]")—*Civitas Dei* XIII, 14.

[446] R. Joseph Albo (1380-1444) also interprets the story of the Garden of Eden allegorically, regarding it as a "symbolic allusion to man's fortune in this world." In his interpretation, Adam represents humankind; the Garden of Eden—the world; Eve—the physical; the Tree of Life—the Torah (cf. Prov. 3:18); and the serpent—the evil inclination. The placing of Adam in the Garden, in the midst of which stands the Tree of Life, symbolizes the fact that man is placed in the world in order to observe the commandments of the Torah. Adam's expulsion from the Garden of Eden contains an allusion to the punishment that will befall man if he disobeys the Divine commandments (*Sefer ha-Ikkarim*, 1:11). *Torah Shelemah* cites numerous parallels to Albo's non-literal approach and maintains that it is a dispute between commentators as to whether this passage is to be understood literally or allegorically.

beings still experience this Adamic drama on a daily basis whenever tempted to violate certain boundaries of proscribed behavior.

❖ *The Yearning For Edenic Peace*

With the help of Eliade's broad knowledge of primal religions, let us expand on Ibn Ezra's insight. Eliade believes that a vague residual memory of Eden can be traced to many of the mythic traditions of the world. These myths describe a primordial world where heaven and earth were ontologically accessible to one another. Primordial man lived in a state of bliss, of spontaneity and freedom, and communicated in friendship and in innocence with God and with nature.

Eliade further explains that humanity's memory of the Fall exists independent of any tradition recorded or reinterpreted by the Judeo-Christian faiths of the world. The memory of the Fall is rooted in something far more subtle and universal. The alienation, anxiety, and restlessness that human beings feel come from a sense of spiritual homelessness stretching back to the earliest periods of human history, a pre-historical time when human beings first became self-aware of their existential predicament. As the memory of this primordial oneness with the universe fades, he can now only faintly remember that something priceless is lost—possibly forever:

> [M]an's deep dissatisfaction is with his actual situation, with what is called the human situation. Man himself feels torn and separate. He often finds it difficult to properly explain to himself the nature of this separation, for sometimes he feels cut off from "something" *powerful*, "something" utterly *other* than himself . . . an indefinable, a timeless "state", of which he has no precise memory, but which he does remember from the depths of his being: a primordial state which he enjoyed before Time, before History. This separation has taken the form of a fissure, both in him and in the World. It was the "fall," not necessarily in the Judeo-Christian meaning of the term, but a "fall" nevertheless since it implies a fatal disaster for the human race and at the same time an ontological change in the structure of the World. From a certain point of view one may say that many beliefs implying the *coincidentia oppositorum* reveal a nostalgia for a paradoxical state in which the contraries exist side by side without conflict and the multiplications form aspects of a mysterious Unity.[447]

But since the Fall, humans have never given up their nostalgia and yearning for the unitive world characterized by this ontological reality faintly remembered as "Paradise." The collective unconsciousness of humankind yearns for a time when we will eventually return to the primal state of oneness with God and with nature. Memories of Eden's primordial images continue to exert an influence on human consciousness through religious and mythic imagery, literature, artistic expression, meditation, and political thought. Could this be the secret Ibn Ezra was alluding to?

---

[447] Mircea Eliade, *The Two and the One* (Chicago: University of Chicago Press, 1965), 122.

2:9 וַיַּצְמַח יְהוָה אֱלֹהִים מִן־הָאֲדָמָה כָּל־עֵץ נֶחְמָד לְמַרְאֶה וְטוֹב לְמַאֲכָל – **Out of the ground the LORD God made to grow every tree that is pleasant to the sight and good for food** – Every part of the tree was completely edible for food, from its wood to its leaves. The verse also intimates that there was no lack of attractive fruit in the garden that was permitted; as the Talmud itself observes, "Everything the Compassionate One prohibited, he permitted something similar" (BT Hullin 109b), and yet, despite the ample availability of desirous fruit, it was the forbidden fruit that was most enticing.

❖ *The Cosmic Tree and the Axis Mundi*

וְעֵץ הַחַיִּים בְּתוֹךְ הַגָּן – **the tree of life also in the midst of the garden** – In virtually every place of the ancient world, images of the tree of life bear striking similarity. In Egypt, the tree of life is pictured as a tall sycamore upon which the gods sit and obtain immortality from eating. Greek mythology speaks of the sacred "ambrosia" fruit that confers immortality to anyone who eats it. The mythology of India describes a tree in heaven from which Yama and the other gods partake of the life-giving drink, "soma." Among the Sumerians, we find the "gishkin" tree in the Temple of Eridu, also representing a mythical tree of life. Ibn Ezra[448] and James Kugel suggest that perhaps the fruit of the tree was meant to rejuvenate the couple every few hundred years or so. Hence, the denial of the Tree of Life's fruit deprived the primal couple of living an immortal existence.[449]

In many of these primal traditions, the ancient ones spoke of a cosmic tree that they believed was the central axis of the universe and of the world that is commonly referred to by anthropologists and mythologists as the *axis mundi*. This tree is often seen as connecting the mundane world of everyday life with spirit worlds that lie both above and below the ordinary world. Some traditions portray the cosmic tree functioning as a ladder on which the priest or shaman can climb up or down into the spirit worlds.[450] The cosmic tree is often depicted as an enormous tree with its roots in the subterranean deep and its top in the clouds, a shelter for every living being. It is a separate motif from that of the tree of life, although the two were often linked, but the ancient imagery can help us better understand the cultural backdrop against which the Edenic narrative was presented.[451] Eliade explains further:

---

[448] See Ibn Ezra's commentary on Genesis 3:6.

[449] See James Kugel, *How to Read the Bible*, *op. cit.*, 50-51.

[450] See Mircea Eliade's *Myths, Dreams, and Mysteries* (New York: Harper Torchbooks, 1959), 64–65.

[451] The cosmic tree's roots extend down into the underworld below the earth, and its upper branches reach up

> [W]e may note at once that the tree represents—whether ritually and concretely or in mythology and cosmology, or simply symbolically—*the living cosmos*, endlessly renewing itself. Since inexhaustible life is the equivalent of immortality the tree-cosmos may therefore become, at a different level, the tree of 'life-undying' and as this inexhaustible life was—in primitive ontology—an expression of *absolute reality*, the tree becomes for it a symbol of that reality (the 'centre of the world'). . . .[452] To the primitive mind, nature and symbol were inseparable. . . . The sacred tree of Mesopotamia is more a symbol than a cult-object. . . . It is in virtue of what it *expresses* (which is something beyond itself) that the tree becomes a religious object. . . . [453] The tree came to express the cosmos fully in itself, by embodying, in apparently static form, its "force", its life, its periodic regeneration.[454]

The Canaanite veneration of the sacred tree is well-known and documented and their worship of the tree is undoubtedly related to the Mesopotamian memory of the cosmic tree that appears throughout their mythology. Despite the biblical proscriptions not to plant an *ăšērâ* tree or a sacred grove by the Tabernacle altar[455], or to use sacred poles that may have contained sacred images of the Canaanite goddess Asherah, nevertheless, the biblical imagination still retains a residual memory of the Edenic tree in much of its symbolism, e.g., the Menorah, which resembles a golden tree (Exod. 25:34)—and ultimately wisdom herself (which later became symbolized by the Torah), is likened to a "tree of life to those who lay hold of her" (Prov. 3:18 RSV). The tree of life may be read as a metaphor for the fulfilled and blessed life that every human being yearns for—all of which contains a residual memory of a time that has long vanished.

❖ *No Ordinary Tree*

וְעֵץ הַדַּעַת טוֹב וָרָע - and the tree of the knowledge of good and evil – Many scholars think that the phrase "good and evil" is a merism (a rhetorical device used to describe the whole by enumerating its parts) for total knowledge. However, other scholars contend that "good and evil" is legal language denoting the authority to decide an issue (cf. 1 Kgs. 3:4–28, especially vv. 9, 28). Thus, in Genesis 3, by eating the fruit taken from the Tree of the Knowledge of good and evil, humanity claims for itself the

---

into the world above the sky. Cf. Eliade, *Patterns in Comparative Literature* (New York: Sheed & Ward, 1958), 271–73.

[452] Mircea Eliade, *Patterns In Comparative Religion* (New York: Sheed & Ward, 1958), 267.

[453] Ibid., 268.

[454] Ibid., 273.

[455] Cf. Exod. 34:13; Deut. 7:5; 12:3; 16:21; Judg. 6:25, 28.

right to make decisions independently from God (to whom these decisions properly belong) and the right to self-determine what is good and what is evil.

The storyteller does not suggest that there is anything inherently evil in this tree. In fact, nowhere in this primal story does the Torah intimate that God is the author of evil. While it is certainly true that in making man as He did, God made the possibility of evil, creating the possibility of evil is not the same as actualizing it. Some medieval rabbinic commentaries regarded the tree as quite an ordinary tree, which was selected by God to provide an ethical test for the man. The passage does not say it is a mere tree of knowledge, but rather that it is a tree of a *special kind* of knowledge. The Tree of Knowledge of good and evil may not have conveyed any kind of "magical" knowledge at all.

Maimonides offers a different spin to the narrative. Prior to the incident of the forbidden tree, Adam experiences reality in purely binary black and white terms. Everything in the garden was either considered permitted or forbidden, true or false. There were no intellectual distinctions, or shades of gray, or any kind of ambiguity. Only truth and falsehood existed, which are defined by God alone. Good and evil, on the other hand, stem more from humankind's subjective point of view. If at first Adam had the incisive ability to see things objectively with perfect clarity—by learning to choose, he lost his objectivity.[456]

Ramban goes one step further than Maimonides. He asserts that had Adam not eaten of its fruit, humankind would always naturally be drawn toward the good. Partaking of its fruit resulted in the blurring of our cognitive ability to distinguish between right and wrong. As a result of his choice, Adam comes to experience and evaluate things in terms of their immediate perceived benefit, resulting in a more subjective rather than objective experience of reality.[457]

On the other hand, Abarbanel argues that the Tree of Knowledge serves as a stimulant for the sexual appetite. The reason for his explanation is because he believes that the noun דַּעַת (*dá^caṯ*) connotes a carnal kind of knowledge (cf. 4:1). However, this interpretation smacks of Augustinian overtones. The verb יָדַע (*yāda'*) connotes an intimate knowledge of something that is rooted in experience, hence, "experiential knowledge" is a much more precise definition.

❖ *Locating Eden*

Many a myth has its basis in historical fact. One might wonder: What specific location may have inspired this biblical myth? Eden has sometimes been identified with

[456] Maimonides, *Guide* 1:2.

[457] As Seforno observes, "to choose the sweet even when it is harmful, and reject the bitter, even when it is for one's own benefit."

the island of Bahrain. Some scholars located the site of Eden just north of Babylon, where the Euphrates and Tigris rivers come close together. Some believe Eden was located somewhere near Eridu along the Persian Gulf because of the parallels to the Babylonian myth of *Adapa* and the Fall of man in Genesis 3.

2:10 וְנָהָר יֹצֵא מֵעֵדֶן לְהַשְׁקוֹת אֶת־הַגָּן וּמִשָּׁם יִפָּרֵד וְהָיָה לְאַרְבָּעָה רָאשִׁים – **A river flows out of Eden to water the garden, and from there it divides and becomes four branches** – Vv. 10-14 form a long parenthetical statement about the geography of the four rivers. As a geographical description, it is fraught with numerous difficulties that have eluded scholars for millennia. The biblical writer appears to be describing the geography of ancient Sumer just north of the Persian Gulf in what is present-day Iraq. Ancient Mesopotamian legends recall a paradise at the northern end of the Persian Gulf. The text seems to suggest that the known historical world is watered by four rivers, which are branches of the one great river originating in Eden, though it clearly does not originate inside the garden, but rather outside the garden or perhaps beyond Eden. The identity of this river remains a mystery. The river may have originated from the subterranean ocean (2:6), which flows out to the four corners of the known historical world, particularly the Mesopotamian valley of the Tigris and Euphrates, or alternatively, this verse may be indicating a river formed by a confluence of four rivers rather than branching into four.

Of the four rivers, only the third and fourth branch rivers have been identified, as the Tigris and the Euphrates. Their known sources in the mountains of Armenia could suggest that Eden may have been located in the north rather than in the east. There is less certainty as to the other rivers' identities. By process of elimination, it may be possible to surmise that the Pishon and the Gihon were in the general vicinity of the Tigris and the Euphrates. Speiser was of the opinion that since we know that the Tigris and the Euphrates are upstream rivers, the other two rivers must therefore have also been upstream sources or tributaries, as the downstream waters are too salty to be of any benefit for a terrestrial garden.

❖ *The Mythical Significance of the Number Four*

There is another mythical significance to this verse. Jung and Eliade have brought to our attention how the number four is laden with symbolism. Four stands for a material and cosmic number: the four phases of the moon; the four cardinal points of the earth; the four elements of earth, wind, water and fire; the four sides of a square. According to the Pythagoreans, the tetrad is a numerical symbol of the world order and totality. The ancient Babylonian rulers, as early as the middle of the 3rd millennium B.C.E., went by the epithet "King of the Four Quarters," i.e., "king of the earth."[458] In terms of biblical

[458] Even King Cyrus of Persia later described himself as "King of the world, great king, mighty king, king of Babylon, king of the land of Sumer and Akkad, king of the four quarters . . . King of the world" (quoted from the famous Cyrus Cylinder). Henri Frankfort, Samuel Noah Kramer, *Kingship and the Gods: a study of Ancient*

symbolism, the number four corresponds to the four corners of the earth (Isa. 11:12; Ezek. 46:21); the four winds (Jer. 49:36); the four chariots patrolling the earth (Zech. 6:1–5); the four living creatures surrounding the divine throne (Ezek. 1:10). In the furniture of the Tabernacle (Exod. 25–39), we similarly find four rings of gold, four cups, four pillars, four horns, four bronze rings and four rows of precious stones; the Tabernacle also has four rectangular dimensions making up its sacred precincts (1 Kgs. 7:5, 19, 27, 30, 34, 38)—all of which convey a mystical quality of completeness and totality. Most importantly, there are four letters in the Hebrew spelling of YHWH, which is frequently referred to as the "Tetragrammaton," a derivation from the Greek τετραγράμματον [τετρα = tetra (four) + γράμμα = *gramma* (letter].

Many centuries later, in the *Wisdom of Sirach*, the four rivers become the voice of Lady Wisdom who symbolizes the Torah:

> All this is the book of the covenant of the Most High God,
> The law that Moses commanded us
> As an inheritance for the congregations of Jacob.
> It overflows, like the Pishon, with wisdom,
> And like the Tigris at the time of the first fruits.
> It runs over, like the Euphrates, with understanding,
> And like the Jordan at harvest time.
> It pours forth instruction like the Nile,
> Like the Gihon at the time of vintage.
> The first man did not know wisdom fully,
> Nor will the last one fathom her.
> For her thoughts are more abundant than the sea,
> And her counsel deeper than the great abyss
> Sirach 24:23-29

2:11 שֵׁם הָאֶחָד פִּישׁוֹן – The name of the first is Pishon – The precise meaning of פִּישׁוֹן is unclear. Some think it might be derived from the root פוש "to leap" or "jump" (HALOT: 189). Pishon has sometimes been identified with the Indus or a river in Arabia. The Septuagint, Josephus[459] and the Midrash[460] each identify Pishon with the Nile River (Νεῖλος),[461] while Augustine believes it was the Ganges in India.[462]

Near Eastern Religion as the Integration of Society & Nature (Chicago: University of Chicago Press, 1978), 228-230.

459 *Ant.* 1. 37-39.

460 Cf. *Midrash Gen. Rabbah* 16.

461 S. F., Mason and L. H. Feldman observe that Josephus derives this interpretation from the Septuagint verse in Jeremiah 2:18 (*Flavius Josephus: Translation and Commentary*, Volume 3: Judean Antiquities Books 1-4 (Boston; Leiden: Brill, 2000), 562.

הוּא הַסֹּבֵב אֵת כָּל־אֶרֶץ הַחֲוִילָה – it is the one that flows around the whole land of Havilah – The name חֲוִילָה most likely is a diminutive that means "a stretch of sand" and derives from the root חול (*ḥôl* = "sand"), and was the dwelling place of Ishmael and his descendants (Gen. 25:18). Havilah is the biblical form of the name of the large and old tribal federation of Haulan in southwestern Arabia (Gen. 10:7, 29, 25:18; 1 Sam. 15:7), which is divided into two or three branches. It is possible that there may have been two places named Havilah, the other place being near the Pishon River (or the Indus River) in the general vicinity of western Pakistan. Most modern scholarship thinks that Havilah is located somewhere in southern Arabia, or eastern Africa, and is blessed with valuable resins and precious stones (cf. 10:6-7, 29).[463]

2:12 וּזֲהַב הָאָרֶץ הַהִוא טוֹב שָׁם הַבְּדֹלַח וְאֶבֶן הַשֹּׁהַם – and the gold of that land is good; bdellium and onyx stone are there – The noun בְּדֹלַח (*bĕdōlaḥ* = "bdellium") may also possibly be a pearl or a precious gum resin. It has most often been placed in western Saudi Arabia near Medina along the Red Sea, an area that does produce gold, bdellium, and onyx. Genesis 10:29 describes Havilah as the "brother" of Ophir, a region also reputed for its wealth in gold.

2:13 וְשֵׁם־הַנָּהָר הַשֵּׁנִי גִּיחוֹן– The name of the second river is Gihon – Richard E. Friedman conjectures that the name גִּיחוֹן involves a wordplay, for all snakes must crawl on their גָּחוֹן (*gāḥôn* = "belly", cf. Gen. 3:14 and Lev. 11:42).[464] However, this interpretation is more of a midrashic type of exposition—one that all the medieval rabbinic exegetes purposely ignore with respect to this particular word and passage. Rashi conjectures that the name גִּיחוֹן (Gihon) comes from יִגַּח (*yiggaḥ* = "gores"), since the river "roars and gores" like a raging ox. Westermann more correctly renders it as "the turbulent one."[465] It may also derive from from the verb גִּיחַ (*gîaḥ* = "burst forth,"

---

[462] Among other scholars, Delitzsch identifies it with the Indus. Some scholars believe the Pishon River may have existed in the northeast sector of Saudi Arabia, which runs through the country from the Hijaz Mountains near Medina to the Persian Gulf in Kuwait, near the mouth of the Tigris and Euphrates. John Gill (1697-1771) thinks that the Pishon may correspond to Pliny's Phasis, which today is better known as the Rioni River, which is the main river located in western Georgia. The Rioni originates in the Caucasus Mountains, in the region of Racha and flows west to the Black Sea. Cf. *Natural History* l. 6. c. 4; *Strabo Geograph* l. 11, 343, 345, 364.

[463] See BDB 296:2 and the *Anchor Bible Dictionary* Vol. 3, 82.

[464] Friedman's insight was already anticipated in Gen. Rabbah 1:16.

[465] *Genesis*, Vol. I, 218.

"bubble," or "gush"; see Job 40:23). A similar meaning also exists in the Arabic *jāḫa* = "burst forth" (HALOT: 189). Westermann explains that the philology of Pishon and Gihon are not descriptions well-suited to the great rivers, but rather to springs, e.g., the spring of Gihon in Jerusalem—the place where Solomon was anointed king (1 Kgs. 1:33; 38, 45; 2 Chron. 32:30; 33:14).[466]

Jon D. Levenson examines the underlying mythic interpretation that these biblical verses only hint at. He astutely explains that the Gihon served as the principal source of water serving the entire city of Jerusalem. According to Isaiah 7-8, Jerusalem's water system "held transcendent significance in the religious consciousness of those who lived there." To the mythic imagination of ancient Israel, "The sacramental spring that functioned as the source of Jerusalem's miraculous waterworks was conceived as the cosmic stream which issues from that mountain and sheds its fertilizing waters upon the face of the whole earth."[467] This connection, reasons Levenson, shows how the Temple of Jerusalem and the Edenic Paradise are directly related.[468]

הוּא הַסֹּובֵב אֵת כָּל־אֶרֶץ כּוּשׁ – it is the one that flows around the whole land of Cush – The name כּוּשׁ (*k̲ûš* = "Cush") is similar to the Egyptian *K'š*, which has sometimes been identified with the Nile or "Nubian Nile," located in southern Egypt and northern Sudan.[469] This view, also advocated by Claus Westermann, proposes that this meaning is plausible.[470] (For a further description of Cush, see notes to Gen. 10:8–10). Some scholars think that Cush may be referring to the Kassites, with the land of the Kassites (*k̲ûšû* in Babylonian). Historically, the Kassites (ca. 18th century B.C.E.) lived in the mountains east of Mesopotamia in Luristan, east of the Tigris, in what is now

---

466 *Genesis*, Vol. I, 217.

467 Jon D. Levenson, *Sinai and Zion: An Entry into the Jewish Bible* (New York: Harper and Row, 1985), 130.

468 Centuries after the Temple's destruction, the prophet Ezekiel foretells of a wonderful and superabundant stream that will flow from the Temple, which will restore to fertility traditionally arid ground, and is symbolic of the return of the conditions of primeval paradise (Eze. 28:13-14; 47:1-12). A similiar paradisiacal motif is also found in Joel 3:18 and Zech 13:1-3; 14:8. Indeed, the imagery of the "living waters" suggests an eschatological dimension that will lead to the eventual purification of humankind as well as a return to a new Edenic state of purity—which neatly fits Levenson's theory.

469 HALOT: 467

470 Some scholars have proposed that the name Pishon derives the name from the Egyptian root *p'-hnw*, "the canal." The sun god Re landed each day at this canal, adjacent to the Nile, establishing it in a context of paradise, and from thence it was associated with the Garden of Eden. Cf. John C. Munday Jr., "Eden's Geography Erodes Flood Geology" *WTJ*-Vol. 58 #1-Spr. 96, 124-155.

western Iran.[471] The latter seems to be the more logical choice since the Nile does not join with the Tigris and the Euphrates.[472] Gihon River is mentioned specifically as one of the three rivers that flow out of Eden along with the Tigris and the Euphrates Rivers. Possible candidates include: the Diyala or the Kerkha, however, precise identification is uncertain since the rivers may have changed their course over the millennia.[473]

2:14 וְשֵׁם הַנָּהָר הַשְּׁלִישִׁי חִדֶּקֶל הוּא הַהֹלֵךְ קִדְמַת אַשּׁוּר — **The name of the third river is Tigris, which flows east of Assyria** — Onkelos identifies this river as דִּגְלַת (*Diglat*) a name that is Sumerian and Akkadian in origin.[474] The Septuagint translates חִדֶּקֶל (*ḥiddéqel*) as Τίγρις (Tigris River) and in Latin as *Tigri*. This river rises in eastern Turkey, flowing about 1,150 miles southeast through Iraq to the Euphrates River. It functioned as a major transportation route in ancient times.

וְהַנָּהָר הָרְבִיעִי הוּא פְרָת — **And the fourth river is the Euphrates** — The Septuagint identified פְּרָת (*pōrāṯ*) as Εὐφράτης (Euphrates). In Akkadian it was known as *Purattu*. The Euphrates flows some 1,700 miles from central Turkey through Syria and into Iraq, where it joins the Tigris River to form the Shatt al Arab. The waters were a major source of irrigation for the flourishing civilizations of ancient Mesopotamia. It is fed by tributaries from the Persian hills, the Greater and Lesser Zab, Adhem, and Diyala Rivers.

❖ *Protecting Eden: Its Ecological Implications for Today*

2:15 וַיִּקַּח יְהוָה אֱלֹהִים אֶת־הָאָדָם וַיַּנִּחֵהוּ בְגַן־עֵדֶן לְעָבְדָהּ וּלְשָׁמְרָהּ — **The LORD God took the man and put him in the garden of Eden to till it and keep it** — Genesis places humanity at the pinnacle of God's bio-centric creative activity. With

---

[471] E.A. Speiser, "The Rivers of Paradise," in *Oriental and Biblical Studies*, University of Pennsylvania, 1967, 23–34. See H. Eising's article in the TDOT, Vol. 2, 466-68.

[472] Marcus Kalisch argues that the biblical writer shares some of the common mistaken views of ancient geography that many of ancient Israel's neighbors subscribed to, namely that the Nile Euphrates and Tigris were all believed to be conjoined-despite the fact that these rivers flow in opposite directions (cf. *Antiquities* 1:36 for an example). While this may be perhaps the simplest reading of the text, it certainly is not the only interpretation.

[473] D. R. W. Wood., ed., *New Bible Dictionary* (Downers Grove, IL. InterVarsity Press 1996, c1982, c1962), 412.

[474] As observed in the HALOT: 293. Josephus in *Antiquities* i: 1, 3 also refer to the Tigris Διγλαθ; cf. Pliny *Nat. Hist.* vi: 127.

humankind's appearance, the progression of Creation—from its state of non-being and chaos that followed—to the present moment, marks the highest evolution of consciousness having emerged thus far.

Another Interpretive View: The LORD God took the man and put him in the garden of Eden to till it and keep it. – The Babylonian creation myth underscores, in the minds of its believers, that they were no more than mere slaves to the gods.[475] In contrast, the Torah's view of humankind is portrayed in radically different terms. God created humankind to act as His vice-regent and steward over Creation. God did not create Adam to be a mere receiver of divine benefits; like the Creator, Adam too, must contribute toward the process and improvement of Creation. Even prior to the Fall, Adam was created to work; but his work was of a different sort entirely. Adam's workload was not burdened with futility or frustration; his work was creative and satisfying and he was required to put forth minimal effort for his food and sustenance. Nowhere does the Torah intimate that Adam was created to relieve God of tedious labor, but rather he was made to reflect God's care of the natural world. The Bible radically redefines the role of Adam in ways that contrast with other Near Eastern traditions. In the literature of the ancient Near East, work is regarded as a curse, a dreary burden to be at best tolerated; humankind was created to relieve the gods of their burden of running and maintaining the universe. According to Tablet VI of *Enuma Elish*, man was created from the blood of Kingu, an insurgent deity, for the purpose of providing for the needs of the gods in doing their work.

> They bound him [Kingu] holding him before Ea;
> They imposed on him guilt and severed his blood (vessels).
> Out of his blood they fashioned mankind;
> He [Ea] imposed the service and let free the gods.
> After Ea, the wise, had created mankind,
> Had imposed upon it the service of the gods—
> That work was beyond comprehension.[476]

By embracing the ethic of work, humankind joins God in preserving and propagating creation. This thought finds elegant expression in the Midrash:

> When the Holy One, blessed be He, created the first man, He took him and led him round all the trees of the Garden of Eden, and said to him, 'Behold My works, how beautiful and commendable they are! All that I have created, for your sake I created it.

---

[475] N. Sarna observes, "The position and function of man in the scheme of creation paralleled precisely the status of the slaves in Mesopotamia" *Understanding Genesis* (New York: Schocken Books, 1972), 7.

[476] James B. Pritchard, ed., *Ancient Near Eastern Texts (ANET) Relating to the Old Testament* (Princeton, NJ: Princeton University Press, 1955), 68.

> Pay heed that you do not corrupt and destroy My world. For if you do spoil her, there will be nobody to repair her after you.[477]

This Midrashic interpretation highlights the importance of stewardship, not only for the Garden of Eden, but for our taking care of the earth, God's garden. By taking care of the primordial garden, Adam learns to recognize that all of life is God's unique design, endowed with spirit, consciousness, and intelligence. Adam's respect for Creation makes him realize that the human species is a part of the great web of life, which he must nurture for the world to be self-sustaining and productive. Indeed, the degradation of the environment damages the original balance that Adam and his progeny must maintain. Through toil, Adam would realize how all of Creation depends on the Divine as the source of life for its sustenance and continued existence.

Understanding the implications of Adam's stewardship is vital for our contemporary society. The science of ecology has shown how ecosystems of the world are delicately balanced; should human beings ruin them through abusive acts (ecocide), future generations will have to endure the consequences. Through work and stewardship, humankind comes to emulate God's own work and creativity as *Imitatio Dei* (imitation of God). It was the divine intent from the beginning for humankind to elevate and ennoble itself by means of work, and in so doing, elevate Creation to the realm of the spirit, leading all Creation in song and joyous exaltation of the Divine. Note that God intended to make Adam not a "master" over the Garden of Eden, but rather, its caretaker and steward. Once Adam forgets that he is only a steward of the garden, the boundaries established by the Creator became unclear and ultimately violated.

2:16 וַיְצַו יְהוָה אֱלֹהִים עַל־הָאָדָם לֵאמֹר מִכֹּל עֵץ־הַגָּן אָכֹל תֹּאכֵל – **And the LORD God commanded the man, "You may freely eat of every tree of the garden"** – It is remarkable that the first precept Adam receives is a dietary law. An important purpose of all the Scriptural dietary restrictions is to teach humankind discipline and self-control, while instilling holiness.

❖ *Respecting the Boundaries of Creation*

2:17 וּמֵעֵץ הַדַּעַת טוֹב וָרָע לֹא תֹאכַל מִמֶּנּוּ – **but of the tree of the knowledge of good and evil you shall not eat** – Note that God does not impose His will upon Adam, nor does He coerce him to obey. Even Paradise has its rules. The Torah teaches that freedom is not the license to do whatever one wants. The Divine proscription also instructs Adam to differentiate between a God-centered world and a human-centered one. In a God-centered world, it is God Who determines the boundaries between right

---

[477] Eccles. Rabbah 7:20.

and wrong; in a human-centered world, humans define values, and in a sense act like God. The willful blurring of these divine defined boundaries is, in a mythical sense, an invitation to chaos and non-being. The power to choose must not be abused; it must be yoked to a spiritual discipline that coheres with the cosmic order.

Freedom always comes with responsibility; Israel's spiritual development does not end with the Exodus, but it continues with receiving the covenant at Sinai. When viewed from this perspective, the Torah wishes to impress upon us that the first obligation of any mortal (great or small) must be to obey God unconditionally—even if one happens to be as wise as King Solomon himself. Even the pursuit of wisdom must have its limits and must be yoked to a higher morality. No man or woman is ever "above the law" even if one happens to be a sovereign of the world's most powerful nation. Each human being is answerable to a Higher Authority. In the case of Adam, his refusal to respect the boundaries that God ordained resulted in dangerous consequences for the world he lived in, affecting every species of life.

❖ *Did God Intend for Humankind to Live Forever?*

כִּי בְּיוֹם אֲכָלְךָ מִמֶּנּוּ מוֹת תָּמוּת – for in the day that you eat of it you shall die – One of the Judaic translators of the Septuagint, Symmachus (*ca.* 2nd-3rd century), translates the text most appropriately as "you shall be mortal." But Ibn Ezra raises a timeless theological question: Were human beings ever intended to live forever? It has often been alleged that God created humanity to be immortal, but as a result of the "Fall," humankind "fell" into mortality.[478] One such proponent, Bahya Ibn Asher (ca. 14th cent.) argues that the Torah never states that Adam would die *immediately*, but rather that he would only *begin* to die. As a result of his disobedience, Adam forfeits his right to live an immortal existence on this earth. Now in effect, God forewarns Adam and his descendants about the possibility of a potential death sentence. Homiletically, Bahya (and later Kugel) claims that the word בְּיוֹם (*bĕyôm*) implies a day in the "life" of God, the equivalent of a thousand years, "For a thousand years in your sight are like a day that has just gone by, or like a watch in the night" (Ps. 90:4). Adam lived only seventy years shy of 1000 years.[479]

---

[478] Ramban contends that had Adam never sinned, he would never have died, since the higher soul bestows life forever, and the will of God was present within Adam at the time of his creation. Whether a person lives forever or not is a matter solely dependent on the will of God; "for in the day that you eat of it you shall die" means that "once you have eaten the fruit you will be condemned to die, since you will no longer exist forever by My will." Adam's loss of immortality comes as a punishment.

[479] Lastly, Bahya cites the Kabbalistic approach, which sees the wording מוֹת תָּמוּת (*môt tāmût* = "you shall surely die") as alluding to two kinds of death: physical death and the death of the soul.

Ibn Ezra rejects this viewpoint. He argues that humankind was never intended to live an immortal existence; like the animals, human beings too must die. This debate seems to have antecedents in the Talmud[480] and in the Midrash. Like Ibn Ezra,[481] Maimonides, in his *Guide to the Perplexed* (3:12), asserts that death was a natural and an inevitable part of the creation process. Death is a necessary ingredient to the whole order of Creation: Without death, human beings would never bother to improve; death reminds humans that they must make the most out of their time in this world.[482] Thus, death itself brings to completion all of Creation and was built into the scheme of nature from the very beginning. It is fascinating to compare the debate between Ibn Ezra and his critics to the fourth-century controversy that engulfed much of ancient Rome between the elderly Augustine of Hippo and Julian of Eclanum (*ca.* 386–454)—the outstanding protégé of Pelagius, both of whom were Augustine's nemeses. Augustine maintains that through an act of will, Adam and Eve altered and changed the fabric of the physical universe, which resulted in the corruption of the entire human race. Through his disobedience, Adam decreed death upon the human race. Had he not sinned, our physical nature would be radically different from what it presently is.[483]

Unlike Augustine, Julian rejects the commonly held notion that death came to this world as a punishment from God. The death that God bequeaths to Adam was different from the type of mortality all other creatures shared. Even if Adam had never sinned, he still would have died, if only because his physical being could not endure forever. The verse "for in the day that you eat of it you shall die" does not refer to the death of the body, but to the death of the soul that takes place in sin. According to Julian, Adam's death was essentially a spiritual one, for he does not physically die immediately after he ate the forbidden fruit.

Is death a blessing? Or is it a curse? Of what, finally, does human life consist? Does not the Wisdom Literature of the Bible tell us that life is a thing as vaporous as the dew, which is driven away and disappears with the wind; that, like a field of grass dried up in the heat of the sun, its withering is a mere fact of life? And all because we must die—or, more to the point, because we alone *know* we must die. Animals do not appear to consciously know the meaning of mortality; they do not entertain thoughts of impending extinction unless they are in direct danger from a predator.

---

[480] Cf. BT Shabbat 55a-b and BT Avodah Zarah 5a.

[481] Cf. Ibn Ezra on Genesis 3:6.

[482] Cf. *Torah Temimah* on Genesis 1:31.

[483] For an example of Augustine's trenchant attempt to refute Julian's viewpoint, see Augustine's Anti-Pelagian classic *On the Merits and Remission of Sins* 1:30.58; 3:6.12; *On Baptism against the Donatists* 4:24.31; 51:259; *Julian* 3:149; 18:20 *Epistles* 157:22; *On Original Sin* 4:3; 19:21.

Thus death is at once the most commonplace of all happenings, and at the same time the most painfully incomprehensible, the least tolerable or welcome of all the things that conspire to overtake and destroy us. Human uniqueness is also paradoxical in that not only are we mindful that we will someday die, but we also deny that it will happen to us. Nothing seems to invalidate our very existence like the thought of death looming over us, like a predatory animal lying in wait to consume us. The comedian Woody Allen may have surmised our angst best: "The only thing I have against death is that I don't want to be there when it happens."

Another Interpretive View: for in the day that you eat of it you shall die – How can Adam or his wife have known what death was, if it was not a part of their existential experience? They could have deduced it from nature; i.e., by watching animals die, certainly they must have realized that death exists for clearly there is nothing in the text to suggest that animals were privy to an immortal existence.

Alone in an Edenic Paradise
(2:15-25)

[15]The LORD God took the man and put him in the Garden of Eden to till it and keep it.
[16]And the LORD God commanded the man, "You may freely eat of every tree of the garden;
[17]but of the tree of the knowledge of good and evil you shall not eat, for in the day that you
eat of it you shall die."

[18]Then the LORD God said, "It is not good that the man should be alone; I will make
him a helper as his partner." [19]So out of the ground the LORD God formed every animal of
the field and every bird of the air, and brought them to the man to see what he would call
them; and whatever the man called every living creature, that was its name. [20]The man gave
names to all cattle, and to the birds of the air, and to every animal of the field; but for the
man[b] there was not found a helper as his partner. [21]So the LORD God caused a deep sleep to
fall upon the man, and he slept; then he took one of his ribs and closed up its place with
flesh. [22]And the rib that the LORD God had taken from the man he made into a woman and
brought her to the man. [23]Then the man said,

"This at last is bone of my bones
and flesh of my flesh;
this one shall be called Woman,[c]
for out of Man[d] this one was taken."

[24]Therefore a man leaves his father and his mother and clings to his wife, and they become
one flesh. [25]And the man and his wife were both naked, and were not ashamed.

The deepest need of man is the need to overcome his separateness, to leave the prison of his aloneness.

—ERICH FROMM, *The Art of Loving*

One is the loneliest number that you'll ever do . . .

—THREE DOG NIGHT, lyrics to "One"

Why does the Torah say: If a man takes a wife (Deut. 22:13) and not If a woman is taken by a man? — Because it is the way of a man to look for a wife, but it is not the way of a woman to look for a husband. You can compare it to a person who lost an article: who goes looking for the lost item?

---

[b] Or *for Adam*
[c] Heb *ishshah*
[d] Heb *ish*

Surely the loser will look for the thing he has lost. [Ever since Adam has lost his rib, every man is trying to retrieve it by looking for a wife.]

—Rabbi Shimon, BT Kiddushin 2b

No fitting companion was found for Adam among all the animals, because his nature was fundamentally different from theirs. We humans share 99 per cent of our genes with our closest primate relative, the chimpanzee. But that 1 per cent difference represents a gaping chasm of consciousness separating our species. Humans will always interact with animals, but never on equal footing. And as this story emphasizes, we can transcend our aloneness only in a relationship between equals.

—NAOMI ROSENBLATT, JOSHUA HORWITZ, *Wrestling with Angels*

Is love pleasure, is love merriment? No, love is longing constantly; love is persevering unweariedly; love is hoping patiently; love is willing surrender; love is regarding constantly the pleasure and displeasure of the beloved, for love is resignation to the will of the possessor of one's heart; it is love that teaches man: Thou, not I.

—HAZART INAYAT KHAN, *Introduction to Alapas*

If names are not correct, language is not in accordance with the truth of things. If language is not in accordance with the truth of things, affairs cannot be carried on to success. When affairs cannot be carried on to success, proprieties and music will not flourish. When proprieties and music do not flourish, punishments will not be awarded. When punishments are not properly awarded, the people do not know how to move hand or foot. Therefore a superior man considers it necessary that the names he uses may be spoken appropriately, and that what he speaks may also be carried out appropriately. What the superior man requires is just that in his words there may be nothing incorrect.

—CONFUCIUS, *Analects* 13.3.5-7

To impress upon Adam the need for *human* companionship, God brought him all the animals so that he might notice that each one had a partner. This parade of God's creatures was intended to lead to a deepening of Adam's own consciousness and personal reflectivity. Adam thought to himself: "The world may be 'very good' from YHWH's perspective, but from *my* perspective something *is missing*." Now, for the first time in the creation story, Adam discovers something that is not "good" in Eden—human aloneness. The nature of Adam's loneliness is not just physical; it is also existential. He wonders, "Am I destined to journey throughout my existence all alone?" The Midrash captures this thought beautifully: "When He brought them, He brought them before him male and female of each and every kind; then he said: 'every creature has a mate, but me!' So the LORD God caused a deep sleep to fall upon the man, and he slept."[484]

---

[484] This particular Midrashic homily is definitely preferable to the Aggadic passage that claims Adam copulated

A biblical narrative is told about Adam; yet, at this point Adam has no personal narrative to speak of. As a solitary being, Adam exists as a two-dimensional individual. Bewildered by his loneliness, Adam does not understand why God made him alone. Rabbinic tradition teaches that Eve's creation accentuates a very important point that is pivotal to the theme of love and to all interpersonal relations: A person must not exist as an isolated entity living solely for oneself. No human individual is complete in oneself. The quest for human fulfillment can come only once a person reaches out beyond the walls of the individual self by entering into a relationship with a *significant Other*. As Buber and Lévinas have noted, by encountering the *Other* as *thou,* one comes to know the *Eternal Thou*. Once he meets Eve, Adam finally finds the remedy to his loneliness.

Throughout history, one essential question has confronted man: How can I overcome my abiding sense of separateness? Is there something more than my own individual existence? Love alone is the only power that can break down the walls of the self that separate humans from others. Love alone provides the elixir that makes separateness and creaturely isolation vanish while still preserving one's uniqueness and individuality.

❖ *One is the Loneliest Number*

2:18 וַיֹּאמֶר יְהוָה אֱלֹהִים לֹא־טוֹב הֱיוֹת הָאָדָם לְבַדּוֹ – **It is not good that the man should be alone** – The image of God is also an intensely relational concept. Although Adam is made in the Divine image, Adam senses that there is something missing from his being. Ultimately we do not fully reflect God's image on our own but in relationship with each other. According to Martin Buber (1878–1965), the knowledge and experience of God are mediated through the human community. Relationships must also be predicated upon a principle of mutuality and dialogue. It is in the sphere of the interpersonal, "the lines of relationships are extended, and intersect in the eternal You."[485] All relationships mysteriously touch one another in a divine embrace. For Buber, God is the Eternal Thou who is addressed in every personal relationship, and is the hidden third partner who is present in every dialogue. More directly stated, in order for the Divine and human interactive relationship to unfold, man must learn to relate to the Other.[486] This thought is elegantly expressed in the book of Ecclesiastes:

---

with all the animals of the garden. Regarding the legend of Lilith, see Excursus 22.

[485] M. Buber, *I and Thou,* W. Kaufmann (tr.) (New York: Scribner's, 1970), 123.

[486] The concept of the Other in Jewish thought has been expertly explored in the many works of Emanuel Lévinas. See his book of essays *Difficult Freedom* (Baltimore: Johns Hopkins UP, 1990), and his essay on forgiveness in "Toward the Other" in *Nine Talmudic Readings* (Bloomington: Indiana University Press, 1990), 12-29. For an important philosophical parallel to Lévinas's thought, see Jean Paul Sartre's *Being and Nothingness*

Better two than one alone, since thus their work is really rewarding. If one should fall, the other helps him up; but what of the person with no one to help him up when he falls? Again: if two sleep together they keep warm, but how can anyone keep warm alone? Where one alone would be overcome, two will put up resistance;

Eccles. 4:9–12 (NJB)

❖ *The Nature and Origin of Adam's Loneliness*

Without a female counterpart, Adam feels fragmented, and unable to properly relate to the world around him. For that matter, his estrangement extends not only to his own humanity, but also to his Creator. Friedrich Schleiermacher (1768-1834), well ahead of his time, intuited the existential nature of Adam's loneliness and the feeling of agitation he experienced in Eden:

> Let me disclose to you a secret that lies concealed in one of the most ancient sources of poetry and religion. As long as the first man was alone with himself and nature, the deity did indeed rule over him; it addressed the man in various ways, but he did not understand it, for he did not answer it; his paradise was beautiful and the stars shone down on him from a beautiful heaven, but the sense for the world did not open up within him; he did not even develop within his soul; but his heart was moved by a longing for a world, and so he gathered before him the animal creation to see if one might perhaps be formed from him. Since the deity recognized that his world would be nothing so long as man was alone, it created from him a partner, and now, for the first time, the world rose before his eyes. In the flesh and bone of his bone he discovered humanity, and in humanity the world; from this moment on he became capable of hearing the voice of the deity and of answering it, and the most sacrilegious transgressions of its laws from now on no longer precluded him from association with the eternal being. All our history is contained in this holy saga.[487]

Another Interpretive View: It is not good that the man should be alone – The text raises an interesting theological and mystical question: How would God know that loneliness is a bad thing? Is it because God "suffers," so to speak, from the same ontological condition? God's desire to reach out and touch the Other is exactly what the Creator wishes to instill within Adam—a desire to reach out toward an Other who is similar but different from himself. Jewish mystics sometimes speak of God creating the cosmos out of His own self; this process is also realized when God creates a mate for Adam, who in turn is derived from himself. (For further comments on this theme, see Excursus 11a-b).

(New York: The Philosophical Library, 1956), 301-400 and 471-558. A relevant comparison of these two thinkers is found in Christina Howells' chapter, "Sartre and Lévinas," in R. Bernasconi and D. Wood (eds.) *The Provocation of Lévinas: Rethinking the Other,* (London and New York: Routledge), 91-99.

[487] Friedrich Schleiermacher, *On Religion: Speeches to Its Cultured Despisers* (Cambridge: Cambridge University Press, 1996), 10.

❖ *Companion and Adversary*

אֶעֱשֶׂה־לּוֹ עֵזֶר כְּנֶגְדּוֹ — I will make him a helper as his partner — Many modern Bible translations tend to offer a bland rendering of this particular text. Both the NRSV and NJPS[488] translations fall into this category. Rashi offers an intriguing interpretation using a more literal translation of the Hebrew phrase עֵזֶר כְּנֶגְדּוֹ (*'ēzer kĕnegdô*) as "a helper against him." The noun "helper" (עֵזֶר = *'ēzer*) is often used in the Tanakh with respect to military assistance "helping" or "rescuing" Israel from its enemies.[489] It sometimes connotes strength and might.[490] Illustrative of this idea is the use of עֵזֶר in connection with Egypt (Ezek. 30:8, 32:21). When used as a verb, it denotes the common action or joint cooperation when the strength of one person is insufficient. עֵזֶר (*'ēzer*) can involve assistance that is either human or divine. Nowhere does the word ever imply inferiority, that there is anything inherently inferior in the person who is assisting. God, too, is called a "Helper."[491] The intent here simply means that man and woman complement each other in what the other person lacks. There is nothing to suggest that the woman has a subservient role in relation to her husband:

> "I will make a helper against him" (Gen. 2:18)—If he is worthy, she will be a help; if not, she will be against him.[492]

The older KJV translation, "I will make a helper against him," may seem to imply a certain degree of cultural negativity, since to be "against" someone implies a conflictive relationship. However, conflicts in a relationship need not be viewed as something inherently bad. The rabbis view tension in a marriage as perfectly normal and even healthy at times. It is important that spouses confront each other, especially when one sees the other acting wrongly. Criticism, questioning, and the ability to communicate are healthy and necessary if a couple is to have a really strong marriage.

Thus, if interpreted literally, the Torah intimates there are times a wife can best be a helper by being *against* her husband. A little dialectic tension between spouses is as important as love. Like salt on a meal, a small measure of contention between husband and wife can be good, but too much can lead to spoiling. Indignation, minus the self-

---

[488] The NJPS reads: "It is not good for man to be alone; I will make a fitting helper for him . . ."

[489] 1 Sam. 7:11–13; Isa. 30:5; Ezek. 12:14; Hosea 13:9.

[490] Pss. 33:20, 115:9, 10-11.

[491] *Cf.* Psalms 33:20; 70:5; 115:9.

[492] T. B. Yevamot 63a.

righteousness, is both purposeful and honest—but it must never lead to viciousness or cruelty. Learning to do battle with one another is healthy and constructive, for it brings to a marriage the principle of equal partnership.

Every marriage challenges couples to strive for the best in their relationship. Each partner must learn to acknowledge the needs of the other in which giving and taking are equal; in which each accepts the other, and where the "I" confronts the "Thou." God intended that their relationship is no less important than procreation per se. Each one exists as a singular being: their relationship to each other is implicit and yet perfectly matched to one another. Man and woman coexist as equals, regardless of role definition in terms of procreation or any other mark of distinction. Although the man was created first, relationships between the sexes are asymmetrical because of the gender differences existing between one another—*equality* is not necessarily synonymous with *identity*.

As a "helper" to the man, the woman became his partner spiritually in the overwhelming task of obedience to God and dominion over the earth. She was also intended to be a vital part of extending the generations (1:28). As man's mate, the woman would always prove to be man's ultimate friend and companion (2:23-24). No one else can challenge—or provoke man to think critically and self-reflectively—while encouraging and inspiring him to be the best he can be, as she was created to do. Woman was not intended to be merely man's helper or servant. She was to be instead his partner. As one scholar notes, "Woman is a power equal to a man; she is his match; she corresponds to him in every way."[493]

❖ *Even As the Strings of a Lute are Alone*

The concept of עֵזֶר כְּנֶגְדּוֹ (*'ēzer kĕnegdô* = "a helpmate opposite him") may suggest another insight: a poetics of space is necessary in any kind of sustainable loving relationship. The poet Kahlil Gibran, in his book *The Prophet*, speaks of the need for lovers to respect each other's differences. Love does not require one partner to give up his or her individuality—even in the name of love:

> Sing and dance together and be joyous, but let each one of you be alone,
> Even as the strings of a lute are alone,
> though they quiver with the same music.
> Give your hearts, but not into each other's keeping.
> For only the hand of Life can contain your hearts.
> And stand together, yet not too near together:
> For the pillars of the temple stand apart,
> And the oak tree and the cypress grow not in each other's shadow.[494]

---

[493] R. David Freedman, "Woman, A Power Equal to Man," *Biblical Archeological Review* 9 (1983), 56-58.

[494] Kahil Gibran, *The Prophet* (New York: Alfred A. Knopf, 1923), 15-17.

Love is the mysterious quality that enables two people to be intimate and one with one another, yet maintain their own sense of individuality as Gibran poetically illustrated above. True love does not demand that the beloved surrender his or her own individuality in order to be loved; this is not love but servitude. In an "I and Thou" relationship, one person affords the other the ability to freely grow and develop rather than using one's influence to mold or control the other person to fit a more desirable or fixed ideal. In healthy relationships, there needs to be a balance between intimacy and independence. This psychological space must be forged and maintained between two people who are bonded in a loving relationship. For this to happen, each person must have a healthy self-identity in order to merge that self with another without losing oneself in the process of developing closeness and intimacy.

❖ *Discovering the Animal World*

2:19 וַיִּצֶר יְהוָה אֱלֹהִים מִן־הָאֲדָמָה כָּל־חַיַּת הַשָּׂדֶה וְאֵת כָּל־עוֹף הַשָּׁמַיִם – **So out of the ground the LORD God formed every animal of the field and every bird of the air** – On the surface of the text, there appears to be a contradiction to the order of creation as described in Genesis 1:24-26, which states that the animal kingdom preceded humankind's creation, while this text suggests that humankind was made first! However, this is not necessarily the case. The verb וַיִּצֶר (*wayyīṣer*) is rendered by the NRSV as "formed," but the verb could just as easily be read as pluperfect, "had already formed," implying that the animal world was indeed created before humankind as indicated in the first chapter.

וַיָּבֵא אֶל־הָאָדָם לִרְאוֹת מַה־יִּקְרָא־לוֹ – **and brought them to the man to see what he would call them** – The Torah stresses that there was a time when human beings lived at peace with the animal kingdom. Adam's personality exuded love and compassion for God's creatures great and small. Originally, the animals came to Adam as they would to a loving shepherd. They were afraid neither of him, nor of each other. Violence did not exist in Eden and it is no accident that the prophet Isaiah foresees a time in human history when humanity would return to an Edenic world where every creature would live in peace and without fear (Isa. 11:6-9). Even the predatory animals would coexist peacefully with domestic animals.

There may have been another reason why God paraded the animal kingdom before Adam. Man was in the most literal sense a late arrival on the scene of Creation; man is not a creature who stands completely apart of the animal kingdom—in fact, his earthly being is rooted in theirs. The inanimate, the vegetative and animal kingdoms are all combined into Adam's makeup. He is a composite of all Creation. This agrees with evolutionary theory stressing that humanity is on a path of evolution. As the early 20th century mystic Rabbi Abraham Isaac Kook (1865-1935) observes, humanity has the capacity to raise not only its own consciousness, but also the consciousness of the planet around it.

❖ *The Biblical Origin of Taxonomy*

וְכֹל אֲשֶׁר יִקְרָא-לוֹ הָאָדָם נֶפֶשׁ חַיָּה הוּא שְׁמוֹ – and whatever the man called every living creature, that was its name – Etymologies of many common animals will often reveal that originally, people identified an animal by its appearance, behavior, or sound.[495] In Hebrew for example, the verb פִּרְפֵּר (*pirpare* = "flutter") thus became פַּרְפַּר (*parpar*) "butterfly." In Hebrew a raven is called עֹרֵב (*'ōrēb*) because it derives from the word עֶרֶב (*'ereb*) "darkness." This pattern exists in other cultures as well. In Latin, the raven was called *corvus* which was derived from the Greek κόραξ (*korax*). The raven's name derives from the root κράζω *(krazō* = "cry") because of its harsh sounding screech. The word *dolphin* derives from the Greek δελφίν (*delphin*) which in turn originates from δελφuj *("delphus* = "womb"*)* because of the mammal's womb-like shape. The word *deer* comes from German *tier* or *deor* ("wild animal") since it was the animal of choice to hunt. The fox derives its name from the Indo-European base *pua,* "thick-haired," "bushy" and so on. Keil focuses on the structural thinking involved in naming:

> Language is . . . the organ of the inner being, or rather the inner being itself as it gradually attains to inward knowledge and expression. It is merely thought cast into articulate sounds or words. The thoughts of Adam with regard to the animals, to which he gave expression in the names that he gave them, we are not to regard as the mere results of reflection, or of abstraction from merely outward peculiarities which affected the senses; but as a deep and direct mental insight into the nature of the animals, which penetrated far deeper than such knowledge as is the simple result of reflecting and abstracting thought. The naming of the animals therefore, led to this result, that there was not found a help meet for man.[496]

---

[495] During the classical era the Roman philosopher, Plutarch (*ca.* 46-120 C.E.), recognized that the common names used by people were originally based on the person's physical characteristics or personality traits. "The Greeks used to give surnames from an exploit, as for instance, Soter ("Savior") and Callinicus ("Of noble victory"); or from a bodily feature, as Physcon ("Fat-paunch") and Grypus ("Hook-nosed"), and so on. See *The Parallel Lives* by Plutarch published in Vol. IV, trans. Thomas North, (New York: Loeb Classics, 1916), Caius Martius Coriolanus, 143-145.

Unlike Plutarch, Plato's dialogues discuss the widely held Oriental and Egyptian view that every name corresponds to the nature or reality it represents—a view that was set forth by Cratylus who said, "He who knows names knows also the things which are expressed by them" (*Cratylus*, 435). However, Plato mentions in the name of Socrates that the logic of this popular position is incorrect. What if the name is falsely attributed? What then? To be able to name in such a manner requires that one must be able to distinguish between the essence and the names that are applied, which is certainly a difficult undertaking!

[496] *Biblical Commentary on the Old Testament, op. cit.,* 88.

Judaic mystical writings add that Adam's naming of the animals derives from his knowledge of the animal kingdom's spiritual essence. Adam's uniqueness is his ability to see the spiritual essence of the creatures he is naming—ability that even the angels did not have! This is the first act that makes Adam truly God-like in his ability to discern the nature of God's creatures. God endows Adam with the ability to see the world symbolically and to understand the symbolic realm by means of his intelligence and knowledge. The term "symbol" is derived from the Greek σύμβολον (*sýmbolon*= συν- [*syn*-] meaning "together" while βολή [*bolē*] translates as "throw"; hence, "throw together" that serves as a force that unifies both spirit and matter.

2:20 וַיִּקְרָא הָאָדָם שֵׁמוֹת לְכָל־הַבְּהֵמָה וּלְעוֹף הַשָּׁמַיִם וּלְכֹל חַיַּת הַשָּׂדֶה – **The man gave names to all cattle, and to the birds of the air, and to every animal of the field** – In the Tanakh, to be without a name is to be condemned to the most marginal kind of existence. All meaningful and ordinary interactions people experience occur through the vehicle of the name which marks the beginning of a relationship. By giving each animal a name, Adam discovers that God's creatures are more than just objects.[497] In general, naming is an acknowledgement of the namer's relationship with another entity, as when an owner names a pet or when the shepherd names his sheep (John 10).

By naming the animals, Adam realizes that animals are also conscious beings too. Learning to relate to an animal by name also serves to prepare Adam for receiving a mate, whom he would also address by name. God shows Adam all the creatures who inhabit the earth so that he might realize how precious each entity is in God's eyes and not exploit them in a reckless or mindless way. Martin Buber posits that an "I and Thou" relationship can exist between humankind and the animal world, as anyone who has ever owned a beloved pet can easily attest to.[498]

❖ *Philo of Alexandria: Adam's Myopia*

Another Interpretive View: The man gave names to all cattle, and to the birds of the air, and to every animal of the field. – Philo raises a fascinating question: Why didn't Adam also give a name to himself? One could answer Philo's question by simply saying that God had already named Adam, as He did the rest of Creation.

> The mind which is in each of us is capable of understanding all other things, but it is incapable of understanding itself. For as the eye sees all other things, but cannot see itself, so

[497] That would explain why people often feel slighted when their names are forgotten by a familiar person which is tantamount to being considered a non-person. During the Holocaust, the Nazis depersonalized the Jews by depriving them of their names and identities.

[498] Cf. Buber's *Between Man and Man* tr. Ronald Gregor Smith (London and New York: Routledge, 2002), 72.

> also the mind perceives the nature of other things but cannot understand itself. For if it does, let it tell us what it is, or what kind of thing it is, whether it is a spirit, or blood, or fire, or air, or any other substance: or even only so much whether it is a substance at all, or something incorporeal. Are not those men then simple who speculate on the essence of God? For how can they who are ignorant of the nature of the essence of their own soul, have any accurate knowledge of the Soul of the universe? For the Soul of the universe is according to our definition—God.[499]

The irony that emerges from his insight is startling. Although Adam discerns the character and nature of God's creatures, he appears to be a man who is oblivious to his own godly image. The human penchant for denying the most obvious and simple spiritual truths about the mystery of one's innermost being is sardonically as amazing as it is perplexing. As Thomas Merton notes, had Adam and Eve realized their uniqueness in the scheme of Creation, they would never have given into the serpent's guile.[500] Philo's point speaks to the existential confusion that still grips the postmodern condition as we grapple in the dark for ultimate answers concerning our place and purpose in the cosmos.

לֹא־מָצָא עֵזֶר כְּנֶגְדּוֹ וּלְאָדָם – **but for the man there was not found a helper as his partner** — The context of the story makes it clear that Adam's need for companionship could not be satisfied by the beasts of the field. Adam senses that he is a different kind of being. His solitude was sexual on the one hand, and yet at the same time, it was also existential. He feels something incomplete about his existence, an emptiness yearning to be filled. Having closely observed the animal world, Adam is for the first time conscious of what he really needs. The Midrash suggests (Gen. Rabbah 17:4) God did not make Eve until Adam asked for her. At that moment, "God caused a deep sleep to fall upon the man, and he slept" (Gen. 2:21).

2:21 וַיַּפֵּל יְהוָה אֱלֹהִים תַּרְדֵּמָה עַל־הָאָדָם וַיִּישָׁן – **So the LORD God caused a deep sleep to fall upon the man, and he slept** — To cure Adam of his chronic state of loneliness, God created another person, perfectly suited to complement Adam and to meet his need for companionship and belonging. Like a skilled surgeon, God applies anesthesia to Adam so that there is no pain. The noun תַּרְדֵּמָה (*tardēmā* = "deep sleep") comes from the root רָדַם (*rādam* = "slumber"). By itself, the verb connotes "to fall asleep" (cf. Job 4:13); however, the context of the verse defines it as a deep sleep (cf. Gen. 15:12). Sometimes it can denote a hypnotic trance or a coma induced by supernatural agency.[501]

---

[499] Philo, *Allegorical Interpretations* 1.91.

[500] See Excursus 24.

[501] The verb is often used in conjunction with prophecy and visionary experiences. The Septuagint renders this word as ἐκστῆναι (*ekstasin* = "ecstasy"), in which a person's consciousness is partially or entirely non-operative through the work of a supernatural power. God reveals Himself to a person while he or she is in a state of

As in Dante's *Inferno*, woman is portrayed as the very embodiment of a human Eros, who is man's salvation. Kierkegaard expresses the idea in poetic terms: "When God created Eve, he caused a deep sleep to fall upon Adam; for woman is the dream of man."[502]

❖ *The Trouble with Trible*

Another Interpretive View: So out of the ground the LORD God formed every animal of the field and every bird of the air, and brought them to the man to see what he would call them – Phyllis Trible proposes an egalitarian interpretation of the story that does not offend contemporary sensibilities. According to her, the meaning of the designation אָדָם (*'ādām)* should be understood as a human being without sexuality—a non-sexual being who had no distinct physical sexual characteristics. Only after creating a mate, does Adam suddenly discover that he *is* male. In creating a second being, God introduces sexual differentiation for the very first time. Trible claims that the biblical writer thus introduces a degree of ambiguity into the term אָדָם for it was only after Eve was created, did the word אָדָם come to mean "a male creature"[503] As Keil and Delitzsch have already pointed out many years before, "The distinction drawn between אֹתוֹ ("in the image of God created He *him"* [Gen. 1:27]) and אֹתָם, (as man and woman created He *them*) must not be overlooked. The word אֹתָם, which indicates that God created the man and woman as two human beings, completely overthrows the idea that man was at first androgynous (cf. Gen. 2:18ff.)."[504]

וַיִּקַּח אַחַת מִצַּלְעֹתָיו – **then he took one of his ribs** – An alternative translation to צֵלָע *(ṣēlā'* = "side)."[505] The term צֵלָע typically refers to the side of something, e.g., the

sleep, when all traces of wakeful consciousness of the outer world cease, while the sense of one's own existence seems to vanish beyond the corporeal realm of existence. When in such a state, the human imagination moves about unrestrictedly and ceases to be bound by the boundaries of the conscious mind, thus becoming receptive to God's revelations.

[502] *Either/Or,* Vol. 1, 425.

[503] *God and the Rhetoric of Sexuality, Overtures to Biblical Theology* (Philadelphia: Fortress, 1978), 94-105.

[504] C. F. Keil & F. Delitzsch, *Commentary on the Old Testament,* Vol. 1 (Peabody, MA: reprinted by Hendrickson, 2001), 30. Marcus Kalisch makes this same identical point as well (*A Historical and Critical Commentary on the Old Testament, op. cit.*, 80).

[505] In Akkadian, the word *ṣēlu* can mean "side" or "rib," as with Hebrew.

sides of the Ark of the Covenant (Exod. 25:12, 14; 37:3, 5), or to the sides of the Tabernacle (Exod. 26:20, 26, 35; 36:25, 31); to the sides of the brass altar (Exod. 27:7; 38:7); to the sides of the altar of incense (Exod. 30:4; 37:27), and to the side of the Temple (1 Kgs. 6:8).

From this association, certain Gnostic[506] and rabbinic texts claim that God originally made Adam as an androgynous being, i.e., based on the myth depicted in Plato's *Symposium*.[507] Aside from Keil's earlier remarks, there are other grammatical considerations that go against Trible's reading of the text. The Torah says that God utilized מִצַּלְעֹתָיו (*miṣṣalʿōṯāyw* = "one of his ribs"), implying that only one of many ribs was used, which would have been impossible if he had been an androgynous entity. The only difference is *his* missing rib. The text says nothing else about the mysterious appearance of other bodily organs.

Contextually speaking, it seems more logical to say Adam felt all *alone* (from the Middle English "all" + "one").[508] By observing the animal kingdom's mating habits,

---

[506] The Gnostic Christians believed that the purpose of Christ's coming is to reunite Adam and Eve. See *The Nag Hammadi Library in English* (Leiden; New York: E.J. Brill, 1996), 70, 12–17. In the literature they left behind, this sect believed that all the woes of human existence occurred after the androgynous unity was broken. Thus, in the *Gnostic Gospel of Phillip*, we find: "When Eve was still in Adam death did not exist. When she was separated from him death came into being. If he enters again and attains his former self, death will be no more" (68, 22–26). It should be noted that in the second century, a group of Gnostic ascetics were known as *Enkrateia* ("self-control"), ascetics who abstained from sexual intercourse as a means of regaining the humanity's primal innocence (cf. 1 Cor. 6:15–17 and Irenaeus's *Against the Heresies c.* 28). According to this group, the serpent introduced Adam and Eve to animal sexuality, and encouraged the couple to imitate them. By doing so, they lost their spiritual excellence. This movement may have helped shape the emergence of Christian monasticism. For an intriguing Jungian exposition of the myth of the androgyne, see Stephen A. Hoeller's *Jung and the Lost Gospels* (Wheaton, IL.: Quest, 1989) 207-209 and Charles Ponce's *Working the Soul: Reflections on Jungian Psychology* (Berkeley, CA:, North Atlantic Books, 1988), 91-124. Although the myth of the androgyne fails to adequately explain the more straight-forward meaning of the text (despite Trible's attempt to prove the contrary), the myth of the androgyne does have mystical significance in the ideas of the Kabbalah, Jungian psychology, and Hermetic wisdom. The basic principle of the androgynous archetype suggests that in the beginning of every psychological or spiritual process, there is a union of opposites that co-exist in a state of harmony; afterwards, something disrupts that harmony and produces a state of division. It is the differentiation of these opposites that ultimately leads to the birth of consciousness. With this acquisition of consciousness, the broken unity is eventually restored and made whole again.

[507] Plato regards Aristophanes as the author of a complex myth of the primeval androgyne: "In the ancient times there were three kinds of beings, each with four legs and four arms: male, female, and androgynous. They grew too powerful and conspired against the gods, and so Zeus sliced them in two. The parts derived from the whole males are the ancestors of those men who tend to homosexuality and pederasty; the parts derived from the whole females are the ancestors of women who incline to be lesbians. The androgynes, who are nowadays regarded with scorn, gave rise to men who are woman-lovers, and adulterers and to women who are man-lovers and adulteresses" (*Symposium* 189e–191e).

[508] In defense of the Midrashic explanation, the androgyny that the Sages were speaking of was more likely meant as a psychological metaphor—depicting the inseparable nature of a husband-wife relationship.

Adam realizes that he does not have a comparable female counterpart to the animal world that resembles him in a purely human way.[509] The loneliness described in Genesis 2:18–20 would make little sense for a sexually undifferentiated creature to be aware of the lack of a sexual counterpart. When God formed him, it was in expectation of his future mate and life partner. Lastly, the creation story was written in a patriarchal culture, and the reader should not be surprised that the narrative would reflect a male perspective of the world. The creation stories found in other Mesopotamian myths also tell the story from a patriarchal perspective. In short, God did not create man as an androgynous being, but rather He created two distinct beings—one male and one female.

❖ *"Lady of the Rib" the Sumerian Eve?*

Some modern scholars see a parallel between Eve's creation from her husband's rib and the Sumerian myth involving the god Enki, the Sumerian name of the Mesopotamian god of wisdom and water (known as Ea in Akkadian). After suffering an illness from eating poisonous plants, the mother-goddess Ninhursaga comes to his aid by producing from his ailing rib (which in Sumerian is termed "*ti*") the goddess Nin-ti, which in Akkadian means "lady of the rib," but in Sumerian also means "to make live" or alternatively means "the lady who makes alive." The Sumerologist Samuel Noah Kramer comments, "It was this, one of the most ancient of literary wordplays, which was carried over and perpetuated in the biblical paradise story, although here, of course, it loses its validity, since the Hebrew word for צֵלָע: 'rib' [*ṣélaᶜ*] and that for 'who makes alive' [*hoveh*] have nothing in common."[510] The similarities between Sumerian and the Genesis stories point to a common creation motif that was well-known to the people of the ancient Near East.[511]

❖ *"Your God is a Thief . . ."*

וַיִּסְגֹּר בָּשָׂר תַּחְתֶּנָּה — **and closed up its place with flesh** – Historically, misogynist readings and interpretations of this text exist in both Christian[512] and

---

[509] This observation was also noted by Rashi.

[510] Samuel Noah Kramer, *From the Tablets of Sumer* (Indian Hills, CO: Falcon's Wings Press, 1957), 170–72.

[511] Samuel N. Kramer, "Enki and Ninḫursag: A Sumerian Paradise Myth" *(BASOR* Supplementary Studies 1), 1945, 8–9; *History Begins at Sumer*, 1958, 195–196; I. M. Kikawada, 'Two Notes on Eve', *JBL* 91, 1972, 33–37; 1969 'Enki and Ninhursag: A Paradise Myth' in ANET, 37–41.

[512] "The image of God in its principle signification, namely the intellectual nature, is found both in man and in woman. However, in a secondary sense the image of God is found in man, and not in woman; for man is the beginning and end of woman, as God is the beginning and end of every creature" (Aquinas, *Summa Theologica* 1.

Jewish traditions[513] and have often been used to justify the exploitation of women. Some of these theologians taught that women are inherently flawed creatures, secondary in terms of importance when compared to men. Unfortunately, many great men in history suffered from the sins of their age when it came to accepting women as equal partners in the area of religion and ethics. Yet, despite the cultural sexism that pervaded their societies, many rabbis expressed deep caring and had a great deal of respect for women in general.[514] One Midrash depicts the birth of Eve in the most glowing terms:

> Caesar once said to Rabban Gamaliel: "Your God is a thief, for it is written, 'And the LORD God caused a deep sleep to fall upon Adam, and He took one of his ribs'" (Gen. 2:21). Rabban Gamaliel's daughter said, "Leave him to me and I will answer him." [Turning to Caesar], she said, "Send me a police officer." "Why do you need one?" he asked. She replied, "Thieves came to us during the night and took a silver pitcher from us, leaving one of gold in its place." "Would that such a thief came to us every day," he exclaimed. "Aha!" said she, "was it not Adam's gain that he was deprived of a rib and given a wife to assist him?" (BT Sanhedrin 39a).

❖ *Searching for Wholeness*

The Talmudic tractate Kiddushin (2b) points out that the reason a man looks for a wife is because he is in search of a lost part of himself, which he must recover to become whole again. Simply put: no man is complete without a wife. As for Adam's "lost rib," God intended for Adam to recover that part of himself that he had lost. In return, God gave him something of infinitely more value. By losing a rib, he gains a life partner with whom he could share life's good and bad moments. Whereas in the past Adam saw himself as essentially incomplete and imperfect, God provides him with a mate to help him become complete and whole; by the same token, the reverse is also true.

The sacred text not only deserves but demands a more egalitarian explanation for our times. As the 18th century biblical commentator Matthew Henry writes: "Not made out of his head to top him, not out of his feet to be trampled upon by him, but out of his side to be equal with him, under his arm to be protected, and near his heart to be

---

Q. 93. A. 3 cf. Q. 96, A. 3.).

[513] For references that pose problematic teachings regarding a skeptical rabbinic view of women see BT Shabbat 33b; BT Ketuboth 61b; BT Bava Metzia 71a; BT Kiddushin 30b; 80b; Rashi's commentary to BT Avodah Zara 18b; BT Sotah 20a; 21b and MT *Hilchot Biah* 22:16.

[514] Some of the best rabbinic teachers extol the greatness of love, marriage, and women in the most glowing terms, "R. Tanhum stated in the name of R. Hanilai: Any man who has no wife lives without joy, without blessing, and without goodness" (BT Yebamoth 62b-63a).

beloved."[515] Alternatively, Cassuto also notes: "Just as the rib is found at the side of the man and is attached to him, so too is the good wife; as the rib of her husband, she stands at his side to be his helper-counterpart, and her soul is bound up with his."[516] Let us propose another thought: Just as the rib-cage serves to protect the heart, lungs and other internal organs from external danger or collapsing, in the same manner, the good wife protects the heart and the breath of her husband through her capacity to express love and devotion. By the same token, since his wife comes from *his* rib, it is *his* duty to love her and protect her from harm's way.

2:22 וַיִּבֶן יְהוָה אֱלֹהִים אֶת־הַצֵּלָע אֲשֶׁר־לָקַח מִן־הָאָדָם לְאִשָּׁה – **And the rib that the LORD God had taken from the man he made into a woman** — In the Akkadian and Ugaritic languages, the verb *banû* means "to create." In Biblical Hebrew בָּנָה (*bānāh*) conveys creating something substantive, e.g., houses, cities, towers, the building of the Temple, and other sacred objects. As the carrier of life, the making of Eve's body involves careful planning. As Rashi notes, "A woman's bodily structure had to be wide enough below and narrower above for bearing the child, just as a wheat-store is wide below and narrower above so that its weight should not strain the walls."

❖ *Eros Awaits*

וַיְבִאֶהָ אֶל־הָאָדָם – **and brought her to the man** — The expression וַיְבִאֶהָ (*wayĕbî 'ehā* = "and he brought her") denotes marriage, as in וַיְבִאֶהָ יִצְחָק הָאֹהֱלָה שָׂרָה אִמּוֹ "and Isaac brought her into his mother Sarah's tent" (Gen. 24:67; cf. 1 Kgs. 3:1). Talmudic legend depicts God braiding Eve's hair so she would be beautiful to Adam. The verse highlights a basic belief that finds ample expression in the rabbinic literature, namely, that since the beginning of the human race, God has functioned as a matchmaker in bringing men and women together in the name of holy matrimony and that this task is as great of a miracle as the splitting of the Red Sea.[517]

> A Roman matron asked R. Jose: "In how many days did the Blessed Holy One, create His world?" "In six days," he answered. "And what has He been doing since then?" "He sits and arranges matches," he answered, "assigning this man to that woman, and this woman to that

---

[515] Matthew Henry, *Matthew Henry's Commentary on the Whole Bible* (Peabody, MA: Hendrickson, 1996, c.1991), 58.

[516] *Genesis,* Vol. 1, 134.

[517] Leviticus Rabbah 8:1. Variants of this story can be seen in; Gen. Rabbah 68:3-4; BT Sotah 2a; BT Moed Katan 18b; BT Sanhedrin 22a; Midrash Shmuel, Chapter 5; Zohar I, 91b.

man." "If that is difficult," she gibed, "I too can do the same." She went and matched She sent for a thousand male slaves and a thousand female slaves, placed them in rows, and introduced them to their perspective mates. In the morning they came to her; one had a wounded head; another had an eye taken out; another had an elbow crushed; another had a broken leg. One woman said: "I don't want *this* man!" Another man protested, "I don't want *that* woman." She immediately summoned R. Jose b. Halafta and said to him: "Rabbi, your Torah is true and excellent; everything that you have said has proven to be accurate."[518]

2:23 וַיֹּאמֶר הָאָדָם זֹאת הַפַּעַם עֶצֶם מֵעֲצָמַי וּבָשָׂר מִבְּשָׂרִי – Then the man said, "This at last is bone of my bones and flesh of my flesh" – The phrase זֹאת הַפַּעַם (*zōʾṯ happáʿam* = "This one now . . .") implies great anticipation, hope, and excitement (for a similar usage, cf. Gen. 29:34). The noun פַּעַם (*páʿam*) also denotes a measure of time; sometimes it connotes a step (Psa. 17:5; 58:11; 85:13).[519] One modern Israeli biblical commentator poetically depicts Adam visualizing Eve in a dream, and when he awoke, behold! Eve stood there before him. Eve was exactly as he had imagined her to be.[520] Unlike the animal world which Adam examined and found lacking, Adam instantly recognized Eve to be the partner he yearned to have, who most resembled himself, composed from his own flesh and bone, and whose footsteps he yearned to hear.

The term עֶצֶם (*ʿéṣem*) connotes three distinct meanings: "self," "bone," and "might." With this statement (v. 23), Adam announces that he does not regard the woman as an inferior being, but rather he regards his mate as a part of his very being and might—an equal with himself. By creating her from Adam's rib, God intended that there would be a sharing of power between them. While bone represents strength, flesh represents weakness; in a marriage each spouse brings strengths that can offset each other's weaknesses. In the Tanakh, the expression "bone and flesh," exemplifies a kinship that will strengthen and make each partner more resilient to adversity. For example, when David arrives in Hebron to be crowned, the tribes of Israel proclaim: הִנְנוּ עַצְמְךָ וּבְשָׂרְךָ אֲנָחְנוּ (*hinnû ʿaṣməḵā ûḇəśārḵā ʾănāḥnû*), "Behold, we are your bone and flesh" (2 Sam. 5:1). The people of Israel demonstrate a willingness to share their king's destiny as they face adversity together. This would seem to be the same point implicit in the Adam and Eve pericope as well. Adam shows a willingness to be a covenantal partner to his mate. Human oneness, happiness, and perfection depend on a man and woman looking to each other to help enhance and complete his or her own divine image. Our likeness to God is predicated on our capacity to experience love, and love can occur only if there is

---

[518] Gen. Rabbah 68:4.

[519] In Old English, counting paces is used as a way of measuring time.

[520] See R. Yehuda Keil, *Da'at Mikra on Bereshit* Vol. 1 (Jerusalem: Mosad HaRav Kook, 1997), 67-68.

someone outside the self.

❖ *Keeping the Flame of Love Alive*

לְזֹאת יִקָּרֵא אִשָּׁה – **this one shall be called Woman** – It is interesting to note that at this stage, it appears that Adam called his new partner אִשָּׁה (*Iššāh* ="Woman") and *not* "Eve"! This may be in part due to his ignorance of his mate's procreative capabilities. Both Abarbanel (ca. 15th-16th century) and 17th century American theologian, Jonathan Edwards, suggest that it is only after the Fall that Adam begins to refer to her by a new name, Eve, since he now finds solace and reassurance in knowing that the human race would not cease as a result of their disobedience, but to the contrary—they would literally live through her, even though they were (presumably) no longer immortal.[521]

This eisegetic interpretation, however, is based on the unwarranted theological assumption that they were both immortal to start. The text explicitly states the primal couple would become immortal, only if they ate from the Tree of Life (3:22), implying that God made them mortal from the start. The Talmud adds a homiletical meaning. Aside from the common letters they share, the two letters (י = y and ה = h) are unique to these nouns אִישׁ and אִשָּׁה ("man" and "woman") when combined together (ה + י) form the Divine Name יָהּ (*Yah*). From this permutation the Sages deduce the following ethical lesson: "when a husband and wife are worthy, the *Shekhinah* (Divine Presence) dwells with them; when they prove unworthy—they are left with אֵשׁ (*ʾēš* = "fire"), a fire consumes their marital relationship.[522] The Midrash poetically expresses this thought as, "A man should not be without a woman, nor should a woman be without a man; and neither of them should ever be without the Divine Presence."[523]

כִּי מֵאִישׁ לֻקֳחָה־זֹּאת – **for out of Man this one was taken** – Initially, a woman came out of a man, but from this moment forward, a man shall come out of the body of a woman (Hizkuni). Alternatively, in this instance, God formed woman from man, but in

[521] Jonathan Edwards writes: "While Adam is under the terror of this sentence of death, he comforts himself with the promise of life couched in what God had said to the serpent. Adam gave Eve a new name on this occasion from that new thing that appeared concerning her after the Fall" *CW*, Vol. 2, *Notes on Genesis*, 1643. An almost identical interpretation can also be found in the well-known early 20th century rabbinic commentary, *Meshech Chochmah* and in Abarbanel's Torah commentary.

[522] T. B. Sotah 17a.

[523] Genesis Rabba 8:9.

the future all human beings will be born only through sexual intercourse with a woman (Bahya). With the advent of in vitro fertilization, the initial creation of human beings takes place outside of a woman's body improves. As science evolves, someday human beings may be completely gestated outside of a woman's body; this phenomenon will inevitably force a serious reinterpretation of this passage.

2:24 עַל־כֵּן יַעֲזָב־אִישׁ אֶת־אָבִיו וְאֶת־אִמּוֹ – **Therefore a man leaves his father and his mother** — This parenthetical expression is the biblical narrator's remark rather than Adam's (Rashi). The Torah wants to provide an etiological explanation about the origin of marriage. As young people come of age and no longer look to their parents as their primary companions and helpers in life, the young couple comes to depend upon on each other for mutual support. Parents have the responsibility to help prepare their children for the time when parental ties are severed and adult children establish their own independent homes.

וְדָבַק בְּאִשְׁתּוֹ – **and clings to his wife** — The verse would seem to at least etiologically imply that God intends for man and wife to be a monogamous union, as is intimated by the famous verse, "I belong to my beloved and my beloved belongs to me" (Song 6:3).[524] Beyond that, the entire Song of Songs reflects the special love that one man and one woman must share with one another and may well illustrate the Edenic marriage expressed in Song of Songs 2:16.[525] The Torah always regards the monogamous marriage to be the ideal and preferred form of family life. In contrast, whenever a polygamous marriage is described in the Tanakh—especially in the Book of Genesis—the union invariably leads to disastrous and sorrowful consequences.

The love between a man and wife will later serve to symbolize the covenantal bond between God and Israel, as romantically depicted in the book of Hosea (Hosea 2:14–23). Human beings become most God-like when they pledge themselves in love and fidelity. God made man and woman so that each would need and be dependent on the other. According to R. Joseph B. Soloveitchik, the notion of "clinging" also implies that both Adam and Eve will share a common moral responsibility toward one another along with a sense of ethical solidarity, i.e., what affects one will affect the other. As a result, each will share in the other's destiny and live a life of ethical sympathy—the kind of relationship that characterizes an "I and Thou" commitment.[526] See Excursus 21 for a

---

[524] Historically, this sentiment has long been a part of the Jewish wedding ceremony as well, "Gladden these beloved companions just as You have gladdened Your creatures in the Garden of Eden. Blessed are You, Adonai, Who gladdens both the groom and bride."

[525] See the notes on Genesis 2:25 with respect to Phyllis Trible's novel reading of the *Song of Songs*.

[526] R. Joseph B. Soloveitchik, *The Emergence of Ethical Man* (Hoboken, NJ: Ktav, 2005), 96.

more elaborate examination of this important Judaic concept.

וְהָיוּ לְבָשָׂר אֶחָד - **and they become one flesh** — Both parents become one with the creation of a child (Rashi). Ibn Ezra questions the veracity of this interpretation—animals also become one flesh with the birth of their offspring, yet this statement is said only of human beings and not of animals. Ramban adds that animals mate only when they have a biological urge to reproduce and leave one another after consummating the mating, but humans are different. Rather, the intent is that they shall live together *as if they were one flesh*; alternatively, the primal couple was originally made up of one flesh, so they should love each other *as if* they were one flesh. This last interpretation is most astute, for in Jewish tradition, marriage is *not* solely for the sake of having children; if that were the case, elderly people would never be allowed to marry. Human beings need companionship. Ramban and Wenham add that in practical terms, becoming one flesh through marriage has certain legal implications that pertain to forbidden relations of those who are כָּל־שְׁאֵר בְּשָׂרוֹ *(kol-šəʾēr bəśārô)* "near of flesh" (Lev. 18:6).[527]

Another Interpretive View: and they become one flesh — the verse raises a practical question about the nature of human procreation. Rabbinic tradition deduces the precept to engage in sexual intimacy from this verse. However, what exactly does this mean? Are we to assume that human sexuality exists solely for the purpose of procreation? Is birth control permitted? Should every sexual act exist for the perpetuity of the human race? No such concept exists in Jewish law or tradition. Jewish tradition stresses more the importance of companionship than it does procreation. Christian theological tradition is less clearly defined. Augustine asserts that the *only* godly purpose found in sexuality is the procreative component—a point that Thomas Aquinas strongly opposes. Like his rabbinic counterparts, Aquinas argues that the union of a husband and wife serves to emotionally bond the couple more closely together. Moreover, it also brings great pleasure to its participants; sexual intimacy strengthens the fabric of a marriage.

According to Augustine, the joys of sex are rooted in a selfish form of love; people engaging in sexual relations are not concerned with the Godly purpose behind it, but are only concerned with the pursuit of their own selfish pleasures. Fortunately for Christians, Aquinas considers this position to be utter nonsense. On the other hand, he

---

[527] G. Wenham develops this theme more clearly than Ramban, and he shows that the marriage between a man and a woman affects a whole web of consanguineous (blood) relations: "'They become one flesh.' This does not denote merely the sexual union that follows marriage, or the children conceived in marriage, or even the spiritual and emotional relationship that it involves, though all are involved in becoming one flesh. Rather it affirms that just as blood relations are one's flesh and bone . . . so marriage creates a similar kinship relation between man and wife."(*Genesis*, Vol.1, 71).

considers masturbation to be a more severe sin than premarital sex since the latter does not serve any emotional purpose in binding a man and a woman together. Aquinas' adherence to the principle of natural law may explain why the Catholic Church has historically opposed birth-control, since it violates the purpose of marriage, which is to have children.[528]

❖ *Original Innocence*

2:25 וַיִּהְיוּ שְׁנֵיהֶם עֲרוּמִּים הָאָדָם וְאִשְׁתּוֹ וְלֹא יִתְבֹּשָׁשׁוּ – And the man and his wife were both naked, and were not ashamed — It is well-known that the Hebrew text contains an important word-play. The word for naked, עָרוֹם (*ʿārôm*) bears striking similarity to the Hebrew word for "craftiness," עָרוּם (*ʿārûm*). To convey the flavor of this pun to the English-speaking reader, Wenham cleverly paraphrases the verse: "They will seek themselves to be shrewd (cf. 3:6) but will discover that they are 'nude' (3:7, 10)." Nakedness can have many meanings aside from the most obvious. Some commentaries suggest that after they ate the forbidden fruit, they suddenly lusted after each other's body. Metaphorically, being "naked" also suggests being exposed to harm and exploitation. In their naiveté Adam and Eve were prone to deception. This verse also seems to imply that they were at ease with their bodies and their sexuality. Both man and wife were as innocent as newborn babies, who were utterly oblivious to their state of nakedness.

Phyllis Trible further develops this theme arguing that the Song of Songs must be read as a metaphor and intra-biblical commentary on Genesis 2-3. What was lost in the Edenic world is regained through the love a man and a woman share and experience together. Contrary to Augustine and some of his cohorts, the Garden of Eden is where human sexuality is first introduced.[529] The pervasive garden theme in the Song evokes memories of the garden before the Fall.[530]. The Song of Songs, then, describes a lover and his beloved rejoicing in each other's sexuality in a garden. This poem is a story of sexuality as God originally intended it to be. Adam made Eve the focus of his delight and joy; Eve made Adam her focal point of love and attention. The Song of Songs celebrates Original Innocence; every human intimate relationship is capable of becoming Eden-esque in purity and holiness.

---

[528] Thomas Aquinas, *The Basic Writings of St Thomas Aquinas*, ed. A. C. Pegis, 2 vols. ii. (New York: Random House, 1945), *Summa Theologica*, Q. 81, Art. 1; Q. 85 Art. 2; Q. 85 Art. 3.

[529] Phyllis Trible, *God and the Rhetoric of Sexuality: Overtures to Biblical Theology* (Philadelphia: Fortress, 1978), 72-105.

[530] Song of Songs 4:12, vv. 15-16, 5:1, 6:2.

The End of Dreaming Innocence (3:1-7)

3 Now the serpent was more crafty than any other wild animal that the LORD God
had made. He said to the woman, "Did God say, 'You shall not eat from any tree in
the garden'?" [2] The woman said to the serpent, "We may eat of the fruit of the trees
in the garden; [3] but God said, 'You shall not eat of the fruit of the tree that is in the
middle of the garden, nor shall you touch it, or you shall die.'" [4] But the serpent said
to the woman, "You will not die; [5] for God knows that when you eat of it your eyes
will be opened, and you will be like God,[a] knowing good and evil." [6] So when the
woman saw that the tree was good for food, and that it was a delight to the eyes, and
that the tree was to be desired to make one wise, she took of its fruit and ate; and
she also gave some to her husband, who was with her, and he ate. [7] Then the eyes of
both were opened, and they knew that they were naked; and they sewed fig leaves
together and made loincloths for themselves.

These things are not mere fabulous inventions in which the race of poets and sophists delight, but are rather types shadowing forth some allegorical truth, according to some mystical explanation.

—PHILO of ALEXANDRIA, *On the Creation,* 55:157

The lamb that belonged to the sheep whose skin the wolf was wearing began to follow the wolf in the sheep's clothing.

—AESOP'S *Fables, The Wolf in Sheep's Clothing*

No man chooses evil because it is evil; he only mistakes it for happiness, the good he seeks.

— MARY WOLLSTONECRAFT, *A Vindication of the Rights of Men.*

It's often safer to be in chains than to be free.

—FRANZ KAFKA, *The Trial*

No one, saint or sinner, escapes suffering, which remains unavoidable in nature.
Yet each of us holds in our hands our spiritual destiny.

—JULIAN of ECLANUM

Lord! We know what we are, but know not what we may be.

—SHAKESPEARE, *Hamlet (4.5.43)*

[a] Or *gods.*

❖ *Deciphering the Contours of Mythic Thought*

To read the story of Genesis 3 as though it were an actual historical event is to miss the point of the ancient drama. Critical awareness of history and science leaves no room for such a primordial event. To decipher the power of this story, it is imperative to understand the role and importance that mythic thought plays in the life of a society—both ancient and modern. By the term *myth*, we do not mean a fictional account or ignorant notions as is commonly assumed today.[531] "Myth," as its name indicates, is an inter-generational tale that reflects a society's core values and metaphysical beliefs.[532]

One of the frequent critiques about myth attributes personality to non-human entities and objects, as is the case with anthropomorphism. However, this assumption is wanting. To the primal mind, everything in nature—both animate and inanimate—exudes personality and presence and rules of subject-object relation have no meaning in the world of myth.[533] The purpose of myth aims to disclose the sacred character of existence for reality is an amalgam of existential meanings. Typically, the function of myth focuses on the origins of the universe as it pertains to: (1) a lived experience in a world that is saturated with an awesome awareness of a mysterious cosmic Presence; (2) the sacred and the profane; (3) myth inviting people to abandon themselves to its immediacy and transpersonal power; (4) myth teaching a people that there is a greater reality that exists beyond human control and comprehension, making the experience of the sacred possible and giving *ultimate meaning to human existence.*

❖ *Unearthing the Archaeology of Consciousness*

Reading the story of Genesis 3 as though it were an actual historical event is clearly missing the point of this ancient drama. Yet, is it possible for a person, steeped in science and secular culture, to derive meaning from such a mythic account of human

---

[531] James Frazer in his *Golden Bough* describes myth as a primitive form of science or pseudo-science.

[532] The French anthropologist Claude Lévi-Strauss explains that myth functions as a basic element of a culture's underlying system of symbolic communication; through its amalgam of archetypal characters, myths reflect the hopes, dreams, fears, and conflicts of the human condition aiming toward the reconciliation of opposites within a given culture. In the final analysis, myths define a community's identity and core values, providing a vision of how a community sees itself within the greater picture of reality (*Structural Anthropology* [New York: Basic Books, 1968], 224).

[533] Scholars who see the mythic world in those terms are really retrojecting their own cognitive distinctions much like James Frazer did in his *Golden Bough*. Ludwig Wittgenstein curtly dismisses Frazer with this pithy summary: "What narrowness of spiritual life we find in [Sir James] Frazer! And as a result: how impossible for him to understand a different way of life from the English one of his time! Frazer cannot imagine a priest who is not basically an English parson of our times, with all his stupidity and feebleness" (*Remarks on Frazer's Golden Bough* [Nottinghamshire: The Brynmill Press, 1979], 5e).

history? A nostalgic return to innocence is impossible. According to Paul Ricoeur's exposition of myth, every person begins at the level of a "first naiveté," where the listener or reader becomes spellbound by the power of the myth; in such a mindset, one views the world unreflectively. Developing a deeper grasp of the myth's meaning requires that one apply a "hermeneutic of suspicion" that subjects the naïve experience of the mythic content to the rigors of critical thought and examination. During the Age of Enlightenment, the great minds of the 18th century subjected the mythic and religious belief system to the steely logic of scientific analysis. However, in the centuries following, Western culture has found the results of a scientific, economic and technocratic world dissatisfying, filling people's lives with a sense of existential angst and despair. To help remedy this problem, Ricoeur (as well as Jung, Lévi-Strauss, Malinowski, Eliade, and many others) urges that modern society considers a return to the world of myth. However, he is not suggesting returning to the first naiveté; i.e., suspending critical thinking faculties, based on the mistaken notion that such action would guarantee a pure and instinctual existence.

Instead, Ricoeur recommends turning toward a "second naiveté" where discursive thought is employed to decipher the language of mythic reality, while concurrently adhering to those beliefs and values that have stood up to critical scrutiny and time. Symbol, metaphor, and myth express the deepest human yearnings through the experience of the primordial self. Hence, "The plunge into the archaic mythologies of the unconscious brings to the surface new signs of the sacred. The eschatology of consciousness is always a creative repetition of its own archaeology."[534] Ricoeur further notes that through a process of demythologization, we can differentiate the historical from the pseudo-historical, by exorcizing the *logos* from the *mythos*. This process of critical distillation can still allow us to experience the inner and transformative power of the symbol as a primordial sign of the sacred, which continues to impact the lives of a faith community.[535]

❖ *Our Primal Longing for Life*

Genesis 3 also contains several etiologies concerning how the world came to be as it is. One of the most important questions is this: Why did God create boundaries governing human behavior? Since the beginning of time, humanity has always struggled with issues of boundaries and limitations. This problem continues to exist in contemporary society, manifesting itself, in one way, as an insatiable need for acquiring possessions. Yet, even this modern condition is also a foreshadowing of Genesis 3. With the abundance of choices in the mythical garden, the primal couple must live with only one restriction and

---

534 Paul Ricoeur, *The Conflicts of Interpretation* (Evanston, Ill: Northwestern University Press, 1974), 334.

535 Ibid., 352-353.

limitation. God's restriction tantalizes their imagination and awakens an erotic and seductive curiosity for the forbidden fruit. Suddenly, they feel compelled to furtively seize the fruit and taste it! We feel a certain affinity with Eve's struggle, resonating with our own libertarian way of experiencing the world—one without ethical or religious boundaries. A well-known Jewish moralist expresses the moral dilemma in succinct terms: "Our wish to fulfill our earthly desires stems directly from our primal longing for life itself—for the basic will to live implants within us a feeling of want and desire that does not discriminate between valid and illegitimate need."[536] Why does this seemingly harmless dietary taboo bother us so? Perhaps the human fascination with the forbidden is precisely what lies at the heart of this timeless story.

❖ *The Serpentine Trickster of Eden*

3:1 וְהַנָּחָשׁ הָיָה עָרוּם מִכֹּל חַיַּת הַשָּׂדֶה – Now the serpent was more crafty than any other wild animal — To decipher the symbolic and mythic significance of the serpent, one must understand its role as personifying the trickster archetype. According to Jung, the trickster archetype is invariably associated with wisdom and the beginnings of spiritual endeavor. Sometimes, as is the case with Genesis 3, it represents the first obstruction to true self-knowledge.[537] Traditionally, there are four aspects of the trickster's identity that include: the divine, the profane, the human, and the animal. Its powers in many myths seem to be more of a supernatural order, and as such, tricksters possess the uncanny ability of frustrating the Supreme Being's creative plans. From a literary perspective, the present text suggests that the Creator is not present or is possibly a silent observer. In light of this dramatic staging, the trickster always lives up to its potential for creating mischief—often to its own detriment.

By many mythic depictions, the trickster has an enormous capacity for lust and sensuality, as well as a hearty appetite for the forbidden (which would explain why in many Midrashic traditions, the serpent had sexual relations with Eve). In many tales of its exploits, the trickster's deception consists of feigning ignorance, while laying a trap for its adversary worthy of a hunter. Quite often, the trickster is the unwitting victim of his own complicated plots. Although it is an intelligent being, it usually does not think of the consequences of its behavior. Throughout human history, the trickster parodies the norms of society; their expertise is to evoke paradox, self-reflection, unpredictability, and alternate visions of reality. As a contrarian spirit, the trickster lives to break down a society's taboos, although they are certainly capable of creating mischief. In the final analysis, they are catalysts of change.

---

[536] Rabbi Yisrael Salanter, *Ohr Yisrael*, Letter 2.

[537] Carl G. Gustav, "The Archetypes of the Collective Unconscious," Collected Writings Vol. 9i. (Princeton: Princeton University Press, 1959/1968a).

❖ *Determining the Serpent's Motivation*

True to the trickster archetype, the serpent in Eden blurs the boundaries between the categories of animal, human, and divine. Although the Torah describes the primordial serpent as an animal, it differs from its fellow creatures in that it possesses the ability to speak and reason. In addition, it has an esoteric grasp of knowledge that makes it more akin to God and the angels. The serpent's mysterious personality leaves the reader wondering what its motivation might have been. Like other such myths, the pay-off for the trickster is both a gain and a loss for which humans pay the price (this pattern also occurs in the Greek myth of Prometheus, who steals the celestial fire of the gods to give it to the mortals). Frequently, it is the trickster who pays the price for his deceit.

In many cultures throughout the world, the serpent acts as the instrument and catalyst of change. Ancient Mesopotamian and Oriental literature associates the serpent with the destructive forces of chaos that threaten to unravel the fabric of creation.[538] When the serpent was untamed, it symbolized destruction and evil; when it was conquered and subdued, it assumed the role of a protector.[539] In other mythic traditions, serpents symbolize esoteric wisdom, as portrayed in Genesis 3, *The Epic of Gilgamesh*, and Buddha and the Boda Tree. For the unwary desert traveler, serpents were frequently associated with danger and death.[540] The ancients utilized snakes in many of their oracular magical rites; the serpent's ability to rejuvenate itself by shedding its skin gave

---

[538] Among the Hittites, the Storm-god wages war against the forces of chaos represented by the serpent Illuyanka. In "The Great Hymn to the Aten," the Egyptian sun god Re, does battle with his worst enemy—the primordial serpent—Apopis. The Babylonian epic *Enūma Elish,* describes how the monstrous Tiâmat—the goddess of the oceans and chaos—creates the serpents, demonic beings, and dragons to do her bidding. In the eastern and gnostic traditions, the serpent is associated with wisdom and enlightenment. The serpent is not always associated with death in mythic traditions—it is also associated with life and transformation. Even in the Torah, the serpent reappears as a conduit for healing and life (Num. 21:6-8). Although Re does battle with Apopis, he finds unexpected protection from the serpent, Mehen, during his journey in the underworld. Hindu mythology depicts Kaliya as the "prince of serpents," who epitomizes evil and is eventually defeated by Krishna; yet, the serpent Sesa serves as Vishnu's companion and sofa. In Hinduism, the *kundali* (derived from the Sanskrit *kundala,* "coil" of rope), is the name given in Tantric literature to the divine cosmic energy (*sakti*) and is likened to the serpent that lies at the base of the spine. When a person becomes spiritually awakened the *kundalini* arises and facilitates enlightenment and total freedom from the world (see *Encyclopedia of Religion,* Vol. 13:270-272).

[539] According to Egyptian mythology, whenever the sun deity Ra travels in his solar boat through the underworld, dragon-like creatures that guarded the tomb of Osiris—god of the underworld, assist him. When Ra is confronted by his mortal enemy, Apepi, a giant sea-serpent (symbolizing the primordial darkness and chaos), Ra slays the entity and dismembers it. Afterwards, Ra sails up from the east as the sun shines for the next twelve hours. However, after Apepi is slain, it is resurrected and lives to do battle again with Ra at nightfall.

[540] *Cf.* Gen 49:17; Amos 5:19, and Isa 14:29.

rise to the widely held belief that the serpent was immortal, as seen in *The Epic of Gilgamesh*, which dates back to about 2700 B.C.E. However, based on the appearance of serpents crafted onto numerous cultic objects dating back as early as the 6th millennium B.C.E., some recent archeological discoveries indicate that the python was worshiped in African caves dating back 70,000 years ago—30,000 years earlier than the oldest previously known human rites.[541]

To decipher the symbolic and mythic significance of the serpent, one must understand its role as a personification of the trickster archetype. According to Jung, the trickster archetype is invariably associated with wisdom and the beginnings of spiritual endeavor. Sometimes, as is the case of the Genesis 3, it represents the first obstacle to true self-knowledge. [542] The serpent also epitomizes masculine potency and sexuality—a notion that Sigmund Freud would later heartily endorse. Across the cultural divide, mythic depictions of the serpent reveal a creature endowed with a mysterious knowledge, power, and wisdom. In Greek mythology, "being licked" by a serpent's tongue was considered a good omen; it meant that the gods would bless a person with supernatural gifts such as prophecy or extraordinary strength. Snakes were also associated with Athena, the Greek goddess of wisdom, and later in the Middle Ages with Prudentia, the personification of prudence or practical wisdom. Then again, there is the well-known saying of Jesus: "Be wise as serpents" (Mt. 10:16).

The primordial serpent's role as trickster in this narrative raises many questions that remain unanswered by the biblical narrator. Why does the serpent resent humankind? Why would it want to deprive God's choice creation of the gifts of immortality? Was its intention sincere, or did it have ulterior motives? What did the serpent stand to gain by Adam's disobedience? Exegetes propose several plausible answers. The serpent may have been motivated by envy. If this early exegetical insight is accurate, one could argue that the serpent projects onto Eve its own inner and unresolved conflict with the Divine, and by doing so, the serpent triangulates the couple into a personal struggle with God. When triggered, a psychological defense mechanism may cause a person to project certain objectionable traits, feelings, desires, or motivations onto another person as a means of protecting the walls of one's ego. It logically follows that when the serpent asserts that YHWH is "jealous" of His foremost creation obtaining this esoteric knowledge of good and evil, the serpent's accusation actually reveals more about its own jealousy and its contempt toward the Creator.[543] Josephus explains that the serpent grew

---

[541] *"Python Cave" Reveals Oldest Human Ritual, Scientists Suggest,* National Geographic News, December 22, 2006.

[542] *The Archetypes of the Collective Unconscious* (CW9i). Princeton: Princeton University Press, 1959/1968a.

[543] Some Midrashic texts do not view the serpent as wishing to dethrone God; its envy was of a more crass nature. Evidently, the serpent lusts after Eve when it sees the primal couple having sexual intercourse. Therefore, it schemes of ways to eliminate Adam, so that it will have Eve all to itself (Genesis Rabba 18:6). This interpretation alludes to the assonance of the Aramaic word for "serpent" חויא (*Hiyûwa*), which is similar

jealous of the happiness Adam and his wife enjoyed by virtue of obeying the Divine commandments. The serpent realized that "these gifts would be lost if it could persuade the woman to taste of the tree of wisdom."[544] Another variant of this idea is explored centuries later in Milton's *Paradise Lost.* Milton writes that after a failed *coup d'état* against Heaven, Satan is expelled and later enters into the body of the serpent in order to estrange Adam and Eve from their Maker.[545] Ultimately, both stories of the Edenic "Fall"—as depicted in Genesis and in *Paradise Lost*—can be attributed to failure to live in accordance with the hierarchy that YHWH established for all of His Creation.

Some of the early Christian exegetes offer a number of possible motivations. John of Damascus (ca. 650-750) argues that the serpent did not wish to be under Adam's dominion. Ambrose (ca. 333-397) makes a similar point: the serpent did not like the human couple's special standing in the world of Paradise. Some Jewish mystics propose that the serpent acted out of jealousy for it sensed its existence was only temporary. It knew that God intended for Adam and Eve to live forever. By means of a cleverly laid trap,[546] it hoped to "even the playing field," thus making them mortal, like itself.[547]

---

in sound to חַוָּה (*Hawwâ* ="Eve"). Other Midrashic traditions contend that Satan felt jealous of Adam's ability to name the animals—a talent that not even the angelic beings possessed! L. Ginzberg cites a number of ancient Midrashic texts that depict the origin of Satan's struggle with God and humankind.

> After Adam had been endowed with a soul, God invited all the angels to come and pay him reverence and homage. Satan, the greatest of the angels in heaven, with twelve wings, instead of six like all the others, refused to pay heed to the behest of God, saying, "Thou didst create us angels from the splendor of the Shekhinah, and now Thou dost command us to cast ourselves down before the creature which Thou didst fashion out of the dust of the ground!" God answered, "Yet this dust of the ground has more wisdom and understanding than thou." Satan demanded a trial of wit with Adam, and God assented thereto, saying: "I have created beasts, birds, and reptiles. I shall have them all come before thee and before Adam. If thou art able to give them names, I shall command Adam to show honor unto thee, and thou shalt rest next to the Shekhinah of My glory. But if not, and Adam calls them by the names I have assigned to them, then thou wilt be subject to Adam, and he shall have a place in My garden, and cultivate it."

Ultimately, Adam wins the contest; Satan shows his contempt for God and His favored creation by rebelling against Heaven. Satan is ultimately cast down into the depths of Hell. Ginzberg includes among his sources: *Yalkut* I, 44; *Aggadat Bereshit* (introduction) 38; *Pugio Fidei,* 837–838, BHM V, 156 (*Legends of the Jews*, 61-62).

[544] *Ant.* 1.1.4 (1.41).

[545] *Paradise Lost,* Book 9.

[546] Whenever confronted by dangerous foes capable of inflicting harm, the trickster achieves through *chutzpa* what brute strength could not accomplish. In the ancient literature of the Mediterranean world, Odysseus resorts to all types of trickery in his ten-year struggle to reach home after the Trojan War. The Tanakh, portrays protagonists as tricksters obtaining advantages over their foes, e.g., Jacob and Esau (Gen. 25:33; 27:28–29); Jacob and Laban (Gen 30:37–43); Abraham /Pharaoh /Abimelech (Gen 12:10–20; 20) and once by Isaac (Gen 26:6–11); Lot and his daughters (Gen. 19:30-38). The trickster continues to play a significant role in the other books of the Tanakh, e.g., Ehud and the king of Eglon (Judg. 3:15–25), Samson and the Philistines (Judg. 14–16), David and Uriah (2 Sam 11:6–13). Tricksters are beloved characters in the ancient Near East,

There is one answer the early exegetes did not consider—the serpent wished to appropriate for itself the very blessing that it had thought to deny the first couple—the gift of immortality. By diverting their attention away from the Tree of Life, and persuading them to eat from the Tree of Knowledge, the serpent hoped that it alone would eat of the Tree of Life and live forever. *The Epic of Gilgamesh* definitely resonates with this latter interpretation and provides the key to answering many of the questions thus far raised in the Genesis story. In this ancient tale about the origin of death, a serpent steals a magic plant from Gilgamesh that would have given him immortality, while he was bathing in a nearby pool. Although the story does not say that the serpent ate the coveted plant, the narrator implies that it did. However, in the Edenic narrative, the serpent does not achieve its goal. Unlike the Gilgamesh serpent, which disappears with the coveted prize, the serpent of Genesis suffers a talionic fate, and becomes the "most cursed of creatures."[548]

Another Interpretive View: Now the serpent was more crafty than any other wild animal – The verse does not say that the serpent was חָכָם (*ḥăḵam* = "wiser") than all the beasts upon the earth. Instead, the biblical narrator chooses a nuanced idiom for עָרוּם (*ʿārûm*) for reasons that will soon become obvious. The Sages of Alexandria render this expression as φρονιμώτατος[549](*phronimotatos*), "sly," "prudent", or "mindful of one's interests."[550] The Greek translation suggests that the serpent may have had a vested interest in causing Adam to stumble, even though the text offers no obvious reason. Richard E. Friedman explains that the serpent knew that of all the species of animals on earth, only human beings would aspire toward the divine.[551] Friedman's exposition seems logical. Perhaps, as mentioned earlier, the serpent perceived Adam as having hubris, and wished to knock him down a few notches.

---

among Native Americans in their folklore, and continue to be revered in contemporary American literature and film.

[547] Dov Baer of Lubavitch, *Torat Chayim s.v.* וְהַנָּחָשׁ הָיָה עָרוּם מִכֹּל חַיַּת הַשָּׂדֶה (New York: Kehot, 1974), 29-32.

[548] Rashi intimates this point as well, "Commensurate with its cunning and its greatness, so was its downfall, since it was the most cunning of animals, in the end it became the most cursed of all animals (Gen. Rabbah 19:1).

[549] Derived from φρονεω (*phroneo): to think, to be careful; to be thoughtful or anxious* (*Thayers Greek Lexicon* 5635). The notion of anxiousness might have been at the root of the serpent's intervention. Adam's numinous character made him innately superior to all the creatures.

[550] According to the NT, *phronimos* appears several times, typically connotes a positive sense "prudent," see of (Matt. 10:16, 24:45; Luke 12:42, 16:8). Conversely, in Romans 11:25 and 12:16, however, it means "arrogant" and is probably derived from the cognate noun *phronēsis*, meaning "arrogance".

[551] Richard Elliot Friedman, *Commentary on the Torah, op. cit.*, 21.

According to Milton, the serpent is really the Devil in disguise. As a fallen angel, the Devil aims to get even with its Maker for its failed *coup d'état* that resulted in the Devil and his minions being casted to Hell.[552] Ultimately, it is the sin of hubris that leads to the Devil's downfall, and to spite its Creator, the Devil takes aim at God's favorite handiwork: humankind! Although this interpretation has a distinctively Christological quality, it does have antecedents in the Apocryphal and Pseudepigraphal writings (*ca.* 250—200 C.E.) from which James Kugel extracts examples to illustrate how early Christianity derived its concept of Satan as a rebellious angel:

> For God created us for incorruption,
> and made us in the image of his own eternity,
> but through the devil's envy death entered the world,
> and those who belong to his company experience it.
>
> *Wisdom of Solomon* 2:23-24
>
> [Later Eve recalls] "The devil answered me through the mouth of the serpent."
>
> *Apocalypse of Moses* 16:4, 17:4
>
> The devil is of the lowest places . . . . And he became aware of his condemnation and of the sin which he had sinned previously. And that is why he thought up of the scheme against Adam. In such a form he entered paradise and corrupted Eve.
>
> 2 Enoch 31:4-6)[553]

Another Interpretive View: וְהַנָּחָשׁ הָיָה עָרוּם מִכֹּל חַיַּת הַשָּׂדֶה – **Now the serpent was more crafty than any other wild animal.** – With an eye for nuance, the rabbis of the Midrash hint at the talionic justice the serpent would eventually receive. The serpent has a mark of distinction due to its crafty nature. However, in the end the "craftiest" of God's creatures becomes "the most cursed."[554] Historically, since the time of the Pseudepigrapha, exegetes—Jewish[555] and Christian alive[556]—frequently blame Eve for the Fall of humanity and all of the human woes that

---

[552] *Paradise Lost*, Book IX, lines 700 and 704.

[553] James Kugel, *The Bible as It Was* (Cambridge, MA: The Belknap Press of Harvard University, 1997), 74.

[554] See Genesis Rabbah 19:1, as cited by Rashi.

[555] See Excursus 28 for parallel examples.

[556]Tertullian (ca. 202 C.E.) boldly writes:

> Do you not know that you are (each) an Eve? The sentence of God on this sex of yours lives in this age: the guilt must of necessity live too. You are the devil's gateway; you are the unsealer of that

follow.[557] In contrast, contemporary feminists praise Eve as the heroine of the biblical story, for she takes the initiative and shows far greater courage and intellectual curiosity than does her compliant husband.[558] Both these eisegetical interpretations fall short of the mark and certainly reveal more about *our* cultural reading of the story than does the original text. Was Eve alone at the time of this exchange with the serpent? Some feminists claim that while Adam was with her, he stood by mutely and passively watched. Rabbinic tradition also suggests that perhaps Eve was more susceptible to disobedience since she did not directly hear God give the original commandment regarding the Tree of Knowledge; in her innocence and naiveté, Eve was more vulnerable to the serpent's seductive ploys. However, these elucidations presuppose that Eve was alone. Such diverse interpretations illustrate the myriad layers of possible readings.

Note that, from the Gnostic perspective, it is Eve and not Adam who responds to the serpent because the feminine persona represents the intuitive wisdom that seeks illumination (as depicted by William Blake's image of Eve and the serpent) and enlightenment, whereas Adam signifies the more rational faculties that see the world in noetic terms.[559] Jungian analyst Charles Ponce points out that according to the Gnostic traditions it is the feminine aspect of the soul that seeks to direct, guide, and produce enlightenment. As the symbol of the soul, the feminine gender is often described as the bearer of divine messages in the form of dreams and visions. "It is the inquisitiveness of this soul principle that consciousness is won from the unconsciousness, that it is Eve who leads Adam to the Tree."[560]

It is also possible that Adam was "with her," as v. 6 plainly says: "she took of its fruit

---

> (forbidden) tree; you are the first deserter of the divine law; you are she who persuaded him whom the devil was not valiant enough to attack. You destroyed so easily God's image man. On account of your desert—that is death—even the Son of God had to die.
>
> —Tertullian, "On the Apparel of Women, "

557 *Apocalypse of Moses* 14:2, 21:6; *Sibylline Oracles* 1:42-43.

558 Carol Meyers writes, "It [Genesis] portrays the female rather than the male as the first human being to utter language, which is the utterly quintessential mark of human life" *(Discovering Eve: Ancient Israelite Women in Context* [New York: Oxford University Press, 1988], 91). It is true that the female is the first and dominant speaker in chapter 3, but her male counterpart definitely has the first word in Gen. 2:23. As Mieke Bal notes, "If the woman is the first to be signified, the man is the first to speak" (*Lethal Love: Feminist Literary Readings of Biblical Love Stories* [Bloomington: Indiana University Press, 1987],116). "Nonetheless, it may be significant to note that it is the presence of woman that renders speechless earthling into eloquent man." Cited from Reuven Kimmelman's "The Seduction of Eve and Feminist Readings of the Garden of Eden" in *Women in Judaism: A Multidisciplinary Journal* 1 (1998), 2.

559 See notes on v. 3 for further explanations.

560 Charles Ponce, *Working the Soul: Reflections on Jungian Psychology* (Berkeley, CA.:, North Atlantic Books, 1988), 63.

and ate; and she also gave some to her husband, who was with her, and he ate." If this interpretation is correct, then we may assume that Adam was present throughout the entire event, but acting like a compliant husband—he never opens his mouth. This would indicate that he did in fact listen to every word but acquiesces by virtue of his silence. Subsequently, when the critical hour of decision finally arrives and he is offered the fruit by Eve, Adam takes the fruit and eats it.

אַף כִּי־אָמַר אֱלֹהִים לֹא תֹאכְלוּ מִכֹּל עֵץ הַגָּן – "Did God say, 'You shall not eat from any tree in the garden?'" – Like Rashi and Ibn Ezra who came after him, Saadia assumes that Eve spoke to a genuine serpent; an interpretative reading that several modern scholars also endorse.[561] Some rabbinic exegetes point out that God endowed the serpent with the power of speech, whereas other scholars think that Adam and Eve understood the language of the animals, much like the shamans who would visit the spirit world and converse with the spirits of the animal kingdom. According to the ancient text, the *Book of Jubilees* (3:25), God enabled all earthly creatures with a capacity to understand and converse with one another. All of this changed once Adam and Eve disobeyed their Maker, and after the "Fall," the "language" of Creation became forgotten. Western folklore attributes this unique kind of knowledge to remarkable people such as St. Francis of Assisi and R. Israel Baal Shem Tov, the founder of the 18th century Hassidic movement.

Another Interpretive View: He said to the woman, "Did God say, 'You shall not eat from any tree in the garden?'" – Some of the early Christian exegetes propose an intriguing interpretation as to the serpent's motivation. The serpent, wishing to discern from Eve what God discloses to her husband about the mysteries that existed in the garden, utilizes this information to bring about their ruination. [562] Once the serpent is apprised of the fact that they were not to approach this particular tree, it realizes exactly the way to ensnare them.[563]

3:2 וַתֹּאמֶר הָאִשָּׁה אֶל־הַנָּחָשׁ מִפְּרִי עֵץ־הַגָּן נֹאכֵל – The woman said to the serpent, "We may eat of the fruit of the trees in the garden." – The Hebrew verse is difficult to decipher; the text appears as though it were missing verbiage. Professor Everett Fox adds: "even though God said: You are not to eat from any of the trees in the garden." This figure of speech is termed an *aposiopesis*; namely, a sudden disruption of a thought in the middle of a sentence, as though the speaker were

---

[561] See for example, the commentaries of Sarna, Brueggemann, Gowan, and Wenham on this passage.

[562] See Ephrem the Syrian's *Hymns on Paradise* 3:4-5 cited in the *Ancient Christian Commentary* on the Scriptures (Downer's Grove, Il: InterVarsity Press, 2001), 75.

[563] Ibid., 76.

unwilling or unable to continue. This literary device relies on the imagination of the listener to fill in the details. There is obviously more to the conversation with the serpent than the Torah actually discloses.[564] As to the content of the "missing" dialogue, Kimchi adds a homiletical spin that clarifies the essence of the verse. As Eve defends God, the serpent casts aspersions on the Creator. While the serpent concedes that God had made humankind superior to the other animals, he also suggests that the Creator wishes to keep them inferior to Himself. Therefore, if Eve and her husband were to partake of the forbidden fruit, they would immediately realize why God views them so contemptuously. The serpent purposely exaggerates the reason for the divine proscription, in order to prompt a reaction from Eve that would result in the couple's downfall (see notes to Gen. 3:4).[565]

❖ *Eden's First Attorney*

3:3 וּמִפְּרִי הָעֵץ אֲשֶׁר בְּתוֹךְ־הַגָּן אָמַר אֱלֹהִים לֹא תֹאכְלוּ מִמֶּנּוּ וְלֹא תִגְּעוּ בּוֹ פֶּן־תְּמֻתוּן – **but God said, 'You shall not eat of the fruit of the tree that is in the middle of the garden, nor shall you touch it, or you shall die.'** — Rabbinic tradition teaches that by adding to God's proscription, Eve ultimately diminishes its original power. The command not to eat the fruit is given before Eve was created, but Adam later tells her not to touch the tree as a safeguard to keep her from eating its fruit. This would explain why the serpent never approaches Adam; the serpent knows that Adam heard, firsthand, what God had said. Eve is different because she heard the commandment only secondhand, and therefore, she is more vulnerable to the serpent's cunning.[566] Evidence supporting this rabbinic reading can be found in 2:16. However, it is possible God later repeated this proscription to Eve so that she too would refrain from eating the forbidden fruit.

3:4 וַיֹּאמֶר הַנָּחָשׁ אֶל־הָאִשָּׁה לֹא־מוֹת תְּמֻתוּן – **But the serpent said to the woman, "You will not die"** — How did the serpent know they wouldn't die? Hizkuni (*ca.* 13th century) suggests that the serpent may have spoken from experience—it had eaten the forbidden fruit (which the animals were never forbidden to do), and it was living proof that it did not die. Thus, the serpent convinces her that God's death threat

---

[564] Even though the serpent saw them eating of the other fruits, he spoke to Eve at length in order that she answer him and come to speak of that tree (based on *Pirkê de Rabbi Eliezer*, ed. Horowitz, ch. 13; *Avot d'Rabbi Natan*, ch. 1).

[565] Kimchi's Midrash is very similar to the Gnostic version of the story; see note to 3:5.

[566] As noted in the *Keter Torah* commentary. This idea also appears in Genesis Rabbah 19:3, where the serpent pushed Eve against the tree: "Have you then died?" he said to her; "Just as you were not stricken through touching it, so will you not die when you eat it, but For God knows that in the day you eat from it . . ."

was meant to intimidate them not to eat; but in actuality, they would not really die.[567] The serpent disarms Eve's objections with the arguments of a skilled attorney. By focusing her attention to the forbidden tree, it becomes even more appealing. Eve feels a natural reticence to even touch the tree per Adam's instructions; the serpent proceeds to dispel her ambivalence, encouraging her to taste the forbidden fruit. However, M. Eliade proposes a different response:

> On the one hand animals are charged with a symbolism and a mythology of great importance for the religious life [i.e., in shamanic encounters—MS]; so that to communicate with animals, to speak their language and become their friend and master is to appropriate a spiritual life much richer than the merely human life of ordinary mortals. And, on the other hand, the prestige of animals in the eyes of the 'primitive' is very considerable; they know [i.e., intuitively—MS] the secrets of Life and Nature, they even know the secrets of *longevity and immortality*. By entering into the condition of the animals, the shaman shares their secrets and enjoys their plentitude of life."[568]

Eliade's exposition raises an important question—at least from a mythical perspective: Did Adam possess shamanic-like abilities that enabled him to communicate with the animals? The biblical texts seem to imply that Adam and Eve may have possessed a natural ability to speak with the animals (shamans still do this by imitating the animal's actions and sounds[569]), and this capability enabled them to identify each creature by its specific name.

When the woman introduces the words פֶּן־תְּמֻתוּן (*pen-təmuṯûn*), "lest you will die" instead of the original wording in 2:17 מוֹת תָּמוּת (*môṯ tāmûṯ*), "you *shall* surely die," this seemingly minor change actually softens the strength of the Divine imperative. One must remember that in the absence of punctuation, the use of doubled-verb construction in Biblical Hebrew is the ancient equivalent to writing something in bold-faced lettering or using an exclamation point. Doubled verb constructions also indicate an intensity of action that lends drama to a text. More importantly, the change in wording allows the serpent to introduce the element of doubt into her mind. The serpent claims that God is unsure as to what *might* befall them should

[567] For a similar line of reasoning, see *Aboth d'Rabbi Nathan*, Chapter 1: "Now you say that God has forbidden us to touch the tree. Well, I can touch the tree and not die, and so can you." What did the wicked snake then do? He touched the tree with his hands and feet and shook it so hard that some of its fruit fell to the ground. . . . Then he said to her, "[You see? So likewise] you say that God has forbidden us to eat from the tree. But I can eat from it and not die, and so can you." What did Eve think to herself? "All the things that my husband has told me are lies." Whereupon she took the fruit and ate it and gave to Adam and he ate, as it is written: 'The woman saw that the tree was good to eat from and a delight to the eyes [Gen. 3:6].' Translated by James L. Kugel, *The Bible as It Was* (Cambridge, MA: Belnap Press of Harvard University Press, 1997), 77.

[568] M. Eliade, *Myths, Dreams, and Mysteries* (New York: Harper Torchbooks, 1959), 63.

[569] M. Eliade, *Shamanism: Archaic Techniques in Ecstasy* (Princeton: Princeton University Press, 1964), 93.

they disobey. The particle conjunction פֶּן (*pen* = "lest") is used in this instance to convey the meaning of "might occur," i.e., it is unclear whether God will really hold you responsible for your behavior, perhaps He won't! To make his point sound more convincing and the tree more appealing, the serpent speaks most emphatically: "You will *not* die!"

The serpent asserts that God knows that eating the fruit of the tree will not result in death. In fact, instead of dying they will attain knowledge, specifically the knowledge of good and bad. Suddenly, the woman's eyes focus on the tree's attributes (3:6). The biblical narrator provides the reader with an inside look as to how Eve arrives at her decision to obtain the fruit. Like a seductive sonnet, Eve can hear the serpent's word echo in her mind: לֹא־מוֹת תְּמֻתוּן – "you shall not die!" According to one pseudepigraphal work, the serpent criticizes Eve's reluctance to eat the fruit:

> "I am grieved over you," the serpent replies, "that you are like animals, for I do not want you to be ignorant; but rise, come and eat, and observe the fruit of the tree." Eve backs off: "I fear lest God be angry with me, just as he told us." But the serpent presses her: "Fear not; for at the very time you eat, your eyes will be opened and you will be like gods, knowing good and evil. But since God knew this, that you would be like him, he begrudged you and said, 'Do not eat of it.' But come to the plant and see its great glory." Partially convinced, Eve admits, "It is pleasing to consider with the eyes"; yet she remains frightened. The serpent urges her: "Come, I will give it to you. Follow me." [570]

3:5 כִּי יֹדֵעַ אֱלֹהִים כִּי בְּיוֹם אֲכָלְכֶם מִמֶּנּוּ וְנִפְקְחוּ עֵינֵיכֶם וִהְיִיתֶם כֵּאלֹהִים – For God knows that when you eat of it your eyes will be opened, and you will be like God – More so than the Septuagint, the Aramaic translations attempt to soften the obvious anthropomorphism here. The Targum of Onkelos loosely renders כֵּאלֹהִים (*kēʾlōhîm*) as כְּרַבְרְבִין ("like masters" or "the great ones") while Targum Pseudo-Jonathan opts for כְּמַלְאָכִין רַבְרְבִין "great angels." Lastly, the Targum of Neofiti prefers, כְּמַלְאָכִין ("like angels)." The serpent argues that once they eat the fruit, both of them will be masters of their own destiny and not be accountable—even to God!

According to R. Joseph B. Soloveitchik, the serpent aims to minimize the Divine threat, countering that God's admonition was less than truthful—He would never carry out His threat. However, the serpent's real objective is to silence or possibly destroy the ethical conscience within man that inspires a moral sense of duty; it is this stirring within the heart of man that awakens him to pursue a spiritual ethos that enriches and

[570] *The Life of Adam and Eve,* printed in James Charlesworth, ed., *The Old Testament Pseudepigrapha*, 2 vols. (Garden City, NY: Doubleday, 1983). Vol. 2, 279.

deepens human existence.[571]

יֹדְעֵי טוֹב וָרָע – knowing good and evil – The expression "good and evil" is a merism and it connotes a knowledge of all things—good and bad. Martin Buber encourages us to view this merism within the backdrop of antiquity and offers the following structuralist approach to the text. To the ancients, the knowledge of "good and evil" was another way of expressing the nature of fortune and misfortune that we experience in the world. Buber argues that the key to deciphering this mystery requires that we develop an adequate awareness of the binary opposites that God established in creation.

❖ *The Dangers Implicit in "Knowing Evil"*

Another Interpretive View: "For God knows that when you eat of it your eyes will be opened, and you will be like God, knowing good and evil." – A more interesting translation reads, "God knows in fact that the day you eat it your eyes will be opened and you will be like gods, knowing good from evil" (NJB). The serpent induces feelings of inferiority and longing in the woman, as to if to say, "Wouldn't you like to have the freedom of a divine being, and do whatever pleases you? With your defiance, you will be completely uninhibited and free." In so many words the serpent implies that they would soon possess omniscience, and this knowledge would immediately enable them to attain God-like power. The primal couple accepts this allegation without question, risking repercussions for their disobedience.

In what way is God's knowledge of good and evil different from that of humankind? According to Martin Buber, God's knowledge derives from the fact that He created the opposites of being. Human beings, on the other hand, can never be "creators" in the literal sense; they can only "beget" what is already in existence. As Buber writes, "God knows the opposites of being, which stem from His own act of creation; He encompasses them, untouched by them; He is absolutely familiar with them as He is superior to them; He has direct intercourse with them." In contrast, humanity's knowledge of evil derives from having "intercourse and direct contact" with evil. Buber notes that this nuance which was the original meaning of the verb יָדַע (*yāḏa*ᶜ = *know*) also means, "to be in direct contact."[572] So long as evil mesmerizes their attention, goodness becomes

---

[571] *The Emergence of Ethical Man, op. cit.*, 97.

[572] Buber notes:

> This knowledge as the primordial possession of God, and the same knowledge as the magical attainment of man are worlds apart in their nature. God knows the opposites of being, which stem from his own act of creation. He encompasses them, untouched by them; He is absolutely familiar with them as he is superior to them. He has direct intercourse with them (this is obviously the

inaccessible to them until they extricate themselves from its grip. In his innocence, Adam cannot imagine how such knowledge would alter his experience of reality. In his excitement, he cannot conceive of being alienated from God, or imagine a darkness that envelops and stifles. The allure of evil might seem difficult to grasp or comprehend. However, for the person who experiences a desire for the forbidden, evil is sweetly tantalizing and overwhelming. The repercussions of choosing the forbidden during the time of an offense do not register in the sinner's critical faculties, and may even be completely unimaginable to the person caught in its grip. After Adam experiences the taste of the forbidden, he begins to comprehend a life without God, which immediately fills him and his wife with anxiety and confusion. What they discover is not a knowledge that enriches their life or the world; instead, it is a knowledge that impoverishes the knower with an experience of alienation and spiritual anxiety.

❖ *From Where Does Evil Derive?*

Nahum Sarna tackles this problem head-on in his Genesis commentary. He explains that *moral* evil derives solely from the misuse of human freedom:

> The biblical answer to this fundamental question, diametrically opposed to prevalent pagan conceptions, is that there is no inherent, primordial evil at work in the world. The source of evil is not metaphysical but moral. Evil is not transhistorical but humanly wrought. Human beings possess free will, but free will is beneficial only insofar as its exercise is in accordance with divine will. Free will and the need for restraint on the liberties of action inevitably generate temptation and the agony of choosing that only man's self-mastery can resolve satisfactorily. The ensuing narrative demonstrates that abuse of the power of choice makes disaster inescapable.[573]

According to this position, evil's existence does not derive from a pre-cosmic primordial chaos in which the various deities struggle against this chaos to be born. Divine power does not act unilaterally, but only in conjunction with human freedom. The Divine is eternally present in shaping history together with His covenantal partner—humankind. Although Sarna's answer has its appeal, the facts of the story indicate that evil, as symbolized by the serpent, also exists as a potentiality that is outside of man. Unlike Sarna, Paul Ricoeur asserts that "evil" has a different kind of ontology, deriving from the primordial chaos of Creation. Ricoeur seems to indicate that there is an important distinction to be drawn between evil, which exists as a primordial force *vis-à-vis* evil that is externalized by human choice. When it comes to moral evil, only man can

---

original meaning of the Hebrew verb 'know' means 'to be in direct contact with'), and this in their function as the opposite poles of the world's being. Thus He who is above all opposites has intercourse with the opposites of His own making. . . . The 'knowledge' acquired by man through eating of the miraculous fruit is of an entirely different order" *Good and Evil*, (New York: Prentice Hall, 1952), 75-76.

[573]N. Sarna, *JPS Genesis,* 16.

make it a part of his psyche. Nevertheless, as the personification of chaos, evil remains as a potentiality within the created order. Ricoeur adds:

> The serpent represents the following situation: in the historical experience of man, every individual finds evil *already there;* nobody begins it absolutely. . . . Evil is part of the interhuman relationship, like language, tools, institutions; it is transmitted, it is tradition and not only something that happens. There is thus an anteriority of evil to itself, as if evil were that which always precedes itself. . . . That is why, in the Garden of Eden, the serpent is already there; he is the other side which begins.
>
> Let us go further; behind the *projection* of our lust, beyond the tradition of evil already there, there is perhaps even more radical externality of evil, a cosmic structure of evil—not, doubtless the lawlessness of the world as such, but its relation of indifference to the ethical demands of which man is both author and servant. From the spectacle of things, from the course of history, from the cruelty of nature and men, there comes a feeling of universal absurdity, which invites man to doubt his destination. . . . There is thus a side of our world that confronts us as chaos and that is symbolized by the chthonic[574] animal. For a human existent, this aspect of chaos is a structure of the universe. . . . Thus the serpent symbolizes something of man and something of the world, a side of the microcosm, a side of the macrocosm, the chaos *in* me, *among* us, and *outside*. But it is always chaos for me, a human existent destined for goodness and happiness.[575]

Unlike Ricoeur, Sarna's exposition does not adequately explain why the serpent is in the garden in the first place or how it knew something about the nature of evil, that Adam and his wife did not know; nor did it occur to Sarna to connect the serpentine imagery to its Mesopotamian parallels. Ricoeur, on the other hand, makes a compelling case for his argument. The story of the primordial serpent in Eden leaves us with an understanding that there are two aspects of evil; one form derives from a primordial source outside of Adam (and by extension, every human being); the other derives from within man himself whenever he actualizes that possibility. Ricoeur adds that the biblical writer purposely kept the serpent, which had not been demythologized, as the sole survivor of the Mesopotamian theogony myths.[576]

❖ *Telling the Serpent's Side of the Story—Rashi and the Gnostics*

Another Interpretive View: for God knows that when you eat of it your eyes will be opened, and you will be like God, knowing good and evil —The serpent

---

[574] In Greek mythology, "chthonic" pertains to the underworld and derives from the Greek *khthōn* "earth."

[575] Paul Ricoeur, *The Symbolism of Evil* (Boston: Beacon Press, 1967), 257-258.

[576] Ibid., 255.

equates godly knowledge with authority and control. By defying God, Adam and Eve become equal to the Creator, capable of standing up to the Him with open defiance and independence. Rashi expresses this thought in clearer terms, "Every artisan detests his fellow artisans; the serpent suggested to her, God ate of the tree and created the world implying that if you eat—you will become like God, creators of worlds."[577]

The serpent claims that God was keeping this knowledge *from* humankind, just for Himself and His angelic hosts (v. 5). Rashi's interpretation has merit; since the beginning of Genesis, the Creator is at work separating and distinguishing one being from another. The serpent suggests that they too could create worlds with the special knowledge that God keeps only for Himself and His heavenly retinue. As one skilled in the art of deception, the serpent makes God appear petty, insecure, and jealous. The serpent claims that God had lied to Adam when He told him that he would die if he ate of the tree's fruit. This Midrashic idea reflects a motif from Gnostic literature, which expands this theme in detail. In one of the early Gnostic treatises, *The Testimony of Truth*, the Gnostic narrator tells the story of Eden from the serpent's viewpoint. In this Gnostic Midrash, the serpent embodies the principle of divine wisdom; the entity persuades Adam and Eve to partake of the knowledge and portrays the Creator God as a malevolent and ignorant demon who intimidates them with the threat of death. Furthermore, the serpent contends that God is only trying to prevent them from acquiring knowledge, and will expel them from Paradise at the first opportunity.[578]

> But of what sort is this God? First [he] maliciously refused Adam from eating of the tree of knowledge. Secondly he said, "Adam, where are you?" God does not have foreknowledge; (otherwise) would he not know from the beginning? [And] afterwards he said, "Let us cast him [out] of this place, lest he eat of the Tree of Life and live forever." Surely he has shown himself to be a malicious grudger. And what kind of a God is this? For great is the blindness of those who read, and they did not know him. And he said, "I am the jealous God; I will bring the sins of the fathers upon the children until three (and) four generations." And he said, "I will make their heart thick, and I will cause their mind to become blind, that they might not know nor comprehend the things that are said." But these things he has said to those who believe in him [and] serve him![579]

---

[577] Gen. Rabbah 19:3.

[578] The Ophites (a.k.a. "Serpent-Brethren") taught the Gnostic doctrine concerning the serpent. They identified the serpent with the Logos, or the mediator between the Father and Matter, bringing down the powers of the upper world to the lower world, and leading the return from the lower to the higher. The serpent represents the whole winding process of development and salvation.

[579] J. M. Robinson and R. Smith, *The Nag Hammadi Library in English*, 4th rev. ed. (Leiden; New York: E.J. Brill, 1996), 455.

❖ *Omitting to Mention the Fine Print*

Many Gnostics assert that far from being the seducer of the human race, the serpent serves as humanity's first teacher and civilizer by teaching it the difference between good and evil.[580] The serpent symbolizes the γνῶσις (*gnosis* = an intuitive apprehension of spiritual truths), the emerging consciousness in nascent humanity that evolves toward individuation. The gnostic seeks to overcome his or her basic alienation from the world by means of a special *gnosis* that aims to transform the inner person—not through cognitive or theoretical thought, but through the revelation of a hidden light that imbues the gnostic with an abiding sense of peace, well-being, joy, and divine grace promising salvation. The gnostic perspective claims that there exists a radical dualism governing the relationship between God and the world, and analogously, between humans and the world. Gnosticism compares the human attachment to the terrestrial world with a form of spiritual servitude, i.e., shackles of earthly existence from which the soul yearns to be free and liberated. The acquisition of this coveted knowledge liberates the gnostic from the created world, one that includes both history and nature. The serpent appears to possess an instinctual awareness of the tree's properties and intuitively knows that its role in the creative drama is to awaken the couple from their state of unconsciousness into a wakeful state of consciousness—regardless of the consequences it would personally have to suffer. For this reason, in the Gnostic myths of the Fall, it is the serpent who defiantly acts as the catalyst of change.

The serpent promises they will soon possess these spiritual qualities, but the serpent neglects to mention the immense cost humanity would have to pay to obtain this enlightenment. The author of Ecclesiastes may have had the Edenic experience in mind when he expresses the thought: "Much wisdom, much grief; the more knowledge, the more sorrow" (Ecc. 1:18). Wisdom never comes to us without cost and tuition. What are some of the moral lessons we can learn from this? The mistakes that we make in life have the potential to serve as valuable life-lessons that can help us renew our spiritual life. The miscues and ill-conceived decisions are a source of suffering–until we make a decision not to repeat these errors. Without cultivating an authentic humility, we condemn ourselves to the insanity of mindless repetition.

3:6 וַתֵּרֶא הָאִשָּׁה כִּי טוֹב הָעֵץ לְמַאֲכָל – **So when the woman saw that the tree was good for food** – The fruit looked as appetizing as any other fruit in the garden. There was nothing externally wrong as far as she could ascertain; however, there may be

[580] Anthropologist Ioan P. Cauliano points out that the character of the serpent varied depending on the specific gnostic group. Among the Orphites, the serpent epitomizes evil and the Nassenes refer to the creature as the "Angel of Iniquity." Elsewhere it is called "the Devil" or "Moluchtas." In the Gospel of Eve, the serpent becomes Sophia, Eve's spiritual instructor. For the Perates, the serpent is the Savior of humankind. In contrast, the Sethians identify the Demiurge and Logos as serpent-like (*The Tree of Gnosis: Gnostic Mythology from Early Christianity to Modern Nihilism* (San Francisco: Harper Collins, 1992), 128.

a subtle allusion embedded in the text. The wording "she saw the tree was good" is reminiscent of the familiar "and the Lord saw that it was good." However, her attempt "to see" what is "good" results in failure. The implication is that only God can *define* the parameters of what is good and evil, and by faithful deference, humanity can only *discern* the difference.

וְכִי תַאֲוָה־הוּא לָעֵינַיִם – **and that it was a delight to the eyes** – When Eve pays too much attention to what she sees, she no longer *hears* the divine Word telling her what is right and wrong, true or false. The only thing that grips her imagination *is what she sees.* Eve fails to understand that appearances can be deceptive. The serpent intentionally does not tell the woman that she *must* eat the fruit. The only thing the serpent suggests was that she *could* eat the forbidden fruit with impunity. The serpent makes the forbidden fruit seem tantalizing, if not erotic. She looks at the tree with a new longing—its fruit was good to eat, a delight to the eyes, and it would give her wisdom. Then she brings it to Adam and repeats everything the serpent had told her. The connection between "word" and "sight" is a motif pivotal to understanding numerous other themes of the Bible. Sight must not exist outside of the Divine Word that commands and demands human obedience (Num. 15:39). "Seeing," when left to its own, often leads to distortion. Hence, when the Israelites later *see* the mighty inhabitants of Canaan, their visual understanding of the situation leads to their despair and cynicism (13:33).

❖ *An Ancient Buddhist Version of the "Fall"*

Another Interpretive View: and a tree to be desired to make wise (MKJV) – While there are several versions of the Fall narrative in ancient Semitic literature, it is not widely known that a mythic memory of a primordial Fall is also recorded in the Oriental world and this phenomenon is especially interesting when examined from the perspective of Jung's theory of the archetype; i.e., the common and universal patterns of thought that spontaneously appear in the stories and myths gathered from all around the world.

Although the Buddhist tradition does not speak of a Fall in the Western theological sense, it does speak of a state of Original Ignorance that occurred at the dawn of human creation. From ignorance came greed, anger, jealousy, and pride; and from these emotional energies come misdeeds that lead to suffering. The first sin among the ancients that perpetuated the Fall was the prejudice of appearance—those of brighter skin began to look down on those with darker skin. Ignorance led to the formation of gender, which eventually gave rise to desire and passion.

One ancient Pali Buddhist text [known as the Pâli Aggañña-suttam and the Prâkrit Mahâvastu, also known as "Aphorism on the Knowledge of the Beginning"] dating back somewhere between the 5th and 1st century B.C.E., records an ancient memory of humanity's original spiritual descent that invites comparison to the Fall narrative of Genesis 3:

> Then the organ of womanhood appeared in the woman and the organ of manhood in the man. And the woman offered to the man strong drink in excess, and the man unto the woman. And as they did so, passion arose, and suffering entered into their bodies. By reason of the suffering they indulged in the act of sex.[581]

Like the Augustinian perspective, the Buddhist doctrine believes that desire is a principal manifestation of the selfish craving, grasping, or a blind state of want. And it is for this reason, desire is considered to be at the root of human suffering; the ultimate goal of Buddhism since is the extinguishing of all desire. In Judaism, desire in itself is neutral—providing one learns how to sublimate it and master it. Jewish tradition also teaches that without desire, the human race would have died in its infancy.

וְנֶחְמָד הָעֵץ לְהַשְׂכִּיל – and that the tree was to be desired to make one wise – All of Eve's senses are kinesthetically engaged and stimulated; she has a lust for wisdom and must sate her curiosity.

❖ *"Stolen Waters are Sweet . . ."*

וַתִּקַּח מִפִּרְיוֹ וַתֹּאכַל – she took of its fruit and ate – Human nature has always found something tempting about illicit pleasure, as "Stolen waters are sweet, and bread eaten in secret is pleasant." (Prov. 9:17). That is to say, forbidden delights are sweet and pleasant especially since they come with risk and danger. Without giving even a moment of further thought, quickly she grabs the fruit and devours it with delight. According to one exposition dating back to Late Antiquity, the serpent manipulates her to eat the fruit and give it to her husband:

> And I opened (the gate) for him, and he entered into Paradise, passing through in front of me. After he walked a little, he turned and said to me, "I have changed my mind and will not allow you to eat." He said these things wishing in the end to entice me and ruin me. And he said to me, "Swear to me that you are giving it also to your husband." And I said to him, "I do not know by what sort of oath I should swear to you; however that which I do know I tell you By the throne of the LORD and the cherubim and the tree of life, I shall give it also to my husband to eat."[582]

וַתִּתֵּן גַּם־לְאִישָׁהּ עִמָּהּ – and she also gave some to her husband, who was with her –Midrashic texts raise the question: Once she tastes the fruit, surely Eve became aware of the alienation and shame which she now experiences. Why would Eve purposely wish to mislead her husband? As previously mentioned, one possible

---

581 Albert J. Edmunds, *A Buddhist Genesis* (Chicago, IL: The Open Court Publishing Company, 1904), 211-213.

582 *Life of Adam and Eve, op. cit.*, 279.

explanation, based on the text in the Pseudepigrapha, suggests that she was following the serpent's orders. However, Rashi writes that Eve fears that God would soon punish her and give Adam a new and improved wife (just like God did with Lilith, Adam's first wife—according to certain Semitic myths). To avoid this scenario, she sets out to make Adam a co-conspirator so that their fate will be as one. On the other hand, it is possible that Adam was not in range of his wife, for had he been present at Eve's conversation—he could have contested the serpent's argument. It is probable that Eve later brought the fruit to Adam, and in his ignorance, he ate it. This interpretation might also explain why Adam did not indict the serpent when he was confronted by God.

❖ *Paradise Lost: Adam's Undying Devotion for Eve*

וַיֹּאכַל - **and he ate** — Note how passively Adam stood in relation to Eve, in contrast to the latter's activity: "*she took* of its fruit and ate . . . *she also gave* some to her husband." In terms of culpability, Jewish tradition asserts that Adam should have known better, but he gave in to his desire to be something more than what he already was. Adam should have responded immediately with a firm reply: "Eve—put the fruit down!" The Christian poet, John Milton, however, has a very different approach. According to him, Adam chooses to eat the fruit not of a desire to become God-like, but so that he too would share the same fate as his beloved.[583] Their destiny was intertwined from the beginning until the end. Although his interpretation is certainly not the contextual meaning of the text—especially in view of the acrimonious charges Adam levies against his beloved afterwards—none the less, Milton's interpretation resonates with Midrashic beauty and is worthy of special mention:

How art thou lost! How on a sudden lost,
Defaced, deflowered, and now to death devote!
Rather, how hast thou yielded to transgress
The strict forbiddance, how to violate
The sacred fruit forbidden! Some cursed fraud
Of enemy hath beguiled thee, yet unknown,
And me with thee hath ruined; for with thee
Certain my resolution is to die:
How can I live without thee! How forego
Thy sweet converse, and love so dearly joined,
To live again in these wild woods forlorn!
Should God create another Eve, and I
Another rib afford, yet loss of thee
Would never from my heart: no, no! I feel

[583] Nicholas of Lyra (1270-1349) offers a somewhat less romantic exposition. According to him, Adam did not eat the fruit out of a desire to attain God-like knowledge; he acquiesced to his wife's wishes so that he would not sadden her. Adam did not believe that breaking this law would actually constitute a mortal sin. Cf. Lesley Smith and Philip D. W. Krey (ed.), *Nicholas of Lyra: The Senses of Scripture* (New York: Leiden: Brill, 2000), 30.

The link of Nature draw me: flesh of flesh,
Bone of my bone thou art, and from thy state
Mine never shall be parted, bliss or woe.
So having said, as one from sad dismay
Recomforted, and after thoughts disturbed
Submitting to what seemed remediless . . .

Paradise Lost, Book IX 900-915

Another Interpretive View: and he ate — Rashi adds she gave the fruit to the animals as well.[584] According to Lurianic Kabbalah, all of Creation underwent a spiritual descent as a result of Adam and Eve's disobedience. Simply put: every human deed can elevate Creation, or bring ruination to what God has created. For this reason, each religious precept of the Torah focuses on unleashing the spiritual potential that is latent in the physical realm, thus correcting the breakage within Creation caused by the first human beings.

❖ *From "Shrewd" To "Nude"*

3:7 וַתִּפָּקַחְנָה עֵינֵי שְׁנֵיהֶם – Then the eyes of both were opened — According to Philo, the Torah uses the word "eyes" figuratively to express the vision of the soul, which alone has the capacity to discern good from evil.[585] At this moment, they experienced pangs of conscience for the first time (Theodoret).

וַיֵּדְעוּ כִּי עֵירֻמִּם הֵם — and they knew that they were naked — Rashi raises an important point from the Midrash, "Even a blind man 'knows' when he is naked. They had one precept to observe, and they stripped themselves of it." Their *fait accompli* could not be rectified regardless of their feelings after the deed. But do Adam and Eve associate their embarrassment with their failure to follow God's proscription? Do they realize the gravity of their duplicitous behavior? It seems that they did, which may explain the play on words: "naked" עָרוֹם (*ʿārôm*) and עָרוּם (*ʿărûm*) meaning "craftiness," or "deceit." Along with their defiance, Adam and Eve become self-conscious of their situation, feeling ill at ease with themselves, with each other, and ultimately with God.

The verse does not say וַיִּרְאוּ (*wayyirʾû*) "and they *saw* . . ." but rather, וַיֵּדְעוּ (*wayyēḏʿû*) "and they *knew* . . . ," i.e., they understood their nakedness in a way that was different from before. Evidently, Adam and Eve both became sexually aroused

---

[584] Gen. Rabbah 19:5.

[585] Philo, *Questions and Answers* 1:39.

immediately after eating the forbidden fruit, which unexpectedly functioned much like an aphrodisiac.[586] Both Augustine and Ramban claim that until this point in the narrative, Adam and Eve's sexuality resembled that of the animal kingdom, insofar as they mated for the purpose of procreation and not for pleasure per se. As a result of their newly acquired sexual consciousness, Adam and Eve enjoy their sexuality in a manner independent from procreation. After experiencing and then acknowledging these new kinds of feelings, they timidly withdraw from one another in embarrassment.

❖ *Like the Hands that Write a Torah Scroll . . .*

Augustine's attitude toward human sexuality is well known—he contends that it is inherently sinful, writing:

> Seeing then, that even in this mortal and miserable life, the body serves some men by many remarkable movements and moods beyond the ordinary course of nature. What reason is there for doubting that? Before man was involved by his sin in this weak and corruptible condition, his members might have served his will for the propagation of offspring without lust. Man has been given over to himself because he abandoned God, while he sought to be self satisfying; and disobeying God, he could not obey even himself. Hence, it is that he is involved in the obvious misery of being unable to live as he wishes. For if he lived as he wished, he would think himself blessed; but he could not be so if he lived wickedly."[587]

Initially, Ramban's commentary shows a remarkable affinity to Augustine's exposition:

> Now at the time sexual intercourse between Adam and his wife was not a matter of desire; instead, at the time of begetting offspring, they came together and propagated. Therefore, all the limbs were, in their eyes, as the face and hands, and they were not ashamed of them, but after he ate of the fruit of the tree of knowledge, he possessed the power of choice; he could now willingly do evil to himself or to others. This on the one hand, is a God-like attribute; but as far as man is concerned, it is bad through it, he has a will and desire."

However, it is important to note that unlike Augustine's austere view of Edenic procreation, Ramban never says that sexual desire is inherently evil—so long as it is sublimated to the worship of God.[588] A medieval work attributed to Ramban[589] re-

---

[586] This point is stressed by Ibn Ezra, Kimchi, Ramban, and Malbim. Cf. Augustine, *City of God* 14:24.

[587] Augustine, *City of God* 14:24.

[588] Cf. Malbim's commentary on Genesis 3:7.

[589] A number of scholarly views argue that the composer of the "Holy Letter" was not really Ramban, but actually somebody else. For a discussion of the literature concerning the authorship of this work, see

enforces the point he writes in his Genesis commentary. According to this text, when human sexuality is dedicated to a holy purpose, the act of intimacy becomes akin to the hands that write a Torah scroll—"honored and worthy of praise." By the same token, if the hands are misused, e.g., a person who uses his hands to do something unethical (e.g., forgery, or violence and robbing) they become defiled and loathsome. The author develops his theological understanding based on the narrative of Genesis 3:7:

- Prior to their sinning, it was one way, but after their sinning, it (human sexuality) became different. What is true with respect to the sexual organs is no less true with any other organ of the human body. When properly used, the organ is praiseworthy, but when misused, it becomes degraded. It follows that all of God's ways are just, holy, and pure. Ugliness comes only by man's misuse of his actions. . . . Nothing He created was shameful. The evidence deduced from Scripture bears this out, "The man and his wife were both naked, yet they felt no shame" (Gen. 2:25). Prior to their sinning, their consciousness was dedicated solely to higher spiritual pursuits solely for the sake of Heaven. For them, their sexual organs were like the eyes, hands, or other organs of the body. However, after they lusted after materialistic pleasures, their intentions were no longer for the sake of Heaven, "Then eyes of both of them were opened, and they realized that they were naked" (Gen 3:7)[590]

If a man and woman subordinate their sexuality to the service of God, sexual desire is like the act of sanctified eating. Ramban, a Kabbalist and his followers stress the importance of maintaining holy thoughts in the act of intimacy—the power of intentionality raises every deed to the sphere of holiness.

❖ *Further Reflections on Shame, Nakedness, and Fleeing*

Another Interpretive View: and they knew that they were naked – Nakedness in the Tanakh, as previously noted, is often used as a metaphor for fragility, weakness, and humiliation.[591] Before transgressing, Adam and Eve are the same as naive children; following the taste of the forbidden, they become adults instantaneously, bypassing puberty. Their eyes are opened, but not quite in the way they anticipated. Having hoped for divine omniscience that would give them power, they realize that the serpent hoodwinked them. Their feelings of nakedness trigger a

---

Gershom Scholem, "Did Ramban Write the *'Iggeret haQodesh?*" *Kiryat Sefer* 21 (1944-45), 179-86 and in *Kiryat Sefer* 22 (1945-46), 84; M. Harris, "Marriage as Metaphysics: A Study of the *Iggeret haQodesh*," *Hebrew Union College Annual* 33 (1962), 197-220.

[590] Seymour Cohen tr., *The Holy Letter: A Study in Jewish Sexual Morality* (Northvale, NJ: Jason Aronson Inc. 1993), 76-80.

[591] In ancient times, victorious armies used to humiliate captives in war by stripping them naked (Isa. 20:4; 47:1–3; Hab. 2:15). David's emissaries to the Ammonite king were humiliated by having half their beards removed and their clothing lopped off to the buttocks (2 Sam. 10:4).

visceral response of confusion, dismay, and embarrassment. Even their relationship to one another is altered, as they see each other from a new perspective and reality. Neither one can freely gaze into the other's eyes. The couple's reaction indicates they experienced blushing (or perhaps they felt sexually flushed) for the first time. Blushing helps convey the emotions that we might be too reticent to express in verbal terms. As Mark Twain once comically wrote, "Man is the only animal that blushes or needs to."

French philosopher Jean Paul Sartre writes that the fear of looking at the Other comes as result of knowing that one is truly vulnerable "before the Other's freedom."[592] The remark fits well with this particular biblical text. After their act of disobedience, Adam and Eve realize that they are not gods; the serpent's promise of them both "knowing good and evil" is misrepresented; they fear "facing" God, for they can barely "face" one other without feeling shame and accountability.

While Emmanuel Lévinas is not commenting on Adam and Eve's realization of their nakedness and alienation, his psychological insights, nevertheless, clarify the close relationship of nakedness, shame, and fleeing from oneself.

> Shame arises each time we cannot make others forget (*faire obliare*) our basic nudity. It is related to everything we would like to hide and that we cannot bury or cover up. The timid man who is all arms and legs is ultimately incapable of covering the nakedness of his physical presence with his moral person. Poverty is not a vice, but it is shameful because, like the beggar's rags, it shows up the nakedness of an existence incapable of hiding itself. This preoccupation with dressing to hide ourselves concerns every manifestation of our lives, our acts, our thoughts. We accede to the world through words, and we want them to be noble. . . . If shame is present, it means we cannot hide what we should like to hide, the necessity of fleeing, in order to hide oneself, is put in check by the impossibility of fleeing oneself. The necessity of fleeing in order to hide from oneself is held in check by the impossibility of fleeing oneself. What appears in shame is thus precisely the fact of being riveted to oneself—the radical impossibility of fleeing to hide from oneself. . . . Nakedness is shameful when it is the sheer invisibility (*patence*) of our being, of its ultimate intimacy, and the nakedness of our body is not that of a material thing.[593]

Although guilt and shame are similar in many ways, there are important distinctions. From a physiological perspective, shame evokes a response of blush and redness in the face. Unlike guilt, shame also involves greater body awareness. The person who experiences shame will typically cover his face, or sink into the ground, or feel a desire to flee. Guilt tends to be more isolated and specific, whereas shame attacks one's entire sense of self. Guilt is a self-imposed judgment of something one did or did

---

[592] Jean Paul Sartre, *Being and Nothingness: An Essay on Phenomenological Ontology* (New York: Routledge, 1969), 268.

[593] Emmanuel Lévinas, *On Escape: De l'evasion (Cultural Memory in the Present)* (Palo Alto, CA: Stanford University Press 2003), 64.

not do, while shame is a revelation of something that one *is*. Shame also guards the boundary of privacy and intimacy, while guilt limits the expansion of power; shame exposes the vulnerability of the self—a state in which one feels inherently defective or inferior, while guilt is concerned with the appropriateness of one's actions. In light of this discussion, Adam and Eve's immediate reaction indicates that they experienced more shame than they did guilt—uneasy with their unexpected sensuality and bodies. Although the word for "shame" is conspicuously absent in v. 7 of this narrative, the Torah strongly implies its presence by the fact that the couple resorts to covering themselves.

Although Adam and Eve's sense of shame may seem like a negative consequence, in effect, their sense of shame opens their eyes to the experience of living a life of virtue and temperance. Thomas Aquinas, like Lévinas, is of the view that the experience of shame can sometimes be morally edifying for the individual who suffers it. "Sentiments to shame, when repeated, set up a disposition to avoid disgraceful things"[594] and protects one from engaging in debasing and destructive behavior. Aquinas further argues that in a society where no sense of shame is experienced, the results are disastrous for everybody—resulting in moral insensitivity and numbness—even brazenness.[595] Without the fear of shame, there might be little incentive to strive toward a virtuous life and temperance.

❖ *Identifying the Forbidden Fruit*

וַיִּתְפְּרוּ עֲלֵה תְאֵנָה וַיַּעֲשׂוּ לָהֶם חֲגֹרֹת – and they sewed fig leaves together and made loincloths for themselves – One might wonder why didn't God reveal Himself while Adam and Eve were naked? Rabbinic scholar Louis Ginzberg explains that according to a well-known rabbinic Midrash,[596] "As long as Adam stood naked, casting about for means of escape from his embarrassment, God did not appear unto him, for one should not "strive to see a man in the hour of his disgrace." He waited until Adam and Eve had covered themselves with fig leaves.[597]

Rabbinic tradition extrapolates from this passage the identity of the mythic Tree of Knowledge: R. Nehemiah remarks: "The tree from which Adam and Eve ate was a fig tree, so that the thing with which they sinned, the fig, became the means through which

---

[594] *Summa Theologia* II-II, q. 144, a. 1.

[595] Ibid., a. 4.

[596] *Midrash Yelammedenu* cited in *Midrash HaGadol* I 91 and in *Yalkut* I, 744; *Likkutim*, IV, 31b.

[597] Louis Ginzberg, H. Szold, H., & P. Radin, *Legends of the Jews* (2nd ed.) (Philadelphia: Jewish Publication Society, 2003), 73.

the damage was repaired, for it says, 'They sewed together fig leaves'" (BT Sanhedrin 70b).[598] However, most popular depictions of the Tree of Knowledge portray the fruit as the apple tree *(pyrus malus)*. The Septuagint renders the word μήλωψ *(melon)* and the Vulgate *malum* as "apple", which also happens to be the Latin word for evil, an association which has reinforced the notion that the forbidden fruit was the apple; a similar parallel exists in ancient Greek literature.[599] The Edenic apple has always been a favorite image among medieval writers and artists alike.[600] Not only does modern literature endorse the apple as the forbidden fruit, but the apple is also a symbol of love in much of the world folklore and mythology.[601] Various ancient Near Eastern art-forms depict their love-goddesses with an apple or quince. In the Song of Songs, the apple is a metaphor for love and lovesickness (Song. 2:3, 8:5). New evidence suggests that the apple also appears in early Sumerian literature.[602]

> My sister, I would go with you to my apple tree.
> I would go with you to my pomegranate tree.
>
> *A Love Song of Shulgi,*

---

[598] Rashi offers a homiletical interpretation: All of the other trees refused to let their leaves except for the fig tree. Why didn't the text disclose the tree's identity? God did so that the tree would not be shamed, lest it be said, "This is the one through which the world was stricken."

[599] In the mythology of ancient Greece, Eris was the least popular of the gods. As the sister of Aries (the god of war), she revels in seeing the torment and destruction of others. At the wedding of Peleus and Thetis (the parents of Achilles), everyone is invited except Eris, the goddess of discord and her brother Ares. Determined to have her way, Eris decides to introduce discord on the couple's wedding day. She waits for the wedding feast to begin and then rolls a golden apple into the banquet room, saying "for the fairest." An argument ensues, and Paris chooses Aphrodite because her bribe was superior. As a reward, he desires to have the most beautiful woman in the world, who turns out to be Helen of Troy.

[600] The image of the poisoned apple figures prominently in the fairy-tale of Snow White, which induces her to fall into a deep and dangerous sleep.

[601] The apple of Eden occurs as an image of deceiving beauty in one of Shakespeare's sonnets to the Dark Lady: ("How like Eve's apple doth thy beauty grow, / If thy sweet virtue answer not thy show" (93.13–14). The apple appears in Chaucer's *Canterbury Tales* in a variety of contexts, including folk proverbs (*Cook's Tale*, 1.4406; *Canon's Yeoman's Tale*, 8.964). Byron likens the apple to the gift of reason (*Cain*, 2.364, 529, 614, 664; cf. Gen. 3:5); The English poet William Blake describes in "A Poison Tree" the fruit of secretly nurtured wrath as "an apple bright"—a more truly evil fruit than that of Eden. The poisoned apple, familiar in other contexts (e.g., the tale of Snow White), recurs as the fruit of the Tree of Mystery in Book 7 of *The Four Zoas* (228–306); the Tree of Mystery appears also in *America* and *Jerusalem*, under the names Urizen's Tree and Albion's Tree. The apple of Eden appears several times in Browning's *The Ring and the Book* (3.169–73; 4.851–59; 7.761–66, 828–29; 9.448–52). Selections cited are from D.L Jeffrey's *A Dictionary of Biblical Tradition in English Literature* (Grand Rapids, MI: W.B. Eerdmans, 1992), 49-51.

[602] According to D. Zohary and Maria Hopf, during the late Neolithic and Bronze Ages between 6000 and 3000 B.C.E., the first fruits ever grown and domesticated were the date, olive, grape, fig, sycamore fig, and pomegranate (*Domestication of Plants in the Old World: The Origin and Spread of Cultivated Plants in West Asia, Europe, and the Nile Valley* [New York: Oxford University Press, 2001], 174-176).

(Segment B, lines 10-19)

Of course there are alternative possibilities to consider. The apricot and the quince have been especially favored, with the quince having the advantage of being a fruit indigenous to the area.[603] Other traditions identify the forbidden fruit with the grape, apple, wheat[604] and the citron.[605] The Kabbalists[606] seem partial to the citron *(citrus medica),* sometimes known as the "apple of paradise." Other distinctive possibilities include the golden orange *(citrus sinensus)* and the carob. Ginzberg conjectures that the grape was also a popular candidate in the writings of antiquity, since the ancients considered wine to be the beverage of the gods.

603 New ISBE, Vol. 1, 214.

604 This Midrashic interpretation was based on the assonance of חִטָּה (*ḥiṭṭā*^{h} = "wheat") and חַטָּאת (*ḥaṭṭā*ʾ*ṯ* = "sin."Cf. Ramban's commentary on Lev. 23:40.

605 Gen. Rabbah 19.5; BT Berakhot 40a; BT Sanhedrin 70a; Gen. Rabbah 10:2 and 8; Esther 2:1; Targum Song of Songs 7:9.

606 Ramban, in his commentary to Lev. 23:40, cites in the name of the Kabbalah that the primordial fruit was the citron.

The Moment of Truth (3:8-13)

8 They heard the sound of the LORD God walking in the garden at the time of the
evening breeze, and the man and his wife hid themselves from the presence of the
LORD God among the trees of the garden. 9 But the LORD God called to the man,
and said to him, "Where are you?" 10 He said, "I heard the sound of you in the
garden, and I was afraid, because I was naked; and I hid myself." 11 He said, "Who
told you that you were naked? Have you eaten from the tree of which I commanded
you not to eat?" 12 The man said, "The woman whom you gave to be with me, she
gave me fruit from the tree, and I ate." 13 Then the LORD God said to the woman,
"What is this that you have done?" The woman said, "The serpent tricked me, and I
ate."

Conscience is God's presence in man.
—EMANUAL SWEDENBORG

It was taught: Before a man sins he inspires awe and fear, and creatures are afraid of him. Once he has sinned, he is filled with awe and fear, and becomes fearful of others. The proof for this is as Rabbi [Judah HaNasi] said: 'Before Adam sinned he listened to the divine utterance while standing upright and without fear. After he sinned, the Divine voice made him fearful and so he hid, as it says, "I heard the sound of you in the garden, and I was afraid, because I was naked; and I hid myself" (Gen. 3:10); 'And the man and his wife hid themselves (3:8).' R. Aibu said: On that occasion Adam's stature was lessened and reduced to a hundred cubits. R. Levi said: Before Adam sinned, the sound of the divine utterance did not disquiet him in the least, but after he sinned it came to him like a ferocious wild creature.
—SONG OF SONGS RABBAH 3:18

The Midrash depicts the spiritual and psychological transformation that occurs with the primal couple's loss of innocence as well as their experience of alienation. The terse but dramatic language of the opening verses conveys the irony and tragedy of human existence. Humankind is changed. Eden no longer feels like home. Prior to their disobedience, the thought of God "taking a stroll" in the Garden, and conversing with Adam and Eve may not have been out of the ordinary. What distinguishes this particular encounter is the fearful reaction it elicits.

❖ *The Shekhinah's Heavenly Ascent*

Rabbinic tradition asserts that the change in Adam and Eve is immediate; they can no longer discern the Presence of the Divine as they once could.[607] For the first time, the

[607] See Zohar 1:12b.

divine Presence fills them with dread and anxiety. In Adam's overactive imagination, God becomes a stalker from whom they must flee. Another Midrashic text contains a different but no less intriguing deconstruction of the passage. In Adam's mind, God does not seem to be walking *toward him*, but *rather away from him*. The verb מִתְהַלֵּךְ (*mithallēk* = "walking") means "leaping and ascending," departing, as it were, from the world.[608] While this teaching may not agree with the simple contextual meaning of "walking," the rabbis want to show how differently Adam now experiences the world of Eden. Their "nakedness" is more than being bereft of clothes; they feel exposed and vulnerable to the world.

On a deeper psychological level, reality suddenly becomes opaque and heavy; what was originally clear and transparent has now become disjointed, unintelligible and existentially confusing. Adam and Eve discover a fragmented world—their connection with the Divine effectively severed. In the aftermath, they feel alienated from the deepest dimension of their lives for they have all but lost their original spiritual intuition. The aforementioned Midrash stresses the awkwardness that paradoxically affects God and humankind alike; in fact, it is God who has been exiled to Heaven by humankind as a direct result of their emerging self-consciousness. But what Adam and Eve fail to realize is that God dwells not only in Heaven or earth, but also within the deepest recesses of the human soul, before Whom, there can be no escape. However, in their naiveté, they try.

3:8 וַיִּשְׁמְעוּ אֶת־קוֹל יְהוָה אֱלֹהִים מִתְהַלֵּךְ בַּגָּן – **They heard the sound of the LORD God walking in the garden** – The passage describes the Presence of the Divine in tangible human-like terms. The "sound" of God conveys an intensification and concentration of God's presence akin to Rudolph Otto's concept of the "numinous" (incapable of being described or understood).[609] As a rule, revelation always accommodates the cognitive and imaginative faculties of the individual receiving the revelation.[610]

לְרוּחַ הַיּוֹם – **at the time of the evening breeze** – This idiom refers to the time of day when the breeze is felt, about an hour before sunset. The Song of Songs alludes to this phenomenon "until the day breathes cool" (Song 2:17 and 4:6). Some of the more

---

[608] The Midrash further shows how the forces of violence and oppression would later cause the *Shekhinah*, the Divine Presence, to withdraw from the world until it had all but completely disappeared from the earthly realm. With the efforts of the seven righteous men, Abraham, Isaac, Jacob, Levi, Kohath, Amram, and Moses, the *Shekhinah* reemerged in the world at Sinai (Gen. Rabbah 19:8).

[609] Rudolf Otto, *The Idea of the Holy*, (New York: Oxford University Press, 1958), 5-12.

[610] See Maimonides' MT, *Hilkhot Yesodei HaTorah* 1:9; *Guide* 2:42. Aquinas also concurs, "The thing known is in the knower according to the manner of the knower" (*Summa* 2:2, Q. 1 and 2).

modern translations take note of this insight and render the phrase as "at the time of the evening breeze" (REB), "in the cool of the day" (NJB), or "at the breezy time of day" (NJPS, NAB).[611] In scientific terms, this occurs when the angle of the sun is parallel with the surface of the earth, which heats the air at the surface while the air that is above has already cooled off. This process creates the kinetic energy that causes a pleasant breeze.

וַיִּתְחַבֵּא הָאָדָם וְאִשְׁתּוֹ מִפְּנֵי יְהוָה אֱלֹהִים בְּתוֹךְ עֵץ הַגָּן – **and the man and his wife hid themselves from the presence of the LORD God among the trees of the garden** — Buber notes that every person who has ever tried to hide himself from God has found himself in the same dilemma: "Every man hides for this purpose, for every man is Adam and finds himself in Adam's situation. To escape responsibility for his life, he turns into a system of hideouts. . . . A new situation thus arises, which becomes more and more questionable every day, with every hideout. The situation can be precisely defined as follows: Man cannot escape the eye of God, but in trying to hide from Him, he is hiding from himself."[612]

❖ *The Divine Beckoning*

3:9 וַיִּקְרָא יְהוָה אֱלֹהִים אֶל־הָאָדָם — **But the LORD God called to the man** — According to the Tanakh, the origin of humankind's spiritual quest for God also corresponds to God's search for a relationship with humankind (Job 10:36). Aside from being a Creator, the Torah reveals that God is also a relational Being.

Another Interpretive View: But the LORD God called to the man — Benno Jacob notes that God spoke to Adam and not to Eve, for only Adam was personally commanded *not* to eat from the tree.[613] The Divine Voice is not revealed in a terrifying thunderstorm threatening Adam's very existence. Instead, the revelation assumes the form of the "still small voice" (1 Kgs. 19:12); it is audible enough for Adam to hear, yet easy to drown out if he chose to do so.

The still small voice describes the call of God that leads humankind to identify with God, and to follow in His ways. God causes this awareness to emerge not from the outside in, but rather from the inside out. The beginnings of human conscience become viable when an individual is capable of making a moral self-assessment; a function of

---

[611] J. L. Niehaus conjectures that the noun יוֹם (*yom* = *"day"*) may be related to the Akkadian cognate *umu* ("storm"), and he translates the phrase לְרוּחַ הַיּוֹם "in the wind of the storm"(see his article in "In the Wind of the Storm: Another Look at Genesis III 8, " *VT* 44 [1994]: 263–67).

[612] Martin Buber, *The Way of Man: According to the Teachings of Hasidism* (New York: Citadel Press, 1948), 10.

[613] *Genesis,* 26.

which is to guide one's behavior toward what is ethically right.[614] In some ways, the feeling of guilt functions as a warning-system whenever these basic and ethical values are being violated. The call of the Divine comes to teach Adam a lesson of vital importance: ethical maturity means becoming aware that God is intricately involved with human responsibility. As it is with Adam, so it is with all humanity.

❖ *The Eternal Question: Where Art Thou?*

וַיֹּאמֶר לוֹ אַיֶּכָּה – and said to him, "Where are you?" — Heschel's comments majestically capture the pathos and power of this exquisitely existential question: "Faith comes out of awe, out of the awareness that we are exposed to His Presence, out of anxiety to answer the challenge of God, out of an awareness of our being called upon. Religion consists of *God's question and man's answer*. The way *to* faith is the way *of* faith. The way to God is *of* God."[615]

Another Interpretive View: – and said to him, "Where are you?" — The purpose of the question is to stimulate a reflective state of mind that will bring Adam back to his senses. Although the Voice of God does not come out and condemn him outright, it does confront him. Adam has every opportunity to confess and repent.[616] Martin Buber develops existential insights intimated by this question, which in a broad theological sense applies to all human beings of all ages, by relating a well-known Hassidic story:

> The old rabbi was once put in jail because the Mitnagdim (defenders of the status quo) had denounced his principles and way of living to the government. He was arrested and sent to St. Petersburg to stand trial for treason. The old rabbi stood accused of sending monies abroad to Israel, which was controlled by the Ottoman Empire, an enemy of Russia. As the very pious man stood in jail, he was very engrossed in meditation. He had hardly noticed the visitor, who happened to be a high-ranking official in the Russian government. He asked the Rebbe, "I have a question on the Bible, and would be most grateful to you if you could give me an adequate answer."
>
> The Rebbe said to him: "Ask whatever you would like, and with God's help, I hope to be able to answer your problem." "How are we to understand that God, the All-Knowing, said to Adam: 'Where art thou?' (after he ate the fruit and hid with Eve)." The Rebbe asked, "Do you believe that the Scriptures are eternal and forever relevant in any time and in any place?" The official said that he did.

---

[614] This concept may be arguably may be the biblical origin of Kant's Categorical Imperative.

[615] Abraham Joshua Heschel, *God in Search of Man: A Philosophy of Judaism* (New York: Harper and Row, 1955), 137.

[616] For other scriptural examples where God prompts individuals with an obvious question, see Numbers 22:9 and Isaiah 39:3.

The Rebbe replied: "The Torah tells us: 'And God called to the Man [Adam]' (Gen. 3:9). This teaches us that God speaks to every individual and asks him, 'Where are you; i.e., where do you stand in relationship to this world?' God has allotted each of us a certain number of days and years, each of which is to be utilized for the doing of good in relation to both God and humankind. Therefore, ask yourself: How many days have you lived already and how much good have you accomplished during that time? You, for instance, have lived already 46 years, how did you use your time?" The official was deeply amazed and thrilled by the fact that the Rebbe had guessed his right age and put his hand on the prisoner's shoulder, while nervously exclaiming: "Bravo!"[617]

❖ *When the Soul Feels Stirred, God is calling . . .*

3:10 וַיֹּאמֶר אֶת־קֹלְךָ שָׁמַעְתִּי בַּגָּן וָאִירָא כִּי־עֵירֹם אָנֹכִי וָאֵחָבֵא – **He said, "I heard the sound of you in the garden, and I was afraid, because I was naked; and I hid myself."** — Adam answers God incorrectly—he should have confessed his sin immediately. Instead, he compounds his disobedience by making even more lame excuses. Heschel explains that Judaism teaches that the human quest for God must also involve a spiritual return unto Him. The Hebrew word for "repentence" תְּשׁוּבָה (*tešuvah*) is "answer," as Heschel notes: "Return to God is an answer to Him . . . the stirring in man to turn to God is actually a 'reminder by God to man.'"[618] This heightened state of feeling is God's beckoning to the individual, urging him or her to let go of the ego and embrace spiritual growth.

The verse in Proverbs 28:13 might serve as an intratextual principle for interpreting this passage yet further: "No one who conceals transgressions will prosper, but one who confesses and forsakes them will obtain mercy." Had Adam taken responsibility in this matter, he may well have been forgiven. Unfortunately, this was not to be the case. Adam's awareness of his nakedness seems to matter more to him than his act of disobedience. As Cassuto observes further, "He does not dare lie before his Creator, but he is not yet willing to avow his sin; hence he strives to turn the conversation to another subject, the last thing that happened after his transgression."[619] Adam then offers an excuse for hiding himself—"because I was naked" (cf. v. 7)—without perceiving that his very excuse provides evidence of his misdeed.

3:11 וַיֹּאמֶר מִי הִגִּיד לְךָ כִּי עֵירֹם אָתָּה – **He said, "Who told you that you were naked?"** — "How did you come to this startling new realization that nakedness is shameful? Who made you aware that you were naked? No one is called "naked" unless

[617] Martin Buber, *Way of Man, op. cit.*, 8.

[618] Abraham Joshua Heschel, *God in Search of Man: A Philosophy of Judaism, op. cit.*, 141-142

[619] Cassuto, *Genesis Vol. 1, op. cit.*, 156.

that person has reason to clothe himself or herself. One would never say that an animal is 'naked' because it lacks clothes, so who informed you that you must wear clothing?"[620]

3:12 וַיֹּאמֶר הָאָדָם הָאִשָּׁה אֲשֶׁר נָתַתָּה עִמָּדִי הִוא נָתְנָה־לִּי מִן־הָעֵץ וָאֹכֵל — "The woman whom You gave to be with me, she gave me fruit from the tree, and I ate." — As a last resort, Adam indirectly accuses God as a primary cause of his offense since He made Eve in the first place! This is indicated by the wording, "the woman *You* gave me." As Rashi astutely notes, "Here Adam shows his ingratitude by blaming his sin on the fact that God gave him a wife."[621]

❖ *A Comic Midrash*

Another Interpretive View: – The man said, "The woman whom You gave to be with me, she gave me fruit from the tree, and I ate." — Adam refuses to accept personal responsibility; he acts as though he has done nothing wrong. Like a child pinning the blame on a sibling, he points his finger at Eve and exclaims: "She did it!" Years ago, comedian Bill Cosby offered a brilliant interpretation explaining the straightforward meaning of the text in a way that is clearer than most rabbinic and non-rabbinic commentaries:

> Whenever your kids are out of control, you can take comfort from the thought that even God's omnipotence did not extend to God's kids. After creating heaven and earth, God created Adam and Eve. And the first thing he said was, "Don't."
>
> "Don't what?" Adam replied.
>
> "Don't eat the forbidden fruit," God said.
>
> "Forbidden fruit? We got forbidden fruit? Hey, Eve...we got forbidden fruit!"
>
> "No way!"
>
> "Don't eat that fruit!" said God.
>
> "Why?"
>
> "Because I am your Father and I said so!" said God (wondering why he hadn't stopped after making the elephants). A few minutes later God saw his kids having an apple break and was angry. "Didn't I tell you not to eat the fruit?" God asked.

---

620 As suggested by Bechor Shor, compare his interpretation with the supra-commentaries of Mizrachi and *Sefer HaZikaron*'s reading of Rashi.

621 BT Avodah Zarah 5b.

"Uh huh," Adam replied.

"Then why did you?"

"I dunno," Eve answered.

"She started it!" Adam said.

"Did not!"

"Did too!"

At least he didn't say, "No problem."

All right then, "Get out of here! Go forth and be fruitful and multiply."

Having had it with the two of them, God's punishment was that Adam and Eve should have children of their own.[622]

On a more sobering note, God is constantly giving the first human couple the chance to do better, but in the end they do worse! Ironically, Adam outsmarts himself by adding to God's prohibition not to *eat* of the tree, and instead, instructs Eve not to *touch* the tree (v. 3)—thus teaching that once we add to God's commandments, we risk perverting them (Deut. 4:2; 13:1). Richard Elliot Friedman correctly observes that these two scriptural passages "are the most violated commandments in the entire Torah."[623] After Eve eats the forbidden fruit, she seeks to assuage her guilty conscience by minimizing the severity of her behavior. After all, if everyone is guilty, then her actions become less morally objectionable. Her behavior is no different than the naughty school child that looks to get other kids in trouble so that everyone will be "equally guilty," when she is found out. Eve doesn't want to be the only one who is guilty before God.

Once they realize they both did something wrong, it never occurs to them to ask God for forgiveness. So instead, they hide. God confronts them with the question: "Who told you that you are naked?" They respond with a guilty silence. One sin leads to another. Rather than confessing, they abdicate responsibility by blaming one another. Ultimately everyone is punished. The moral of the story: When God gives you advice, listen to Him! One would have thought that having learned their lesson, their children would benefit from their parents' mistakes, yet the same pattern occurs again in the Cain and Abel story. After God gives Cain a chance to improve his behavior, Cain goes on to kill his

---

622 Bill Cosby, *Fatherhood*, (White Plains, NY: Peter Pauper Press, Inc., 2002), 64-65.

623 Richard Elliot Friedman, "Ancient Biblical Interpreters vs. Archaeology & Modern Scholars" *BAR*, Vol. 34:1, 2008, 62.

brother. God still gives him another chance to confess his crime, but he still abdicates responsibility. The same pedagogical pattern continues as humanity becomes increasingly more violent. The early chapters of Genesis offer a birds-eye-view into how the sins of the fathers affect the children—children learn by example.

3:13 וַיֹּאמֶר יְהוָה אֱלֹהִים לָאִשָּׁה מַה־זֹּאת עָשִׂית וַתֹּאמֶר הָאִשָּׁה הַנָּחָשׁ הִשִּׁיאַנִי וָאֹכֵל —
Then the LORD God said to the woman, "What is this that you have done?" The woman said, "The serpent tricked me, and I ate." — Adam's lack of caring and devotion to Eve, his acrimony and self-righteousness, reveal a sin that is more serious than the original infraction of eating the fruit of a forbidden tree. The sin of disobedience is certainly minor when compared to the sin of acrimony: Adam blames Eve, Eve blames the serpent, and the serpent (for lack of a better expression) doesn't have a leg to stand on. A sin against God can be atoned for with sincere regret, but a sin against one's fellow human being demands more arduous expiation. Moreover, every sin against another person is also a sin against God. The triangulation of their sin leads to their expulsion. The lack of empathy marks the beginning of a post-Edenic consciousness. One Midrash suggests that had she prayed for pardon, both of them would have been forgiven.[624]

---

624 *Midrash Tanhuma* (S. Buber ed.), 3:39; *Tanhuma*, Tazria 9; Gen. Rabbah 20:2; 19:11.

"The Glory of God is a Human Fully Alive"

3:14-24

14 The LORD God said to the serpent, "Because you have done this, cursed are you among all animals and among all wild creatures; upon your belly you shall go, and dust you shall eat all the days of your life. 15 I will put enmity between you and the woman, and between your offspring and hers; he will strike your head, and you will strike his heel." 16 To the woman he said, "I will greatly increase your pangs in childbearing; in pain you shall bring forth children, yet your desire shall be for your husband, and he shall rule over you."

17 And to the man[b] he said, "Because you have listened to the voice of your wife, and have eaten of the tree about which I commanded you, 'You shall not eat of it,' cursed is the ground because of you; in toil you shall eat of it all the days of your life; 18 thorns and thistles it shall bring forth for you; and you shall eat the plants of the field. 19 By the sweat of your face you shall eat bread until you return to the ground, for out of it you were taken; you are dust, and to dust you shall return."

20 The man named his wife Eve,[c] because she was the mother of all living. 21 And the LORD God made garments of skins for the man[d] and for his wife, and clothed them.
22 Then the LORD God said, "See, the man has become like one of us, knowing good and evil; and now, he might reach out his hand and take also from the tree of life, and eat, and live forever"— 23 therefore the LORD God sent him forth from the garden of Eden, to till the ground from which he was taken. 24 He drove out the man; and at the east of the garden of Eden he placed the cherubim, and a sword flaming and turning to guard the way to the tree of life.

> *With Adam's fall human history begins. The original, preindividualist harmony between man and nature, and between man and woman, was replaced by conflict and struggle. Man suffers from this loss of oneness. He is alone and separated from his fellow man, and from nature. His most passionate striving is to return to the world of union which was his home before he disobeyed. His desire is to give up reason, self-awareness, choice, responsibility, and to return to the womb, to Mother-Earth, to the darkness where the light of conscience and knowledge does not yet shine. He wants to escape from his newly gained freedom and to lose the very awareness which makes him human.*
>
> —ERICH FROMM, *You Shall Be As Gods*

[b] Or *to Adam*
[c] In Heb *Eve* resembles the word for *living*
[d] Or *for Adam*

We are sinful not only because we have eaten of the Tree of Knowledge, but also because we have not yet eaten of the Tree of Life. The state in which we are is sinful, irrespective of guilt.
—FRANZ KAFKA, *The Third Notebook*

It's not always easy to be living in this world of pain
You're gonna be crashing into stone walls again and again
It's alright, it's alright
Though you feel your heart break
You're only human, you're gonna have to deal with heartache

Just like a boxer in a title fight
You got to walk in that ring all alone
You're not the only one who's made mistakes
But they're the only thing that you can truly call your own
—BILLY JOEL, "*You're Only Human*"

❖ *The Consequences of the Fall*

As is often the case with other narratives in the early chapters of Genesis (Gen. 4:9-10; 11:5; 18:21), Genesis 3 has the appearance of an investigative trial. After gathering the evidence and receiving testimonies from the accused, God now shifts His role as interrogator to that of prosecuter. Rabbinic tradition derives an important lesson from these narratives: judges should not rush to make a decision without first considering all the evidence. Prior to that time, there is always a presumption of innocence.[625]

3:14 וַיֹּאמֶר יְהוָה אֱלֹהִים אֶל־הַנָּחָשׁ כִּי עָשִׂיתָ זֹּאת – The LORD God said to the serpent, "Because you have done this — Rashi raises an obvious question, "Why didn't God interrogate the serpent for its role in causing Adam and Eve to stumble?" Rashi answers:

> From here we learn that we may not intercede in favor of one who entices people to idolatry, for had He asked him, "Why did you do this?" he could have answered, "The words of the Master and the words of the pupil—whose words do we obey?" In other words, Adam and Eve should have obeyed God rather than the serpent.[626]

Rashi's insight serves as a paradigm for anyone who willfully entices his fellow to apostasy (Deut. 13:6–9). The basis of this interpretation comes from this text right here.

---

625 On Genesis 11:5, Rashi notes: "He did not need to do this, except to teach judges not to condemn a defendant until they have seen the case and understood it" (Midrash Tanhuma Noah 18 [S. Buber ed.]). *Cf.* Rashi's notes on Genesis 18:21 concerning the fate of the Sodomites.
626 See BT Sanhedrin 29a.

Seducing an innocent to commit a crime is a morally punishable offense in the eyes of the Divine. The serpent's punishment is consistent with a later notion: animals that harm human beings are accountable.[627] Benno Jacob adds that is the first passage in the Tanakh that speaks about the importance of divine justice, the principle of "measure for measure" for "as you have done so shall it be done to you."[628] Ephrem the Syrian (306-373) proposes a different answer:

> When Adam and Eve were questioned, and were found to be lacking in remorse or true contrition, God went down to the serpent—not with a question—but in order to exact punishment. For whenever there is an opportunity for repentance, it is appropriate to ask questions, but to someone who is a stranger to repentance, He employs a language of retribution. Thus, when God says to the serpent "Because you have done this . . ." The serpent does not reply, "I did not do so," because it was afraid to lie; nor does it say "I did it," because it was a stranger to repentance.[629]

אָרוּר אַתָּה מִכָּל־הַבְּהֵמָה וּמִכֹּל חַיַּת הַשָּׂדֶה – **cursed are you among all animals and among all wild creatures [of the field]** – "Cursing," when invoked, results in the withholding of divine blessing. Peaceful coexistence with the animal kingdom was about to come to a sudden end. Rashi cites one old rabbinic opinion attributed to an Amora, Rav Yehuda, who claims that the gestation period of certain species of serpents lasts seven years, compared with other creatures whose gestation period is much shorter (cf. BT Bekhorot 8a). This interpretation seems hard to believe, for the Talmud itself was certainly well aware of the fact that almost all reptiles lay eggs.[630]

עַל־גְּחֹנְךָ תֵלֵךְ – **upon your belly you shall go** – The only parallel to this phrase is Leviticus 11:42, which brands all such creatures as unclean.[631] Rashi deduces that originally the serpent had legs, but they were cut off. It is interesting to note that certain species of serpents possess vestigial hips and shoulders and have the ability to make a large portion of their bodies erect. Many archeological excavations at Assyrian sites have shown "clay figurines of the Mush-rushshu, or red dragon, a composite creature with the body of a lion, head and neck of a serpent, and a long tail."[632] In *Enuma elish*, the

---

[627] Cf. Gen. 9:5-6; Exod. 21:28; Lev. 20:15-16.

[628] *Genesis*, 48.

[629] *Christian Commentary on the Scriptures* op. cit., 88.

[630] See BT Hullin 64a. In *Torah Shelemah,* R. Menahem Kasher seems to sense the awkwardness of this passage and suggests that over time, the nature of snakes "changed." Kasher's strained comment takes the story too literally, rather than parabolically.

[631] G. Wenham's commentary on Genesis 3:14.

[632] As noted by Pauline Albenda in "Of Gods, Men and Monsters on Assyrian Seals," *BA*, 41:1-4, 17.

monster Tiamat defeated by Marduk is depicted as a dragon or some form of serpent. It stands to reason that our passage most liklely contains a veiled polemic against the existence of such hybrid mythical creatures that represent the forces of chaos present in the universe.[633] All creatures, great and small, serve God's purpose in the grand scheme of Creation.

The serpent's punishment corresponds to its crime, as Rashi observes: "In proportion to its cunning and greatness was its downfall. What was the most cunning of God's living beings[634] became in the end the most cursed of all God's creatures."[635] Since it had exalted itself above man and creature alike, it was only appropriate that it should be condemned to move along on its belly. Its arrogance led to its debasement among God's creatures, as indicated by lowliness of rank in the hierarchy of animal existence.

וְעָפָר תֹּאכַל כָּל־יְמֵי חַיֶּיךָ – **and dust you shall eat all the days of your life** – "Dust" in this instance symbolizes abject humiliation.[636] The ancients believed that serpents subsisted on the dust of the earth. Among the Arabs there is a similar belief regarding demonic beings known as *jinn*, who are also described as eating dirt. However, the Torah is merely stating that serpents could survive by eating small rodents and creatures that move about on the "dust of the earth." The text thus provides an etiological explanation for why snakes crawl on the ground.

In the gentle spirit that is the trademark of so many Hasidic homilies, the Kotzker Rebbe (1787–1859) once commented on the serpent's fate of having to crawl on its belly and eat the dust of the earth. If the serpent had to derive sustenance from gold and silver, which are rare, we could understand the curse. But the abundance of dust means that the serpent would never go hungry. The Rebbe answers that this very abundance is itself the curse. Every other creature knows that its sustenance comes from the Divine. The serpent, totally self-sufficient from the dust, need never turn to anyone. For when one's daily fare is so plentiful, why turn to God?

---

633 Dragon imagery is often applied to Egypt (so Rahab, Isa. 30:7; and quite possibly 51:9, cf. v. 10; Ps. 87:4) or Pharaoh (Ezek. 29:3–5; 32:2–8). The imagery of YHWH battling with the dragon and the sea is found in the book of Job (3:8; 7:12; 9:8, 13; 26:12–13; 38:8–11; and 40:15–41:26).

634 The Targum of Pseudo-Jonathan paraphrases the text differently, "And the serpent was wiser to evil." Jerome reads, "Now the serpent was wiser than all the beasts upon the earth." Aquila and Theodotion understood the עָרוּם to mean *panourgon*, that is, "worthless" and "sly." So by means of this word are described cunning and slyness rather than wisdom" cited from *St. Jerome's Hebrew Questions on Genesis*, trans. Robert Hayward, (Oxford: Clarendon Press, 1995, 32).

635 Cf. Gen. Rabbah 19:1.

636 Cf. Pss. 44:25; 72:9; Isa. 49:23; Amos 2:6–7; Job 30:19; 42:6, Mic. 7:17, *et al.*

3:15 וְאֵיבָה אָשִׁית בֵּינְךָ וּבֵין הָאִשָּׁה וּבֵין זַרְעֲךָ וּבֵין זַרְעָהּ הוּא יְשׁוּפְךָ רֹאשׁ וְאַתָּה תְּשׁוּפֶנּוּ עָקֵב – **I will put enmity between you and the woman, and between your offspring and hers; he will strike your head, and you will strike his heel."** – As long as the serpent remains on its belly, it poses little threat. However, should it raise its head, it is a sure sign that it is ready to attack. Thus, treading on the serpent is used in this sense as a metaphor for overcoming or defeating it.

3:16 אֶל־הָאִשָּׁה אָמַר הַרְבָּה אַרְבֶּה עִצְּבוֹנֵךְ וְהֵרֹנֵךְ – **To the woman he said, "I will greatly increase your pangs in childbearing"** – Several wordplays are present. The pain of childbirth (עִצָּבוֹן = *ʿiṣṣāḇôn* and עֶצֶב = *ʿéṣeḇ*) that a woman experiences (Gen. 3:16), is linked with the pain of manual labor (עִצָּבוֹן) that a man experiences (Gen. 3:17). Both results come about as a direct consequence of eating the fruit of the forbidden tree. Cassuto points out another subtle wordplay in the text. The word *tree* עֵץ (*éṣ*) has the same first two radicals as the word for pain עָצֶב *(ʿāṣēḇ).* Cassuto further explains: "It was with respect to עֵץ that the man and the woman sinned, and it was with עַצֶּבֶת *(ʿăṣeḇah* = "pain") and עִצָּבוֹן *(ʿiṣṣāḇôn* = "toil, suffering") that they were punished." [637] Each of these puns points to common etiology regarding the origin of human suffering, resulting as a direct consequence of human disobedience.

The NRSV converts the entire Hebrew text הַרְבָּה אַרְבֶּה עִצְּבוֹנֵךְ וְהֵרֹנֵךְ into one salient theme focusing on the pangs of childbearing. However, the older translations take a different approach, which lend themselves to a greater variety of nuances: "I will greatly multiply your pains and your groanings" (LXX); "I will multiply your sorrows, and your conceptions" (VUL); "I will greatly multiply thy sorrow and thy conception" (KJV); "I will greatly multiply your pain" (ASV). Newer translations read more like the NRSV: "I will intensify the pangs of your childbearing" (NAB); "I will greatly increase your pains in childbearing" (NJB); "I will make most severe your pangs in childbearing" (NJPS); "I shall give you great labor in childbearing" (REB).

Rashi and Ibn Ezra once again spar on the meaning of this passage and see the text as more nuanced than these noted newer biblical translations. Ibn Ezra breaks up the verse to encompass two major aspects of a woman's life, explaining that עִצְּבוֹנֵךְ *(ʿiṣṣəḇônēḵ)* denotes the initial pain a woman experiences when she loses her virginity, whereas the second aspect of וְהֵרֹנֵךְ (*wəhērōnēḵ*) suggests the pain she experiences during childbirth.

637 *Genesis,* Vol. I, 165.

Like Ibn Ezra, Rashi, also sees the woman's pain in two distinct stages: עִצְּבוֹנֵךְ denotes the pain of rearing children, while the aspect of וְהֵרֹנֵךְ connotes the pain of pregnancy. Rashi's position is correct insofar as the noun עֶצֶב is sometimes used to convey mental discomfort, emotional grief, and sorrow as well (see Gen. 6:6), while Ibn Erza is correct in accentuating the physical pain (Prov. 5:10; 14:23) associated with being a woman.

It is surprising that neither Ibn Ezra nor Rashi considers the possibility that עִצְּבוֹנֵךְ can denote the experience of menstruation—a point that was raised by Seforno and later by Malbim (1809-1879). This interpretation has advantages over both Ibn Ezra and Rashi in that there is a flow and evolution to a woman's pain that begins with her experiencing the discomfort of her menstrual cycle, the accompanying pain with the loss of her virginity, and leading to the physical pain of giving birth. Psychological pain is also associated with raising children; even after the children are grown, the mother never ceases to worry about her offspring—or for that matter the grandchildren! The pain of childbirth is such that the bonds of mother and child are deeply etched into the mother's soul for having endured so much for her infant. As Erich Fromm has noted on several occasions, the depth of love is determined by the degree of labor one exerts.[638] One cannot have a deep love for something one has not labored for, as God told Jonah:

> But God said to Jonah, "Is it right for you to be angry about the bush?" And he said, "Yes, angry enough to die." Then the LORD said, "You are concerned about the bush, for which you did not labor and which you did not grow; it came into being in a night and perished in a night." (Jonah 4:9-10)

❖ *Etiological Explanations and Their Limitations*

As the 15th century Jewish thinker, R. Joseph Albo notes, the stories of the Edenic garden are meant to account for the difficulties of life that human beings experience.[639] More often than not, etiologies[640] in the Tanakh correspond to a

[638] Erich Fromm, *The Art of Loving: An Enquiry into the Nature of Love* (San Francisco: Harper and Brothers, 1956), 26.

[639] *Sefer ha-Ikkarim*, 1:11.

[640] An etiology concerns itself with the study of causes and origins. As a philosophical investigation, the philosopher tries to understand the nature of existence and how it came to be. In Genesis, etiologies serve to explain the origin of a custom, an event, a name, a geographical formation, an object, a shrine. Other etiologies include: the first act of Creation, the first day, the first week, the first Sabbath, the origins of marriage, menstruation, pregnancy, family dysfunction, the first dietary law, the first farmer and shepherd, the first conflict between the shepherd and a famer, the origin of sibling rivalry; the first fratricide, the first fugitive, the first city, the first ship-builder, the first natural catastrophe, and so on.

negative evaluation and many people throughout the ages have read this particular story as a justification for a hierarchy where women are subordinated to men. This is precisely the point of encounter where a modern reader must insist that while etiologies provide explainations for the causes and origins of a social attitude, they should not be read as prescriptions *for how the world ought to be.* To go one step futher, many of these prescriptions characterize a world as it ought NOT to be. Etiological explanations have their limitations, especially when ethical issues are involved; they should never prevent a person or a community from critically reexamining the basis of the etiological explanation's internal logos. The failure to do so can sometimes lead to disastrous consequences.

One example that comes to mind is the use of anesthetics in childbirth. In 1847, Church leaders quoted God's curse to Eve: "in pain shall you bring forth children." How could she fulfill the biblical punishment of bearing children in pain while being under the influence of chloroform? One wise doctor countered that scripturally, there was no harm in giving anesthetics to men, because God Himself put Adam into a deep sleep when He extracted his rib. However, the ecclesiastical bodies remained unconvinced when it came to the suffering of women who were in childbirth.[641]

Former Chief Rabbi of the British Commonwealth Immanuel Jakobovits writes in his *Jewish Medical Ethics* that as late as 1853, even before the discovery of anesthesia, there was an incident in France where two women—one pregnant and one who aided her with some artificial means to ease the pain of her delivery—were both burnt to death for attempting to circumvent Eve's curse. Toward the end of the nineteenth century, chloroform was banned by the Catholic Church. The ban remained in effect until 1949, when painless births were permitted.[642] A society's etiological explanations when left unanalyzed, can become a source for social dysfunction. There are broad implications that go beyond just the Edenic story, and a contemporary believer ought to take etiological explanations of any practice and hold them up to ethical scrutiny.

Lastly, in the Pseudepigraphal *Book of Adam and Eve*, the ancients propose a surprisingly sensitive reading of the text that demonstrates a willingness to deconstruct the text in a manner that is respectful toward women in general, and Eve in particular: "And he went and found her in great distress. And Eve said: 'From the moment I saw thee, my lord, my grief-laden soul was refreshed. And now entreat the Lord God on my behalf to hearken unto thee and look upon me and free me from my awful pains.' And Adam entreated the Lord for Eve."[643]

---

[641] See Andrew D. White, *A History of the Warfare of Science with Theology in Christendom*, originally published by Appleton in 1896, reprinted in 1993 as part of the Great Minds Series by Prometheus Books, Vol. II, 60.

[642] Immanuel Jakobovits, *Jewish Medical Ethics* (New York: Bloch Publishing, 1959), 104.

[643] *Book of Adam and Eve,* 20.1.

❖ *The Nexus of Creativity, Work, and Love*

Why should childbearing or physical labor be so painful? All acts of true creativity come with a degree of pain and struggle. The eighteenth century Italian Kabbalist, R. Moshe Hayim Luzzato, describes the "bread of shame" as a metaphor for one who receives the benefits of God's blessings without ever having to expend effort; self-respect is always linked to work and labor. Regarding this truth, the Jerusalem Talmud further says: "When a man receives charity from the hand of another, he cannot look at him straight in the face without feeling a residue of embarrassment."[644] God, in His infinite wisdom, wants human beings not to be mere receivers of blessing and goodness, but to earn their own way—both physically and spiritually. The greater effort one exerts, the more beloved does the product of one's work become. There is no doubt that a mother loves her child so dearly because of the pain she has had to endure for her young. The same is also true with fathering—the more a father gives of his time and attention toward his children, the deeper he feels connected to them. Certainly, when a man struggles at his work, he too, can take great pride in earning his bread.

As Fromm explains, love grows and matures in proportion to the labor that is expended, for true creativity is an expression of our own human uniqueness and is therefore an everlasting source of pride—whether it be giving birth and nourishing new life, our jobs, tending our garden, our personal artistic ventures—human beings love what they personally create. Fromm emphasizes this point, "Love is the active concern for the life and the growth of that which we love. Where this active concern is lacking, there is no love." [645]

❖ *Are Infants "Born in Sin"?*

בְּעֶצֶב תֵּלְדִי בָנִים – in pain you shall bring forth children – Observe how the verse says "in pain," and not "in sin you shall bring forth children." The notion of innocent children being born in a state of sin is one of the most important distinctions separating Judaism from the salvation oriented faith of post-Augustinian Christianity. In Augustine's theological worldview, to exist in an unbaptized state is to risk being condemned to eternal damnation. For all the countless billions of human beings not born Christian or even exposed to Christianity, the message is ominously clear. There is only one place all nonbelievers will end up—and it's certainly not Heaven. Even

---

[644] See J.T. Orlah 1:3; and R. Moshe Hayim Luzzato, *Sefer Tevunot Hashem*, Chapter 1.

[645] Erich Fromm, *The Art of Loving: An Enquiry into the Nature of Love, op. cit.*, 26.

unbaptized infants were condemned to experience a "second death" (Augustine's pseudonym for Hell).[646] "Infants are from birth subject to the wrath of God because they belong, as born of Adam, to the mass of perdition."[647]

As mentioned earlier, Julian of Eclanum was a devoted follower of Pelagius, and he called Augustine's God "a persecutor of infants, who throws tiny babies into the eternal fire."[648] While Augustine's position has remained the official stance of the Vatican, nevertheless, there are some thinkers within the Church who have second thoughts on how this debate should be resolved. Karl Rahner (1904–84), one of the Catholic church's foremost twentieth century thinkers, felt compelled to ask, "Was it all false, the case made by Pelagius and Julian of Eclanum against the universally triumphant Augustine? Were they not in many respects vindicated afterward in a slow development that has lasted to our day?"[649] For a more extensive examination of Rahner's view, see Excursus 25.

Sometimes the view of an outsider can add to a discussion. As a Jewish researcher, I wonder whether Augustine might have been partially correct, considering the violent history of the 20th century. As the 21st century unfolds, there is no lessening of genocidal tendencies among those rogue nations seeking to undermine civilization through whatever fierce means possible. One must pause before passing judgement on Augustine. Perhaps there are people who are born (for whatever the reason might be) morally defective, yet a human being is and must remain capable of transcending his biological, societal and parental programming. Ultimately, every person can choose, as Maimonides once wrote, to be as righteous as Moses himself, or as wicked as Pharaoh. We are what we choose to be.

❖ *Sexism is not Pre-ordained*

וְאֶל־אִישֵׁךְ תְּשׁוּקָתֵךְ – yet your desire shall be for your husband– This famous scriptural passage has long served as a justification for male dominance. Reflective of this point of view are the opinions of Ibn Ezra and Calvin, who write that in a post-Edenic world, a woman's desire will be totally subject to that of her husband and that she must be under his authority to do his bidding. "Her desire, whatever it may be, will not be her own. She cannot do what she wishes, for her husband rules over her like a despot and whatever she wishes is subject to his will."[650] Rashi views the dominance of

---

646 Based on Rev. 2:11; 20:6,14; 21:8 cf. *Concerning the Necessity of Grace for All*, Chapter 40.

647 *Retractations*, Book 2, Ch. 36.

648 Augustine, *Against Julian* I, 48.

649 Karl Rahner, *Theologie der Gergenwart*, 1977, 2, 76.

650 John Calvin's *Commentary on Genesis* 3:16.

men over women in purely sexual terms, for it is the way of men to dictate when they will have marital relations.

Like other Semitic societies, Biblical Hebrew typically refers to the husband as the בַּעַל (*bá῾al*) signifying "owner," or "lord," of his wife only in a formal and legal sense, but not necessarily in an intimate context.[651] However, the prophet Hosea envisions a time when the ideal spiritual model of an intimate relationship will not be predicated upon power and lordship, but rather based upon a loving relationship between equals who cherish one another as life-mates (Hos. 2:18). This is indicated by the term Hosea uses, אִישִׁי (*ʾîšî*) "*my* man" or "*my* husband" (emphasis added) and denotes genuine mutuality and deep affection—all of which is implied in Genesis 2:24. For further discussion on this point, see Excurses 21 and 29.

Another Interpretive View: yet your desire shall be for your husband – R. Avraham Saba (15th century) makes an interesting if not controversial homiletical interpretation based upon Kimchi's interpretation of Isaiah 26:16-17. Saba observes that God imbued women with a wondrous quality—at the time they give birth, they crave for the presence of their husbands to be with them—despite the fact that the husbands may be regarded by some wives as the perpetrators of their current painful condition. By the same token, argues Kimchi, "Israel too craves for God's Presence as they suffer in exile, despite the fact that it is God, Who is the ultimate cause of their dilemma." In the case of the woman who is in travail, she endures great pain, but knowing that her husband is lovingly present makes her pain more bearable. Israel's birthpangs are no different; she can endure great sufferings, but having the knowledge that God is still with her, enables Israel to bear her pain as she witnesses God's Presence to the world.

וְהוּא יִמְשָׁל־בָּךְ – and he shall rule over you — The verb for "rule" (מָשַׁל = *mašl*) implies a lord/servant type of relationship (Gen. 37:8). However, there are numerous biblical precepts that restrict the master's treatment of his slave. Even if a master so much as slaps a slave, and makes his skin red (21:25), he goes free. In numerous cases, a מוֹשֵׁל (*môšēl* = "ruler") is often used metaphorically to describe a tyrant, one who rules with disregard for the governed.[652] John Skinner writes, "The idea of tyrannous exercise of power does not lie in the verb; but it means that the woman is wholly subject to the man, and so liable to the arbitrary treatment sanctioned by the marriage customs of the East. It is noteworthy that to the writer this is not the ideal relation of the sexes."[653]

---

651 See J.C. de Moor and M.J Mulder's article on בַּעַל (TDOT: Vol. 2, 181-200).

652 Cf. Isa. 3:4,14:5,19:4; Jer. 51:46; Prov. 29:12; Ecc. 9:17, passim.

653 John Skinner, *A Critical and Exegetical Commentary on Genesis*. ICC. 2d ed. (Edinburgh: Clark, 1930), 83.

Another Interpretative View: and he shall rule over you — Soloveitchik points out a psychological nuance to the text. As a result of the Fall, Adam and Eve experience loneliness in their "otherness." Each one yearns for companionship and emotional intimacy. In the post-Edenic world, Adam's relationship to Eve takes on a "subject-object relationship seeking to dominate and subordinate" the Other (comparable to Buber's "I and It" relationship).[654] Philosopher and Rabbi, Joseph B. Soloveitchik notes:

> Adam of today wants to appear as master-hero and to subject Eve to his rule and dominion, be it ideological, religious, economic, or political. As a matter of fact, the divine curse addressed to Eve after she sinned, "and he shall rule over thee" has found its fulfillment in our modern society. The warm personal relationship between two individuals has been supplanted by a formal subject-object relationship which manifests itself in a quest for power and supremacy.[655]

Soloveitchik's description fits the historical way in which Western culture has treated its women until recent times. The simple fact is that men have always tried to control and repress a women's sexuality. The women's liberation movement which began in the early part of the 20th century has radically altered cultural perspectives on how men are expected to treat women. In light of the changing social paradigm, feminist theologian Phyllis Trible and others advocate newer hermenutical approaches to the text that allow for more egalitarian interpretations—especially when viewed through the lens of Song of Songs, which sees this book as an intrabiblical commentary on Genesis 2. From this perspective, the institution of marriage is based on loving, caring, and mutuality rather than power and superiority. [656] When men exploit women and justify this ill-treatment as being "biblically endorsed," they are in effect giving their stamp of approval to a fallen world that has infected the most intimate of human relationships and at the same

---

[654] Phyllis Trible contrasts the nature of the male-female relationship depicted in Genesis and the Song of Songs in the manner that is somewhat reminiscent of Soloveitchik's theological insight: "In Eden, the yearning of the woman for harmony with her man continued after disobedience. Yet the man did not reciprocate; instead, he ruled over her to destroy unity and pervert sexuality. Her desire became his dominion. But in the Song, male power vanishes. His desire becomes her delight. Another consequence of disobedience is thus redeemed through the recovery of mutuality in the garden of eroticism. Appropriately, the woman sings the lyrics of this grace: 'I am my lover's and for me is his desire'" (*God and the Rhetoric of Sexuality*, *op. cit.*, 160).

[655] See R. J.B. Soloveitchik, "Confrontation," (*Tradition*, 1964), 55-80, 63-64.

[656] Although the marital metaphor is used elsewhere in the Tanakh, the relationship of God and Israel is often depicted in patriarchal terms (cf. Exod. 34:15–16; Lev 17:7; Hos. 2:2; Ezek. 23:9-10, 20). In contrast, the male-female relationship depicted in the Song of Songs is of an egalitarian quality. Together, they celebrate the fullness of their love in love's entire splendor. The Edenic story sees the woman as being more intelligent and aware, whereas in the Song of Songs, the woman initiates lovemaking; man and woman also appear to have a more shared responsibility in the garden (Song. 1:6-8; 7:12).

time alienates humans from God. God's intention from the time of the Fall, is for men and women to reconstitute their roles as helpers and supporters for one another through their relational life-journeys. The process of individuation seeks to restore humanity to the state of original blessing—not to keep humanity shackled to a retrogressive theology of human fallenness.

3:17 וּלְאָדָם אָמַר – And to the man He said – A more correct rendering is – **And unto Adam He said** (NJPS) – For the first time, the noun is used here in the Masoretic text as a personal name without the definite article. As previously mentioned, when the noun אָדָם (*ʾāḏām*) has the prefix of the definite article, it is to be considered as an appellative, and is the equivalent to "the human race."

כִּי־שָׁמַעְתָּ לְקוֹל אִשְׁתֶּךָ – Because you have listened to the voice of your wife – God refuses to accept Adam's feeble justification. Adam has no excuse for his behavior—she did not force him to eat, he ate freely of his own volition. It is no coincidence that later on in Genesis 21:12, God instructs Abraham to *listen to his wife Sarah* concerning the expulsion of Hagar and her son. Already, the biblical narrator wishes to intimate a point that the Jewish mystics would later explicitly acknowledge: Abraham and Sarah's relationship is akin to Adam and Eve's—Abraham is like the new Adam, while Sarah is the new Eve, and his acquiescence to her will in this one respect, represents a correction (a *tikkun*) of Adam's sin.[657] Expressing this thought in a more practical way, Oliver Wendell Holmes observes: "Man has his will—but woman has her way."[658]

Another Interpretive View: – **Because you have listened to the voice of your wife** – Adam did not eat the forbidden fruit because he believed that the serpent's words were correct, rather, he ate the fruit so that his wife would not be upset with him for refusing.

וַתֹּאכַל מִן־הָעֵץ אֲשֶׁר צִוִּיתִיךָ לֵאמֹר לֹא תֹאכַל מִמֶּנּוּ – and have eaten of the tree about which I commanded you, "You shall not eat of it" – Rabbinic tradition argues that Adam can not plead innocence since he heard the proscription directly from God. However, Eve is different since she never hears the prohibition directly from YHWH. In her defense, one could argue that it was understandably easy for the serpent to seduce her because she had only heard the prohibition secondhand, whereas Adam has no such excuse.

---

[657] There are several other analogies which we will later point out when we examine the Abraham cycle.

[658] Oliver Wendell Holmes, *The Autocrat of the Breakfast-Table* (Boston: Houghton, Mifflin, 1916,) 42.

אֲרוּרָה הָאֲדָמָה בַּעֲבוּרֶךָ בְּעִצָּבוֹן תֹּאכְלֶנָּה כֹּל יְמֵי חַיֶּיךָ – **cursed is the ground because of you; in toil you shall eat of it all the days of your life** – Labor is not a consequence of the Fall; Adam has been given the task of tending the garden even before the Fall. It is the monotony and difficulty of labor that are the consequences of the Fall. Because both Adam and Eve fail to show proper stewardship of God's creation, Adam has to contend with the reality of struggling for a living. The narrative wishes to demonstrate that by violating the boundaries originally established by God, Adam disrupts the harmony that exists in the celestial garden. It is interesting to note that the estrangement from the Divine leads to an estrangement from nature. Primal man gives up his natural innate ability to feel at one with the world of Creation. The scriptural narrative wishes to stress that to grasp the significance of the Fall, one must pay heed to the separation and alienation caused by this violation of divinely prescribed boundaries.

On a deeper level, Adam's new tension with nature comes as a direct result of allowing his "false self" to stand between him and the Divine. For humans to find harmony in the universe and in the world of nature around them, they must first cultivate harmony within themselves. Failure to do so will and must perpetuate the struggle humans have with everything around them. Thomas Merton focuses on the existential dilemma that has long characterized the discord between science and religion:

> After Adam had passed through the center of himself and emerged on the other side to escape from God by putting himself between himself and God, he mentally reconstructed the whole universe in his own image and likeness. That is the painful and useless labor which has been inherited by his descendants—the labor of science without wisdom; the mental toil that pieces together the fragments that never manage to coalesce in one completely integrated whole: the labor of action without contemplation, that never ends in peace or satisfaction, since no task is finished without opening the way to ten more tasks that have to be done.[659]

3:18 וְקוֹץ וְדַרְדַּר תַּצְמִיחַ לָךְ וְאָכַלְתָּ אֶת־עֵשֶׂב הַשָּׂדֶה – **thorns and thistles it shall bring forth for you; and you shall eat the plants of the field.** – Whenever you sow any kinds of seeds, it will sprout thorns, thistles, artichokes and cardoons, which are edible only after preparation (Rashi).[660]

❖ *The Semantics of Bread and War*

3:19 בְּזֵעַת אַפֶּיךָ תֹּאכַל לֶחֶם – **By the sweat of your face you shall eat bread** – The Mishnah says the production of bread involves eleven distinctive steps: sowing,

[659] Thomas Merton, *The New Man* (New York: Farrar, Straus, and Cudahy, 1961), 117–118.

[660] Cf. Gen. Rabbah 20:10. See also BT Beitzah 34a.

plowing, harvesting, binding sheaves, threshing, winnowing, selecting, grinding, sifting, kneading, and baking—all to produce one loaf of bread (BT Shabbat 73a).

It is no linguistic accident that the word for bread, לֶחֶם (*leḥem*), is also the root word of מִלְחָמָה (*milḥāma*)—the Hebrew word for war. Almost three millennia before Marx wrote his biting critique on Western society, the Torah recognized that the source of all human conflict is the eternal battle to find bread and scratch out a living. Medieval Hebrew grammarians point out that the meaning of לָחַם (*laḥām*) not only connotes "battle," but may also mean "join together," which has parallels in other Semitic languages, e.g., the Arabic words *lāḥhama* ("solder," "weld") and *luḥma* ("relationship"), which suggest the idea of coming together for a common meal, or for the purpose of combat.[661] Kimchi theorizes war is referred to as מִלְחָמָה (*milḥāma*) since the sword "consumes" the flesh of its warriors.[662]

While it is true that man would earn his bread by the sweat of his brow, he had to guard himself from thinking that he was the sole source of his livelihood. Indeed, material prosperity may lead to a complacency which encourages the thought that God is no longer necessary for one's life. To be spiritually impoverished is to be nothing more than a "wage slave"—someone who merely exists rather than someone who truly lives. Indeed, such an attitude could lead one away from God. While bread gives physical sustenance, it cannot nourish the needs of the soul. Human beings require meaning and a sense of purpose to experience a sense of true fulfillment. "One does not live by bread alone, but by every word that comes from the mouth of the LORD" (Deut. 8:3).

While one may read this passage (3:19) as a curse, in another sense it is a great blessing. Self-actualization of the soul cannot be achieved without conscious effort being expended. Rabbinic wisdom bears this principle out: "If a man says to you, I have laboured and not found, do not believe him. If he says, I have not laboured but still have found, do not believe him. If he says, I have laboured and found, you may believe him" (BT Megilla 6b). In simple terms, spiritual accomplishment is accorded to the person who expends the greatest degree of effort.

❖ *Should Death be Construed as a Punishment?*

עַד שׁוּבְךָ אֶל־הָאֲדָמָה כִּי מִמֶּנָּה לֻקָּחְתָּ כִּי־עָפָר אַתָּה וְאֶל־עָפָר תָּשׁוּב – until you return to the ground, for out of it you were taken; you are dust, and to dust

---

661 TDOT, Vol. 7, 521-533.

662 *Sefer HaSherashim*, 359

you shall return —The verse implies that death was construed not as a curse but as a natural occurrence. There is no illusion here that man would have lived forever had he not eaten of the forbidden fruit.[663] Death itself, as already noted,[664] is a part of nature's original design. Death is what human beings share with everything else that has ever lived; it is a part of the created order. Benno Jacob expresses a similar thought:

> *To dust shall you return*—It has been claimed that this sentence changes the former constitution of man and that death entered only through Adam's sin. The Bible very clearly indicates the opposite; the death of man is the consequence of his creation—everything returns to the place from which it has been taken; life is only a temporary separate existence of a piece of soil. The sinner and the innocent both die; the difference between them is only when and for what reason. This is certainly a somber view of man's destiny, but a necessary supplement to the happy view of chapter one. Life has the aspect of day and night; the Bible teaches the complete truth and can therefore not limit itself to one or the other.[665]

Having originated from the earth, it is only natural that age and deterioration would return man to his origin. Had Adam not sinned, his departure from the physical world would not have been filled with anxiety or pain; his soul would have made a peaceful transition to the next level of human existence.[666] So too, were our relationships with God, nature, and our fellow beings more hallowed, our fear of death would diminish considerably and we would experience oneness with God at our time of death. The fear of death comes as a result of the disorder that pervades so much of our relationships, creating a feeling of anxiety in ourselves and in the world around us. Were Adam less of a consumer, and more of a dispenser of the divine blessing to all of God's creations, he would have regarded death not as the last fearful frustration but as the natural end of a well-lived life.

3:20 וַיִּקְרָא הָאָדָם שֵׁם אִשְׁתּוֹ חַוָּה כִּי הִוא הָיְתָה אֵם כָּל־חָי – The man named his wife Eve, because she was the mother of all living. — We have already noted in 2:23 that Eve's orginal name may have been *Isha* ("woman"), but the new name takes on a special meaning in light of the primal couple's newly acquired existential awareness as Pelagius so noted. "Eve" means "life," and her name has become a mark of respect and honor for she would soon become the first primal mother of humankind. Perhaps Adam confers this new name upon her after she had already become pregnant; otherwise this whole passage would have little contextual meaning. Name-changing is never a fortuitous event in the scriptures; when it occurs, it always marks a profound change in

---

[663] Cf. *Aderet Eliyahu*, H. Gunkel, and John Skinner, *Genesis*, ICC, 2nd ed. (Edinburg: T. & T. Clark L.T. D., 1930), 88.

[664] See notes on Gen. 1:9; 2:9; 3:22.

[665] Ibid., 31.

[666] BT Sotah 14a.

the biblical character's personal destiny, as we will soon see in the cases of Abraham, Sarah, and Israel.

❖ *The World's First Designer Wear*

3:21 וַיַּעַשׂ יְהוָה אֱלֹהִים לְאָדָם וּלְאִשְׁתּוֹ כָּתְנוֹת עוֹר וַיַּלְבִּשֵׁם – **And the LORD God made garments of skins for the man and for his wife, and clothed them.** – Is there something more to this story than just an etiology as to why people wear clothes instead of walking around naked, or to inform the reader how the fashion industry first began? Everett Fox notes, "Once punishment has been pronounced, God cares for the man and the woman. Both aspects of God comprise the biblical understanding of His nature, and they are not exclusive of each other." Fox's point is well taken. The skin garments with which God clothed Adam and Eve would serve to remind them perpetually of God's provision. However, Benno Jacob sees God's provision of clothes as a mark of distinction that separates humankind from the animal world.[667] The rabbis deduce a beautiful ethical lesson from this verse. Later on, God would demand that the faith community of Israel emulate God's own behavior in clothing the naked:

> If you take someone's cloak in pledge, you will return it to him at sunset. It is all the covering he has; it is the cloak he wraps his body in; what else will he sleep in? If he appeals to me, I shall listen. At least with me he will find compassion.
>
> Exod. 22:26–27

> Is it not to share your bread with the hungry, and bring the homeless poor into your house; when you see the naked, to cover them, and not to hide yourself from your own kin?
>
> Isaiah 58:7

The rabbis stress the importance of emulating God's graciousness. Indeed, God's own ethical behavior must become the template for human righteousness and compassion.

> R. Hama son of R. Hanina [4th cent.] said: "After the LORD your God, shall you walk" (Deut. 13:5). But is it possible for a man to walk right behind the Divine Presence? Has it not already been said, "The LORD your God is a consuming fire"? (Deut. 4:24) True, but this is what the verse means: you are to emulate the ways of the Holy One. Just as He clothes the naked: "And the LORD God makes garments of skins for the man and for his wife, and clothed them" (Gen. 3:21), so must you clothe the naked. Just as the Blessed Holy One visits the sick regarding which is written, "The LORD appeared to Abraham near the great trees of Mamre" (Gen. 18:1), so should you visit the sick. Just as Blessed

---

[667] *Genesis,* 31.

> Holy One buries the dead: "He buried [Moses] in the valley" (Deut. 34:6), so should you bury the dead. Just as the Blessed Holy One comforts mourners: "And it came to pass after the death of Abraham that God bestowed blessing upon Isaac his son" (Gen. 25:11), so should you comfort mourners (Sotah 15a).[668]

Theologian John Shea explains: "To tell a story of God is to create a world, adopt an attitude, suggest a behavior. But the stories are first, while we are second. We are born into a community of storytellers. In interpreting our traditional stories of God we find out who we are and what we must do."[669] Every story compels reflection and dialogue. These simple but poignant narratives offer hope and ethical balance that can enrich the inner life with a sense of peacefulness.

❖ *From "Garments of Ethereal Light" to "Garments of Skins"*

Another Interpretive View: And the LORD God made garments of skins for the man and for his wife, and clothed them. — In contrast to the scholars that see the primal couple's clothing as a sign of divine grace and provision, some rabbinic and non-rabbinic sources set forth a radically contrarian view. A number of Midrashic texts have a strong affinity with the Gnostic writings of the second century.[670] One tradition, attributed to Rabbi Meir, purports that originally God had given Adam and Eve "garments of ethereal light."[671] However, after their disobedience, God gives them "garments of skins" instead. Some esoteric rabbinic texts maintain that Adam's ethereal nature was the sole reason the primordial serpent becomes jealous.[672] This Midrashic reading is, in part, based on a word play in Gen. 3:21 where the term עור (*ʿôr* ="skin") is explained as though it were written אור (*ʾôr*= "light").[673]

---

[668] In Jewish tradition acts of mercy consist of the following virtues: feeding the hungry; giving drink to the thirsty; clothing the naked; hospitality; visiting the sick; ministering to prisoners; burying the dead; feeding the hungry, supporting those who have fallen unto bad times, clothing the naked. Cf. (Isa. 58:7; Ezek. 18:7, 16; Tob. 1:16–17; 4:16; cf. Sir 7:34–35; 2 Enoch 9:1; *Abot* d'Rabbi Natan 7; Derech Eretz Raba 99. Derech Eretz Zutra 2; Mt. 25:35. Cf. Mat. 25:31-46).

[669] John Shea, *Stories of God* (Liguori, MO: Liguori Publications, 2007), 9.

[670] *The Nag Hammadi Library* VII 1, 8:14; I 4, 45:30-31.

[671] *Cf. Pirkê de Rabbi Eliezer* 14:20 and the Jerusalem Targum to Genesis 3:21.

[672] See *Ben Ish Chai, Parshat Berashit.*

[673] Evidently, R. Meir's Torah scroll must have had a scribal error, for it was found written "garments of light"(*ʾôr*). The Midrash reads, "This refers to Adam's garments, which were like a torch [shedding radiance], broad at the bottom and narrow at the top. Isaac the Elder said: They were as smooth as a fingernail and as beautiful as a jewel. R. Johanan said: They were like the fine linen garments which come from Bethshean (Gen. Rabbah 20:12). The Talmud also alludes to this in tractate Niddah: "R. Joshua b. Hananiah: *And the LORD God*

According to one Midrash, God overlaid Adam and Eve's bodies with a special ethereal skin, suffused with divine radiance. No sooner had they violated the command given them then this special outer layer dropped from them, and they realized their "naked" situation. There is a scriptural verse that supports this kind of gnostic interpretation. In Psalm 8:5, we read: "You made him a little lower than the heavenly beings and crowned him with glory and honor" (NIV)—but as a consequence of Adam's disobedience, humankind lost a part of its spiritual innocence. A different intrabiblical interpretation may also be found in Ezekiel's prophecy to the King of Tyre, whom he likens to Adam. The prophet Ezekiel describes Adam's garment as consisting of precious gems, e.g., carnelian, topaz, and beryl, chrysolite, onyx, and jasper, sapphire, garnet, and emerald (Eze. 28:13). This entire description is obviously meant to be metaphorical, conveying how Adam's body possessed a certain kind of iridescence that one would see in a precious gem. Both these scriptural passages may help explain why Adam and his wife felt so "naked," for they lost the celestial gifts with which God had endowed them, that distinguished them from the animal kingdom. This nakedness of soul consisted of not only feeling transparent before the Divine, but persisted even after he and his wife sewed for themselves a fig leaf girdle.

An interesting Christian parallel to this Midrashic reading is found in the writings of Origen (ca. 185-254). Origen, a neo-Platonic Christian thinker, envisions Paradise as an ethereal realm that was more spiritual in substance than it was physical. Jerome and some of the other Early Church Fathers found Origen's theory scandalous.[674] After their sin, God covered their bodies with skins of flesh because Adam and Eve had become fallen and earth-bound creatures.[675] Due to his adherence to the simple meaning of the Scriptures (which is evident from the Vulgate), Jerome rejects Origen's philosophical exposition of the Garden. Jerome views the story of the Fall primarily as an event that occurs in *real time*. In contrast, Origen sees the Fall as an event that symbolically takes place in *mythical time*. There is good reason to think that Rabbi Meir and Origen may have been well acquainted with some of the same Gnostic teachings pertaining to Adam and his spiritual transformation as a result of the Fall, whereby Adam loses his spiritual luminosity.

---

made garments of skins for the man and for his wife, and clothed them (Gen. 3:21). This teaches us that the Holy One, blessed be He, makes no skin for man before he is formed" (BT Niddah 25a). See Zohar I 71a and R. Isaac Luria's *Torah Commentary* on this passage.

[674] Jerome writes: "But if the water is visible and real, then the fig-tree and the rest of the timber must be real also, and Adam and Eve must have been originally formed with real and not phantasmal bodies, and not, as Origen would have us believe, have afterwards received them on account of their sin" (*Letters of Jerome, Letter 51.from Epiphanius*).

[675] Origen adds, "And the expulsion of the man and woman from Paradise and their beings clothed with tunics of skins (which God, because of the transgression of men made for those who had sinned) contain a certain secret and mystical doctrine (far transcending that of Plato) of the souls losing their wings, and being born downwards to earth, until it can lay hold of some stable resting-place" (*Origen Against Celsus,* Book 4, Ch. 40).

❖ *Conversion and the Return to Lost Innocence*

According to Jewish tradition, conversion to Judaism has long involved ritual immersion in a pool of water by the individual seeking cultic purification and spiritual renewal. When emerging from the ritual bath, the convert is considered to be in a state resembling that of a newborn baby—bereft of any vestige of one's former sinful condition. Early Christianity incorporated this ritual in its baptism ceremony, where nakedness and the absence of shame are considered vital for those who are being reborn in Christ. Anthropologist Jonathan Z. Smith explains that the symbolic undressing of the prospective convert represents the primal nudity of Adam and Eve—a return to lost innocence. The emergence from the baptismal pool also functions as a prefiguration of the resurrection (cf. Romans 6:1-5)—a time when the ordinary garments will have no significance; at this juncture of human evolution, the original ethereal garments Adam and Eve had lost will be returned to the human race once more. Citing the early church father Theodore, Smith notes:

> There are, thus, two different states of nakedness according to Theodore: The first is the nakedness of shame—of Adam and Eve after the Fall—a nakedness in which the postulant stands on the *cilicium* whose pricks remind him of his sinful state, a nakedness like that of a slave. The second state, which is like that of Adam and Eve before the Fall, is a nakedness without shame, a nakedness which will be fully realized by the believer only at the resurrection and for which a white shining garment is the anticipatory sign, a nakedness of transcendence.[676]

3:22 וַיֹּאמֶר יְהוָה אֱלֹהִים הֵן הָאָדָם הָיָה כְּאַחַד מִמֶּנּוּ לָדַעַת טוֹב וָרָע – **Then the LORD God said, "See, the man has become like one of us, knowing good and evil"** – To whom was God referring to? It has often been suggested that it is either meant as a plural of majesty or as a deliberative plural in which God directs the statement to Himself and is used in the way of self-encouragement. Some argue that God and His heavenly angelic court are endowed with the ability to discern good from evil, unlike the animal kingdom, which operates by instinct alone.[677] A strong argument could be made that these words uttered by God to the Heavenly retinue are said in the Lilliputian spirit of sarcasm and irony, as if to say, "Look at this tiny little earthling! This man acts as if he really knows about good and evil! Does he really believe that he has become like us?" Irony and sarcasm are frequently used in the Tanakh when speaking about how God reacts to humankind's hubris.

Aristotle explains that the philosopher conceives of εἰρωνεια (*eironeia* = "irony") as "the contrary to boastful exaggeration; it is a self-deprecating concealment of one's

---

[676] Jonathan Z. Smith, *Map is not Territory: Studies in the History of Religions* (Chicago: University of Chicago Press, 1993), 12.

[677] See notes on Gen. 1:26.

powers and possessions; it shows better taste to deprecate than to exaggerate one's virtues."[678] In all such instances of irony, the intention of the speaker is the exact opposite of what is actually being said.[679] The notion of God having "a sense of humor" also occurs in Genesis 21:6, with the birth of Isaac, and with Exodus 10:2.

וְעַתָּה פֶּן־יִשְׁלַח יָדוֹ וְלָקַח גַּם מֵעֵץ הַחַיִּים וְאָכַל וָחַי לְעֹלָם – and now, he might reach out his hand and take also from the tree of life, and eat, and live forever – It is remarkable that it never occurs to Adam or his wife to take a "taste" from the Tree of Life; throughout the story of Genesis 3 this superb tree plays no part. The fruit is there—ready to pluck. Unlike the Tree of Knowledge, there are no prohibitions banning the first couple from enjoying its fruit. Paradoxically, no one thinks it worthwhile to taste the succulent fruit and live forever. Instead, their eyes focus only on the Tree of Knowledge. Why is this so? My own suggestion is that one of the greatest illusions human beings have harbored since the beginning of time is the idea that we will physically live forever. Anthropologist Ernest Becker (1924-1974) explains that the fear of death is not something that comes naturally to a person. It is not a quality human beings are born with. Studies indicate that a child has no perception of death per se until the ages of five or six years old. The concept of an absolute negation, such as death, is foreign to the psyche at this age and the child only comes to realize the inevitability of death when reaching nine to ten years of age. What a child does experience firsthand are the feelings of separation anxiety whenever his caregiver is unavailable to provide him with his immediate wants and needs.[680] Even though we rationally know that we will not live forever, the denial of our death is a natural part of our psychological makeup. We get it honestly from our primal parents who, like us, could not imagine that they too would someday die. This could explain why it never occurs to Adam and Eve to eat the fruit of immortality, even though it is right there in front of them.

Another Interpretive View: and now, he might reach out his hand and take also from the tree of life, and eat, and live forever – This statement may be a continuation of the last comment (Then the LORD God said, "See, the man has become like one of us"), which God said in sarcasm, as if to say, "Look what this pathetic little earthling is looking to do next—he wants to become immortal by eating the fruit of the Tree of Life." So what does God do to drive home the point that man and woman will have to work hard for the rest of their life? "The LORD God sent him forth from the garden of Eden." Perhaps God forbids Adam to eat of the Tree of Life more out of a sense of concern and pity. Without developing and improving his nature, Adam would never

[678] *Nichomachean Ethics*, 1108a—1119d.

[679] Elsewhere in his tract on *Rhetoric (*Book 3), Aristotle also notes that irony involves self-deprecating humor, "a mockery of oneself . . . the jests of the ironical man are at his own expense."

[680] Ernest Becker, *The Denial of Death* (New York: Free Press, 1973), 13-14.

have derived satisfaction from his newly achieved immortality. Such a gift might have proven to be more of a curse than a blessing. Without death, man would stagnate, remaining forever as an immature *puer aeternus* (eternal youth).

3:23 וַיְשַׁלְּחֵהוּ יְהוָה אֱלֹהִים מִגַּן־עֵדֶן – therefore the LORD God sent him forth from the garden of Eden – The garden of Eden is now off limits to him. However, because Adam enjoyed the garden so much, he finds it difficult to leave and might even desire to return; therefore, "He drove out the man; and at the east of the garden of Eden he placed the cherubim" (v. 24). Like a landlord whose tenants refuse to pay the rent, God evicts His tenants. Here is one of the first examples of "tough love" in the Tanakh. God does not function as an enabler, nor does He foster spiritual or moral co-dependency. The Creator does not rescue the primal couple from the consequences of their moral choices. Their acquistion of freedom comes with a price; spiritual growth and evolution cannot occur unless both the man and woman suffer the consequences of their actions. Once again, we see what is true with the first human couple, has remained true with every human being since.

לַעֲבֹד אֶת־הָאֲדָמָה אֲשֶׁר לֻקַּח מִשָּׁם – to till the ground from which he was taken – M. Henry notes that Adam and Eve are not subject to any further punishment.

> He was sent to a place of toil, not to a place of torment. He was sent to the ground, not to the grave, to the work-house, not to the dungeon, not to the prison-house, to hold the plough, not to drag the chain. His tilling the ground would be recompensed by its fruits. Observe, then, that though our first parents were excluded from the privileges of their state of innocence, yet they were not abandoned to despair. God's thoughts of love designed for them a state of probation on new terms.[681]

3:24 וַיְגָרֶשׁ אֶת־הָאָדָם – He drove out the man – The root גָּרַשׁ (*garš*) denotes an effective separation between persons (as in divorce) or groups (as in exile and expulsion).[682] Ugaritic and Moabite languages also attest to the meaning "to drive out." In Arabic, *jaraša* means "expose publicly,"while *zajara*, connotes "drive away" (HALOT: 204). In terms of our text, God had driven man out of a paradisiacal existence where he has lived in close proximity to God, to a profane and secular existence where he must struggle to find the meaning of his existence.

---

[681] Matthew Henry, *Commentary on the Whole Bible: Complete and Unabridged in One Volume* (Peabody, MA: Hendrickson, 1996, c.1839), 35.

[682] Cf. Gen. 21:14, 25:6, 28:5, 45:7.

❖ The Existential Meaning of Adam's Expulsion

The Zohar sees a talionic purpose to this expulsion: Since humankind chooses to "divorce the Shekhinah" (the Divine Presence) from their lives, the primal couple must live with the consequences of their spiritual divorce. More often than not, humankind still divorces the Divine from becoming the center of his/her life. What has happened long before, continues to reverberate with every defiant decision to live a life without God. Erich Fromm writes:

> But he cannot go back. The acts of disobedience, the knowledge of good and evil, self-awareness are irreversible. There is no way to turn back. Man . . . can solve this dichotomy only by going forward. Man has to experience himself as a stranger in the world, estranged from himself, and from nature, in order to be able to become one again with himself, with his fellow man and with nature, on a higher level. . . . Man creates the historical process which began with the first act of freedom—the freedom to disobey—to say "no."[683]

The Edenic Fall is an unalterable event in nascent humanity's evolution toward becoming self-conscious of its spiritual destiny. Ironically, the serpent's words ring true. With their act of disobedience, humanity acquires the ability to see their existence in terms of opposites—*but this knowledge results in immediate and far-reaching consequences*. Humankind no longer feels an instinctual oneness with Creation; the bifurcation of good and evil, past and future, God and humanity uncovers a world riddled with contradiction, dissonance, and paradox. However, despite the polarities warring from within the soul, humankind never loses its nostalgic yearning to regain an Edenic existence—a return to the Divine womb. Spiritual homelessness is now poised to give rise to a more conscious evolution born from blood, sweat, and tears.

וַיַּשְׁכֵּן מִקֶּדֶם לְגַן־עֵדֶן – **and at the east of the garden of Eden he placed** – As with other references to "east" found in the book of Genesis (e.g., 4:16. 11:2; 13:11) the term *east* signifies the withdrawal of the Divine Presence.[684]

אֶת־הַכְּרֻבִים – **the cherubim** – Western art since the time of the Renaissance traditionally depicts the cherubim as chubby-faced angel-children with wings, but such a description hardly seems to fit the contextual meaning of the present text, which indicates

---

[683] Erich Fromm, *You Shall Be As Gods* (New York: Harcourt, Rinehart, Winston, 1966), 87-88.

[684] Rabbinic tradition makes this same point, ויהי בנסעם מקדם - הסיעו עצמם מקדמונו של עולם "R. Leazar b. R. Simeon interpreted the passage regarding the tower builders, "They betook themselves away from the Ancient One (*Kadmon*) of the world, saying, 'We refuse to accept either Him or His Divinity'" (Gen. Rabbah 38:7).

they appeared to Adam and Eve as frightening creatures![685] Where did this notion come from? Actually, it derives from the Babylonian Talmud. The Sages ask, "What is the derivation of a cherub? "R. Abbahu construes כְּרוּב, as כְּרַבְיָא—a contraction of כּ "like" and רוֹבֶה (*roveh* = "child") for in Babylon they call a child רַבְיָא (*rabia*); thus, a cherub is an angelic being that has a face resembling a child (Rashi).[686] This rabbinic conjecture gave rise to the medieval imagery of chubby little angels, which appealed to Christian artists.

The actual origin of the cherubim remains controversial. It has been proposed that the cherubim may possibly be related to the Akkadian *kurabu*, denoting celestial interceding beings. Later in Israelite history, the cherubim guard the sacred objects housed in the Ark of the Covenant. A representation of the cherubim was fastened to the mercy seat of the ark[687] in the Holy of Holies[688] and functioned as the bearers of God's heavenly throne.[689] During the time of The First Temple, Solomon placed two enormous and elaborately carved images of winged cherubim, inside the innermost sanctuary of the Temple.[690] When placed together, they covered one entire wall; their outstretched wings providing a visible pedestal for the invisible throne, serving as a heavenly chariot from which the Divine ascends.

However, the cherubim imagery of Genesis probably resembled the mythic creatures portrayed in the art and literature of the various peoples living in the ancient Near East and Mediterranean world. They have often been likened to the winged bulls and lions of Babylonia and Assyria: colossal figures with human faces standing guard at the entrances of temples and palaces, or to the sphinxes of Egypt, whose task was to guard the sacred sanctuaries against encroaching evil spirits or other undesirable beings.[691] Some scholars believe the cherubim may have been wind-demons similar to the harpies of Greek mythology, while others think that the cherubim may have resembled the mythical griffins of Scythia that zealously kept watch over the country's gold. Similar conceptions are found in the Hittite culture as well.

---

[685] In contrast to his interpretation on Exodus 25:18, here, Rashi interprets cherubim here as "destructive angels" (cf. BT Sanhedrin 82a).

[686] Philo gives a different exposition, and suggests they represent God's creative and kingly power, but in Greek, Χερουβίν means "vast knowledge and science" (*Life of Moses* 2:97).

[687] Exod. 25:18 ff.

[688] 2 Chron. 3:7–14.

[689] Cf. 1 Sam 4:4; cf. 2 Sam 6:2; Isa 37:16; Eze. 10:20.

[690] 1 Kgs. 6:23–28.

[691] At Calah in the palace of Ashurnasirpal II, images of two-winged goddesses stand on either side of a sacred tree *The Ancient Near East in Pictures* (ANEP), Princeton 1954 (second ed. 1969), 656.

John Skinner cites an opinion that the cherubim of the Torah may have resembled the winged *genii* that are often depicted as standing by the tree of life in Babylonian art. "These figures are usually human in form with human heads, but sometimes combine the human form with an eagle's head, and occasionally the human head with an animal body."[692] Archeological finds have discovered neo-Assyrian seals portraying a fruit tree flanked by two such mythical creatures with deities standing on their backs supporting a winged sun disk. Such imagery may be found in many places in the Tanakh where God's chariot in the heavens is described as a winged sphinx or cherub and it is upon the cherub wings that the chariot soars unto the heavens (cf. Psa. 18:10).[693]

וְאֵת לַהַט הַחֶרֶב הַמִּתְהַפֶּכֶת לִשְׁמֹר אֶת־דֶּרֶךְ עֵץ הַחַיִּים – and a sword flaming and turning to guard the way to the tree of life – These angelic beings assume fearsome appearances that may have possibly taken on the sudden appearance of lightning so that the primal couple would not trespass and eat the from the Tree of Life. As in any transition into adulthood, loss of innocence represents a psychological wound that opens the door for individuation and personal growth. Whereas in primitive societies personal and often painful physical marks are inflicted to indicate the permanent transition to adulthood, the loss of Adam's innocence serves as a psychological wound, always reminding him of his organic oneness with the world which he willfully gives up in his quest to become fully human. Were Adam to continue in an unconscious state, he would never have evolved to become truly human. His existence would not have been much different from the animals he befriends in the primal garden. Without the trauma of loss, a soul's individuation would be impossible–Adam would have remained in an infantile state, a pathetic shadow when compared to what he would someday become.

❖ *The Rabbinic Remythologization of Eden*

Jacob Neusner offers a most penetrating analysis, differentiating between the Jewish and Christian view of the expulsion as it pertains to both respective faith communities. He notes that in classical Christian terms, Jesus personifies the "Last Adam" (or perhaps more accurately–the "New Adam"), who restores humanity to its Edenic innocence and purity. In Rabbinic Judaism, the nation of Israel stands as Adam's counterpart, while the land of Israel corresponds to Eden. Historically, both the Babylonian exile in 586 B.C.E. and the Roman exile in 70 C.E. represent Adam's fall from grace that came about by disregarding God's law to not eat the forbidden fruit. The various prescriptions of Rabbinic Judaism thus aim to mythically restore the individual and the Jewish people to a state of Original Innocence. Neusner further explains:

---

692 *Genesis,* ICC, 90.

693 Thus for example, when Ezekiel later saw the presence of God in a vision, he saw that God's Presence was above the cherubim, riding as it were in the chariot they constituted (Eze.10:18–19; cf. 2 Kgs. 2:11–12; 6:17).

> The political myth of Rabbinic Judaism now emerges in the Mishnah in all of its tedious detail as a reprise—in now-consequential and necessary, stunning detail—of the story of God's commandment, humanity's disobedience, God's sanction for the sin or crime, and humanity's atonement and reconciliation. The Mishnah omits all explicit reference to myths that explain power and sanctions, but invokes in its rich corpus of details the absolute given of the story of the distinction between what is deliberate and what is mitigated by an attitude that is not culpable, a distinction set forth in the tragedy of Adam and Eve, in the failure of Moses and Aaron, and in countless other passages in the Pentateuch, Prophetic Books, and Writings. Then the Mishnah's is a politics of life after Eden and outside of Eden. The upshot of the matter is that the political myth of Rabbinic Judaism sets forth the constraints of freedom, the human will brought to full and unfettered expression, imposed by the constraints of revelation, God's will made known.[694]

Neusner goes on to make an even more striking illustration of his thesis and explains that the framers of the Mishnah aimed to confront the Fall from Eden through the introduction of the Sabbath laws. The original peacefulness of Creation—before it was disturbed by Adam's disobedience—returns each week with the arrival of the Sabbath, and concludes:

> The Mishnah's framers have posited an economy embedded in a social system awaiting the seventh day, and that day's divine act of sanctification which, as at the creation of the world, would set the seal of holy rest upon an again complete creation. There is no place for action and actors when what is besought is no action whatsoever, but only unchanging perfection. . . . All the action lies within, in how these statements are made. Once they stand fully expressed, when nothing remains to be said, nothing remains to be done.[695]

One might add that in rabbinic literature, the Sabbath contains an eschatological dimension that also finds expression in the Sabbath liturgy that often links the grace of the Sabbath peacefulness with the arrival of the Messianic era—an age when every day will possess the quality of the Sabbath.

❖ *An Edenic Postscript*

Woundedness, trauma, wandering, and loss are all part and parcel of the process of becoming a spiritual adult. What we see here in the first chapters of Genesis is the birth of human consciousness; yet there can be no birth without enduring pain and adversity. These same psychological motifs become increasingly evident in many of the subsequent narratives of Genesis and beyond, e.g., Isaac's traumatic close brushes with death, Jacob's wrestling with an angelic being, Joseph's experience as a slave sold to traders in Egypt, the Israelites' collective experience of suffering in Egypt, David and Job's

---

[694] Jacob Neusner and Bruce Chilton, *Types of Authority in Formative Christianity and Judaism* (London: Routledge, 1999), 29.

[695] Ibid., 37.

hardships, and so on. In each of these narratives, the experience of danger and loss plays an important role in determining and shaping every protagonist's opportunity for expansion and growth. In the greater scheme of things—in order for Adam to mature spiritually—he has no choice but to eat the forbidden fruit. But far from being a Fall, we should refer to life in Eden as the great Awakening.

In the spirit of Pelagius and the Judaic mystics, the poet Rainer Maria Rilke believes that humankind's expulsion from Edenic existence paves the way for humanity's ultimate transformation—a pathway to authentic self-discovery that leads to spiritual maturity. Paradoxically, the absence of God becomes the arena that allows for the possibility of soul-making.

> The Christian experience enters less and less into consideration; the primordial God outweighs it infinitely. The idea that we are sinful and need to be redeemed as a prerequisite for God is more and more repugnant to a heart that has comprehended the earth. Sin is the most wonderfully roundabout path to God—but why should *they* go wandering who have never left him? The strong, inwardly quivering bridge of the Mediator has meaning only when where the abyss between God and us is admitted—but this very abyss is full of the darkness of God; and where someone experiences it, let him climb down and howl away inside it (that is more necessary than crossing it). Not until we can make even the abyss our dwelling-place will the paradise that we have sent on ahead of us turn around and will everything deeply and fervently of the here and now, which the Church embezzled for the Beyond, come back to us; then all the angels will decide singing praises, in favor of the earth.[696]

Holocaust survivor and psychologist, Victor Frankl, affirms that the power of human freedom can consciously make a positive difference in the world. In this regard, Frankl's philosophy continues the theological tradition already established by Pelagius, Julian of Eclanum, Kant, Rilke, and Jewish thinkers stretching back to ancient times. Frankl believes that one of the most dangerous aspects of traditional psychoanalysis (which we will call psychology's "Original Sin") is the mistaken belief that human behavior is governed by a principle of *pan-determinism.* Such a view sees the human being as though he is incapable of taking a stand toward realizing his capacity for creativity and happiness. Frankl asserts that no human being is fully conditioned or determined.

Quite the contrary: each person must determine for themselves whether he or she wants to surrender to life's difficulties or rise above them. *To be truly human is to ultimately be self-defining and self-determining.* As Frankl notes, "Human freedom is not freedom from conditions but rather, freedom to take a stand, to face whatever

---

[696] Maria Rilke and Stephen Mitchell (tr.), *Ahead of All Parting: The Selected Poetry and Prose of Rainer Maria Rilke*, (New York: Random House, 1995), 572.

conditions might confront him."[697] Man's existence is never a given; each person must decide what one will be at any hour and at any minute. The capacity to change can occur even in the twinkle of an eye. The possibility of redemption always remains for those wishing to make a sincere change for the better. However, human beings are responsible only for the evils they commit—*they are not accountable for the sins of others*. While it is true human existence is influenced by a variety of forces, e.g., biological, psychological, and sociological, nevertheless, everyone has the power to transcend the conditions one is confronted with. And in doing so, each individual ultimately transcends one's self. Once that occurs, only then does a person emerge as a self-transcending being.

[697] Victor Frankl, *The Will to Meaning*, (New York, Penguin 1988).

Excursus 1: The Nature of Biblical Interpretation

In R. Ishmael's School it was taught: 'And like in hammer that shatters the rock in pieces' (Jer. 23:29) i.e., just as the rock is split into many splinters, so too one biblical verse may convey many teachings.

Sanhedrin 32a

A. In Praise of Textual Fluidity

The field of hermeneutics raises a number of soul-searching and thought-provoking questions that have great relevance to the study and interpretation of the Bible. Does the text shape the interpretation? Or, is it the interpretation that shapes the text? If an author is no longer present and can no longer explain the purpose of his or her composition, how does one discern the author's original vision that inspired his or her work? Alternatively, if discerning the author's outlook proves to be impossible, can a reader's inner voice illuminate a text as a substitute? Aside from how an individual encounters Scriptures, what role does a faith-tradition or religious community play in mediating or shaping a contemporary understanding of a sacred text? In what ways can a religious tradition expand and embellish, or limit and impede, the scope of the text's meaning? At the end of the day, how do we determine the meaning of a text?

The first modern scholar to critically address many of these issues was German theologian Friedrich Schleiermacher (1768-1834). In his theory of hermeneutics, Schleiermacher argues that an interpreter should always attempt to understand the mind of the author as much as possible, and view the work within the context of the author's life. "The belonging together of hermeneutics and rhetoric consists in the fact that every act of understanding is the inversion of a speech-act, during which the thought which was the basis of the speech must become conscious."[698] As a tool, Schleiermacher claims that a psychological hermeneutic can sometimes enable an interpreter to understand the author's original work even better than the original author himself!

A contemporary of Schleiermacher, Friedrich Schlegel, went even further than Schleiermacher, adding that sometimes a literary work contains confusions, which needs to be corrected by the reader: "It is not enough that one understands the actual

---

[698] Schleiermacher adds, "The putting of oneself in the place of the author is implicit in what was just been said. And it follows first of all that we are the better equipped for explication the more we have assimilated it, but second that nothing which is to be explicated is to be understood all at once, but it is only each reading which makes us capable of better understanding it by enriching that previous knowledge. Only in relation to that which is insignificant are we happy with what has been understood all at once" (Friedrich Schleiermacher and Andrew Bowie, *Hermeneutics and Criticism: And Other Writings*, (Cambridge: Cambridge University Press, 1999), 24.

sense of a confused work better than the author understood it. One must know, *characterize*, and even *construe* the confusion even down to its very principles."[699] This latter point plays a significant role in how the "hermeneutic of suspicion" impacts feminist exegesis and liberation theology,[700] where the express goal is to expose the false projections and other cognitive distortions of the human will-to-power.

In Anthony C. Thiselton's encyclopedic study chronicling the history of hermeneutics and religion, the author points out that Schleiermacher believes the act of interpretation involves "listening," and stepping out of one's own frame of mind. This is not a concern with "the subjectivity of the isolated individual," but the relationship between individual consciousness and an individual's capacity for inter-personal communication on the basis of shared language. Schleiermacher presupposes "a linguistic and inter-personal interaction in which the individuality of the self was not only enhanced but also transcended and perhaps transformed."[701]

Attentive listening to the biblical text provides an essential requisite for spiritual transformation. The hermeneutical task also "involves the author's thought, experience, and situation; the content, context, language, and effects of the text; the first readers of the text, including their linguistic and other capacities and competences; and the consciousness and experience of later interpretation."[702] Furthermore, Schleiermacher subscribes to what may be considered a holistic approach to scriptural interpretation. "Complete knowledge is always in this apparent circle, that each particular can only be understood via the general, of which it is a part, and *vice versa*. And every piece of knowledge is only scientific if it is formed in this way."[703]

---

[699] See Michael Forester's article on Schleiermacher in *The Stanford Encyclopedia of Philosophy Online Edition*. (http://plato.stanford.edu/entries/schleiermacher/#4).

[700] The psychological and critical view of religious texts and their social underpinnings began with the philosophers Feuerbach, Marx, Nietzsche and Freud. According to Paul Ricoeur, these men argued that interpretation must involve a "hermeneutic of suspicion" that exposes the hidden biases that exist against certain ideas or groups of people within a given faith's history that continue to influence societies in unconscious repressive ways. Feminist liberation theologians assert that a modern reader needs to question even the integrity of the biblical text itself and acknowledge the existence of problematical passages endorsing women's oppression.

[701] Anthony C. Thistleton, *New Horizons in Hermeneutics: The Theory and Practice of Transforming Biblical Reading* (Grand Rapids, MI: Zondervan, 1992), 207.

[702] Ibid., 208.

[703] Friedrich Schleiermacher and Andrew Bowie, *Hermeneutics and Criticism: And Other Writings op. cit.*, 24.

Thus, every facet of interpretation—from the textual, the historical, and the interpretive—serves to re-present the biblical text anew to the reader each time the text is encountered. There is much to admire about Schleiermacher's approach to Scripture, and this commentary has made practical use of Schleiermacher's unique interpretive style which combines exegesis with psychological and holistic insight. However, modern methodologies also offer alternative ways of experiencing the Tanakh in a manner that he did not anticipate.

B. Expanding Our Hermeneutical Horizons

Among current hermeneutic approaches, the ideas of Hans-Georg Gadamer (1900-2002) deserve special consideration for the field of biblical exegesis. According to Gadamer, texts possess an "excess of meaning" that move *beyond* whatever may have been the original intention of a literary author. Unlike Schleiermacher, who was more concerned with the original author's intent, Gadamer focuses on the reader's *experience* of the text. The great literary classics of history offer insight on the contemporary human condition. The genius of a classic lies in its ability to transcend its original cultural milieu, while blending two different cultural worlds that create a dialogue between the text and the interpreter.

Gadamer refers to the fruit of this exchange as a "fusion of horizons" in which the world of the author and the reader meet.[704] Although it is fixed in the sky, the horizon possesses movement; it expands and changes. "The horizon is, rather, something into which we move and which moves with us. Horizons change for a person who is moving."[705] Regardless of the type of world the author(s) inhabits, the literary or artistic message evokes a response across the ages that is continually being reinterpreted by readers who listen and question the narrative in light of their own historical circumstances. As with art, the true aesthetic experience does not revolve or focus on the historical circumstances and context that produced the original work but rather involves *a living relationship* that relates to the work in the present. Whatever may have been on the artist's or author's mind is not as important as the *subjective* impact it has upon its viewers or readers.[706]

According to Gadamer, the act of interpretation does not so much unlock the past meaning of the text but rather establishes a dialogue with the text in the present. For Gadamer, the authorial intent of the writer is not decisive in determining the meaning of

---

[704] Hans-Georg Gadamer, *Truth and Method* (New York: Sheed and Ward, 1975), 242-54 and 302-7.

[705] Ibid., 304.

[706] Similarly, musical composition will always vary depending upon a musician's skill and interpretation.

the text for a particular reader. However, his position is not completely without his share of critics, for some scholars reject some of the basic premises Gadamer uses in his philosophical approach[707]

Thiseleton explores the theological implications of Gadamer's "horizon" metaphor as it pertains to the community of faith and its historical relationship to its past. The horizon of the present can never exist apart from the influence of tradition:

> The horizon or the pre-intentional background is thus a network of revisable expectations and assumptions which the reader brings to the text, together with the shared patterns of behavior and belief with reference to which processes of interpretation become operative. The term "horizon" calls attention to the fact that our finite situatedness in time, history, and culture defines the present (though always expanding) limits of *our world* of what we *can see.* The term "background" calls attention to the fact that these boundaries embrace not only what we can draw in conscious reflection, but also the pre-cognitive dispositions or competences which are made possible by our participation in the shared practices of a social and historical world. [708]

Whenever a human being attempts to understand a text or a cultural object from the past, there can only be a convergence of the horizons of the past and present, but never a complete fusion of them. Meaning emerges only as the text and interpreter engage in dialogue; i.e., a "hermeneutical conversation."[709] This two-way dialogue creates a nexus that binds the worldview of the text with the worldview of the reader. Thus, the discovery of meaning is not embedded in the text per se, but is rather

---

[707] E. D. Hirsch argues that it is possible to determine the rightful place of authorial intention when it pertains to deciphering a text's meaning. Hirsch argues that it is important to make a distinction between the "meaning" and "significance." Meaning is precisely what the author intended his work to mean—it is what is represented by the text. What is not expressed by the author in the text is impossible to know. Hirsch explains, "Meaning is that which is represented by a text; it is what the author meant by his use of a particular sign sequence; it is what the signs represent. Significance, on the other hand, names a relationship between that meaning and a person, or a conception or a situation, or indeed anything imaginable" (E.D. Hirsch, *Validity of Interpretation* [New Haven: Yale, 1967], 8). Thus, significance is more subjective—it entails a relationship between the verbal meaning and what exists outside of it—hence, it goes beyond anything that the author may have intended. There is a distinct social dimension to significance that is born out of the reader's personal experience and interaction of the text. The interpretation may have significance for the community and its culture—but it has no bearing whatsoever on original intent. However, one could counter that it is unclear how Hirsch differentiates determining the meaning of a text from its significance, for the very act of doing so, Gadamer explains, becomes relative to the starting point or "pre-understanding" of the individual. Regardless how one approaches the text, the reader's biases will always color the way one reads a text—hence arriving at a truly objective reading of a text may be for all practical purposes impossible.

[708] Anthony C. Thiselton, *New Horizons in Hermeneutics: The Theory and Practice of Transforming Biblical Reading* (Grand Rapids, MI: Zondervan, 1992), 46.

[709] Hans-Georg Gadamer, *Philosophical Hermeneutics,* trans. and ed. David E. Linge (Berkeley, California: University of California Press, 1976), xix.

discovered in the act of reading, which continues to extend the original text's meaning. In the final analysis, the goal is to allow the narrative text to transform the world of the reader.

Hermeneutic philosophers of the postmodern era often stress that meaning is not inherent in a text itself, but emerges only as the interpreter enters into dialogue with the text.[710] A text's meaning depends largely on the perspective of the one who enters into dialogue with it, so that there are as many interpretations of a text as there are readers willing to engage it. Moreover, without a reader, the text becomes irrelevant—regardless who the author happens to be. A static view of a text does not allow for creative interaction, but a text that is approached as dynamic and living, allows for a creative application of its overall message. Perhaps one of the most essential points made by the postmodernists is that the cultural differences between eras are so sweeping and complete that even the most meticulous historical study cannot fully recapture the meaning of past documents. We cannot escape the conditioning of our own historical situation, and for this reason, the process of understanding demands that two perspectives be taken into consideration: the view of the writer and the view of the interpreter. Since all texts remain open and subject to the possibility of new interpretation, this process cannot be reduced to a set method but rather one that remains fluid at all times. According to philosopher Paul Ricoeur, all texts and all objects flow and transmit a "surplus of meaning" which can never be exhausted either by the objective text itself or by any one particular generation's interpretation. Interpretation is always a living and ongoing process.[711]

C. Entering the Hermeneutical Spiral

Hermeneutic scholars often point out that the process of understanding is not linear or a finite, but rather a spiraling trajectory in which the same elements are encountered repeatedly, leading to new and different levels of understanding with each reading of the text.[712] There is a blending of the generations that touch one another whenever a text is encountered and studied. That is to say, the past can only

---

[710] Ibid., 261.

[711] A good example of this dynamism is reflected in how rabbinic interpretation has historically redefined the Torah's message through utilizing the thirteen hermeneutical rules of interpretation. See The Introduction to the Sifra Mechilta of Rabbi Shimon bar Yohai to Exodus 21:1; for a more comprehensive exposition, see *Encyclopedia Judaica Vol.* 8, 366–72); Hermann L. Strack, *Introduction to the Talmud and Midrash* (New York: Athenaeum, 1969), 95-96.

[712] In Jewish tradition, when the Torah is completed during the holiday of Simchat Torah, it is re-wound to the beginning and reading begins anew.

be understood in light of the present, and by the same token, the present can only be understood in light of its past. This blending of the text and the subjectivity of the reader create an arching of the text, which is sometimes referred to as a "hermeneutical circle." Another hermeneutical scholar, Grant R. Osborne, describes this dynamic image of a "hermeneutical spiral" to describe vibrant movement from the horizon of the text to the reader's horizon.

> [I]t is not a closed circle (i.e., the process) but rather an open-ended movement from the horizon of the text to the horizon of the reader. I am not going round and round a closed circle that can never detect the true meaning but am spiraling nearer and nearer to the text's intended meaning as I refine my hypotheses and allow the text to continue to challenge and correct those alternative interpretations, then to guide my delineation of its significance for my situation today. The sacred author's intended meaning is the critical starting point, but not an end in itself. . .[713]

However, the reader's lack of objectivity need not be considered an obstacle; indeed, as Gadamer has already noted, our "prejudices" of the text are a necessary part of the interpretive process—provided we can free ourselves from their influence when it is warranted. When the reader moves into the hermeneutical circle and learns to discern his/her own biases and prejudices, new meanings can be gleaned from the work as it encounters present culture. Rabbinic interpretation has never felt particularly bound to the literal word of the Torah per se, but each generation of rabbinic scholars develops newer approaches to scriptural interpretation that expand the meaning of a text, sometimes through the path of Halacha[714]and sometimes through the Aggadah.[715] Reinterpretation of scriptural texts requires an intertextual process of questioning, comparing, and contrasting older paradigms of exegesis to contemporary models. In doing so, they refuse to slavishly follow just the "letter of the law," and in many ways expand beyond the Pentateuch's historical and literal trajectory.

---

[713] Grant R. Osborne, *The Hermeneutical Spiral: A Comprehensive Guide to Biblical Interpretation (*Downers Grove, IL: InterVarsity Press, 1991), 6.

[714] A good example of this dynamism is reflected in how rabbinic interpretation has historically redefined the Torah's message through utilizing the thirteen hermeneutical rules of interpretation. See The Introduction to the Sifra Mechilta of Rabbi Shimon bar Yohai to Exodus 21:1. For a more comprehensive exposition, see *Encyclopedia Judaica Vol.* 8, 366–72); Hermann L. Strack, *Introduction to the Talmud and Midrash* (New York: Atheneum, 1969), 95.

[715] Jacob Neusner explains, "Rabbinic Judaism in documents of exegesis, narrative ("Aggadah"), exhortation, extension, and amplification of Scripture, sets forth a system that translates into governing principles the implications of Scripture's narratives, laws, and prophecies. That system recasts Scripture's mythic monotheism—monotheism set forth through the narrative of Scripture—into a working theology for holy Israel's cosmic and social order" *Handbook of Rabbinic Theology: Language, System, Structure* (Boston: Brill, 2002), 107.

D. Implications for Biblical Exegesis

As with all great works of literature, every student of the Bible should approach the material with questions that arise from one's own horizons and "pre-understanding" of the world which would affect how the text is engaged and ultimately interpreted. R. Bultmann (1884–1976), an early 20th century exponent of hermeneutical exegesis, went even further by claiming that no one examines a Scriptural text as an impartial observer without a pre-understanding of what the sacred text says.[716] While objectivity ought to be viewed as the goal of the exegete, nevertheless, each person brings a perspective to the text that must be consciously accounted for. In addition, he notes, "The demand that the interpreter must silence his subjectivity . . . in order to attain an objective knowledge is therefore the most absurd one that can be imagined."[717] Thus prejudices do not necessarily invalidate interpretation, so long as one is cognizant and honest about them.

Going beyond Bultmann and Gadamer's novel insight, Thiselton notes that postmodernism must find a more secure philosophical base that recognizes the ability of texts to communicate and transform life-worlds. From the religious perspective, "the text itself progressively corrects and reshapes the interpreter's own questions and assumptions."[718] That is to say, rather than making the text relativistic and bereft of a spiritual epicenter, as postmodern criticism claims, it is the sacred text that molds and defines the faith community to its vision of what the world may be.[719]

As previously mentioned, some scholars insist that hermeneutical approaches to the Scriptures need to try and take in account the biblical author's intentions, as well as to establish a consensus of interpretation as defined by the faith community over its historical development and its relevance to the present. Ultimately, interpretation does

---

[716] Rudolf Bultmann, "Is Exegesis without Presuppositions Possible?" in *Existence and Faith: Shorter Writings of Rudolf Bultmann,* ed. Schubert M. Ogden (New York: World Publishing, 1960), 289-96.

[717] Rudolf Bultmann, "The Problem of Hermeneutics" in *Essays Philosophical and Theological* (London: SCM, 1955), 255.

[718] Anthony C. Thiselton, *The Two Horizons* (Grand Rapids, MI: Eerdmans, 1980), 439.

[719] The interpreter of Scripture may in some ways even be analogous to the role of the observer in a scientific experiment. According to the Heisenberg Principle, the result of a given experiment is unavoidably influenced by the observer. In the field of quantum mechanics, both the observer and the system being observed are mysteriously connected. Whatever the results of an observation happen to be, they will to some extent be determined by the choices of the observer, as portrayed in the famous example of "Schrodinger's Cat." The point of this illustration is to show that the old paradigm of absolute objectivity is not possible in the scientific world based on how we experience reality. The same principle applies no less to how the Scriptures ought to be interpreted. Regardless who the interpreter happens to be, every interpreter approaches his material from his or her unique perspective, or as Gadamer says, "prejudice," that colors the way one experiences a classical text such as the Bible.

not conclude with just the reader and the text; an ongoing dialogue must occur between the interpreter and one's fellow interpreters forming a new horizon of insight and understanding that will inevitably converge with future generations of readers. Together with the participants of the present, the voices of past generations can experience a recasting and rebirth for the present. It is my personal belief that the power of the Divine continues to mediate between the horizons of past and present—God is the communicative Force and Presence that keeps the message of the Bible eternally relevant.

While it is commonly believed that the Source of Scripture is inerrant, the human transmitter of the Divine Word is, at times, an imperfect agent bound by the cultural constraints of the age s/he lives in. A discriminating eye for objectivity and truth are necessary for a modern reader to ascertain distinctions separating the social world of the past from the social world of the present. Today, there is more awareness of the social conditioning of texts and their hidden biases that may be lurking in a given biblical text. In the spirit of the Sages who believe that the Torah speaks in the language of people, it behooves the reader to see the Torah not as a relic of the past, but as a crucible whose spiritual luminescence continues to purge societies from the shackles that bind and constrict the human spirit.

E. Derrida and the Midrash

As surprising as it may seem, traditional midrashic exegesis finds remarkable affinity and support from Jacques Derrida and his unique postmodern theory of "deconstructionism."[720] According to Derrida, text and commentary co-exist and are of equal value regardless of what the original author may have intended, serving to generate new matrixes of interpretive meaning. Paradoxically, Derrida adds that just as

---

[720] Deconstructionism is a difficult term to define, as Derrida himself has admitted on many occasions: To simplify "deconstructionism in a nutshell, is a contradiction in terms." Firstly, the purpose of the nutshell is to contain the nut, whereas the purpose of deconstructionism is "to free the nut," by removing the walls surrounding the hidden nuances of language. "Nutshells enclose and encapsulate, shelter and protect, reduce and simplify, while everything in deconstruction is turned toward opening, exposure, expansion, and complexification" (John Caputo, *Deconstruction in a Nutshell: A Conversation with Jacques Derrida* [New York: Fordham University Press, 1997], 31). Once shattering the textual "nutshell" is accomplished, new and endless possibilities of meaning are born. The philosophy of deconstructionism *is not interested in destroying the meaning of a text*, but attempts to reconstruct its meaning. It does so by exploring the unconscious side of language much like psychoanalysis, which Derrida's philosophy is related to. The concept of meaning cannot be conveyed by the writer to a reader; indeed, *the reader is ultimately more important in deciphering meaning than is the author*. Therefore, no text can ever be fully explained; it will—by its very existence—always yield to further deconstructionism. As a postmodern phenomenon, deconstructionism regards all meaning as being relative to a cultural milieu and situation—and can often lead to an attitude of moral relativism or multiculturalism. Nevertheless, Derrida feels that all truth is conditioned by the individual's perspective. One important insight Derrida makes is the idea that there is no such thing as a perfect reference or one-to-one correspondence between words and the meaning they confer. With the curiosity of a detective, a reader is encouraged to view any text with suspicion—there's always more to a text than what meets the eye.

a reader cannot know the author's real objective, by the same token, *neither can the author!* The author may not even be consciously aware of the possible impact of his words and what they mean to a potential reader.

There is an interesting antecedent to Derrida's theory in the Talmud. One well-known rabbinic story reads:

> Rab Judah said in the name of Rab, "When Moses ascended on high he found the Holy One, blessed be He, engaged in affixing coronets to the letters. Moses exclaimed, 'Lord of the Universe, [why are these crowns necessary?] God answered, 'Many generations from now a man named Akiba b. Yosef will expound upon each crown heaps of laws.' Moses requested, 'Master of the Universe, let me see him.' God replied, 'Turn around.' Moses went and sat down eight rows, and listened to the discourses of the Law. Unable to follow their arguments, Moses felt ill-at-ease, but when they came upon a certain topic, the students asked their teacher, 'From where do you derive your teaching?' Akiba replied: 'It is a law given unto Moses at Sinai.' Moses found comfort in Akiba's answer" (BT Menachot 29b). The Talmudic narrative stresses that not even the writer of the Torah himself was consciously aware of what he had written at Sinai. God informs Moses that each generation of Sages would add immeasurably to the revelation that occurred at Sinai. From this and other rabbinic teachings, we may discern that revelation of the Divine Word is never static or monolithic; it is dynamic, pulsating and ever-changing. While the human writer is unaware of the fullness of his composition, it is the Divine hand that guides the biblical writer in ways that far transcend his conscious mind.

Like this story of Moses, a future interpreter (like R. Akiba) may see beyond the vision of the original author.[721] This concept applies no less to poetry, art, music, biblical prophecy, and philosophy.[722] Moreover, the author himself may read the text at varying points in time

---

721 As mentioned earlier, the Russian philosopher and literary theorist, Mikhail Bakhtin, arrives at a similar conclusion with respect to classical literature: " . . . it is immensely important for the person who understands to be located outside the object of his or her creative understanding—in time, in space, in culture. For one cannot even really see one's own exterior and comprehend it as a whole, and no mirrors or photographs can help; our real exterior can be seen and understood only by other people, because they are located outside us in space, and because they are others." Mikhail Bakhtin, *Speech Genres and Other Late Essays* (Austin, TX: University of Texas Press, 1986), 7.

722 A good example of this is found in the philosophical works of Plato, which resonate with more wisdom than the author could have dared to imagine. Sometimes in philosophy, as is true with prophecy, glimpses of the future may often be conveyed in words which could hardly have been understood or interpreted at the time when they were uttered. For this reason, Alfred North Whitehead exuberantly characterizes the entire Western philosophical tradition as nothing more than "a series of footnotes to Plato." Perennial questions such as: Is reality stable and permanent or is it always changing? Is the universe infinite or does it have a beginning? What is the nature of reality? Are ethical values like justice and courage relative? Are values considered "absolute"—simply and forever right and true? What constitutes justice? What is the nature of happiness? How shall we best live our lives? Plato and other Greek thinkers of his age would have been amazed at the new directions and trajectories their philosophical ideas have taken. The same point could just as easily be made of any of H. G. Well's famous novels, e.g., *The Island of Dr. Moreau* or *The Time Machine*, and *The War of the Worlds,* or especially Gene Rodenberry's *Star Trek* series.

and derive completely different meaning(s) from his original thoughts (as all authors can easily attest to). Derrida contends there is an *itérabilité* (transcendence) which characterizes the nature of the text. Based on this paradigm, deconstruction focuses on the "received text," i.e., the final form of a particular text and not its earlier recensions.

Such an approach views the text holistically rather than reductively. Whether one speaks or writes, something is always conveyed through the medium of the word, revealing aspects that we may only be subconsciously aware of. Language speaks most eloquently when it is aware of its own imaginative status, and therefore, is a fluid means that naturally produces a tempestuous sea of contradictory meanings and interpretations.[723] For Derrida, it is not so much what a given text originally meant—for both the reader and interpreter play a role that is no less important than the author's. Consequently, the search for meaning from a text has no value unless the interpreter's individual history is triangulated in the exegetical equation.

On a critical note, one must wonder whether it is necessary to completely accept Derrida's notion that it is impossible to determine the intent of a deceased author. Unless Derrida is suggesting that his readers become omniscient, one must wonder whether it truly is impossible as he maintains. Arriving at the root of authorial intent may not always be as difficult to arrive at as Derrida claims. In terms of biblical exegesis: Linguistics, history, and archaeology contribute relevant insight into the worldview of an author; these disciplines provide hard data as to what an original author might have had in mind before transcribing his words. With these tools, it is possible to arrive at the plain or contextual meaning of the text, i.e., the *peshat*. In short, Derrida's attack on the absence of objective meaning is not without criticism. Yet, despite these limitations, Derrida is correct in including the reader as an important part of the interpretive process. Meaning is never quite context-free, it is to a large extent—inter-subjective and is therefore, connected to the subjective world of the reader.

Notwithstanding Derrida's idiosyncratic style of thought, in some ways, his unorthodox methods capture the essence of rabbinic hermeneutical thought. The Sages of ancient Israel observe, "The Torah *speaks* in the language of humanity." [724] They did not say, "The Torah *spoke* in the language of humanity." Nor did the Sages say that "The

---

[723] Derrida adds, "That writing [is] *epekeina tēs ousias*. . . . *Nonpresence is presence. Différance,* the disappearance of any originary presence, is at once [*la fois*] the condition of possibility and the condition of impossibility of truth. 'At once' means that the being-present [*ōn*] in its truth . . . is doubled as soon as it appears, as soon as it presents itself. It appears, in its essence, as the possibility of its most proper non-truth, of its pseudo-truth reflected in the icon, the phantasm, or the simulacrum. What is, *is not* (*sic*) what it is . . . unless it adds to itself the possibility of being repeated as such. And its identity is hollowed out by that addition, withdraws itself in the supplement that presents it." *Dissemination,* tr. Barbara Johnson (Chicago: University Press Chicago, 1981), 168.

[724] BT Berakhot, 31b; *Sifre*, Numbers 112.

Torah is *written* in the language of humanity." From a Derridian perspective, the distinction is critical. Ancient Israel understood that the interpretive dimension of the Torah transcends what is merely *written* in the Torah. As previously mentioned, throughout the Talmud, rabbinic Judaism often ingeniously inverts the simple meaning of a text from what is actually written.[725] When we allow the Torah to "speak" to the present, we can discover newer insights that address our contemporary social conditions.[726] The rabbis' metaphor of a "speaking Torah" contains yet another important insight. Since Torah requires human language for its interpretation, it follows that its language is—by its very nature—never a complete and fixed system. Like all other scientific, literary, or philosophic areas and disciplines involving human communication, the language of Torah must remain open and dynamic to innovative and new creative expressions.

This process has always been an integral part of intrabiblical exegesis, and this same methodology continues well into the Talmudic era and beyond.[727] The rabbis have taught that a biblical text or a rabbinic text cannot fully come alive unless it is questioned, deconstructed, interpreted and intertextually re-interpreted.[728] The interpretive processes of the past may have served the needs of earlier generations, but laws and traditions require periodic re-visioning and judicial review. This mechanism applies to rabbinic law as well, preventing it from becoming stale, or at worst—obsolete. To

---

[725] Here are just a few examples: the Mishnah regarding the biblical law pertaining to *lex talionis* in Exodus 21:24-25, which the majority of the Sages interpret in terms of compensation—contra Rabbi Eliezer, who insists on a more literal interpretation (Bava Kama 8:1; cf. T. B. Bava Kama 83b-85b); the Torah prescribes death to the wayward and rebellious son (Deut. 21:18-21) which the Sages effectively abolished, along with the biblical laws regarding the apostate city in Deuteronomy 12:12-18 (BT Sanhedrin 71a).

[726] Throughout the Talmud the Sages are frequently depicted as speaking in the present tense, e.g., "Rava says . . ." or "Rabbi Shimon says . . ." It would seem to be more appropriate to say that "Rava said. . . or Rabbi Shimon said . . ." However, the Talmudic redactors intentionally created a text that would allow the voices of the past to always remain connected with the future. In this sense, any discussion of the Talmud continues to speak to the present, producing a "fusion of the horizons" as noted by Gadamer.

[727] Daniel Boyarin writes, "We will not read midrash well and richly unless we understand it first and foremost as *reading*, as hermeneutic, as generated by the interaction of rabbinic readers with a heterogeneous and difficult text, which was for them both normative and divine in origin" cited from *Intertextuality and the Reading of Midrash* (Bloomington/Indianapolis, IN: Indiana University Press, 1990), 5. Another intriguing work illustrating the theological diversity of early Tannaitic thought is Daniel Boyarin's "On the Status of the Tannaitic Midrashim" *The Journal of the American Oriental Society*, Vol. 112, 1992, where Boyarin presents a trenchant attack against Jacob Neusner's approach to rabbinic theological thought.

[728] There is a famous Yiddish story about a rabbi who was once asked to take a pulpit in a far-away community. When he visited the town, the synagogue leaders told the rabbi, that in their town, many of the great rabbis were buried in their cemetery. Upon visiting the cemetery, the rabbi was surprised to see that was not true. When he asked the leaders what they meant, they told him the following: "Many of the great rabbis are, in a sense, really buried here since there is nobody left to teach their words and carry on their legacies." The rabbi understood the town leaders' wisdom and accepted their pulpit.

prevent this from occurring, rabbinic exegesis allows for a periodic re-evaluation of its sacred texts and their long-standing traditions—especially when the need for alternative solutions is demanding.[729] This phenomenon is especially well attested in the rabbinic literature known as Responsa.

Like Gadamer and Bakhtin, Derrida encourages readers to disallow any tradition that limits one's interpretive freedom. Ultimately, meaning is defined *not* by the text but by the reader (which, incidentally, is what Judaic tradition has encouraged for the greater part of its history). For this reason and more, Judaism has generally eschewed fundamentalist approaches that take the Bible literally. While this viewpoint goes far beyond the "fusion of horizons" suggested by Gadamer, Derrida's viewpoint allows for immense possibilities of meaning, providing one does not let the text dictate what that meaning is. Derrida revels in what he perceives to be the beauty of *ambiguity*, a term that until the 20th century generally had a pejorative connotation. Yet, ambiguity lies at the heart of all Midrashic discourse. Indeed, the medievalists' obsession with nuance has greatly engendered the biblical exegesis that we now enjoy today. Ricoeur's definition of interpretation is especially helpful for understanding the Midrashic exegete's methodology: "Interpretation we will say is the work of thought which consists of deciphering the hidden meaning in the apparent meaning, and in the unfolding the levels of meaning in the literal meaning"[730]

F. "Death of the Author"

Structuralist Roland Barthes's essay on *The Death of the Author* raises a number of important issues that have vital implications for biblical exegesis. While his ideas bear similarity to Derrida's, Barthes goes one step further. He insists that after the death of the author, *nobody can lay claim or authority over a text*:

> The death of the Author means that nobody has *authority* over the meaning of the text, and that there is no hidden, ultimate, stable meaning to be deciphered: Once the Author is removed, the claim to decipher a text becomes quite futile. To give a text an Author is to impose a limit on that text, to furnish it with a final signified, to close the writing. Such a conception suits criticism very well, the latter then allotting itself the important task of discovering the Author (or his hypostases: society, history, psyche, liberty) beneath the work: when the Author has been found, the text is "explained" – victory to the critic. . . . In the multiplicity of writing, everything is to be disentangled, nothing deciphered; . . .

[729] Normally, the way a Jewish marriage is dissolved is either through divorce or through the death of the spouse. However, annulment is also an alternative that has been used throughout much of Jewish history. Rabbinic scholars continue to debate over whether this method should be used in cases where the husbands refuse to grant their wives a proper religious divorce. See Mordechai's novella to BT Yevamot, *siman* 30; cf. *Responsa Maharam Mintz*, number 105, cited in *Responsa Seridey 'Eish* 3:25, 71.

[730] *The Conflict of Interpretation: Essays in Hermeneutics* (Evanston, Ill: Northwestern University Press, 1974), 13.

> the space of writing is to be ranged over, not pierced; writing ceaselessly posits meaning ceaselessly to evaporate it, carrying out a systematic exemption of meaning.[731]

In short, if there is no reality behind the text, then the Author of the text is irrelevant. Theologically speaking, if the Author (God) is "dead" and is no longer accessible, does this diminish the importance of the Bible as a Divine work? Does the "death of the Author" imply that there is no longer any source for meaning to be discovered from the Author's work, and that all meaning is relatively imposed unto the text? Anthony Thiselton explains, "If, as we suggest, that the Bible is a love letter from the heart of God, to read the words, 'I love you' as the words of a dead or an anonymous lover, would destroy this act of love, and transpose it into a tragedy."[732] Barthes writes that the refusal to assign a fixed meaning either to the world or to texts "liberates an activity we may call counter-theological, properly revolutionary, for to refuse to halt meaning is finally to refuse God." However, from the biblical perspective, the biblical writers affirm just the opposite: God is the ultimate Author and Source of meaning and object of reference.

One literary scholar, Nike Kocijancic Pokorn, responds to Barthes's critique by referring to a well-known medieval classic that was written anonymously known as "The Cloud of Unknowing." This work was written by someone from a monastic order that had the practice of leaving his text unsigned. Although this practice might seem to be in harmony with the postmodern view that the author is dispensable, Pokom points out that this was not the case with this celebrated mystical classic. Whereas Barthes's argument only pertains to an actual known author; it does not pertain to an anonymous author:

> The author of the Cloud was convinced that his text did not remain open to endless interpretation, if his intended message was accessible only to those who shared with him a sincere wish for the experience of mystical union. And finally, the Cloud author expressed his belief in the existence of the final, transcendental truth, which ensures the meaning of the text. The "right" understanding of the message of the text is thus guaranteed by the faith shared by the author and his readers, by their common faith in the hyper-essential God, who revealed himself in the person of Jesus Christ. And if in the poststructuralist world "the absence of the transcendental signified extends the domain and the play of signification infinitely,"[11] in the world of our fourteenth-century mystic the presence of the Transcendental God, of the divine *auctor*[733], the source of *auctoritas*, ensures the meaning, if the author and the reader of the text share the same horizon of understanding and faith.

---

731 Roland Barthes, "The Death of the Author" printed in *Image-Music-Text* (New York: Hill and Wang, 1978), 146-147.

732 Anthony C. Thiselton, *Thiselton on Hermeneutics* (Grand Rapids: MI: Eerdmans, 2006), 206.

733 The word "author" derives from the Middle English *auctour*, from Old French *autor*, from Latin *auctor* ("creator") deriving from *auctus*, and the past participle of *augēre*, to "to originate, increase" from which the English verb augment comes from.

> The reasons for the authorial disappearance are then essentially different in the two cases; while Roland Barthes proclaims the death of the author because he wants to announce the birth of the reader and above all that of the critic with his/her own interpretation of the text, the medieval author of the *Cloud* conceals his name because he thinks that his authority is not needed, and that the shared experience with the reader of his book will grant access to the divine transcendental authority, which bestows meaning on the text.[734]

One could similarly argue that the absence of an author's name in the biblical books indicates that the writer's identity is not what is really important: but the message certainly is. By sharing the stories of faith in the Tanakh, one can arrive at the same shared experience by those who live by the prophetical values of these seers and moral teachers.

That being said, Barthes's premise may have a basis in Aggadic and Midrashic thought, which frequently describes what may be termed as "an absence of God." Kabbalistic thought especially crystallizes this concept in the *tsimtsum* where God relinquishes some of His power, in order for human beings to make their own decisions pertaining to right and wrong—without any coercion from Above. For this goal to occur, God "withdraws" from the world, and this "absence" allows for human free will to define a pattern of religious and moral behavior, as the Sages say, "All is in the hands of Heaven—except the fear of Heaven."

An important antecedent to the doctrine of the *tsimtsum* can be seen in the following Talmudic account, where Rabbi Eliezer ben Hyrcanus debates the Sages over the ritual status of a certain type of newly designed oven that could be disassembled. "Could such an oven become ritually impure? The Sages ruled that it could be ritually defiled, but Rabbi Eliezer differed. Despite attempts to persuade his colleagues, Rabbi Eliezer does not succeed. After resorting to several miraculous interventions to prove his point, R. Eliezer saves his greatest proof for last:

> Then R. Eliezer raised his voice and said, "Let Heaven itself attest that the law is in accordance with my opinion!" Suddenly, a Heavenly Voice declared, "Why do you disagree with R. Eliezer? Do you not realize that law is always in accordance with his opinion?"
> R. Joshua arose from his place and declared to God, "Is it not written that, 'The Torah is not in Heaven?" R. Jeremiah said, "This means that we do not adjudicate law on the basis of a Heavenly Voice, for the Torah was already given to humankind at Mt. Sinai." R. Joshua continued his speech, "We do not listen to a Heavenly Voice because You God already wrote in the Torah at Sinai, 'The matter shall be decided according to the majority" (Exod. 23:2). Later, one of the Sages, R. Nathan, had a dream where he encounters Elijah the Prophet. He asks him, "What did God say after this argument?" Elijah replies, "God was laughing and proudly said, "My children defeated me, My children defeated me!" [735]

---

[734]Nike Kocijancic Pokorn, *The Cloud of Unknowing in Dialogue with Post-modernism,* http://www.kud-logos.si/knjiznica-religija/nike-cloud.htm.

[735] BT Bava Metzia 59b.

The Aggadic passage intimates that God's displacement to the Heavenly world after Sinai is a necessary and critical act in order to allow others to reinterpret on their own what was given to them at Mt. Sinai. Some Sages express the thought in different terms, "From the day the Temple was destroyed, the only thing the Holy Blessed One has in His world is the four cubits of the Halacha."[736] This rabbinic teaching does not mean that God necessarily abandons the world for other creative pursuits, but rather God's Presence is triangulated and present whenever people of like mind come together to discuss His Law. To the Jew who studies the Torah, the process of revelation never ceases. Even liturgically, God is still considered the "Giver of the Torah." For when a people live by the Torah's teachings, the Author remains forever alive—despite Barthes's theological claim to the contrary.

G. Exegesis vs. Eisegesis: Concluding Remarks

Returning to our original discussion in the Introduction, strictly speaking, there is no way to "objectively" distinguish exegesis from eisegesis. People of all faiths and academic backgrounds experience God through a commitment to their faith of choice; a spiritual self-understanding is mediated through a person's interpretive lens and theological worldview. Each approach, paradoxically, creates the mirror reflecting the interpretation one wishes to impose unto the text. Despite obvious differences and dissents, one methodology supplies what the other lacks; hence, both techniques must be integrated by the interpreter. Indeed, a balance between the exegetic and the eisegetic keeps one intellectually honest—and humble. To rephrase a well-known aphorism from Einstein, *eisegesis without exegesis is blind; exegesis without eisegesis is lame*. This applies no less to the contemporary historical and critical theories that understand the biblical text essentially as a human work, rather than as the "Word of God." From a religious vantage point, one can still believe in the divinity of the Torah's message without having to subscribe to a theological doctrine of literalism that limits its scope of theological or existential interpretation.

Excursus 2: The Dynamics of Textual Criticism

The Torah speaks in the language of humankind.
BT Berakhot 31b

A. Why is Textual Criticism Important?

It is interesting to note that the Septuagint reads: καὶ εἶδεν ὁ θεὸς τὰ πάντα, ὅσα ἐποίησεν, καὶ ἰδοὺ καλὰ λίαν. καὶ ἐγένετο ἑσπέρα καὶ ἐγένετο πρωί, ἡμέρα ἕκτη. "And God

---

[736] BT Berakhot 8a.

called the firmament Heaven, and God saw that it was good, and there was evening and there was morning, the second day." Could this be a more accurate reading than the Masoretic Text? One might argue that this possibility should not be ignored. However, whoever introduced this editorial gloss in the Septuagint, failed to take into consideration that the divisions of waters were not completed until the separation of the dry land from the water had occurred—all of which took place on the third day—as Rashi correctly concludes. Therefore, the most appropriate place to conclude with this refrain is at the end of the third day.

Just as the interpretation of the text flows with dynamic movement, so too does the actual transmission of a text. Textual scholar Ronald S. Hendel explains, "The task of textual criticism begins with a recognition of the validity of Heraclitus's maxim in the transmission of texts: πάντα ῥεῖ (*panta rei*), 'all things flow.' All texts transmitted by scribes, as by other means, change over time."[737] Fluidity is by no means limited to how to interpret a text; it pertains no less to how a traditional text has been transmitted over the generations since its redactional inception. Earlier we used the metaphor of the tapestry to denote the weaving of strands of interpretations that were contributed by past generations; this same idea applies no less to the area of textual transmission, which is also made up of strands of tradition. Granted, many of these strands are frayed and even tattered, while others remain remarkably intact. Without considering the textual condition of a text, interpretive efforts by a literary critic or commentary may prove to be founded on a faulty understanding of the text.

There are a number of Orthodox rabbinic scholars of the Lithuanian and Hassidic variety who tend to view textual criticism with suspicion, for an immaculate text—one that is dictated by God to Moses—allows no room for error. According to Maimonides' *Thirteen Principles of Faith*, every word, every letter of the Torah is inerrant. Jewish law later substantiated this theological view. If, during the Torah reading, a single letter isfound to be defective, damaged, or missing from a Torah scroll, it cannot be chanted at a Torah service until the scroll is repaired.[738]

Several of today's most pious rabbinic scholars confidently deduce from this ruling that there is no such thing as a redactional history of the Pentateuch. These textual variants and discrepancies alone refute the notion that current Torah scrolls we now

---

[737] Ronald S. Hendel, *The Text of Genesis 1-11: Textual Studies and Critical Edition* (Oxford: Oxford University Press, 1998), 3.

[738] Mishnah Berurah expounds upon R. Yosef Karo's ruling: "If an error is discovered during the Torah reading . . ." The majority of Halachic scholars ruled that if a Torah Scroll lacks even a single word or a single letter or has an error in it, the Scroll is invalid for the reading. According to them, if one discovers an error in the Torah Scroll, even after seven people who were called to the reading already read from it, it is necessary to go back to the beginning of the portion and read it again from a valid Torah scroll and say the blessings for that reading" (*Mishna Berurah* on O.H. 143:4, note 13).

have are bereft of errors. To assert the contrary is to presuppose the inerrancy of the scribe—which in the final analysis is a near impossibility—that would require a miracle of biblical proportions! Historically, as Hendel observes, the vast weight of rabbinic opinion indicates that in effect, there is no single manuscript that could ever qualify as *the* Masoretic Text; in fact, each of these variant texts could arguably be considered "Masoretic."[739]

What we have here, are, as Hendel notes, ". . . texts, editions, translations, manuscripts, and fragments. Each of these preserves a version of the text, and each version has been affected by the vicissitudes of time and transmission."[740] Moreover, Hendel elsewhere elaborates, "Every known ancient Hebrew manuscript of the Bible—including every ancient manuscript of the traditional Masoretic text—has a different number of letters."[741] For those who advocate the using of the Torah as a gigantic anagram, the textual discrepancies of the MT demolish any theory that the there is a hidden "code" embedded within the Torah text than can only be understood with the help of computer technology.

Historically, the Masoretic Text was first established by the Karaite Aharon ben Moshe ben Asher (ca. 10th century), and later by R. Jacob ben Hayyim of Venice in 1524-1525. These manuscripts reveal dramatic differences in the area of spelling, vocalization, and Masoretic marginalia.[742] Textual criticism (commonly referred to as "lower criticism"[743]) concerns itself with the task of restoring the original text based on the oldest manuscripts that are currently in existence. Scholars sift and weigh the variant readings and scientifically attempt to arrive at what may have been the original text that was first written.[744]

---

[739] Marc Shapiro brilliantly writes, "It is only natural that Me'iri, to mention one example of many, speaks of 'Masoretic works' rather than a single Masoretic text (*Beit HaBehirah* on BT Kiddushin 30a). In fact, he could not have spoken of the Masoretic text because this characterization is not part of traditional Jewish terminology, but is, rather, a relatively recent invention of printers and editors" *The Limits of Orthodox Theology* (Oxford: Littman Library of Jewish Civilization, 2004), 92-93, see also 91-123.

[740] Ronald S. Hendel, *The Text of Genesis 1-11: Textual Studies and Critical Edition, op. cit.*, 5.

[741] Ronald S. Hendel,"The Secret Code Hoax," *Bible Review* 13 (August 1997), 23.

[742] The term "marginalia" refer to the notes that are written along the margins.

[743] The science of textual criticism has often been called "lower criticism," since it is concerned with the preliminary task of producing a clearer Hebrew text as the basis of which historical-critical method, or "higher criticism," does its work. Since the terms "lower" and "higher" are likely to suggest judgments of worth or value, these designations are gradually falling into disuse.

[744] An excellent resource: Jacob Weingreen: *An Introduction to the Critical Study of the Text of the Hebrew Bible* (Oxford University Press, New York, 1981).

Generally speaking, there are three kinds of anomalies affecting the physical integrity of a text. Sometimes they are of an unintentional nature; other times, the ancient scribes purposely tampered with the text itself. Here are some other orthographic anomalies that include:

- Dots written over certain letters[745] and words[746] (known as *puncta extraordinaria)* which are found in fifteen places in the Tanakh[747], ten of which are in the Pentateuch.

- Large lettering (*literae majuscula)*[748] and small lettering (*minusculae*).[749]

- Suspended lettering indicates a scribal insertion.[750]

- Mutilated *wāw* in שלום (Num. 25:12) and ק (Exod. 32:25) and Num. 7:2).

- The use of inverted *Nûns* in Numbers 10:35–36, indicate a bracketing of the text, much like the way a parenthesis is now used.[751]

- Missing consonants.

B. Kethib and Kêrî Readings and Debates

Indeed, prior to the Renaissance, Jewish scholars had already begun debating some of the theological implications involved with textual criticism: concerning the traditions,

---

[745] Cf. Gen. 16:5, 18:9, 19:33, 35, Num. 9:10.

[746] Gen. 33:4, 37:12, Num. 3:39, 21:30, 29:15, Deut. 29:28.

[747] 2 Sam. 19:20, Isa. 44:9, Eze. 41:20, 46:22, Ps 27:13.

[748] Gen. 1:1; Lev. 11:42.

[749] Gen. 2:4.

[750] One of the most interesting cases involving a deliberate insertion of a letter occurs in Judges 18:30, וַיָּקִימוּ לָהֶם בְּנֵי־דָן אֶת־הַפָּסֶל וִיהוֹנָתָן בֶּן־גֵּרְשֹׁם בֶּן־מְ֫נַשֶּׁה "The Danites set up the carved idol for themselves, and Jonathan, son of Gershom, son of Manasseh . . ." It is obvious the biblical narrator wished to protect Moses's reputation on account of his grandson's apostasy, ergo, the scribe changes the name of the culprit's grandfather! For other verses involving suspended lettering see Ps. 80:14; Job 38:13, 15.

[751] These letters indicated that the passage does not belong in the present context (cf. *Sipre* 84 on Num. 10:35). In the Masoretic tradition these signs developed into that of inverted *nuns,* but originally they had the form of a sigma [(] and an antisigma [)].also found in 11QpaleoLev, 1QS, 1QM, and in the writings of the Alexandrian textual critics indicating elements that did not belong to the text. These are the forerunners of our modern parentheses.

concerning the *kethib* and the *kêrî*, i.e., the written text vs. the pronounced text. According to R. David Kimchi (1160-1235), one of the medieval Jewish world's greatest commentators, there is a simple explanation for why there are orthographic variants in the text.

> Oftentimes, words in the Tanakh are written one way in the main text known as כְּתִיב (*kethib* = "written"*)*, while variant "pronounced" reading known as קְרִי (*kêrî* = "to be read") is indicated in the outer margins of a text. Undoubtedly, a prophet or some other divinely inspired speaker must have spoken one version—not two! It seems to me that the reason for this ambiguity can be historically traced back to the period of the first Exile. During that time, books were misplaced and lost; scholars who were familiar with the Torah died. When the men of the Great Assembly restored the Torah to its former glory, they discovered variant readings in the manuscripts and went according to the majority. Concerning textual passages they could not decide, sometimes they wrote one version of the text but did not vocalize it; other times they wrote it in the margin but not inside the text, or, they wrote it one way and another way in the margin.[752]

Kimchi was not alone; Isaac ben Moses ha-Levi (c. 1350 – c. 1415), also known by his Latin name, "Profiat Duran" (Efodi), concurs with Kimchi, and admits that the textual variants are due to the difficulties of Jewish life in the Diaspora.[753] It was only natural that there would be some degree of textual uncertainty as to the Kêrî and *Kethib* variants.

> During those seventy years of the Babylonian exile, loss (*hefseḏ*) and confusion (*bilbul*) began to overtake them [i.e., the holy books], so that the people forsook them. And, because the chief of the Scribes, Ezra the Priest, the Scribe, realized this, he armed himself and mustered all his strength to correct the errors (*ha-me*ʿ*uwaṯ*); and all the Scribes who followed him did likewise. They corrected those scrolls as well as possible, this being the reason for their remaining complete in the number of *parašiyyoṯ*, and of verses, and of words, and of letters, and of plene and defective spelling, and of irregular and regular usage, etc. And for this reason, they were called Scribes; and they wrote books containing this [information]—the books of the Masorah. And in those places where loss and confusion encroached [upon the text], they left [variant: they made] the *Kêrî* and the *Keṯiḇ* for it to record the doubt about what was found.[754]

---

[752] *Kimchi's Commentary* on 2 Samuel 15:21.

[753] M. Me'iri notes, "Certain matters became doubtful with the passage of time. Today we no longer know whether the *waw* in *gahon* (Lev. 11:42) belongs to the first half of the Torah or in the second half. Consequently, this issue cannot be resolved by counting the letters of Torah. Although we rely on generally accepted Torah scrolls, we can no longer be certain as to which words are the silent letters written, and which words are the silent letters dropped" (*Beit HaBehirah* on BT Kiddushin 30a).

[754] See Barry Levy, *Fixing God's Torah* (Oxford: Oxford University Press, 2001), 81.

However, not all subsequent rabbinic scholars accept Kimchi's matter-of-fact explanation. Dan Isaac Abarbanel takes Kimchi to task. The idea of rabbis tampering with the sacred text, Abarbanel argues, diminishes the essential sanctity of the prophetic books.

> The opinion these scholars advance seems utterly incomprehensible to me! How can I believe or dare suggest the possibility that Ezra the Scribe found questionable books of God's written Tanakh in state of neglect and confusion? If a Torah scroll that is missing one letter is considered ritually invalid, how much more should if a *kêrî* and *kethib* came together in the Torah, which would imply that sundry letters are missing. Our sole comfort, it would seem, is the fact that the Torah remains with us—even in a state of exile! If we concurred with these scholars (Kimchi and Efod) we will have nothing else to rely upon. The prophet Isaiah exclaims, "He shall come to Zion a redeemer to those of Jacob who turn from sin, says the LORD. This is the covenant with them which I myself have made, says the LORD: My spirit which is upon you and my words that I have put into your mouth shall never leave your mouth, nor the mouths of your children Nor the mouths of your children's children from now on and forever, says the LORD" (Isa. 59:20). The verse bears witness to us that the physical integrity of the Torah, along with the words of the prophets and holy inspiration will not suffer from even the slightest deviation at all. Maimonides too, in his commentary to the Mishnah demands that every believer to accept that the Torah we have today is the same as that given to Moses on Mount Sinai, with no changes whatsoever—as specified in his Eighth Principle of Faith.[755]

Abarbanel justifies the differences of the *kêrî* and the *kethib* by arguing that the prophet deliberately wrote down an unusual form, and by doing so, wished to allude to some of the hidden mysteries of the Torah—depending on the degree of his prophecy. In light of this, Ezra never presumed to alter the text out of a respect that there may have been a hidden reason why a missing or an extra letter or peculiar idiom was added.

Professor Marc B. Shapiro skillfully argues that historically, numerous rabbinic scholars over the last millennium concur with Kimchi's view of the *kêrî* and the *kethib*[756] over Abarbanel and his cohorts. Yet, for most religious Orthodox Jews living today, it is the view of Abarbanel that prevails.[757] Barry Levy cites a well-known question that one scholar posed to one of the greatest Halachic scholars of the mid-20th century, R. Avraham Yeshya Karelitz a.k.a. "the Hazon Ish" (1878-1953): If a Torah scroll were discovered that differs from those that are currently used—even if it had belonged to

---

[755] *Abarbanel's Introduction to his Commentary on Jeremiah.*

[756] See Barry Levy, *Fixing God's Torah, op. cit.,* 15–6, 22, 32, 68, 76–81, 143–9, 151, 153–4, 174. See also Marc B. Shapiro, *The Limits of Orthodox Theology* (Oxford, G. B.: Littman Library of Jewish Civilization, 2004), 91-123.

[757] Rabbi Moses Feinstein reinterprets a view expressed by Maimonides, "Anyone who denies the Torah is not Divine—even if he says this about just one sentence or word—or if he says that Moses made the Torah up all by himself, such a person is a denier" (MT, *Hilkhot Teshuvah 3:8).* According to R. Feinstein, this applies even to a person who denies so much as one letter of the Torah (*Iggerot Moshe, Orah Hayyim*, Vol. 4 [New York: Moses Feinstein, 1981], no. 24, 39–42). It is important to note that R. Moshe Feinstein evokes the epithet of "denier" more than any Halachic scholar has done in history.

Rabbi Akiba or to Moses himself, would all current Torah scrolls have to undergo revision? The saintly rabbi replied that even if such a scroll were discovered, it would be totally inconsequential for the Halacha. Levy points out that another scholar who knew the Hazon Ish quite well, refused to accept such an anecdotal story as evidence of what the scholar really thought[758]. However, Levy seems dubious whether anything can alter the spirit of conservativism that is endemic to the Orthodox community.

One of the greatest living Talmudic scholars of our age, R. David Weiss Halivni, explains that the question whether one follows the written text versus the variant pronounced tradition, has practical implications in a variety of Talmudic discussions.[759] Among the early rabbis, some felt that *kêrî* takes precedence over *kethib* while others argued the opposite. Practically speaking, Weiss Halivni points out that the *kethib* must be kept intact—a Torah scroll is never corrected to reflect the *Qere* pronunciation of the text. Rather than recall all the questionable Torah scrolls, Ezra and his committee decided to allow for the possible errors in transmission by an unwitting scribe who erred. Weiss Halivni writes:

> The Radak's[760] opinion places the ambiguity between *Kêrî* and *kethib* in the period of exile and attributes the transmission of both forms to Ezra himself. Some, however, may also say that instances of *kêrî* and *kethib* arose through the gradual and accidental accumulation of errata in the text, following canonization. If a word was recorded in error, following a scribal error or an error of mistaken hearing, the altered text might have been circulated and accepted as holy writ before the error became apparent. Someone with knowledge of the previous unaltered text might then have noticed the discrepancy. Even so, the altered text could not be replaced, since conscious tampering with the written word would not have been acceptable. Therefore the previous, unaltered text would have been reintroduced, at a later date, as an adjunct oral tradition, to be pronounced aloud as a *kêrî*, but not to displace the written word, the *kethib*. Alternatively, it may have happened that a small group within the chain of textual transmission, somehow unwittingly introduced alterations in its text. Over time, this divergence from the textual mainstream may have resulted in two or more subtly different versions of the canon, circulating at the same time. The variant readings of either group may then have been added marginally to the text of the other, as *kêrî*, leaving the text in place as *kethib*.

C. Emendations of the Scribes -- תִּקּוּנֵי סוֹפְרִים *(Tiqqûnê sôpêrîm)*

One day, a scribe came across an unusual passage that piqued his interest and curiosity. As he was reading Genesis 18:22, he realized that the text read: עוֹדֶנּוּ עֹמֵד לִפְנֵי

[758] Barry Levy, *Fixing God's Torah, op. cit.*, 173.

[759] Cf. BT Sukkah 6a; BT Sanhedrin 4a.

[760] R. David Kimchi.

וַיהוָה אַבְרָהָם "And YHWH was standing before Abraham." This anthropomorphic expression seemed so shocking— he wondered: How could God, the Creator of the world, stand as though He were a servant waiting upon a mortal? The sheer audacity of it all! The scribe felt it was his duty, as it were, to "correct the text" and so he changed the order of the text to read: וְאַבְרָהָם עוֹדֶנּוּ עֹמֵד לִפְנֵי יְהוָה "Abraham stood before YHWH." According to tradition, there are eighteen passages[761] where the early scribes essentially emend the text to avoid making it appear inappropriate to a reader or community who understand the text as it was being read.[762] The Sages were not unanimously clear as to what these eighteen texts might have been, and it is possible they are mentioned, to illustrate the fact that such emendations (תִּקּוּנֵי סוֹפְרִים) have taken place. According to Ernst Würthwein, moreover, there may indeed be even more, which were added sometimes for theological and other motivations.[763]

D. *Some of the Modern Techniques Used in Textual Criticism*

Here are some of the typical errors found in manuscripts:

- *Haplography* — a scribal slip involving the writing of any word, single letter, or syllable only once when it should have been written more than once.[764]

- *Dittography* — is the phenomenon of writing a letter or word twice instead of once.[765] One of the best examples can be seen in Leviticus 20:10, which reads:

[761]The list of *Tiqqûnê sôpĕrîm include:* Gen. 18:22; Num. 11:15; 12:12; 1 Sam. 3:13; 2 Sam. 16:12; 20:1; 1 Kgs. 12:16; Jer. 2:11; Ezek. 8:17; Hos. 4:7; Hab. 1:12; Zech. 2:8 (MT 12); Mal. 1:12; Ps. 106:20; Job 7:20; 32:3; Lam. 3:20; 2 Chr. 10:16.

[762] Ellis R. Brotzman offers an even more graphic illustration based on a text in Habakkuk 1:12: "The Masoretic Text of which is translated, 'Are you not from of old, YHWH [sic], my God, my Holy One? We will not die.' According to the scribal tradition, the text originally stated that 'You [YHWH] will not die.' Christian D. Ginsburg argues from the parallelism and from the Targum rendering that this is the clear meaning of the passage, but apparently the scribes' sensibilities would not allow them to let the text stand as written" Ellis R. Brotzman, *Old Testament Textual Criticism: A Practical Introduction* (Grand Rapids, MI: Baker Books), 117.

[763] See Ernst Würthwein and Erroll F. Rhodes (tr.), *The Text of the Old Testament: An Introduction to the Biblia Hebraica Ernst Wurthwein* (Grand Rapids, MI: Eerdsmans, 1991), 17-18.

[764] See for example, in the MT of 2 Sam. 22:41 a *nun* is missing, giving the nonsense form תַּתָּה instead of the obviously required נָתַתָּה, "you have given."

[765] According to 1 Chronicles 8:4, וַאֲחוֹחַ "Ahoah" is listed as the sixth son of Bela and grandson of Benjamin; the name is most likely should read אֲחִיָּה Ahijah.

וְאִישׁ אֲשֶׁר יִנְאַף אֶת־אֵשֶׁת אִישׁ אֲשֶׁר יִנְאַף אֶת־אֵשֶׁת רֵעֵהוּ מוֹת־יוּמַת הַנֹּאֵף וְהַנֹּאָפֶת And the man that committeth adultery with another man's wife, **even he that committeth adultery with his neighbor's wife,** both the adulterer and the adulteress shall surely be put to death (OJPS), while in most modern translations, the text simply reads: "If a man commits adultery with his neighbor's wife, both the adulterer and the adulteress shall be put to death" (NAB).

As the reader will observe, the above portion that is highlighted in bold-faced lettering could just as easily have been left out of the text. Modern translations are much more aware of the text's awkwardness, than were many of the older biblical translations.

- *Metathesis* — involves a reversal of the order of two sounds or letters in a word, either as a mispronunciation or as a historical, dialectical variant or orthographic development.[766]

- *Fission* — occurs whenever a single word is divided into two separate words.

- *Fusion* — occurs whenever two words become fused as one word.[767]

- *Homophony* — involves one of two or more words pronounced alike[768] but different in meaning or derivation or spelling.[769]

---

[766] For example, the word for "lamb" may sometimes appear as in the usage, אִם־כֶּשֶׂב הוּא־מַקְרִיב (*ʾim-keśeḇ hûʾ-maqrîḇ* = "if he offers a lamb") as in Leviticus 3:7); sometimes lamb may be spelled: כֶּבֶשׂ as in the expression וְאִם־כֶּבֶשׂ יָבִיא (*wəʾim-keḇeś yāḇîʾ* = "if he brings a lamb" as in Leviticus 4:32.

[767] A good example of fusion can be seen in the passage from Amos 6:12, הַיְרֻצוּן בַּסֶּלַע סוּסִים אִם־יַחֲרוֹשׁ בַּבְּקָרִים כִּי־הֲפַכְתֶּם לְרֹאשׁ מִשְׁפָּט וּפְרִי צְדָקָה לְלַעֲנָה "Do horses run upon the rocks? Doth one plough *it* with oxen?" (YLT). However, most modern translations read, "Do horses run on rocks? Does one plow the sea with oxen?" (NRSV). Here is the reason for the difference. The question posed by the prophet Amos, "Can one plough with oxen" –the answer is only too obvious: People do all the time! But this kind of reading totally subverts the sarcasm of the prophet. Clearly he wanted to make the exact opposite point, therefore, modern commentators since the time of 18th century commentator J. D. Michaelis argue that the text needs to be changed from בַּבְּקָרִים (*babbəqārîm* = "with oxen") to בְּבָקָר יָם (*babbəqār yām*) With this emendation the parallelism is kept intact since one obviously cannot plow the sea!

[768] In English there are many such examples, such as *to, too,* and *two.*

[769] The HALOT (pg. 511) points out several examples of how homophony works: ". . . לֹא read as לוֹ (cf. Tractate Soferim 6:5, 6; Bardtke *Fschr. Alt* 2:22) Exod. 2:18 (יעד) Lev. 11:21; 1 Sam. 2:3; 2 Sam 16:18 2 Kgs. 8:10; Isa. 49:5; Ps 100:3; Job 13:15; Ezra 4:2; 1 Chr. 11:20; read as לֹא(= לוֹ) Gen 23:11; Ps 407 Job 9:33; 23:6; Ruth 2:13."

- *Misreading similar letters* — tired scribes sometimes confused one letter of a word for another of similar shape.[770]
- *Homoeoteleuton* — occurs when an intervening passage due to one line, has a similar ending on another line, e.g., as between two sentences.[771]
- *Homoeoarktoz* — this could involve the omission of an intervening passage from the beginning of two similar sentences.[772]

Excursus 3: Discerning the Purpose of Creation

This whole creation is essentially subjective, and the dream is the theater where the dreamer is at once: scene, actor, prompter, stage manager, author, audience, and critic.
—CARL GUSTAV JUNG, *Psychological Reflections*

Genesis chronicles how God created the universe and the world. Yet, one obvious question remains a mystery: Why does God create? What kind of "desire" prompts God to create? Surely had there been no "desire" on the part of God, there would not be a world. Of course, by the term "desire," we are speaking only in analogical terms. As one modern philosopher noted, the presence of desire does not always flow from a "rational source" with respect to human behavior:

---

[770] One of the best examples involves the enlarged אֶחָד of Deuteronomy 6:4 and Exodus 34:14, לֹא תִשְׁתַּחֲוֶה לְאֵל אַחֵר; The reason these two letters were enlarged was to avoid a possible transposition of the ר and the letter ד that convey the antithetical meaning of the verse –"You shall not worship the **One** God!" I suspect a scribal error of this sort became the reason why these two letters were enlarged, so that the scribes would be more conscious of what they were doing! A mistaken transposition in Deut. 6:4 might read, "Hear O Israel, the LORD is a pagan god!" Such a scribal error in all likelihood caused alarm when a Torah reader mistakenly read the text before a community. However, such mistakes were not that uncommon. A similar example can be seen in Genesis 10:4 and 1 Chronicles 1:7 concerning the identification of the **D**odanim and the **R**odanim.

[771] A good example of a homoeoteleuton can be seen in G Wenham's notes to Gen. 4:1; he explains: [The] "Samaritan Pentateuch adds נלכה השתה "let us go into the field" and this is supported by the ancient versions except by Targum, Onkelos, and the Syriac, which says "let us go down into the valley." The clause may have been omitted in MT because of a homoeoteleuton with "in the field." But the difficulty of MT may have prompted the expansion found in the other texts" G. Wenham, *Vol. 1: Word Biblical Commentary: Genesis 1-15. Word Biblical Commentary, op. cit.*, 94.

[772] As a possible example, E. R. Brotzman writes, "The Masoretic Text has a four-word sequence יוֹם לַשָּׁנָה יוֹם לַשָּׁנָה ("a day for a year, a day for a year" [Num. 14:34]), but some medieval manuscripts containיוֹם לַשָּׁנָה only once instead of twice[772] *Old Testament Textual Criticism: A Practical Introduction* (Grand Rapids, MI: Baker Books, 1994), 113.

> Indeed, we don't form them; they form themselves from within us. They simply pop into our heads, uninvited and unannounced. While they reside there, they take control of our lives. A single rogue desire can trample the plans we had for our lives and thereby alter our destinies.[773]

How is the nature of divine desire akin to human desire? Would it be more theologically correct to suggest that God's "desire" be considered "transrational" in nature? Some Hassidic thinkers assert that a divine desire is a transrational category that is beyond human comprehension. Before we contemplate the reality of creation itself, we must ask other questions: Why did God create *this particular world?* Does creation serve a purpose beyond itself? These questions are simple enough, yet the *Book of Genesis* does not offer a direct answer.

Despite the reticence of the earlier generations to supply a clear and cogent answer to this simple but baffling question, several theological, scriptural, or philosophical answers have been proposed throughout the ages that attempt to answer this question. The Cambridge historian and philosopher Arthur Lovejoy writes that God's creation derives from the "Principle of Plentitude." This notion has its roots in ancient Greek thought, and various permutations of the concept have appeared throughout the history of Western metaphysics and science. Lovejoy points out that in Plato's *Timaeus,* the transition from the eternal to the temporal, or from the ideal to the sensible—every possible form that exists becomes actualized.[774] Aristotle agrees that "no possibilities which remain eternally possible will go unrealized."[775]

The first century Judaic philosopher Philo of Alexandria also concurs. God creates because creativity is part of His Divine nature. "For God never ceases from making something or other; but, as it is the property of fire to burn, and of snow to chill, so also it is the property of God to create."[776] Over two centuries later, the neo-Platonic philosopher Plotinus expounds a similar thought: it is the nature of the One in its perfection to "overflow," producing in its exuberance the existence of the "Other."[777] All beings, then, participate in the nature of the Good in such measure as they may, according to their individual capacity. The implications of this theory as it pertains to the reality of evil cannot be understated. In the grand scheme of reality, every facet in the universe serves a specific function and purpose. Plotinus explains:

[773] William Irvine, *On Desire: Why We Want What We Want* (New York: Oxford University Press, 2006), 11.

[774] *Timaeus* 30c, 39e, 42e, 51a, 92c.

[775] *Metaphysics,* Book IX, 1047b 3.

[776] *Allegorical Interpretations* 1:3.

[777] *The Six Enneads* 5:21.

> Are we, then, to conclude that particular things are determined by Necessities rooted in Nature and by the sequence of causes, and that everything is as good as anything can be? No: the Reason-Principle is the sovereign, making all: it wills things as they are and, in its reasonable act, it produces even what we know as evil: it cannot desire all to be good: an artist would not make an animal all eyes; and in the same way, the Reason-Principle would not make all divine; it makes Gods but also celestial spirits, the intermediate order, then men, then the animals; all is graded succession, and this in no spirit of grudging but in the expression of a Reason teeming with intellectual variety. We are like people ignorant of painting who complains that the colors are not beautiful everywhere in the picture: but the Artist has laid on the appropriate tint to every spot. Or we are censuring a drama because the persons are not all heroes but include a servant and a rustic and some scurrilous clown; yet take away the low characters and the power of the drama is gone; these are part and parcel of it.[778]

In more recent times, Alfred North Whitehead regarded the principle of plentitude as God's aesthetic desire to create beauty in the cosmic order. Since God's power is conceived only in relational terms, the Creator requires conscious participation on the part of every entity in the cosmos to realize the fullness of its divine potential.

> The order of the world, the depth of reality of the world, the value of the world in its whole and in its parts, the beauty of the world, the zest of life, the peace of life, and the mastery of evil, are all bound together—not accidentally, but by reason of this truth: that the universe exhibits a creativity with infinite freedom, and a realm of forms with infinite possibilities: but . . . this creativity and these forms are together impotent to achieve actuality apart from the completed ideal harmony, which is God.[779]

From a different perspective, the following paradox emerges from Genesis 1:1. Prior to God's act of Creation (assuming that we can even liberate ourselves from speaking of Creation in temporal terms, which is nearly impossible since we are born and exist solely in sequential time and have no other means of speaking about God except through human speech—with all of its limitations) God was not a Creator! God becomes a "Creator" only by virtue of creating and entering into a relationship with Creation. Jewish mystics have long recognized that God's true oneness is best reflected through diversity and opposites and in reality is a paradoxical state in which the polarities of being exist side by side without conflict. This would also suggest that the cosmos, in some mysterious way, has a determining effect upon the Creator. Ordinarily, traditional theology emphasizes creaturely dependence upon the Creator. The act of creation externalizes a God's fullness of being as the philosophers Plato, Aristotle, Philo, and Plotinus intuited. For a fuller treatment of this subject see the Excursus 4 on the theme of *Romantic Theology*.

---

[778] *The Six Enneads*, 3:11.

[779] Alfred North Whitehead, *Religion in the Making* (New York: World Publishing, 1960), 115.

Excursus 4: Romantic Theology: Creation Flows from Love

Love gives naught but itself and takes naught but from itself.
—KAHIL GIBRAN, *The Prophet*

For much of Jewish tradition, mystics and spiritual teachers alike have believed that the purpose of Creation derived from Divine love. These primal intuitions are present throughout the Bible itself, which chronicles a plethora of metaphors depicting how God relates to the world and all of its creatures, out of love, compassion, and concern.[780] While some thinkers argue that these scriptural depictions are a concession to the popular imagination, others differ.

According to Michael Wyschogrod, there is real danger lurking behind rationalistic faith when God ceases to be a "Thou" Who enters into a relationship with human beings. Instead, the Divine is ontologically reduced to nothing more than a grand theological abstraction, or the "God-idea" as John Dewey, M. Kaplan and their followers were fond of saying. Wyschogrod chronicles the historical progression that originally began when Judaism first encountered the wisdom of the Greeks, "And gradually the philosophic God comes to permeate Jewish consciousness. The real God whom Adam feared and loved fades, to be replaced by a philosophical principle. The real estrangement between God and man has begun."[781]

A. *Hasdai Crescas – Creation Reveals Divine Love*

Fortunately, many medieval Judaic thinkers[782] realized the dangers of a cognitive faith that appeals solely to the mind at the expense of the heart. The Spanish thinker R. Hasdai Crescas (1340-1410) rejected Maimonides' stoic theological attitude[783]and

---

[780] *Cf.* Exod. 15:13; 33:19; 34:6–7; Deut. 4:31; 7:6–8, 13; 10:15, 18; 13:17–18; 23:5; 34:6; 1 Chron. 16:34; Pss. 6:4; 8:3, 4; 18:50; 25:6,8; 32:10; 36:7; 42:8; 59:17; 63:3,9; 78:38; 86:5; 89:30–34;103:17; 106:1; 107:1, 8, 43; 136:1–5, 26; 138:2, 8; 145:8, 17; 146:8; Isa. 38:17; 55:7; Jer. 3:12; 31:3; 33:11; Lam. 3:22–23; Job 7:17; Joel 2:13; Jon. 4:2; Mic. 7:18; Mal. 1:2; Zech. 1:16, et al.

[781] Michael Wyschogrod, *The Body of Faith* (San Francisco: Harper & Row Publishers, 1983), 83.

[782] Bahya ibn Pakuda and Meir ibn Gabbai were among the earlier exponents of romantic theology as well.

[783] Crescas asserts that according to Maimonides, the reason Divine love did not factor into Maimonides' theology was to speak of "God's love" only has anthropomorphic value as a figure of speech, which is intended solely for the ignorant masses who cannot imagine God being indifferent to humankind. B. Spinoza concurs with Maimonides (*contra* Crescas and J. Abarbanel), plainly noting: "He, who loves God, cannot endeavor that God should love him in return" the reason being, love is caused for the purpose of one's pleasure, but God is perfect and has no need for pleasure" (*Ethics,* 5:19). In light of this, one is also compelled to say that God is incapable of *feeling* a human being's pain, since God is beyond emotion. On the matter of "God's love," Spinoza writes in a classic neo-Maimonidean manner, that (1) Were God to "love man," He

stressed that all of Creation exists solely due to God's infinite capacity to express and manifest love. God's act of love is something that is never complete; it flows with continuity each moment and is immediately present—whether we consciously realize it or not. God's creation speaks to us through a grammar of Eros. Divine love is embedded into the fabric of the created order, without which nothing could exist:

> From the nature of love in general, it is clear that the love for God results in a union with God, for even in the case of physical objects, it is evident that love and concord among them are the causes of their perfection and unity. In fact, among the ancients was the opinion that the origin of *generation* is love and union, whereas the origin of decay is hatred and separation. If this is so in the case of physical objects, how much more so must it be so in the case of spiritual beings, namely, that union and unity result from the love and concord that exists between them.[784]

Crescas alludes to a philosophical theory that was originally advanced by the great pre-Socratic philosopher Empedocles (492-432 B.C.E.), who describes the entire cosmos as being ruled by two competing processes: Strife—which tears things apart and finds its representation *par excellence* in sacrificial dismemberment; Love—the force that reunites those things rent asunder by Strife. In monotheistic terms, God's love is the glue that keeps the universe intact.[785]

---

would be subject to passions that would jeopardize His immutability (2) If God loved man, then this would lead to man serving God on condition that God love him in return, and this would violate the wisdom that man should worship God without any anticipation of receiving a reward for his worship (3) the belief in an impersonal God also contributes to the social welfare of humanity, "since it teaches us to hate no one, to be angry with no one, and to envy no one and eliminates the mistaken notion of divine favoritism" (cf. Henry A. Wolfson's *The Philosophy of Spinoza: Unfolding the Latent Processes of His Reasoning* [Cambridge: Harvard University Press, 1934], 283-288). Paradoxically, it is significant that not even Spinoza could afford to dispense using anthropomorphism in his writings. According to Spinoza, "Hence it follows that God, in so far as he loves himself, loves man, and, consequently, that the love of God toward men, and the intellectual love of the mind towards God are identical."(*Ethics* 5:36). One could argue in defense of Maimonides, Maimonides is not as cerebral as Spinoza imagined him to be. Maimonides plainly writes that human morality, as envisioned in the Torah, *is possible only because it resembles God's own morality.* The entire theological concept of *Imitatio Dei* is inextricably related to anthropomorphism—a view that Maimonides, despite his fondness of Aristotle, endorsed in his MT, *Hilchot De'ot* 1:5-7 and in the conclusion of his *Guide to the Perplexed* (3:34). E. Lévinas points out that according to Maimonides' *Guide* 3:54, the greatest intellectual perfection of humankind comes when humanity emulates God's ethical attributes! Cf. Lévinas's *In the Time of the Nations* (Bloomington, IN: Indiana University Press, 1994), 172. For a similar position see M. Samuel, *The Lord is My Shepherd: The Theology of the Caring God* (Northvale, NJ: Jason Aronson Inc., 1996), 69-104 and Michael Wyschogrod, *The Body of Faith* (San Francisco: Harper & Row Publishers, 1983), 82-86.

[784] *Ohr Hashem* II, 6:1, cited in Henry A. Wolfson's *The Philosophy of Spinoza*, 276-277. See also *Ohr Hashem* I-iii-3, 24b.

[785] For Crescas, the entire Bible is a love-story about God's incessant concern for humanity. Since Abraham loved God, God reciprocated by loving Abraham. God's love of Israel is much like the love that father displays towards his son. Crescas understood the power of metaphor, but there are some biblical metaphors about God that ought to be taken literally, such as love.

B. *Judah Abarbanel's Dialogues of Love*

Another one of the great Jewish humanists of the Renaissance period, Judah Abarbanel (ca. 1460-1523), believed that a human being's intellectual love of God is reciprocated and complemented by God's love for that person. God freely creates the universe out of love. Abarbanel writes in his *Dialogue of Love* III 43a:

> *Sophia*: What then does this term love mean with reference to God?
>
> *Philone*: It means the will to improve the beings created by Him as well as the universe and to increase their perfection to the extent of which their nature is capable. The love which is in God presupposes a deficiency in the beloved, but not in the lover . . . though the Deity rejoices and joys (if the word is suitable) in the increase of the perfection of the created beings because of the love of God for them; in this, supreme perfection becomes more resplendent.[786]

Abarbanel further wrote that love is the impulse that adds to the splendor of God's infinite being. God's love and desire for Creation does not flow from anything that is lacking in Divine nature but from the object of God's affection. He desires that all entities produced may come to perfection primarily through their own efforts and deeds. From the divine perspective, God's love extends across the entire created order and is inclusive of all entities great and small, prodding each being to achieve the highest degree of perfection possible. To actualize this possibility, the Creator gives humanity unceasing help and encouragement to realize, develop, and nurture its creative potential.[787]

C. *Moshe Hayim Luzzato – Creation as Divine Giving*

Jewish mystics and Romantic theologians (such as Crescas, Judah Abarbanel, and others) have supposed that love, as an attribute, seeks to engender life through giving and nurturing. Humanity can only strive toward *imitatio dei* by developing its capacity of giving rather than receiving. R. Moshe Chaim Luzzato (18th century, Italy) made this particular point the centerpiece of his mystical theology:

> The blessed Creator is the ultimate personification of good, and it is the nature of the kind to act kindly. This is the reason God created entities, so that He might bestow favor upon them. For without the receiver, there is no benefactor of good. In His exalted

786 S. Pines, *Sources of Leone Ebreo's Doctrines* reprinted in *Jewish Thought in the Sixteenth Century*, Bernard Dov Cooperman, ed. (Cambridge, MA: Harvard University Press, 1983), 382-383.

787 Leone Ebreo, *Dialogues of Love (Dialoghi d'Amori)*, tr. F. Friedeberg-Seeley and Jean H. Barnes, (London: Soncino, 1937), 299.

> wisdom, the Divine knew that in order for this goodness to truly become complete, the receiver must be worthy to receive this goodness, through the effort of one's own hands. Only then would the beneficiary realize that he has truly earned that good and would not be humiliated in having received God's blessing, as if he were receiving a handout, for the Sages said, "One who does not eat of his own cannot look in the face of his benefactor."[788]

Luzzato makes an important point: Without Creation, God only has the potential for "good"; it is only through Creation that "goodness" becomes actualized. Central to Luzzato's mystical theology is the belief that Divine love can only be expressed through the act of giving, a Divine outpouring toward Creation.[789] Creation expresses God's infinite love. God created the universe so that all of Creation might grow and evolve, and become freely and fully conscious of its origin and ultimate being. Most importantly, of all God's earthly creatures, human beings are unique in that they are driven by a desire to discover meaning and transcendence. From the biblical text of Genesis it is clear that God never intended for people to be mere receivers and consumers in the cosmic scheme of things. The experience of transcendence can come only through personal effort and accomplishment, "by the sweat of one's brow." The key to spiritual growth and awareness comes through our capacity to act, as the Creator does, for the betterment of Creation.

D. *Abraham Joshua Heschel: God in Search of Man*

More than any recent Jewish theologian of the 20th century, Abraham Joshua Heschel points out that most theories of religion begin the search for God with a notion of Him as detached, distant, and hidden from humankind. Biblical religion is concerned with not only our search for God, but also with God's search for man, motivated by a sense of Divine pathos and concern, which seeks to evoke a human response:

> From the very first Thou didst single out man and consider him worthy to stand in Thy Presence (Yom Kippur liturgy). This is the mysterious paradox about biblical faith: God is pursuing man. It is as if God were unwilling to be alone, and that He had chosen man to serve Him. Our seeking Him is not only man's but also His concern, and must not be an exclusively human affair. His will is involved in our yearnings. All of human history as described in the Bible may be summarized in one phrase: God is in search of man. Faith in God is a response to God's question. . . .

---

[788] *Da'at Tevuvat,* Chapter 1.

[789] The motif of God creating the world out of love is central to Christian theology as well. Aquinas writes regarding the purpose of prayer: "God loves his creatures, and he loves each one the more, the more it shares in his own goodness, which is the first and primary object of his love. Therefore he wants the desires of his rational creatures to be fulfilled, because they share most perfectly in the goodness of God. And his will is an accomplisher of things, because he is the cause of things by his will. . . . So it belongs to the divine goodness to fulfill the desires of rational creatures that are put to him in prayer" (*Summa Contra Gentiles* 3:95).

. . . When Adam and Eve hid from His Presence, the LORD called: "Where art thou?" (Genesis 3:9). It is a call that goes out again and again. It is a small echo of a still small voice, not uttered in words, not conveyed in the categories of the mind, but ineffable and mysterious, as ineffable and mysterious as the glory that fills the whole world. It is wrapped in silence; concealed and subdued, yet it is as if all things were the frozen echo of: Where art thou? . . . Religion consists of *God's question and man's answer*. The way *to* faith is the way *of* faith. Unless God asks the question, all our questions are in vain.[790]

E. Norman Lamm – Creation as Divine Agape

More recently Rabbi Dr. Norman Lamm, Chancellor of Yeshiva University, expressed a similar mystical thought that resonates with Heschel's insights:

"The LORD is one" implies that God is, as it were, a lonely God. This loneliness and sadness are reflected in the divine image, humans, of whom He said, "It is not good that man should be alone" (Gen. 2:18). Both God and human beings deserve *rachmones,* pity—we, for our failure and pain and suffering, and God, for being abandoned by this creature created in God's very own image and endowed with the gift of free will that we misuse and abuse. And so each waits and longs for the other. The way to bridge the brooding cosmic loneliness, to find our way to each other, is through love.

It is this sense of mutual sympathy that gives rise to love. God reaches out for us with love—as affirmed in the blessing immediately preceding the Shema: "Blessed are You, O LORD, who chooses His people Israel *in love*"—and we, recognizing that "the LORD is One," [Deut. 6:4] that the Creator is lonely, yearning for our companionship, respond with love immediately after proclaiming God's utter oneness: "You shall *love* the LORD your God with all your heart . . ." [Deut. 6:5]. Those thinkers whose interpretations of the Love of God we discussed in chapters 10 to 14 all worked on the premise that God is transcendent and perfect: we need God, but God does not need anyone or anything. He is utterly self-sufficient. But here we are speaking of God in a different way. Conceived of in poetic and psychologically human terms, the divine-human relationship takes on a different dimension, best understood through distinction between two types of love usually referred to in theological writings by their Greek names, *eros* and *agape*. Agape is the love that a protective parent feels for his or her child. It is a selfless love: the parent asks nothing in return, not even to be loved by the child. Eros, in contrast, is romantic love, such as that felt by husband and wife for each other. Such love is expected to be not only reciprocal, but also mutually pleasurable. The love we feel for and from God is agape, not eros.[791]

The term *agape* indicates a love that is unconquerable and determined to outlast any opposition; it always seeks the occasion to express the highest goodness and

[790] Abraham Joshua Heschel, *God in Search of Man: A Philosophy of Judaism* (New York: Harper and Row, 1955), 136-137.

[791] Norman Lamm, *The Shema: Spirituality and Law in Judaism* (Philadelphia, PA: JPS, 1998), 122.

benevolence whenever the opportunity presents itself. This love remains steadfast even in the face of ill-treatment and insults; it seeks nothing but the highest good and welfare in others at all times—even in the face of rejection and humiliation. Talmudic wisdom bears this out. R. Yochanan states: "Wherever you find mentioned in the Scriptures the power of the Blessed Holy One, you will also find His humility."[792] By God limiting His power, humanity has the ability to do what angelic beings would find impossible—the denial of their Creator's existence. This becomes possible because God's Divine Love allows for the Other to exist with a sense of total freedom. (See Excursus 11 B-C.)

An important distinction between eros and agape is missing in Lamm's otherwise fine exposition. No romantic theology concerning God's love for Creation can be based on anything other than agape love. Analogically speaking, most human beings spend a lifetime searching for the perfect Other to possess and experience personal fulfillment and satisfaction. However, true agape love—whether it flows from a human or divine source—transcends the boundaries of eros because it risks complete vulnerability and faces the possibility of rejection. In contrast, eros seeks in others the realization of its own desire, but agape love does not focus solely upon the beloved for its own personal enrichment or fulfillment.[793] Agape love is concerned with the good and welfare of the Other, while revealing a different kind of love that is oppositional to any kind of self-love. For these reasons, agape is the apt metaphor when expressing Divine Love. In the prophetic literature of the seventh century, the prophets invariably express God's love for Israel in terms of agape and not eros.

F. Alfred North Whitehead: The Eternal Urge of Desire

Humanity's existential loneliness may not be a fluke. In some mysterious way, God too may "suffer" (anthropomorphically speaking) from the same condition. The Hebrew word for "one" may also mean "alone" (which incidentally comes from the Old English "all one"). Creation occurs because of God's desire for alterity. In poetic terms, would it be inconceivable to suggest that it is the nature of the Divine to outflow love on an infinite scale? Love cannot help but unfold in an endless array of finite worlds, of almost infinite diversity. This concept finds considerable support by British physicist and process philosopher Alfred North Whitehead, who views God's activity through the prism of love. The nature of love allows for the space of the Other. According to Whitehead, God is "the lure for feeling, the eternal urge of desire"[794] that propels each

---

[792] BT Megillah 31a.

[793] There is a well-known and oft quoted NT passage that captures this concept well, "Love (ἀγάπη) is patient; love is kind; love is not envious or boastful or arrogant or rude. It does not insist on its own way; it is not irritable or resentful; it does not rejoice in wrongdoing, but rejoices in the truth. It bears all things, believes all things, hopes all things, endures all things. Love never ends . . ." (1 Corinthians 13:4-8).

[794] A. N. Whitehead. *Process and Reality,* Corrected Ed. (New York: Free Press, 1978), 346.

entity in the created order to realize its divine purpose. Divine love is faithful, abiding, and is always at work:

> God's role is not the combat of productive force with productive force, of destructive force with destructive force. It lies in the patient operation of the overpowering rationality of his conceptual harmonization. He does not create the world, he saves it, or more accurately, he is the Poet of the world, with tender patience leading it by his vision of truth, beauty, and goodness.[795]

Whitehead's enchanting metaphor, "Poet of the world," teaches us that there is something profound about the nature of existence that cannot be reduced to an equation or scientific formula. The works of the Bible likewise possess an essence and quality that transcends binary code or other mathematical algorithms. The divine design of this beauty is most obvious when human beings learn to discern Creation as an aesthetic masterpiece.

G. Franz Rosenzweig: From Creation to Revelation

The early 20th century Jewish thinker, Franz Rosenzweig, offers a different approach with respect to his particular view of romantic theology. Rosenzweig believes that Creation per se does not really disclose God's Presence to the world. Creation is not an end in and of itself; but rather, the purpose of Creation is revelation. Without revelation, we cannot recognize the world as God's Creation. When God reveals Himself to humankind as "I," the Divine Presence awaits for a response, which allows for the possibility of dialogical relationship. Unlike Adam, who is reticent to engage God in a meaningful dialogue, Abraham responds to the Divine beckoning with the one and only truly meaningful response: "Here I am," i.e., "I am present to You." The "I" once it is called by name, enables the process of revelation to move beyond the impersonal discourse of creation which allows for ongoing relationship.[796]

Martin Buber later drew an important inference from Rosenzweig's nexus of creation and revelation: If there is a Creator Who is also a Revealer, then human life takes on a radically important meaning:

> The man of today knows of no beginning, As far as he is concerned, history ripples toward him from some prehistorical cosmic age. He knows of no end; history sweeps him on into a posthistorical cosmic age. What a violent and foolish episode this time between the prehistorical and the posthistorical has become! Man no longer recognizes an origin or goal

---

[795] Ibid., 344.

[796] "The immediate determinacy of the proper name appears in place of the article. With the call of the proper name the word of revelation steps into real dialogue; the proper name makes the breech in the fixed wall of thinghood" (*Star of Redemption*, 208/186).

because he no longer wants to recognize the midpoint. Creation and redemption are true only on the premise that revelation is a present experience. Man of today resists the Scriptures because he cannot endure revelation. To endure revelation is to endure the moment full of possible decisions, to respond to and be responsible for every moment. [797]

H. Emmanuel Lévinas: *Beyond the Metaphysics of Creation*

Similar to Rosenzweig, Emmanuel Lévinas believes that Creation reveals God's infinite capacity to relate toward something Other than Himself. As great as the endless chasm separating the Divine from the human truly is, this divine distance does not destroy the conscious awareness of the Other. Lévinas's definition of transcendence is especially important to keep in mind, for there is a tendency among modern thinkers to define transcendence as a state of being beyond our sensory perception and experience of the physical world. For Lévinas it is quite the opposite: "Transcendence designates a relation with a reality infinitely distant from my own reality, yet without this distance destroying this relation and without this relation destroying this distance as it would happen with relations within the same." [798] Far from being trapped within a static state of ontological "sameness," God's Being is paradoxically relational; God possesses an infinite capacity to situate Himself, so-to-speak, *beyond Himself,* that allow for the possibility and reality of ethics.[799] The capacity to relate to us as "the Other" is what enables us as human beings to relate toward another entity outside of our individual Self–just as God relates toward Creation.

In summary, some theologians (both ancient and modern) think that there may be no logical explanation for why God creates; humankind cannot grasp what lies beyond the phenomenal realm of nature.[800] With the eyes of faith, a different perception of

---

[797] Martin Buber, *Israel and the World: Essays in Time of Crisis* (New York: Schocken Books, 1948), 95.

[798] *See Totality and Infinity,* (Pittsburgh: Duquesne University Press, 1969), 43-44.

[799] Lévinas expounds: "A calling into question of the Same—which cannot occur within the egoistic spontaneity of the Same—is brought about by the Other. We name this calling into question of my spontaneity by the presence of the Other ethics. The strangeness of the Other, his irreducibility to the I, to my thoughts and my possessions, is precisely accomplished as a calling into question of my spontaneity as ethics. Metaphysics, transcendence, the welcoming of the Other by the Same, of the Other by Me, is concretely produced as the calling into question of the Same by the Other, that is, as the ethics that accomplishes the critical essence of knowledge" (*op. cit.*, 33).

[800] In Kantian terms, we only know the sensory world (i.e., the world of appearance) from within a continuum of time, space, substance, and causality. However, time, space, substance, and causality are not objective realities that exist apart from what we normally experience. They are creations of our own mind or intuition, without which we could not grasp the awesome nature of the cosmos. As to the question, "What kind of reality exists beyond the temporal and spatial realm?" This question, according to Kant, can never be answered. What lies beyond the phenomenal and temporal reality we experience, is the world of *Ding an sich*, "the thing-in-itself", which transcends whatever human beings are capable of grasping, since it is intrinsically unknowable" (*The Critique of Pure Reason,* trans. Paul Guyer and Allen Wood [Cambridge: Cambridge University

reality occurs. Creation reveals something mysterious and profound about God's capacity to relate toward something Other than Himself. Theologians who advocate the concept of "romantic theology" intuitively feel that God's involvement with Creation, paradoxically, expresses a "desire" for "relationship," which the ancients conceived of in the poetic terms of love and fulfillment. For Jewish tradition, as Franz Rosenzweig already notes, this love of God is most visible in the precepts that were given at and after the great Sinai theophany. From the early chapters of Genesis we discover how the Torah speaks in a language that ordinary people can understand and discover something paradoxical about the Creator, or at least our understanding of the Creator: aside from being the Author of all existence, He also has personality![801]

Excursus 5: Re-reading Genesis 1:1

Why adapt a translation that has been aptly described as a verzweifelt geschacklose [hopelessly tasteless] construction, one which destroys a sublime opening to the world's greatest book?

—Hershel Shanks, "How the Bible Begins"

A. *The Odyssey of a Translation*

In the beginning God created—The preamble to Genesis has been the subject of considerable debate since the very first appearance of the Septuagint, which translates the opening verse of Genesis as, Ἐν ἀρχῇ ἐποίησεν ὁ θεὸς τὸν οὐρανὸν καὶ τὴν γῆν "In the beginning God created the heaven and the earth." The Latin Vulgate, the King James Version (KJV), and numerous other translations have made this translation the most popular of all time. More recently, an alternative translation has emerged, which has drawn considerable support from both the medieval and modern scholars[802]: "When God began to create the heaven and the earth" (NJPS). Other contemporary Bible translations aim at a new synthesis, merging older and newer translations into a single tapestry: "In the beginning, when God created the heavens and the earth" (NRSV, NAB) or, "In the beginning of creation, when God made the heaven and the earth" (REB). Karaite scholar Hakham Avraham Ben-Rahamiël Qanaï offers this pluperfect rendering: "When at first God had created the heaven and the earth . . ."[803]

Press, 1998), A17 B31.

801 For another variant on this theme, see Excursus 2.

802 G. Wenham, Victor Hamilton, G. R. von Rad, N. Sarna, Claus Westermann, to name just a few.

803 Qanaï further argues that the ample use of the *waw conversive* in the first five chapters indicates the entire section needs to be read in the pluperfect: "and the earth had been desolate and empty, and darkness had been upon the face of the sea, and a mighty wind had been blowing over the face of the water, and God had said, "let there be light", and there was light, and God had seen that the light was good, and God had differentiated between the light and the darkness, and God had called the light Yom, and He had called the darkness *Lailah*, and there had been evening and there had been morning, one *Yom* . . ." (Gen. 1:2-5). This interpretation is very similar to Rashbam's interpretation on Genesis 1:1, who explains the opening verse to mean, "After God

A modern reader may ask: What difference does it make which translation is followed? Why change the old KJV? Why is there a discrepancy among the translations? Older translations of the Bible are based on the Septuagint, which render the text Ἐν ἀρχῇ (*en arche* = "in *the* beginning"). In Greek thought, ἀρχῇ connotes not only point at which something new begins in time, but also implies its end (τέλος).[804] Since the "beginning" of something arose out of the Infinite, so too will its end dissolve itself into the Infinite much like a droplet of water that falls into the ocean. The power of the Divine is thus necessary for each moment of creation's continued existence. These ancient Judaic scholars of Alexandria grammatically read the word בְּרֵאשִׁית (*bərēʾšîṯ*) in the absolute state (i.e., which functions independently of any other word) and this translation indicates that there is a chronological order to the process of creation. Thus, when the Torah says, "In the beginning God created the heaven and the earth," this is truly *the absolute* beginning.

Are there any explicit scriptural references supporting the Septuagint's translation in the Masoretic Text? Expressed in different terms, is the noun רֵאשִׁית (*rēʾšîṯ*) ever written in the absolute state in the Tanakh? By understanding verse 1 as an independent clause and a complete sentence, it is possible that these ancient translators wished to allude to the doctrine of *creatio ex nihilo*. Philo of Alexandria also argues strongly against the older view held by some of his peers that the world had been created *in* time: "It would be more correct to say that the world was not created *in* time, but that time had its existence *in consequence* of the world. It is the motion of the heavens that has displayed the nature of time."[805]

In other words, time has just as much reality in its own right as the cosmos does; it is by no means ever independent of it. Thus, "in the beginning" means that it is the Creator Who initiates the beginning of time and space. Such a conception would have made a profound impression on non-Jewish readers of the Septuagint who were interested in learning about Judaic cosmology and the Jewish theological view of monism, which stood in stark contrast to views espoused in Greek philosophy—especially by Aristotle. Later Jewish thinkers such as Saadia Gaon, Maimonides, Ramban, Kimchi, and others have all endorsed this theological reading of Genesis 1:1.[806]

---

had created the heavens and the earth . . . when the uppermost heavens and earth *had already* been created." See Martin I. Lookshin, *Rashbam's Commentary on Genesis* (Lewiston, NY: Edwin Mellon Press, 1989), 31.

[804] In Classical Greek the term ἀρχῇ functions both in an ordinary sense and in a philosophical sense ("First Cause"). It "always signifies 'primacy,' whether in time: 'beginning,' *principium*, or in rank: 'power,' 'dominion,' 'office' " (*TDNT*, 1:499). According to the BDAG, ἀρχῇ denotes the commencement of something as an action, process, or state of being, beginning, i.e., a point of time at the beginning of a duration (BDAG 111-112).

[805] *Allegorical Interpretations* 1:2.

[806] Some scholars add that the presence of the disjunctive accent commonly referred to by Torah readers as

B. Creation from Chaos?

There are some ancient and medieval views that differ from the theologians, arguing that the creation of the world does not imply an absolute beginning, but suggests a beginning where God worked with pre-existent matter in forming the heavens and the earth. The first century Aramaic translation known as Targum Neofiti, renders בְּרֵאשִׁית as מלקדמין "from antiquity"[807] or "from time immemorial" or "from primeval times," and is similar to Onkelos's paraphrase of the text where the word בְּרֵאשִׁית is rendered as בְּקַדמִין "in antiquity." Neither of these terms allude to an absolute beginning—as suggested by the Septuagint—but rather to an indefinite point in time; this reading also agrees with the rabbinic attitude that God created other things prior to the creation of the heavens and the earth (see Gen. 1:1 regarding "Wisdom's Role in Creation").

During the medieval period, several rabbinic and Karaite commentators took sharp grammatical exception with the opinion that Genesis 1:1 speaks of an absolute beginning. According to Rashi, Ibn Ezra, and Aharon ben Eliahu, whenever רֵאשִׁית appears in the Tanakh, it is always written in the construct state ("the beginning of"). Based on this understanding בְּרֵאשִׁית ought to be read and understood as an adverbial phrase meaning: "When at first God created the heaven and earth . . ."[808] Rashi's most convincing proof that the Torah was *not* interested in teaching the reader about the order of Creation is found in verse 2, "and the Spirit of God hovered over the face of the water." The strength of Rashi's argument draws from the fact that there is no mention anywhere in the Torah of God bringing water into existence and calling the dark watery nebulous state in verse 3 "water." From this perspective, one might argue that Rashi deduces that water preceded the earth in Creation. However, Rashi warns the reader against making such a conclusion, later explaining that the Torah does not teach us anything about the sequence of the earlier or later acts of Creation. Therefore, Rashi (and similarly Ibn Ezra) argue that the correct reading of

---

the *tipha* proves that in the oral tradition handed down by the Masoretic scribes, the word was understood as an absolute. Qanaï counters that the purpose of the *tipha* is chanted so that the words will not be slurred together when read by the Torah reader—and nothing more than that—as every skilled Torah reader certainly knows.

[807] In biblical literature, קֶדֶם (*qéḏem*) is used in a number of poetic passages connoting the original created condition of the world (cf. the Targum's translation of Psa. 68:33, and Deut. 33:15).

[808] Examples of other adverbial phrase include: אָמֹר אָמַרְתִּי כִּי־שָׂנֹא שְׂנֵאתָהּ which is translated as "I certainly said, that thou didst certainly hate her," (Judg. 15:2 —YLT) or שָׁמוֹעַ שָׁמַעְתִּי – "I have surely heard . . ." (Jer. 30:18). Adverbial phrases add intensity to the text.

vv. 1-3 ought to be read: "In the beginning of God's creating the heavens and the earth—now the earth was without form . . ." [v.2]. God said, "Let there be light . . ." This translation suggests that the first thing God created was light.[809]

If the biblical narrator wanted to inform his reader or listener about the chronological order of Creation, how would this have been expressed in Biblical Hebrew? Rashi and Ibn Ezra assert that the narrator would have had to use a less ambiguous term, e.g., בָּרִאשֹׁנָה (*bārîšōnāh* = "at the beginning" or "at [the] first") or בְּרֵאשִׁית (*bərēʾšîṯ* = "in the beginning"). In any case, it would be obvious that the word רֵאשִׁית (*rēʾšîṯ*) should be read as an absolute noun.

Several contemporary biblical scholars likewise assert that in all but fifty other places where the noun רֵאשִׁית is used, it is always written in the construct state (i.e., in the beginning of . . ."), the only exception is found in Isaiah 46:10 מַגִּיד מֵרֵאשִׁית אַחֲרִית (*maggîḏ mērēʾšîṯ ʾaḥărîṯ*) "declaring the end from the beginning."[810] However, this is not quite accurate; there is one other verse, אַחֲרִית דָּבָר מֵרֵאשִׁיתוֹ (*ṭôḇ ʾaḥărîṯ dāḇār mērēʾšîṯô)* "Better is the end of a thing than its beginning" (Ecc. 7:8). Marcus Kalisch cites several other examples, some of which include: וַיַּרְא רֵאשִׁית לוֹ (*wayyár*ʾ *rēʾšîṯô*) "He chose the best for himself . . ." (Deut. 33:21), or לָרֵאשִׁית (*lārēʾšîṯ*) "for the first fruits" (Neh. 12:44). Still and all, the theological implications are significant. Based on the text's syntax, if the "beginning" is not absolute, then it could imply that Creation did not come into being instantaneously, instead, God used pre-existent materials to form

[809] Several modern scholars often cite and endorse Rashi and Ibn Ezra's interpretation—albeit, for entirely different reasons. For them, such a reading of the preamble of Genesis 1:1 implies that the cosmology of the Bible is both conceptually and linguistically influenced by the Babylonian creation epic, *Enuma elish*, which employs a similar beginning:

> When in the height heaven was not named,
> And the earth beneath did not yet bear a name,
> And the primeval Apsu, who begat them,
> And chaos, Tiâmat, the mother of them both . . .
>
> (*Enuma elish*, L.W. King (tr.), *The Seven Tablets of Creation,* London, 1902).

This hermeneutic approach presupposes that the Torah's opening salvo borrows from a theme that had been well familiar to other Semitic peoples. While there are bound to be similarities in the cosmologies of antiquity, there are differences that should not be glossed over or homogenized. The Tanakh posits one simple truth that stands apart from the theogony myths of the pagan world, namely, God is the Sole Source and Preserver of all Creation. The pagan pantheon of the Mesopotamian world did not so much as receive an honorable mention and for this reason, their names are conspicuously absent.

[810] For a survey of references on this point, see V. Hamilton's *The Book of Genesis: Chapters 1-17, op. cit.,* 104;

the extant universe, which is by its very nature—eternal.

C. Is there an Alternative Solution?

Perhaps the Sages of Alexandria had a different consonantal tradition that would certainly have affected how the Torah was read in the Alexandrian synagogues. Unlike the current Masoretic pronunciation, where the word בְּרֵאשִׁית (*bǝrēʾšîṯ*) is read, the Alexandrian Jews chanted בָּרֵאשִׁית (*bārēʾšîṯ*) instead. Although this interpretation is only conjecture, it would account for the Septuagint's translation in a way that is streamlined, simple and theologically understandable.

Although there may be little linguistic justification on the traditional translation, it does have some theological cogency. The early 20th century Italian commentator, Benno Jacob (1862-1945), argues for the older and more traditional translation:

> It is the first great achievement of the Bible to present a divine creation from nothing in contrast to evolution or formation from a material already in existence. Israel's religious genius expresses this idea with monumental brevity. In all other creation epics the world originates from a primeval matter which existed before. No other religion or philosophy dared to take this last step. Through it God is not simply the architect, but the absolute master of the universe. No sentence could be better fitted for the opening of the Book of Books than "In the beginning God created the heavens and the earth." Only an all pervading conviction of God's absolute power could have produced it.[811]

So which translation should the reader prefer? Gordon Wenham explains that the greatest strength of the old translation "rests in its antiquity, those closest in time to the composition of Gen. 1 may be presumed to be best informed about its meaning."[812] The Septuagint's original translation is also consistent with the series of terse sentences found throughout the first chapter. In terms of its literary significance, the opening preamble, "In the beginning God created the heavens and the earth" (Gen. 1:1) dovetails neatly with the verse, "This is the account of the creation of the heavens and the earth" (2:4)—especially if the original Hebrew text the Septuagint based itself on, reads בָּרֵאשִׁית (*bārēʾšîṯ*) instead of בְּרֵאשִׁית (*bǝrēʾšîṯ*).

In addition, the literary form supports the conclusion that Genesis 1:1 is an independent and central presentation of God's total creative activity from the world's inception to its Sabbath wholeness. From "In the beginning God created . . ." it is clear

---

811 *The First Book of the Bible: Genesis, Interpreted by B. Jacob* (New York: Ktav, 1974, 2007), 1.

812 *Genesis* Vol. 1, *op. cit.,* 13.

that God is the Source of all Creation and nothing could exist without God's power to bring something into existence that did not formerly exist. As mentioned earlier (see notes to 1:1), the phrase "the heavens and the earth" constitute a pair of contrasting opposites, or a merism, which includes everything in between.[813]

While many modern scholars justifiably take issue with this point, nevertheless, the biblical text, as it is, allows for both interpretive readings. It is the opinion of this commentator, that there is certainly nothing inappropriate with affirming the older translation based on the Septuagint text. However, the newer readings do enjoy considerable support from modern and medieval scholarship as well, and thus warrant respectful consideration.

Excursus 6: The Mystery of Divine Personhood

When all within is dark, and
former friends misprize,
From them I turn to Thee, and
find love in Thine eyes.
When all within is dark,
and I my soul despise,
From me I turn to Thee, and
find love in Thine eyes.
When all Thy face is dark, and
just angers arise,
From me I turn to Thee, and
find love in Thine eyes.

—*SOLOMON IBN GABRIOL, Royal Crown, 11c'*

Judah HaLevi (ca. 1075-1141) was the first Jewish thinker to differentiate the God of the patriarchs from the God of the philosophers. For Halevi, the God of the Bible is a God who has a stake in human history and is concerned with humankind. Despite the linguistic limitations of an anthropomorphic language—without which it would beimpossible to speak about God—there can be little doubt, that in the Tanakh, YHWH is more than the Eternal Being that creates and sustains the created order, but is in a mysterious way—*personal.* But what does this term exactly mean? In analogical terms, to claim that God is a personal Being, implies that God possesses the capacity to purposefully carry out His will. Most dictionaries explain that "person" derives from the Greek word πρόσωπον (*prósōpon*= "face" or "mask"). In ancient Greek dramas, the

[813] Since ancient times, the philosophical relationship between a "part versus the whole," or "the many and the one" fascinated and stimulated the growth of Western thought. The principle of approaching a whole from the perspective of its parts and treating the whole as the sum of its individual parts became known as merism.

mask would signify a specific role that an actor played; often an actor would take on several roles, hence changing masks to denote the varying "personas."

According to C. G. Jung, the *persona* represents the external and social aspects of an individual's identity that one reveals to the outer world. [814] In theological terms, when speaking about God possessing "personality," it is critical to keep in mind that this is only a metaphor that best describes God's "social" being; i.e., how God relates toward each entity within creation, as noted by Whitehead.[815] Despite the inherent limitations of the term, there are aspects of personhood that are very important—especially when pertaining to our direct relationship with the Divine. In the final analysis, personhood is deeply rooted in the uniqueness of the individual's identity. This same concept may be analogically employed when speaking about God's "personal" identity, noted correctly by Thomas Aquinas.[816] When describing God as "personal," we assert that there cannot be an "I and It" (to borrow a term from Martin Buber) relationship with God's ultimate

[814] In Jungian psychology, problems occur whenever the ego over-identifies with the *persona*, which becomes the core identity, i.e., the inner person becomes a reflection of what others expect, leaving one's inner identity empty and vacuous. Men in particular, tend to identify their core identities by the professional roles that they play in society. When that role is destroyed (as is the case with burn-victims, or when someone is publically shamed), this often creates a psychological crisis where the individual must re-discover and re-define his core identity. Cf. *Anima and Animus,* CW 7, par. 318; *Concerning Rebirth*, CW 9i, par. 221.

[815] Alfred North Whitehead argues that life contains three ingredients: self-enjoyment, creative activity, and purpose. It would be wrong to consider the light of the sun, or the formation of mountains, as mere abstractions; a kind of setting or environment for life. Life is all-pervasive, whether it be in the form of a snow flake or in the cry of an injured animal. Human beings, like the rest of nature, absorb what is outside themselves into their own being; therefore, all things are interrelated. Whitehead does not view the building blocks of the universe as tiny particles that are fixed and permanent. The underlying substance of matter is not a substance at all, but rather a system of interrelated events. Nature is composed of endless numbers of entities that share relationships (protons, electrons, neutrinos, etc.) with other entities while growing in infinite ways. Each atom, molecule, cell, organ, organism, and community receives stimulus from the other and in turn influences other patterns of activity. The relationship between God and the universe is one of immanence and interpenetration. God presents novel possibilities for each creation, thus enabling even the smallest of creation to reach its potential toward harmony and integration (A. N. Whitehead, *Process and Reality: An Essay in Cosmology* (New York: Free Press, 1979, c.1929). For a more recent development of this concept, see Ben Goertzel, *From Complexity to Creativity Explorations in Evolutionary, Autopoietic, and Cognitive Dynamics* (New York: Springer, 1997), 306-310. Also, see Paul Davies and John Gribbin, *The Matter Myth: Dramatic Discoveries That Challenge Our Understanding of Physical Reality* (New York: Simon and Schuster, 2007), 1-30.

[816]According to Aquinas, anthropomorphism teaches that there is, in a manner of speaking, a family resemblance between humanity and its Maker. A person can only interpret in terms of patterns stemming from one's individual experiences. Aquinas teaches that religious language *must* facilitate relatedness to God. "And in this way some things are said of God and creatures analogically, and not in a purely equivocal nor in a purely univocal sense for we can 'name' God only from a creaturely point of view. Hence, whatever is said of God and creatures is said according to some relation of the creature to God as to its principle and cause, wherein all the perfections of things pre-exist excellently" (*Summa Theologia* 1. Q. 13, art. 5). Elsewhere Aquinas adds: "For the words of *God is good*, or *wise,* signify not only that He is the cause of wisdom or goodness, but that these exist in Him in a more excellent way. Hence as regards what the name signifies, these names are applied primarily to God rather than to creatures" (*Summa Theologica* Q. 13, Art. 6).

reality. His existence compels relationship. If we assume that God is a "personal being," then I, as His creation, can choose to have a dialogical relationship with Him—or not. Buber argues that in the "I and Thou" relationship, we interiorize God's reality in a manner that becomes immediately triangulated in every conceivable relationship.

While many thinkers like Baruch Spinoza, David Hume, Mordechai Kaplan, and John Dewey scoff at this concept, I would encourage persons today to consider re-visioning this pivotal but elusive concept. To say that "God is personal" expresses the idea that the Creator has an interest in our destiny and that our existence is not some cosmic fluke. However, there is a negative aspect to God's personhood that must be acknowledged. Justly, Maimonides warns that there always exists the danger that we might be imagining that God is nothing more than a glorified human-like being, who resembles an old man with a long white beard (as often depicted by William Blake in his famous etchings), a creature who is, in reality, fabricated by our imagination (as Feuerbach and Freud later deduced).[817] Maimonides would have certainly endorsed Francis Bacon's view regarding superstition: "It would be far better to have no opinion of God at all, than to have such an opinion as is unworthy of him: for the one is unbelief, the other is contumely: and certainly superstition is the reproach of the Deity."[818]

According to Maimonides, the idea of a monotheistic person entertaining a pagan concept of the Divine is worse than being a practicing pagan. But in analogical terms, there are many benefits in affirming that God is truly "personal." To say that God possesses "personhood" indicates that we must never let God be reduced to a mere theological abstraction or formula; the act of prayer should not become like dictating a memo "To whom it may concern." The Tanakh teaches that God has an identity; God is moral; God is not indifferent to human suffering and corruption. Moreover, He can be summoned by name through reflective prayer. Lastly, God has a name. But what exactly is in a name? Just as a human being possesses a unique identity that is reflected by the numerous roles one plays in the world, so too does God. One can be a mother, a father, a teacher, a brother or sister, an uncle, a spiritual leader, a poet, a fireman, and so on. No matter what role one plays in life, there is something mysterious about one's being that is never exhausted by the persona one wears to the outside world. Each of our names conveys something paradoxical about our individual nature. Although a name might seem as though it were nothing more than a cipher of the personality, paradoxically, it also participates in the fullness of being. If names possess a mysterious and almost

[817] For this reason, Maimonides believes that human beings are incapable of determining *what precisely God is; the most that the human mind can ascertain is what God is not.* Maimonides teaches that we cannot know anything about God per se; He is completely incomprehensible. At the very most, human beings can only describe what God does in the world but will never be able to discern what God is (cf. Maimonides, *Guide* 1:58; Thomas Aquinas, *Summa Theologica* Q13.2, I, 60 ff; M. Samuel, *The Lord is My Shepherd: The Theology of the Caring God, op. cit.*, 78-94.

[818] *The Essays or Counsels of Civil and Moral* (New York: Barnes and Nobles, 2005, 1595), 41.

contradictory quality, as is the case with human beings, how much more so does this apply when one speaks about the nature of the Divine Reality. God's own "personhood" can be no less of a mystery, for God, too, has many names—each of these names representing a unique kind of relationship with the world.[819]

Excursus 7: Chaos Bound, Chaos Unbound, Chaos Redeemed

Chaos is a name for any order that produces confusion in our minds.
—George Santayana (1863-1952)

What became of the primordial chaos that exists in the beginning of Creation? Did God's creation of the cosmos dispel the chaos altogether, or was it merely kept in abeyance? Is chaos mysteriously co-eternal with God? Jon D. Levenson believes that God did not eliminate chaos; accordingly, creation is neither stagnant nor completed, but rather, it is an ongoing process of structuring and ordering reality by defining and maintaining the boundaries that characterize its existence. Thus, chaos is not eliminated by God—He only keeps it in check. Levenson explains further:

> In each case, the confinement of chaos, rather than its elimination, is the essence of creation, and the survival of the ordered reality hangs only upon God's vigilance in ensuring that those cosmic dikes do not fail, that the bars and doors of the Sea's jail cell do not give way, that the great fish does not slip off his hook. That vigilance is simply a variant of God's covenantal pledge in Genesis 9 never to flood the world again. Whatever form the warranty takes, it testifies to both the precariousness of life, its absolute dependence upon God, and to the sureness and firmness of life under the protection of the faithful master. The world is not inherently safe; it is inherently unsafe. Only the magisterial intervention of God and His eternal vigilance prevent the cataclysm. Creation endures because God has pledged in an eternal covenant that it shall endure and because he has, also in an eternal covenant, compelled the obeisance of His great adversary. If either covenant (or are they one?) comes undone, creation disappears.[820]

To buttress his argument, Levenson demonstrates that the mythopoetic imagery of the Psalms depicts a metaphysical battle between the forces of evil represented by the primordial darkness and the waters of chaos versus YHWH, a motif that has many parallels with the Mesopotamian creation stories. The psalmist characterizes these obstinate forces as chaos-monsters that threaten and undermine God's rule of the cosmos. Israel's history has taught it that the chaotic forces still permeate the world.
Chaos survives the Creation. When Israel is confronted by chaos's irrepressible energies,

---

[819] In one well-known Midrashic exposition on Exodus 3:14, R. Abba b. Mammel says: "God said to Moses, 'You wish to know My Name? I am called according to My deeds . . .'" (Exod. Rabbah 3:6).

[820] Jon D. Levenson, *Creation and the Persistence of Evil: The Jewish Drama of Divine Omnipotence* (San Francisco: Harper & Row, 1988), 17.

its faith community demands that God "awaken" Himself and reassert His Presence in the world in accordance with the covenant He has established with Israel. Levenson writes:

> The God to whom this theology bears witness is not the one who continually acts in history, but one whose acts are clustered in the primordial past or in the eschatological future, or both, that is, the God who will reactivate his mighty deeds and close the horrific parenthesis that is ordinary history. . . . Rather, YHWH in this theology is a deity who can still be aroused, who can still respond to the anguish cry of his cultic community to effect a new victory.[821]

In summary, according to Levenson, the biblical writers intimate there is a cosmic struggle occurring in the Genesis creation narratives that is more manifestly expressed elsewhere in the Tanakh. Although this aspect is greatly demythologized in the Genesis text per se, the cosmic myth still remains intact. This battle depicts the forces of the Divine versus the forces of chaos, whose power must always be kept in check by YHWH. Periodically, these unbridled forces run amok and require God to do His celestial maintenance upon them. Eventually, however, YHWH will triumph over the forces of chaos. Levenson is not alone; there are many other modern biblical theologians who concur with him. Most notably, W. Brueggemann personifies the chaos as "Nihil" as though it is an entity comparable to YHWH and explains:

> First, it is possible to conclude, with some Israelite texts, that this power of the Nihil is still loose in the world and still actively opposes Yahweh. That is, in the sovereign act of creation, whereby Yahweh orders chaos, Yahweh provisionally defeated the power of Nihil but did not destroy or eliminate the threat of chaos. As a result, this power of Nihil from time to time gathers its force and conducts forays into creation to work havoc, for it has not yet come under the rule of Yahweh. Thus is posed a primordial dualism in which Yahweh has the upper hand but is not fully in control, and so from time to time creation is threatened.[822]

While there are some aspects to Levenson's process theology that are admirable, I must differ with him in a number of significant theological areas.

(1) Firstly, chaos and evil are not the same; this is a premise that Levenson never didactically proves. What these two forces share in common are dissolution and non-being, but there is a subtle difference. In physics—chaos—when seen in terms of entropy, aims toward a perfect equilibrium of its forces (through decay and dissolution), until it reaches a state of static and inert uniformity. Such is the nature of the physical universe; however, evil is not determined by nature per se, but rather, by an act of *choice*. In

---

[821] *Ibid.,* 50.

[822] W. Brueggemann, *Theology of the Old Testament: Testimony, Dispute, Advocacy* (Minneapolis: Fortress Press, 199), 534.

choosing evil, man wields the freedom and power to subvert his original purpose, as Paul Ricoeur writes: "to undo (*défaire*) and unmake himself (*se défaire*), after he has been made (*fait*) and made perfect (*parfait*)."[823] According to the basic teachings of Process Theology, chaos functions as a midwife determining how human potential within the human drama should unfold. Harmony is best achieved through intensity and the struggle of *becoming* and from this perspective "evil is the half-way house between perfection and triviality. It is the violence of strength against strength."[824] Nevertheless, Divine creativity is best manifested when entities work toward a common unitive purpose, as is evident throughout the matrix of nature.[825]

(2) The Torah stresses the inherent goodness of all of Creation and for this reason, the term *good* appears seven times in the Creation narrative (cf. Gen. 1:10, 12, 18, 21, 25, 31). Creation in Genesis 1-2 flows with an elegance and grace. From God's perspective, even the chaos serves as a positive function[826] in the scheme of Creation.[827]

(3) To suggest that chaos is mysteriously coeval with the Creator postulates a metaphysical dualism that makes the biblical theology of Genesis virtually

---

[823] Paul Ricoeur, *The Symbolism of Evil* (Boston: Beacon, 1967), 233-234.

[824] A. N. Whitehead, *Adventures of Ideas* (New York: The MacMillan Company, 1940), 355.

[825] Whitehead observes that evil arises when "The mutual obstructiveness of things" prevents entities from actualizing their inner potential and thrust toward self-realization" *Process and Reality, op. cit.*, 517.

[826] This latter point is widely recognized by the scientific disciplines of quantum mechanics and modern cosmology. The inherent paradoxical nature of physical reality allows for the infinite possibilities of creation to simultaneously exist as Plotinus and others originally envisioned.

[827] Beauty from chaos can also be seen in fractal geometry, which reveals a remarkable order in chaos that is reflected in meteorological systems both in this world as well as in other planets. Fractal patterns defy predictability and possess behavioral complexity that often cannot be deduced from the knowledge of its individual parts. This hidden fractal order underlies all of nature's seemingly "chaotic" events, revealing to the mathematician intricate and dazzling patterns that contain an infinity of variations and forms. Indeed, the traditional definition of "chaos" as simply "randomness" or as "a state of confusion," or "lacking any order" and similar definitions may prove to be too imprecise., A new understanding of chaos may take on entirely new meaning in the world of modern mathematics that question the Newtonian belief that the laws of physics are completely deterministic. One of the most intriguing concepts advanced by the meteorologist Edward Lorenz, is the "Butterfly effect." Lorenz asserts that the flapping of a butterfly's wings in one city would be enough to change the course of all future weather systems elsewhere on the planet. The theological and metaphysical implications of this significant concept have yet to be adequately assessed, but it would seem to suggest the manner in which God utilizes chaos to achieve His purpose which may be far more profound than many biblical scholars and theologians are willing to admit. For a selection of scientific writings dealing with the novel applications of chaos theory, see James Gleick, *Chaos: Making a New* Science (New York: Penguin, 1988); K. J. Falconer, *Fractal Geometry: Mathematical Foundations and Applications* (New York: John Wiley & Sons, 1997); B. B. Mandelbrot, J. Damerau, M. Frame, and K. McCamy; *Gaussian Self-Affinity and Fractals* (New York: Springer, 2001); *Chaos and Fractals: New Frontiers of Science* H.-O. Peitgen, H. Jurgens, and D. Saupe, (New York: Springer; 2nd ed. Edition 2004).

indistinguishable from other Mesopotamian creation myths, as well as those of Zoroastrian theology[828] and Gnostic syncretism[829] that were pervasive in the early centuries prior to the birth of Christianity and shortly afterwards. It seems that a number of Christian scholars openly embrace Levenson's theory, largely perhaps, because it helps to ontologically substantiate their belief in the continuous struggle between God and the demonic forces represented by Satan, who is credited with causing Adam's Fall, and subsequently that of all humanity. The only way to completely eliminate the possibility of dualism is to embrace the notion of *creatio ex nihilo*.[830] Moreover, a series of merisms scattered throughout the Tanakh pertaining to "heaven and earth," forms an intra-textual commentary that supports this argument,[831] which cannot easily be dismissed. Regardless of whatever happens to be the scholarly consensus *du jour*, several respectable biblical scholars[832] uphold the traditional translation of Genesis 1:1 in an unabashed way. Therefore, when the Torah says, "In the beginning God created the heavens and the earth," this merism neatly sums up all of Creation.

(4) Assuming that Jeremiah and Ezekiel were historical figures who confronted their nation about the challenges they were facing, there can be no doubt that when the prophets spoke of these mythic creatures, they were only speaking metaphorically and not mythically. They chose these metaphors because Israel's political foes identified with these mythic entities, who served as national and religious symbols of their military power and hegemony. Here are three examples:

> He has consumed me, routed me,
> (Nebuchadnezzar, king of Babylon,)
> he has left me as an empty vessel;
> He has swallowed me like a dragon:
> filled his belly with my delights,
> and cast me out.
>
> —Jer. 51:34 (NAB)
>
> Son of man, set your face against Pharaoh,
> King of Egypt, and prophesy against him

[828] See notes on Genesis 1:2 for a more comprehensive examination of the subject.

[829] See Henry A. Wolfson's chapter on "Gnosticism" in *The Philosophy of the Early Church Fathers* (Cambridge, MA: Harvard University Press, 1956), 495-574.

[830] From the opening salvo of Genesis 1:1, "In the beginning God created the heavens and the earth" (KJV), as many scholars note, this merism, implies that God created everything—even the chaotic waters and darkness of Creation. The Torah begins with the general principle, and proceeds to explain the rest of the story in what is a long parenthetical statement, as observed by Qanaï.

[831] "In six days the LORD made the heavens and the earth, the sea and all that is in them" (Exod. 20:11). Indeed, an intra-biblical commentary on Genesis 1:1 can be gleaned from numerous other biblical passages supporting the doctrine of *creatio ex nihilo*, e.g., Nehemiah 9:6; Psalms. 90:2; and especially Proverbs 8:22–31. Merisms about "heaven and earth" abound in Psalms 115:15; 121:2; 124:23.

[832] E. Speiser, U. Cassuto, B. Jacob, C. Westermann, G. Wenham, V. Hamilton, and others.

and against all Egypt.
Say this to him: Thus says the Lord GOD:
See! I am coming at you, Pharaoh, King of Egypt,
Great crouching monster
amidst your Niles.
—Ezek 29:2-3 (NAB)

Son of man, utter a lament over Pharaoh,
the king of Egypt, saying to him:
Lion of the nations, you are destroyed.
You were like a monster in the sea,
spouting in your streams,
Stirring the water with your feet
and churning its streams.
—Ezek. 32:2-4 (NAB)

To the ancient psyche, wars in the ancient world assumed a metaphysical dimension; when an earthly battle occurred, the warriors believed that a spiritual clash between tutelary beings simultaneously raged on behalf of their earthly subjects. The defeat of an enemy nation represented the defeat of its gods as well. To some extent this pattern is repeated in the wars even of the present. Today, Jihadist Islam regards its battle in precisely the same metaphysical terms that the ancients once envisioned; and to a lesser degree, the same phenomenon is evident among people living in Western countries, who proclaim that "God is on our side." In biblical times this became apparent in the conquest of Canaan, for Israel's triumph was also YHWH's. But when Israel lost its homeland and Temple, it was only natural that this experience produced a state of cognitive dissonance that is articulated in many of the Psalms of complaint. However, these references found in Psalms do not necessarily pertain to abstract mythical forces, but to the enemies of Israel who identify with these mythic beings. Thus, the reference to these chaotic entities must be understood metaphorically rather than literally. The difference is a subtle one, but it is one that is in keeping with the plain meaning of the *peshat* without having to resort to dualism.

(5) For Levenson to assert that God "no longer acts in history" except in the eschatological era, I believe he misses the point of how God's omnipotence really functions in the world. Divine power does not act unilaterally, but only in conjunction with human freedom. Human agents more often than not, serve in this capacity (e.g., Moses, Miriam, the Judges, King David, King Cyrus of Persia, Esther, Mordechai, and so on). The Divine is eternally present in co-shaping history through the witness of Israel, His chosen people, and more specifically, through the agents of transformation that God utilizes. Sometimes, God uses a gentile king to achieve His purpose, e.g., Cyrus of Persia (Isa. 44:24-28), whom the prophet Isaiah even called "the anointed of God" (Isa. 45:1). This passage, incidentally, is the only place in the entire Tanakh where a non-Israelite monarch is called "God's anointed one." Such a term is usually designated for the Kings of Israel (cf. 1 Sam. 24:6;

Lam. 4:20), for high priests (Lev. 4:3, 5, 16; 6:22), and priests (Exod. 28:41; Lev. 10:7; Num. 3:3). In our own day, after the greatest devastation of Jewish lives since the fall of Jerusalem, we have witnessed how two thoroughly secular Jews, Theodore Hertzl and David Ben Gurion, played a pivotal role, as did President Truman in helping to create the Third Jewish Commonwealth, which in biblical terms, is arguably one of the greatest political miracles of Jewish history.

Perhaps one of the most poignant biblical illustrations stressing this theological theme derives from the prophetic story in Jeremiah 18:1-11. God instructs Jeremiah to visit and observe the local potter working at his craft. His visit to the potter reveals the intensity of the artist's work. When the potter first takes the clay, he throws it down on to his wheel as hard as he can. This process occurs repeatedly until he gets rid of the bumps and air pockets that are in the clay. Unfortunately for the potter, his clay is of an inferior variety. Instead of discarding it, the potter remains unwavering and determined to utilize his material until he completes his work of art. The clay is not passive for the centrifugal force produced by the wheel keeps the clay in a state of perpetual motion; however, the potter always keeps the clay firmly in his grip. Of the several lessons one can draw from this incident, (a) God's involvement with Israel is analogous to an artistic challenge; (b) God is always at work in shaping His people's destiny; (c) God, like the potter, is patient and determined to achieve His purpose. One way or the other, Israel will serve as God's instrument to the world. Yet throughout this drama, divine power is never coercive; it takes into account the limitations of human freedom.

Rabbinic wisdom also understands this ancient intuition, and views Israel's survival in subtle but supernatural terms:

> R. Joshua b. Levi said: "Why were they called men of the Great Synod? Because they restored the crown of the divine attributes to its ancient completeness.[833] For Moses had come and said: "The great God, the mighty, and the awful" (Deut. 10:20). Then Jeremiah came and said: "Aliens are destroying His Temple" (Jer. 32:17). Where are the manifestations of His "awesome" deeds? Therefore, he omitted saying the attribute of divine awesomeness. Daniel came and said: "Aliens are enslaving his sons. Where are the manifestations of His 'mighty deeds?'" Therefore, he omitted saying the attribute "mighty." But the Great Synod came and said: "On the contrary! Here are His mighty deeds! God suppresses His wrath, in that He extends long-suffering to the wicked. This is His awesomeness! If not for the awe of the nations for the Holy One, how could one single nation persist among the many predatory nations!"[834]

---

833 The crown of God's praise, by reintroducing the divine attributes that Jeremiah and Daniel had omitted.

834 BT Yoma 69b. Rashi adds in his notes to the Talmud that despite the numerous attempts by her enemies to destroy Israel, she has still managed to survive! A different version appears in the Midrash Esther Rabbah 10:11; Pesikta Rabati 9; Midrash Tanchuma (Warsaw) *Parshat Toldot* 5: "How great is the lamb that survives the seventy wolves! How great is their Shepherd!"

Historically, as the Jewish people became more self-conscious of their miraculous survival, it became obvious to them that God has never abandoned them—such is the paradox of faith. Over time, Jewish leaders and teachers have come to appreciate a different kind of omnipotence unlike the experience of their prophetic forbearers. As their perception of God evolved, the Israelites came to discover that divine power is subtle, paradoxical and open-ended.

(6) The biblical belief in redemption is *not* limited to an eschatological era when the cultic community finally gets its spiritual act together. Redemption is a process that silently unfolds without much fanfare.[835] It begins with a sincere change of heart and a change of behavior; rabbinic wisdom reiterates this truth, "R. Jonathan states: Great is repentance, because it brings about redemption."[836] Or consider the Midrashic comment, "Redemption, like a livelihood, must be earned every day."[837] Heschel expresses the same concept in slightly different terms: "Man's good deeds are single acts in the long drama of redemption, but not only the people of Israel, but the whole universe must be redeemed."[838] He further adds, "But man holds the keys that can unlock the chains fettering the Redeemer."[839] Hassidic teachers have always emphasized that the redemption of the world always begins with the redemption of the human soul.[840]

The biblical theologian J. Richard Middleton shares many ideas that resonate with my own reflections on this subject. In one article, he concludes on an elegant and

---

[835] "Three things occur when one least expects it: the Messiah, a found article and a scorpion" (BT Bava Metzia 97a).

[836] BT Yoma 86b.

[837] Gen. Rabbah 20:9.

[838] Abraham Joshua Heschel, *The Earth is the Lord's: The Inner World of the Jew in Eastern Europe* (New York: Farrar, Straus & Giroux, 1950), 72.

[839] Ibid., 53.

[840] Levenson explains that, "[T]he rabbis of the Talmud usually did not believe the end-time to be imminent. In consequent, their thought lacks the excruciating sense of urgency characteristic of apocalyptic literature and displays a relaxed and often playful attitude. The latter would have been abhorrent to those who believed themselves to be stand at the end of the aeon. They would have considered it frivolous. . ." (*Creation and the Persistence of Evil: The Jewish Drama of Divine Omnipotence, op. cit.*, 36-37). This is certainly a valid point, but I would add, many Sages felt that the entire premise of apocalyptic faith is based on a profound misunderstanding of the biblical theology of redemption. If anything, when the Sages re-examined the concept of redemption, they realized that the eschatological dimension does not unilaterally occur from God per se, but occurs once the inner person allows himself to become a vessel for the Divine. A similar concept also exists in the Gospel narratives, when Jesus tells his disciples that "the kingdom of heaven is ἐντὸς ὑμῶν ("within you") (Luke 17:21).

uplifting note. In his view, the combat motif advocated by Levenson and Gunkel ought to be considered spiritually dysfunctional and discarded:

> [T]he creation account of Gen 1 does not just relativize the creation-by-combat motif. Rather, by its alternative depiction of God's non-violent creative power at the start of the biblical canon, Gen 1 signals the Creator's original intent for shalom and blessing at the outset of human history, prior to the rise of human (or divine) violence. As the opening canonical disclosure of God for readers of Scripture, Gen 1 constitutes a normative framework by which we may judge all the violence that pervades the rest of the Bible.
>
> If the portrayal of God's exercise of non-violent creative power in Gen 1 is taken in conjunction with its claim that humanity is made in the image of *this* God, this has significant implications for contemporary ethics. This opening canonical disclosure of God and humanity constitutes, not only a normative framework for interpreting the rest of Scripture, but also a paradigm or model for exercising of human power in the midst of a world filled with violence.[841]

In summary, human evolution is a long painstaking process with no short-cuts. Chaos, while similar to evil in some respects, differs in others; its ontology is not infinite and one could argue that while chaos is embedded in the fabric of creation, evil's existence is not. God acts uniformly in every event; but the degree in which God's Presence is experienced or realized, ultimately depends more on our perception and interpretation of how we see and *allow* the divine continuum to unfold, beginning first with us, and ultimately the world. As a process, redemption is a co-creative venture with God that requires human mindfulness and focus. If any metaphor best conveys the power of God's determination, it is *patience*. "The human mind may devise many plans, but it is the purpose of the LORD that will be established" (Prov. 19:21).

Excursus 8: Further Reflections on Creation ex Nihilo

In His goodness, He renews each day the work of Creation.
—A Pre-Maccabean Prayer

A. How ancient is the Doctrine of Creatio ex Nihilo?

Is the origin of the *creatio ex nihilo* doctrine truly a post-biblical theological concept introduced during the Hellenistic era, as many scholars in the last hundred years wish to

[841] "Created in the Image of a Violent God? The Ethical Problem of the Conquest of Chaos in Biblical Creation Texts" (*Interpretation,* 2004), 341-355. For a more extensive treatment of his theme, see Middleton's book *The Liberating Image: The Imago Dei of Genesis 1* (Grand Rapids, MI: 2005), 250-269.

assert? The Tanakh itself does not speak of such an explicit philosophical idea; in fact, it appears for the first time in 2 Maccabees 7:28, in a text written in Greek and originating in the 2nd century B.C.E. In this famous passage, a mother pleads with her son who is about to be executed for his faith, exclaiming: "I beg you, child, to look at the heavens and the earth and see all that is in them; then you will know that God did not make them out of existing things; (οὐκ ἐξ ὄντων ἐποίησεν - *ouk ex onton epoiesen)*, and in the same way the human race came into existence" (NAB). That is to say, the same God that creates the universe out of nothingness also possesses the power to raise a person from the ashes and non-being of death. It seems highly unlikely that such a story would not have also been based on a common attitude that Jews subscribed to for many, many centuries, nor is it a huge conceptual leap for those already believing that God created the universe!

Another one of the oldest references to the doctrine of *creatio ex nihilo* comes from the *Letter of Aristeas*, which is believed to have been written sometime between 150-100 and 1st century B.C.E., and records: "For it would be utterly foolish to suppose that anyone became a god in virtue of his inventions. For *the inventors* simply took certain objects already created and by combining them together, showed that they possessed a fresh utility: they did not themselves create the substance of the thing." [842]

On the other hand, a different perspective appears in *The Wisdom of Solomon*, a work believed to have originated between the 3rd century B.C.E. and the early 1st century C.E. The author was very adept in Judaic and Greek thought, and expresses the biblical story of Creation in terms that appear in Plato's *Timaeus,*[843] "And indeed Your all-powerful hand which created the world from formless matter . . ." (καὶ κτίσασα τὸν κόσμον ἐξ ἀμόρφου ὕλης—*kai katisasa ton kosmon ex amorthou hyles*). It is commonly assumed that the author was referring to Genesis 1:1; however, the author may have been referring to Genesis 1:2 and not 1:1!

From Philo of Alexandria's writings, it is unclear whether he actually subscribes to *creatio ex nihilo* or not. Some argue that Philo believes that God created all things—including the pre-existing matter—from nothing.[844] Subsequently, once the

---

[842] *Letter of Aristeas,* 136.

[843] According to Plato, when God "took over all that was visible, seeing that it was not in a state of rest but in a state of discordant and disorderly motion, He brought it into order out of disorder" (*Timaeus* 30a, trans. R.G. Bury, Cambridge: Harvard University Press, 1929, 9:55 Creation, for Plato, does not occur out of *creatio ex nihilo*, but involves the ordering of pre-existing matter. The novelty of God's creation consists of the cosmos being endowed with reason and soul (*ibid.*), i.e., which produces a *telos* (the end of a goal-oriented process) and *logos* to the cosmos. Cf. Plato, T*imaeus* 50d and Aristotle, *Physics* 191a, 10.

[844] Philo writes, "Just as the sun divides day and night, so too—according to Moses—did God divide the light from the darkness; for 'God made a division between the light and the darkness.' And above all, just as the

creative process begins, God acts more like an Artist than an actual Creator by utilizing the raw materials that already exist. Others read Philo differently, contending that Philo does not believe in *creatio ex nihilo,*[845] and that his theological position derives from Plato and Aristotle. As Wolfson observes, the difference in perspective may have been attributed to Philo's listening audience. To those of a Platonic mindset, Philo "Platonizes" his doctrine; to those more traditionally oriented, he emphasizes the doctrine of *creatio-ex nihilo*. It may well be that Philo sees no theological or philosophical problem with either viewpoint—provided it is properly articulated. Alternatively, Philo may have personally hedged on this issue at different stages of his thinking.[846]

On the other hand, Josephus is a different matter, he substitutes the verb ἔκτισεν (*ektisen* = "created") in place of the Septuagint's ἐποίησεν (*epoiēsen,* "made"). With this alteration, Josephus makes it obvious to his readers that God continuously creates the world *ex nihilo* and has no need to form it out of preexistent matter.[847] One famous Midrash records a discussion between a Gnostic philosopher and R. Gamaliel (1st century C.E.), who uses an intratextual approach in explaining the opening lines of the Genesis creation narrative:

> "Your God was indeed a great artist, but surely He utilized good materials that assisted Him!" Rabbi Gamaliel asked: "And what do you think they are?" He replied, "*Tohu, bohu,* darkness, water, wind (*ruah*), and the deep." Rabbi Gamaliel exclaimed, "Woe to that man . . ." while adding, "The term *creation* is used by Scripture in connection with all of them. Regarding *tohu* and *bohu* is written, "I make peace and create evil" (Isa. 55: 7).[848] Concerning darkness is written, "I form the light, and create darkness" (ibid.). Concerning the creation of water, is written, "Praise him, you highest heavens, and you waters above the heavens! (Ps. 148: 4) How so? "For He commanded, and they were created" (ibid. 5); concerning wind is written, "For lo, the one who forms the mountains, creates the wind . . . (Amos 4:13); and concerning

sun's rising reveals bodies that were hidden, so too does God, who created all things. Not only did He bring them all to light, but He even created what before had no existence, acting not only as their Artificer (δημιουργός - ***dēmiourgos)***, but also as their Creator (Κτίστης - ***Ktistēs)***" (*On Dreams*, 1.76).

[845]Philo, *The Eternity of the World* 5.

[846] *Philo*, 304ff.

[847] Josephus, *Antiquities,* 1.1.1 §27.

[848] Rabbi I. Epstein explains an unarticulated theological question that motivated the Gnostic philosopher's question in his notes to the Soncino translation, "By tohu and bohu the philosopher meant primeval matter, without form. Thereupon R. Gamaliel quoted: I make *shalom* (that which is whole, i.e. what contains both matter and form) and evil, i.e., that which is defective, consisting of matter only without form. Thus, that too was created. V. Husik, *A History of Mediaeval Jewish Philosophy*, (New York: Macmillan, 1916, 175.) Perhaps too this is an allusion to the view that matter is a source of evil."

the depths is written, "When there were no depths I was brought forth, when there were no springs abounding with water. (Prov. 8: 24).[849]

This pagan philosopher of the Midrash expresses a thought that is reminiscent of a comment made by a second century Neo-Pythagorean philosopher named Numenius, who sought to demonstrate how the wisdom of Pythagoras and Plato could be found in the Torah of the Jews. Numenius has been often quoted as saying, "What else is Plato but Moses speaking Attic Greek?"[850] Like the Midrash of the pagan philosopher, the story of God creating the world from pre-eternal matter seems compatible with the teachings of Plato.

One might wonder why the doctrine of *creatio ex nihilo* is not widely discussed in the Talmud itself, however, the rabbis were certainly familiar with much of the philosophical and Gnostic speculation concerning the universe's cosmology, and they felt this was not a topic that ought to be discussed in public. The study of philosophy was considered to be potentially dangerous, thus it was to be avoided. The *Ma'aseh Berashit* ("The Work of Creation") was not to be studied in the academies or in public.[851]

Still and all, the cosmology of Genesis does find occasional expression in the Midrashic literature. Recorded in a 3rd century Midrashic text, R. Yochanan and Resh Lakish discussed the difference between a human and divine creativity.

> R. Yochanan said: When a mortal king builds a palace, after having built the lower stories he builds the upper ones; but the Holy One, blessed be He, created the upper stories and the lower stories within a single act. R. Simeon b. Lakish said: When a human being builds a ship, first he brings the beams, then the ropes; after this he procures the anchors, and then erects the masts. But the Blessed Holy One, created them [i.e., heaven and earth] and their crew, as it is written, "Thus says God the LORD, Who created the heavens and stretched them out"—*we-notehem* (Isa. XLII, 5); this is written *we-nawtehem* ("and their mariners").[852]

Although the proof text of Resh Lakish is not at all grammatically convincing, the theological point both these Sages make is a valid one: both stress the sheer novelty in how God creates the world—with complete simultaneity in accordance with His will.

---

[849] Gen. Rabbah 1:9.

[850] As cited in the writings of Clement of Alexandria, *Stromata,* i. 342; Eusebius, *Praep. Evang.*, xi. 10; *Suda*, Numenius.

[851] Mishnah in Hagigah 2:1 and the Tosefta Hagigah 2:1. Rashi explains in one may not inquire beyond the extent of heaven, it follows that one may not inquire beyond the time of its existence, i.e., concerning what happened prior to the six days of Creation (BT Hagigah 11b; cf. *Taror HaMor* on Gen. 1:1).

[852] Gen Rabbah 12:12.

Just as the early rabbinic writings provide some evidence that they accepted the theory of *creatio ex nihilo*, so too, did the Early Church Fathers. The one lone exception was Justin Martyr (ca. 100-165 C.E.), who saw no conflict between Plato's view of creation and the Genesis story. The theme of the early 2nd century work, *The Shepherd of Hermas*, expresses God's oneness as being basic to the early Church, and was undoubtedly influenced by the *Shema Prayer* recited by Jews twice daily: "First of all, believe that God is one, who created everything and maintained it, and who made everything to be out of what was not, who contains everything but alone is not contained."[853]

With the rise of the Kalam school of Muslim philosophy, which developed during the late 9th century, R. Saadia Gaon, head of the Sura Academy in Babylon, articulated Jewish philosophy in a way that was not seen since the days of Philo. According to him, the belief in *creatio ex nihilo* had long been accepted by the Jewish communities of his time.[854]

B. *The Emergence of Judaic Neo-Platonic Thought in the Medieval Era*

A millennium later, a number of significant medieval rabbinic thinkers moved away from the *creatio ex nihilo* doctrine believing that the Platonic notion of creation from pre-eternal matter is, at the very least, logically compatible with the biblical story of Creation.[855] Some of the renowned names include: Judah Halevi,[856] Ibn Ezra,[857] Solomon Ibn Gabirol,[858] and especially Gersonides.[859] On the basis of Maimonides' own

---

[853] C. Osiek, and H. Koester, *Shepherd of Hermas: A Commentary. Hermeneia—A Critical and Historical Commentary on the Bible* (Minneapolis: Fortress Press, 1999), 103.

[854] Saadia Gaon, *Emunot ve-Deot,* Part 1 Ch. 2.

[855] For a good survey of the literature dealing with this theme, see, I. Husik, *A History of Mediaeval Jewish Philosophy;* Isidore Epstein, *The Faith of Judaism* (London; Soncino,1954); Louis Jacobs, *The Principles of the Jewish Faith* (London; Jason Aronson, 1964, *1988).* The best recent work on the subject is Marc B. Shapiro's *The Limits of Orthodox Theology: Maimonides Thirteen Principles Reappraised* (Portland: The Littman Library of Jewish Civilization, 2004), 70-86.

[856] Judah Halevi notes, "If a believer in the Torah feels compelled to acknowledge and admit that God had created the world out of pre-eternal matter, and that there were many worlds prior to this one, he would not harm his belief that God created this world at a given point in time (*Kuzari,* 1:67).

[857] Ibn Ezra dismisses the idea that בָּרָא (*bārā*ʾ) implies *creatio ex nihilo.* Many of his expositors think Ibn Ezra did not believe in this doctrine on the basis of his comments on Genesis 1:1.

[858] This brilliant idiosyncratic philosopher and mystic subscribes to the Platonic distinction between matter and form, which manifest themselves in the phenomenal universe—from the highest spiritual entity to the lowest within the created order; degrees vary within Creation depending upon how spiritual an entity is. Ibn Gabirol also believed that the Divine Will acts as the intermediary between God and the emanative processes that make up the world.

theological writings, some scholars argue that he hedges on this question.[860] Nowhere in the Mishnah Torah does he ever mention the doctrine of *creatio ex nihilo*, nor does he list the individual who denies this belief among the heretics who forfeit the Afterlife.[861] In addition, Maimonides actually considers the Platonic idea of the material universe as having the same eternal relationship to God, in much the same way as the shadow of a tree is to the tree, or as heat is to fire, or as light is to the sun. Even if it could scientifically be proven that the universe has always existed, this would not necessarily contradict the contextual meaning of the Scriptures, which clearly states that God created the world. In his *Guide* (2.13-15), Maimonides boldly admits that there is ample support, from both biblical and rabbinic texts[862] for a Platonic view of the universe as being derived from pre-eternal matter.

Yet, Maimonides' personal position is not completely clear, nor is it consistent. In his opening statement to *Laws of Torah Fundamentals*, he writes:

> If one could imagine that God does not exist, then nothing else could exist either. But if it could be imagined that no other beings—apart from God—enjoyed existence, then God alone would still exist and would not cease existing once they have ceased to exist. For all beings require God for their existence, but God does not require Creation—not even a single entity—for His existence. It logically follows that God's true existence remains *sui generis* from that of any created entity.[863]

---

[859] While many Jewish thinkers (cf. Ramban's commentary on Gen. 1:1) subscribe to this doctrine of pre-eternal matter, they consider this substance to be "pre-eternal"—relative only to the earth itself. However, it is God Who brings forth pre-eternal matter from out of utter nothingness. One of Gersonides' most novel theological and philosophical concepts was that God creates the universe out of an eternal, unformed matter, which is unlike any kind of matter known to humankind. Indeed, Gersonides took a far more radical step in believing that God had created the world from eternal and uncreated matter. According to him, the beginning of Genesis refers to two types of matter: גֶּשֶׁם (*ḡéšem,* the primordial and chaotic matter from which the universe was formed from), which is associated with the chaotic waters of creation in Gen. 1:2 and חֹמֶר הִיוּלִי (*ḥomer hyle* = ὑλικοὶ), i.e., hylic matter that is capable of receiving form and impression). This latter type of matter does not possess any independent ontological existence—it is amorphous but malleable by nature and corresponds to what Aristotle refers to as the material "substratum" that underlies all physical things (cf. Aristotle, *On the Heavens,* 1:2-3; *Metaphysics,* IX:8). According to Gersonides, God created the universe out of this pre-existent eternal matter. See Levi ben Gershom and Seymour Feldman (tr.), *The Wars of the Lord,* Vol. 3 (Philadelphia: Jewish Publication Society, 1984), 39.

[860] David Hartman, *Maimonides: Torah and Philosophic Quest* (New York: JPS, 1976), 122-123.

[861] MT *Hilchot Teshuvah* 3:7-8.

[862] Maimonides specifically refers to the *Pirkê de Rabbi Eliezer* 3:7b—a work he believed dated back to the second century, but in reality only goes back to the ninth century.

[863] Maimonides' MT *Hilchot Yesodei HaTorah* 1:3.

Thus, Maimonides leaves no doubt that every aspect of Creation—ranging from pre-existent matter to the world of humankind—depends upon God's existence.

Maimonides' influence can also be seen in Thomas Aquinas' deliberations; Aquinas, like Maimonides, believes that this question cannot be philosophically decided, and that Christians should hold that the world is created—and that it has not always existed—as an article of faith based upon revelation.[864] Although the Patristic sources affirm that the cosmos was created *ex nihilo,* Justin Martyr proved to be that one notable exception, arguing that Plato took his idea on this matter from Moses!

> And that you may learn that it was from our teachers—we mean the account given through the prophets—that Plato borrowed his statement that God, having altered matter which was shapeless, made the world, heard the very words spoken through Moses who, as above shown, was the first prophet, and of greater antiquity than the Greek writers; and through whom the Spirit of prophecy, signifying how and from what materials God at first formed the world, spoke thus: "In the beginning God created the heaven and the earth. And the earth was invisible and unfurnished, and darkness was upon the face of the deep; and the Spirit of God moved over the waters. And God said, 'Let there be light; and it was so.'" So that both Plato and they who agree with him, and we ourselves, have learned, and you also can be convinced, that by the word of God the whole world was made out of the substance spoken of before by Moses. And that which the poets call Erebus, we know was spoken of formerly by Moses. [865]

C. *Modern Perspectives on Creatio ex Nihilo*

Paul Tillich offers one of the more interesting expositions on *creatio ex nihilo.* According to Tillich, the term *ex nihilo* points to something fundamentally important about the creature (any entity within the created order); namely, that it must take over what might be called 'the heritage of non-being' (all entities at one time of its existence will cease to exist). "Creatureliness" by its very definition implies non-being since every entity depends upon its Creator for its continued existence. However, creatureliness involves more than non-being; and as such, it possesses the power to transcend its momentary existence. The power of being implies a capacity for humankind to self-reflectively meditate upon its unique nature, and this power of being enables it to participate in the Ultimate Being of God, Who is the Ground and Bedrock of all Being.

Tillich further adds that being a "creature of God" by necessity includes coming to terms with the eventual reality of non-being, which in turns produces the common anxiety stemming from the realization that we will someday cease to exist. Rather than passively

---

[864] *Summa Theologica* 1. Q. 46, Art. 2.

[865] *Apology* 59, *The Ante-Nicene Fathers,* ed. Alexander Roberts and James Donaldson (reprint Grand Rapids, MI: Eerdman's, 1989), 1:182. For a similar view see Clement of Alexandria in *Stromata* 14.

submit to this inevitable outcome, humankind can choose to face its existence heroically rather than with existential despair and resignation. The paradox of all of human existence nevertheless carries an aspect of God's own Being within him that cannot be destroyed by virtue of every human being made in the likeness of the Divine Image.[866]

For a rabbinic parallel to Tillich's concept, R. Sheneir Zalman of Liadi (1745-1813), repeatedly explains that the notion of *creatio ex nihilo* is really a misnomer, since everything derives solely from God. The "nothingness" that we experience is really an illusion.[867] Sheneir Zalman further asserts that the distinction between the Creator and Creation is unlike the analogy of a water droplet and the ocean, for while the gulf between the ocean and the droplet is relatively incomparable, theoretically, the ocean could be subdivided repeatedly until the precise amount of droplets are accounted for. In mathematical terms, the difference between God and the Creation is more analogous to the relationship between zero and one. Should a person add one zero to zero, the value of zero will always remain constant—even if the number of zeros subsequently added are endless in number. Like the mathematical symbol zero, Creation will never be something that is ever self-derivative.[868]

Creation derives its ontology solely from the power of the Divine that brings it into constant being; indeed, this involves a radical leap that for all practical purposes introduces something that is altogether novel and different. From the human perspective, God *seems* as though He is a "non-being," in that humankind is not consciously aware of the Divine Reality that surges throughout every fiber of Creation. Without this veil of divine obscurity, freedom could never be realized—for everything would be transparent and obvious. From the Divine perspective, the existence of the universe is comparable to a ray of light that remains and is always replenished within the sun itself—it has no ontology apart from God.[869]

---

[866] Paul Tillich, *Systematic Theology* Vol. I, (Chicago: University of Chicago Press, 1957), 253.

[867] R. Sheneir Zalman's exposition bears a striking resemblance to the Hindu concept of *mäyä*—the manifest reality of the Absolute that creates the sensory world we experience. Shankara, compares *mäyä* to the *mäyävi*—an illusionist who possesses the ability to create a reality that does not really exist. However, for those who can perceive the trick, they see the truth as it really is. Shankara concludes, "As the magician is not affected by the *mäyä* which he himself has created, since it is unreal, so also the Supreme is not affected by the *mäyä* of *samsara* (rebirth)" (Arvind Sharma, *The Philosophy of Religion and Advaita Vedanta: A Comparative Study in Religion and Reason* [University Park, PA: Pennsylvania State University, 1995], 8-9). A similar thought is also expressed in Mahayana Buddhism, which purports that the nature of this "derived reality" really obscures the true undifferentiated spiritual reality from which the world originates; in short, *mäyä* exists by an act of a divine illusion. This metaphysical construction of our existence is purposely designed to hide and constrict the cosmic consciousness of God.

[868] *Tanya*, 1:48; 4:20; *Likutei Torah, Parshat Devarim* 46c, 20d.

[869] See *Sh'ar Yichud V'Emunah* chapters 1-7 where R.S. Zalman elaborates on this theme and R. M. M. Schenersohn's *Derech Mitzvotecha émunat élohut,* (Poltava, 1901; reprinted in Brooklyn, Kehot 1976*)*, 42-62.

D. Creatio per Verbum – Creation by the Word

Like Levenson, theologian Bernhard W. Anderson considers the notion of the *creatio ex nihilo* as being too abstract of a philosophical idea for the ancient Hebrew mind.[870] Unlike Levenson, Anderson is not willing to say that God creates the universe from a co-eternal chaos, noting: "[I]n any case, the idea of a created chaos would seem strange in a narrative that is governed by the view that creation is the antithesis to chaos (cf. Isa. 45:18)." He further adds:

> The main intention of the writer is to emphasize the absolute sovereignty of God. There is no suggestion that God is bound or conditioned by the chaos, as in the *Enuma elish myth,* which portrays the birth of the gods out of the waters of chaos. Nor does God have the character of a demiurge who works with material that offers some resistance or imposes limitations. On the contrary, God creates with perfect freedom by the commanding word—a view underscored by the use of the verb *bārāʾ.* In the Old Testament, this verb is used exclusively of God's action and expresses the effortless divine creation that surpasses any human analogy such as the potter or the architect (cf. Pss. 51:10[12]; 104:30; Isa. 43:1,7, 15; 48:7). Since, however, this verb is used in conjunction with the verb *ʿāśāh* ("make") in Gen. 1:16-17 and elsewhere is linked with *yāṣār* ("mold," e.g., Isa. 43:1; 45:18) it was undoubtedly employed to support the view of creation by the Word, rather than creation *ex nihilo*.[871]

Anderson's notion of *creatio per verbum* is certainly more theologically preferable to the concept of creation from chaos, nevertheless, one must wonder: is it really that much different from *creatio ex nihilo?* It seems at least from the biblical narrator's subconscious or conscious perspective, the phenomenal universe does not have an independent existence, but depends upon the divine fiat that brings it into existence (v. 1:3), and sustains it (cf. Psa. 33:6, 9; Isa. 40:8). Although the ancient Israelite priests ("P") had never conceived of *creatio ex nihilo* in a philosophical vein, they mythopoetically intuited that the universe is (1) not co-eternal with God (2) one expression of God's infinite power.

It is presumptuous to think of primal societies as suffering from ineptitude and incapability of abstract thought (as Levenson and Anderson seem to allege). The

---

[870] R.K. Harrison makes the same identical assertion: ". . . a philosophical postulate is undoubtedly too abstract for the Hebrew mind to entertain, and while it is not specifically stated in Genesis 1, it is certainly implicit in the narrative. The reader is meant to understand that "the worlds were not fashioned from any pre-existing material, but out of nothing"; 'prior' to God's creative activity, "there was thus no other kind of phenomenological existence." R.K. Harrison, "Creation" *The Zondervan Pictorial Encyclopedia of the Bible*, (Grand Rapids: MI: Zondervan), 1975, 1023.

[871] Bernhard W. Anderson, *From Creation to New Creation: Old Testament Perspectives* (Minneapolis, MN: Augsburg Press, 1994), 30.

French anthropologist and social critic Claude Lévi-Strauss observes that the *deep structures* found in the myths of "primitive" cultures show a profound capacity for thinking in abstract terms—comparable with any modern society. Rather than discarding the biblical passage as pure myth (in the most common or even pejorative sense of the term), it behooves us to wonder whether the biblical mythos might suggest a higher truth than is commonly assumed. Cultural hubris sometimes prevents people from looking at a sacred text from a new perspective (much like the way Sir James Frazer pejoratively views primal societies in his research). The concept of *creatio per verbum* is no less abstract than the notion of *creatio ex nihilo*. Clearly, the ancient Hebrew storyteller uses mythopoetic imagery in expressing a theological view of reality that is every bit as sophisticated as modern theological thought—one that has numerous parallels in cultures around the ancient world (see notes on 1:3 and Excursus 8C).

The concept of *creatio per verbum* is not entirely new to Jewish theology (see notes to Gen. 1:3). Jewish thinkers since the time of Philo of Alexandria have always recognized Creation as the dynamic expression of Divine speech. It is no coincidence that in the Greek language, λόγος (*logos*) signifies not only divine reason or order, but also the spoken word. God's logos is nothing more than a manifestation and revelation of God's "mind," God creates through the Word, and this concept finds ample expression in the liturgy that affirms, "Blessed is the One Who spoke, and the world came into being!" R. Sheneir Zalman (1745-1812) develops this leitmotif in his brand of mystical theology of Creation. According to him *creatio per verbum* is the vehicle through which *creatio ex nihilo* occurs:

> Let this point serve as an answer to the deists, who deny God's creation. . . . In their error, they foolishly imagine that creation is akin to the work and design of mortals as when a smith completes fashioning a vessel, that vessel no longer requires the smith to ensure its existence. Even when its maker is physically removed from it, the vessel remains intact—just as it was when he fashioned it. By the same token, these thinkers foolishly imagine that since heaven and earth exist, the cosmos no longer depends upon the Creator for its *raison d'être*.
>
> However, their eyes are covered for they do not differentiate between Divine and human creativity; the latter consists of improving upon something that is already in existence; that is to say, human creativity can only change an object's form and appearance. Returning to our original analogy of the smith, he merely takes a silver ingot and transforms it into a vessel. Human creativity always consists of altering the form of some pre-existing matter. . . . After finishing his handiwork, the smith leaves it alone to its own device. Similarly, the smith knows that once his work is finished, it no longer requires his attentiveness . . .
>
> . . . In contrast, God's creation is different. He literally wills the cosmos into being from a state of utter non-being. In reality, physical existence is a novelty that occurs each

moment of its duration. . . . If this creative flow ceases—even for a single moment—everything that exists would instantaneously return to its original state of non-being. From this perspective, one must say that *creatio ex nihilo* is a far greater miracle than even the Splitting of the Sea of Reeds (Exod. 14:21-22; 15:8). For in this case, God merely drove back the sea through the force of a strong east wind that blew throughout the night. The waters at the Sea of Reeds stood immediately erect as if they were a wall. Had God withdrawn the wind, the waters would instantly revert to their natural flowing state. . . . The element of novelty was obvious to all who witnessed the miracle, they recognized how the Divine power kept the water's temporary structure intact. . . . However, after the last of the Israelites finished crossing, the waters of the Sea of Reeds reverted back to its natural state. What is true with regard to a great biblical miracle applies all the more so when comparing it to a miracle like Creation. The entire cosmic reality depends upon its Creator to provide it with being each moment it exists. . . . Ethereal letters expressed by the Divine Word continue animating and renewing Creation for all time. This would explain why the Psalmist proclaims, "Your Word stands in the Heavens. . . ." (Psa. 33:6)

. . . From the human perspective, the only reason why the universe and all of its entities appear as though they are self-derivative is due to our inability to recognize the Divine Source that is animating the cosmos. We do not comprehend, nor do we see with our corporeal eyes how the Divine power of God and the "breath of His Mouth," assume the form of Creation. However, if the human eye were able to see and comprehend the life-force and spiritual flow infusing Creation directly, "from the mouth of God" and "His breath," then physical and tangible world would cease to exist, and all would be exactly as it was before the Six Days of Creation—when all was naught. . . . We would see reality as it truly is—a manifestation of Godliness.[872]

E. *Similarities between Divine and Human Creativity*

Russian theologian Nicolai Berdyaev (1874-1948) would probably consider Sheneir Zalman's distinction between human and divine creativity as being two-dimensional. Divine freedom is manifested in human freedom as well, and is rooted in a mutual ontology that God and humankind paradoxically share. Berdyaev explains:

Through creation there always arises something perfectly new that has never existed before; i.e., the "nothing" becomes "something." Hegel discovered in his own way the truth—that dynamism—becoming the appearance of the new, presupposes non-being. . . . Man's creativeness is similar to God's, but God does not need any material for His creation, while man does. A sculptor makes a statue out of marble. Without marble, without material, he cannot create. In the same way, man needs cosmic matter for all his creation. A philosopher's creative thought needs the world for its matter and without this a philosopher's creative thought would hang in the void.

---

[872] R. Sheneir Zalman, *Tanya*, *Shaar HaYichud ve Emunah*, Chapters 2 and 3).

All this leads people to believe that human creation is never out of something. But the creative conception itself, the original creative act, does not depend upon any material. It presupposes freedom and arises out of freedom. It is not the marble that gives rise to the sculptor's conception, nor is that conception entirely determined by the statues or human bodies which the sculptor has observed and studied. An original creative work includes an element of freedom and that is the "nothing" out of which the new, the not yet existent, is created. . . .

. . . The faculty of imagination is the source of all creativity. God created the world through imagination. In Him, imagination is an absolute ontological power. Imagination plays an enormous part in the moral and spiritual life of man. There is no such thing as the magic of imagination. Imagination magically creates realities. Without it there can be no works of art, no scientific or technological discoveries, no plans for ordering the economic or the political life of nations. Imagination springs from the depths of the unconscious, from fathomless freedom. Imagination is not only imitation of timelessly existent patterns, as Platonism in all its forms interprets it, but creation out of the depths of non-being of images that never existed before.[873]

Berdyaev's perspective explains why the doctrine of *creatio ex nihilo* is more than just a theological abstraction; in fact, this doctrine serves to reveal the true power and pure freedom of the Divine—an important point that Gersonides and Levenson seem to overlook. This quality is not altogether absent with respect to human creativity, for human beings summon their creativity from the bowels of their being. Such qualities are present in all works of genius and inspiration, as manifested in the works of great musicians, artists, poets, and writers.

Excursus 9: The Power of the Word in Pre-Biblical Cultures

A. The Word in Mesopotamian and Oriental Traditions

The Hindu philosopher Bhartrihari writes,

All knowledge of what is to be done in this world depends upon the word. . . . There is no cognition in the world in which the word does not figure. All knowledge is, as it were, intertwined with the word. . . . If this eternal identity of knowledge and the word were to disappear, knowledge would cease to be knowledge; it is this identity which makes identification possible . . . It is this that is the basis of all the sciences, crafts and arts. Thanks to it, whatever is produced can be classified. . . . The consciousness of all living beings is of the nature of the word; it exists within and without. (1.121, 124, 125, 126).[874]

---

[873] Charles Hartshorne and William L. Reese (ed.), *Philosophers Speak of God* (Chicago: University of Chicago Press, 1953), 291.

[874] Cited from Ben-Ami Scharfstein, *Ineffability: The Failure of Words in Philosophy and Religion, op. cit.,* 75.

Every culture that has ever lived seems to have recognized and even exalted the power of words. Among primal peoples, the power of the word is demonstrated by the suggestive and magical properties of a word or phrase (e.g., *abracadabra*[875]) or name. For instance, when a young man is deemed a warrior via tribal ritual, he assumes a new name: perhaps one like "Wild Stallion." More than just a label, a warrior's nature may be much like that of a wild-stallion; thus, his newly given name reinforces in his own persona the qualities of his namesake.

In much the same way, when the biblical narrator introduces the thought that God creates through the Word, he must have consciously or unconsciously used imagery familiar to people coming from a Mesopotamian region. Throughout the Semitic and Oriental world (as well as in ancient Egypt), the spoken word was not only perceived as an expression of thought, but also conveyed a potent power and force of energy. The Mesopotamian priests believed that names and incantations literally ordered the structure of the phenomenal universe. The Babylonian deity, Marduk-Ellil, is depicted as transforming the natural forces of the world by means of his commanding word. Marduk's word was considered to be so powerful, that he possessed the ability to rescind and recreate a constellation. His worshippers exclaim:

O Marduk, you are our champion,
We bestow upon you kingship of all and everything . . .
To Marduk their firstborn said they (these words),
"Your destiny, O Lord, shall be foremost of the gods',
Command destruction or creation, they shall take place.
At your word the constellation shall be destroyed,
Command again, the constellation shall be intact."
He commanded and at his word the constellation was destroyed,
He commanded again and the constellation was created anew.
When the gods his fathers saw what he had commanded,
Joyfully they hailed, "Marduk is king!" [876]

In Egypt, too, it was believed that the name of a thing or person was its equivalent and held the key to that entity's destiny. To know the secret name of an enemy or even a god enabled that individual to gain mastery over him. Incantations, when properly chanted, could create order and dissipate it; these spells could even kill a person and restore him to life. According to the mythology of Memphis, Ptaḥ was the supreme creator god who conceived of the world in his heart, created the primordial chaos, and brought it forth by speaking it with his tongue.[877]

---

[875] *Abracadabra* is an expression that means, "I will create, as I speak." The original Aramaic was either עַבְדָא כְּדַבְרָא, (*avda kedavra,*) which means, "what was said has been done," or עברא כדברא (*avra kedavra*) which means "what was said has come to pass" or "caused to perish like the word" or "I will create what is told."

[876] W. W. Halo and K. L. Younger, *The Context of Scripture* (Leiden; New York: Brill), Vol. 1, 397.

[877] S. Langdon, "Works (Sumerian and Babylonian)"and G. Foucart, "Names (Egyptian)," in J. Hastings, ed.,

In the Egyptian mythology of the Old Kingdom (2686-2181 B.C.E.), *Pyramid Texts* describes how Atum—the primal deity of the Heliopolitan pantheon—after pleasuring himself, swallows his seed, and then vomits forth the first pair of deities: Shu and Tefnut. The British theologian Don Cupitt attempts to explain the subtle theological underpinnings of this idea as it relates to the doctrine of *creatio ex nihilo*:[878]

> The phrase "spitting image," still in use in modern English, preserves a group of very ancient ideas. Male semen was once thought of as charged with sacred casual and creative power, for by ejaculating his semen, a man could apparently project out and create a small image of himself—his offspring. But human spittle resembles semen, and is associated with the mouth, the tongue, the teeth and the lips, by which speech is formed. And as a productive, forming and organizing principle, speech is even more powerful than semen. Through speech we express ourselves, thoughts formed deep in our hearts emerging through the tongue to control the self, guide social life and organize the world of experience. So spittle, because of its associations—metaphorical and metonymic—both with semen and speech, has been widely credited with magical properties. A spitting image is a likeness so close that it could have been produced by one's own semen/spittle. And spittle is used around the world to form things, and in healing . . .[879]

According to Cupitt, the Egyptian myth stresses the creative and magical power of the deity's mouth, which possesses the ability to summon forth creation. In the pre-philosophical consciousness of the Old Kingdom, the ancients understood or intuited the idea that Creation is an act of self-expression—not unlike the creative power of human speech. Language and reality are thus dynamically interrelated.

This pattern is also visible in Sumerian culture. Sumerologist Samuel Noah Kramer observes that the Sumerians also exhibited a profound respect for the divine word:

> As for the creating technique attributed to these deities, Sumerian philosophers developed a doctrine which became dogma throughout the Near East—the doctrine of the creative power of the divine word. All that the creating deity had to do, according to this doctrine, was to lay his plans, utter the word, and pronounce the name. Probably this notion of the creative power of the divine word was the result of an analogical inference based on observation of human society. If a human king could achieve almost all he wanted by command—by no more than the words of his mouth—the immortal and superhuman deities in charge of the four realms of the universe could achieve much more.[880]

Encyclopedia of Religion and Ethics. Cf. James Pritchard, *Ancient Near Eastern Texts Relating to the Old Testament* (2d ed.; Princeton, NJ: Princeton University Press, 1955), 5.

[878] Although Cupitt's theory is interesting, it hardly demonstrates the point he wishes to make. The Egyptian creation myth of Atum does not prove the notion of *creatio ex nihilo* at all—but it does prove that Egyptians believed in a doctrine of creation from chaos, since Atum arises out of the primordial waters of chaos (*ANET*, 3).

[879] Don Cupitt, *Creation Out of Nothing* (London: SCM Press, 1990), 1-2.

[880] Samuel Noah Kramer, *History Begins at Sumer: Thirty-Nine Firsts in Recorded History* (Philadelphia, PA.:

B. The Hebraic Vision: A Cosmic Word Echoes throughout the World

Biblical writers regarded the Divine Word as a cosmic force reverberating throughout the created order. According to Psalms 33:6, the Word of God animates the cosmos: בִּדְבַר יְהוָה שָׁמַיִם נַעֲשׂוּ "By the Word of the LORD the heavens were made." To the Hebraic (as well as the Semitic) imagination, words are powerful—it is the stuff reality is made of. In Biblical Hebrew, among its various nuances, דָּבָר (*dabhar*) connotes a "thing" (Exod. 35:1); or a "promise" (Deut. 15:6); and a "decree" (Jer. 51:12) or "affair" or "history" (1 Kgs. 14:12).[881] In each of these examples, דָּבָר connotes something substantive and real. Everything that exists in the world is viewed as a manifestation of the Word of God that animates it.

Primal cultures regarded the word as an instrument of power; in fact the power of the word was considered to be the ultimate weapon—a fact that is especially evident in the pericope about King Balak of Moab and Balaam (Num. 22:6ff). In this narrative Balak hires the soothsayer Balaam of Pethor to curse the Israelites who are approaching his land. Like other ancients, Balaam believes in the power that suffuses the spoken word to change and alter physical reality. With Balaam's assistance, Balak believes that he can help him avoid certain defeat, and advise him how to defeat the Israelites (Num. 22:6). Similarly, this theme is also present in the beginning of Genesis 12:2-3, where God verbally blesses Abram with the power to convey a blessing or curse at his discretion. Another illustration occurs when Jacob asks for the name of his mysterious assailant; he refuses to grant Jacob that knowledge—since to know the name of an angelic being or deity is to have mastery over it (Gen. 32:30).

C. The De-valued Word in Modern Culture

It is tragic that our appreciation of the spoken word pales in comparison to how the ancients enshrined it in their mythologies and cultures. As a result, the word in contemporary society tends to be devalued. There are many practical reasons for this phenomenon. Since the invention of the printing press, the world has become more literate than at any other time of recorded history. Along with the proliferation of literacy, the word has become increasingly more secularized due to advances made by technology. Cell phones, radio/TV, the Internet, and all other forms of electronic digital media and telecommunication devices have inundated civilization with a continuous stream of words—wherever and whenever—twenty-four hours a day.

University of Pennsylvania Press, 1981), 78.

[881] For other meanings of דָּבָר, see BDG: 182:1; HALOT: 209; *Gesenius* 185-188.

Spiritual impact stemming from this inundation of verbiage renders the Divine Word fleeting and banal; this may in part help explain why many people find it difficult to hear the Divine Voice in our daily lives. Amidst our busy schedules, and the pressures of everyday existence, it is essential for us to create the space inside our hearts to search our thoughts and examine our potential for spiritual awakening. Oftentimes our thoughts get tangled with false perceptions and other cognitive distortions. To avoid this state, we must bring silence to the mind and senses. The peacefulness of stillness or silence allows for the possibility of spiritual awakening flowing from the higher regions of consciousness. To discover the mystery of our being, we must sometimes withdraw (a kind of reverse "tsimtsum"; see Excursus 11) from the outer world and create a space for God to enter and embrace our inner world. This is exactly what the prophet Elijah did, who found God in "the stillness of being" (2 Kgs. 2: 1-2, 6-14). In this sacred space, we can safely listen, wonder, question, and dialogue about our place in the cosmos.

D. Re-Sacralizing the Word

> *When you speak, cherish the thought of the secret of the voice and the word, and speak in fear and love, and remember that the world of the word finds utterance through your mouth. Then you will lift the word.*
>
> *Remember that you are only a vessel, and that your thought and your word are worlds that spread out: the world of the word-that is the Divine Presence which, when it is uttered, desires something from the world of thought. And when you have drawn the light of God into your thought and word, pray that something of the abundance and blessing from the world of thought may pour over the world of the word. Then you too will receive what you need. That is why* we say: *"Let us find you in our prayers!" God can be found in our very prayer.*
>
> —*MARTIN BUBER, The Ten Rungs, Collected Hassidic Sayings*

The biblical prophets understand the power of the Word and utilize it to challenge a lazy and religiously pretentious status quo: armed with the power of the Word, the prophets set out to transform and recreate their society anew. More than just an abstract and metaphysical principle, the inherent power of the spoken word takes on special ethical significance. Norwegian theologian Thorlief Boman explains why word and deed must be yoked together—especially when it comes to the realm of the interpersonal.

> The word is the highest and noblest function of man and is, for that reason, identical with his action. "Word" and "deed" are thus not two different meanings of *dabhar*, but the "deed" is the consequence of the basic meaning inhering in *dabhar*. If the Israelites do not distinguish sharply between word and deed, they still know of very promising words which did not become deeds; the failure in such instances lies not in the fact that the man produced only words and no deeds, but in the fact that he brought forth a counterfeit word, an empty word, or a lying word which did not possess the inner strength and truth

for accomplishment or accomplished something evil. An Israelite would not therefore be able to burst out contemptuously like Hamlet, "Words, words, words!" for "word" is in itself not only sound and breath but a reality. Since the word is connected with its accomplishment, *dabhar* could be translated "effective word" (Tatwort); our term "word" is thus a poor translation for the Hebrew *dabhar* because for us "word" never includes the deed within it.[882]

With respect to personal integrity, a promise or vow "legally" binds not only the individual, but also affects the soul's relationship to the Divine (Num. 30:3). Evidence from the Tanakh clearly indicates that a personal verbal assault on another is considered to be the same as physically harming someone with a lethal weapon (Ps. 120:3-4).[883] For this reason and more, gossip is frequently considered the causative agent for premature death and immense suffering. According to the biblical consciousness, life, creation, and language are profoundly intertwined. Words—at least in a figurative sense—can create or impact the world of the listener. Violent treatment of the word most often leads to the violent treatment of people. Recent history has shown how dangerous the spoken word can be in creating an ideology that inspires acts of genocide, random acts of terrorism, or other forms of social violence. The most depraved leader of the 20th century mobilized an entire country to commit genocide against the Jews and other minorities through hate speech. Today, the rhetoric of Jihadism evokes the same pathos of hatred, instigating countless acts of mayhem against Israel's citizens and other peace-minded peoples of the world who embrace Western pluralism and tolerance. If words have sacred power, then they must be appropriately and ethically expressed.

Excursus 10: Time, Creation, and Theology

> *I know well enough what it is, provided that nobody asks me;*
> *but if I am asked what it is and try to explain, I am baffled.*
> —AUGUSTINE, *Confessions, Book XI*

Rabbinic wisdom teaches that there are some aspects to creation that are hidden; we cannot presume to know the mind of God. "Why does the Torah begin with the

---

[882] Thorlief Boman, *Hebrew Thought Compared with Greek* (Philadelphia: Westminster Press, 1960), 65-66.

[883] The scriptural references regarding the sins of character defamation, oral deception, and deceitfulness are vast: Exod. 20:16; 23:1, 6, 7; Lev. 19:11, 16. Deut. 5:20; 19:15-21; 1 Sam. 22:8-19; 1 Kgs. 21:10-13; Pss. 5:6; 15:3; 19:16-19; 27:12; 41:5; 50:20; 52:2-4; 55:20-21; 62:4; 63:11; 101:5-7; 116:69; Prov. 2:12-15; 6:19; 10:18; 11:13; 12:17; 14:5; 16:28; 18:8; 19:5, 9; 20:19; 25:18, 23; 26:20-26; Isa. 59:2-4; Jer. 5:2; 6:27-28; 7:8; 9:3-6; Hos. 4:1-2; 11:12; Ezek. 22:9; Zech. 8:16-17.

letter ב (*beth* = "b")? Just as the letter ב is closed at the sides but is open in front, so you are not permitted to investigate what is above and what is below, what is before and what is behind."[884] The Judean sage Jesus ben Sirach (is 200–180 B.C.E.) offers this practical advice to those who speculate about the "hidden matters" alluded to in the Creation story:

Neither seek what is too difficult for you,
nor investigate what is beyond your power.
Reflect upon what you have been commanded,
for what is hidden is not your concern.
Do not meddle in matters that are beyond you,
for more than you can understand has been shown you.[885]

Sirach 3:21-23

Such an answer may have been intended to keep the masses away from Gnostic speculations. Rabbinic wisdom teaches that there can be no definitive answer to such a question since time and space did not yet exist, except as a mere potentiality.[886]

With a dry wit rarely seen in theologians, Augustine writes about a certain person who inquired what God was doing *before* He created the world. Augustine replied: "He was preparing hell, for those who pry into such mysteries."[887] However, neither Sirach,

---

[884]Gen. Rabbah 1:10.

[885] This passage is cited in the Talmud in BT Hagigah 13a and in T.J. Hagigah 77C, and in Gen. Rabbah 8:2. "R. Leazar said in Bar Sirach's name: 'About what is too great for thee inquire not; what is too hard for thee investigate not; about what is too wonderful for thee know not; of what is hidden from thee ask not; study what was permitted thee; thou hast no business with hidden things'." Sirach's responses is reminiscent of God's response to Job 38:1-7:

Then the Lord answered Job out of the whirlwind:
"Who is this that darkens counsel by words without knowledge?
Gird up your loins like a man,
I will question you, and you shall declare to me.
Where were you when I laid the foundation of the earth?
Tell me, if you have understanding.
Who determined its measurements—surely you know!
Or who stretched the line upon it?
On what were its bases sunk,
or who laid its cornerstone
when the morning stars sang together
and all the heavenly beings shouted for joy?

[886] For an alternative response, see Excursus 3.

[887] *Confessions,* Book 11.

nor the Sages, nor Augustine really address a more relevant question: When did the existence of time first begin? One of the most brilliant theological insights concerning the nature of time was first proposed by Philo of Alexandria, who explains that at the moment when Creation occurred, time also simultaneously came into existence.[888] Augustine wasn't always so flippant with his theological comments; elsewhere, following in Philo's path, Augustine echoes an almost identical thought:

> Then (Moses) says that "in the beginning God made the heaven and the earth," taking "the beginning" not, as some think, in a chronological sense, for there was not time before there was a world. Time began either simultaneously *with* the world or *after* it. For since time is a measured space determined by the world's movement, and since movement could not be prior to the object moving, but must of necessity arise either after it or simultaneously with it, it follows of necessity that time also is either coeval with or later born than the world. And since the word beginning is not here taken as the chronological beginning, it would seem likely that (only) the numerical *order* is indicated, so that "in the beginning He made" is equivalent to "He made the heaven first."[889]

Philo and Augustine's intuition has received confirmation from Einstein's theories of relativity. According to Einstein, time and space came into existence with the world and its laws of nature, and could not be defined or measured apart from it and them. British theologian Keith Ward offers an intriguing exposition of Augustine's alternative answer. In Augustine's *City of God* (Book 11:4), he raises the question once more: "No time passed before the world, no creature was made by whose course it might pass." Ward adds: "Time is a sort of relations between objects, and where no objects exist which are related by that relation, then the relationship does not exist either. The temporal series extends back, as a relation, T [= time], between objects, to an object which simply does not have T, or anything preceding it.[890] Elsewhere, Augustine suggests that there might have been an infinite number of

---

[888] See Philo, *On the Creation*, 7. In addition, both Rashi and Ibn Ezra also assert that Genesis 1:1 depicts Creation occurring within time.

[889] Augustine interpreted Jerome's *in principio* as referring to the beginning of time, thus, time did not exist until God created time and that there was, therefore, no time during which God had not created (*On Genesis: Two Books on Genesis against the Manichees; And, on the Literal Interpretation of Genesis, an Unfinished Book,* Trans. J. S. Roland and J. Teske [Washington, DC: Catholic University of America Press, 1990]), 50. Origen writes that time did not come in existence until the after the creation of the second, third, and fourth days (Origen and Ronald E. Heine trans., *Homiles on Genesis and Exodus* [Washington DC: Catholic University of America Press, 1982], 45). L. Ginzberg, points out (*The Legends of the Jews,* [Philadelphia: The Jewish Publication Society of America, 1909-38], 5.6-7) that certain Midrashic texts suggest that time is actually older than the world (cf. Genesis Rabbah 3.7 and Koheleth Rabbah 3.11). This viewpoint has antecedents in Epicurean thought as well (cf. Cicero, *De Natura Deorum.* 1.21).

[890] Geoffrey Wigoder, *The Meditation of the Sad Soul: Abraham Hiyyah* (Routledge& Kegan Paul (London: 1969), 39.

universes before this one, in which case, time would have no beginning."[891]

Augustine's argument is resurrected later by the 12th century Jewish philosopher Abraham Hiyah, who writes: "'Time' is used here inexactly and according to human usage, but in fact, until things went from potentiality to actuality, there was no such thing as Time, because Time existed in potentiality when all beings existed in it, for Time has no substance and is only a measure signifying the duration of existing things. Without such things, there is no duration on which Time is dependent." It is quite possible that Hiyah may have heard this interpretation from a Christian monk with whom he was friendly.[892]

The British physicist and theologian A. R. Peacocke raises a number of important theological questions regarding God's reality in relation to time and space:

> But if God's mode of being is not within the temporal process, does this not mean that God is "timeless"? This is a particular form of the problem of the relation between transcendence and immanence which always arises in any discussion of the various models of the activity and nature of God as Creator. How can God be thought to act *in* time and yet be the creator *of* time? Recent analyses of this question show that a number of important traditional attributes of God (e.g. his personhood,[a,b] his ability to act in the cosmos,[b] his ability to know the world as temporal and changing[a,c]) lose coherence and meaning if God is regarded as "timeless" in the sense of being "outside" time altogether in a way which means time cannot be said to enter his nature at all, so that he can have no temporal succession in his experience. But similar remarks pertain to space in relation to God: how can God be thought to act *in* space, and to be the creator *of* space, and yet to be non-spatial, to have no spatial location? We appear to have less difficulty with space in relation to God than with time, presumably because the content of mental life includes the sense of temporal succession. We must therefore posit *both* that God transcends space and time, for they owe their being to him, he is their Creator; *and* that space and time can exist "within" God in such a way that he is not precluded from being present at all points in space and time, a way of speaking of the world's relation to God we shall have cause to employ again.[893]

Maimonides already seems to have anticipated Peacocke's conclusions. For Maimonides, God's existence is not merely eternal—but is also timeless and unaffected by the temporal constraints that might conceivably restrict Divine omniscience. Each of the questions Peacocke grapples with reveals the problems that are associated with language itself. Simply put, human beings have no other way of expressing reality except

---

[891] Keith Ward, *Religion and Creation,* (Oxford: Clarendon Press, 1996), 289-290. The concept of alternate universes was also anticipated by Philo and later by R. Hasdai Crescas in the 15th century. The Midrash too, also speaks of God "creating universes and destroying them" (Zohar 1 24b).

[892] *The Meditation of the Sad Soul: Abraham Hiyya, op. cit.,* 28.

[893] A. R. Peacocke, *Creation and the World of Science* (Oxford: Clarendon Press. 1979), 80-81.

in the terms drawn from their temporal spatial worldview. Yet, God's perception of the universe transcends the boundaries constricting human consciousness, which is inherently limited, as Maimonides explains:

> God is self-aware of His own reality, knowing Himself as He truly is—but not with an external knowledge that is analogous to how *we* extrinsically perceive reality, since we and our perception of the world are not one.[894] Were God's knowledge [i.e., self-awareness] predicated upon something that is [temporally or spatially] "external" to Him, there would be a plentitude of godlings co-existing with God [thus producing a henotheistic reality composed of entities characterizing the objects of], His "life" and His "knowledge"—[God's absolute oneness would be severely ontologically compromised]. Rather, the blessed Creator's knowledge [self-awareness] and existence—combined with His knowledge and life are indeed [ontologically] One and can only fittingly be described as the Knower, the Known, and Process of Knowing—all wrapped up in one. Human speech can barely articulate this truth, while the ear is incapable of rationally comprehending this— but the human heart can scarcely sense such a reality, but not in all of its fullness.[895]

Perhaps an illustration can be drawn from a 19th century Hindu philosopher who explains why human reason cannot fathom the nature of God's reality, according to the theology of the renowned 8th century Hindu philosopher Shankara:

> The entire world lives in the mind of man, and it is the movement of the conscious mind that produces the distinctions of perception, the perceiver and the perceived, a differentiation where in fact there is none, as everything is part of the vast ocean of unity. This state does not recognize the distinctions of knower, known and knowledge, all of which are but relative terms with no finality about them. Similarly, the three states of the human experience (waking, dreaming and the dreamless) are unreal, for none of them lasts long enough, and each gives place to the other in turn, as the mind passes from state to state. Each of them has a beginning and an end and exists only in the absence of the others. The term "relativity" in itself implies its antithesis, the "Reality," and beyond the three states specified above is the Atman, as the basis of them all. It alone is and constantly remains, behind the ever changing panorama of life, the ever unborn, eternally awake, the dreamless and self-illumined, by its very nature a pure cognition

---

[894] Elsewhere, Maimonides illustrates his point by pointing out how when a person sees a tree, its image is etched in the mind's eye, reproducing a mental image of it which enables him to comprehend the tree as it exists in actuality. Thus, there are three aspects to consider: the perceiver (man), the object (the tree) and the act or process of comprehension—all of which are contingent upon each other in this analogy. However, God's perception of the object (i.e. Creation) never occurs "outside" of Him, but within the Divine Consciousness, for God is always self-aware (*Guide* 1:68).

[895] MT, *Hilchot Yesodei HaTorah* 2:10 (my translation and commentary); Maimonides' concept also bears a striking comparison to Shankara, who also asserts that a pure state of consciousness of God-realization produces the awareness that the knower, known and knowledge are indeed one (*nirvikalpaka samadhi*) (William S. Haney II, "Deconstruction and Sanskrit Poetics" [Manitoba: *Mosaic* Volume 28, Issue 1, 1995], 336).

distinct from the non-cognition of the sleep state.[896]

With this thought in mind, the theological implications of Genesis 1:1 are now clear: If God is the Author of time, then it stands to reason that from the biblical perspective, God's existence and reality stand completely apart from the temporal reality we experience as entities. By the same token there is a tendency among our contemporaries to speak of the "God within" or the "God who is beyond." Such epithets reflect the temporal and spatial perceptions of the Divine, which are metaphors drawn from our human perspectives of the world. The simple truth is we cannot imagine a reality transcending time and space. We do not exist in such a continuum; we can only barely grasp the existence of such a timeless state of being; ergo, we tend to utilize theological language to describe how we imagine God to be, which reflects our dependence upon the time-space continuum. Lastly, Maimonides' conclusion concerning the power of the heart is replete with mystical significance. Reason per se can only take an individual so far, but the heart can sense an altogether different Reality; moreover, it is genuinely capable of responding to the Spirit's beckoning.

Excursus 11: Creation Through "Tsimtsum" — A Divine Kenosis

Once a simple supernal light irradiated all existence. . . . There was no emptiness of space—only the light of the Infinite One. . . . As the Infinite One desired to create worlds and emanations, the Infinite One focused upon the central point of the light, removing the light from all sides as it were. As an empty space emerged, a complete vacuum appeared. . . . Now, this withdrawal (tsimtsum) was equal all around that central, empty point, in such a manner that that empty space formed a circle which was totally equidistant all around. It was not in the form of a square, with right angles, for the Infinite One withdrew Itself in the form of a circle, equidistant on all sides . . .

—R. HAYYIM VITAL, *Etz Hayyim* (*The Tree of Life*)

To paraphrase the well-known saying of St. Irenaeus, the religio perennis is fundamentally this: the Real entered into the illusory so the illusory might be able to return unto the Real. It is this mystery, together with metaphysical discernment and contemplative concentration that are its complement, which alone is important in an absolute sense from the point of view of gnosis: for the gnostic—in the etymological and rightful sense of the word—there is in the final analysis no other "religion." It is what Ibn Arabi called "the religion of love", placing the accent on the element of "realization."

—SEYYED HOSSEIN, FRITJOF SCHUON, *The Essential Frithjof Schuon*

Theologians and philosophers have long wondered how God created a world that

[896] Kirpal Singh, *The Crown of Life: A Study of Yoga* (Brooklyn: Swan House Pub Co; 4th edition, 1990), 123-124.

possesses a separate sense of self—one that seems apart from God. The renowned 16th century Kabbalist, Isaac Luria, explains that in order for a world to exist—both finite and self-conscious of its own being—God has to "diminish" the light of His own infinite Being, by "withdrawing," as it were, "to the periphery." Luria metaphorically describes this creative process as צמצם *"tsimtsum"* – a word that means "contraction" or "constriction." Luria's *tsimtsum,* to a large degree, is based on the rabbinic notion of the Shekhinah. Historically, Luria's myth of the *tsimtsum* is not without its antecedents. One recent study traces the origin of the *tsimtsum* to certain Gnostic traditions (of the Valentinian variety), which seeped their influence into the Zohar. The notion of "God withdrawing into Himself" prior to emanation, derives from the 2nd century Christian Gnostic thinker, Basilides of Alexandria, who established a Gnostic sect known as the Basilideans.[897]

According to one 5th century Midrashic text, the notion of God's Presence is said to have been contained (מצמצם שם שכינתו) within the parameters of the Ark of the Covenant (15:10).[898] Other rabbinic teachings of the Midrash and Talmud regarding a concept of *tsimtsum* include: "Since the day that the Temple was destroyed, the Blessed Holy One, has nothing in this world but the four cubits of Halacha [Jewish Law] alone" (BT Berakhot 8a).[899] The renowned historian of Kabbalah, Gershom G. Scholem, differentiates between the earlier rabbinic models of the *tsimtsum* from the concept that he championed:

> The Midrash—in sayings originating from third-century teachers—occasionally refers to God as having concentrated His Shekhinah, His divine presence, in the Holiest of Holies, at the place of the *Cherubim*, as though His whole power were concentrated and contracted in a single point. Here we have the origin of the term *Tzimztum*, while the thing itself is the precise opposite of this idea: To the Kabbalist of Luria's school, *Tsimtsum* does not mean the concentration of God *at* a point, but his retreat *away* from a point. [900] What does this mean? It means briefly that the existence of the universe is made possible by a process of shrinkage in God. . . . Something of the Divine Being is exiled out of Himself, whereas the Tsimtsum

[897] Lawrence Fine, *Physician of the Soul, Healer of the Cosmos: Isaac Luria and His Kabbalistic Fellowship* (Stanford, CA: Stanford University Press, 2003), 144-149. Midrash Tanchuma, Vilnas Parshat Vyakhale 7.

[898] S. Buber, *Midrash Tanchuma* (Vilnas, 1885) Parshat Vyakhale 7.

[899] Rav J. B. Soloveitchik explains this rabbinic aphorism in terms of the *tsimtsum* doctrine. According to him, the entire Halachic enterprise is dedicated to realizing the Divine Presence into the lowly material world, "In the ideal world of Halacha, the concept of holiness means the descent of Divinity into our concrete world. This is how laws become the building blocks of the purely spiritual." As a support for this theological premise, he quotes a biblical passage which reads: "For the Lord thy God walks in the midst of your camp" (Deut. 23:15) and the Rav further explains: "It is the contraction of the Infinity within a finitude of laws bound to laws, measures, and standards; the appearance of transcendence within empirical reality" cited from Zvi Kolitz's *Confrontation: The Existential Thought of Rabbi J.B. Soloveitchik* (Hoboken, NJ: Ktav, 1993), 15.

[900] Gershom Scholem, *Major Trends in Jewish Mysticism,* Third edition (New York: Schocken, 1974), 260.

could come to be considered as an exile into Himself.[901]

Most Kabbalists point out that the concept of צמצם is only meant metaphorically since space (and time) has no ontology prior to Creation.[902] Had the Infinite God not restricted His light, then everything would be overwhelmed by God's totality. Yet conversely, the *tsimtsum* does not represent a complete withdrawal of God—only a partial one. Were the *tsimtsum* a total withdrawal, creation as we presently know it, would never have even an inkling of anything pertaining to Divinity and our sense of cosmic unity would be totally undifferentiated, i.e., without any sense of separate identity. More to the point, for human beings to have the freedom to become self-aware of their nature and origin of being, God must accommodate human freedom by withdrawing a part of His infinite power. God "contracts" some of His infinite essence in order to create the ontological space for a finite universe and world to exist.

The withdrawal of the Divine is not altogether complete, and may be analogous to a type of spiritual "black hole" where the divine energy is kept in check. Some Kabbalists compare this progression to the residual fragrance that is left in a perfume bottle after its contents has been emptied. More importantly, there is a second aspect of the *tsimtsum* that is equally as important to the initial withdrawal of God—to Himself, so to speak: the reintroduction of the Divine light into the ontological void that reveals God as the Creator within the primordial space of this new emergent creation. As the celestial light of the *Ein Sof* (the Endless One) flows and contracts, and flows and contracts, it gradually brings order into the chaotic space until each dimension of Creation becomes increasingly more tangible and limited. Thus, new levels of phenomenal reality are created, finally producing this material universe with all of its diverse expressions.[903] There is a mystical verse in the Psalms that captures this imagery—the notion that God creates the universe by wrapping Himself in a garment of light (Psa. 104:2).[904] (See notes on Genesis 1:3).

---

901 Ibid., 261.

902 Even "light" itself, is only a metaphor since spiritual light has no separate ontology apart from the Divine and is only meant to illustrate the primordial oneness that suffused all existence prior to the Creation of the universe.

903 See Gershom Scholem, *Major Trends in Jewish Mysticism*. 3d ed. (New York: Schocken, 1961), 260-265.

904 This idea is also alluded to in *Me'or HaShemesh Parshat Bereshit*: : והנה, אמרו חז"ל (ב"ר ג ד) על פסוק (תהלים קד ב) עֹטֶה אוֹר כַּשַּׂלְמָה, שנתעטף הקב"ה באור וברא את העולם. ורמזו בזה, כי השי"ת צמצם אורו שיהיה מקום לעמידת העולמות

In analogical terms, almost any kind of creative human activity requires a "clearing" of mental "space" so that the power of the imagination will reveal new creative thoughts and concepts. As the power of conceptualization unfolds, the nascent concept may seem like a thin beam of light entering into the conscious mind. Once this light appears, the intellect will expand upon the concept and eventually seek to manifest itself into an inspired product of creativity or a new idea—this process ought to be especially familiar to anyone who has ever attempted to write a book! Some Jewish mystics say that the process of *tsimtsum* can be recognized whenever a conscientious teacher clears his or her mind and distills a sophisticated thought so that even a young child may comprehend its new wisdom.

A. *Tsimtsum as Mystical Pedagogy*

The metaphor of the *tsimtsum* may even be deduced directly from the Tanakh. One important passage in Isaiah 30:20 which fits well within the theological schema of the *tsimtsum,* "No longer will your Teacher hide himself, but with your own eyes you shall see your Teacher." The metaphor of God as "teacher" may explain the *tsimtsum* more lucidly than other approaches. Pedagogically speaking, it is often said there is no such thing as a "bad student" but only "bad teachers," who are incapable of articulating their thoughts to a student. At any rate, as the educator attempts to distill the concept, he cannot afford to ignore the child's undeveloped cognitive abilities. Failing to ignore the child's limitations will only result in confusing the student. As an *effective* communicator, a teacher should find a way to distill an abstract concept for the student by utilizing concepts that are familiar to the student's frame of reference, making sure that the material is not overwhelming the student.

Delivering academic material too enthusiastically or ambitiously may actually overwhelm the student. Over the course of time, as the student becomes more proficient, the subject matter also becomes increasingly more complex. As a student encounters difficulties, the teacher should respond with patience. In this way, the student may finally master the material in order to make practical use of the knowledge that he can now share with others. Much of this analogy can also be applied to a parent-child relationship. Parents may not always approve of the child's choices; nevertheless, an effective parent "creates the space" that allows the child (hopefully!) to express his will wisely. In the same manner, God hides His own Being from Creation, so that one will not be overwhelmed by the light of God's infinite Being and Presence.

Like the teacher/ parent/child analogy, God also gives us the space to be who we are, while creating the opportunity for us to incrementally expand and define our own spiritual consciousness of *who and what we are.* In a paradoxical sense, the *tsimtsum* is a cosmic illusion, for even when God seems hidden—He is still present everywhere.

B. Tsimtsum as a Metaphor for Divine Love

Another analogy of the *tsimtsum* may also be deduced from the model of love. As Lévinas observes, God in His Infinite nature, allows for the existence of the Other to emerge: God is first and foremost a relational Being. How does this occur? As mentioned earlier, self-limitation is the pre-condition God adheres to in creating human beings endowed with freedom of choice. This act of self-limitation is for the good and interest of the entity, so that it will have the capacity to grow in the direction it chooses. God's self-limitation in allowing us to experience self-determination analogically resembles behavior we describe as *agape* (unconditional) love. As such, love is humble, kind, patient and accepting; it has the capacity to endure periods of distance and difficulty so that the loved one has the space to grow and develop. Love acts faithfully and is trustworthy. Love anticipates hope. Love is redemptive.

On the Divine scale, God imposes limitations on His power and on His omnipresence in allowing individuals to act as though there is no Ultimate Reality. Judaic wisdom recognizes that the greatness of the Creator does not lie in His ability to create the world, but in His divine "humiliation" to tolerate its defiance and apathy toward the "One Who spoke and all things came into being" (*Siddur*). One of the paradoxes of the *tsimtsum* is the idea that the Talmud expresses the same thought, although in different terms: "R. Yochanan says, 'Wherever you find mentioned in the Scriptures the power of the Blessed Holy One, you will also find His humility.'"[905] By limiting His power, humanity has the ability to do what angelic beings would find impossible—denial of their Creator and Maker.

C. Tsimtsum and Theodicy

The doctrine of the *tsimtsum* has special significance with respect to the issue of theodicy. Briefly stated, evil's existence derives directly from the diminishment of light that is directly caused by result of the *tsimtsum*. The concealment of the Divine Light is necessary if humankind is to develop as an entity endowed with freedom. Martin Buber stresses that the origin of evil is ontologically related to the Lurianic Kabbalah notion of the "breaking of the vessels," a cosmic event that upsets the order and harmony of Creation.

> As a result of the breaking of the vessels, the divine harmony is disrupted, the Shekinah is exiled, and sparks of divinity fall downward into physical creation. In the physical world the sparks are surrounded by hard shells of darkness (*qelipot*), a type of negative evil. This whole process is further confirmed by the fall of man, but it is also within man's power to liberate the divine sparks from their imprisonment in the shells and send them upward again to union with their divine source. Through this liberation the power of

---

[905] BT Megillah 31a.

darkness is overcome and *tikkun*, the restoration of the original harmony, is effected.[906]

Unlike other Gnostic systems that advocate a retreat from the physical world, the Kabbalah is grounded in the traditional Judaic beliefs that the physical world has a great capacity to be spiritually elevated through the practice of the *mitzvot* (commandments of God). Judaism teaches: "Someday, a human being will have to give account for all that his eye beheld and he did not eat."[907] When viewed from this perspective, the world can seem, at times, as if God's Presence has receded from humanity. Yet, God's Reality is still present, waiting for humankind to release the Divine energy that is concealed in all things. In this mystical way, humanity has the potential to fix the cosmic rupture that has occurred within the spiritual world and as a result of the "Fall" of Adam.

Excursus 12: Anthropocentric Theology and Its Contemporary Permutations

A junkyard contains all the bits and pieces of a Boeing-747, dismembered and in disarray. A whirlwind happens to blow through the yard. What is the chance that after its passage a fully assembled 747, ready to fly, will be found standing there?

—FRED HOYLE, *The Intelligent Universe*

The eternal silence of these infinite spaces frightens me.

—Blasé Pascal, *The Pensées*

A. Saadia Gaon and the Anthropic Principle

Centuries before Copernicus, the medieval world believed in a Ptolemaic view of the universe. In Saadia Gaon's (ca. 10th century) theology, humankind is the center-piece of Creation. The earth's centrality to the cosmos is likened to a kernel that is lodged in the center of the fruit, or to a yolk at the center of the egg. By the same token, Saadia argues that earth occupies the center of the universe.[908] Withouthumankind's

---

[906] Maurice S. Friedman, *Martin Buber, Life of Dialogue* (Chicago: University of Chicago Press, 1956), 18.

[907] Jerusalem Talmud, *Kiddushin* 4:12.

[908] It would be remarkable if in the modern era, one could still find a geocentric advocate for Ptolemaic science, yet the late Lubavitcher Rebbe, R. Menachem Mendel Schneersohn, advocated just such a position. Here is an extraordinary letter the Rebbe wrote (September 16, 1968):

> I am in receipt of your letter of September 10th, in which you touch upon the question of whether the sun revolves around the earth or vice versa, in view of the fact that you heard from a college student that the truth is that the earth revolves around the sun. It greatly surprises me that, according to your letter, the student declared that science has resolved that the earth revolves around the sun. The surprising thing is that a person making such a declaration would be about one half century

existence, everything in the cosmos would be purposeless and meaningless. Despite Maimonides' critical opinion of Saadia's anthropocentric view, a partial defense for Saadia's philosophical cosmology may be drawn today from modern physics.

Many contemporary physicists argue that the presence of a sentient and self-conscious species in the universe is actually based upon a marvelous number of delicately balanced physical "coincidences." The recent discussion over the "Anthropic Principle" was first initiated by the physicist, Brandon Carter, in 1973. During a conference honoring Copernicus's 500th birthday in Cracow, Carter advanced the thesis that the position of humankind's status in the universe is privileged in the sense that the development of living organisms could not have taken place in just any physical conditions, but actually required special conditions dependent on such properties of the universe such as age, rate of expansion, and the values of particular parameters.[909]

The Anthropic Principle shows that the organization of matter in the universe is not a slipshod or haphazard affair—the universe reflects symmetry and order. Physicist Paul Davies observes that there are more than two dozen essential prerequisites that must be satisfied if life is to exist on the earth. A hidden principle seems to be organizing and structuring the cosmos in a coherent way. Concisely stated, the universe's dynamics are calibrated for creating *conscious* life. Had there been the slightest variance from the moment of the Big Bang, no life of any kind would exist.[910]

Davies explains that if the strong nuclear force holding protons and neutrons together were just slightly stronger than what it actually is, protons and neutrons would have such an affinity for one another that they would clump together to form only heavy elements, which are absolutely essential to support life, and omit light elements such as hydrogen. On the other hand, if the strong nuclear force was slightly weaker, then there would only be hydrogen in the universe and that would not suffice either. If the gravitational force was too strong, stars would burn out too quickly and their behavior would become erratic. For instance, our sun has just the right rate of burning and is very

behind the times insofar as the position of modern science is concerned. This belief is completely refuted by the theory of Relativity, which has been accepted by all scientists as the basis for all the branches of science. One of the basic elements of this theory is that when two bodies in space are in motion relative to one another (actually the theory was initiated on the basis of the movements of stars, planets, the earth, etc.), science declares with absolute certainty that from the scientific point of view both possibilities are equally valid, namely that the earth revolves around the sun, or the sun revolves around the earth. Herman Branover, Joseph Ginsburg, and Menachem Mendel Schneersohn (trans. Arnie Gotfryd) *Mind over Matter: The Lubavitcher Rebbe on Science, Technology and Medicine* (Jerusalem: Shamir 2003), 75-77.

909 Brandon Carter, "Large Number Coincidences and the Anthropic Principle in Cosmology," in *Confrontation of Cosmological Theories with Observational Data*, ed. M. S. Longair (Dordrecht, 1974), 291-298.

910 Paul Davies, *Other Worlds* (New York: Touchstone, 1980), 143-144. *Cf.* J.D. Barrow and F.J. Tipper, *The Cosmological Anthropic Principle* (Oxford: Oxford University Press, 1986).

steady in the emission of heat and light, which is of course vitally necessary for sustaining life on earth. Moreover, the balance of gravitational and electromagnetic forces is crucial in determining the character and life of stars. Again, the electromagnetic forces play the most important role in the formation of molecules (where atoms come together in groups that have particular chemical properties) and of course, if we don't have the right molecules, biological systems such as plants, animals and people could not come into existence.

As a physicist, Davies would go somewhat further than Saadia, the theologian. He asserts that the mere fact that we are aware of our cosmological and ontological origins is indeed significant:

> We human beings have been privy to the deepest workings of the universe. Other animals observe the same natural phenomena as we do, but alone among the creatures on this planet, *Homo sapiens* can also *explain* them. How has this come about? Somehow the universe has engineered not just its own awareness, but also its own *comprehension*. Mindless, blundering atoms have conspired to make not just life, not just mind, but *understanding*. The evolving cosmos has spawned beings who are not merely to watch the show, *but to unravel the plot*. What is that enables something as small and delicate and adapted to terrestrial life as the human brain to engage with the totality of the cosmos and the silent mathematical tune to which it dances? For all we know, this is the first and only time anywhere in the universe that minds have glimpsed the cosmic code. If humans are snuffed out in the twinkling of a cosmic eye, it may never happen again. . . . Could it be just a fluke? Might the fact that the deepest level of reality has connected to a quirky natural phenomenon we call "the human mind" represent nothing but a bizarre and temporary aberration in an absurd and pointless universe? *Or is there an even deeper subplot at work?*[911]

Thus, as remarkable as the appearance of life is—even on the most pristine level—it is astounding how human consciousness possesses the ability to contemplate itself in relation to the universe. Not only does it have the ability to objectively reflect upon this cosmic process, it can even report on its own character and nature! Similar in principle to Davies' penetrating inquiry, Oxford scholar Richard Swinburne and molecular biologist and theologian Alister McGrath, both assert that the inherent intelligibility of the universe in itself requires an explanation. Why should we be able to understand the universe at all? This question, McGrath argues, points to the notion of a Creator God. McGrath further asserts that Swinburne's novel concept renders the old "God of the gaps" theory of the cosmos to the dustbin.[912]

---

[911] Paul Davies, *Cosmic Jackpot: Why Our Universe is Just Right for Life* (New York: Houghton Mifflin, 2007), 5.

[912] The "God of the gaps" theory is a theological approach that appeals to God's existence as the only plausible explanation for the universe's immense complexity. The term originated with the 19th century evangelical scholar Henry Drummond.

It is therefore not the *gaps in our understanding of the world* which point to God but rather the very *comprehensibility* of scientific and other forms of understanding that requires an explanation. In brief, the argument is that *explicability itself requires explanation*. The more scientific advance is achieved, the greater will be our understanding of the universe—and hence the greater need to explain this very success. It is an approach which commends and encourages scientific investigation, [and does] not seek to inhibit it. [913]

Although nearly a thousand years have passed since the time Saadia proposed his novel but geocentric and anthropocentric view of the universe, the essence of his position has been resurrected and reaffirmed by modern physicists, philosophers, and theologians alike. In short, it is safe to suggest that had Saadia Gaon been aware of the philosophical and scientific permutations of the contemporary era, he would have certainly endorsed the Anthropic Principle as being consistent with his own personal view of humankind and the world.

B. Maimonides' Rejection of Anthropocentric Theology

We know that Maimonides took sharp exception with Saadia's theological cosmology. First of all, Saadia's claim that this world is the "center of God's universe" cannot possibly be scientifically established. Nevertheless, one must wonder if Maimonides would have embraced the cosmological implications of the Anthropic Principle. Perhaps he might have reconsidered taking a second look at Saadia's geocentric theology; it is also possible that he would still maintain his original position, namely, that the creation of the universe is essentially rooted in the inscrutable will of God, a concept which may elude human understanding. The fact that there is life on this planet does not preclude that God may have created many types of life-forms on other planets—such a view does have some support in the Midrash.[914]

For the discordant atheist or agnostic, the universe exists as a brute fact. It simply "is what it is." In his bestselling book *The First Three Minutes,* Nobel Prize winning physicist Steven Weinberg deflates some of the often heard theological expositions endorsing the Anthropic Principle as a proof for Genesis:

It is almost irresistible for humans to believe that we have some special relation to the universe, that human life is not just a more-or-less farcical outcome of a chain of

[913] Alister McGrath, *The Dawkins Delusion? Atheistic Fundamentalism and the Denial of the Divine* (Downer's Grove, IL: Inter-varsity Press, 2007), 31.

[914] According to one 5th century Midrashic text: "R. Tanhuma taught: 'He has made everything suitable for its time' (Ecc. 3:11). R. Tanhuma said, 'The world was created exactly when it was appropriate to do so, for it was not fit to be created earlier.' R. Abbahu adds, 'From this teaching we may deduce that the Blessed Holy One, went on creating worlds and destroying them until He created this world, and then God said: 'These please Me; however, those worlds did not please Me"' (Gen. Rabbah 9:2).

> accidents reaching back to the first three minutes, but that we were somehow built in from the beginning. As I write this I happen to be in an airplane at 30,000 feet, flying over Wyoming en route home from San Francisco to Boston. Below, the earth looks very soft and comfortable — fluffy clouds here and there, snow turning pink as the sun sets, roads stretching straight across the country from one town to another. It is very hard to realize that this all is just a tiny part of an overwhelmingly hostile universe. It is even harder to realize that this present universe has evolved from an unspeakably unfamiliar early condition, and faces a future extinction of endless cold or intolerable heat. The more the universe seems comprehensible, the more it also seems pointless.[915]

Oddly enough, Maimonides might have concurred with Weinberg up to a certain point. For humankind to advance spiritually, it must learn to give up its belief that "man is the measure of all things," and substitute that "God is the measure of all things" instead. Maimonides has no difficulty explaining the creation narrative's distinctive geocentric perspective of the world; this is more due to the fact that Torah speaks in the language of the common person, who experiences the world through anthropocentric eyes. However, a deeper metaphysical grasp of God's relationship to the world indicates that the vastness of the celestial heavens serves a higher purpose that has little to do with humankind's strivings and its sense of self-importance.

Indeed, there may be countless worlds in the universe where other beings are no less sentient and aware than we are, even though such inhabited extraterrestrial civilizations have yet to be scientifically proven. Physicist Steven Hawking thinks the "weak anthropic principle" better explains the emergence of sentient life than the "strong anthropic principle" which claims that the entire cosmos exists simply for our sake. Hawking notes:

> [T]he conditions necessary for the development of intelligent life will be met only in certain regions that are limited in space and time. The intelligent beings in these regions should therefore not be surprised if they observe that their locality in the universe satisfies the conditions that are necessary for their existence. It is bit like a rich person living in a wealthy neighborhood not seeing any poverty.[916]

The concept of parallel earths is actually discussed in a number of ancient Judaic writings: Philo, the Sages of the Talmud and Midrash did not rule out such a possibility. It is conceivable that prior to the creation of this world, God was involved in other creative enterprises, namely—creating and destroying other worlds.[917] In another

---

[915] Steven Weinberg, *The First Three Minutes: A Modern View of the Origin of the Universe* (New York: Basic Books, 1993), 154.

[916] Stephen Hawking and Leonard Mlodinow, *A Briefer History of Time* (New York: Bantam, 2008), 130.

[917] According to one 5th century Midrashic text: "R. Tanhuma taught: 'He has made everything suitable for its

rabbinic text, the Talmud suggests that God "rides upon a light cherub, and floats in eighteen thousand worlds."[918] This rabbinic interpretation has theological implications concerning the potential discovery of sentient extraterrestrial life.

In R. Norman Lamm's well-known study,[919] he emphatically argues that when Maimonides wrote his *Guide* toward the end of his life, he believed that anthropocentrism was one of the three most basic errors preventing humankind from developing an authentic understanding of God, and the universe; it is these cognitive distortions that are so typical of popular conceptions which prevent a person from actualizing a fully-developed faith in the Divine. For Maimonides, Creation is *theocentric* and not an anthropocentric venture.[920] This idea was originally conveyed by the prophet Isaiah who proclaimed, "Everything that is called by My Name, I have created for my Glory" (Isa. 43:7); i.e., *for God's glory and not for the glory of creation.* Since humankind is *not* the measure of all things, there are mysteries that no human mind will ever be able to fully fathom, since they are grounded in the will of God.

Physicist Harold Schilling offers a deeply profound understanding of the term "mystery" that is reminiscent of Rudolph Otto's notion of the "numinous." By the term *mystery*, Schilling explains it is not to mean an unsolved puzzle or a gap in our knowledge. Rather, mystery refers to something that is inherently unknowable and inexplicable. No amount of

---

time' (Ecc. 3:11). R. Tanhuma said, 'The world was created exactly when it was appropriate to do so, for it was not fit to be created earlier.' R. Abbahu adds, 'From this teaching we may deduce that the Blessed Holy One, went on creating worlds and destroying them until He created this world, and then God said: 'These please Me; however, those worlds did not please Me''' (Gen. Rabbah 9:2).

[918] BT Avodah Zarah 3b.

[919] Norman Lamm, *Faith and Doubt: Studies in Traditional Jewish Thought* (New York: Ktav, 1986), 107-160.

[920] Maimonides, *Guide* 2:13:

> For no part of the creation is described as being in existence for the sake of another part, but each part is declared to be the product of God's will, and to satisfy by its existence the intention [of the Creator]. . . . You must not be misled by what is stated of the stars [that God put them in the firmament of the heavens] to give light upon the earth, and to rule by day and by night. You might perhaps think that here the purpose of their creation is described. This is not the case; we are only informed of the nature of the stars, which God desired to create with such properties that they should be able to give light and to rule. In a similar manner we must understand the passage, "And have dominion over the fish of the sea" (Gen. 1:28). Here it is not meant to say that man was created for this purpose, but only that this was the nature which God gave man. But as to the statement in Scripture that God gave the plants to man and other living beings, it agrees with the opinion of Aristotle and other philosophers. It is also reasonable to assume that the plants exist only for the benefit of the animals, since the latter cannot live without food. It is different with the stars, they do not exist only for our sake, that we should enjoy their good influence; for the expressions "to give light" and "to rule" merely describe, as we have stated above, the benefit which the creatures on earth derive from them (*Guide* 2:13).

knowledge can ever diminish or eliminate the sense of mystery. On the contrary, our desire to grasp the nature of the cosmic mystery is only intensified as our knowledge of it expands with each scientific discovery. In religious terms, the sense of mystery we experience when gazing at the heavens is the source of all wonder, and is the bedrock of true worship and devotion. This sense of mystery that pervades Creation evokes existential questions that point us toward ultimate issues and ultimate concerns, as Schilling writes:

> An important role of ritual and liturgy in religion is to keep alive in the worshipper a keen sense of awe and wonder in the presence of ultimate mystery. . . . No doubt this is why the language of religion is influenced so much by a sense of a reality and power of mystery and is, to a large extent, symbolic and mythical in character. The discursive and technical languages of, say, the sciences are not capable of adequately communicating the transrational and noncognitive meanings and implications of insights that comes out of man's encounter with ultimate mystery.[921]

Throughout our existence as a species, we have been driven by an impulse to understand and wonder about our relationship with the world around us and with our Ultimate Reality. Although we as human beings are bound by the shackles of time, each one of us can endow every day with spiritual meaning that transcends our own temporal limitations. In the language of the ancient Psalmists, man's awareness of his "smallness" can induce a sense of awe, wonder, and humility as he beholds Creation and exclaims:

> What is man that you are mindful of him,
> the son of man that you care for him? (Psa. 8:4)

In one of Maimonides' most mystical thoughts, the great master illustrates how meditation can lead to an awareness of the Divine, by redirecting one's focus to a theocentric view of reality that shatters our childish notions of anthropocentrism. A look into the universe reveals an altogether different reality from the world we experience daily. Obviously, had Maimonides been aware of the Hubble Space Telescope, his discovery of the universe's vastness would have only re-enforced his intuition, in the grand scheme of Creation, that humankind is not as important of a species as it imagines itself to be.

> What is the way to attain the love and fear of God? When a man contemplates His great and wondrous deeds and creations, and sees in them His unequaled and infinite wisdom, he immediately loves and praises and exalts Him, and is overcome by a great desire to know the great Name; as David said, "My soul thirsts for God, for the living God" (Ps. 42:3). And when he considers these very matters, immediately he withdraws and is frightened and knows that he is but a small, lowly, dark creature who, with his inferior and puny mind, stands before Him who is perfect in His knowledge; as David said, "When I consider Your heavens, the work of Your fingers . . . what is man that You are mindful of him?" (Ps. 8:4, 5). Thus do I

[921] Harold Schilling, *The New Consciousness in Science and Religion* (Philadelphia: Pilgrim Press, 1973), 48-56.

explain many great principles concerning the actions of the Master of the Worlds [namely] that they provide an opportunity for a wise person to love God. As the Sages said concerning love, "as a result of this you will come to know Him by whose word the world came into being." [922]

By adopting a theocentric view of the universe, Maimonides also evades the issue of theodicy, since the problem of evil is generated by the perception that the universe exists for the sake of the individual. If humanity is not the center of the universe, then all the various tribulations and evils that a person experiences throughout his or her life are part and parcel of living in a world that is governed by natural law. Ultimately, each person must find meaning in his or her own life and by doing so, will learn to transcend the limitations of creaturely existence.

Excursus 13: A Theological View of Evolution

Miracles abound everywhere, but man closes his eyes with his hand and sees nothing.

—RABBI ISRAEL BAAL SHEM TOV, *attributed*

There are only two ways to live your life: as though nothing is a miracle, or as though everything is a miracle.

—ALBERT EINSTEIN

וַיְהִי־עֶרֶב וַיְהִי־בֹקֶר יוֹם הַשִּׁשִּׁי — **And there was evening and there was morning, the sixth day.** — Ever since Charles Darwin originally introduced his Theory of Evolution, the traditional belief in a universe created by God in "six days" has been chided and discarded in our culture as being scientifically obsolete. Clearly, the biblical writers did not deliberately regard the Torah as a textbook about science, but rather first and foremost as a guide for living an ethical and holy life. Nevertheless, it is worth citing one of the greatest Jewish mystics of the early 20th century, R. Abraham Isaac Kook, whose opinion of the Theory of Evolution is described in positive terms. Kook notes that evolution is compatible with many ideas found in early Kabalistic writing:

> The concept of evolution of existence, of all that has being, lowers man's spirit and elevates him. A life-enhancing and a life-negating principle are embodied in it. When a person looks backward and sees the lowly state in his past, and considers his own present moral, intellectual and physiological condition, so fortunate, so happily in contrast to the past, his mind becomes disoriented on the one hand. His moral discipline is weakened. Whatever moral sensibility he may feel in himself when the evil inclination of some lust should assail him he will say that it is too much for a creature like himself, whose origin is from dumb beasts and crude savagery.

922 MT, *Hilchot Yesodei ha-Torah*, 2:2.

> In contrast to this the concept of evolution in relation to the future elevates man to the moral height that one envisions in the account of man's greatness at the time of his creation, when he dwelt with God, before his banishment from the Garden of Eden. As a person rises in knowledge and understanding, in the study of Torah and in the cultivation of good attributes, in his intellectual and moral propensities, he marches forward toward the future. Automatically the doctrine of evolution works on him to set him on the right course and to strengthen his moral senses, until he will enter the domains of holiness and purity with a higher vigor full of the strength of the Lord. Theconcept of the past will inspire him with fear, as he will reflect on the frightful lowliness of the past and feel that by corrupting his ways he may fall to that dark, lowly state. By contrast, by perfecting his ways and actions, personal and social, there is open to him a great light that directs him to endless progress.[923]

Other Modern Orthodox scholars[924] have adopted a similar view to Kook's, agreeing that the Theory of Evolution has a place in Jewish theology provided one does not view evolution as a random and blind process. Evolution merely reflects the wisdom of how God endows Creation with a sense of purpose and direction. The processes of adaptation, variation, and natural selection reflect how consciousness expands from the micro to the macro.

A. The Debate Concerning "Intelligent Design"

In recent times, there has been considerable debate concerning teaching the theory of Intelligent Design also known as "ID." Advocates of this theory argue that Darwin's theory of natural selection over time, cannot fully explain the origin of life or the emergence of highly complex life forms. It implies that life on earth was the product of an unidentified intelligent force. For example, as a biological computer, the brain is capable of multi-tasking, and outperforming anything a human being can technologically produce. The brain has the capacity to store between 100 trillion and 280,000 quintillion bits of information—all within the encasement of just a measly three pounds that is protected by a hard bony armor, serviced by a fluid and complex network

---

[923] Ben Tzion Bokser, *Abraham Isaac Kook: The Lights of Penitence, the Moral Principles, Lights of Holiness, Essays, Letters, and Poems* (New York: Paulist Press, 1978), 231-232.

[924] Prominent Orthodox rabbis who affirm that the world is older, and that life has evolved over time, include R. Aryeh Kaplan, R. Israel Lipschitz, R. Sholom Mordechai Schwadron (a.k.a. MaHaRSHaM), R. Zvi Hirsch Chajes, R. Isadore Epstein, R. Louis Jacobs, and more recently R. Naftali Slivkin. These rabbis propose their own versions of theistic evolution, in which the world is older, and that life does evolve over time in accord with natural law, yet also holding that God has a role in this process. Rabbi Slivkin's ideas, although not original, have been banned by many leading Ultra-Orthodox rabbis and have been the subject of considerable debate. See G. Safran's article, "Gedolei Yisroel Condemn Rabbi Nosson Slifkin's Books" *Dei'ah Ve Dibur,* March 30, 2004.

of blood vessels. Without the brain as the seat of intelligence, a person could not live for more than four minutes. A typical human being's survival depends upon the harmonious functioning of this sophisticated bio-computer. Should any one of these functions be impaired, death could occur. As Michael Behe likens the biological complexity to a simple mousetrap, William Dembski briefly summarizes Behe's position:

> A good example of such a system is a mechanical mousetrap. . . . The mousetrap depends critically on the presence of all five of its components; if there were no spring, the mouse would not be pinned to the base; if there were no platform, the other pieces would fall apart; and so on. The function of the mousetrap requires all the pieces: you cannot catch a few mice with just a platform, add a spring and catch a few more mice, add a holding bar and catch a few more. All of the components have to be in place before any mice are caught. Thus the mousetrap is irreducibly complex.[925]

Dr. Francis C. Collins, one of the country's leading geneticists and the head of the Human Genome Project, points out several weaknesses in the ID argument. For one thing, many Christian scientists (like himself) have not found acceptance in the general scientific community, and is considered to be a "fringe movement" without much credibility. More seriously, the ID does not allow for scientific experimentation, as Collins observes:

> All scientific theories represent a framework for making sense of a body of experimental observations. But the primary utility of a theory is not just to look back but to look forward. A viable scientific theory is not just to look back but to look forward. A viable scientific theory predicts other findings and suggests approaches for further experimental verification. ID falls profoundly in this regard. Despite its appeal to many believers, therefore, ID's proposal of the intervention of supernatural forces to account for complex multi-component biological entities is at a scientific dead end. Outside the development of a time machine, verification of the ID theory seems profoundly unlikely.[926]

Collins claims that the ID argument ultimately appeals to the "God of the Gaps" theory; i.e., utilizing a deity to explain the things we are currently unable to, but whose role grows smaller with every scientific discovery. In the end, as science expands human knowledge, the need to resort to supernatural interventions for how the cosmos functions—shrinks, thus ultimately undermining faith.[927] Paul Davies concurs, while adding,

---

[925] William A. Dembski, *Mere Creation: Science, Faith & Intelligent Design* (Downers Grove, IL: InterVarsity Press, 1998), 178. See also Michael Behe, *Darwin's Black Box: The Biochemical Challenge to Evolution.* (New York: Free Press, 1996), 43-45.

[926] Francis Collins, *The Language of God* (New York: Free Press, 2006), 187.

[927] One is reminded of the time when the French astronomer and mathematician Marquis Pierre Simon de Laplace (1749-1827) presented Napoleon with his work about the motion of the planetary bodies. Napoleon asked him what place God had in his system. The scientist replied, "I have no need of that hypothesis."

> Many features of the human body contain design flaws, such as the dangerous convergence of food and air pathways in the throat and the inadequate robustness of the spine. If there is a designer, then this being is not micromanaging the process very well. The weak point in the "gaps'" argument of the Intelligent Design movement is that there is no reason why biologists should immediately have all the answers anyway. . . . One of the confusions surrounding the Intelligent Design movement is a failure to distinguish between the fact of evolution and the mechanism of evolution. . . . Another possible mechanism is self-organization. Many non-living systems evolve complex patterns and organizational structures from featureless beginnings . . . snowflakes form distinctive hexagonal patterns. Nobody suggests that there are genes for a snowflake, but nobody suggests that they are made by an intelligent designer either.[928]

Without empirical proof, ID may face the same "ultimate demise" that the teleological argument did in the 19th century.[929] As an alternative, Collins proposes a model that is similar to Kook and Chardin's. The concept he refers to as "BioLogos," expresses the belief: "God is the Source of all life and that life reveals the will of God."[930] It should be noted that newer peer-reviewed studies of the Intelligent Design argument will continue to keep this controversy alive for some time to come.[931]

On the other hand, Davies contends that William Paley's teleological arguments, pertaining to the organization of the cosmos, present a much stronger case for a Designer universe that is immune to Darwinian attacks: "The Darwinian mechanism of variation, inheritance, and selection cannot be easily adapted to cosmology."[932] British theologian Richard Swinburne also concurs noting:

> If we can explain the many bits of the universe by one simple being which keeps them inexistence, we should do so—even if inevitably we cannot explain the existence of that one simple being. . . . I am not postulating a "God of the gaps," a god to merely explain the things which science has not explained. I am postulating a God to explain what

---

[928] Paul Davies, *Cosmic Jackpot: Why Our Universe is Just Right for Life, op. cit.*, 196-197.

[929] Classical thinkers since the time of Philo of Alexandria have often used the "Teleological Argument" (a.k.a., the "Argument from Design") to prove God's existence as the Creator of the universe. In Darwin's own day, philosopher William Paley (1743-1805) was best known for his famous "watchmaker's argument," which Darwin refuted.

[930] *The Language of God, op. cit.*, 203.

[931] See Stephen Meyer's *Signature in the Cell: DNA and the Evidence for Intelligent Design* (New York: HarperCollins, 2009). Meyer contends that the digital code embedded in DNA points powerfully to a designing intelligence and helps unravel a mystery that Darwin did not address: how did the very first life begin? The newest scientific discoveries in genetics strongly suggest that intelligent design is the best explanation for the complexity of life and the universe.

[932] Paul Davies, *op. cit.*, 198.

science explains. The very success of science in showing how deeply orderly the natural world is provides grounds for believing that there is an even deeper cause of that order.[933]

The wondrous mystery of the universe always fascinated Einstein, who observed, "The eternal mystery of the world is its comprehensibility."[934] Human consciousness possesses a marvelous capacity to discover and appreciate beauty and order in nature. To the eyes of faith, this phenomenon is due to humankind created in the image of the Divine.

While these arguments pose a new and significant wrinkle to the debate concerning evolutionary theory, critics of today's Intelligent Design Argument remain unconvinced and defiant as they have been since the days of Darwin and others. Perhaps we would be wise to follow the dictum of the early 20th century Jewish moralist, R. Yisrael Meir Kagan, who quips, "To the believer there are no questions, and to the unbeliever, there are no answers." That is to say, if one sees the world and the universe through the prism of faith, one can appreciate God's handiwork. If one sees the universe though the lens of scientific reductionism, one can just as easily attribute everything that exists to solely materialistic causes. In the end, it is all in the eye of the beholder and in the heart of the believer.

Davies, like many other cosmologists and physicists, also questions the supposition of a random universe and its capacity to create life-forms that are sentient and self-aware: "The very fact that the universe is creative, and that the laws have permitted complex structures to emerge and develop to the point of consciousness—in other words, that the universe has organized its own self-awareness—is for me powerful evidence that there is 'something going on' behind it all. The impression of design is overwhelming."[935]

Excursus 14: The Image of God in Early Hellenistic and Rabbinic Thought

Man is the measure of all things.

—PROTAGORAS, *attributed*

It is a pity that rabbinic schools of all Judaic denominations typically neglect to teach

933 Richard Swinburne, *Is There a God?* (New York: Oxford University Press, 1996), 68.

934 Albert Einstein, *Ideas and Opinions* (New York: Crown Publishers, 1954), 285.

935 Paul Davies, *The Cosmic Blueprint: New Discoveries in Nature's Creative Ability to Order* (West Conshohocken, PA: Templeton Foundation Press; New Edition, 2004), 203.

their students about the role of the Septuagint and its historical importance in being the very first "Targum" (translation) of the Tanakh. When studying the Septuagint's finer nuances, it is like discovering a message in a bottle that was washed along the shore after being lost for millennia. The Alexandrian Jews were the first community of the Diaspora to encounter the beginnings of Western culture. It was also the place where Jews created the first symbiosis of Judaic and Greek thought. In light of this, the insights of the Alexandrian Judaic community contain invaluable insights that can only enrich our contemporary appreciation of Jewish history and our ability to adapt, synthesize new ideas, and survive as a people.

The Septuagint translates צֶלֶם as εἰκών (*eikon=icon)* and דְּמוּת as ὁμοίωσις (*homoiosis* = "likeness"). Words associated with ὁμοίωσις express a clear and essential resemblance, hence a correspondence to particular characteristics, i.e., a specific or a generic likeness. Sometimes, the Septuagint uses this word synonymously with εἰκών, which can be defined as a visual or a mental picture of something, e.g., a painting, a statue, a figure on a coin. It may also denote a comparison or a simile. [936]

One reason the Septuagint chose these terms, was to convey that in a figurative sense, humankind is only a "copy" of the Supreme Reality. However, God is not a copy or a "projection" of the human imagination, nor is God an objectification of man's subjective state of mind as atheistic thinkers purport. Actually, it is quite the opposite; the physical world exists as a mirror image of the spiritual realm, which is the true source of the phenomenal world we live in. The analogy of the mirror is an apt one for the mirror that I gaze into reflects *my* image and likeness; it depends upon *me* for its existence but not *vice versa.* In Plato's conception of the universe, every great or small phenomenon that exists depends upon its spiritual essence for its tangible existence and expression.

Plato believes that the entire physical world derives its being from archetypal forms that function as the ethereal templates from which the material world is derived. He refers to these forms as εἶδος (*eidos=idea),* in the sense of a model; i.e., "mental image," τῆς ψυχῆς (*tes psuches*).[937] According to Plato's metaphysics, the *idea* exists

[936] The term εἰκών (*eikōn)* means "image, picture, reflection," derives from ἔοικα (*eoika)*, "becoming like." In Classical Greek, *eikōn* could refer to "pictures" or "statues" or "idols." See, BDAG: 280; TDNT 2:381.

[937] For other references in Plato and the other Greek classics regarding the Platonic use of εἶδος (*eidos*) in the sense of "model," "idea," "essence of a thing" cf. *Symposium,* 210b; *Meno* 81; *The Republic Hippias, I,* 289d; *Phaedo,* 74-76; 100-103e; *Theaetetus,* 148d; *Parmenides* 129-135; *Timaeus* 30; cf. Philo's *Opus Mundi.,* 103; *Vita Moses,* II, 76;: Aristotle *Physics,* I, 4, 187a, 18; *Metaphysics* VI,3, 1029a, 29. Aristotle rejects Plato's doctrine of the εἶδος and concludes that the most basic substrates are also the essences of things, and that both of these are identical with the εἶδος of a thing as a member of a certain species.

independently of its copy or image discerned in space and time.[938] Once physically actualized, the idea becomes a shadow of the archetypal realm it reflects. The *eidos* represents the essence of a thing. To use an analogy, the car I now drive was conceived from an ethereal car that constitutes its essence; i.e., the car began as a concept that derived from a person's idea long before it ever became a physical reality. Consequently, even if the car I drive is imperfect in some way—it is missing a mirror or a fender—anyone looking at my car would still recognize it as a car since all cars share the same conceptual essence. The closer my car is to the realm of the *eidos*, the more beautiful and perfect my car is.

A. Philo, the Kabbalists and Adam Kadmon

One of the most important Jewish thinkers of all time, Philo of Alexandria, took this concept one step further and applied it to the biblical text concerning the Divine image, which he termed as ἀρχέτυπος (*arkhetupos* = archetype).[939] The divine archetype—literally the Godly image—is endowed in every human being. It is this divine force that is responsible for spiritually molding, directing, and influencing human development. Philo goes to great lengths to distinguish between what he calls the "heavenly man" (the man of the *eidos*) which God created *vis-à-vis* the "earthly" Adam (who lives in the *real* physical world). Philo explains why the human soul bears witness to God's divine image:

> Moses says that man was made in "the image and likeness of God" . . . for there is nothing born on the earth that resembles God more than man. Let no person think that he is capable of judging a being that possesses the form of a man, nor does the human body resemble God. The "resemblance" metaphorically spoken of in the Scriptures, refers only to the most important part of the soul, namely, *the mind*. . . . In the same status that the great Governor occupies in the universal world, in a manner of speaking, that same quality also exists in the mind of man. Like God, the mind is invisible and sees everything; the mind also possesses an indiscernible essence, which enables it to discern the essences of all other things, whether it be art, science—all kinds of roads leading to diverse directions . . . whether by land or by sea—the mind investigates everything that is found in the elements. . . . But not every image necessarily resembles its archetypal model, since in actuality—most people are unlike.[940]

[938] Plato, *Republic*, VI, 509a.

[939] The etymology of ἀρχέτυπος is significant when examined in light of its Greek origins. The nominal prefix ἀρχή (*archē*) denotes a point that originates in a temporal and ontological sense while the term τύπος (*tupos*= "type") connotes a template, impression, or example which anticipates or precedes a later realization—hence it connotes an archetype and symbol.

[940] Philo, *On the Creation*, 69-70.

The Platonic resemblances in Philo's writings are most striking; as mentioned earlier, Plato taught that all images—whether they are mental or material—are to be regarded as inferior reflections, as it were, of eternal, abstract, ideal Forms or Ideas. Since not all people actualize this image, this accounts for the differences among people—some are more God-like, while others are less so. By the same token, when God created Adam, He did not fashion him just from the clay but from a spiritual template. Hence, humankind is more than just an earthly creation—he is a spiritual creation as well. According to Philo, the image of God thus represents the idealistic image the Creator used to form "the earthly Adam," whose spiritual being, paradoxically and mysteriously, stands apart from the rest of all of Creation. Over a millennium later, Rashi came to the same conclusion, noting that the term "image" refers only to the "mold" God used to create him, and does not refer to having made humankind in "God's image."

The mystics of the Kabbalah borrowed from this Platonic theme and refer to the archetype as אדם קדמון (*ādām qadmôn* = "Primordial Man"). According to the Kabbalah, the realm of *ādām qadmôn* is depicted as androgynous in nature and in much the same way, God's creativity and manifestation within the creative order incorporates the aspects of both the male and female genders; *ādām qadmôn* is considered to be a macrocosm in the great "chain of being" and that mediates between the Creator and Creation. In later Kabbalistic writings, *ādām qadmôn* is regarded as a type of "world soul" in as much that all of Creation is—to a greater or lesser degree—a manifestation of this macro-spiritual reality that is moving toward the goal of self-awareness and self-actualization.

B. *A Rabbinic Synopsis on the Image of God*

Rabbinic views pertaining to "likeness of God" vary. Due to sectarian interpretations in their day, the Sages grappled over the meaning of "Let us make man in our image . . ." (Gen. 1:26). These interpretations can be neatly summed up:

- God took consul with the Torah itself.[941]

- Some Midrashic texts suggest that God took counsel with the heavens and the earth much like a king consults with his architect.[942]

- All of Creation participates in humankind's formation and creation.[943]

---

[941] Pirqe R. Eliezer, 11.

[942] Gen. Rabbah 8:3.

[943] Gen. Rabbah 8 on 1:26, according to R. Joshua.

- God was speaking with the angelic beings and solicited their approval.[944]

- God was "speaking to Himself."[945]

Rabbinic tradition teaches that this image is never forfeited, despite Adam's Fall. One midrashic text relates: "When Hillel the Elder parted from his students, he used to accompany them. His students asked him, 'Rabbi, where are you going?' He answered, 'To fulfill a *mitzvah*.' They asked, 'What kind of *mitzvah*?' He answered that he was going to take a bath. They asked him, 'Since when is that a *mitzvah*?' He answered, 'If the statues of kings placed in theaters and circuses are washed and polished, and as a reward the cleaner earns his living and is honored in the company of the royal household, how much more so should I, who was created in the image of God, (אני שנבראתי בצלם ובדמות), take care of myself, as it is written: 'for in the image of God made He man."'

Ethical implications of the Divine image are no less significant. Murdering a human being is considered like one who has harmed the figure of the king; i.e., the likeness of God. R. Tanchuma points out the relational dimensions of the Divine image have important practical implications: Anyone who despises his fellow man is considered as though he despises the Creator, in Whose image he is created.[946] Going one step further, there is a poignant rabbinic story that illustrates this important idea:

> Rabbi Shimon ben Elazar, returning from a trip in Migdal Eder, from his teacher's house met a certain man who was exceedingly ugly. Rabbi Shimon said to him, "*Raka* (simpleton), how ugly are the children of Abraham our father." The other man replied, "What can I do for you? You may want to speak to the Craftsman Who made me." Rabbi Shimon immediately alighted from his horse and bowed before the man and said, "I apologize to you, please forgive me." He replied to him, "I will not forgive you until you go to the Craftsman Who made me and say, "How ugly is the vessel which You have made!"
>
> Rabbi Shimon walked behind him for three miles. When the people in town heard of Rabbi Shimon's arrival, they came out to meet him and greeted him with the words, "Peace be unto you, rabbi." The other man said to them, "Who are you calling *Rabbi*?" They answered, "The man who is walking behind you." Thereupon he exclaimed, "If this man is a rabbi, may there not be any more like him in Israel!" He told the people the whole story, and the townspeople begged him to forgive the rabbi, and he agreed, only on the condition that he never act in this

[944] God creates Adam in the image of the angels so that there would be no jealousy among the angels. The Midrash depicts God as saying, "Among the celestial beings, there are some in My likeness. However, if there are none in My likeness among the earthly beings, there will be envy among the creatures of the Creation." See Rashi's Commentary on Genesis 1:26; Tanhuma, Shemoth 18; Gen. Rabbah 8:11, 14:13.

[945] Gen. Rabbah 8:3 according to R. Ammi.

[946] Genesis Rabbah 24:7.

manner again toward anyone.[947]

The story highlights an important truth: the willful mistreatment of another human being in effect, devalues the image of God because we are all created in the Divine Image. The human face—regardless how disfigured it may be—commands that we show respect to the uniqueness of the human person which transcends one's physical attributes.

C. Rabbi Akiba and Ben Azzai's Famous Debate

The Sages of the first two centuries wondered: What is the most important principle of the Torah? Rabbi Akiba argued that it is the precept of "you shall love your neighbor as yourself" (Lev. 19:18). Akiba's brilliant student, Ben Azzai, differed: "You must not say: 'Since I have been put to shame, let my neighbor also be put to shame, for if you do so, know that you are shaming someone who is made in the likeness of God.'"

Put in simple and more contemporary terms: If you cannot respect the Divine image that you are made in, the odds are that you will not be able to respect the Divine image in others. Even if one were shamed, such disparaging treatment does not entitle the victim to reciprocate in kind—not even in the face of provocation.

To insult or harm the divine image in any of its forms is to deny the essential brotherhood and sisterhood of humankind. This is why Ben Azzai felt that the verse affirming the Divine image is by far the most comprehensive principle of the entire Torah—the bedrock of all biblical morality.[948] For R. Akiba, love is the supreme value for interpersonal relationships. However, for Ben Azzai, the most supreme ethical principle in the Torah is the teaching of Divine equality. Respecting the godly image in oneself and in others ensures that society will be just and moral.

In summary, Ben Azzai's attitude about the uniqueness of the human individual expresses the same ethical concept in a slightly different context. As we find in another Mishnah, Ben Azzai says: "Do not despise any human being and do not consider anything as improbable—for there is not a man who does not have his hour, and there is not a thing which does not have its place."[949] There is no human being in this world that cannot leave a positive mark in the world.

---

[947] Tractate *Derech Eretz* (Chapter 4).

[948] Sifra, Kedoshim 4:12. In Genesis Rabba 24:7, the order is reversed, but there can be little doubt that the Sifra represents the older of the two traditions.

[949] Mishnah Aboth 4:3

Excursus 15: The Image of God in Medieval Rabbinic Thought

Man never acts in a way more resembling God than when he bestows kindness.
—PHILO of ALEXANDRIA, *Special Laws* IV

A. Saadia: Image as a Mark of Distinction

Saadia points out in his philosophic classic that בְּצֶלֶם אֱלֹהִים (*bəṣélem ʾĕlōhîm*= "in the likeness of the Divine image") is figurative language for God bestowing special honor unto humankind, which He did not confer unto the rest of Creation. This distinctiveness is visible in humanity's ability to exert dominion over the earth (Gen. 1:26).

Among modern scholars, biblical theologian D.J.A. Clines clarifies the meaning of Divine image by pointing to the nuanced difference between "representative" and "representation" which in many ways complements Saadia's original insight on the subject:

> Man is created not *in* God's image, since God has no image of His own, but *as* God's image, or rather *to be* God's image, that is to deputize in the created world for the transcendent God who remains outside the world order. That man is God's image means that he is the visible corporeal representative of the invisible, bodiless God; he is representative rather than representation, since the idea of portrayal is secondary in the significance of the image. However, the term "likeness" is an assurance that man is an adequate and faithful representative of God on earth. The whole man is the image of God, without distinction of spirit and body. All mankind, without distinction, are the image of God. . . . Mankind, which means both the human race and individual men, do not cease to be the image of God so long as they remain men; to be human and to be the image of God are not separable.[950]

B. Maimonides: "Image" as Reason

Like Philo and Saadia, Maimonides takes sharp issue with scholars who believe that God actually possesses a humanoid shape.[951] The image of the Divine is most present in the

---

[950] D.J.A. Clines, "The Image of God in Man," *Tyndale Bulletin* 19 (1968), 101.

[951] Maimonides' great critic, R. Abraham Ibn Daud (*ca.* 1110-1180), rebuked him: "Why has he called such a person a heretic? וכמה גדולים וטובים ממנו — Many people *greater and better than him* adhered to such a belief on the basis of numerous Scriptural passages [that indicate Divine corporeality]. Just as the Tanakh can be so easily misunderstood, how much more so can the Aggadot [Talmudic ethical and theological teachings] confuse the mind!" (R. Avraham Ibn Daud's notes on MT *Hilchot Teshuvah* 3:7). A more polite re-wording of Ibn Daud can be found in R. Joseph Albo's version: "Although the component part of belief is indeed so, nevertheless, he who believes that His Being is corporeal—as a result of anthropomorphic phrases found in the Scriptures and in the Midrash—does not deserve to be identified as a "heretic" (*Sefer Halkarim* 2:41). For a comprehensive survey on the literature dealing with this issue, see Marc Shapiro's "The Limits of Orthodox Theology" (Oxford, G. B.: Littman Library of Jewish Civilization, 2004), 45-70.

human being's capacity to reason[952] and ascertain abstract spiritual truths so that human beings may in part, resemble angelic beings.[953] Moreover, the soul's eschatological standing in the Afterlife depends upon the cultivation of the human intellect in grasping these higher truths.[954] Maimonides begins his *Guide* by theologically defining what exactly "image" and "likeness" mean, so that an average person—whether Jew or non-Jew—can develop an acceptable and rational conception about the true nature of God[955] Maimonides states that without a rational and theologically correct understanding of God, even one who claims to be monotheistic is essentially not much different from the pagan who imagines the gods resembling human beings. In some ways, he is worse, for he is guilty of transforming the God of Israel into a pagan fetish. Like Aristotle, Maimonides believes that the faculty of reason enables one to become most God-like when that person develops the capacity to partially grasp the nature of God's ultimate reality.[956]

C. Ibn Caspi: Humankind as Creation's First Hybrid

Ramban explains that humankind resembles creatures of the earth since his origin comes from the earth, but he also resembles the spiritual realm, since he derives his soul from God's breath. The Spanish Judaic philosopher and commentator, R. Yosef Ibn Caspi (*ca.* 1297-1340), views humanity as possessing unique qualities that blend both the spiritual and physical realms.

> A human being is not an angel that his reason should always be working perfectly. Nor is he a mule, that his reason should never be active at all. In some respects a human being may be metaphorically likened to a hermaphrodite—half angel and half mule. Hence, neither angel nor mule was bidden to wear fringes! As our honored Rabbis said, God asked the angels, "What have you to do with the Torah?"[957] Humankind, however, received this and similar commandments, because he occupies an intermediate position, with his mind sometimes active, sometimes quiescent. The investiture of the fringed garment does recall all the

---

[952] Like Maimonides, Rashi wrote in his Torah commentary that the excellence of the divine image is seen in the human capacity to discern and understand.

[953] *Guide* 1:26.

[954] MT, *Hilchot Yesodei HaTorah* 4:8,12.

[955] MT, *Hilchot Shemitah V'Yobel* 13:13.

[956] In addition, Maimonides further argues, that in Biblical Hebrew, the term תֹּאַר (*tō°'ar*) is used to describe physical shape or form that is perceived with the five senses. In the fifteen places (Gen 29:17; 39:6; 41:18; 41:19; Deut 21:11; Judg. 8:18;1 Sam. 16:18; 25:3; 28:14; 1 Kgs. 1:6; Est. 2:7; Isa 52:14; 53:2; Jer. 11:16; Lam 4:8) where this expression appears, it is never used in the Tanakh with respect to God.

[957] See T. B. Shabbat 88a and BT Berakhot 28b.

precepts, until ultimately he remembers that God . . .[958]

On the one hand, humankind resembles the angels in their capacity to reason. Yet, humanity possesses the quality of freedom and self-determination. However, unlike God Who acts only for the good, humankind possesses the ability to misuse freedom for evil purposes. Every human being that is born has the potential to ascend to a lofty status, should one so desire to attain it. Conversely, misusing one's reasoning powers renders a human being indistinguishable from an animal, which at least lives in harmony with its instincts—in full accordance with how God intended it to be. R. David Kimchi notes that humanity has the potential to realize the Divine image within, for each person decides whether to become angelic-like or bestial-like. Ultimately, it becomes a matter of choice.

D. The Nexus of Creation—Kimchi's Novel Understanding of the Divine Image

A number of Judaic scholars explain בְּצֶלֶם אֱלֹהִים to mean "in the image of the angels."[959] However, some rabbinic scholars differ. In the spirit of Midrashic exegesis, Kimchi and others[960] take a different approach, suggesting that God solicited all of Creation to participate in humankind's formation; the Creator intended for a human being be a composite of the spiritual and the terrestrial realms. Jewish mystics also tend to see all parts of Creation—from the spiritual heights of the heavenly realm to the nether regions of the earth—converging in humankind.

Modern anthropology illustrates the wisdom of Kimchi's insight. Humankind also derives many of its basic personality traits not only from God—but from nature.[961] The

---

[958] Israel Abrahams, *Hebrew Ethical Wills* (Philadelphia: JPS, 1948), 307.

[959] Cf. the commentaries of Pseudo Targum-Jonathan; Midrash Tanchuma Shemoth 18; Gen. Rabbah 8:11, 14:13; Rashi, Seforno, Rashbam and Ibn Ezra.

[960] Theodoret cites this view with approval in his *Questions on Genesis and Exodus*, "After completing the material and the spiritual creation, the God of the universe formed man last and set him like an image of himself in the midst of the inanimate and the animate, the material and the spiritual, so that the inanimate and the animate might offer their service as a kind of tribute, and spiritual beings, by caring for him, might manifest their love for the Creator" (*op. cit.*, 51).

[961] The Sages appear to have understood this truth as well, for they candidly said, "If the Torah had not been given we could have learnt modesty from the cat, honesty from the ant, chastity from the dove, and good manners from the cock who first coaxes and then mates"(BT Eruvin 100b). While the Talmud delineates the positive traits humankind could have learned from nature, it goes without saying that our ancestors could just as easily have learned many negative character traits from nature, e.g., from the ant we would have derived the principles of totalitarianism; from the cat we would have developed certain predatory traits showing no mercy toward the weak and defenseless such as a male lion's tendency to destroy his offspring; from the chicken, our ancestors might have learned how to be scavengers who prefer to live in filthy habitats, and so on.

philosopher, Michael Shermer, observes that morality is not unique to human beings, per se, but can be seen in the animal kingdom as well:

> The following characteristics appear to be shared by humans and other mammals, including and especially the apes, monkeys, dolphins and whales: *attachment and bonding, cooperation and mutual aid, sympathy and empathy, direct and indirect reciprocity, altruism and reciprocal altruism, conflict resolution and peacemaking, deception and deception detection, community concern and caring what others think about you, and awareness and response to the social rules of the group.* Species differ in the degree to which they express these sentiments, and with our exceptionally large brains (especially the well-developed and highly convoluted cortex) we express most of them in greater degrees than other species. Nevertheless, the fact that such premoral sentiments exist in our nearest evolutionary cousins may be a strong indication of their evolutionary origins. Still, something profound happened in the last 100,000 years that made us—and no other species—moral animals unprecedented in nature.[962]

Biologist Lyall Watson also takes a scientific look at the existence of evil, and like Shermer, he sees a mutual affinity between human and animal behavior. Watson once observed a group of young penguins standing on the edge of an ice floe, learning how to swim. Fearful that there might be a leopard seal lurking in the murky waters, the penguins stood their ground and refused to go into the water. As thousands of penguins crowded on the floe, some pushing occurred from the back of the ranks until one of the penguins slipped into the water. After the lone penguin entered the water, a leopard-seal suddenly appeared and ate the small creature. Reticent, the other penguins backed off until eventually, the group pushed another one of its members into the water. Sure enough, the leopard-seal reappeared and swallowed the second penguin as well. The same process occurred again, and by the fourth time, apparently, the leopard-seal had eaten enough and the fourth penguin was left safe and sound. Afterwards, the entire penguin group jumped in and enjoyed the swimming as if they hadn't a care in the world. From this incident, Watson deduced that selfishness and cowardice are not just human traits; there are many other species of animals that share these qualities as well.[963]

From a theological perspective, one could say that since God created humanity as a microcosm of the created order, it is only natural that humankind would possess all these traits as part of its moral and evolutionary constitution. Our genetic makeup as a species is hardwired for survival. Driven by a ruthless and determined desire to survive, the success of a species depends upon its ability to reproduce itself, in spite of the odds that face it. Only by understanding the nature of our genetic history, as Watson and Shermer (and others) have formidably argued, will we ever be able to rise above our genetic heritage. Our ability to see life in synergistic terms is another

---

[962] Michael Shermer, *The Science of Good and Evil* (New York: Owl Books, 2005), 31.

[963] Lyall Watson, *Dark Nature: A Natural History of Evil* (New York: Harper Collins, 1995), 54-56.

aspect that makes us different from the rest of Creation. This self-awareness enables us as a species to transcend our own biological evolution by probing the mystery and nature of our being. The actual source of evil does not exclusively derive from the "Fall." On a deeper level, evil may also emanate from a natural source, which humankind shares with the rest of the animal kingdom.[964] Our will to survive by any means possible, at least in neo- Darwinian terms, may *partially* explain why human tragedies of the Holocaust and other genocides continue to plague civilization even in the 21st century.

So, how does one define the uniqueness of the Divine image in an age of scientific awareness and incredulity? How do human beings differ from their evolutionary predecessors? Shermer notes there are several aspects that make human beings different from the rest of the animal world, and they are (1) self-awareness and knowledge that others are also self-aware; (2) possessing the ability for human choice and freedom; (3) awareness of one's own consciousness; (4) the ability to utilize symbolic logic in evaluating and determining ethical behavior; (5) recognizing the consequences of one's deeds; (6) taking responsibility for one's decisions. From a religious perspective, I would add that humankind's ability to respond to a Higher Authority outside of one's own psyche is also indicative of a human spiritual vocation. In the final analysis, the ability to experience personal transformation, individuation and transcendence is what makes human beings more God-like than animal-like.

E. Ontological Implications

The *image of God* concept in the Bible is no less radical today than it was in biblical times. Whereas the emperors of the ancient world regarded themselves as god-incarnated beings and avatars, Judaism came and democratized the idea of the divine image; every human being is endowed with the Divine spirit that is the ultimate source of our identity and higher self. What are its practical implications? For one thing, Judaism teaches that we as human beings cannot be content living an animal-like

[964] Some recent genetic experiments indicate that people may have a genetic predisposition toward altruism. The researchers of this study posed an online task in which participants had to decide whether or not to give virtual money away, and found that those who chose to give away some or all of their money differed genetically from those who were tightfisted. Participants who behaved more generously had the gene, called AVPR1a. "The experiment provided the first evidence, to my knowledge, for a relationship between DNA variability and real human altruism," said Ariel Knafo, a researcher at Hebrew University's Psychology Department in Jerusalem, who helped lead the study. "Those who had the AVPR1a gene gave away on average nearly 50 percent more money than those without it. The research, published online in the research journal, "Genes, Brain and Behavior" may help biologists discover why humans developed the trait, the scientists said today in an e-mailed statement." Some animal species such as the voles (a type of rodent found mostly North America and Eurasia), argued Knafo, "possess the same gene, which has been tied to social bonding in earlier experiments" (*Jerusalem Post*, December 5th, 2007).

existence. Because of the soul-breath and divine image with which God has endowed us, we feel ontologically different from the rest of Creation. This experience of being different is the source of our anxiety. Although we live as physical beings and are bound up with the physical universe, we can never discover our identity *within it*. To know who we really are, we must look *beyond* the physical realm. To grasp the mystery of our human existence, we must look *inward* to the God whom we imagine, not down to the dust from which we were formed. The human being is thus a symbol and visible sign of a spiritual and transcendental divine reality.

At the deepest existential level, God created us to experience a relationship with the Divine; therefore, the human soul reflects and partakes in God's nature. Though the lives of all creatures are suffused with mystery and wonder, human beings are different in that we are granted the ability to understand the secret of that wonder and mystery; we have the capacity to search the enigma of our beings by plumbing the depths of our souls. Human fulfillment depends on recognizing that God alone gives meaning and purpose to life. Even if we were to possess every imaginable creaturely comfort and convenience modern society could provide, we would still feel there was something *missing* from our lives, because at the root of our very being burns a desire to find peace and serenity in something Other than ourselves. Jewish mystics teach that nothing can fill the inner emptiness and homelessness the soul feels, other than a relationship with the Divine. Our inability to achieve perfect comfort in the finite, together with unquenchable longing for consummate spiritual fulfillment, is reflective of our lofty destiny.

The divine origin of the soul explains the perennial dissatisfaction that we so often feel throughout our lives on earth. When we respond to the deepest yearnings of the heart, we realize the truth of Augustine's (354–430 C. E.) words: "You have made us for yourself, O Lord, and our hearts are restless until they rest in you."[965] Being made in the image of God is the most intimate and distinctive aspect of being a human, and we cannot destroy the divine image without ceasing to be what we are. Should we succeed in cutting ourselves off from this most sacred dimension, we inevitably cut ourselves adrift, resulting in alienation and disintegration at the very heart of our being. If we were actually aware of our true spiritual nature, were we more mindful of the Divine image we carry inside us, we would surely guard this precious image from anything that might diminish or tarnish its radiance and light. The thirteenth century German mystic, Meister Eckhart likened the image of God to a reflection cast from the sun against a mirror:

> I take a basin of water and place a mirror in it and put it under the wheel of the sun. The sun casts its luminous radiance upon the mirror, and yet it is not diminished.

[965] Augustine, *Confessions* 1, 1: CCL, 27, 1.

> The reflection in the mirror is the sun, and yet the mirror is what it is. Thus it is with God. God is in the soul with His nature and in His being and His divinity, and yet He is not the soul. The reflection of the soul in God is God, and yet the soul is what it is.[966]

One Sufi[967] master metaphorically explains the same concept in slightly different terms: "The spirit is likened to the sun and what we call souls are the rays of the spirit. If the spirit is eternal, then the souls are eternal. If the sun is eternal, the rays are eternal because the sun and the rays are not two things; rays are the unfoldment of the sun and souls are the unfolding of the spirit."[968] This spirit that each of us possesses has the ability to transcend the boundaries that circumscribe our earthly existence. To accomplish this goal, we must resolve to live morally, and responsibly, recognizing the spirit of God that is ever present within all of Creation, which demands our best and most authentic ethical response at all times.

Lastly, humankind not only possesses a capacity for spiritual perfection, but also has the potential to bring the world to its ultimate fulfillment. God created humankind with unlimited possibilities for creative expression. In a partnership with God, humankind must learn to transform the chaos of creation into a cosmos, the profane into the sacred, the natural into the spiritual, the ordinary into the extraordinary, and the momentary into the eternal (see notes on Gen. 1:2). But to accomplish this requires that a person recognize the darker regions of the soul, and the frailties that retard spiritual development. Emulating God's positive attributes[969] provide a template for realizing this objective through random acts of compassion, as well as a commitment to the laws of equity and justice as defined by the Torah and its teachers.

Excursus 16: Reflections on Genesis 1:21: Do Animals Have a "Soul"?

The just man knows the soul of his beast, but the heart of the wicked is merciless.
—Proverbs 12:10

A. Soul as the Sentience of Life

The author of Proverbs stresses an important ethical lesson: a humane person

[966] This notion bears a remarkable likeness to Sheneir Zalman of Liadi's theory of *bittul hayesh*, "negation of the self." See *Sha'ar Yichud Ve'Emunah* chapters 1-7.

[967] The designation "Sufi" refers to a group of Muslim mystics. In Arabic *sufi* means "man of wool."

[968] *Hazrat Inayat Khan, The Message Volumes of Hazrat Inayat Khan* Volume VII, "*In an Eastern Rose Garden*" (Alameda, CA: Hunter House, 1979, 2nd rev. ed.), Introduction to Chapter 3.

[969] Whenever the Sages of the Midrash and Talmud refer to emulating God's attributes, they almost invariably stress His positive traits, e.g., mercy, compassion, concern, and so on (cf. Maimonides MT *Hilchot De'ot* 1:5-7).

considers the needs of his animals and acts kindly towards them.[970] The world of Creation is full of sentient beings, which also experience many of the joys and blessings that people commonly enjoy: like humankind, these creatures also experience pain. Suffering is a common language that links humanity with other species of animal life. Therefore, Jewish ethics take sharp issue with French philosopher Rene Descartes (*ca.* 1596–1650), who compares animals to machines that service people, stating that their suffering "means nothing more than the creaking of a wheel."[971] In physiological terms, according to Descartes, what human beings and animals share is that their bodies function by the laws of mechanics. One might respond: How then do human beings differ from animals? Descartes argues that the Creator endows human beings with a divine soul and a moral conscience—qualities that are lacking in animals. In addition, unlike animals, human beings possess the ability to conceptualize and verbalize ideas. Most importantly, only human beings are capable of conscious and rational thought since they are uniquely endowed with the ability to be self-reflective. Only a human being is capable of exclaiming, "Cogito ergo sum."

Philo of Alexandria explains that the Mosaic proscription prohibiting the boiling of a kid in its mother's milk aims to teach Israel that mercy and self-restraint should govern people's relations with animals no less than with each other.[972] According to biblical law, a person may not satisfy his or her appetite disregarding the feelings of animals, especially where mothers and their young are concerned. A worshipper in ancient times, for example, is barred from sacrificing a newborn animal until it is at least eight days old (Exod. 22:28–29; Lev 22:27). "Nothing could be more brutal," writes Philo, "than to add to the mother's birth pangs the pain of being separated from her young immediately after giving birth, for it is at this time that her maternal instincts are strongest." In other respects, too, the Law calls for self-restraint. Thus, it would be an act of unnatural excess, Philo argues, to cook a young animal in the very substance with which nature intended it to be sustained. In a similar vein, the Law prohibits one from sacrificing an animal together with its young (Lev 22:28), since this would again involve an unnatural combination of that which gives life and that which receives it.[973]

---

[970] R. Yehuda HaHasid of Regensburg notes: "The cruel person is he who gives his animal a great amount of straw to eat and on the morrow requires that it climb up high mountains. Should the animal, however, be unable to run quickly enough in accordance with its master's desires, his master beats it mercilessly. Mercy and kindness have in this instance evolved into cruelty." Quoted from Noah Cohen's *Tsa'ar Ba'ale Hayim — The Prevention of Cruelty to Animals* (New York: Feldheim Publishers, 1959), 45–46.

[971] *Discourse on the Method of Rightly Conducting the Reason, and Seeking the Truth in the Sciences,* ch. 5, 92-93.

[972] Philo, *Virtues* 125-44.

[973] Philo's explanation is later found in the commentaries of Ibn Ezra, Rashbam, Ramban, Bechor Shor, Abarbanel, Aharon Eliyahu and S. Luzzato. On the other hand, Bechor Shor supposes that it also refers to the cooking of the kid, before it has been weaned from its mother's milk.

Pursuing a similar approach found in Philo, Maimonides comments on a number of biblical precepts dealing with preventing cruelty towards animals in his *Guide*:

> It is also prohibited to kill an animal with its young on the same day (Lev. 22:28), the reason being, is so that people should be restrained and prevented from killing the two together in such a manner that the young is slain in plain sight of the mother; the pain of the animals under such circumstances is very great. There can be no difference in this case between the pain of man and the pain of other sentient beings, since the love and tenderness of the mother for her young ones is not produced by reasoning, but is a matter determined by instinct and this faculty exists not only in man but in most living beings. This law applies only to ox and lamb, because of the domestic animals used as food these alone are permitted to us, and in these cases the mother recognizes her young. . . . If the Torah provides that such grief should not be caused to cattle or birds, how much more careful must we be that we should not cause grief to our fellow human beings![974]

According to Maimonides, an animal's ability to feel emotional pain gives it moral standing; it is for this reason that the Torah prohibits these acts. Not all Jewish thinkers concur with Maimonides. Ramban claims that the prohibitions against cruelty to animals are not so much for the animal's benefit, but for the sole moral development of humankind. Cruelty towards animals is desensitizing (commenting on Deuteronomy 22:6 and Leviticus 22:28), which will eventually produce brutality and insensitivity to the pain and suffering of others.

> The ruling on the mother bird is not predicated upon the Almighty's "pity" for the animal. Otherwise, God would have forbidden their slaughter altogether! The reason, however, for the prohibition is to instill within us compassion and the avoidance of cruelty; butchers and slaughterers often become insensitive to the suffering on account of their occupation. Therefore, to avoid engendering these negative traits, the Torah proscribed precepts that a person should not slaughter the mother and its young on the same day (Lev. 22:28) and sending away the mother bird (Deut. 22:6). Such laws are not inspired by feelings of consideration for their suffering but are decrees to inculcate humanity in us. [975]

[974] Maimonides elsewhere explains his position: "Some scholars think the precepts have no objective at all, and exist only as arbitrary decrees of God. Others say that all the precepts—both negative and positive—are dictated by Divine wisdom, and contain a basic *telos*. Ergo, there is a reason for each precept, they are enjoined because they serve a purpose" (*Guide* 3:26).

[975] Ramban's position bears an almost uncanny likeness to his contemporary, Thomas Aquinas, who writes:

> Affection in man is twofold: it may be an affection of reason, or it may be an affection of passion. If a man's affection be one of reason, it matters not how man behaves to animals, because God has subjected all things to man's power, according to Psalm 8:8, "Thou hast subjected all things under his feet": and it is in this sense that the Apostle says that "God has no care for oxen"; because God does not ask of man what he does with oxen or other animals. But if man's affection be one of passion, then it is moved also in regard to other animals: for since the passion of pity is caused by the afflictions of others; and since it happens that even irrational animals are sensible to pain, it is possible for the affection of pity to arise in a man with regard to the sufferings of animals. Now it is

Would this mean that an animal's feelings are, for all practical purposes, not considered by God? Ramban's response is twofold:

(1) Clearly the Torah does not consider animals to possess the same degree of self-awareness and status that people do. Consequently, the Torah does not want people to act cruelly towards animals, not because such behavior would cause pain and suffering to the animal per se, but specifically because such insensitive acts reinforce destructive behavior in human beings, resulting in their diminished moral standing.

(2) The issue here is not that an animal is bereft of feelings. Certainly one should acknowledge animals experience pain, but one must also acknowledge that people have the right to utilize their labor, and may also slaughter them for their personal needs.[976]

Is it possible for man to accept Ramban's claim that humanity can develop compassion for all sentient life and yet ignore their pain and suffering when it is within humankind's self-interest to do so? In contrast to Ramban, Maimonides sees a more profound web of connectedness which all sentient life forms share with one another, particularly with respect to pain and suffering. As a general rule, mother animals suffer when witnessing the destruction of their young, while the young suffer anxiety upon seeing the death of their mother.

From the Maimonidean perspective, the ethical intent is to prevent humankind from causing needless pain and suffering to those creatures who are entrusted to its care and stewardship. Like human beings, most of God's creatures experience some degree of

---

> evident that if a man practices a pitiful affection for animals, he is all the more disposed to take pity on his fellowmen: wherefore it is written (Prov. 11:10). (*Summa* 2 Q. 102 Art. 6).

Aquinas' theological position regarding animals eventually became part of the canon of the Roman Catholic Church. Even as late as the mid-18th century, Pope Pius IX refused to allow a society for the Prevention of Cruelty to Animals to be established in Rome on the grounds that to do so, would imply that human beings have duties towards animals. Such a view is diametrically different from Judaism with respect to the rights of animals.

[976] Ramban would not necessarily agree with Descartes' mechanistic view of life; nevertheless, if the practice of vivisection serves to better enhance the quality of human life, it is reasonable to say that Ramban would have endorsed it, as do most contemporary Halachic scholars. Medical experimention with animals for the purpose of curing illness does not constitute a violation of the laws proscribing cruelty to animals. However, this only applies if efforts are made to minimize animal pain and suffering. Hunting animals for either sport or pleasure involves numerous biblical and rabbinic violations. See Avraham Steinberg, *The Encyclopedia of Jewish Medical Ethics* (New York, Jerusalem: Feldheim, 2003), 259-272.

sentience, pain and suffering. Despite its exalted privilege in the created order, a human being cannot ignore senseless animal suffering resulting from cruelty or indifference without causing danger to one's own soul.[977] When slaughtering animals for food, the act of kosher slaughter must always be performed competently and humanely. Ramban is also correct in asserting that these precepts aim to develop humanity and moral decency; the inculcation of compassion serves as an important by-product that comes as a direct result from treating animals as sentient creatures.

There is ample Scriptural support for Maimonides' view: טוֹב־יְהוָה לַכֹּל וְרַחֲמָיו עַל־כָּל־מַעֲשָׂיו – "The LORD is good to all, compassionate to every creature" (Ps. 145:9). That is to say, God's goodness and compassion extend to animals because they are *not* bereft of feelings—and that is why they are worthy of consideration! In addition, the Book of Proverbs makes it even clearer: "A righteous man considers the *soul of his beast*, but the tender mercies of the wicked are cruel" (Prov. 12:10). Here, too, the text clearly intimates that the Creator nurtures life in the animal world because they are worthy of divine compassion for their own sake, and not just for the sake of man – in sharp theological contrast to the anthropocentric view advocated by Ramban.

As indicated earlier, Ramban claims that if compassion and mercy were the basis for sending the mother bird away, then the Torah would have forbidden their slaughter. However, this argument too, does not hold up to scrutiny. Perhaps, in an idealistic Edenic or Messianic world, this would undoubtedly be true. In reality, humankind is far from reaching that mark. For now, the eating of meat must be viewed as a temporary concession to humankind's baser nature.

Although the Torah permits the consumption of meat, there are numerous restrictions and limitations that restrict its use. For instance, the method of how the animal is slaughtered matters greatly. The law does not entitle a slaughterer to cut a limb off from a living animal to satisfy his appetite for flesh, nor can he consume the animal's blood. Even before the act of slaughter, the butcher must test the blade's sharpness in order to minimize the animal's pain. Special attention must also be taken not to cause an animal any excess stress or physical injury. After the animal has been ritually slaughtered, special care must be taken not to cause the animal any unnecessary harm, e.g., by not placing a metal hook in its throat to facilitate bleeding immediately after the incision is made or cutting off an animal's ears for tagging while the animal is still conscious.

[977] On the issue concerning vivisection, it seems likely that Maimonides' belief that animals were created to serve man is compatible with animal experimentation for the cause of science, provided that necessary steps are taken to ensure minimal pain.

Of all the medieval scholars whose ideas come closest to Maimonides, the wise words of Ibn Caspi (ca. 1280-1340, Spain) best reflects this kind of modern ecological sensitivity:

> We are, as it is known, composed of four substances—mineral, vegetable, animal and human—these are the four categories of created things. In our pride we foolishly imagine that there is no kinship between us and the rest of the animal world, how much less with the plants and vegetation. To eradicate this thoughtless notion, God gave us certain precepts defining the parameters of our relationship; hence some precepts concern the mineral kingdom, while others pertain to vegetative kingdom; other precepts relate to the animal kingdom and others human–all of which define our responsibilities toward each of these created orders of existence. . . . For this reason the Torah commanded us to show pity toward these entities, e.g., to send away the mother bird (Deut. 22:6), or not seethe a kid in its mothers' milk (Exod. 23:19). . . . In conclusion, the Torah inculcates in us a sense of our modesty and lowliness that we should be ever cognizant of the fact that we are of the same stuff as the ass and mule, the cabbage and pomegranate and even the lifeless stone.[978]

Zoologists Jeffrey Moussaieff Masson[979] and Donald R. Griffin[980] have written extensively on the nature of animals' attitudes toward their families, and their similarity to humans. In fact, they claim animal behavior resembles human behavior more than many scientists might care to admit. Moussaieff Masson writes that the fathering instincts of birds are in many ways, far superior to that of human fathers! For example, the father sungrebe—a water fowl from Guatemala—has pouches beneath his wings, with which he carries his young chicks when he flies, ten days after they are born. Regarding human newborns and their fathers, studies indicate that new fathers spend only approximately 37.7 seconds a day interacting with their infants in the first few months of their lives! The simple truth is, humankind can look to some positive role models amongst the animal world for how fathers and mothers care for their young.[981]

Scientists prefer to withhold the application of human terminology to animals in the lab, denying their test subjects of having any kind of "emotion," in order to prevent interfering with an experiment. Even "naming" an animal is considered to be taboo, since a name establishes a sentient relationship with the creature. Moussaieff Masson points out that since "names have a humanizing effect . . . it is a lot harder to kill a

---

[978] Cited from Nechama Leibowitz's *Studies in Devarim* (Hebrew edition), 221

[979] Jeffrey Moussaieff Masson, *The Emperor's Embrace: Reflections on Animal Families and Fatherhood* (New York: Pocket Books, 1999).

[980] Donald R. Griffin, *Animal Minds* (Chicago: University of Chicago Press, 1992).

[981] Jeffrey Moussaieff Masson, *The Emperor's Embrace: Reflections on Animal Families and Fatherhood* (New York: Pocket Books, 1999), 106-109.

friend."[982] He goes on to say, that this is the greatest obstacle preventing scientists from investigating the emotional life of animals. Anyone who has ever cared for a beloved pet knows how complex their personalities are, and would be stirred by the words of Ecclesiastes: "For the fate of humans and the fate of animals is the same; as one dies, so dies the other. They all have the same breath, and humans have no advantage over the animals; for all is vanity" (Ecc. 3:19).

B. *A Soul that Speaks and Communicates*

According to Rashi, one of humanity's chief distinctions from the animal world lies in its unique ability to formulate speech in expressing ideas about itself, the world, and God. As proof, Rashi cites the Aramaic translation (Targum) of Onkelos (2nd cent. C.E.), who paraphrases the verse to mean: וַהֲוָת בְּאָדָם לְרוּחַ מְמַלְּלָא "and it became within man, a speaking spirit," as if to say humanity represents the most evolved of all created entities, for humankind alone was granted the power of understanding and speech. These traditional interpretations regarding the human capacity for complex and abstract speech raise important questions in light of our contemporary knowledge of zoology, comparative linguistics, anthropology, and neuroscience. Simply put, how unique is the human capacity to speak and communicate through language? Is human language the by-product of a long evolutionary history, or is it more the result of spontaneous development that is unique to people?

There is a large scientific interdisciplinary debate about the nature of human communication going back to the time of Darwin, who originally theorized that human language is simply an evolved form of communication, no different in principle from the grunts, gestures, and calls generated by other non-human species. Darwin posits, "I cannot doubt that language owes its origin to the imitation and modification of various natural sounds, the voices of other animals, and man's own instinctive cries, aided by signs and gestures."[983] While natural selection argues for a gradualist account for language, the appearance of organized language makes its mysterious but spontaneous appearance only in humankind. Until the 20th century, the origin of language remained a forbidden topic in certain academic circles, probably because of its highly speculative nature.[984]

Still and all, some linguistic scholars like Noam Chomsky reject the Darwinian idea

---

[982] Jeffrey Moussaieff Masson, *When Elephants Weep: The Emotional Lives of Animals, (New York: Delta, 1995)*, 36.
[983] Charles Darwin, *The Descent of Man*. New York: Crowell, 1874, 89-90.

[984] Only several years after Darwin's publication, a ban on the topic was incorporated into the founding statues of the Linguistic Society of Paris, arguably, the most important academic linguistic institution of its time: "The Society does not accept papers on either the origin of language or the invention of a universal language." J. Aitchison, *The Seeds of Speech: Language Origin and Evolution*, (Cambridge, MA: Cambridge University Press, 2000), 5.

that language could have evolved by natural selection. Chomsky asserts that the human language instinct is fundamentally incompatible with the modern Darwinian theory of evolution, in which complex biological systems arise by gradual accumulation over generations of random genetic mutations that enhance reproductive success. As such, language is a skill limited strictly to humans, who are the sole possessors of the cognitive hardware which makes language possible.

Chomsky contends that human language is radically different from primate communication and draws attention to the incredible ease with which children learn to communicate (as opposed to learning, for instance, mathematics) far beyond the intellectual capacity of their years.[985] Such ability is actually hardwired within the brain itself, which enables it to grasp the words along with its grammar, intuitively knowing how to make symbolic sense of the words that are spoken. Chomsky refers to this mental faculty as the "Language Acquisition Device" or simply "LAD." The child's innate ability to acquire the grammar necessary for a language can best be explained only if one assumes that all grammars are variations of a single, generic "universal grammar," which is a cross-cultural phenomenon that reveals how all human brains come "with a built-in language organ that contains this language blueprint." He postulates that there is an "organ" within the brain that enables it to effortlessly learn the meaning of symbolic language. It is this "instinct" or "innate facility" that makes human language unique.

Among modern linguists, M.I.T. Professor Steven Pinker offers one of the most controversial theories about human language in his book, *The Language Instinct.*[986] While Pinker is sympathetic to many of Chomsky's original insights regarding the uniqueness of human language, he also sides with the Darwinian view that the brain's innate grammatical abilities are not necessarily incompatible with natural selection and mutation. He writes, "There must have been a series of steps leading from no language at all to language as we now find it, each step small enough to have been produced by random mutation of genes and with each intermediate grammar being useful to its possessor."[987]

One could argue that once a person defines language from a purely human perspective, other forms of non-human language are at a disadvantage from the start. It is perhaps more relevant to ask ourselves, how do animal species communicate with one another? Or, can human beings, for example, train primates to understand or speak human language? If in fact, the understanding of symbols is a vital prerequisite to the

---

[985] Noam *Chomsky, Aspects of the Theory of Syntax,* (Cambridge: MIT Press, 1965).

[986] Steven Pinker, *The Language Instinct: How the Mind Creates Language* (New York: Harper Perennial Modern Classics, 2000, c.1994).

[987] Steven Pinker and Paul Bloom, "Natural Language and Natural Selection." *Behavioral and Brain Sciences*, vol. 13, 721.

development of language, then, is the phenomenon of syntax, as Chomsky argues, the most important defining feature that is exclusive to human language?

Some scientists, like primatologist Sue Savage-Rumbaugh, contend that certain species of primates are capable of developing a basic sense of syntax. She offers an altogether different approach to the relationship of animals and language, through the use of lexigrams and computer-based keyboards, the same kind of technology that is used for children and adults with language deficits. With this method, each lexigram or symbol represents a word; however, a symbol is not necessarily characteristic of the words it represents. Remarkably, the information gathered at the center regarding the primates' abilities to acquire symbols, comprehend spoken words, decode simple syntactical structures, learn concepts of number and quantity, and perform complex perceptual-motor tasks have revolutionized the way scientists understand primate communication.[988] Other researchers have also managed to teach gorillas how to utilize sign language.[989]

Studies with the African Grey Parrot, named "Alex," have been studied for the past thirty years by animal psychologist Irene Pepperberg, initially at the University of Arizona and later at Harvard and Brandeis University. Prior to her studies, most scientists believed that birds were only capable of mimicking human speech, but were incapable of using words creatively. According to Pepperberg, birds actually possess a capacity to reason and utilize words in expressing themselves and can even count! Alex's intelligence is believed to have been comparable to that of dolphins and great apes, if not that of a five-year-old human child. Had it not died prematurely because of illness, it might have developed an even greater capacity to express itself through human language.[990]

Marine biologists have also discovered that the humpback whales' songs continue to change as the season progresses. The New Year's song will start off where last year's song has ended, providing evidence of an enormous memory capacity. As the season progresses,

---

[988] Her studies include: "Perception of Personality Traits and Semantic Learning in Evolving Hominids," in *The Descent of Mind: Psychological Perspectives on Hominid Evolution* (New York: Oxford University Press, 1999), 98-115; *Ape Communication: Between a Rock and a Hard Place in Origins of Language: What Non-Human Primates Can Tell Us*, Santa Fe, NM: School of American Research Press, 1999. "Continuing Investigations into the Stone Tool-Making and Tool-Using Capabilities of Bonobo (Pan paniscus)" in *Journal of Archaeological Science, 26 1999*, 821-832. "Linguistic, Cultural and Cognitive Capacities of Bonobos (Pan paniscus)" *Culture & Psychology, Vol. 6(2) 2000*, 131-153.

[989] Elephants are also among the most intelligent animals of nature. In addition to being capable of possessing memory, sympathy, artistic expressiveness, humor, altruism, the ability to use tools, they are self-aware of others—especially of their families. Elephants also appear to possess the complexity of language that makes them comparable to primates. Some zoologists think there is evidence showing that elephants may possess complex language-skills as well (See D.L. Parsell, *In Africa, Decoding the "Language" of Elephants*, National Geographic News, 2003-02-21).

[990] Irene Pepperberg, *Alex & Me: How a Scientist and a Parrot Uncovered a Hidden World of Animal Intelligence--and Formed a Deep Bond in the Process.* New York: Harper Collins, 2008.

the song will gradually change. New pieces will be added while other sections will be dropped. One whale may carry a note a bit longer than another whale, but the structure and components are the same. One recent study points out that their language sophistication is so great, that some whales seem to sing in different dialects depending on their place of origin. For example, blue whales off the Pacific Northwest sound differently from blue whales in the western Pacific, which sound differently from those living off of Antarctica. Moreover, they all sound differently from the blue whales living near Chile (some experts claim that it's all in the accent). Whales in the eastern Pacific are purported to emit lower-pitched sounds followed by a tone, while other whale populations use a different variety of pulses, tones, and pitches. Perhaps the regional differences in their tones are similar to the distinctions between French and Italian, or are variations of the regional accents found in this country). In addition, whales even have a grasp of grammar when they communicate.[991]

The implications of these studies are as far reaching as they are practical. By studying how non-human species participate in language, we will, in the process, better understand more about the nature of human learning, since many of the same principles are involved. The more knowledge we gain from this process will also help to effectively communicate and teach people who have communication disorders, besides expanding our understanding of the creatures that co-inhabit our world with us. In any event, with the ever-growing expansion of human knowledge in our day, we ought to humbly acknowledge the words of the Psalmist who exclaimed ages ago:

מָה־רַבּוּ מַעֲשֶׂיךָ יְהוָה כֻּלָּם בְּחָכְמָה עָשִׂיתָ מָלְאָה הָאָרֶץ קִנְיָנֶךָ

How manifold are your works, LORD!
You have made them all with wisdom;
The earth is full of your creatures

(Psalm 104:24)

Excursus 17: Does the Biblical Concept of "Dominion" Endorse Exploitation of the Environment?

When the Holy Blessed One created the first man, He took him and led him round all the trees of the Garden of Eden, and said to him, "Behold My works, how beautiful and commendable they are! All that I have created, for your sake I created it. Pay heed that you do not corrupt and destroy My world, for if you corrupt it there will be nobody after you to repair it."

—Ecclesiastes Rabbah 7:20

---

[991] See Bjorn Carey, *Grammar Revealed in a Whale's Love Song,* MSNBC News, 2006-03-22.

The expression, וְיִרְדּוּ *(wəyirdû = "have dominion") may imply dominion as well as declension. Should he prove worthy, he will dominate the beasts and cattle; if he proves unworthy, he will sink lower than them, and the beasts will rule over him.*

—Rashi's Commentary on Genesis 1:26

A. Is the Biblical Notion of Dominion "Anti-Nature"?

The biblical story of Creation is often criticized for endorsing an attitude that promotes the exploitation of the environment. During the 1960's and throughout the next decade, biblical scholars of all different stripes have claimed that Genesis 1:28 is largely responsible for many of the ecological problems currently facing our planet: the extinction of numerous species, ongoing deforestation, and potentially dangerous global climate changes are just a few of the controversial issues. Some intellectuals continue to criticize the "Judaeo-Christian" tradition (conveniently, but incorrectly conflating these two different faiths) as being "anti-Nature" and by extension, even "anti-female," since man's domination of woman is viewed within the context of man's domination over nature (Gen. 3:17).

Mythologist and philosopher Joseph Campbell, as well as his admirers, contend that patriarchal religions tend to be violent and out of control. In contrast, the female goddess religions, regarded as paragons of civility, are characterized as violence-free, and evoking an aura of peacefulnes. Campbell further asserts that the Eastern religiouperspective of nature is infinitely more advanced and spiritual than views proposed by the West. In one book, Campbell nostalgically recollects a conversation he once shared with the popular Buddhist apologist and missionary, D. T. Suzuki:

> I remember a vivid talk by the Japanese Zen philosopher Dr. Daisetz T. Suzuki, which opened with an unforgettable contrast of the Occidental and Oriental understandings of the God-man-nature mystery. Commenting first on the Biblical view of the state of man following the Fall in Eden, "Man," he observed, "is against God, and Man, and Nature, are against each other. God's own likeness, (Man), God's own creation (Nature) and God himself—all three are at war. [992]

Similar attitudes are also expressed by the 20th century historian of medieval history, Lynn White, Jr., who also blames humanity's ecological woes on the old biblical notion of dominion. White believes that this Scriptural passage entitles and empowers people with the right to utilize the natural world however they see fit. Furthermore, he alleges that Genesis 1:26-28 teaches that man has a right to dominate, subdue, and control

[992] Joseph Campbell, *Myths to Live By* (New York: Bantam New Age Books, 1973), 95-96.

nature with no regard for the welfare of the environment.[993]

White believes that primitive and Eastern religions show more sensitivity toward the welfare of the environment than Christianity, and in much the same way are better sources for environmental ethics. Unlike the ancient Oriental and Greco-Roman religions, or Native American Indian faiths that venerate animals, trees, rivers, and mountains in the belief that all entities are endowed with guardian spirits which need to be placated—biblical religion was very different. White asserts that once Judaism and Christianity overcame primitive animism, these religions made it possible to exploit nature with an attitude of indifference toward all natural objects. As a solution to our current ecological dilemma, White suggests:

> Since the roots of our trouble are so largely religious, the remedy must also be essentially religious, whether we call it that or not. We must rethink and re-feel our nature and destiny. The profoundly religious, but heretical, sense of the primitive Franciscans for the spiritual autonomy of all parts of nature may point out a direction. I propose Francis as the patron saint for ecologists.[994]

The examples of Franciscan and Dominican stewardship that the Catholic Church promotes are indeed excellent models, as White wisely recommends. However, White's analysis makes a number of unproven assumptions that are suspect and questionable. When speaking about Judaism's ethos, reference must also be made to the entire corpus of religious beliefs—especially those found in classical rabbinic texts, which contain some of the most detailed expositions of stewardship found in the ancient world. As a case in point, theologian Louis Jacobs presents a clear summary of how Judaism follows a philosophy that is "eco-sensitive":

> Waste-disposal, for instance, was a major concern in rabbinic times. Care was to be taken, the Rabbis urged, that bits of broken glass should not be scattered on public land where they could cause injury. Saintly men, the Talmud (*Bava Kama* 30a) remarks, would bury their broken glassware deep down in their own fields. Other rubbish could be deposited on public land, but only during the winter months when, in any event, the roads were a morass of mud because of the rains. In the Mishnah (*Bava Batra* 2), rabbinic concern for a peaceful and clean environment was given expression in definite laws. . . . Carcasses, graves, and tanneries must be kept at a distance of at least 50 cubits from the city. A tannery must not be set up in such a

---

[993] Lynn White, Jr., *"The Historical Roots of Our Ecological Crisis" Science 155* [1967], 1203-7 Reprinted in Barrett de Bell, ed., *The Environmental Handbook*. New York: Ballantine Books, 1970. Joseph Campbell's *Myths to Live By* (New York: Bantam New Age Books, 1973), 95-96, Peter Marshall's *Nature's Web: Rethinking Our Place on Earth* (New York: Paragon House. 1994), 97-108. These writers show a lack of knowledge of the subject matter they claim to have academically mastered. Scriptural, ethical and poetic underscores the importance of stewardship toward all of God's creatures. Jewish tradition must not to be lumped together with the Christian faith on this issue.

[994] Lynn White Jr,. *op. cit.,* 1207.

> way that the prevailing winds waft the unpleasant odor to the town. A prohibition known as *bal tashḥit,* 'do not destroy' is based by the Rabbis on the biblical injunction not to destroy fruit-bearing trees (Deuteronomy 20:19), but it is extended by them to include wasting anything that can be used for the benefit of mankind. For instance, while it was the custom to rend the garments on hearing of the death of a near relative), to tear too much or too many garments violates this rule (*Bava Kama* 91b). Maimonides formulates this as: "It is not only forbidden to destroy fruit-bearing trees but whoever breaks vessels, tears clothes, demolishes a building, stops up a fountain or wastes food, in a destructive way, offends against the law of "thou shalt not destroy". Maimonides' qualification, "in a destructive way" is intended to convey the thought that if, say, a fruit-bearing tree is causing damage to other trees, it may be cut down since then the act is constructive. A Midrashic homily has it that the reason why the wood used for the Tabernacle in the wilderness was not from fruit-bearing trees, was to teach human beings that when they build their own homes they should use wood from other than fruit-bearing trees.[995]

The gaps in White's critique of the Judeo-Christian faiths are alarming and his article is a good example of someone who utilizes a straw man for making what is truly a specious and one-sided argument. One of the best responses to the allegation these men raise can be found in a seminal work, written by a man who is often described as the "father of environmentalism," René Dubos (1901-1981). Dubos offers a number of pointed criticisms aimed at White's article and to D. T. Suzuki (whom he credits with originating this polemic back in the 1950's).

> In my opinion, the theory that the Judeo-Christian attitudes are responsible for the development of technology and for the ecological crisis is at best a historical half-truth. Erosion of the land, destruction of animal and plant species, excessive exploitation of natural resources, and ecological disasters are not peculiar to the Judeo-Christian tradition and to scientific technology. At all times, and all over the world, man's thoughtless interventions in nature have had a variety of disastrous consequences or at least have changed profoundly the complexion of nature . . .[996]

Dubos also shows how even Oriental societies treated the environment with recklessness and indifference. He notes that China was ahead of the West in science and technology which in turn caused massive ecological damage to their region. The barren hills of central and northern China were once heavily forested. Dubos added that human ecological problems were not just limited to the Occidental countries, but were also felt throughout other communities in Asia as well.

---

[995] Cited from: *The Jewish Religion: A Companion* (Oxford: Oxford University Press, 1995), 140. For another work dealing with a Judaic exposition of the ecological principles, see Norman Lamm's *Faith and Doubt: Studies in Traditional Jewish Thought* (New York: Ktav, 1983), 162-185.

[996] René Dubos, *A God Within* (New York: Charles Scribner's Books, 1972), 158.

> Even the Buddhists contributed largely to the deforestation of Asia in order to build their temples; it has been estimated that in some areas they have been responsible for more than half of the timber consumption. The Chinese attitude of respect for nature probably arose, in fact, as a response to the damage done in antiquity. . . . In Japan also, the beautifully artificial gardens and oddly shaped pined trees could hardly be regarded as direct expressions of nature; they constitute rather a symbolic interpretation of an intellectual attitude towards scenery. Wildlife has been so severely reduced in modern Japan that sparrows are the only kind of birds remaining of thc dozens of species that used to pass through Tokyo a century ago.[997]

Many of the ecological problems occurred when early Neolithic man struggled mightily for survival, and killed any animal that posed a threat to his existence. In ancient Egypt, the Pharaohs and their Assyrian neighbors killed large numbers of wild animals just for the pleasure of the sport as is well-documented on many ancient drawings. Even in the farthest regions of the world such as Australia, the native Aborigines' penchant for setting off fires contributed toward its semi-arid climate. If anything, Dubos notes that "the Judeo-Christian peoples were probably the first to develop a pervasive concern for land management and an ethic for nature."[998]

Dubos, of course, is referring to the institutions such as the sabbatical year and the Jubilee Year that treat the earth similar to that of a sentient being, which is entitled to the benefits of "rest" and cessation from human hands (Exod. 23:11; Lev. 25:4; 25:49). It is remarkable that each ecological-based precept exerts profound sociological ramifications for the entire faith community as well. During the Sabbatical year, debts are cancelled (Deut. 15:1–9); the Jubilee Year provides release for Hebrews who had become servants through poverty (Lev. 25:39–41, 54). During these festivals the poor are free to eat the produce from all of the fields (Exod. 23:11; Lev. 25:6–7, 12). Likewise, the Torah aims at curtailing human violence against the environment—notably during a time of war (Deut. 20:19-20); as well as the laws restricting the commingling of different seeds when sowing a field (Deut. 22:9-11), and the law against mixing meat and milk together. (Exod. 23:19).

B. The Noble and Ignoble Savage

Philosopher Michael Shermer adds a *coup de grace* to the arguments made by the eco-thinkers (e.g., Suzuki, Campbell and their legion of doting admirers). Shermer traces the modern myth of the "noble savage" in Western culture to the English poet, John Dryden (1631-1700), who wrote, "I am free as Nature first made man/When wild in the woods the noble savage ran." What stirred Dryden to pen these words? In all likelihood, the notion of the "noble savage" was inspired by the Europeans' discovery

---

[997] Ibid., 160.

[998] Ibid., 161.

of the indigenous peoples of America and Africa. Struck with awe and fascination, European intellectuals believed they discovered societies of people that were not tainted by greed, anxiety and human evil, which they regarded as the by-products of urban civilization. The French philosopher Jean-Jacques Rousseau was largely responsible for popularizing the "noble savage" in his philosophical thought. Rousseau further observes:

> And it is for want of sufficiently distinguishing ideas, and observing at how great a distance these people were from the first state of nature, that so many authors have hastily concluded that man is naturally cruel, and requires a regular system of police to be reclaimed; whereas nothing can be more gentle than he in his primitive state, when placed by nature at an equal distance from the stupidity of brutes, and the pernicious good sense of civilized man; and equally confined by instinct and reason to the care of providing against the mischief which threatens him, he is withheld by natural compassion from doing any injury to others, so far from being ever so little prone even to return that which he has received. For according to the axiom of the wise Locke, Where there is no property, there can be no injury.[999]

Indeed, admiration and culture envy of the "noble savage," as illustrated in James Fennimore Cooper's, *The Last of the Mohicans*, continue to be dramatized in the cinematic imagination of Hollywood. To Shermer's credit, he challenges the premise of this thought and considers it to be "one of the last creation myths of our times," which he dubs as the "Beautiful People Myth." Shermer begins his vivid tale:

> Long, long ago, in a century far away, there lived beautiful people coexisting with nature in balanced ecoharmony, taking only what they needed, and giving back to Mother Earth what was left. Women and men lived in egalitarian accord and there were no wars and few conflicts. These people were happy, living long and prosperous lives. The men were handsome and muscular, well-coordinated in their hunting expeditions as they successfully brought home the main meals for the family. The tanned, bare-breasted women carried a child in one arm and picked nuts and berries to supplement the hunt. Children frolicked in the nearby stream, dreaming of the day when they too would grow up to fulfill their destiny as beautiful people.
>
> But then came the evil empire—European White Males carrying the diseases of imperialism, industrialism, capitalism, scientism, and the other "isms" brought about by human greed, carelessness, and short-term thinking. The environment became exploited, the rivers soiled, the air polluted, and the beautiful people were driven from their land, forced to become slaves, or simply killed. The tragedy, however, can be reversed if we just go back to living off the land where people would grow just enough food for themselves and use only enough to survive. We would then all love one another, as well as our caretaker Mother Earth, just as

[999] Jean-Jacques Rousseau, *A Discourse upon the Origin and Foundation of the Inequality among Mankind,* Part 2, ch. 17.

they did long, long, ago, in a century far, far away.[1000]

Unfortunately, no such idealized world ever existed—at least in a historical sense. Our ancestors were not the eco-stewards we imagine them to be. Flawed with the same type of nature human beings have possessed since the beginning of their existence, our prehistoric ancestors did not behave with much regard for the ecoharmony of the earth. As one example, Shermer notes that the indigenous peoples of North America were responsible for "destroying the wooly mammoths, giant mastodons, ground sloths, one-ton-armadillo-like glyptodonts, bear-sized beavers, and beefy saber-toothed cats, not to mention American lions, cheetahs, camels, horses, and many large mammals; all went extinct at the same time that Native Americans first populated the continent in the mass migration from Asia some 15,000 to 20,000 years ago. The best theory to date as to what happened to these mammals is that they were overhunted into extinction."

Patterns of ancient ecocide can be seen throughout the prehistorical world. Violence, aggression, and warfare are characteristics we share with most of the primate species. These violent impulses can be seen throughout the animal world, and Shermer cites dozens of other examples illustrating this phenomena. After surveying the anthropological literature, he concludes:

> There is nothing beautiful about the Beautiful People. Given them the plants, animals, and technologies—and the need through population pressures—to exploit their environment and they would do so; indeed, those that had that particular concatenation of elements did just that. In other words, centuries before and continents away from modern economies and technologies, and long before European White Males (dead or alive), humans consciously and systematically destroyed each other and their environments. The ignoble savage lies within.[1001]

C. Appreciating the Ecological Principles of Leviticus

The Book of Leviticus adds another dimension to our discussion that many theologians and academics tend to completely overlook. The slaughter of animals has no context outside the realm of holiness—especially as mirrored through the practice of the Jewish dietary laws. The anthropologist, Mary Douglas, writes that the laws of cultic purity serve to help impose God's order and control in the world of creation. On some level, the dietary laws remind us about the sanctity of all life which demands from us humane treatment.

[1000] Michael Shermer, *The Science of Good and Evil, op. cit.,* 95.

[1001] Ibid., 101.

> Unclean is not a term of psychological horror and disgust, it is a technical term for the cult, as commentators have often pointed out. To import feelings into the translation falsifies, and creates more puzzles. The technique of delayed completion postpones the meanings until chapter 17. At that point Leviticus commands the people not to eat blood, not to eat an animal that has died an unconsecrated death, that is, an animal that has died of itself, or an animal torn by beasts, presumably with its blood still in it (Lev 17:8-16; see also Deut 14:21). The dietary laws thus support the law against unconsecrated killing. The Leviticus writer's reverential attitude to life, animal and human, explains the animal corpse pollution rules. 'Thou shalt not stand upon [profit from] another's blood' (Lev. 19:16). The case of the animal's blood and the case of the human's blood are parallel. Ritual impurity imposes God's order on his creation.[1002]

Levitical laws protect the vast number of animals by limiting the permitted species to just a few. In her introduction to her classic study on the dietary laws of Leviticus, anthropologist Mary Douglas writes:

> The religion of Leviticus turns out to be not very different from that of the prophets which demanded humble and contrite hearts, or from the psalmists' love of the house of God. The main new feature of this interpretation is the attitude to animal life. In this new perspective, Leviticus has to be read in line with Psalm 145:8-9: the God of Israel has compassion for all that he made. His love for his animal creation lies behind his laws against eating and touching their corpses. The flocks and herds of the people of Israel are brought under the covenant that God made with their owners, and the other animals benefit from the promises he made in Genesis after the flood, that he would guarantee the regularity of the seasons and the fertility of the ground. The more closely the text is studied, the more clearly Leviticus reveals itself as a modern religion, legislating for justice between persons and persons, between God and his people, and between people and animals.[1003]

In short, although his statements concerning "dominion" on the surface seem to imply that humankind may act toward Creation with indifference, White's eisegetic reading fails to take into account the entire corpus of biblical and post-biblical literature, which clearly stresses the importance of stewardship.

Excursus 18: When Precisely Did the Six Days of Creation End?

R. Shimon said, "A human being who is flesh and blood, who cannot precisely know his times and moments, must add from the profane to the holy. On the other hand, God, who precisely knows His times and moments, can enter into it by a hairbreadth, and it appears as if He concluded His work on that very day, i.e., the Sabbath.

[1002] *Leviticus as Literature* (New York: Oxford University Press, 2000), 151.

[1003] Ibid., 1-2.

Genesis Rabbah 10:10

Genesis 2:2 poses one of the greatest questions of Judaic antiquity: *When precisely did Creation end?* The wording of the text poses a serious question that has troubled scholars since ancient times. Judging by the precise wording of the verse אֱלֹהִים בַּיּוֹם וַיְכַל הַשְּׁבִיעִי מְלַאכְתּוֹ אֲשֶׁר עָשָׂה ("and God completed by the seventh day from all the work that He done"), the Masoretic Text seems to imply that God finished creating the universe *on* the seventh day!

A. Early Responses: The Septuagint

Numerous attempts have developed over the millennia to solve this textual and theological conundrum. The Septuagint version reads differently from the Masoretic Text: καὶ συνετέλεσεν ὁ θεὸς ἐν τῇ ἡμέρᾳ τῇ ἕκτῃ τὰ "And God finished his works that he had made *on the sixth day* . . ." Support for this variant reading can be found in the Samaritan Pentateuch, along with the Peshitta, the Book of Jubilees (2:1), Josephus (37 C.E.–100 C.E.), and *Jerome's Questions on Genesis*. Among modern scholars: John Skinner, A. Dillman, and more recently, Ronald S. Hendel argue that the Septuagint's text is probably based on an older Hebrew manuscript that we no longer possess.[1004] Accordingly, Hendel thinks the Hebrew text should read: הַשִּׁשִּׁי (*haššiššî*) instead of הַשְּׁבִיעִי *(haššəḇîʕî)* "And on the ***sixth*** **day** God finished the work that he had done."

B. Con-versing with Hendel

Although Hendel's overall thesis may have great merit, the logic of some of his arguments is not compelling. Referring to the early 20th century biblical scholar, John Skinner, Hendel claims that the Hebrew preposition ב (= "b") seldom means "by"—it usually connotes "on" or "in." To begin with, this statement is not quite accurate. Word for word renderings seldom hit the mark. Prepositions are used differently in each language; no two languages use prepositions in quite the same way.

Useage of prepositions is inherently idiomatic. For example, the expression "take a bath," might sound confusing to any foreigner who does not speak English as a first language. Even in similar languages like Hebrew and Arabic, the differences in each language's prepositions vary considerably. Whereas in English one would say, "read the

[1004] Ronald S. Hendel, *The Text of Genesis 1-11: Textual Studies and Critical Edition* (Oxford, NY: Oxford University Press, 1998), 32-34.

book," in Hebrew, one would say לקרא בספר which literally means "to read in the book" In English, one would say, "wash it with water" but in Hebrew one would say, לרחץ במים "to wash in water." Whereas in English, these prepositions are not a part of our usage in the examples given, in Hebrew they are. In English one could say, "With the coming of sunset, the day is over." Such a statement would mean that at the arrival of sunset the day is over; one would not presume to say, "After sunset, the day is over." By the same token, when translating the וַיְכַל אֱלֹהִים בַּיּוֹם הַשְּׁבִיעִי the text plainly means "and He ceased *by* the seventh day from all the work that *He had done*."

In defense of the Septuagint's deviation from the Masoretic Text, the Sages of Alexandria realized the Hebrew text was potentially confusing, and so they chose a clearer way of expressing the thought in a manner that a Greek reader could easily understand. These translators chose an idiomatic way of reading the text rather than a literal reading which would have proven to be clumsy. One should add that Prof. Emanuel Tov (Hendel, 33) made this same exact point. The Talmudic view that the Sages of Alexandria deliberately changed the text of Genesis 2:2 are rooted in tradition. On the subject of translation, the Talmud reports: "R. Judah said: If one translates a verse literally, he is a liar; if he adds thereto, he is a blasphemer and a libeler" (BT Kiddushin 49a; cf. Tosefta Megillah 3:41 [Lieberman Edition]). Centuries later, Maimonides wrote about the inherent difficulties involved in translating an original work from one language to another in his famous letter to Samuel ibn Tibbon (1150-1230):

> One who wishes to translate from one language to another and tries to translate word by word, while adhering to the original order of words, the subject will ultimately produce a confusing and unreadable translation. Instead, the translator should first try to grasp the sense of the subject matter. He should then proceed to explain the material according to his understanding into the other language. Such an undertaking is impossible without transposing the word order of a text. Sometimes, he will have to utilize several words to express a single idea, while at other times the translator will utilize fewer words to express a more complex thought. Adding and deleting words is necessary—if one wishes to produce a lucid translation of an original work.[1005]

C. The Targum's Interpretation of Genesis 2:2

One variant of the Targum of Onkelos text paraphrases וְשֵׁיצִי וחמיד יוי בְּיוֹמָא שְׁבִיעָאָה עֲבִידְתֵּיהּ דַעֲבַד וְנָח בְּיוֹמָא שְׁבִיעָאָה מִכָּל עֲבִידְתֵּיהּ דַעֲבַד "God was *filled with longing* for His work on the seventh day."[1006] However, more typically, most textual versions of Onkelos read:

[1005] *Maimonides' Letter to Samuel Ibn Tibbon* (my translation).

[1006] Italian mystic R. Menachem Recanti (1250-1310), claims he saw this version in the Jerusalem Targum and suggested that the verb וַיְכַל ***(wayoḵal)*** may be related to the verb כָּלֶה (*kāleh*) "failing with desire" or "longing"

וַיְשִׁיצִי (*wašyẕy*) [God] "finished" [His work], which denotes the sense of ceasing from it.[1007] This reading parallels the Septuagint which emphasizes the importance of the Sabbath being a day when God "ceased" rather than God "rested." On the other hand, one of the oldest of the Aramaic translations, the Targum Neofiti, plainly renders the text as ואשלם ממריה דייי ביום שביעיאשביעאה עיבידתיה די ברא "*On the seventh day* the Word of the Lord *completed the work* which He had created . . ." (Emphasis added.) Apparently, Neofiti's rendering apparently did not create too much controversy, for its writer felt this was the plain meaning of the original Hebrew text.

D. Rashi and the Midrashic Approach

To sidestep the dilemma, Rashi proposes two responses to this question. Firstly, he observes that human beings are not like God Who knows the precise moment when one day ends and when another begins. Because of this ambiguity, it has long been the custom of Jews to begin the Sabbath before nightfall in order to ensure that the Sabbath's sanctity will not be violated. Still, since human beings are not privy to God's perspective of time, it appears as though God actually completed Creation *on* the seventh day—as evidenced by a literal reading of the verse! Defending his point, Rashi then cites the Midrashic opinion that God did in fact, introduce something new on the seventh day—rest![1008] Nevertheless, this Midrashic interpretation fails to convince, for nowhere in the Tanakh is "rest" ever referred to as a new creation. If anything, the notion of מְנוּחָה (*mənûḥāʰ*) always refers to the absence of work. It hardly seems fitting to equate *resting* with *doing*.

Perhaps Rashi's interpretation may be defended by plainly asserting that the arrival

---

(cf. Deut 28:32, Psa. 84:3). However, the real root of this word derives from כָּלָה (*kāla* = "finished," "fulfilled," "complete," e.g., the construction of a house [1Kgs. 6:38]). This type of thinking is analogous to associating דָּבָר (*dāḇār* ="word") and דֶּבֶר (*déḇer* = "plague"). Although both these words share the same consonants, they are nevertheless two entirely different words. In English, it would be like comparing the noun "lead" and the action "lead." Gersonides adds "All the works involved in the construction of Creation are nothing more than a cipher of that divine idea which exists in the mind of the Supreme Artificer. God loves and esteems His works so intensely, that He continuously preserves them through His providential care. Obviously—there can be no room for doubt—the text does not mean that He *ended* on the seventh day. Rather, God desired the preservation of all that He had made" (See Gersonides' Commentary on Genesis 2:2).

[1007] The Targum of Pseudo-Jonathan paraphrased the text differently: וּשְׁלִים יְיָ בְּיוֹמָא שְׁבִיעָאָה עֲבִידְתֵּיהּ דַּעֲבַד וְעִישַׂרְתֵּי עִיסְקִין דִבְרָא בֵּינֵי שִׁמְשְׁתָא וְנַח בְּיוֹמָא שְׁבִיעָאָה מִכָּל עֲבִידְתֵּיהּ דַּעֲבַד "And the creatures of the heavens and earth, and all the hosts of them, were completed. And the Lord had finished by the seventh day the work which He had wrought, and the ten formations which He had created between the suns."

[1008] Rashi derived this reading from Gen. Rab. 10:9.

of the Sabbath marks the completion of Creation.[1009] To both the biblical and rabbinic imaginations it was inconceivable that the week wouldn't have a Sabbath! Creation itself would have missed its most important day! Certainly, in a mythopoetic, liturgical,[1010] and ritual sense, ancient Israel believed that the entire created order centers on the Sabbath. Liturgically, there are numerous allusions to the Sabbath being the "Crown of Creation,"[1011] as one famous Shabbat prayer reads: "What arose last in deed was first conceived!"[1012]

E. Kimchi and Ibn Ezra's Interpretation

In contrast to Rashi's Midrashic interpretation, both Kimchi and Ibn Ezra insist the verb וַיְכַל (*wayə̄kal*) ought to be read as pluperfect, implying that God *had completed* His work "by" the seventh day, and not that He completed His work "on" the seventh day. Further evidence for this interpretation stems from the fact that the letter ב of בַּיּוֹם (*bayyôm*) ought to be read as a preposition that in this verse connotes "with" or "by." Accordingly, the verse ought to be rendered: "And *by* the seventh day

---

[1009] It may be noted that Rashi neglected to mention several other Pentateuchal passages that re-enforce the notion that Creation was *completed in six days* (Exod. 16:26; 20:9,11; 23:12; 24:16; 31:15, 17; 34:21; 35:2; Lev 23:3; Deut 5:13). However, in two places (Gen. 2:2 and Exod. 31:17), Rashi stresses the significance of "rest" in light of the concept of *Imitatio Dei;* human beings learn to rest as a means of emulating their Creator Who also "rested" (more precisely: "ceased") after creating the universe in six days. Unlike Rashi, Ibn Ezra makes the point that whenever Israel observes the Sabbath, she bears witness to this theological belief. Moreover, anyone working on the Sabbath is like one who denies God's role as Creator.

[1010] The cadence of the first chapter of Genesis possibly suggests that it may have played a liturgical role in the Temple service, either as part of the Sabbath liturgy or as part of the New Year Festival—much like the Babylonian *Enuma elish* was chanted at the Babylonian New Year festival. The relationship between the Creation and the Temple, as the center of the cosmos, stresses the primal intuition that sacred cult has the duty to ensure the well-being of the cosmos. See Ed Noort, "Creation in Genesis, Jeremiah, the Ancient near East, and Early Judaism," *The Creation of Heaven and Earth: Re-Interpretation of Genesis I in the Context of Judaism, Ancient Philosophy, Christianity, and Modern Physics* ed. George H. Van Kooten, (Boston, Brill, 2005), 4.

[1011] *Come in peace, soul-mate, Sweet bride adored,*
Greeted with joy, song and accord,
Amidst God's people, the faithful restored,
Enter, O Bride—Enter, O Bride!

Lecha Dodi Shabbat Prayer, Stanza 10.

[1012] *Come! Let us greet the Bride Sublime!*
For She is the Fountain of Blessings, in every clime,
Anointed, regal, since the earliest of time,
What arose last in deed was first conceived!

Lecha Dodi Shabbat Prayer. Stanza 3.

God had completed the work that He had done."[1013] Umberto Cassuto and Gordon Wenham cite other examples where the pluperfect use of the verb וַיְכַל (*wayəḵal*) is sometimes employed (Genesis 17:22, 24:19, and 49:33).

Wenham points out that there is no indication that God created anything new on the seventh day before He finished and I would add as a possible intra-biblical clarification, all the other biblical verses dealing with the six days of Creation[1014] consistently indicate the universe was completed in that time frame and not beyond the sixth day. Cassuto draws attention to Exodus 40:33, where the verb וַיְכַל (*wayəḵal*) is used in relationship to work, "Thus Moses had finished all the work." Samuel Rolles Driver masterfully sums up the traditional exegetical position, "God formally brought His work to its close by not continuing it on the seventh day, as He had done on the preceding days."[1015]

Excursus 19: Con-versing with Heschel: Holiness of Time vs. Holiness of Space

It was only after they succumbed to the temptation of worshipping a thing, a golden calf, that the erection of the Tabernacle, of holiness in space, was commanded.

—*ABRAHAM JOSHUA HESCHEL*, *The Sabbath*

A. Is Sacred Time More Important Than Sacred Space?

While Heschel's premise is appealing, is his assertion that sacred time is intrinsically more important than sacred space accurate? For example, Heschel contends that the precept regarding the Sanctuary was only a concession due to the people's predisposition toward spatial forms of worship. When history began there was only one holiness in the world—holiness of time.

When at Sinai the word of God was about to be voiced, a call for holiness in man was

[1013] Rabbinic tradition lists this particular verse as an example where the Sages deliberately mistranslated the text when they prepared the Greek translation of the Bible for King Ptolemy (BT Megillah 9a-b). Many of these lists found in rabbinic literature vary considerably. See J.T. Megillah 1.1.9; Tractate *Sofrim* 1:8; Tractate Sefer Torah 1; *Mechilta de R. Ishmael Pisha* 14:64-77; ARNb 37; Yalquṭ Shim'oni 3; Midrash Tannaim on Exod. 22; and Midrash HaGadol on Exod. 4:10. Read R. Menachem Kasher's *Torah Shelemah* Vol. 1 on Genesis 2:2. For a NT discussion, refer to the debate between Jesus and the Pharisees in John 5:17, where Jesus asserts that God's creative activity is manifest even on the Sabbath when it pertains to healing.

[1014] Cf. Exod. 16:26; 20:9,11; 23:12; 24:16; 31:15, 17; 34:21; 35:2; Lev 23:3; Deut 5:13,

[1015] S. R. Driver, *The Book of Genesis: With Introduction and Notes. 7th rev. ed.* (London: Methuen, 1909), 17.

proclaimed: "Thou shall be unto me a holy people." It was only after they succumbed to the temptation of worshipping a thing, a golden calf, that the erection of the Tabernacle, of holiness in *space,* was commanded. The sanctity of time came first, the sanctity of man came second, and the sanctity of space came last. Time was hallowed by God; space, the Tabernacle, was consecrated by Moses.[1016]

According to Heschel and others, the Tabernacle was a concession to the people's immature spiritual state. What the Israelites wanted was a God that they could physically see. The precept of constructing the Tabernacle ensured that the people would have a holy place that would ultimately satisfy their physical senses and need for a spiritual locus that was bound to a physical space. These Midrashim assert that the precept to build a Sanctuary was given only after they worshipped the Golden Calf; God had realized that at this nascent level of their spiritual development they were incapable of a more abstract form of worship.

Heschel selects certain rabbinic sources to substantiate his view regarding the supremacy of sacred time over sacred space. While it is true that some of the Sages and medieval rabbinic scholars like Rashi and others suppose that the laws concerning the construction of the Tabernacle had been given *after* the Israelites' moral and spiritual debacle with the Golden Calf, it is important to add that not all rabbinic scholars accept this analysis. For example: Ramban insists that the Torah records these scriptural sections in their proper chronological order as they occur. He maintains that the precepts concerning the Tabernacle's construction come as a direct result of the theophany at Sinai which left the Israelites yearning for a permanent locus with which they could re-experience God's Presence anew.[1017] Thus, it was only natural that the Tabernacle legislation should immediately follow the Sinai theophany; Umberto Cassuto makes the same point.

> In order to understand the significance and purpose of the Tabernacle, we must realize that the children of Israel, after they had been privileged to witness the Revelation of God on Mt. Sinai, were about to journey from there and thus draw away from the site of the theophany. So long as they were encamped in the place, they were conscious of God's nearness; but once they set out on their journey, it seemed to them as though the link had been broken, unless there was a tangible symbol of God's Presence among them. It was the

---

[1016] Abraham Heschel, *The Sabbath: Its Meaning for Modern Man* (New York: Farrar Straus and Young, 1951), xvii.

[1017] Benno Jacob makes this same point in his commentary on Exodus, "God had planned something greater than this; He wished to remove His temporal seat from the peak of Sinai and descend in order to dwell constantly in the midst of *b'nei yisrael. He* whom heaven and earth cannot encompass; *He,* the all-holy in the midst of an unclean people (Lev. 16:16)! They would place Him among themselves by preparing a site (*miqdash*) appropriate for His holiness. Whenever the people moved, this sanctuary became a wandering Sinai which accompanied them, a segment of heaven transplanted upon earth into the midst of the people. We must remember that God had descended onto Sinai from heaven" *The Second Book of the Bible: Exodus* (Hoboken, N.J.: Ktav, 1992), 758-759.

function of the Tabernacle [literally, "Dwelling"] to serve as such a symbol. Not without reason, therefore, does this section come immediately after the section that describes the making of the Covenant at Mt. Sinai. The nexus between Israel and the Tabernacle is a perpetual extension of the bond which was forged at Sinai.[1018]

A careful reading of the Tabernacle laws may also suggest that the notion of sacred space is, in some ways, intended to replicate the kind of spiritual atmosphere that had pervaded Edenic existence prior to the "Fall." The precept of making the *cherubim* in Exodus 25:8 mythically alludes to the *cherubim* that guarded the road to the Tree of Life (Gen 3:24). The Midrashic imagination also makes this point explicitly clear. Commenting on the verse, "I have come to my garden—my sister, my bride. I gather my myrrh with my spices. I eat my honeycomb with my honey. I drink my wine with my milk. Eat, friends! Drink, be intoxicated with love!" (Song. 5:1). One ancient Midrashic text traces how and why the Shekhinah gradually withdrew from the world:

> At the beginning of time, accordingly, the root of the Presence was fixed in the regions of the earth below. After Adam sinned, the Presence withdrew to the first heaven. The generation of Enosh arose: they sinned; the Presence withdrew from the first heaven to the second. The generation of the flood arose: they sinned; the Presence withdrew from the second heaven to the third. The generation of the dispersion of the races of man arose: they sinned; the Presence withdrew from the third heaven to the fourth. The Egyptians in the days of our father Abraham arose: they sinned; the Presence withdrew from the fourth heaven to the fifth. The Sodomites arose: they sinned; the Presence withdrew from the fifth heaven to the sixth. The Egyptians in the days of Moses arose: from the sixth heaven to the seventh. Over against these wicked men, seven righteous men arose and brought it about that the Presence came back to the earth. Our father Abraham arose: the merit he earned brought it about that the Presence came back from the seventh heaven to the sixth. Isaac arose: the merit he earned brought it about that the Presence came back from the sixth heaven to the fifth. Jacob arose: the merit he earned brought it about that the Presence came back from the fifth heaven to the fourth. Levi arose: the merit he earned brought it about that the Presence came back from the fourth heaven to the third. Kohath arose: the merit he earned brought it about that the Presence came back from the third heaven to the second. Amram arose: the merit he earned brought it about that the Presence came back from the second heaven to the first. Moses arose: the merit he earned brought it about that the Presence came back to the earth. Hence [the reference to Moses] in the verse It was on Israel's bridal (*klt*) day that Moses brought to a conclusion (*klwt*) [the coming back to earth that God had begun in the days of Abraham] (Num. 7:1).[1019]

From these Midrashic statements it is clear that the Tabernacle symbolizes a return to an Edenic existence where God's Presence can be tangibly felt and re-experienced by the faith community. This analysis also seems to compliment Ramban's viewpoint better

---

[1018] *Commentary on Exodus*, 319.

[1019] W. G., Braude and I. J *Kapstein Pěsiķta dě-Rab Kahǎna: R. Kahana's Compilation of Discourses for Sabbaths and Festal Days* [2nd ed.] (Philadelphia: Jewish Publication Society 2002), 7-8.

than the interpretation championed by Rashi and Heschel.

B. *More Questions on Heschel's Position*

As further proof for his thesis, Heschel makes special note of how the construction of the Tabernacle comes to a grinding halt out of deference to the Sabbath and its observance by the Israelites (Exod. 31:13-17). Rabbinic support for this case comes from the Mekhilta, which argues that the Tabernacle's construction did not supersede the observance of the Sabbath. On the surface, this interpretation seems logically plausible, but evidence from other biblical passages indicates a different perspective; namely, sacred space and time co-exist equally and also complement each another with regard to holiness (cf. Lev. 19:30a). Some references explicitly point out that this distinction no longer fully applied after the Tabernacle's construction was dedicated. Furthermore, one could argue on the basis of other Scriptural verses, that the holiness of space actually *overrides* the holiness of the Sabbath in ways that differ from the common communal observance. For example, animal sacrifices had to be offered up even on the Sabbath (Num. 28:9), in addition to the regular burnt offerings that were commanded (Num. 28:10), as well as the kindling of fires for the Eternal Lamp, the burning of the incense, and the offering of the holiday and New Moon sacrifices when they coincided with the Sabbath.

According to the Mishnaic tradition, the kneading, rolling, and baking of the High Priests' cakes do override the Sabbath, but on the other hand, their grinding and sifting do not override the Sabbath. R. Akiba laid down a general rule: "Any work that can be performed before the Sabbath does not override the Sabbath, but that which cannot be performed before the Sabbath overrides the Sabbath" (Menachot 11:3-4).[1020] A similar principle applies no less to the precept of circumcision on the Sabbath (Shabbat 19:1) and the law concerning the Pesaḥ sacrifice (Pesachim 6:2). By the same token all sacrifices that are of a more personal nature, e.g., the purification offerings of the leper, or for the woman who has recently given birth—any sacrifice that does not affect the entire community—cannot be offered on the Sabbath, nor can the showbread be baked on the Sabbath (Mishnah Menachot 11:1).

The sacredness of place differs from the sacredness of time in another significant respect: its sacred character is calibrated to Israel's behavior. Jacob Milgrom uses a provocative metaphor that likens the Sanctuary's spiritual condition to the portrait of Dorian Gray, which loses its original splendor as Dorian morally deteriorates, but

---

[1020] Therefore it follows that since grinding and sifting can be done before the Sabbath, they do not override the Sabbath, but the kneading, the shaping and the baking cannot be done before the Sabbath, for since the flour has already been hallowed in the half tenth measure the offering would become invalid if it were kept overnight; accordingly they override the Sabbath. The basic concept that is operative here is the law of "*lina*." If part of a sacrifice is left beyond its prescribed time for its service without that service being performed, that part of the sacrifice becomes invalidated. See BT Pesachim 13b.

returns to its former beauty at his death. In the same manner, the Sanctuary becomes a spiritual barometer reflecting the nation's sins that defile the Sanctuary. Without the purification rites of Yom Kippur, the state of moral and ritual impurity threatens to drive out God's Presence from the nation, spelling doom for Israel's inhabitants (Eze. 1-3; 8-11; and 40-42).[1021] Once the Sanctuary is spiritually detoxified from the people's sins, it becomes immediately re-sanctified, allowing for the sacrifices to resume in a renewed state of cultic purity. Professor Menahem Ben-Yashar, a contemporary Modern Orthodox Israeli biblical scholar adds:

> Our Rabbis learned from this that every public offering which has a fixed time supersedes the Sabbath.[1022] We conclude: building the Tabernacle is preparation for something sacred, yet the work itself is profane, hence not to be carried out on the Sabbath. The place and the structure did not become sanctified until the Divine Presence filled the completed Tabernacle (Exod. 40:34-35). Once the Tabernacle was sanctified a balance was struck: offerings and tasks that could not be put off would supersede the Sabbath, but every offering or task that could be postponed to the next day would not be sacrificed on the Sabbath. This point is made in apposition to the tendencies evident in recent generations towards viewing the sanctity of time in Judaism as preferential over the sanctity of place, since the sanctity which comes from the source of eternal spiritual Being is close to the dimension of time, which is abstract, eternal and spiritual; in contrast, the dimension of space is entirely dependent on matter, is tangible and temporal . . .[1023]

It is important to remember that comparing gradations of holiness are in a sense, analogous to comparing apples and oranges: while they are both fruits that share a mutual sweetness, they are—in the final analysis—two different species of fruit. Rather than seeing the holiness of time and space in hierarchical terms as Heschel envisions, perhaps it would be more accurate to say that the ontology of sacred time co-exists contemporaneously with sacred space–*not above it, but in harmony with it.* Oddly enough, this interpretive reading agrees with Einstein's novel view that there is no difference between space and time, for we exist in a space-time continuum.

The Hebrew term עוֹלָם (*ʿôlām*) suggests both a time-space continuum, for aside from meaning "world" or "universe," עוֹלָם may mean either "time" or "eternity" depending upon its scriptural context. Its Ugaritic cognate is *'lm,* also denotes the realm of

[1021] Cf. J. Milgrom, "Israel's Sanctuary: The Priestly 'Picture of Dorian Gray,'" *RB* 83 ([1976]) 390–99 and in *SCTT*, 75–84.

[1022] See *Mekhilta de-Rabbi Yishmael, Bo,* Tractate *De- Pishah* 5; *Sifre* on Numbers, 65.

[1023] Menahem Ben-Yashar, *Of Time and Place,* (Bar-Ilan University Parashat Hashavua Study Center, Parashat Vayakhel-Pekudei 5764/March 20, 2003 http://www.biu.ac.il/JH/Parasha/eng/pekudei/yas1.html).

"eternity." Typically, עוֹלָם is sometimes used with respect to objects of the world and universe that antedate human existence, e.g., the stars, sun, moon, world, and mountains—all of which were brought into existence because of divine love.[1024] However, unlike the term קָדוֹשׁ (*qādôš* = "holy"), עוֹלָם is never used with respect to God.

Many Hebraic scholars think the term עוֹלָם (*'ôlām*) most likely derives from the word עָלַם (*'ālam*) "be hidden," "concealed," "secret," or "to hide," or perhaps more precisely—the vanishing point—and may pertain to what is hidden in the distant future or in the distant past, e.g., "since time immemorial." Frequently, עוֹלָם is used in reference to God's love.[1025] Some Hassidic thinkers suggest that the world is called עוֹלָם since it represents the realm of physical reality where God's Presence and Being are most profoundly hidden.[1026]

Heschel states: "According to the ancient rabbis, it is not the observance of the Day of Atonement, but the Day itself, the 'essence of the Day,' which, with man's repentance, atones for the sins of man."[1027] This insight is certainly accurate—but only within the context of a faith that was forced to re-define the significance of this most sacred holiday after the Jewish people lost its spiritual center—the Temple. Without a Temple, how else could the holiday of Yom Kippur be observed? Since that time, Judaism has learned to transcend the geographical boundaries that originally defined its religious identity[1028] and in doing so, has become a truly universal faith that is not dependent upon space, like all other nations—as S. R. Hirsch has deduced.

Still, there are occasions when the holiness of time and space converge and become one. The most vivid example is the Day of Atonement which is called "Sabbath of Sabbaths"; yet the holiness of this holiday is contingent upon a series of complex personal preparations as well as priestly rituals that involve sacred space; i.e., the High Priest entering the Holy of Holies; the atonement sacrifices; and the scapegoat rituals. The nexus of sanctified time and space thus make the collective/personal experience of purification and atonement possible. To a lesser degree, the holiness of space (characterized by the "Land of Israel") reflected in the beginning of the Jubilee Year, is also calibrated to the time of Yom Kippur (Lev 25:9). By blowing the shofar at the end of Yom Kippur, the Land of Israel is sanctified anew: slaves regain their freedom, debts are forgiven, and sold parcels of real property revert to their original owners. It is also

---

[1024] Cf. Pss. 73:12; 90:2; 136:7, Ecc. 3:11.

[1025] Cf. Pss. 113:2; 115:18; 121:8; et al.

[1026] See TDOT, Vol. 10, 530-545.

[1027] *The Sabbath*, *op. cit.*, xvi.

[1028] Heschel neglected to mention that the spatial dimension of Yom Kippur was originally intended to serve as a purification of the Tabernacle/Temple.

important to emphasize that anything God confers as "holy" remains holy, such as the innate sanctity of human life[1029] or the holiness of Jerusalem, or the Land of Israel—long referred to as the "The Holy Land." Mt. Zion, likewise, is frequently considered God's "holy mountain,"[1030] as is Mt. Moriah (Gen. 22:14). Whereas Mt. Sinai's holiness was fleeting, lasting only for the duration of the theophany, the prophet envisioned a time when Mt. Zion's holiness would become permanent.[1031]

Here too, I agree with Menachem Ben-Yashar, who observes that the sanctity of time is "also bound up with geography." Israel's spiritual connection with the Land is a connection that remains permanent and inviolate whether Israel is living in the Land or in the Diaspora. Whereas it is true that in some of the priestly texts the Torah says that human beings can "defile" the land (Num. 35:34), God assures that the Land—like a sentient being—can "cough up" its sinful inhabitants whenever the time is ripe (Lev. 18:28). As with the holiness of the Sabbath, it is the responsibility of the nation of Israel to see that the Land remains in a sanctified condition. Whether it is the temporal holiness of the Sabbath and holidays, or for that matter, the spatial holiness of the Land of Israel, people must mindfully imbue the physical and the temporal with a quality of holiness that suffuses life with reverence, purpose, and meaning.

There is also a dimension of space that the Sabbath has always historically and culturally embraced. Whether it be the Temple, the synagogue, or the home, each of these places have served as centers of Sabbath celebration. Specifically, spatial sanctity of the home embraces prayer, song, Torah study, story-telling, and conversation. The Jewish people are called upon to realize the Sabbath's holiness in practical and meaningful ways: by shopping for special foods during the week, wearing special garments for the Sabbath day, setting the table, lighting the candles—all within the context of a spatial realm.[1032] A Sabbath space is also created whenever special efforts are expended for sharing the Sabbath meal with family, friends, and guests. The home functions as a miniature Sanctuary where a family acts in an almost priestly manner by endowing their domicile with holiness, sublimity and love. When God created the Sabbath and made it holy, He also endowed it with the capacity to become a

---

[1029] With regard to human life, there is an irreducible quality that endows every human being with a potential for goodness and holiness; whether these aspects are ever realized becomes a matter of free choice. Indeed, this is one of the common arguments raised against the death penalty in some religious circles. If human life is inherently sacred, then the State has no right to terminate it. By destroying the life of another, one also destroys the goodness that is within oneself.

[1030] Cf. Psa. 2:6; 48:2; Isa. 11:9; 56:7; 57:13; 65:11, 25; 66:20; Joel 4:17; Obad. 1:13, et al.

[1031] For further elaboration of this point, see Jon D. Levenson's study on: *Sinai and Zion: An Entry into the Jewish Bible* (San Francisco: Harper and Row Publishers, 1985).

[1032] Cf. BT Shabbat 119a-119b for examples of how the rabbis prepared for *Shabbat*. Cf. MT *Hilchot Shabbat* 30:5; O.H. 262:1; 268:1.

holy day for all future generations. Practically speaking, it is up to Israel to remember that the Sabbath encompasses that which binds her and God together, integrating both the temporal and spatial dimensions.

C. The Ascendency of Sacred Space in Our Day

Why did such thinkers like Heschel and others maintain that Judaism is a religion that stresses the holiness of time over space if there is a strong component of sacred space within Judaism itself? For centuries, the Jewish people have acclimated themselves to living in a homeless environment. Since the Land of Israel ceased to be the central place in the life of the Diaspora Jewish community, it was only natural for Jewish thinkers to stress the timeless aspect of Judaism over its spatial dimension. Once more, Menachem ben Yashar gets at the heart of the issue:

> The tendency to prefer the abstract sanctity of time over the concrete sanctity of place stems not only from cosmopolitan spiritual trends. Quite the contrary, these trends are sustained among us by the reality of many generations of exile, i.e., actual separation from the places that were sanctified for worship of the Creator, and in religious terms, the removal of the Divine Presence. Ideally, with the Temple standing, the place of the synagogue was side by side with the Temple, primarily as a place of gathering to read the people the Torah; after the destruction of the Temple, the synagogue came to replace the Temple.[1033]

Yale scholar Eitan Levine adds that it was the spacelessness of the European Jew that enabled it to survive numerous attacks made by the Crusaders when they destroyed every synagogue in the Rhine Valley: "[T]his was a faith which could function independent of a special place, national home, religious preserve, or institution. It could flourish in the humblest home, the most exposed field, or most distant land. Judaism (and only Judaism) had succeeded in transcending space, and in that sense, in becoming truly universal." [1034]

Heschel's theological insights capture the kind of attitude that has recast the Jewish holidays as a "cathedral of time," but the re-emergence of Israel as a state has forced the Jewish people to re-evaluate the practical, religious, moral, and political issues that come with living in sacred space. However, now that the Jewish people have returned to their rightful homeland, it is time for modern Jewry to re-evaluate the importance of sacred space within a contemporary context. Such an understanding could have significant implications for Israel—especially in light of the various agricultural and

---

[1033] Menachem ben Yashar, *Of Time and Place, op. cit.* BIU, 2003.

[1034] E. Levine, "Jews in Time and Space" in *Diaspora: Exile and the Contemporary Jewish Condition,* edited by E. Levine (New York: Steimatzsky and Shapolsky, 1986), 4.

cultic precepts that the Jewish people can now observe for the first time in nearly two thousand years.

Liturgically, traditional Jews have long prayed for a restoration of the sacrificial cult and the rebuilding of the Temple, but whether such a religious locus will take place in the decades ahead remains to be seen. This kind of religio-political development will depend largely on the political impact it will have on Israel's neighbors—not to mention on the lives of all of Israel's citizens. How sacred space is ultimately configured and utilized is a matter of great ethical significance; the use and abuse of power in a spatial context challenges Jewish values on every level. The spatial reality of a Jewish State should not come at the risk of abusing the civil rights and personal freedoms of its citizens—whether Jewish or non-Jewish. As Levine concludes, "For better or worse, the Jewish people have re-emerged into the dimension of space; for nearly twenty centuries Jews have survived spacelessness; now they must survive space."[1035]

Theologians might want to reconsider using hermeneutical approaches claiming uniqueness and exclusivity that are, in effect, sometimes theologically self-serving. Judaism makes ample use of the primal patterns, motifs, and symbols concerning sacred time and space that have long functioned as a part of the religious psyche of humankind since the beginning. In biblical tradition, sacred time and sacred space are complementary aspects that work in harmony with one another. While there are historical reasons why the sacredness of time achieved ascendancy in Judaism, there is also a rich spatial dimension that has remained a constant in Jewish history that should not be ignored.

Excursus 20: The Documentary Hypothesis in the Creation Narratives of Genesis 1-2

Rabbi Shimon said: Woe to the person who says that Torah presents mere stories and ordinary words! . . . Ah, but all the words of Torah are sublime words, sublime secrets! . . .

—*ZOHAR, III: 152*

Hitherto, one has generally trusted one's concepts as if they were a wonderful dowry from some sort of wonderland: but they are, after all, the inheritance from our most remote, most foolish, as well as most intelligent ancestors.

—FREIDRICH NIETZSCHE, *Will to Power*

[1035] Ibid., 10.

A. "J" and "P" and Their Exegetical Differences

It is worth noting that no concrete archaeological proof has ever been produced supporting the supposition by biblical critics that the priestly writers ("P") or those of the Yahwist tradition ("J") knew only one Divine Name.[1036] While the Documentary Hypothesis certainly resonates with a strong sense of logic that may be appealing, it cannot be granted a status of superiority to all other alternative and traditional approaches. In fact, it could even be argued from a neo-traditional perspective, that although the Documentary Hypothesis is a novel way of looking at the *peshat*, it is certainly not the only way of examining the contextual meaning of the text.

However, for exegetical purposes, let us accept its premise and attempt to decipher its deeper theological implications. The priestly writers awed by the cosmic order that permeates the universe, possessed an outlook that was more cosmocentric in its focus than the Yahwists who envisioned Creation through a more anthropocentric lens. For P, God defines the limits of the cosmos, the world, the succession of the seasons, and the holiness of the Sabbath. The seven-part, dramatic formation of the universe reveals to the reader that everything in the cosmos could not exist were it not for the power and generosity of the Creator. The writing style of P is eloquent and concise, yet his account of the Creation narrative is nothing less than awe-inspiring and majestic. In Genesis 1:27, man and woman are depicted as equal partners, and are created simultaneously. As such, the verse ought to be translated, "Let us make humanity in our own image . . ." Contrary to many medieval scholars who subscribed to Aquinas' belief that women are innately inferior to men,[1037] the P strand of tradition regards the image of God as possessing both male and female qualities. Furthermore, unlike J, P does not use the Tetragrammaton until the time of Moses, when God makes His Name known to Moses for the first time (Exod. 6:2-3); before that time God is simply known as אֱלֹהִים

[1036] H. C. Leupold quotes the biblical scholar William Moeller, who draws attention to a very remarkable parallel in this connection:

> In 2:4-4:26 it must be observed that *Yahweh 'Elohim* is used successively *twenty* times, with the name *'Elohim* interrupting *five* times, but always for a very definite reason, and the name *Yahweh* is used *ten* times, making a total of *thirty five* (built up out of the sub-totals 20 plus 5 plus 10). Furthermore, it must be observed that these thirty-five correspond exactly to the *thirty five 'Elohim* found in 1:1-2:3, which thirty five names are again contained in the tenfold expression "*and God said*" (*'Elohim*) and therefore also resolve themselves into 25 plus 10. Consequently, the *seventy* divine names of 1:1-4:26 can in no wise be regarded as being used in a purely arbitrary sense . . . (*Exposition of Genesis* [Grand Rapids, MI: Wartburg Press, 1942], 55).

[1037] Thomas Aquinas derived his sexism from Aristotle, who believed that a woman is nothing more than a "misbegotten man" (Aristotle, *The Generation of Animals,* II, 3). Aquinas even adds that women should not have been made in the original Creation (*Summa* I Q. 92: A. 1; for other comparable references, cf. *Summa* I, Q. 98, A. 2 and *Supplement to Part III*, Q, 52, Reply to Objection 2).

('ĕlōhîm).

The priestly tradition views Creation as an expression of God's aesthetic and artistic imagination, sensuously imbued with God's original blessing; indeed, the universe itself exists as a result of God's spoken Word: "God said . . . and it was so." Everything in Creation is made according to perfection, and all are judged by the Creator, Who sees "that this was good." God the Creator is omnipotent and requires no assistance. There is a quality of effortlessness and peacefulness that is pervasive throughout the priestly version.

In contrast, J depicts the Creator in chapter 2 in a far more anthropomorphic manner. God does not create by fiat or word, but by fashioning and forming, like an artisan modeling clay vessels, struggling to give shape and perfect expression to his handiwork. First, God prepares the soil, so that it will produce suitable clay for what will be humanity's construction. Like a human artisan, YHWH creates and works with His hands, fashioning a perfect being until the ultimate human genesis is realized. In other words, unlike chapter 1, all is not "good"—yet! After creating man and infusing him with the breath of life, God reexamines His creation and concludes, "It is not good for man to be alone" (2:18), and He creates a companion for Adam who resembles him. However, this time the creative process is entirely different, for unlike Adam's formation from the earth, He fashions a being from Adam's *own* body. The man recognizes the woman as his mate, and accepts her as a full partner and a fitting helper for him. Whereas J intimates that the woman plays a subservient relationship to her mate, this is not the case with P's narrative.

Another distinction between the two accounts can be seen in how Creation unfolds. J does not assume that the world came into being over seven days, but rather, that everything came into being on the same day. In addition, two names of God appear: Elohim and YHWH, whereas in P, only Elohim appears. P defines God as a Being Who is wholly transcendental and wholly Other, while in J's portrayal, God is described as having a complex humanlike personality; a Being who "walks with man," and Who becomes passionately affected by the foibles of human nature. Overall, J is concerned more with the earthly and the human, in contrast with P's focus on the cosmic and the divine. In addition, J makes use of mythical themes from various extra-biblical sources that were in currency in ancient Mesopotamia. The personalities of the players in this Divine drama are immensely complex—YHWH, by far the most psychologically complicated. Yale scholar Harold Bloom likens YHWH to the figure of King Lear in Shakespeare and claims, "YHWH is powerful, imaginative, and capricious as reality itself, and yet he's also the basis of our understanding of what it is to be human."[1038]

[1038] Harold Bloom, *Jesus and Yahweh: The Names Divine* (New York: Riverhead Trade, 2007).

J concerns himself with the development of human consciousness, as well as God's own developing consciousness and shows how the existence of evil first originated in the world; i.e., J depicts God as being surprised by His own creation's capacity for actualizing evil (e.g., Gen. 3:20, 22, 6:3). J's lucid narrative informs us of the beginnings of humankind's estrangement and alienation from God—sadly, the inextricable destiny for humanity that becomes more profound with each passing generation. From the Yahwist perspective, it becomes necessary for one remnant to bear witness to God's Presence in the world, which leads to the patriarchal narratives and ultimately, to the saving acts of the Exodus. Therefore, the story of Creation as narrated in both the J and P traditions, describes the beginnings of human individuation and the journey towards rediscovering the aboriginal wholeness that is lost after Eden. However, it is important to keep in mind that in P's version of Creation, one discovers that there is no stress or plot that could justly be described as a story. On the other hand, in J's depiction of Genesis 2-3, there exist all the elements one would expect to find in a true story.

One modern scholar's response to these two traditions is reflected in Umberto Cassuto's argument that the two creation stories were most likely penned by the same hand. Others also attribute the entire book to a single redactor who conflated all of the different oral histories that were passed down throughout the generations. Unlike Greek mythology, where narratives are never repeated or duplicated, stories are often repeated in the Semitic tradition, seldom correlating to one another in every detail. In fact, this is more often the norm than not.[1039] The first chapter of Genesis depicts the creation of humankind only in general details, the second chapter depicts humankind's creation in more lucid detail which is in keeping with the ancient Semitic style of writing. Cassuto further notes that Judaic tradition is sensitive to this problem, as Rabbi Eliezer b. Rabbi Yose the Galilean observes, "The listener may think that it is another narrative, whereas it is only the elaboration of the first."

B. *Two Aspects of the Divine Reality*

Certainly, there are strong arguments countering the notion of multiple writers or sources. For instance, consider the premise that the alternating Divine names have nothing to do with different writers or sources, but rather designate two different aspects of God's Being and relationship with the universe and humankind. This question was raised by Judah Halevi in the 11th century and later, as stated above, by U. Cassuto in the 20th century. Granted, this point of view may not be very popular in academic circles, but it does merit some value to the interpretive process. God's name, YHWH, appears whenever He discloses His nature to those with whom He

---

[1039] See Genesis 24ff. regarding Eliezer's retelling of the story of how he met Rebekah.

enters a relationship, and wherever the Bible stresses this personal relationship. In short, YHWH appears in the narrative whenever there is a moral concern or issue at stake. In contrast, Elohim denotes a more abstract philosophical notion of God as it pertains to the nature of ontology. Elohim refers to God as Creator of the universe, Ruler of nature and Source of all life. According to Cassuto, the biblical Redactor's intention was to indicate that the appearance of YHWH/Elohim in this chapter announces to the reader that YHWH and Elohim are one and the same: the transcendent God Who created the cosmos enters into relationship with humankind. For the community of Israel, these names are especially significant—by entering into covenantal relationship with YHWH, Israel affirms that its national God is also the God of the entire created order.[1040]The Midrash also sees the YHWH/Elohim combination as signifying two aspects of God's "character" and "personality." Here, YHWH connotes divine compassion while Elohim indicates justice and law. The Midrashic thinkers understood the Creation of the universe as a manifestation of God's divine justice, as indicated by the name Elohim. However, knowing that the world could not endure, God attached his name "YHWH", which is associated with mercy, so that the physical world would survive by virtue of Divine mercy and compassion. This approach can richly expand our understanding of the sacred text in ways that deserve more attention than academicians are willing to give.

Admittedly, the Sages' perspective and interpretation certainly present contradictions that are not easily resolved. For one thing, YHWH is not always represented in the Tanakh as a merciful and benevolent being. YHWH is consistently portrayed in the Scriptures as demanding some very morally challenging activities (e.g., the laws regarding genocide found in Deuteronomy and other scriptural passages[1041]). In fact, YHWH is often described as the Divine Warrior;[1042] while it is better to be on the winning side of God, being among YHWH's enemies (and they are legion) can prove to be hazardous to one's health. Traditional rabbinical interpretation fails to adequately deal with the asymmetrical apsects of God's providential acts, hence, despite some of its limitations, the Documentary Hypothesis has a style and simplicity that is elegant and intellectually captivating. Its stress on historicity oftentimes makes better sense of the passages' historical context with respect to many of the disturbing biblical texts concerning genocide, than traditional rabbinic exegetes.

[1040] Umberto Cassuto's best known critique of the Graff-Wellhausen theory is found in his short but trenchant treatment of his *Documentary Hypothesis: and the Composition of the Pentateuch* (Jerusalem: English trans. Israel Abrahams, 1961), 15-26.

[1041] Exod. 23:32–33; 34:11–16; Num 21:2–3; and Deut. 7:1–5; 20:16–18; Josh 6:21, 8:26; 10:28; 11:11, passim..

[1042] Cf. Exod. 14 and 15; Numbers 10:35–36; Deut 28:25–26; Joshua 6ff; Josh.6, 7:11; 10:1–15; Judg. 5ff; 1 Sam. 4–7; 17:45–47; 2 Sam. 5:22–25; 2 Kgs. 6:6–23; Lam. 2:15, passim.

C. Con-versing with James Kugel: The Theology of "P"

James L. Kugel, a Modern Orthodox rabbinic scholar, demonstrates a willingness to engage and integrate the historical-critical methods of biblical criticism, especially remarkable when considering his theological background and training. Kugel points out several other differences between the P school *vis-à-vis* the J school, which are deserving of special mention. According to Kugel, P's theology contains some of the most "chilling conceptions" the ancients ever had about the Deity:

> It was already noticed that the God of Genesis 2-3 had a more "hands-on" approach to creating the world than the God of chapter 1, attributed by scholars to P. In chapter 1, God simply speaks and things happen—suddenly there is light, suddenly there is a firmament, and so forth. One would not be wrong to characterize this God as somewhat more impersonal. But even this description is more personal than the God revealed in later portions of the priestly text, according to scholars. Recent analysis has in fact highlighted the difference between the way God is depicted in the priestly parts of Genesis and the way He is depicted after that. In P's part of Leviticus, for example, God does not speak in the first person, "I will do this" or "I have ordered that"—not even to Moses. It is as if P seeks to deny that God can be thought of as a person-like Being, one who can say "I." So too, P's God does not personally punish people; punishment just somehow falls on wrongdoers and they are "cut off" (in the passive voice) or otherwise disciplined (P doesn't say how). Nor does He personally forgive; instead; it is forgiven to the sinner who makes good his infraction. P's version of the giving of the Torah at Mount Sinai is consistent with this picture; Moses *enters the cloud* and hears a voice, but the people outside hear nothing at all. All this seems to correspond to something profound in P's theology.[1043]

Clearly, there is scriptural support to Kugel's theological position. However, closer scrutiny reveals that P's depiction of the image of God is not really as "impersonal" as Kugel asserts. For example, it is no linguistic fluke that the divine epithet אֱלֹהִים (*'ĕlōhîm*) also means "judge," for God creates the universe according to a template of order and justice. When a human being adheres to the divine harmony that pervades the cosmos through observing the precepts of the Torah, earthly existence literally becomes enlightened and unencumbered. Life is a journey where every human act carries within it the seeds of its own well-being and life destiny. Alternatively, the sinful act unleashes forces that will engulf and self-destruct the wrongdoer, or at the very least, make one's life difficult to manage. This thought is captured beautifully in Psalm 1:

> Happy are those who do not follow the counsel of the wicked,
> Nor follow the path of sinners,
> Or has joined the company of the impudent;

[1043] James Kugel, *How to Read the Bible* (New York: Free Press, 2007), 305.

Rather, the teaching of the Lord is his delight,
God's teaching they study day and night.
They are like a tree planted beside streams of water,
That yields fruit in its season,
Whose foliage never wither,
And whatever it produces thrives.
But the wicked are different!
They are like the chaff driven by the wind
Therefore, the wicked cannot survive judgment
Nor will sinners be in the assembly of the just
The LORD loves the way of the just
But the path of the wicked leads to ruination
Psalm 1:1-7

Psalm 1 stresses that throughout our existence we must learn to recognize the difference between the wheat from the chaff, and the real from the illusory; we must consciously choose between the experience of being connected with the divine, or the feeling of being spiritually anxious and homeless. Regardless of our individual choices, one thoughtful or thoughtless action impacts the world. This message runs like a stream of consciousness throughout the Genesis narratives.

However, this theological notion is certainly not at all unique to P but is present in the theology of J as well, a good example being the story of the Exodus. When YHWH commands mighty Pharaoh to release the Israelites, the Egyptian monarch soon discovers that there are consequences to his disobedience. Soon, his entire country is plagued by a series of natural disasters that bring misery and suffering to all of his people. Nature, herself, rebels against the rule of tyranny and attempts to set the record straight once and for all. The great spiritual "chain of being" found in the tradition of P, is equally present in the stories attributed to J and not just P, as Kugel claims.

Kugel further asserts that in Leviticus, God does not speak to mortals in the first person.[1044] Evidence for such a theory seems inconclusive. The fact remains that there are ample instances where God does speak in the first person, as personal pronouns appear throughout Leviticus, which is the *locus classicus* of priestly texts.[1045] These passages are replete with numerous anthropomorphisms that one would not expect to see if P truly had an aversion for using them. Note, also, that whenever God says, "I will . . . ," it is always spoken in the context of a dialogue with His covenantal party. There is absolutely nothing "impersonal" about this exchange between God and Moses, or with Aaron and the Israelite

[1044] Richard Friedman, *How to Read the Bible*, *op. cit.*, 305.

[1045] Cf. Leviticus 6:10; 7:34; 8:31, 35; 9:23; 10:13; 17:10, 12; 18:4-5; 18:26; 18:30; 19:3; 19:19; 19:30; 19:36-37; 20:3; 20:5-6; 20:8; 20:22; 20:24-25; 22:9; 22:31-32; 23:30; 23:43; 25:18; 25:21; 25:38; 25:42; 25:55; 26:2-4; 26:9; 26:11-13; 26:15-19; 26:21-22; 26:24-25; 26:28; 26:30-33; 26:36; 26:41-45.

people. God is also portrayed by the Holiness Code of Lev. 19 as being intensely personal and concerned with ethical human conduct. Therefore, P appears to be more concerned with the human condition than Kugel is willing to acknowledge.

Still, in Leviticus 26-28, P paints a very different picture. God *does* announce that He will take it upon Himself to personally afflict wrongdoers (note the repetitive phrase, "I will . . .") who violate the commandments. Thus, the biblical language illustrated in Leviticus 26-27 is as anthropomorphic in its imagery as any passage found in the J tradition. In each of these passages, the Creator is always depicted as playing an active role in administering retribution whenever it is warranted.

D. Prayer, Sacrifice and the Priestly Theological View

One of the most extraordinary claims Kugel makes pertains to the relationship between sacrifice and prayer:

> Perhaps the most striking thing to scholars about the God of P is that people do not pray to Him. The book of Psalms is full of prayers and songs of praise to God, many of them quite ancient, and scholars have established that the majority of these psalms were composed to be recited in God's "house," the temple where He was deemed to be present. But a reader of P would never guess that this was so. P describes in great detail the offerings in the temple, but he never says a word about prayers or songs being recited there. In fact, in P people never pray; what good would it do? P's God is an almost impersonal force. So, too, the ancient festive hymns praising Him are never mentioned in P either . . .
>
> . . . In our own modern society, such a vision of God might actually appear comforting to some. After all, without quite putting the thought in words, we live in a world that is based on ruling out a role for the divine in daily life. That would suit P just fine—keep supporting the temple, he would say, and we'll keep offering the sacrifices. Meanwhile, political upheavals, natural catastrophes, the suffering of the righteous—these are not problems for P's theology; God is enthroned in splendid isolation. He has no interests in thank-yous, so save your breath.[1046]

Kugel assumes that sacrifice did not co-exist with prayer, yet, in Hosea 14:3 we find: וּנְשַׁלְּמָה פָרִים שְׂפָתֵינוּ (*ûnəšalləmāʰ pārîm śəpāṯênû*) "Instead of bulls we will pay *the offering of* our lips" (NJPS), which suggests that prayer is the equivalent of sacrifice, or, prayer is a replacement for sacrifice. The Talmud bears this wisdom out: "With what shall we replace the bullocks we formerly offered to You? 'Our lips,' in the prayer we pray to thee.[1047] Rabbinic tradition attributes the institution of

---

[1046] James Kugel, *How To Read The Bible, op. cit.,* 305-306.

[1047] A variant of this teaching is also seen in BT Yoma 86b: "R. Isaac said: In the West [Palestine] they said in the name of Rabbah b. Mari: Come and see how different from the character of one of flesh and blood is the action of the Holy One, blessed be He. As to the character of one of flesh and blood, if one angers his fellow, it is doubtful whether he [the latter] will be pacified or not by him. And even if you would say that he can be pacified, it is doubtful whether he will be pacified by mere words. However, with the Blessed Holy One, if a

prayer to the patriarchs[1048] or to a Mosaic decree and this tradition has remained an important part of the sacrificial cult since its inception.[1049] Perhaps it could be said in defense of Kugel's claim, that the Hosea passage represents an evolutionary change in the theological imagination of ancient Israel; Hosea expresses a thought that is not present in P—at least as it is understood in the Pentateuch. However, closer study of the Leviticus texts does not bear this out. If anything, the imagery of Hosea is predicated upon the sacrificial imagery of Leviticus.

The relationship between sacrifice and confession is stressed in numerous passages in the Levitical literature: (1) With regard to the guilt and trespass offerings (Leviticus 5:5), it is significant that the Torah insists spiritual rehabilitation of the sinner must begin with the verbal act of confession, thus preceding the sacrificial act. Atonement begins within the heart and soul of the worshipper in order for Divine forgiveness to become effective (cf. Psa. 51:16). Confession, per se, is crippled unless it is motivated by one's sincere feelings of remorse and contrition.[1050] (2) The Yom Kippur offering referred to in Leviticus 16:21, establishes confession as a pre-condition for atonement and purification, without which the Yom Kippur offering is useless. (3) In Leviticus 26:39-42, we discover that the act of verbal confession atones for sins that can no longer be expiated through sacrifice—a reality that is caused by the state of Israel's expulsion from her homeland. It seems difficult to imagine how any kind of atonement offering could be effective without the verbal declaration of confession. (4) Based on the priestly legislation of Numbers 5:7, all acts of fraud, perjury and embezzlement are no less morally defiling than that of leprosy. In many ways, these moral failings ought to be considered far worse since crimes of moral turpitude require an act of

person commits a sin in secret, He is pacified by mere words, as it is said: 'Take with you words, and return unto the Lord' (Hosea 14:3). Furthermore, God even accounts it to him as a good deed, as it is said: 'And accept that which is good' (Ibid.). Furthermore: The Scriptures account it to him as if he had offered up bullocks, as it is said: So will we render for bullocks the offerings of our lips (Hosea 14:3). Perhaps you will say [the reference is to] obligatory bullocks. Therefore it is said: 'I will heal their backsliding, I will love them freely' (Hosea 14:5).

[1048] T. B. Berakhot 26b.

[1049] The Christian scholar, G. F. Moore (*Judaism* Vol. 2, 218), provides a statement that might on the surface appear to support Kugel's position, "So long as the Temple stood, we used to offer a sacrifice and thus atonement was made; but now we have nothing to bring but prayer" (Midrash Tanchuma Parshat Korah 12). However, the rabbinic interpretation here is merely loosely stated; the intent of the Sages may equally suggest that originally both prayer and sacrifice functioned together. Now, in the absence of the Temple, prayer alone will have to suffice.

[1050] Maimonides makes this point vividly clear in his *Laws of Repentance* "Anyone who verbalizes his confession without resolving in his heart to abandon sin is like a person who immerses in a ritual pool while holding on to a rodent. His immersion is of no value until he lets go of the rodent" (MT. Hilchot Teshuvah 2:3).

will and a denial of conscience; cultic impurity that is due only to physical circumstances pale in comparison. To enter God's Presence, there must be an effort expended to repair the breaches that undermine social justice and personal trust. To facilitate the spiritual renewal of a sinner, one must make a confession and bring the appropriate atonement offering. In the priestly worldview, those individuals who defile the spiritual integrity of the Tabernacle are a far greater affront to its purity than those suffering from physical ailments such as leprosy, unusual body discharges, and corpse contamination. This same point is also repeatedly stressed throughout the prophetic literature.

From this perspective, the collage of verses referenced above prove that prayer, at least in the form of a confession, existed early on in the priestly traditions of Leviticus and Numbers and played a vital role in the sacrificial cult. The evidence for this assertion contradicts Kugel's image of an isolated deity who is indifferent to human offerings. Sacrifice in the Tanakh *always* involves more than just rote ritual; the act of sacrifice adds a sacred dimension to the community and individual, but this sacredness is contingent upon the moral integrity and purity of mind and deed of the person offering the sacrifice. Human morality in the final analysis is, according to P's theology, the benchmark of the Divine Image referred to in Genesis 1:26.

From an anthropological standpoint it is fair to ask, what primal society didn't offer prayer along with its sacrifices? Among nearly all the major religions of the world, the relationship between sacrifice as a means of expiation, always presupposes the existence of a Higher Being, whose moral character demands a change in the worshipper's moral behavior, namely, that individual is personally responsible for the removal of his sin. Human fault may occasionally be traced to a moral lapse, but it can also be due to the failure of properly carrying out a ritual, or may even be the result of an unconscious reason that requires expiation. In terms of the other types of sacrifice, thanksgiving offerings are invariably accompanied with prayers of praise, acknowledgement and gratitude for the goodness the worshipper receives.

E. Priestly Theology and the Priestly Benediction

Perhaps one of the most personal and best known ancient priestly prayers that Kugel does not take into consideration is the Priestly Benediction[1051] of Numbers 6:22-

[1051] The antiquity of this prayer is beyond dispute. In 1979, when Israeli archeologists discovered at family tomb located in Ketef-Hinnom, two silver amulets containing a variant of the priestly benediction in ancient Hebrew script dating back to the 7th century B.C.E. The silver scrolls not only point to the authenticity and antiquity of the Priestly Benediction, it represent the earliest inscriptions containing a text also found in the Bible in addition to containing the oldest attestation to the use of YHWH found to date in Jerusalem. As such, these few verses from one of the books of the Pentateuch predate the earliest biblical copies of the

27:

> The Lord spoke to Moses, saying: Speak to Aaron and his sons, saying, "Thus you shall bless the Israelites: You shall say to them,
> "The Lord bless you and keep you;
> May the Lord make his face to shine upon you, and be gracious to you;
> May the Lord lift up his countenance upon you, and give you peace."
> So they shall put my name on the Israelites, and I will bless them.

The visceral power of this prayer is due to the fact it is shamelessly anthropomorphic. While discursive theological language speaks much ado about the nature of God, it cannot begin to describe in words the actual experience of God. Prayer flows from a heart that is alert and open to the miniature synchronicities which disclose God in the world. Biblical theology stresses that even with all its obvious limitations—anthropomorphism is the language of encounter par excellence throughout the Tanakh. The priests evoke sensuous language. The Priestly Benediction teaches that God is unabashedly personal. The intensity of the Divine-human relation connotes an experience of God's Presence that is all so intensely real, permeating every segment of our being with absolute certainty. In their priestly view of the universe, God is not only the Creator—He is ultimately the Bestower of personal blessing and peace. Such a depiction would certainly contradict Kugel's notion that according to priestly theology God is basically an indifferent deity.

In short, Kugel's comment on P's attitude regarding prayer does not take into consideration other aspects that play a vital role in the priestly theology of worship; this is clearly not limited to just the act of sacrifice. Prayer—whether as a confession or as a paean for times of joy and thanksgiving—also plays an equally important part according to the theology of P. Subsequently, it is doubtful whether P's perception of God and sacrifice is as clear-cut as Kugel claims—if anything, prayer and the act of sacrifice appear to be closely interrelated. By the same token, the Priestly Benediction is grounded in theology that sees God as Giver of all temporal and spiritual blessings, Who blesses His people with the fullness of prosperity.

Excursus 21: The Meaning of "Clinging" (Genesis 2:24)

Two souls with but a single thought,

Dead Sea Scrolls by 400 years and bring us back to the period that preceded the Babylonian exile. R.D. Cole adds that the themes of the Priestly Benediction are consistent with similar blessings dating back to the earliest period of Israelite history:

> Ancient Near Eastern texts from the second millennium B.C.[E.] contain parallels to the themes of divine countenance, the lifting up of the face, and the blessing of well-being (šalem) (p. 128).

Two hearts that beat as one.
—MARIA LOVEL, *Ingomar the Barbarian, II*

The root דָּבַק (*dabaq*) in all Semitic languages translates to mean "cling together" and "stick together." Few English words can convey the emotional power of this Hebraic verb. דָּבַק denotes clinging to someone in affection and loyalty. Man is to cleave to his wife (Gen. 2:24). Ruth clung to Naomi (Ruth 1:14). In a relationship of love and devotion, to cleave to someone means a willingness to share a life and a common destiny. While Shechem is described as being *strongly drawn* to Dinah, daughter of Jacob (Gen. 34:3), the same verb is used to describe King Solomon's unhealthy "clinging" to his pagan wives who influenced him to *cling to* other gods (1 Kgs. 11:2). Elsewhere דָּבַק is used to connote fusing or soldering objects (cf. Isa. 41:7). It is also used to describe how the various parts of the body are attached to one another; Job says that his bone *cleaves* to his skin (Job 19:20). One of the best known verses utilizing this colorful metaphor comes from the Psalms: "If I forget you, O Jerusalem, let my right hand wither; let my tongue stick to my palate if I cease to think of you, if I do not keep Jerusalem in memory even at my happiest hour." (Ps. 137:5-6). In Modern Hebrew, דָּבַק still has the sense of "to stick to, adhere to"; דָּבַק yields דֶּבֶק (*debeq*), the noun form for "glue." As a term of endearment, דָּבַק also implies a bond of loyalty and devotion, or a close relationship. (Gen 2:24).

Understandably, we find the same verb used in Deuteronomy 30:20 to depict the ideal loving relationship between God and Israel.[1052] The fact that the Torah uses it to describe the ideal husband-and-wife relationship is very spiritually suggestive. Jewish mystical texts develop the concept of דְּבֵקוּת (*devekut* = "attachment to God") to also include an ecstatic state of feeling oneness with the Divine. Hasidic mystics teach that one can experience *devekut* by being focused on God in one's daily work and activities. The notion of *devekut* between God and man is predicated upon the metaphor of husband and wife. Ideally, *devekut* never demands the dissolution of the self, the "I" remains an "I" and the "Thou" remains a "Thou." Respect toward the other's individuality is always respected and never is it destroyed by the other.

Excursus 22: Adam's "First Wife" — Lilith in Jewish Folklore: Past and Present

The foolish and cruel notion that a wife is to obey her husband has sent more women to the grave than to the courts for a divorce.

[1052] Cf. Deut. 30:20; Pss.102:6; 119:25; 137:6; Job 29:10.

—Lemuel K. Washburn

A. The Origin of Lilith's Name

One of the most interesting personalities listed in rabbinic and non-rabbinic literature is the figure of Lilith, who is said to be Adam's "first wife" and sometimes referred to as "the first Eve." The only reference to Lilith may be found in Isaiah 34:14 where the term לִילִית *(lîlîṯ)* first appears. Older bible translations render לִילִית as "screech owl."[1053] This interpretation is consistent with the previous stanzas that speak about other wild animals or birds. Newer translations seem to prefer "Lilith" because of its strong connections to Sumerian, Babylonian, and Assyrian mythologies. In Sumerian, the word *lil* "wind" is related to the name; as such, she was also known as a storm-demon. If this definition is correct, then the other creature mentioned in the same verse שָׂעִיר must mean the hairy goat-demon. The fact that Lilith does not appear in any other Scriptural reference is significant—especially given the antiquity of the belief of her existence.[1054] For many years scholars thought that the name "Lilith" was connected to the popular folk etymology לַיְלָה *(laylâ* = "night"). However, the real origin of the name derives from the Assyrian *lilîtu* and Akkadian the *lilū, lilītu* and *ardat lilī*, who were the three storm deities.[1055] In Sumerian, the term *líl* means either "wind" or "spirit." The Jews probably first learned of this feminine demonic being after the Northern Kingdom of Israel was deported to Assyria in 721 B.C.E., and shortly later when the Southern Kingdom was deported to Babylon.[1056]

B. Lilith in the Alphabet of Ben Sirach

Although the origin of Lilith is not mentioned anywhere in the Talmud, she is mentioned in the popular medieval composition known as *The Alphabet of Ben Sira* (ca.

[1053] Cf. the Septuagint, Pseudo-Targum Jonathan and the Vulgate. A modern rendering of this passage would thus be: The wild beasts of the desert shall also meet with the howling beasts; and the shaggy goat shall cry to his fellow. The screech owl also shall rest there, and find for herself a place of rest (*MKJV*).

[1054] The *lil* is also mentioned in the Sumerian epic *Gilgamesh, Enkidu and the Netherworld* (ca. 3rd millennium B.C.E.).

[1055] Cf. BDB 539:1; HALOT 528; cf. Marcus Jastrow's *Dictionary of Targumim, Talmudic and Midrashic Literature*, 707; Numbers Rabbah 16:25.

[1056] According to one rabbinic tradition, Lilith was the daughter of Ahreman, the opponent of Ohrmizd in the Zoroastrian religion (T. B. *Bava Bathra* 73a). See Karel Van der Toorn, Bob Becking, and Pieter Willem Van Der Horst, *Dictionary of Deities and Demons in the Bible* (Leiden; Boston; Grand Rapids, Brill: Eerdmans, 1999), 520. She is also mentioned in the Jerusalem Targum to Num. 6:24; Deut. 33:24; Isa. 34:14 and in T. B. Erubin 18b.

8th century). According to medieval Jewish folklore, God created Lilith from the earth just as He created Adam. From the beginning of their relationship, Adam and Lilith immediately begin to fight. One version of the myth, recounts how Adam insists on making love in the missionary position and Lilith agrees—provided she can be in the dominant position instead:

> After God created Adam, who was alone, He said, 'It is not good for man to be alone (Genesis 2:18). He then created a woman for Adam, from the earth, as He had created Adam himself, and called her Lilith. Adam and Lilith immediately began to fight. She said, "I will not lie below," and he said, "I will not lie beneath you, but only on top. For you are fit only to be in the bottom position, while I am to be in the superior one." Lilith responded, "We are equal to each other inasmuch as we were both created from the earth." But they would not listen to one another. When Lilith saw this, she pronounced the Ineffable Name and flew away into the air. Adam stood in prayer before his Creator: "Sovereign of the universe!" he said, "the woman you gave me has run away." At once, the Holy One, blessed be He, sent these three angels to bring her back.[1057]

The quarrel is profoundly psychologically nuanced, similar in many ways to an ordinary day in the battle of the sexes. The myth draws attention to the pattern of dysfunction that affects the complicated world of human relations. It is conjectured that Adam could not endure having an egalitarian relationship and so their conflicts quickly lead to Lilith's sudden departure—she did not want to be Adam's *underling*! Rather than playing the role of marriage counselor, YHWH sends for three angels to bring her back, issuing the following ultimatum. "If she agrees to return, then fine. If not, she must permit one hundred of her children to die every day." [1058] The ancients believed demons were very prolific beings, populating much more quickly than mortals—a view that many of the rabbis uncritically accepted in the Midrash.[1059]

After the Lilith prototype proves to be a failure, and to make sure that there would never be a problem regarding who would be the "head of the family," God—this time—creates a woman out of Adam's rib to symbolize her subservience to her husband. In short, according to this version of the story, Lilith prefers to stay alone and focus on making infants sick. She threatens to inflict harm upon male infants until the eighth day of life, and female children after twenty days (some variants say twelve). Lastly, Lilith makes one additional vow—not to harm the infant in any way if the infant wears an

---

1057 David Stern and Mark J. Mirisky, *Rabbinic Fantasies: Imaginative Narratives from Classical Hebrew Literature* (Chicago, IL. Publisher's Row/Varda Books, repr. 2001), 183-184.

1058 It seems strange that *The Alphabet of Ben Sira* did not think to ask where Lilith was going to find her new love interests. However, in a different variant of the myth, the angel Samael (not to be confused with Samuel), chief of the fallen angels (a.k.a "Satan"), finds her weeping and falls in love with her. Unlike Adam, Lilith finds Samael to be more egalitarian and appealing; she accepts him as her mate. See Maximilian Josef Rudwin "The Legend of Lilith" *Devil in Legend and Literature* (Chicago: Open Court, 1931), 94-104.

1059 See Gen. Rabbah 20:11.

amulet bearing the name of three special angels. When Lilith sees their names, she remembers her oath, and the child recovers."

C. Lilith as an Archetype of the "Terrible Mother"

Jungian psychologist Erich Neumann argues in his psychological study, *The Great Mother* (2d ed., New York, 1963), that Lilith personifies the archetype of the "Terrible Mother," while also analogous to the Greek Gorgon and harpies. These mythic figures personify the archetypal image of negativity—that of destroyer—latent in the feminine psyche; as such. Horrified by what they saw, the ancients retold this tragedy in the language of myth. Lilith represents the sinister side of femininity. Neumann shows how this pattern develops cross-culturally:

> And the dark side of the Terrible Female is a symbol for the unconscious. And the dark side of the Terrible Mother takes the form of monsters, whether in Egypt of India, Mexico or Etruria, Bali or Rome. In the myths and tales of all peoples, ages, and countries—and even in the nightmares of our own nights—witches and vampires, ghouls and specters, assail us, all terrifyingly alike. . . . Thus the womb of the earth becomes the deadly devouring maw of the underworld, and beside the fecundated womb and the protecting cave of earth and mountain gapes the abyss of hell, the dark note of the depths, the devouring womb of the grave and of death, of darkness without light, of nothingness. For this woman who generates life and all living things on earth is the same who takes them back into herself, who pursues her victims and captures them with snare and net. Disease, hunger, hardship, ware above all, are her helpers, and among all peoples the goddesses of war and the hunt express man's experience of life as a exacting blood.[1060]
>
> It is in India that the experience of the Terrible Mother has been given its most grandiose form as Kali, "dark, devouring time, the bone-wreathed Lady of the place of skulls . . .[1061] But all this—and it should not be forgotten—is an image not only of the Feminine but particularly and specifically of the Maternal. For in a profound way life and birth are always bound up with death and destruction. That is why this Terrible Mother is 'Great,' and this name is also given to Ta-urt, the gravid monster, which is hippopotamus and crocodile, lioness and woman, in one. She too is deadly and protective. There is a frightening likeness to Hathor, the good cow goddess . . ."[1062]

D. Talmudic and Kabbalistic Depictions of Lilith

The Talmud makes ample mention of Lilith's activities. Lilith is described as a

---

[1060] Erich Neumann, *The Great Mother* (New York: Princeton-Bollingen Series XLVII, 1991 ed.), 148-149.

[1061] Ibid., 150.

[1062] Ibid., 153.

female night-demon whose erotic nature evokes a desire for illicit sexual relationships (*succubus*). Lilith's physical attributes are also described in detail; she is depicted as having long hair and wings[1063] and the rabbis warn all men not to sleep alone in a house lest Lilith come and seduce them in their dreams (T. B. Shabbat 151b).[1064] Lilith is especially popular in the Zohar where she appears as the seductress supreme.[1065] In all likelihood the rabbinic stories about Lilith were, in part, intended to prevent young rabbinic scholars from the sins of masturbation and illicit sexual relations which the Zohar equates to the crime of murder. The scholar, Rabbi Joshua Trachtenberg explains:

> As a result of the legend of Adam's relations with Lilit [*sic*], although this function was by no means exclusively theirs, the Lilits were most frequently singled out as the demons who embrace sleeping men and cause them to have nocturnal emissions which are the seed of a hybrid progeny. . . . As the demons whose special prey is lying-in women, it was found necessary to adopt an extensive series of protective measures against her. . . . We seem to have here a union of the night demon with the spirit that presides over pregnancy, influenced no doubt by the character of the Babylonian Lamassu, and the lamiae and *striga* of Greek and Roman folklore.[1066]

Trachtenberg's insight is obviously accurate. According to the Zohar, a man who masturbates in this world will be treated in the next life like one who is worse than a murderer—since he has, in effect, murdered his own seed; in God's eyes he is considered the most reprehensible kind of human being.[1067] In a strange way, the Zohar sees Lilith as the guardian of family purity. Any couple failing to observe the laws governing sexual abstention risks incurring her wrath. Even making love by candle light can result in Lilith causing children to become epileptic and risk being pursued and killed by Lilith.[1068] One may deduce from the Zohar's condemnation that the fate of young men or children dying is a talionic punishment for having spilled seed. The proof text for this is the story of Er and Onan, who died rather than give their seed to Tamar (Gen. 38:1-10).[1069]

1063 BT *Erubin* 100b; BT. *Nidah* 24b.

1064 The origin of the English word "nightmare" has nothing to do with a murderous horse derived from *Grimm's Fairy Tales*; it was an evil female spirit who afflicted sleepers with a feeling of suffocation. "Nightmare" is compounded from "night" + "mare" (Old English for "goblin." In Old Irish, Morrigain is the "demoness of the corpses," lit. "queen of the nightmare" while in Polish, *mora* means "incubus" or "succubus" (the former is a male demonic spirit, the latter is the female equivalent). Each of these stories is based on the Lilith myth.

1065 Cf. Zohar 1:14b; 27b; 33b; 34b; 55a; 169b; 2:27b; 96a; 106a; 3:19a; 76b-77a.

1066 Joshua Trachtenberg, *Jewish Magic and Superstition* (New York: Commentary Classic, 1939; reprint, 2004), 36.

1067 Zohar 1:219b.

1068 Zohar 1:14b.

1069 For a comprehensive treatment of this subject, see David M. Feldman, *Abortion in Jewish Law* (New York:

Archaeology has discovered special incantation bowls that were used to help a person seek protection from "demons, demonesses, lilis, liliths, plagues, evil satanic beings and all evil tormentors that appear." As one scholar notes, "The liliths were but one class of an elaborate taxonomy of malevolent spiritual beings. The sexually aggressive character of the lilis and liliths accounts for the fact that exorcistic texts are often expressed in formal divorce terminology, such as this text (No. 35, Isbell): 'Again, bound and seized are you, evil spirit and powerful *lilith*. . . . But depart from their presence and take your divorce and your separation and your letter of dismissal. [I have written against] you as demons write divorces for their wives and furthermore, they do not return [to them].'"[1070]

E. Recasting Lilith—A Bad Girl Becomes Good—Judith Plaskow's New Midrash

With the advent of women's liberation movements, Lilith has undergone a dramatic make-over; now, Lilith is widely regarded by many women as a heroine who is the first woman to insist on having an egalitarian relationship with her mate. Judith Plaskow blames Adam for the expulsion of Lilith from her home, which gave rise to men's subjugation of women as we have witnessed throughout history. Different from the story recounted earlier from *The Alphabet of Ben Sira,* Plaskow weaves a short neo-midrashic story about Lilith's moral rehabilitation, entitled "Applesource":

> In the beginning, the Lord God formed Adam and Lilith from the dust of the ground and breathed into their nostrils the breath of life. Created from the same source, both having been formed from the ground, they were equal in all ways. Adam, being a man, didn't like this situation, and he looked for ways to change it. He said, "I'll have my figs now, Lilith," ordering her to wait on him, and he tried to leave her the daily tasks of life in the garden. But Lilith wasn't one to take any nonsense; she picked herself up, uttered God's holy name, and flew away. "Well, now, Lord," complained Adam, that uppity woman you sent me has gone and deserted me." The Lord, inclined to be sympathetic, sent His messengers after Lilith, telling her to shape up and return to Adam or face dire punishment. She, however, preferring anything to living with Adam, decided to stay where she was. And so God, after more careful consideration this time, caused a deep sleep to fall on Adam and out of one of his ribs created for him a second companion, Eve . . .
>
> . . . Meanwhile Lilith, all alone, attempted from time to time to rejoin the human community in the garden. After her first fruitless attempt to breach its walls, Adam worked hard to build them stronger, even getting Eve to help him. He told her fearsome stories of the demon Lilith who threatens women in childbirth and steals children from their cradles in the middle of the night. The second time Lilith came, she stormed the

London: New York University and University of London Press Limited, 1968), 109-165.

[1070] The *New ISBE*, Vol. 3, s.v. "Lilith," 536.

garden's main gate, and a great battle ensued between her and Adam in which she was finally defeated. This time, however, before Lilith got away, Eve got a glimpse of her and saw she was a woman like herself . . .

. . . One day, after many months of strange and disturbing thoughts, Eve, wandering around the edge of the garden, noticed a young apple tree she and Adam had planted, and saw that one of its branches stretched over the garden wall. Spontaneously, she tried to climb it, and struggling to the top, swung herself over the wall.

She did not wander long on the other side before she met the one she had come to find, for Lilith was waiting. At first sight of her, Eve remembered the tales of Adam and was frightened, but Lilith understood and greeted her kindly. "Who are you?" they asked each other, "What is your story?" And they sat and spoke together, of the past and then of the future. They talked for many hours, not once, but many times. They taught each other many things, and told each other stories, and laughed together, and cried, over and over, till the bond of sisterhood grew between them.

Meanwhile, back in the garden, Adam was puzzled by Eve's comings and goings, and disturbed by what he sensed to be her new attitude toward him. He talked to God about it, and God, having His own problems with Adam and a somewhat broader perspective, was able to help out a little—but He was confused, too. Something had failed to go according to plan. As in the days of Abraham, He needed counsel from His children. "I am who I am," thought God, "But I must become who I will become."[1071]

F. Afterthoughts

While this author is certainly sympathetic to the contemporary Jewish woman's desire to make the Judaic faith more egalitarian, one might consider whether rehabilitating a dubious character such as Lilith is really a good idea. Re-creating the mythology of what was commonly regarded as a universally sinister creature is ahistorical and spurious; it may even border on the perverse. Constructing a heroine or Judaic icon out of Lilith is like trying to make a folk-hero out of Hannibal Lecter (although Hollywood seems to have already done that!). There are many positive role models of strong women that can serve as a much better example, such as Sarah, Rebekah, Rachel, Shifra and Puah, Miriam, the daughters of Zelophad, Rahab, Deborah, Jael, Esther, and many others.

In the myth described in *The Alphabet of Ben Sira*, it seems obvious that Lilith hates children largely because of her hatred for Adam; her contempt for men is solely because they are the sons of Adam. Lilith's refusal to listen to God, is similar to her refusal to listen to Adam—her husband. As a seductress, she always maintains power and control over a sexual relationship, which she dictates on *her* terms. The myth of Lilith and

[1071] Cited from Sybil Sheridan's book, *Hear Our Voice: Women in the British Rabbinate* (Columbia, SC.: University of South Carolina Press; 1st North American 1998), 107-109.

Adam is intriguing from a psychological perspective, since it seems to encapsulate the difficult way men and women have always related to one another. Psychologically speaking, the rabbinic portrayals of Lilith's rejection of Adam may say more about their tortured relationships with their own wives. Lilith, the succubus, may have been more of a psychological fantasy for what some of the rabbis secretly craved, and a representation of the Madonna/Whore Complex (as evident in the Zohar's somewhat persistent obsession with illicit sexuality).

Excursus 23: A Prelude to "The Awakening"– Modern Theological Perspectives

For what is freedom, but the unfettered use;
Of all the powers which God for use had given?
—*SAMUEL TAYLOR COLERIDGE, The Destiny of Nations*

❖ *Paul Tillich: The Fall as the "End of Dreaming Innocence"*

As a rule, rabbinic tradition did not subscribe to the Christian description of Genesis 3 as the "Fall,"–a term which does not appear at all in this famous story. As well, the Sages rejected the interpretations found in the Pseudepigraphal writings that intimate the cosmic struggle between God and the legions of the Devil (see notes on Genesis 3:1-10). But this theme does appear in the Apocryphal writings, e.g., Sirach 25:23, where the ancient philosopher blames the woman for introducing death to the world. A similar intimation appears in Wisdom of Solomon 2:24, "But by the envy of the devil, death entered the world, and they who are in his possession experience it."[1072] However, neither of these speaks of "Original Sin" as understood in numerous Christian texts.[1073] In fact, from the Christian perspective, Eve becomes the prototype for all women because of her acquiescence to the serpent's seduction.[1074] Jewish exegetical tradition has always felt that the Christian reading committed considerable violence to the text. Lastly, psychologist Theodor Reik (1888-1969) made an amazing observation: "Not before Sirach (200-175 B.C.E.) is there any allusion found to a primeval sin and not before the Apocalypse of Baruch (80-150 C.E.) is there any hint of the story of the Fall

[1072] Some scholars think the passage refers to Cain. Because of the envy he feels toward his brother, he becomes the world's first murderer. However, in 1 Enoch 69:6, the writer believes that Satan caused Eve to sin. See also 2 Esdr. 3:7-22; 7:118.

[1073] See John 1:29; 8:44; Rom. 5:12-21; 1 Cor. 15:21-22, 45-49; Heb. 9:26.

[1074] This would explain why Christians consider Mary, in a sense, the "Second Eve," much like Jesus becomes the "new Adam."

that brought upon man the liability of future punishment. Jesus refers neither to the Garden of Eden nor to the Fall."[1075]

One Protestant thinker, Paul Tillich (1886–1965), prefers to regard the biblical story of the Fall not as a historical account of what happened a long time ago, but as a profound expression of how human beings become existentially estranged from God, from their true selves, and from others. As Tillich writes, "Theology must clearly and unambiguously represent the Fall as a symbol for the human situation universally, not as the story of an event that happened 'once upon a time.'"[1076]

This story in particular serves as a living symbol for the human situation, and must not be reduced to being a mere echo of the past. Human beings possess the freedom necessary to contradict their essential nature; however, along with this freedom comes the anxiety of finitude. The Creator intended for us to embrace the world as God's "Original Blessing," but Adam and Eve cannot live with the limitations imposed on them. They want to be something more than what they are: the Garden with all its beauty lacks what they yearn for the most—the freedom *to be*. What makes us unique in all of earth's creation is our preoccupation with the purpose of our very being. Indeed, to be human is to ask about being. On the deepest ontological level, we are creatures who know that our being is not something that is self-explanatory, but is in essence a riddle. We feel a kinship with all things that exist, yet we are unique in wanting to understand the mystery of our existence and being. We cannot find satisfaction living like animals. We yearn for something deeper and more meaningful. It is this existential reality that makes the heart and soul of the human being restless and ill at ease.

In mythical terms, for Adam, the alternative means a life of nonbeing and meaninglessness. The biblical narrator may have wished to convey the paradoxical message that true freedom comes with discipline; that is to say, being able to indulge in any pleasure represents bondage to one's desires. In this sense, the restriction of Eden serves as a paradigm for the spiritual life. For the community of faith, the story of Eden serves as a metaphor for the arduous path God's people have taken throughout history. All the various proscriptive and prescriptive laws of the Bible, along with all the sundry rabbinic restrictions, aim to elevate the human spirit to the heights of the heavens. Adam and Eve live without any awareness of sin; indeed, for the primal couple, the concept of sin is beyond their grasp.

Tillich characterizes their condition as a psychological state of "dreaming

---

[1075] Theodor Reik, *Myth and Guilt: The Crime and Punishment of Mankind* (New York: George Braziller Inc., 1957), 60.

[1076] Paul Tillich, *Systematic Theology*, Vol. II (London: Nesbet & Co., Ltd., 1955), 33.

innocence.[1077] The term *dreaming* describes the state of essential being, while *innocence* indicates un-actualized potential: "In the state of dreaming innocence, freedom and destiny are in harmony, but neither of them is actualized."[1078] In the very act of actualizing freedom, the state of dreaming innocence comes to a sudden end. The possibility of estrangement from God is inevitable if human freedom is ever to be realized, yet God created the world with this very possibility. Adam and Eve do not live in a state of perfection, because their psychological and spiritual beings lack individuation. For Tillich, the Fall represents "a fall from the state of dreaming innocence": an awakening from *potentiality to actuality.* In short, the Fall was necessary for the development of humankind.

B. Freud: Paradise as a Unitary Existence of Oceanic Oneness

With rare theological insight, Sigmund Freud (1856–1939) was among the first of modern thinkers to suggest that infancy, in a sense, represents a re-dramatization of the Fall from the Paradise story. At the infant's earliest stage of psychological development, the infant experiences an "oceanic oneness." As the baby nurses from its mother's breast, it does not distinguish between itself and the world, but rather the world is an extension of itself, "in which the infantile ego is sufficient unto itself."[1079] The infant's world, however, is only temporary. All parents—sooner or later—will impose restrictions, eventually severing the infant's continuous pursuit of carefree indulgence and desire toward pleasure. As the child matures, s/he develops a sense of self-identity. Soon, the child realizes the impossibility of its former existence. For all practical purposes, paradise has been lost.

C.G. Jung and Erich Neumann add that the Paradise parable points to a preconscious stage of infancy in which the ego's center of human consciousness has not yet been activated.[1080] Neumann refers to the bond of mother and child as "existence in unitary reality" that embraces both mother and child. Neumann believes that at this

---

[1077] Ibid., 33.

[1078] Ibid., 34.

[1079] Sigmund Freud, *The Complete Psychological Works*, (J. Strachey, Trans. London: Hogarth Press Vol. 18), 110.

[1080] Regarding this idea, Neumann writes: "With the emergence of the fully-fledged ego, the paradisal situation is abolished; the infantile condition, in which life was regulated by something ampler and more embracing, is at an end, and with it the natural dependence in that ample existence. We may think of this paradisal situation in terms of religion, and say that everything was controlled by God; or we may formulate it ethically, and say that everything is still good and that evil had not yet come into the world. Other myths dwell on the 'effortlessness' of the Golden Age, when nature was bountiful, and toil, suffering and pain did not exist; others stress the 'everlastingness' of the Golden Age, the deathlessness of such an existence" *The Origins of Human Consciousness*, (Princeton: Bollingen Foundation, Inc, 1954), 114–115.

stage of the child's evolving consciousness, the image of the mother is not perceived as a separate and independent entity. The mother is seen as an extension of the child's body and consciousness. There is no subject, object, ego, or self; the infant has no individual experience or perceptions, except for the one experience with the mother—one of total connectedness.[1081]

While the child is within the womb, the unborn enjoys the bliss and serenity that may be compared to Paradise. According to Neumann, Adam was like an infant in the womb waiting to be psychologically born. Had he not "sinned," Adam would never have experienced pain or pleasure as we know these experiences; one would be the same as the other. He would have existed in a neutral state, a condition without desire, and a state of being that would embrace the opposites. It could, indeed, be called a state of Paradise or what Joseph Campbell (1904–87) referred to as "bliss." In speaking of the birth trauma as an archetype of transformation, Campbell states:

> In the imagery of mythology and religion this birth (or more often rebirth) theme is extremely prominent; in fact, every threshold passage—not only this from the darkness of the womb to the light of the sun, but also those from childhood to adult life and from the light of the world to whatever mystery of darkness may lie beyond the portal of death—is comparable to a birth and has been ritually represented, practically everywhere, through an imagery of re-entry into the womb.[1082]

The "re-entry into the womb" is what may be identified as a psychological return to the function of intuition, whether it is immediately after birth or in any later experience of transformation. It is a way of returning to the mother while in the world, rather than in the womb, which was the original experience. This particular experience is one of the recurring themes of Genesis as is evident in the *Akedah* of Isaac, and the individuation of Jacob and Joseph. Each crisis they experience becomes a crucible for change and spiritual transformation.

C. Mircea Eliade's View of the Fall: The Emerging Contours of Profane Existence

Mircea Eliade also expands the Paradise story in a way that goes far beyond anything Freud, Jung, and Neumann propose. He asserts that it would be wrong to assume that "religious man" existed only in an infantile state of being; Adam was created with intelligence to manage and take care of the Garden. Archaic man believed he contributed to the maintenance of the cosmos. All his interactions with the inanimate, vegetative, and animal worlds made a cosmic difference. The secular

---

[1081] Erich Neumann, *Narcissism, Normal Self-Formation and the Primary Relation to the Mother* (New York: The Analytical Psychological Club of New York, 1966), 108.

[1082] Joseph Campbell, *Myths to Live By* (New York: Penguin Books 1993), 62.

man, who lives in a purely profane mode of existence, lives only for himself and society. "For him, the cosmos does not properly constitute a cosmos—that is, a living and articulated unity."[1083]

Eliade asserts that the Paradise story characterizes a reality in which Heaven and Earth exist in perfect harmony; it is a place where man could communicate with all of nature. Primordial man lived with a closeness that was full of spontaneity and freedom. He did not see himself as *distinct* from nature; within his being he embraced all the forces of nature of which he considered himself to be a part. However, as a result of the Fall, primordial man's super-consciousness receded into a state of unconsciousness. Adam becomes more of a terrestrial being than a spiritual being—out of touch with his ultimate sense of reality, alienated from God, nature, his wife, and finally, himself.

Memory of the Fall exists in myths of all peoples around the world. Every civilization and culture has regarded the human condition as if it were under a spell of unnatural limitations and separateness. All religions try to correct this through dreams of Utopia and Messianism. Even secular humans yearn to reconnect with the world as their ancestors did. Retreats into the country and mountains away from the urban jungles reflect the deeply rooted yearning of moderns to rediscover the cosmic unity that pervades human existence, albeit unrealistic if not impossible to achieve. With respect to the modern secular consciousness, Eliade writes that a new type of "Fall" has occurred in our world—one where human beings are even more disconnected from the depths of their own beings than ever before:

> From the Christian point of view, it could also be said that nonreligion is equivalent to a new "Fall" of man—in other words, that nonreligious man has lost the capacity to live religion consciously, and hence to understand and assume it; but that, in his deepest being, he still retains a memory of it, as, after the "Fall," his ancestor, the primordial man, retained intelligence enough to enable him to rediscover the traces of God that are still visible in the world. After the first "Fall," the religious sense descended to the level of the "divided consciousness;" now, after the second, it has fallen even further, into the depths of the unconscious, it has been "forgotten."[1084]

D. A Fall Forward—Irenaeus's Novel Insight

Irenaeus of Lyons (ca. 180 C. E.) was the first religious thinker to seriously grapple with the theological implications of the Fall. Unlike Augustine and subsequent Christian thinkers, Irenaeus did not believe that God created humankind in a state of sin. On the

---

[1083] *Mircea Eliade, The Sacred and the Profane* (New York: Harcourt, Brace, and Jovanovich, 1959), 93.

[1084] Mircea Eliade, *The Sacred and the Profane, op. cit.*, 213.

contrary, God created humankind with the *potential* for perfection; He did not create humanity already perfect. Irenaeus first developed his theology based on the two metaphors used in the creation of humanity: *image* and *likeness* (Gen. 1:26). The "image" is the raw material that has the potential for further development into the "likeness." Image and likeness represent two distinct aspects of human nature. Whereas the metaphor *image* refers to the natural qualities in humans (reason, personality, and the like) that make them resemble God, in contrast, *likeness* refers to a human capability of becoming truly God-like. Thus, the goal of creation must be realized through human growth and evolution. Humans must graduate from being mere "creatures of God" to becoming "children of God." The path to eternal life involves a commitment to continuous moral and spiritual development. Creation exists in an essentially unfinished state. It is in the constant process of *evolving* and *becoming*.

John Hick, today's foremost exponent of Irenaean theology, explains that in Irenaeus's schema, the Fall is a parabolic story about our existence as imperfect and immature creatures. As disastrous as the primal Fall was in producing the world's first evicted tenants, the drama also marks the beginning of humanity's moral growth. Without the expulsion from Eden, human individuation would not have been possible. The primal couple does not deliberately set out to be "sinful" but rather, their straying is akin to that of young and ignorant children. Irenaeus stresses that without the ability to choose consciously between good and evil, human beings would be less than human:

> Wherefore he has also had a twofold experience, possessing knowledge of both kinds, that with discipline he may make choice of the better things. But how, if he had no knowledge of the contrary, could he have had instruction in that which is good? For there is thus a surer and an undoubted comprehension of matters submitted to us than the mere surmise arising from an opinion regarding them.
>
> For just as the tongue receives experience of sweet and bitter by means of tasting, and the eye discriminates between black and white by means of vision, and the ear recognizes the distinctions of sounds by hearing; so also does the mind, receiving through the experience of both the knowledge of what is good, become more tenacious of its preservation, by acting in obedience to God; in the first place, casting away, by means of repentance, disobedience, as being something disagreeable and nauseous; and afterwards coming to understand what it really is, that it is contrary to goodness and sweetness, so that the mind may never even attempt to taste disobedience to God. But if any one shuns the knowledge of both these kinds of things, and the twofold perception of knowledge, he unaware *divests himself* of the character of a human being.[1085]

[1085] *ECF*, *Against the Heresies*, Book 4, ch. 39.

In Irenaeus's theology of humanity, God invites our cooperation to grow and become like God, but doing so involves a necessary and painful process of learning. God intends for humans to become beings whose moral character has been formed in part by their own conscious actions: assuming responsibility for what they have done, and what they have become. Only through a historical process of trial and error could humankind evolve to a point of maturity and excellence. The fact that evil exists is necessary for the essential growth of humankind. In terms of theodicy, God could have eliminated evil, but at the price of creating a humanity that is infantilized; indeed, a race of pampered children.

Human perfection can occur only through a process of moral and spiritual growth. Although evil exists in man as a weakness and frailty, it does not represent a defect on the part of God. Temptation, sin, and suffering are necessary conditions if egoistic humans are to become loving persons worthy of life with God. History involves a person-making pedagogy in which the world's rough edges and painful growth are needed if people are to develop virtue and turn freely to a hidden, un-coercive God out of love—and not out of a state of compulsion. History is the testing ground and arena for person-making. Sin serves as the context through which the human personality learns to subordinate that untamed part of itself in the service of God.

It is equally important to point out that historically, Irenaeus was not alone in this matter. Clement of Alexandria (*ca.* 150-215) and Gregory of Nazianzus (*ca.* 329-389) also conceived of Adam as a child-like being, whose perfection would occur at a future time.[1086] These early Christian theologians share Irenaeus's point of view that all human beings were made "to adapt to virtue" through which one could gradually evolve toward perfection.[1087] In another important study, Fr. John Meyendorff emphasizes the viewpoint of the Early Greek Church Fathers, that sin always involves a personal act—and is never, per se, an act of nature. Gregory of Nyssa (335-394) understood the passage in Genesis 1:27, *"God created man in His own image,"* as referring to the creation of humankind as a whole. It is obvious therefore, that the sin of Adam must also be related to all men, just as salvation brought by Christ is

---

[1086] It is interesting to note that Clement of Alexandria (150-215 C.E.) also spoke of an "inherited sin" from Adam, i.e., Adam and Eve's children learn from their parents' poor example. He writes, "Contemplate a little, if agreeable to you, the divine beneficence. The first man, when in Paradise, sported free, because he was the child of God; but when he succumbed to pleasure (for the serpent allegorically signifies pleasure crawling on its belly, earthly wickedness nourished for fuel to the flames), was as a child seduced by lusts, and grew old in disobedience; and by disobeying his Father, he dishonored God" (*Stromata*, Book vi, ch. 11-12). Clement probably would have concurred with contemporary theologians who consider sin to be a sociological phenomenon, and not biologically preordained as Augustine would later assert. Unlike the Gnostics of his era, Clement insisted that the sin of Adam and his posterity was due to the purposeful misuse of his freedom. Conversion, for Clement, occurs when the individual dedicates his life to imitating the life of Christ.

[1087] As noted in John Hick's *Evil and the God of Love* (New York: Harper & Row Publishers, 1977), 215-218.

salvation for all mankind; but neither original sin nor salvation can be realized in an individual's life without involving one's personal responsibility."[1088] The patriarch Photius of Constantinople (who served from 858 to 867) regards the Augustinian belief in "Original Sin" (which he refers to as a "sin of nature") to be nothing short of "heresy."[1089]

What are some important implications for today's world that can be drawn from this discussion with respect to the problem of theodicy? If the Early Greek Church Fathers are indeed correct in maintaining that human sinfulness is not hardwired in human nature per se, but instead it is the consequence of human freedom, then human beings must take complete responsibility for the existence of human-generated evil. Evil serves as an important force in driving humankind to realize its inner potential. Theologian John Hick derives his notion of a "soul making" theodicy from Irenaeus and other ancient Greek Christian theologians. He believes God's purpose in Creation is achieved through the evolution of human consciousness. Virtue is not a quality that can be given *carte blanche*; rather, it must be learned and earned. God is not revealed to us as clearly as, say, the material objects we daily perceive. So it is rationally possible for human beings to disbelieve in God and to organize their lives around the absence of God. "The world," Hick says, "is religiously ambiguous, capable both of being seen as a purely natural phenomenon and of being seen as God's creation and experienced as mediating his Presence."[1090]

The world, with its all of its variegated moral challenges and natural obstructions, was never a paradise, but an appropriate environment for the first stage of a process of development toward the perfection and self-actualization of one's spiritual potential. From this standpoint, the world may be called, as the poet Keats describes, "'The Vale of Soul Making,' then you will find out the use of the world."[1091] The world is, in an important sense, a place where the soul is formed and educated, affording each person the potential to become a spiritually aware individual. Based on this insight, it seems as though God, in His infinite wisdom, arranged everything so that the first parents would have to sin. From this perspective, it would seem that the ultimate trickster of Creation is *not* the serpent, *but God Himself!*

[1088] *De Opif Hom* 16; PG 44:185B.

[1089] John Meyendorff, *Byzantine Theology: Historical Trends and Doctrinal Themes* (New York: Fordham University Press, 1974), 143-145.

[1090] John H. Hick, "An Irenaean Theodicy" in *Encountering Evil: Live Options in Theodicy* (Atlanta, GA: John Knox Press, 1980), 43.

[1091] John Keats: *The Major Works: Including Endymion, the Odes and Selected Letters* (New York: Oxford University Press, 2001), 473.

Excursus 24: The Birth of the "False Self"

Once there was a Dog who had gotten himself a piece of meat and was carrying it home in his mouth to eat it in peace. On his way home, he had to cross a plank lying across a running brook. As he crossed, he looked down and saw his own shadow reflected in the water beneath. Thinking it was another dog with another piece of meat, he made up his mind to have that also. So he made a snap at the shadow in the water, but as he opened his mouth, the piece of meat fell out, dropped into the water and was never seen more.

The moral: Beware lest you lose the substance by grasping at the shadow.

—AESOP'S FABLES, *"Dog and the Shadow"*

In the writings of Thomas Merton (1915–68), the notion of the "false self" is central and many of his insights could prove useful in deciphering our tale. Merton defines the false self as "someone I was never intended to be and therefore a denial of what I am supposed to be." The nature of the false self recognizes the world and everything in it as a series of separate, detached entities estranged from God's love and reality. The more immersed a human being is in the world of ego, the less awakened one is to one's real and authentic self.

According to Merton, the serpent dupes the primal couple into thinking that they are not God-like in their nature, in spite of being created in the Divine image. This point encapsulates the irony of the story. The serpent, then, recognizing its opportunity, takes advantage and proceeds to awaken within Adam and Eve the desire to be that which they are unaware of already being. What emerges in Adam and Eve is a "false self" that appeals to the selfishness of each one's illusory ego.

The serpent is, in a sense, the midwife of the false self. Merton further asserts that what makes the serpent's promise so insidious is that it conveys only a half-truth; it sells us a bag of goods that we already own. "And you will be like God, knowing good and evil" (Gen 3:5). Adam and Eve do not recognize that they are already participants and sharers of God's own divine life. The primal man's desire to become God-like comes naturally because of the divinity that already springs from the core of his being. This divinity is the source of his authentic identity. While humanity possesses the potential to become God-like, it cannot hope to be so without God's help. Becoming God-like cannot occur through usurping God's own transcendental sovereignty. As we, the readers, ponder the existential meaning of this mythic story, we realize that the essence of our soul's identity—which is rooted in God's innermost Being—cannot be seized by our compulsive will-to-power. This soul-essence comes as a gift from God, and we cannot hope to seize it from God's hands as though it belongs solely to us. The serpent's offer to help Adam and Eve become God-like was wrong, since his argument was based upon an ontological lie. Adam and Eve are not the source of their own existence, nor the source of their own fulfillment. Accepting the serpent's lie is to commit spiritual suicide; they cannot cut themselves off from the source of their being without doing grave damage to their souls. In short, the serpent wants Adam and Eve to remain forever alienated beings, out of touch with their own spiritual truth, and condemned to live only the most marginal type of human existence.

The serpent acts forcefully to keep Adam spiritually unconscious of his destiny and potential greatness by appealing to his grandiosity and desire for power. By keeping Adam oblivious to the mystery and depths of his own being, the serpent is determined to prevent Adam from discovering the true purpose of his destiny. As it was with Adam's journey, so it is with each human being. When we "lose" God, we also lose the ground of our own being; hence this becomes the root cause of our spiritual alienation. Each of our lives takes us on a soulful journey where we discover our "true" selves in an effort to discern God. As this process unfolds, we discover God who has been present within our being from the very beginning. Merton insists that our true self subsists on a life that is grounded in God's eternal love; it is only the false self that cannot accept this.

> But whatever is in God is really identical with Him, for his infinite simplicity admits no division and no distinction. Therefore, I cannot hope to find myself anywhere except in Him. Ultimately, the only way I can be myself is to become identified with Him in whom is hidden the reason and fulfillment of my existence. Therefore, there is only one problem on which all my existence, my peace, and my happiness depend: to discover myself in discovering God. If I find Him I will find myself and if I find my true self I will find him. [1092]

Merton claims that man's Promethean defiance of God in the name of self-determination and autonomy of the false self is an illusion. Just as Adam's problem can only be solved through a returning to his true self, the same is no less valid with those of us who understand the existential depth of Adam's personal narrative. His story is ours as well. In our eagerness to become masters of our own being and destiny, we cling to every success like an infant holding on to its security blanket. Life becomes self-centered instead of God-centered. Merton concludes that the primordial event of Adam's Fall continues to live in every act we make in the service of the false self. The belief that the false self exists only for the fulfillment of egocentric pursuits entails living an untruthful existence, not only with oneself, but with the rest of reality as well. On the other hand, the true self represents the highest degree of excellence that we—human beings made in God's image—are capable of realizing. To discover the true self, we must personally embark on a spiritual journey that calls for dedicating our lives to the service of God and the betterment of society.

[1092] Thomas Merton, *New Seeds of Contemplation* (New York: New Directions, 1961), 5.

Each of us must realize why we feel and experience spiritual alienation, imbalance, and anxiety. To find the purpose of our being, we must shed the illusions of separateness and alienation that block our vision from ourselves, from God, and from each other. An altruistic act of love and compassion creates a miniature epiphany that liberates us from the shackles of the ego and the false self. To see and experience this reality marks the beginning of a journey toward human redemption.

Excursus 25: The Greatest Theological Debate of Late Antiquity: Augustine of Hippo vs. the "Judaizing" Pelagius

By his sin, Adam, as the first man, lost the original holiness and justice he had received from God, not only for himself but for all human beings. Adam and Eve transmitted to their descendants human nature wounded by their own first sin and hence deprived of original holiness and justice; this deprivation is called 'Original Sin'. As a result of Original Sin, human nature is weakened in its powers, subject to ignorance, suffering and the domination of death, and inclined to sin (this inclination is called 'concupiscence').

—*Catechism of the Catholic Church*

A. *The Loss of Human Innocence*

It is a pity that most Jewish commentators fail to discuss the traditional Augustinian understanding of the Fall narrative. One of the greatest debates in religious history takes place between Augustine and Pelagius (c. 354–418) over the nature of Adam's Fall.[1093] Briefly stated, Augustine considered the Fall to be so radical that human life nearly lost every trace of pure goodness, resulting in the total corruption of human nature. As another direct consequence of Adam's sin, reason and every other aspect of being have become *totally* depraved. This doctrine of total depravity is not intended to imply that fallen humanity is incapable of good works, but rather that there is no aspect of the human being that is unaffected by sin: "There is," as Karl Barth notes, "no relic or core or goodness which persists in man in spite of his sin."[1094] Given the psychological complexity of human behavior, Augustine claims that even good human actions spring up from elements reflecting pride and self-interest; human behavior is, for all practical purposes, intrinsically tainted with

[1093] Augustine's Anti-Pelagian writings include: *The Merits and Remission of Sins and Infant Baptism; The Spirit and the Letter, Nature and Grace; The Perfection of Human Righteousness; The Grace of Christ and Original Sin, Epistle* 194; *Against Julian* (419–30); see *Marriage and Concupiscence; Against Two Letters of the Pelagians; Against Julian; Unfinished Work against Julian*; and against the misnamed Semi-Pelagian monks of Africa and Gaul (427–30), see *Grace and Free Will, Correction and Grace, Epistle* 217; *The Predestination of the Saints*; and *The Gift of Perseverance*.

[1094] Karl Barth, *Church Dogmatics* Vol. IV.1 (New York: T&T Clark International, 1956), 493.

sin. Among modern Protestant theologians, Wolf Pannenberg similarly argues in defense of the traditional Christian view.

> This, then, is the first and fundamental element in the concept of original sin as opposed to actual sin (sin of act). With it a second is closely connected: the radicalness of sin. Sin is located at a deeper level than the individual act, deeper than any transgression. . . . The idea of original sin as a sinfulness that affects the whole of human existence from birth may be taken as an extreme expression of that Jewish spirit of repentance. At the same time, of course, the idea of original sin breaks through the boundaries of the Jewish religion as a religion of law, since the unconditionality of original sin leaves no room for a human righteousness, unless human beings are first redeemed from their sin. . . . The universality of sin, which is the third and decisive element in the concept of original sin, is a presupposition for the universality of the redemption wrought by Jesus Christ.[1095]

Pannenberg's interpretation of repentance in Judaism falls short of the mark. Nowhere does the Tanakh give any credence or support of human beings sinful by virtue of existing. The root of sin, according to Judaism, is in the intention that produces the deed. Judaism teaches that one must take total responsibility for one's actions. This concept is stressed repeatedly in the book of Leviticus, which prescribes sacrifices for committing unintentional sins. There is no sin-offering that is ever offered in Leviticus made for simply existing. Pannenberg's exegetical remarks are a classic example of eisegetical reasoning.

B. "Original Sin" —The World's First Sexually Transmitted Disease

Antecedents to Augustine's doctrine of "Original Sin" appear in the writings of Paul of Taurus. Sin, for Paul, dominated much of his consciousness. The way of Jewish tradition did not seem adequate enough for purging himself from his chronic condition. In the end, Paul discovers that the power of faith in the resurrected Christ alone could guarantee grace and salvation. From this perspective, salvation no longer requires pious deeds or good works, for human frailty being what it is can never eradicate the human proclivity toward sin. Paul's spiritual anthropology can be seen in 1 Cor. 15:21-2, where he declares that just as physical death came to all by the actions of one man (Adam), the belief in Christ's death as a vicarious atonement undoes Adam's primal sin; therefore, the faithful who accept this sacrifice are deserving of being brought back to life after death. [1096] However, this premise is far from being clear and obvious. It is one thing to say that all humankind suffers for the sin of Adam; ergo, we all suffer death as a

---

[1095] W. Pannenberg, *Anthropology in theological perspective*. Translation of: *Anthropologie in theologischer Perspektive* (London; New York: T&T Clark, 1985), 120.

[1096] Cf. 1 Cor. 15:45–58 and Rom. 5:12–20, Paul sees the fate of all humanity as being trapped in the web of human sinfulness, both individually as well as corporately. Only grace in Christ can bring about salvation from the clutches of Adam's sin.

collective punishment. However, it is quite a conceptual leap to presume that every person is afflicted with some hereditary taint or moral impediment that is genetically transmitted to Adam's descendants because of his transgression. With this background information in mind, it will now be clearer how and where Augustine and Pelagius differ when it comes to interpreting the apostle's words.[1097]

According to Augustine, the story of Genesis 3 is an etiology about the world's very first sexually transmitted disease—Original Sin. Augustine characterizes the essence of Adam's sin as concupiscence (*concupiscentia*), a word used to translate the biblical word for "desire" or "lust," which often connotes a distinctively sexual meaning.[1098] Since humans are born in sin, one remains a helpless sinner—regardless of how righteous one might be—without the possibility of salvation, until that time when Jesus is accepted as one's personal savior. The failure to do so results in the eternal damnation of one's soul. As a support text for his belief, Augustine cites the well-known verse from Romans 5:12: "Therefore, as sin came into the world through one man and death through sin, and so death spread to all men because all men sinned." "In Adam's Fall, we sinned all" (*Early New England Primer*).

It is possible that Augustine's dim view of the human condition grew out of his personal struggles as reflected in his *Confessions*, a spiritual autobiography. Despite several futile attempts to correct his licentious ways, Augustine became convinced that it was impossible to escape sin by mere acts of will. His own moral disease reflects a chronic condition inherited from the fallen Adam. Deliverance from this spiritual bondage is possible only through divine grace irresistibly and compellingly breaking upon him.

C. Augustine's Greatest Critic: Pelagius

One critic of Augustine refused to accept such a pessimistic view of humankind. The

---

[1097] R. N. Flew, *The Idea of Perfection in Christian Theology* (Oxford University Press, 1934), 45. For a comprehensive listing of traditional Christian interpretations on Romans 5:12, see C.E.B. Cranfield, *Romans: A Shorter Commentary* (Grand Rapids, MI: Eerdmans Publishing Co., 1985), 112-15; see A. C. Thiselton, *The First Epistle to the Corinthians: A Commentary on the Greek Text* (Grand Rapids, MI: W.B. Eerdmans, 1224); From First Adam to Last: A Study in Pauline Anthropology (New York: Scribner's Sons, 1962), 15-17; R. Bultmann, *Primitive Christianity in its Contemporary Setting*, trans. R. H. Fuller (New York: Meridian Books, 1956), 46-7.

[1098] Other definitions of concupiscence suggest a different meaning, namely, human sensuality. Choosing temporal pleasures over eternal and spiritual values dim the light of the soul and prevent it becoming more God-like. Aquinas later expanded this idea to basically include any corrupt disposition that results in the soul's disharmony and spiritual deformity, leading to its alienation away from God, or, any wrongful disposition that ultimately clouds a person's faculty of reason (*Summa*, Part 2a Q 6. Art. 7). Protestant theology believes that concupiscence is, in itself, sinful and not merely, as in the Roman Catholic understanding, a disordered inclination that may lead to sin. See W. G. T. Shedd &, A. W. Gomes, *Dogmatic Theology* (Phillipsburg, NJ: P & R Pub, 2003), 953.

Christian monk Pelagius taught his followers that Adam's Fall did not directly affect his posterity at all, nor did the behavior of Adam and Eve spiritually transmit a disease to the human race. The primal parents' sins affected only themselves. Every child born into the world is as Adam was at Creation: entirely innocent; each human being is born with the freedom to choose his or her own path in life.[1099] Pelagius contends that Augustine's doctrine of "sovereign grace" went against the biblical belief that God endowed humanity with natural goodness and free will. Even before the advent of Jesus, there were sinless and righteous human beings, "gospel men before the gospel," such as Noah, Melchizedek, Abraham, and Job.[1100] We owe much of the information we have about Pelagius to his critic Augustine, who preserved the words of his adversary:

> Sin is carried on only by imitation, committed by the will, denounced by reason, manifested by the law, punished by justice. . . . If sin is natural, it is not voluntary; if it is voluntary, it is not inborn. These two definitions are as mutually contrary as are necessity and free will. Adam was created mortal and would have died whether he sinned or not sinned; the sin of Adam injured only him, not the human race; the law leads to the kingdom of Heaven, just as the gospel does; even before the coming of Christ there were men without sin; newborn infants are in the same state which Adam was before his transgression; the whole human race does not die with the death and transgression of Adam, nor does it rise again through the resurrection of Christ. . . . One can be neither praised nor blamed, neither rewarded nor condemned, except for one's own acts and self-acquired character, which must be within the compass of one's ability. What is innate, inherent, or infused is clearly not within the power of the will, and therefore cannot have any moral character.[1101]

For Pelagius, it was wrong to convict the entire human race because of one man's sin. On numerous occasions, Augustine felt that Pelagius's "Judaic"[1102] ideas[1103]

[1099] Like Pelagius before him, Immanuel Kant attacked the old Augustinian and Protestant view of Adam's fall from grace, and said that the belief that sinfulness is passed on to a person's posterity was nothing more than a superstition.

[1100] See Augustine's work *The Merits and Forgiveness of Sins* 1:30, 58; *On the Baptism of Sins* 4:24.31; 51.129.

[1101] Translated by Jaroslav Jan Pelikan, *The Christian Tradition: A History of the Development of Doctrine, Vol. 1 The Emergence of the Catholic Tradition* (100-600) (Chicago: Chicago University Press, 1971), 315. *Cf. Anti-Pelagian Writings* 11:23 published in Vol. V of the *Early Church Fathers Nicene–Post/Nicene Part* I (New York: T. & T. Clark, 1887).

[1102] Aside from some of the other Early Church Fathers, Pelagius's views may have also been shaped by his encounters with rabbinic teachers from the Jewish community as he travelled through the Holy Land before settling in Rome. Jerome, who was also a contemporary of Pelagius, learned Hebrew from a rabbi in Palestine. It would seem that despite the polemically-charged era both faiths lived in, Jewish and Christian scholars exchanged theological views of the Bible in the spirit of fellowship and open-mindedness—millennia before the advent of modern Jewish-Christian interfaith relations.

[1103] Augustine, *ECF* 2.5.0.0.3.3.

threatened to undermine the authority of the Church and the Church's claim that it alone could liberate man from the chains of Original Sin.[1104] However, Pelagius countered that the Bible teaches that nature is good, as God created it to be, and that humankind is morally free to chart its own spiritual destiny, because human beings are fashioned in the likeness of the Divine image. Since every human being derives his or her own essential goodness from God, therefore, no newborn infant deserves to be damned because of Adam's sin. Moral goodness or evil are potentialities that each person can choose to realize. If we act righteously, we become righteous; if wickedly, we become wicked. Numerous Scriptural injunctions—make it perfectly clear that "Parents shall not be put to death for their children, nor shall children be put to death for their parents; only for their own crimes may persons be put to death" (Deut. 24:16). This principle precludes the possibility of innate, hereditary depravity such as Original Sin. The severity of Adam's sin ought to be viewed in terms of the deed's pedagogic effect. In effect, Adam becomes a poor role model for subsequent generations. Human corruption is due to the habit of evil that if left uncorrected, spreads like a contagion. Humans are born without virtue or vice, but have the capacity for either type of behavior.

Pelagius's moral strictness is as exacting as it is demanding; his view of human nature is sober and grounded in reality. According to him, the onus of personal responsibility for all sins, both large and small, is upon each of us as individuals; hence there can be no excuse—not even for the most minor or venial of sins. It behooves everyone to know that sin involves a conscious and preventable defiance of God's will; sin is, in the final analysis, an act of deliberate rebellion against God's sovereignty and wisdom. Pelagius believes that even the smallest infraction—since it could be avoided—carries with it the possibility of eternal punishment.[1105] Pelagius writes that God would never impose duties and responsibilities upon people that they could never possibly hope to fulfill. Without freedom of will, humankind is no better than moral idiots. The obligation to live a moral life is in accordance with individual ability. Deny a person of his freedom and capacity to act rationally, and one might just as well give license to all those who—much like the pre-converted youthful Augustine—behave with reckless abandon. After all, couldn't he just as soon wait to "be saved" from Above after enjoying all of the tasty forbidden pleasures of this world? Why, asks Pelagius, should we bother avoiding the sins of this world if, in the final analysis, moral behavior doesn't really matter—so long as one makes a declaration of faith in Christ? Conversely, Augustine

---

[1104] Luther and Calvin understood original sin as "a hereditary depravity and corruption of our nature" See John Calvin, *Institutes of the Christian Religion,* trans. Henry Beveridge, (Edinburgh 1865, II .i.8). Unlike Augustine, Calvin relates Original Sin not so much to heredity, as to an ordinance of God, a heavenly decree from God passed on all humankind.

[1105] With the exception of the Qumran Jewish community, Saadia Gaon and possibly Ramban, no other major Jewish theologian subscribed to the doctrine of "eternal damnation" or more precisely, "the soul that sins shall be cut off from its people" (Num. 15:30). See Ramban's commentary on Leviticus 18:29.

counters that Pelagianism made the saving work of Christ unnecessary, that it undermined the central drama of the New Testament. Pelagius had made men independent of God in the sense that their salvation was entirely in their own hands.

Although historically Augustine's view became normative theology for the next millennium and longer, still and all, Thomas Aquinas did not fully accept Augustine's dim view of human nature. While it is true that human sinfulness weakens our innate capacity to live virtuously—sin, argues Aquinas, cannot eradicate the fact we are, in the final analysis, rational beings. Our human goodness cannot be fully extinguished. In the case of Adam, Original Sin causes him to lose the special gifts that enable him to sublimate and control his lower bodily functions. Prior to his sin, Adam's rational faculties were perfect. That being said, it is possible that this gift can be restored to us by supernatural grace alone for our human efforts to obtain salvation would always fall short of the divine benchmark. Naturally, reasons Aquinas, this infusion of special grace could never happen without the assistance of the Catholic Church and its rich sacramental system. Aquinas understands the implications of his doctrine, and how he virtually hedges on Pelagian teaching. Without the assistance of the Church, its capacity to function as an intermediary agency would have been undermined; its ecclesiastical ability would not have been able to function.[1106]

Jewish thinkers concur with Pelagius's position that no human being is tainted by the sins of Adam—but only by his own sinful deeds. Human nature was not at all corrupted, nor did a human being become an inherently immoral, "evil" creature, outside the realm of "grace" by merely being born. Each of us, through acts of will, freely decides our moral and spiritual destinies. Even when a person has sinned, that breach in his relationship with God is repairable through sincere penitence. Rather than pointing to human depravity, the rabbis sought to encourage their followers to adopt an optimistic approach, thus awakening the capacity for human goodness. The human instinct for pleasure and power becomes a problem only when it runs amok. There is no inherited predisposition that prevents us from becoming virtuous and pious. Only the quality of our behavior can determine whether the light of the Divine image will ever find its reflection in us.

D. The Subsequent Disciples of Pelagius

While the greater majority of Christian thinkers historically followed in the footsteps of Augustine (e.g., Martin Luther (1483–1546), and John Calvin (1509–64), more and more modern Christian thinkers are starting to doubt the veracity of Augustine's

---

[1106] Thomas Aquinas, *The Basic Writings of St Thomas Aquinas*, ed. A. C. Pegis, 2 vols. ii. (New York: Random House, 1945); *Summa Theologica*, Part 1 Q. 81, Art. 1; Q. 85 Art. 2; Q. 85 Art. 3. See also F. C. Copleston, *Aquinas* (New York: Harmondsworth: Penguin Books, 1982), 156-98.

exegetical reading of "fallenness" in our biblical text. Earlier we mentioned how several of the Hellenistic writers among the early Church Fathers (most notably, Irenaeus, Clement) who, along with Pelagius and Julian of Eclanum, regarded Adam's primal act of disobedience as an evolutionary step toward consciousness and spiritual maturity. The tradition of these early scholars resonates in the thought process of Immanuel Kant and Fredrick Schleiermacher.

Immanuel Kant views Adam and Eve's creation as possessing an original innocence. Due to their innocence, their corruption had to occur through an external source of temptation—the serpent—who represents the mysterious principle of "radical evil". Once evil's existence is introduced into their psyches, their blissful condition vanishes like a dream.T heir Fall catapults the first earthly couple into a state of awakened consciousness, as Paul Tillich later emphasizes. As a parable of the human condition, Kant decided that sinfulness cannot be a hereditary condition which man cannot hope to ever change. Like Pelagius, Kant insists that evil comes directly from the misuse of one's freedom. Since "radical evil" originates in human freedom, reason dictates that it cannot be a genetically inherited condition.[1107] Put in different words: If I have an evil disposition, it is because I freely chose to behave in such an anti-social manner early in my moral development. Once I choose to do evil, the heart of my will becomes corrupt; becoming genuinely good is difficult until I undergo a personal conversion. Therefore, since radical evil involves a deliberate misdirection of the human will, I alone am ultimately responsible for my moral rehabilitation and conversion.

As a thinker of the Enlightenment, Kant also believes that society, as a whole, can change and re-program people who possess these atavistic values or impulses through culture and education. For Kant, striving toward moral perfection offers the only cure for overcoming radical evil. Nevertheless, to achieve this, expunging radical evil requires a deliberate and rational "change of heart" i.e., a reorientation of how one chooses to relate toward others. The key to achieving this new integration occurs through practicing the "categorical imperative." Simply stated, Kant regards the categorical imperative as the universal moral law that teaches: treat all persons as ends and never as a means to an end; recognize the moral worth and dignity of each human being; practice virtue for its own sake without any anticipation of receiving reward from others. With respect to the traditional tenets of the Church and its doctrine of Original Sin, Kant offers a radical re-visioning of Christianity: Jesus did not vicariously atone for humanity's sins. Far from being the great exception to humanity, Jesus, according to Kant, is the example of a person who lived by the categorical imperative for all of his rational decision-making processes.

F. Schleiermacher optimistically claims as well that every individual has an innate capacity to realize a consciousness of God. Were this not the case, human nature would

---

[1107] Immanuel Kant, *Religion within the Limits of Reason Alone* (New York: Harper Torchbook, 1960), Book One.

be flawed by its very design. Since the image of God is, in a manner of speaking, indelibly stamped upon the human soul, this tendency toward God-consciousness can never be lost. Like Kant, Schleiermacher asserts that ultimately, each human being is responsible for his or her own sins.[1108]

Among modern 20th-21st century Christian thinkers, like Claus Westermann,[1109] Walter Brueggemann,[1110] and Terrence Freitheim, categorically reject the Augustinian interpretation as being out of touch with the original intention of the biblical story, and have adopted a much more Judaic understanding of the narrative. Freitheim writes in his commentary:

> The metaphor of "fall" does not do justice to these texts. Traditionally, this metaphor has been used to refer to a fall "down." Others typically emphasize the "becoming like God" theme, where human beings strive for and, indeed, assume God-like powers for themselves. This kind of a fall "up" . . . violates the basic thrust of the metaphor. . . . Such an upward move in the texts has been interpreted positively (at least since Irenaeus) in the sense that human beings move out from under the parental hand of God; they are pioneers on the road to moral autonomy and maturity, a necessary move if they are to become truly human. The position reflects the mounting consciousness of the last few decades that rebellion against the yoke of authority is both an inevitable and a necessary element in human maturation.[1111]

As mentioned earlier, the Catholic theologian Karl Rahner (1904–84), rejects the Augustinian understanding of Original Sin as a condition that is biologically transmitted through Adam and Eve. Moral sinfulness is not something that can be genetically

---

1108 Friedrich Schleiermacher, *The Christian Faith,* ed. H. R. Mackintosh and J. S. Stewart (Edinburgh: T. and T. Clark, 1928), 303.

1109 "The narrative of Gen 2-3 does not speak of a 'Fall,' and these chapters know of no human being before sin" Claus Westermann, *Genesis 1-11: A Commentary* (Minneapolis: Augsburg, 1984), 276.

1110 W. Brueggemann explains, "Frequently, this text is treated as though it were an explanation of *how evil came into the world.* But the Old Testament is never interested in such an abstract issue. In fact, the narrative gives no explanation for evil. There is no hint that the serpent is the embodiment of principle of evil. The Old Testament characteristically is more existential. It is not concerned with origins but with faithful responses and effective coping. The Bible offers no theoretical statement about the origin of evil. And, indeed, where the question of theodicy surfaces, it is handled pastorally and not speculatively . . ."*Genesis: A Bible Commentary for Teaching and Preaching* (Atlanta: John Knox Press, 1982), 41. In his Introduction, Brueggemann claims that Genesis is not interested in myth as a *structure* of reality, but rather "is about a memory that is transformed, criticized, and extended each time it is told" and prefers to speak of Israel's narrative as "story" rather than as "myth." However, that is precisely what "myth" is—a symbolic story about a people's origin and values.

1111 S. Towner, "Interpretations and Reinterpretations of the Fall," *Modern Biblical Scholarship*, ed. F. Eigo (Villanova, PA: Villanova University Press, 1984), 78, cited by Terence E. Fretheim, "Genesis: *New Interpreter's Bible* (Nashville, TN: Abingdon Press, 1994), 367.

inherited. In almost Neo-Pelagian terms, Rahner develops his radical revisioning of Original sin yet further:

> "Original sin" in the Christian sense in no way implies that the original, personal act of freedom of the first person or persons is transmitted to us as our moral quality. In "original sin" the sin of Adam is not imputed to us. Personal guilt from an original act of freedom cannot be transmitted, for it is the existential "no" of personal transcendence towards God or against him. And by its very nature this cannot be transmitted, just as the formal freedom of a subject cannot be transmitted. This freedom is precisely the point where a person is unique and no one can take his place, where he cannot be analyzed away, as it were, either forwards or backwards or into his environment, and in this way, he escapes responsibility for himself. For Catholic theology, therefore, "original sin" in no way means that the moral quality of the actions of the first person or persons is transmitted to us, whether this be through a juridical imputation by God or through some kind of biological heredity, however conceived. In this connection it is obvious that when the word "sin" is used for the personal, evil decision of a subject, and when on the other hand it is applied to a sinful situation which derives from the decision of another, it is being used only in an analogous sense, and not in a univocal sense . . . [1112]

From the Judaic perspective, we applaud Rahner's openness. However, Pelagius is hardly alone in his theological sentiments. Men like Irenaeus of Lyons, Clement of Alexandria, and Gregory of Nazianzus all support an alternative reading of the Fall narrative that differs greatly from that of Augustine. It is also clear from these notable examples that at one time or another, the early Catholic Church possessed a less rigid view regarding the nature and impact of Adam's sin than is now commonly assumed. Great thinkers of the pre-Augustinian era and of the rabbinic community found common ground in one of the most puzzling stories of the Bible. There can be no doubt that the Sages of Judea concur with Pelagius and Julian of Eclanum—sinfulness is not an inherited or biological condition.

In conclusion, as stated earlier in Excursus 23, the metaphor *Awakening,* as opposed to *the Fall* might be better suited to the primal moment when the first couple becomes aware of the freedom God had given them. While it is true they misused their freedom by violating the Divine imperative God had given them, they nevertheless learned that freedom involves making conscious choices. One of the great lessons we may glean from this mythical tale of beginnings is that freedom and personal responsibility are inseparable. Every human act, every moral decision made, no matter how trivial it might seem to us at the time, has an impact on the world around us and reverberates into Infinity.

[1112] Karl Rahner, *Foundations of Christian Faith*, (New York: Herder & Herder, 1982), 111.

Excursus 26: The Serpent as a Psychological Metaphor

> *The greedy thoughts of a man are put into the mouth of an animal as they come from the beast in man.*
>
> —BENNO JACOB on Genesis 3:1

A. The Serpentine Metaphor in Gersonides and Ricoeur

Since the days of Philo of Alexandria, some Jewish thinkers and mystics followed in Philo's allegorical footsteps when commenting on the serpent imagery of Genesis 3. Philo's own words best sums up his personal view of the narrative:

> And these things are not mere fabulous inventions, in which the race of poets and sophists delights, but are rather types shadowing forth some allegorical truth, according to some mystical explanation. And anyone who follows a reasonable train of conjecture will say with great propriety, that the aforesaid serpent is the symbol of pleasure, because in the first place he is destitute of feet, and crawls on his belly with his face downwards.[1113]

With keen psychoanalytical insight, Gersonides (1288–1344) writes that the primordial serpent symbolizes φαντασία (*phantasia*) the "power of the imaginative faculty" of man.[1114] In part, Gersonides utilizes Maimonides' theory of the imagination to clarify his point.[1115] While the imaginative faculty has the ability to recall impressions left by incidents of the past that are no longer present, the imagination also has the ability to override or depart from "normal" laws of reality (more commonly associated with dream states and prophetical or mystical experiences). In light of this theory, the dialogue between Eve and the serpent was really an internal dialogue—not with the serpent—but with her imagination.

Gersonides describes the imaginative faculty as "crafty" because it does not abide by the rule of logic. Moral standards derive from the power of reason. In contrast, the psyche's imaginative faculty entertains all sorts of possibilities, which include the permitted as well as the forbidden.[1116] Eve's inner voice prompted her to approach the

---

[1113] Philo, *On the Creation*, 56:157. For a more exegetical commentary of the Fall narrative in Philo, see his *Questions and Answers on Genesis*, Questions 31-50.

[1114] R. Yaakov Leib Levy, *Gersonides's Commentary on Genesis* (Jerusalem: Mosad HaRav Kook, 1962), 62.

[1115] Maimonides, *Guide* 2:42-44. Later toward the end of the *Guide* (3:51), Maimonides takes a critical view of the imagination. Without it being grounded in knowledge and religious worship, the imagination is prone to distort one's understanding of God. However, the study of metaphysics does not necessarily lead or inspire prayerful worship. See David Hartman's *Maimonides: Torah and Philosophic Quest* (New York: JPS, 1976), 189-190.

[1116] Gersonides writes that the imagination is analogous to a horse or camel, which when left to its own, will go in any direction it desires. The power of rational thought is analogous to the rider, who thoughtfully guides

forbidden tree in an effort to grasp the difference between good and evil. Eve's rational self was reticent to enter uncharted waters, but she succumbed to her curiosity and intuition. Eating from the Tree of Knowledge introduced Adam to the notion of binary opposites, e.g., good and evil, male and female, God and humanity, truth and falseness, obedience and rebellion, desire and fear, and so on.

Similar to the allegorical interpretations of Philo, Maimonides, and Gersonides, Seforno also rejects the literalist approach, regarding the narrative as a psychological parable or metaphor about the power of temptation—symbolized by the serpent. The parable of Adam, Eve, and the serpent presents an etiology about the origin of temptation and its destructive effect that befalls the person who submits to its alluring power. Joseph Albo also interprets the Edenic story allegorically but he regards the tale more as an etiology—a "symbolic allusion to humankind's fortune in this world." In Albo's elucidation, Adam represents nascent humanity; the Garden of Eden—the world; Eve—the physical; the Tree of Life—the Torah (cf. Prov. 3:18); and the serpent—the darker impulses of the evil inclination. God situates Adam in the Garden to convey the drama of his earthly existence and the spiritual forces that pull at his existential being—in the midst of which stands the Tree of Life, symbolizing enlightenment and the observance of God's commandments. Adam's expulsion from Eden contains an allusion to the punishment that will befall Israel, should it disobey the divine proscriptions.[1117]

Abarbanel conjectures that Eve saw the serpent climbing the Tree of Knowledge; she notices that it ate the forbidden fruit and that it did not die. It seemed as if the serpent were saying to her, "Look, I ate the forbidden fruit and I did not die; if you eat the fruit that God has forbidden, you will not die either." The serpent merely provided the context for Eve's eventual rebellion. Abarbanel further suggests that the origin of sin does not emanate from outside of man, but comes from within the depths of man himself. In other words, the test of the fruit was merely a test of obedience; there was nothing inherently significant about this particular tree over another. Among modern Judaic exegetes, Cassuto also follows this rationale, that the entire conversation took place in Eve's mind and that the Torah is dressing the dialogue in the "garb of a parable." Sarna expressed the same idea in his commentary to Genesis.

Among recent Christian theologians, Paul Ricoeur opines, "Eve, then, does not stand for women in the sense of a 'second sex.' Every woman and every man are Adam, and

---

and directs the animal toward his ultimate destination (*Gersonides's Commentary* to Genesis 3:1). Philo too, develops this thought in his famous distinction between the rider and the charioteer. Prudence enables one to take control like a charioteer, but when the human mind thinks foolishly, it has no control over the "reins" of his passions; as a result, he is out of control and headed for a disastrous ending. However, a skilled charioteer knows how to take control of a potentially hazardous situation, and always remains in command (*Agriculture* 70).

[1117] *Sefer ha-Ikkarim*, 1:11.

every man and every woman are Eve; every woman sins 'in' Adam and every man is seduced 'in' Eve . . ."[1118] However, unlike the Judaic views cited above, Ricoeur immediately cautions his reader not to assume that the story is purely psychological in character. The biblical narrator wishes to intimate that evil's existence derives from an order that is "wholly Other" than humankind, and therefore, exists "outside of man." He explains further, "This reduction of the serpent to a part of ourselves does not, perhaps, exhaust the symbol of the serpent. The serpent is not only the projection of man's seduction by himself, not only our animal nature goaded by interdictions, maddened by the vertigo of infinity, corrupted by the preference each man gives to himself and to that in which he differs from others, beguiling his human nature . . ."[1119] As Ricoeur claims, the serpent has a different ontology from humankind—one that does not originate from *within* him, but from *beyond* him, "Thus the serpent symbolizes something of man and something of the world, a side of the microcosm and a side of the macrocosm, the chaos *in* me, *among* us, and *outside*. But it is always chaos for me, a human existent destined for goodness and happiness."[1120]

B. *A Jungian Approach to the "Fall"*

Expanding on the story of the Fall, Jung explores this motif in light of his theories pertaining to analytical and depth psychology. Jung regards the narrative of Genesis 3 as a drama that occurs within the soul of every human being. Within the soul's inner structure exists an unconscious aspect of our human nature, which contains our unwanted tendencies and unrealized potentials. Often we are unaware of this aspect of our nature, or we may actively try to disown it. Nevertheless, it stays with us like a shadow; in fact, Jung refers to this archetype of the soul as "the Shadow." In simple terms, the Shadow persona represents the inferior and primitive side of man's nature, the "other person" that a person consciously wishes to hide.

Thus, the snake symbolically represents what is essentially a hidden part of Adam and Eve's personalities that was unconsciously looking for expression. Had Adam and Eve not already been endowed with the Shadow *persona*, the primal couple would never have given in to temptation. This does not make the serpent archetype synonymous with evil; like any other animal of the garden, the serpent is just being true to its wild, unbridled nature. In psychological terms, the serpent represents the part of the human being that is untamed and true to its basic instincts. Jung actually goes one step further and reasons that the antinomy of humankind, "reflects the inner instability of YHWH . . . and is the prime cause not only of the creation of the world, but also of the

---

[1118] Paul Ricoeur, *The Symbolism of Evil* (Boston: Beacon Press, 1967), 255.

[1119] Ibid., 257.

[1120] Ibid., 258.

pleromatic drama for which mankind serves as a tragic chorus." [1121] From the Jungian perspective, the Serpent paradoxically represents the hidden aspect of the Divine that strives for individuation and realization. From a Maimonidean perspective, this type of interpretation might seem to border upon the idolatrous since it presumes that God is in made in the human image, when in reality it is the exact opposite. However, God's "individuation" appears to have ample support in rabbinical and mystical writings.

C. *Two Tales of Temptation: Adam and Job*

The Edenic temptation of Adam and Eve invites a comparison to another well known biblical narrative—the temptation of Job. Indeed, there are a number of intriguing parallels that are striking. Unlike the serpent of Eden that acts in cross-purpose to YHWH, in the Jobian narrative YHWH essentially partners with Satan and allows him to tempt and torture the pious Job. Satan creates the circumstances that will soon push Job to the limits of his faith. Like the serpent of Eden, the satanic angel of Job plays an important role in Job's spiritual evolution and faith development. Whereas Adam is tempted to eat the forbidden fruit, Job is tempted to curse God—which he resists. Ultimately, Job's character is changed as a result of his experience with the "dark night of the soul." Despite enduring ordeal after ordeal, Job experiences God completely anew—up close and personal—unlike his relationship with God in his former prosperous life. Like Adam and later Jacob, Job's encounter with darkness ultimately transforms him for the better—he moves from a person who is unconscious of his spiritual potential, to becoming a self-actualizing human being capable of consciously enjoying his relationship with the Divine.

Excursus 27: Why Did God Create Evil – A Parable from the Zohar

The fact that evil confronts good, gives man the possibility of victory.

—R. YEHIEL MICHAEL OF ZLOTSHOV, *Hassidic Aphorism*

Let us assume for a moment that the rabbis and the allegorical school are correct in identifying the serpent as a metaphor for the evil inclination. But why did God create the impulse for evil? Would humankind have been better off not having to deal with such an urge? The Zohar raises this question, and offers the reader a most intriguing thought-provoking response with respect to the phenomena of moral evil.[1122]

[1121] C.G. Jung, *Answer to Job* (Princeton: Princeton University Press, 1954), 66.

[1122] For more information regarding the relationship concerning natural evil and God, see my notes on Genesis 1:2.

Should it be asked, "How can a man love Him with the evil inclination? Is not the evil inclination the seducer, preventing man from approaching the Blessed Holy One to serve him? How, then, can man use the evil inclination as an instrument of love for God?" The answer lies in this, that there can be no greater service done to the Holy One than to bring into subjection the "evil inclination" by the power of love to the Holy One, blessed be He. For, when it is subdued and its power broken by man in this way, then he becomes a true lover of the Holy One, since he has learned how to make the "evil inclination" itself serve the Holy One. Here is a mystery entrusted to the masters of esoteric lore. All that the Holy One has made, both above and below, is for the purpose of manifesting His Glory and to make all things serve Him. Now, would a master permit his servant to work against him, and to continually lay plans to counteract his will? It is the will of the Holy One that men should worship Him and walk in the way of truth that they may be rewarded with many benefits. How, then, can an evil servant come and counteract the will of his Master by tempting man to walk in an evil way, seducing him from the good way and causing him to disobey the will of his Lord? But, indeed, the "evil inclination" also does through this the will of its Lord.

It is as if a king had an only son whom he dearly loved, and just for that cause he warned him not to be enticed by bad women, saying that anyone defiled might not enter his palace. The son promised his father to do his will in love. Outside the palace, however, there lived a beautiful harlot. After a while the King thought: "I will see how far my son is devoted to me." So he sent to the woman and commanded her, saying: "Entice my son, for I wish to test his obedience to my will." So she used every trick in her book to lure him into her embraces. But the son, being good, obeyed the commandment of his father. He refused her allurements and thrust her from him. Then did the father rejoice exceedingly, and, bringing him in to the innermost chamber of the palace, bestowed upon him gifts from his best treasures, and showed him every honor. And who was the cause of all this joy? The harlot! Is she to be praised or blamed for it? To be praised, surely, on all accounts, for on the one hand she fulfilled the king's command and carried out his plans for him, and on the other hand she caused the son to receive all the good gifts and deepened the king's love to his son.[1123]

The Zoharic passage illustrates a remarkable concept that exists in many of the primal religions of the world, the notion of the *coincidentia oppositorum,* also known as "the reunion of opposites." As Eliade has already noted, the lost memory of this unitive existence with reality emanates from a part of humanity that yearns to overcome th duality and opposites we now experience in a post-Fallen world. He adds that "on the level of presystematic thought, the mystery of totality embodies man's endeavor to reach a perspective in which the contraries are abolished, the Spirit of Evil reveals itself as a stimulant for the Good . . ."[1124]

1123 Zohar 2:162b–163a (all translations of the Zohar are from the Soncino translation).

1124 Mircea Eliade, *The Two and the One* (Chicago: University of Chicago Press, 1965), 123.

Excursus 28: Intimations of "Original Sin" in Early Rabbinic Sources

In woman was sin's beginning,
and because of her we all die.
Allow water no outlet,
and be not indulgent to an erring wife.
If she walks not by your side,
cut her away from you.
—Sirach 25:24

If God created the evil inclination, He also created the Torah as its antidote.
—BT Bava Bathra 16a

The Talmud records a number of conversions that took place between "Antoninus" (believed by the rabbis to be the Roman Emperor Marcus Aurelius) and Judah HaNasi (the redactor of the Mishnah), one of which focused on the question of pre-natal sin:

> Antoninus also enquired of Rabbi, "From what time does the Evil Inclination take hold over person? Is it from the time of the embryo's formation or is it from the time of its birth?" He replied, "From the time of formation." Antonius countered, "If the Evil Inclination began with the formation of the embryo, then the babe would kick in the womb and break its way out! Rather, it must be from the time of its birth." Rabbi Judah admitted, "There is Scriptural support for Antoninus's view, "Sin is couching at the door in wait" (Gen. 4:7), i.e., at the womb where the babe enters into the world.[1125]

It is interesting to compare this passage to the gospel of John 9:1-3 where a similar discussion takes place between Jesus and his disciples:

> As Jesus was passing by, he saw a man who was blind from the day of his birth. "Rabbi," his disciples said to him, "who was it who sinned that he was born blind–this man or his parents?" "It was neither he nor his parents who sinned," answered Jesus, "but it happened that in him there might be a demonstration of what God can do.

Talmudic wisdom records an aphorism that most likely has its roots in antiquity: "There is no death without sin and there is no suffering without iniquity" (BT Shabbat 55a). The subject of pre-natal sin appears to have been widely discussed in Late Antiquity. The NT discussion may very well reflect the kind of theological discussions heard in the 1st century. The statement in John could be read as a condemnation of original sinfulness. Each human being is born with the capacity to transcend one's natural limitations. However, in terms of Jewish folk-beliefs, it is clear that some Jews of that era thought that being born blind or deaf might have been due to the sins of a past life. Others attributed the physical impairment to the sins of the parents as possibly alluded to in Exodus 20:5. However, Ezekiel 18:20 categorically rejects such a notion

---

[1125] BT Sanhedrin 91b. For a variant reading, see Genesis Rabbah 34:11.

and the teachings of Jesus are in harmony with that latter passage. Some Midrashic texts on Genesis 25:22 suggest that the tendency toward evil is a pre-natal condition. The struggle of Jacob and Esau began while they were still inside their mother's womb; the rabbis understood Rebecca's pregnancy difficulties to be a portent of the archetypal struggle between the forces of good and evil that were raging within her.[1126]

It is important to note that Judaism for the most part, never spoke of the experience in Eden in the Christian sense as an "Original Sin." However, a few medieval thinkers tried to modify the Christian concept and re-interpret it from a Judaic perspective. Representative of this opinion is the Zohar, which states that as a consequence of Adam's transgressions, "all men are under the influence of the *yetser hara* (evil impulse)."[1127] Some of the Talmudists were also of the same opinion.[1128] In another rabbinic tradition Eve's name, *Havvah,* is linked with the Aramaic word for "serpent" חִיוְיָא (*ḥ'iyuwwāh*).[1129] This Midrashic correlation indicates that the first sin involved the acquisition of sexual knowledge.[1130] A different Midrashic text suggests that Sammael (Satan) was riding on the serpent, (i.e., utilizing the serpent) when he seduced Eve, so that her firstborn, Cain, the first murderer, was literally the son of the devil.[1131]

[1126] Commenting on the verse "וַיִּתְרֹצְצוּ הַבָּנִים בְּקִרְבָּהּ "And the children struggled together within her" (Gen. 22:6), the Midrash reads:

> R. Johanan said: Each ran to "slay" the other [the root רָצַץ (*rāṣaṣ*) means to "crush," or "oppress"]; Some interpret וַיִּתְרֹצְצוּ as an expression of רוּץ (*rûṣ*) "running." When she passed by the entrances of the Torah academies of Shem and Eber, Jacob would run and struggle to come out; when she passed the entrance of a pagan shrine, Esau would run and struggle to come out (Genesis Rabbah 63:6).

However in a contrasting Midrash, it is clear that some of the Sages felt that no person is shackled by pre-natal sinfulness.

[1127] "R. Abba replied: 'If Adam had not sinned, he would not have begotten children from the side of the evil inclination, but he would have borne offspring from the side of the Holy Spirit. But now, since all the children of men are born from the side of the evil inclination, they have no permanence and are but short-lived, because there is in them an element of the 'other side'" (Zohar 1:61a).

[1128] "R. Johanan said, 'When the serpent came unto Eve, he infused filthy lust into her. If that be so [the same should apply] also to Israel! When Israel stood at Sinai that lust was eliminated, but the lust of idolaters, who did not stand at Sinai, did not cease'" (BT Avodah Zara 22b).

[1129] A version of the Jerusalem Targum actually translates Gen 3:20 as "And Adam called the name of his wife Chavah (Eve) who he named after the snake חִיוְיָא (*ḥeyuwwāh* = "snake"). See R. Menachem Kasher, *Torah Shelemah* 24:214 and *Abarbanel's Commentary* on the Torah 1:102-103.

[1130] Ibn Ezra, Kimchi, and Ramban also regarded Adam and Eve's change in purely sexual terms, see notes on 3:7.

[1131] *Pirkê de Rabbi Eliezer* 21.

There are occasional Midrashic and Talmudic passages that portray another variant of the Christian doctrine of Original Sin. While the rabbis never viewed women as inferior beings, most of the rabbis believed that all women born after Eve must bear the responsibility to undo the harm caused by her; i.e. for introducing death to the world. Rashi points out in his commentary to Shabbat 32a that the failure for a woman to observe the three precepts regarding family purity, taking *ḥallah* for the priests, and lighting the Shabbat candles, could result in tragedy for that particular woman! Thus we read:

> Why does a man go out bareheaded while a woman goes out with her head covered? She is like one who has done wrong and is ashamed of people; therefore, she goes out with her head covered.

In other words, the woman covers her head as a symbol of submission to her husband because of Eve's sin. In attempting to explain why certain communities have the custom of having the women walk in front of the corpse:

> Why do they [the women] walk in front of the corpse [at a funeral]? Because they [women] brought death into the world, they therefore walk in front of the corpse, [as it is written], for he is borne to the grave . . . and all the men draw after him, as there were innumerable before him (Job 21:32).
>
> And why was the precept of menstruation given to her? In a sense, she shed the blood of Adam by causing death, therefore was the precept of menstruation given to her. And why was the precept of taking off "dough" given to her? Because of the fact she corrupted Adam, who was like the "dough" (*ḥallah*) of the world. For this reason she was the precept of dough given to her. And why was the precept of the Sabbath lights given to her? She was responsible for having extinguished the soul of Adam by introducing death to the world. Therefore, it was apropos that the precept of the Sabbath lights given to her.[1132]

Rabbinic commentaries stress that although the human capacity for evil is present from the moment of birth, this does not mean that a human being is compelled to sin. God explicitly told Cain that he can control his natural destructive impulses. Sinfulness is not a given; each human being can make a conscious choice to behave morally. The second century rabbinic sage Rabbi Akiba said, "Although everything is foreseen by God, God has given us free will." Other rabbis adopted R. Akiba's approach that circumcision can overcome the affects of the Fall.[1133] In yet

---

[1132] Gen. Rabbah 17:8, J. T. Shabbat 20a.

[1133] Genesis Rabbah 21:9. Among medieval Jewish thinkers, Hasdai Crescas accepted the notion of original sin, but argued that all *mitzvot* are means of redemption from the "poison" injected into Eve by the serpent (*Or Adonai*, 2:26).

another place, Rabbi Yochanan remarks that the Torah, a spiritual guide, *is* the Tree of Life that can undo the damage of the Fall.[1134] One of the more descriptive Talmudic passages underscores this point:

> R. Simeon b. Levi said, "Man's Evil Desire gathers strength against him daily and seeks to slay him, for it is said: 'The wicked lie in wait for the righteous, seeking their very lives' (Psa. 37:32). Were it not for the Blessed Holy One, he would never be able to prevail against him, for it is said, 'but the LORD will not leave them in their power or let them be condemned when brought to trial' (Psa. 37:33)."
>
> The School of R. Ishmael taught: "My son, if the Repulsive One should assault you, lead him to the House of Study: if he is of stone, he will dissolve; if iron, he will shiver into fragments, for it is said: 'Is not my word like fire,' declares the LORD, 'and like a hammer shattering rocks?' (Jer. 23:29); If he is of stone, he will dissolve, for it is written, 'Come, all you who are thirsty, come to the waters; and it is said: as water wears away the soil of the land' (Job 14:19)."[1135]

One of the most complex doctrines of ancient rabbinic psychology is the doctrine of the two impulses—*yetser hara* and the *yetser tov* ("the urge to do good"). The former they describe as man's natural self and is often associated with the human heart that is the seat of desire. The *yetser hara* is always present in one's thoughts. At worst, the evil inclination can create great evil in the world; on the other hand, it can be a great ally in the service of God.

The Torah represents the archetypal "tree of life" that can tame and redirect the primal energies of the soul to perform the will of the Divine. As mentioned earlier, "Were it not for the evil inclination, nobody would build a house, marry and beget children."[1136] Libido, ambition, desire, and everything else that makes us "human," has a potential of serving a divine purpose in God's plan for creation. In rabbinic literature, life is viewed as a constant struggle, not so much to destroy the impulse for evil as to transform it into a force of goodness. The Sages declare that one must love God with all of one's heart (Deut. 6:4), implying even with the darker elements of the evil inclination.[1137] Thus to love God with all your heart means to love God even as we struggle with our darker impulses and thoughts. This seemingly

---

[1134] Midrash HaGadol on Genesis 3:24.

[1135] BT Kiddushin, 30b.

[1136] Genesis Rabbah 9:7. Other sources include Ecclesiastes Rabbah 3:15; Midrash Tehillim (S. Buber ed.) 9; Yalkut Shimoni Parshat Bereshit 16.

[1137] Rashi writes on Deut. 6:4 "Love Him with your two inclinations, i.e., the good and the evil (cf. Tosefta to Tractate Berakhot 6:7[Liberman Edition]; Sifrei 32; BT Berakhot 54a; Midrash Tennaim on Deuteronomy 6:5 *et al*). Another interpretative view; "with all your heart" implies that your heart should not be divided (i.e., at odds) with the Omnipresent" (Sifrei 32).

paradoxical prescription might seem odd on the surface, but in all honesty, it is quite simple. By learning to say no to our desire to do harm or act in a way that is callous or inconsiderate, we serve God with our whole heart. Domesticating the savage urges from within requires that one consciously serve God with every ounce of our being and energy. The gift of Torah provides an antidote to human pride and sinfulness; the ethos of Torah provides a blueprint for how we can achieve a sense of balance and harmony in our physical, emotional, and spiritual lives.

Excursus 29: The Curse of Eve: Con-versing with Paul of Tarsus on Genesis 3:16

Paul is the eternal enemy of women.

—George Bernard Shaw

Unlike the egalitarianism taught by Jesus in the Gospels, Paul appears to have taken a different kind of approach. One could argue that Jesus's teaching regarding male and female relations is more consistent with the Edenic world that existed before the Fall, whereas Paul's theological view of marriage appears to focus more on a "Fallen" condition of the world. For instance, in Paul's letter to the Christians of Ephesus, he exclaims, "Wives, submit yourselves to your own husbands, as to the Lord, for the husband is the head of the wife, as Christ also is the Head of the Church" (Ephes. 5:22-23).

Modern Christian interpreters are quick to point out that the language used is not quite as harsh in the Greek translation as it appears in most English translations. For example, the Greek term Paul uses for "head" is κεφαλή *(kephale)* and not ἄρχων *(archon),* which would connote more the idea of a ruler, commander, chief, or leader. That is to say, Paul does not wish to suggest that a man should rule like a tyrant or a dictator, but more as a benevolent monarch, whose leadership depends upon the consent of the governed; i.e., the wife.[1138] Nor does Paul seem to insist that a woman be submissive for no other reason than her just being female—a view Josephus himself heartily endorses.[1139] In fairness to Paul, he does encourage that a husband love his wife to the point of even sacrificing his life for hers (v. 25). However, other Pauline statements regarding the husband/wife relationship remain problematic. Elsewhere Paul asserts that the reason why a woman must cover her head is to show her subservience to her husband—whereas for men, it is exactly the opposite:

[1138] W. L. Liefeld, *Vol. 10: Ephesians: The IVP New Testament Commentary Series* (Downers Grove, Il: InterVarsity Press, 1997), 143.

[1139] See Josephus's *Against Apion* 2:24:199.

> A man, on the other hand, should not cover his head, because he is the image and glory of God, but woman is the glory of man. For man did not come from woman, but woman from man; nor was man created for woman, but woman for man; for this reason a woman should have a sign of authority on her head . . . (1 Corinthians 11:7-9).

Paul makes a similar point also in the Book of Timothy, when he once again exhorts, "Let the woman learn in silence with all subjection. But I suffer not a woman to teach, nor to usurp authority over the man, but to be in silence. For Adam was first formed, then Eve. And Adam was not deceived, but the woman being deceived was in the transgression" (1 Timothy 1:11-14). One may argue that Paul's comments ought to be v iewed within the cultural context of his time. There is ample evidence that a number of early rabbinic teachers also took a dim view of women assuming a position of power and authority over men. In one Mishnah, we find: "Rabbi Eliezer says: 'Anyone who teaches his daughter Torah teaches her lewdness.' Rabbi Joshua says: 'A woman prefers one measure of lewdness to nine measures of separation.'"[1140] Despite the fact that the Sages did not follow R. Eliezer ben Hyrcanus because of his excommunicated status[1141], medieval Halachic scholars like Maimonides felt that R. Eliezer's opinion is indeed correct—a man should not instruct his daughter Torah.[1142] In a patriarchal governed society, knowledge represented both status and power, and those in power remained determined to maintain the patriarchal order at all costs.[1143] Even presently there are a number of Orthodox Halachic scholars who still eschew teaching women Talmud—but this trend is now starting to change within more Modern Orthodox communities in accordance with the Mishnaic view of Ben Azzai, who asserted that a father has a duty to teach his daughter Torah.[1144]

[1140] Mishnah Sotah 3:4.

[1141] BT Bava Metzia, 59b; JT Mo'ed Katan, iii. 81a.

[1142] Cf. the various statements attributed to R. Eliezer ben Hyrcanus BT Sotah 20a, 21b and JT Sotah 3: 16a.

[1143] A question was once posed to R. Moshe Feinstein as to whether the widow of a former kashrut supervisor could function in her husband's place as a kashrut supervisor. Since such a position was generally reserved for men, some feared that allowing a woman to work in this capacity might undermine the biblical and rabbinic law: "You will set a king over you" (Deut. 17:14)—the verse specifies only a king—and not a queen! (*Sifre Deut.* 157). R. Moshe Feinstein R. Moshe Feinstein reasoned that if a woman is religiously trustworthy and competent, she could assume any public office short of the monarchy (Pardes, 1960). (*Pardes*, 1960).

[1144] Maimonides writes in his MT *Hilchot Talmud Torah* 1:13:

> A woman who learned Torah is rewarded, although not as much as a man is. The reason is that she was not commanded to do so, and one who does something while not commanded to is not rewarded as much as one who was commanded and carried it out, but is rewarded less. Although she is rewarded, the Sages commanded (*tzivu*) that a father should not teach his daughter Torah, because most women are not oriented to learn but rather transform Torah discussions into trivia due to the poverty of their intellect. The Sages said, "Anyone who teaches his daughter Torah is as if he has taught her *tiflut* (frivolity)." What does this apply to? This applies to the Oral Torah (i.e., the Talmud). However, concerning the study of the Written Torah, he should not teach it to her from the outset

It is important to note that Judaism never denied the prophetic office to women; Miriam, Deborah, and Huldah are three strong examples of women who functioned as spiritual leaders of ancient Israel. While some Christian denominations do not ordain women for this particular reason, the greater number of modern Christian denominations no longer subscribe to a literal reading of these Pauline texts.

Excursus 30: Eden and Jerusalem: A Paradigm of Sacred Space

Emblazoned over the final chapter is the proclamation that in the end of days, "the LORD shall be king over all the earth; in that day there shall be one LORD with one name" (14:9). What was only hinted at earlier now becomes explicit: Jerusalem is and will be proclaimed the center of all the earth, and its Temple will be a fount of blessing and healing waters for all. In a world utterly transformed, the essential holiness and purity of the shrine will affect all pilgrims. Even the bells of the horses will be like objects of priestly purity; even metal pots will be holy vessels for the meat of those who come to Jerusalem for sacrificial worship.

—MICHAEL FISHBANE, *Commentary on Zechariah 14:9*

Jon D. Levenson writes about the close relationship of the Temple to Edenic space in his book, *Sinai and Zion: An Entry into the Jewish Bible*. According to him, the prophet Ezekiel conceives of Zion as the "navel of the world," that functions as the locus between God and humankind. In the mythic imagination of the biblical writers, Zion and Eden are intimately connected (cf. Eze. 28:13-14), as one Midrash depicts:

> Just as the belly-button is positioned in the center of a man, thus is the Land of Israel positioned in the center of the world, as the Bible says, "dwelling at the very navel of the earth (Eze. 32:12), and from it the foundation of the world proceeds. . . . And Jerusalem is in the center of the Land of Israel, and the Temple is the center of Jerusalem, and the Great Hall is the center of the Temple, and the Ark is the center of the Great Hall, and the Foundation

---

(*lekhat'hila*), however, if he already taught her, it is not as if he taught her *tiflut*.

For an example of how a Modern Orthodox Halachic authority reinterprets this controversial ruling, see Rabbi Yehuda Henkin, *She'elot uTeshuvot B'nei Banim, Vol. 3, 12:14, Marcheshvan 5752 "Teshuvot on Women's Issues,"* 2002 http://www.nishmat.net/article.php?id=7&heading=0.

Stone is in front of the Ark, and beginning with it, the word was put on its foundation (*Tanhuma, Kedoshim* 10).[1145]

The Qumran literature and pseudepigraphal writings (cf. Jubilees 3ff.) concur with some early rabbinic sources equating the Garden of Eden with a prefiguration of the Temple.[1146] This view was also shared by an early church father, Ephrem the Syrian (306-373). In his *Hymns on Paradise,* Ephrem explains that Adam lived a very priest-like existence. Subsequently, Adam's prohibition concerning the forbidden tree parallels the priestly restriction of approaching the Holy of Holies (Lev. 162ff.). As such, the Tree of Knowledge separates the outer court of the Edenic paradise from the inner court—the place where the Tree of Life stands. Just as the sanctuary curtain conceals the Holy of Holies, The Tree of Knowledge veils The Tree of Life. Sabastian Brook summarizes Ephrem's midrashic exposition:

> The Paradise Hymns provide us with a number of topographical details which, taken together, can give us some idea of how St. Ephrem conceptualized this Paradisical mountain. We learn that the mountain is circular (I.8) and that it encircles the "Great Sea" (II.6), enclosing both land and sea (I.8-9). The Flood reached only its foothills (I.4), and on these foothills is situated the "fence" or "barrier" (*syaga*), guarded by the Cherub with the revolving sword (II.7, IV.1, based on Genesis 3:24). This fence demarcates the lowest extremity of Paradise. Halfway up is the Tree of Knowledge, which provides an internal boundary beyond and higher than which Adam and Eve were forbidden to go (III.3); this Tree acts as a sanctuary curtain hiding the Holy of Holies, which is the Tree of Life higher up (III.2). On the summit of the mountain resides the Divine Presence, the Shekhina (Syriac *shkinta*).[1147]

[1145] Jon D. Levenson, *Sinai and Zion: An Entry into the Jewish Bible, op. cit.*, 118.

[1146] The Qumran Halacha expert Joseph M. Baumgarten asserts that the Garden of Eden could only be understood in light of the cultic laws governing the Tabernacle. According to *Jubilees* 3, both Adam and Eve are prohibited from eating any fruit of the garden until they have undergone a purification period and wait 40 or 80 days respectively (Cf. *Jub.* 3.12; 1QH[a] 16.10–13) in keeping with the laws specified in Leviticus 12:4-5 (See J.M. Baumgarten, "Purification after Childbirth and the Sacred Garden in 4Q265 and Jubilees" in G.J. Brooke with F. García Martínez (eds.), *New Qumran Texts and Studies: Proceedings of the First Meeting of the International Organization for Qumran Studies, Paris 1992* (STDJ, 15; Leiden: E.J. Brill), 3-10.

The theological implications with respect to the Christian belief in "Original Sin" are especially significant. This teaching appears to derive from Judaic sources dating back to the intertestamental period. As one scholar notes, "Similarly, the Damascus Document suggests that the child will become impure through nursing, which it forbids during the mother's impurity (4Q266 6 ii 11). Scripture explicitly refers only to the mother's impurity (Lev. 12:4–5; but cf. Luke 2:22). A theological principle found in other Qumran texts may be surfacing here as well: humanity is born in an impure condition, coming into the world brings impurity (*even for Adam and Eve*) (cf. 1QH 9.22; 1QS 9.9–10)" cited from H. K. Harrington, *Vol. 5: The Purity Texts. Companion to the Qumran Scrolls* (London; New York: T&T Clark, 2004), 62. Cf. G. J. Brooke, '4Q500 1 and the Use of Scripture in the Parable of the Vineyard', *DSD* 2 (1995), 275–9 and Paul Swarup, *The Self-understanding of the Dead Sea Scrolls Community* (New York: Continuum, 2006), 62-66.

[1147] Ephrem the Syrian and Sebastian P. Brock (trans.), *Hymns on Paradise*, (Crestwood, NY: St. Vladimir's

Interestingly, Ephrem believes that Adam and Eve were unaware of the Tree of Life since it was concealed by the Tree of Knowledge. God purposely hid it for two reasons:

> God had created the Tree of Life and hidden it from Adam and Eve, first, so that it should not, with its beauty, stir up conflict with them and so double their struggle, and also because it was inappropriate that they should be observant of the commandment of Him who cannot be seen for the sake of a reward that was before their eyes.[1148]

In the final analysis, argues Ephrem, God's commandments must be observed for their own sake and not be observed for the sake of receiving a reward. Once Adam sins, he becomes like someone who violates the sacred space of the Sanctuary.[1149]

Among modern scholars, Jacob Neusner also develops this cultic connection between Eden and the Temple of ancient Israel. According to him, Adam's expulsion from Eden contains a paradigm of ramifications that pertain to the cultic legislation found in the other books of the Torah:

> Death is the outcome of the tragedy of Eden. In invisible form death effects uncleanness, which brings about exclusion from what is sacred. In the context of the temple and household, that means removal of person or object from what is to be kept cultically clean and ready (in the temple) to be sanctified. In tangible form, death is represented by such principal sources of uncleanness as the corpse, on the one side, and the gentile, on the other.[1150] The elaborate system of cultic cleanness put forth by the Halakhah of the Mishnah-Tosefta (not much amplified by the

---

Seminary Press, 1997), 52.

[1148] Ephrem the Syrian, *op. cit.*, 60.

[1149] *Hymns on Paradise*, *op. cit.*, 53-60.

[1150] Contrary to Neusner's assertion, there is nothing intrinsic in gentiles that would convey impurity by virtue of them being gentiles per se, rather their cultic impurity is caused by certain activities that render them impure, e.g., touching corpses, sexual intercourse with a menstruant, someone who wore animal skins from impure animals. By the same token, if a person suffered from gonorrhea, or was involved in the cult of idolatry, or ate an animal that died on its own, he or she contracts cultic impurity; however, vegans would not be included since their dietary behavior poses no such cultic problem. The Austrian rabbi and theologian A. Büchler (1867-1939), wrote extensively on this topic and has demonstrated that the Levitical impurity of a gentile did not exist in Judaic practice until the time that preceded the destruction of the Temple in 70 C.E. Its purpose was purely political since Rome and her allies were at war with Judea. The Israeli historian, Gedaliah Alon (1890-1950), argues with Büchler's position and maintains that (1) the tradition of levitical "uncleanness" is fairly ancient (2) the primary basis for the gentile's levitical impurity is due to their worship of paganism (3) there was a dispute regarding whether or not such a ruling should be applied; yet, there can be no denying that there is an ancient basis to this law which is carried out in conversion ceremonies involving ritual immersion in a mikveh (4) the aim of this legislation is to minimize Jewish-gentile relations. Admittedly, the law was never "fixed," and Jews continued to have business dealings with their gentile neighbors long after these laws were promulgated. See *Jews, Judaism and the Classical World* (Jerusalem Magnes Press, reprinted in 1977), 146-189.

> Yerushalmi or the Bavli) contrasts life with death, cleanness or sanctification with uncleanness, represented at the apex of sources of uncleanness by the corpse.
>
> That is just as the narrative of Genesis would lead us to anticipate. Eden stands for eternal life with God, so the loss of Eden brought death in its place; that is the very meaning of the action. And it is articulated by mythic monotheism: Adam will work until he dies. Not surprisingly, then, the principal source of uncleanness is the corpse. The enemies of Eden, the sources of uncleanness, which pollute the Israelite table and bed, are formed in the model of death or in hierarchical relationship to death. From these Israel in its household, like the priests in the temple, is to be protected. Perpetual alertness is required to stand against the sources of uncleanness, representing death.[1151]

The analogy Neusner draws is reminiscent of comments mentioned by Ephrem the Syrian. The expulsion from the Edenic garden may be read as a prefiguration of Israel's expulsion from the Land of Israel. Indeed, the numerous Halachic restrictions found in the sacred rabbinic texts of the first centuries that follow the destruction of the Temple were intended—on a mythical level—to restore Israel to a state of Original Innocence that will ultimately be realized in the Messianic era.

[1151] Jacob Neusner, *The Theology of the Halakhah* (Leiden; New York: Brill, 2001), 233.

An Interpretive Guide to the World of Judaic Commentaries and Thinkers

Abarbanel, Isaac ben Judah (1437–1508) Statesman, bible commentator, and religious philosopher, Abarbanel sometimes preferred Christian interpretations when it came to the contextual meaning of the text (Portugal, Spain, and later Italy).

Abarbanel, Judah (ca. 1460-1523) Philosopher and theologian, this son of Don Isaac was one of the great Jewish humanists of the Renaissance period. His most famous work, *Dialogues of Love*, focuses on the nature of love and its derivation from the Divine. Abarbanel's work is the first Judaic theological tract that deals exclusively with Romantic Theology (Spain and Italy).

Aggadah The body of homiletical expositions and moralistic teachings found in many discussions of the Talmud.

Akiba ben Yosef (ca. 1st-135 C.E.) One of the most notable Jewish figures of the 2nd century, R. Akiba's textual approach to the Bible revolutionized rabbinic interpretation. For Akiba, every orthographic peculiarity, redundancy, particle, preposition, adverb, preposition, and peculiarity of the Pentateuch contained hidden meanings waiting to be deconstructed by an interpreter. Akiba played an important role in the formation of the Mishnah and influenced the development of Jewish mysticism.

Albo, Joseph (ca. 1380–1444) An influential Jewish theologian of the 15th century whose best-known work, *Sefer ha-Ikkarim* ("Book of Principles"), examines the theological fundamentals of Judaism. As a result of his debates with Christian theologians, Albo decided to deemphasize the importance of the Messiah as one of the cardinal beliefs of Judaism, just as Maimonides argued in his *Thirteen Principles of Faith* (Spain).

Aquila (ca. 2nd century) Originally a convert to Christianity, Aquila later came to embrace Judaism. He is believed to have studied under Rabbi Akiba, who appointed him to write a Greek translation of the Tanakh based on the principles of R. Akiba's interpretations. He has often been associated with Onkelos (Pontus, Anatolia).

Azzai, Shimon ben (1st –2nd century C.E.) One of the most important students of the early rabbinic traditions, whose devotion to Torah study was legendary. He held the view that a father is required by Torah law to provide even his daughters with a Torah education—a view that some of his colleagues refused to accept. He was also a student and colleague of R. Akiba.

Baal ha-Turim (*ca.* 1270–1340) His commentary on the Torah, the Arba'ah Turim, "Four Rows," earned R. Jacob ben Asher this moniker. He made ample use of numerological patterns, focusing for the most part, on the contextual meaning in much the same interpretive style as Ramban (Germany and Spain).

Bahya ben Asher (ca. 1250—1340) Spanish exegete, moralist and Kabbalist, who sought to harmonize the various strands of the PaRDeS. His moralistic expositions at the beginning of a biblical pericope always took into consideration the ethical sensibilities of his readers (Spain).

Bekhor Shor (ca. 12th century) A French *tosafist*, exegete and poet, Joseph ben Isaac Bekhor Shor studied under Rashi's renowned grandson, R. Jacob Tam. He became one of the most famous Talmudic and Halachic scholars of his day, championing a contextual approach that is similar to the styles of Rashi and Rashbam. He also stressed the rational nature of the precepts. The author became the first exegete to alert the reader to the biblical use of doublets. He sometimes referred to Moses as the "Redactor" of the Torah (See, for example, his comments on Numbers 20:1-13 and its relationship to Exodus 17:1-7 (France).

Book of Jubilees (ca. 160 B.C.E.) This book represents one of the oldest post-biblical expositions of Genesis and Exodus. *Jubilees* is part of the ancient literature known as the Pseudepigrapha, and its author claims that this book's origins derived from the hand of Moses himself.

Buber, Martin (1878-1965) A Jewish theologian and philosopher born and educated in Vienna. His most famous work, *I and Thou* (originally published in German, 1922) combines theology and modern existentialism (Austria, Berlin, Zurich, New York).

Cassuto, Umberto (1883-1951) A rabbi and biblical scholar, Cassuto is best known for his critique of the Wellhausen documentary hypothesis (Italy).

Crescas, Hasdai (1340-1411) A Jewish philosopher who was medieval Judaism's most outspoken critic of Aristotelian philosophy as championed by Maimonides and Gersonides (Barcelona, Spain).

Dead Sea Scrolls Considered to be one of the most important archeological discoveries of modern times, the Qumran discoveries feature the oldest existing manuscripts of the Tanakh that date back to approximately 300 years after the biblical canon was finally closed. They are considered to be older than any extant version of the Bible by about a thousand years.

Derrida, Jacques (1930-2004) An Algerian-born Jew who immigrated to France where he became a leading French philosopher. He is best known as the founder of deconstruction and many of his theories have important implications for theology in how people read and experience a text. (France).

Dessler, Eliahu (1892-1953) A prominent rabbinic scholar whose ideas bear a remarkable resemblance to the psychologist Erich Fromm. His *Michtav MeEliahu* (*Letters from Elijah*) represents a complete synthesis of the ideas found in Kabbalah, *musar* (Jewish ethics) and Hassidic texts (Great Britain).

Eliahu, Aharon ben (1328-1369) Aharon was widely considered to be one of the most important Karaite thinkers and exegetes of his time; he commanded a wide expertise of rabbinic, Muslim, and Karaite sources (Nicomedia, Turkey).

Epstein, Baruch (1860-1941) Lithuanian Talmud and bible scholar best known for his *Torah Temimah* commentary on the Torah. He was the son of Rabbi Yechiel Michel Epstein, the famous author of the *Arukh HaShulkhan*. The *Torah Temimah* commentary attempts to didactically show how the rabbis of the Talmud and Midrash deduced their interpretations based upon their understanding of how Biblical Hebrew functions.

Fishbane, Michael (1943-) Contemporary Judaic and Biblical scholar whose well-respected works include: *Biblical Interpretation in Ancient Israel, The JPS Bible Commentary: Haftorah,* and a number of works dealing with hermeneutics, mysticism, myth, theology, and Midrash (United States).

Friedman, Richard Elliot (1945-) Widely regarded as one of the best-known modern Jewish advocates of the Documentary Hypothesis. He argues that the P source of the Bible was written during the reign of Hezekiah "emphasizes centralization of religion: one centre, one altar, one Tabernacle, one place of sacrifice. Who was the king who began such centralization? King Hezekiah." Author of *"Commentary on the Torah,"* (SF: Harper Collins, 2001)

Fromm, Erich Pinchas (1900-1980) A 20th century psychologist and social philosopher who wrote extensively on the nature of Nazism and alienation. His most popular books include, *The Art of Loving* and *Being and Having*. Fromm's insights on the nature of biblical theology are sadly underrated, when in actuality he is one of the most important Jewish thinkers of his time (Germany United States).

Freud, Sigmund (1856-1939) Father of psychoanalysis (Austria).

Genesis Rabba Palestinian *aggadic* midrash on the Book of Genesis, edited ca. 425 C.E.

Gordon, Cyrus Herzl (1908-2001) American scholar of Near Eastern and Mediterranean Studies who argued there is a closer historical relationship between the Judaic and Greek cultures than commonly assumed (United States).

Hertz, Joseph (1872-1946) Former Chief Rabbi of Great Britain. R. Hertz's commentary was the first modern Jewish work to combine the scholarship of non-Jewish and Jewish commentators (London)

Heschel, Abraham Joshua (1907-1972) One of the most significant Jewish leaders and scholars of the 20th century whose theology of pathos became visibly clear when he joined Martin Luther King in Selma in the march for civil rights. In terms of his various theological writings, Heschel reexamined and redefined the place of the Sabbath, rabbinical theology, biblical prophecy, revelation, and faith in contemporary Jewish thought (New York).

Hirsch, Samson Raphael (1808–1888) The founder of Modern Orthodoxy, Hirsch creatively attempted to integrate Judaism with modern Western culture as defined by the ethical philosophy of Immanuel Kant (Germany).

Hizkuni (13th century) Hezekiah ben Manoah, named for his kabbalistic commentary on the Pentateuch, Hizkuni combined the styles of Rashi, Ibn Ezra, Rashbam and Bechor Shor with his own very original insights (France).

Ibn Ezra, Abraham (1089–1164) First and foremost a grammarian, Ibn Ezra was especially critical of any interpretation that violated the rules of Hebrew grammar. Ibn Ezra's sensitivity to the contextual meaning of the Pentateuch led him, at times, to believe that certain biblical portions may have been edited after the time of Moses, e.g., Gen. 12:6; 22:14; Deut. 1:1; 3:11, and were possibly interpolations. Ibn Ezra occasionally incorporates a philosophical view throughout his commentaries on the Pentateuch and other biblical books (Spain).

Ishmael ben Elisha (90-135 C.E.) R. Ishmael was one of the most important rabbinic teachers of the beginning of the 2nd century. He and Rabbi Akiba founded two interpretive schools that differed in how they approached a biblical text. R. Ishmael in many ways was the forerunner of the "peshat" method, which focused on the contextual meaning of a passage while R. Akiba attributed meaning to the smallest particles of a text (Judea).

Jacob, Benno (1862-1945) Like U. Cassuto, Benno Jacob's monumental commentaries on the books of Genesis and Exodus take sharp aim at the erroneous and reductionistic assumptions expressed by the early advocates of the Documentary Hypothesis (Germany).

Jacobs, Louis (1920-2006) One of Britain's most prestigious scholars whose former Orthodox background enabled him to critique and redefine Orthodox Jewish theology for the postmodern world. Jacobs repeatedly championed the polydoxy of Judaic thought by demonstrating the inherent flexibility of early and classical medieval rabbinic scholars and their theological and Halachic works (London).

Josephus, Flavius (ca. 37–ca. 100) Born Joseph ben Matthias, Jerusalem born and of Jewish royal and priestly descent, he served during the Judean-Roman war as a commander in the Galilee. Later, he was captured by the Romans, and eventually freed by Vespasian. After the defeat of Judea, Josephus travelled to Rome where he wrote many historical manuscripts that included the first history of the Jewish people, a work that provides a rare first-hand look at the Hellenistic world of Judaism along with the seminal events that occurred in the first century (Judea).

Kalisch, Marcus (1828-1885) Born in Poland, Kalisch was educated at Berlin University where he studied classics and Semitic languages. Later, he immigrated to England where he became a tutor for the Rothschild family. His Torah commentary was the first comprehensive English work to combine philology, classics, and philosophy, Hebrew grammar, Semitic languages, and rabbinic thought. His vast familiarity with Christian sources and comparative religion make him unique in the annals of Jewish intellectual history of that era.

Kasher, Menachem (1895-1983) His greatest work was the encyclopedic Torah commentary entitled *Torah Shelemah.* In this multi-volume compendium, Kasher presents one of the most comprehensive digests of rabbinic literature drawn from ancient, medieval, and modern sources that explore the nuances of the biblical texts along with the explanations of the Targums that accompany them (Poland and the United States).

Kook, Abraham Isaac (1865–1935) A Seminal 19th century and 20th century rabbinic scholar, philosopher and mystic, Kook served as the first Ashkenazi Chief Rabbi of the British Mandate for Palestine. He did not shy away from integrating ideas from secular culture with the mystical notions found in the Kabbalah, e.g., the theory of evolution. In his creative synthesis of science and faith, Kook's ideas bear a strong similarity to those of Henri Bergson (Palestine).

Lamm, Norman (1927—) Chancellor of Yeshiva University, Rabbi Lamm, perhaps more than anyone living today, embodies the spirit of Modern Orthodoxy. One of the most original Jewish thinkers of the 20th -21st centuries, his willingness to engage other branches of Judaism along with canons of Western culture sets him apart from others in his era (Brooklyn, N.Y.).

Levenson, Jon D. (1949-) A foremost biblical scholar focusing on the historical relationship between Judaism and Christianity, he is also one of the few systematic Jewish theologians (United States).

Lévinas, Emmanuel (1906-1995) Widely respected as one of the most important Continental philosophers of the 20th century, his expertise included the fields of philosophy, phenomenology, ethics, and religion. His approach to philosophy was dramatically changed as a result of the Holocaust. Lévinas believed that the true experience of transcendence is not—as the mystics thought—an escape from the world, but to the contrary, involves the commitment to justice and working towards the social and ethical betterment of humankind (France).

Lowe, Yehudah (1525-1609) Also known as MaHaRaL, an acronym for *Moreinu ha-Rav Loew*, "Our Teacher the Rabbi Loew." Maharal was a prolific writer who composed numerous works on Jewish theology, mystical expositions, and works on the Talmud, often taking issue with several famous medieval scholars such as Maimonides and Gersonides. His exposition on Rashi is considered to be one of the most important expositions written in his age (Czechoslovakia).

Luria, Isaac (1534-1572) Considered to be among the most influential, and remarkable Kabbalists of all time, he established a cadre of well renowned students in Safed, Israel. Luria viewed creation as a harmonious coalescence of spiritual and physical forces united in a great "chain of being", whose ultimate perfection depends upon humankind to actualize.

Luzzato, Moshe Chayim (1707-1746) Also known as "RaMCHaL," Luzzato was one the greatest Kabbalists and Jewish philosophers of the early 18th century. His best known work is the ethical tract, *Mesillat Yesharim* (Path of the Just), which delineates how each person can develop a saintly character (Italy).

Luzzato, Samuel David (1800-1865) Also known as SHaDaL, his literary activity set him apart from most of the commentaries of his time. He had the distinction of being the first Orthodox scholar to grapple with the growing science of biblical criticism, frequently citing classical and Christian sources in his commentaries (Italy).

Maimon, Abraham ben (1186–1237) The son of Moses Maimonides, and also a religious philosopher, his philosophy of Judaism sometimes incorporated elements from Sufi thought (Egypt).

Maimonides, Moses ben Maimon (1135-1204) Famously known as "Rambam,"

Maimonides was one of the greatest Jewish thinkers and legal scholars of all time. He consistently interpreted the Bible through the various categories of Aristotelian metaphysics, while stressing the human (linguistic) mode of biblical transmission. Maimonides was one of the first Jewish thinkers to subscribe to a method of demythologization and exerted a great influence over the German Christian mystic Meister Eckhart and Thomas Aquinas (Spain and Egypt).

Malbim (1809–1879) An acronym for Meir Loeb ben Yehiel Michael. Malbim attempted to demonstrate how rabbinic interpretations were grounded in the Hebrew syntax of the Tanakh, claiming that there is no redundancy when it comes to the words, phrases or sentences of a given biblical text. Every word has its unique meaning which he consistently tried to relate to the text's deeper and more conceptual meaning. Malbim frequently integrated ideas from the Kabbalah into his commentary (Russia, Eastern Europe).

Meir (2nd century) Rabbi Meir was one of the main students who helped to reconstitute the Sanhedrin after the failed Bar Kochba revolt. He was responsible for the spread of rabbinic traditions. Many anecdotes about him describe his profound humility and willingness to promote reconciliation whenever possible. His wife was the famous female scholar, Beruriah.

Massoretes Deriving from Heb. מסרת, *Massoreth*, ("tradition"), these were Jewish grammarians who lived between the 6th and 9th centuries C.E. Their efforts preserved the biblical text from accretion, alteration, or corruption, setting up its traditional divisions, pronunciation, and mode of public recitation. The Massoretes also provided marginal notes pointing out the various orthographic, grammatical, and lexicographic irregularities. The text which derives from the work of the Massoretes is known as the "Massoretic text".

Midrash The Midrash generally serves as a pedagogic device for the purpose of teaching morals and ethical lessons based on the lives of the various biblical figures. Most notable among biblical collections is Midrash Rabba ("Great Midrash"), a composite of commentaries on the Pentateuch and five Megillot (Song of Songs, Ruth, Ecclesiastes, Esther, Lamentations) differing in nature and age. Its oldest portion, the 5th-century Genesis Rabba, is largely a verse-by-verse commentary, while the 6th-century Leviticus Rabba consisting of homilies and Lamentations Rabba (end of 6th century) is mainly narrative. The remaining portions of Midrash Rabba were compiled at later dates.

Mishnah The name מִשְׁנָה, ("repetition," hence, "instruction") is a collection of rabbinic laws that became the basis of the Jerusalem and Babylonian Talmud. The subject matter is divided into six sections pertaining to all aspects of Jewish life as it existed in the centuries prior to the Temple's destruction. The six sections are "Seeds" (laws on agriculture), "Festivals," "Women" (marriage laws), "Injuries" (civil and criminal law), "Holy Things" (laws pertaining to priestly sacrifices), and "Purification" (Levitical laws of cultic purity). The redactor of the Mishnah was Rabbi Judah the Prince, who assembled the materials sometime during the year 200 C.E.

Mizrachi, Eliahu (1455-1525) served as chief rabbi of the Ottoman Empire and authored a voluminous commentary on Rashi's exposition.

Neusner, Jacob (1932-) A modern Talmudic theologian, historian and translator of rabbinic texts, Neusner's prolific writings and translations of the Babylonian and Jerusalem Talmud reveal how rabbinic tradition is rooted within the conceptual world of the biblical text. He asserts that Judaism creates categories of thought that integrate certain core values and ideologies, which in turn enable the rabbis to preserve and redefine Judaism in the centuries following the Temple's destruction. In addition, Neusner argues that each rabbinic work reveals the type of Judaism that existed in a given historical era and community.

Philo of Alexandria (ca. 15 B.C.E.–50 C.E.) A famous Jewish philosopher of Alexandria, he was also the first major Jewish thinker to attempt a grand synthesis of Greek and Judaic thought. Like subsequent Judaic commentators, Philo offered multiple interpretations of the same verse. Philo believed that the Scriptures had to be interpreted in two ways—in accordance with its literal meaning and its allegorical meaning. Philo was the first Jewish exegete to consistently interpret the precepts of the Torah, which he believed instilled virtue in the faith community.

Radak (1160-1235) The acronym for Rabbi David ben Joseph Kimchi. He asserted that the rationalist approaches to the Bible, concerning miracles or prophecy are nothing more than an extension of the original efforts of the classical rabbis. Wherever possible, Kimchi argued that rigorous examination of biblical language yielded the most satisfactory explanations of figurative language (Spain).

Ralbag (1248–1344) The acronym for Rabbi Levi ben Gershom, who was also widely known as "Gersonides." He was a Renaissance type scholar who excelled in areas of such diverse disciplines as mathematical sciences, astronomy, medicine, biblical exegesis and especially Jewish and Greek philosophy. He was also known as a brilliant Talmudist, and as an expert in all areas of Judaic law. His astronomical knowledge was extensive and contributed toward the development of the telescope. Historians of science commonly regard Gersonides as one of the most important European astronomers before Galileo (Southeastern France).

Ramban (ca. 1194-1270) The acronym for R. Moses ben Nahman. Ramban was also known as Nahmanides. He did not limit his exegetical insights to just philological analysis and the meaning of the *peshat*. For him, the moral and ethical lessons were no less important than the *peshat*. On the one hand, he greatly admired Ibn Ezra, yet he did not hesitate to criticize him for showing a lack of reverence with some of his dismissive remarks of the early rabbinical Sages. He was one of the first exegetes to integrate the Kabbalah into his interpretation of the Torah (Spain and Israel).

Rashbam (ca. 1080–1174) The acronym for Rabbi Samuel ben Meir. Rashbam was the grandson of Rashi. As a young man, he frequently argued with his grandfather about the meaning of the peshat in the Torah. He later came to prefer a more linguistic and nuanced approach over the Midrashic style of exegesis that Rashi advocated (France).

Rashi (1040–1105) The acronym for Rabbi Solomon ben Isaac. Rashi is regarded by many as the author of the greatest rabbinic commentaries. Rashi was careful to choose only those interpretations which came closest to the simplest meaning of the text. (France).

Responsa The body of written decisions and rulings given by *poskim* ("decisors" of Jewish law) that covers a period of about 1800 years and contains a storehouse of information about the times of Jewish life in the medieval era and beyond. Some of the types of questions dealt with in the Responsa literature pertain to areas as diverse as ethics, marital issues, family problems, community laws, Jewish-gentile relations, historical issues, theological concerns, science, and the Tanakh, expanding on a number of discussions and conclusions found in the Talmud, Midrash, and philosophical texts.

Saadia Gaon (892—942 C.E.) In his time, Saadia ben Yosef distinguished himself as an exceptional theologian and biblical commentator. Saadia wrote the first translation of the Hebrew Bible into Arabic *(Tafser)*. Far from being a literal translation, Saadia wrote a very literary rendition. Each book was preceded by an Arabic preface, explaining its structure and contents. Faithful to the rationalist tendencies of the Mutazila, Saadia tried to soften the Scripture's use of anthropomorphism. Saadia's translation is still used even to this day, among Yemenite Jews (Babylonia).

Sarna, Nachum (1923-2005) American Bible scholar known for his commentaries on Genesis and Exodus. Sarna believed that there is a cultural commingling of Semitic motifs in the Bible. (United States).

Schneersohn, Menachem Mendel (1902-1994) Schneersohn's analysis on Rashi, *Biurim L'Pirush Rashi* ("Expositions on Rashi's Commentary") are didactic expositions that aim to explain the conceptual differences between Rashi and other medieval rabbinic scholars and their successors, in the style of Talmudic *pilpul*. In his commentary on Rashi, Schneersohn tried to demonstrate why Rashi's commentary is the most complete and inerrant of all the medieval exegetical works (Brooklyn, N.Y.).

Seforno, Obadiah ben Jacob (ca. 1475–ca. 1550) Bible commentator whose rationalistic approach examined the biblical text in light of Jewish philosophy and ethics. In Rome, he taught Hebrew from 1498 to 1500 to the famous Christian humanist Johannes Reuchlin (Italy).

Septuagint The Greek translation of the Torah made for the Jewish community of Alexandria, Egypt, 3rd century B.C.E. Its translators believed that their work would serve as a vehicle through which the Torah's message would be conveyed to a modern world.

Soloveitchik, Joseph Ber (1903-1993) One of the most influential American Orthodox rabbis of the 20th century, and a first-rate Jewish theologian who combined Kantian existentialism with his unique philosophy of Halacha (Jewish Law).

Spinoza, Baruch (1632-1677) One of the most original Jewish thinkers of the 17th century, whose ideas on God, nature, revelation and ethics exerted a profound impact on Western culture and subsequent Judaic thought. He is also credited as being one of the very first scholars to question the Mosaic authorship of the Pentateuch. His controversial views ultimately led to his excommunication from the Portuguese Jewish community (Netherlands).

Symmachus (ca. 170 C.E.) Translator of the Bible into Greek. According to Epiphanius, Symmachus was a convert to Judaism, but Jerome and Eusebius identify him as an Ebionite Christian. He has also sometimes been identified as a disciple of Meir. Unlike Aquila's literalistic translation, Symmachus composed a literary rendering of the Septuagint, and took into consideration the literary style of the Greek intelligentsia. He was intimately familiar with Jewish midrashic exegesis as well as with Greek writings. His translation of the Bible is included in Origen's Hexapla.

Talmud This body of rabbinical literature consists of the Mishnah (c. 200 C.E.), and the Gemorah (c. 500 C.E.), and contains a record of discussions and controversies pertaining to Jewish law, ethics, and history. The Sages claim that their teachings and authority derive from an oral tradition that was given to Moses at Sinai by God, which he handed down to his successor, Joshua and the Elders, who in turn passed the traditions to the next generation until it reached Ezra and the Scribes. The Scribes were then succeeded by the Sages in the First Century.

Targum The Targum is an Aramaic translation of the Tanakh that was compiled sometime during the Second Temple era. The Targum of Onkelos became the official Targum by the 3rd century C.E. and is considered to be the most authoritative Targum of the Pentateuch.

Targum Neofiti A Targum of the Torah preserved in the Vatican Manuscript, "Neofiti 1," discovered in 1956. This particular Targum may be the oldest of all the Targums, dating back to the pre-Christian era and may even be possibly much older.

Targum Jonathan This Aramaic translation of the Torah was erroneously ascribed to Jonathan ben Uzziel through a misreading of the initials "T.Y." (= Targum Yerushalmi). Rabbinic tradition believed he was the author of the Targum to the Prophets. Unlike the Targum of Onkelos, this Targum frequently incorporates Midrashic ideas in its paraphrasing of the biblical text.

Wisdom Literature Throughout the ancient Near East, various thinkers of antiquity composed literary genres dealing with how to live a good and successful life. These writings eventually influenced several famous books in the Tanakh. Perhaps the most obvious example of deliberate cross-cultural borrowing is evident in "The Words of the Wise Men" from Proverbs 22:17-24:22 and 24:33-34, which appear to have been strongly influenced by the *Teachings of Amenemope.* In the Tanakh, Wisdom Literature consists of two general types: short and pithy prescriptions for achieving personal happiness and success (Proverbs), and exploration into what constitutes the ultimate fulfillment with respect to God and human existence (Ecclesiastes and Job).

Wyschogrod, Michael (1928-) One of Orthodox Judaism's most notable contemporary theologians, his best known works are *The Body of Faith: God and the People Israel* and *Abraham's Promise: Judaism and Jewish-Christian Relations.* Wyschogrod, perhaps more than any other Modern Orthodox thinker, has explored the importance of Jewish and Christian dialogue from a theological and historical perspective (United States).

Zalman, Sheneir (1745-1812) Sheneir Zalman was one of the Hassidic movement's most original thinkers who originated the dynasty of Chabad. His best known work was the *Tanya,* which was one of the first mystical tracts dealing with personal growth (Russia).

Zohar ("splendor," or "radiance") Written by Moshe de León (1240-1305), the Castilian Kabbalist claimed that his work dated back to the esoteric teacher R. Shimon Bar Yohai (ca. 3rd century). The Zohar is considered to be Jewish mysticism's greatest work often rivaling both the Tanakh and the Talmud as Judaism's most important text (Spain).

BIBLIOGRAPHY

Abarbanel (Isaac ben Judah). *Commentary on the Torah* [Hebrew] 3 volumes: Jerusalem: Bnai Arbel.

Abarbanel (Isaac ben Judah). *Commentary on Genesis*. Tr. Yehudah Sheviv. Jerusalem: Hotza'at Seforim, 2007.

Abrahams, Israel. *Hebrew Ethical Wills*. Philadelphia: JPS, 1948.

Aharon ben Eliahu, *Keter Torah*. Eupatoria, 1866.

———. *Etz Hayyim*. Publication date: Unknown

Alter, Robert. *The Art of Biblical Narrative*. New York: Basic Books, 1981.

Anderson, Francis I. and Dean Forbes. "Spelling in the Hebrew Bible." Rome: BibOr, 1986.

The Ante-Nicene Fathers, ed. Alexander Roberts and James Donaldson. Grand Rapids, MI: Eerdmans, 1989.

Augustine, *Confessions*, XI, xii, ed. Whitney J. Oates, *Basic Writings of Saint Augustine*. New York: Random House, 1948.

———. *The Literal Meaning of Genesis*. Tr. John Hammond Taylor. New York: Newman Press, 1982.

———. *On Genesis: Two Books on Genesis against the Manichees; and, on the Literal Interpretation of Genesis, an Unfinished Book.* Tr. Roland J. Teske. Washington, D.C.: Catholic University of America Press, 1991.

Auerbach, Erich. *Mimesis: The Representation of Reality in Western Literature*. Princeton, NJ: Princeton University Press, 1953.

Aven Shoshan, Avraham. *HaMilon HaIvri HaMercaz*. Jerusalem, Kiryat Sefer, 1998.

Aviezer, Nathan. *In The Beginning: Biblical Creation and Science.* Hoboken, NJ: Ktav, 1990.

Bakhtin, Mikhail. *Problems of Dostoevsky's Poetics*. Tr. Caryl Emerson. Minneapolis: University of Minnesota Press, 1984.

———. *Speech Genres and Other Late Essays.* Tr. Caryl Emerson. Austin, University of Texas Press 1986.

Aesthetic Activity. Art and Answerability: Early Philosophical Essays (University of Texas Slavic Series, 9). Austin: University of Texas Press, 1990.

Balz, H. R. and G. Schneider. *Exegetical Dictionary of the New Testament.* Grand Rapids, MI: Eerdmans, 1990.

Barth, Karl. *Church Dogmatics.* New York: T & T Clark International. Vol. IV, 1956.

Becker, Ernest. *The Denial of Death.* New York: Free Press, 1973.

Behe, Michael J. *Darwin's Black Box: The Biochemical Challenge to Evolution.* New York: Free Press, 1996.

Bokser, Ben Tsion. *Abraham Isaac Kook: The Lights of Penitence, The Moral Principles, Lights of Holiness, Essays, Letters, and Poems.* Philadelphia: Paulist Press, 1978.

Bonhoeffer, Dietrich. *Creation and Fall,* and *Temptation: Two Biblical Studies.* New York: Simon and Schuster, reprinted in 1989.

Botterweck, G, Johannes, Helmer Ringgren, and David Green. *Theological Dictionary of the Old Testament.* Grand Rapids, MI. Volumes 1-16, 1977-2007.

Branover, Herman, Joseph Ginsburg, and Menaḥem Mendel Schneersohn. *Mind over Matter: The Lubavitcher Rebbe on Science, Technology and Medicine.* Tr. Arnie Gotfryd. Jerusalem: Shamir 2003.

Brown, Francis. *The New Brown-Driver-Briggs-Gesenius Hebrew-English Lexicon.* Peabody, MA: Hendrickson Publishers, 1979.

Brueggemann, Walter. *Genesis: A Bible Commentary for Teaching and Preaching.* Atlanta: John Knox Press, 1982.

———. *Theology of the Old Testament: Testimony, Dispute, Advocacy.* Minneapolis: Fortress Press, 1997.

Buber, Martin. *The Way of Man: According to the Teachings of Hasidism.* New York: Citadel Press and Kensington Publishing Corp, 1948.

———. *Good and Evil.* New York: Prentice Hall, 1952.

———. *Between Man and Man.* New York: Macmillan, 1965.

———. *I and Thou.* Tr. W. Kaufmann. New York: Scribner's, 1970.

Budge, E.A. Wallis, *The Book of the Dead.* Dover, DE: Dover Publications Inc. 1899, reprint 1967.

Bultmann, Rudolf and ed. Schubert M. Ogden *Existence and Faith: Shorter Writings of Rudolf Bultmann,* New York: World Publishing, 1960

———. *Essays Philosophical and Theological.* London: SCM, 1955.

Bokser, Ben Tzion *Abraham Isaac Kook: The Lights of Penitence, the Moral Principles, Lights of Holiness, Essays, Letters, and Poems.* Philadelphia: Paulist Press, 1978.

C. M. Gayley, *Classic Myths.* Boston: Ginn & Company, 1902.

Calvin, Jean. *Commentary on Genesis.* Tr. John King. Grand Rapids, MI: Eerdmans, 1948.

Campbell, Joseph. *Myths to Live By.* New York: Bantam New Age Books, 1973.

Caputo, John. *Deconstruction in a Nutshell: A Conversation with Jacques Derrida.* New York: Fordham UP, 1997.

Carmell, Areyeh and Cyril Domb. *Challenge: Torah Views on Science and its Problems.* New York: Feldheim Publishers, 1978.

———. *Strive For Truth* (Vol. 4), *Sanctuaries in Time: The Scriptural Aspects of the Festivals, Fasts, and Holy Days in the Jewish Year.* Jerusalem: Feldheim, 2002.

Cassuto, Umberto. *From Adam to Noah: A Commentary on the First Chapters of Genesis.* Tr. Israel Abrahams. Jerusalem: Hebrew UP, 1944.

Cauliano, Ioan P. *The Tree of Gnosis: Gnostic Mythology from Early Christianity to Modern Nihilism.* San Francisco: Harper Collins, 1992.

Charlesworth, James, ed., *The Old Testament Pseudepigrapha,* 2 vols. Garden City, NY: Doubleday, 1983.

Charles B. Chavel. *Ramban's Commentary on the Torah.* Shiloh, NY: 1971.

———. Rambam and (ed). *Rambam l'Am* (20 volumes). Jerusalem: Mosad HaRav Kook, 1989.

Cohen, Seymour. *The Holy Letter: A Study in Jewish Sexual Morality.* Northvale, NJ: Jason Aronson Inc., 1993.

Cohen, Noah. *Tsa'ar Ba'ale Hayim: The Prevention of Cruelty to Animals.* New York: Feldheim Publishers, 1959.

Collins, Francis. *The Language of God.* New York: Free Press, 2006.

Josephus. *Complete Works of Flavius Josephus.* Tr. William Whiston. Grand Rapids: Kregel Publications, 1964.

Davies, Paul. *Other Worlds.* New York: Touchstone, 1980.

———. *God and the New Physics.* New York: Schuster and Schuster, 1983.

———. *The Cosmic Blueprint: New Discoveries in Nature's Creative Ability to Order.* West Conshohocken, PA: Templeton Foundation Press; New Ed edition, 2004.

———. *Cosmic Jackpot: Why Our Universe is Just Right for Life.* New York: Houghton Mifflin, 2007.

Davidson, *Commentary on Job.* New York: Williams and Northgate, 1862.

Davidson, Robert. *Genesis 1-11.* Cambridge University Press, 1973.

———. *Genesis 12-50.* Cambridge. New York: Cambridge University Press, 1979.

Delitzsch, Franz. *A New Commentary on Genesis.* Edinburgh: T. & T. Clark, 1899.

Derrida, Jacques. *Dissemination.* Tr. Barbara Johnson Chicago: Chicago University Press, 1981.

Dershowitz, Alan. *The Genesis of Justice.* New York: Time Warner, 2000.

Descartes, Renée. *Discourse on the method: and, Meditations on First Philosophy.*
Tr. David Weissman, William Theodore Bluhm. New Haven: Yale University Press: 996

Dillmann, August, *Genesis, Critically and Exegetically Expounded.* Tr. August Knobel and William Black Stevenson. Edinburgh: T. & T. Clark, 1897.

Douglas, Mary. *Leviticus as Literature.* New York: Oxford University Press, 2000.

Driver, S. R. *The Book of Genesis : With Introduction and Notes. 7th* rev. ed. London: Methuen, 1909.

———. *Additions and Corrections in the Seventh Edition of the Book of Genesis.* London: Methuen, 1909.

———. *The Book of Genesis.* 11th ed. London: Methuen, 1920.

Dubos, René. *A God Within.* New York: Charles Scribner's Books, 1972.

Ebreo, Leone. *Dialogues of Love (Dialoghi d'Amori).* Tr. F. Friedeberg-Seeley/Jean H. Barnes London: Soncino, 1937.

Edwards, Jonathan. *The Works of Jonathan Edwards,* Volume Two, *Notes on the Bible.* Carlisle, PA: Banner of Truth, 1984.

Einstein, Albert. *Ideas and Opinions,* Crown Publishers, New York, 1954.

Eliade, Mircea, *Patterns in Comparative Literature.* New York: Sheed & Ward, 1958.

———. *Myths, Dreams, and Mysteries.* New York: Harper Torchbooks, 1959.

———. *The Sacred and the Profane.* New York: Harcourt, Brace, and Jovanovich, 1959.

———. *Shamanism: Archaic Techniques in Ecstasy.* Princeton: Princeton University Press, 1964.

———. *The Two and the One.* Chicago: University of Chicago Press, 1965.

———. *Encyclopedia of Religion.* New York: Macmillan Publishing Company, 1986.

———. *Images and Symbols.* Princeton, NJ: Princeton University Press, 1991.

Epstein, Isidore. *The Soncino Talmud (*27 volumes*).* London, Soncino, 1947.

Epstein, Baruch. Pentateuch and Five Megillot: Torah Temimah (Hebrew), 5 vols. Tel Aviv: Am Olam, 1955–1956.

Etheridge, J. W. *The Targums of Onkelos and of Jonathan ben Uzziel on the Pentateuch with the Fragments of the Jerusalem Targum.* London: 1862–65; reprinted New York: Ktav, 1968.

Fishbane, Michael, *Biblical Interpretation in Ancient Israel.* Oxford: Clarendon, 1985.

———. *The Garments of Torah: Essays in Biblical Hermeneutics* (Indiana Studies in Biblical Literature). Bloomington, IN: Indiana University Press, 2000.

Fox, Everett. *The Five Books of Moses: Genesis, Exodus, Leviticus, Numbers, Deuteronomy; a New Translation with Introductions, Commentary, and Notes.* Schocken Books, 1995.

Frazier, Sir James. *Folklore of the Old Testament.* Vol. 1. New York: Tudor Publishing, 1923.

Freedman, David Noel. *Anchor Bible Dictionary.* New York: Doubleday, 1992.

Friedman, Maurice S. *Martin Buber, Life of Dialogue.* Chicago: University of Chicago Press, 1956.

Friedman, Richard Elliot. *Commentary on the Torah.* San Francisco: Harper Collins, 2001.

———. *The Bible with Sources Revealed: A New View into the Five Books of Moses.* San Francisco: Harper Collins, 2003.

Fretheim, Terence E. "Genesis" *New Interpreter's Bible.* Nashville, TN: Abingdon Press, 1994.

Freud, Sigmund, *The Complete Psychological Works.* Tr. J. Strachey. London: Hogarth Press. Vol. 18.

Fromm, Eric. *You Shall Be As Gods.* New York: Harcourt, Rinehart, Winston, 1966.

———. *The Art of Loving: An Enquiry into the Nature of Love.* New York: Harper and Brothers, 1956.

Gadamer, Hans-Georg. *Truth and Method.* New York: Sheed and Ward, 1975.

Gelbard, Shmuel. *Lipshuto Shel Rashi* (5 volumes). Petach Tikvah: 1993.

Gibran, Kahil. *The Prophet*. New York: Alfred A. Knopf, 1923.

Gill, John. *Gill's Commentary*, Vol.1. Grand Rapids, MI: Baker Book House, 1980.

Graves, Robert, and Raphael Patai. *Hebrew Myths: The Book of Genesis*. London: Cassell, 1964.

Griffin, Donald R. *Animal Minds*. Chicago: University of Chicago Press, 1992.

Gunkel, Hermann, *Genesis*. Tr. Mark E. Biddle. Macon, GA: Mercer UP, 1997.

Hallo, William and K. L. Younger. *The Context of Scripture*. New York: Brill, 1997.

Hamilton, Victor P. *The Book of Genesis, Chapters 1-17*. "The New International Commentary on the Old Testament." Grand Rapids, MI: Eerdmans Publishing Co., 1990.

Harris, R. L., G. L. Archer, and B. K. Waltke. *Theological Wordbook of the Old Testament*. Chicago: Moody Press, 1999, c. 1980.

Hartman, David. *Maimonides: Torah and Philosophic Quest*. New York: JPS, 1976.

Hartman, Yehoshua David. *Gur Aryeh HaShalame L'Maharal M'Prague* (9 volumes). Jerusalem: Mechon Yerushalayim 1989—1995.

Heidegger, Martin *Introduction to Metaphysics*. Tr. R. Manheim. Garden City, NY: Doubleday, 1961.

Heidel, Alexander Heidel. *The Gilgamesh Epic and Old Testament Parallels*, 2nd ed. Chicago: Chicago UP, 1963.

Hendel, Ronald S. Hendel. *The Text of Genesis 1-11: Textual Studies and Critical Edition*. Oxford, NY: Oxford University Press, 1998.

Henry, Matthew. *Matthew Henry's Commentary. 6 Volumes*. Old Tappan, NJ: Fleming H. Revell Co., n. d.

Herodotus and Aubrey De Sélincourt (tr.). *The Histories*. Baltimore: Penguin Books, 2003, 1954.

Heschel, Abraham Joshua. *The Earth is the Lord's: The Inner World of the Jew in Eastern Europe.* New York: Farrar, Straus & Giroux, 1950.

———. *Man Is Not Alone.* New York: Harper and Row, 1951.

———. *The Sabbath: Its Meaning for Modern Man.* New York: Farrar Straus and Young, 1951.

———. *God in Search of Man: A Philosophy of Judaism.* New York: 1955.

——— and Gordon Tucker. *Heavenly Torah: As refracted through the Generations.* New York: Continuum, 2006.

Hertz, Joseph H. *The Pentateuch and the Haftorahs.* 2 vols. New York: Metsudah, 1941.

Hick, John. *Evil and the God of Love.* New York: Harper & Row Publishers, 1977.

Hizkuni (Hezekiah ben Manoah). *The Torah Commentary of R. Hezekiah b.* Manoah [Hebrew] ed. H. D. Chavel. Jerusalem: Mosad HaRav Kook, 1981.

Ibn Ezra, Abraham ben Meïr. Ibn *Ezra's Commentary on the Pentateuch.* Tr. Norman Strickman, and Arthur M. Silver. New York: Menorah Pub. Co., 1988.

Ibn Ezra and J. L. Krinski (ed.)

Genesis with Ibn Ezra's Commentary. [Hebrew] Mechokake Yehudah Banai Brak, 1961.

Jacob, Benno, Ernest I. Jacob. *The First Book of the Bible: Genesis.* Tr. Walter Jacob. New York: Ktav Publishing House, 1974.

———. *The Second Book of the Bible: Exodus* Hoboken, NJ: Ktav, 1992.

Jakobovits, Immanuel. *Jewish Medical Ethics.* New York: Bloch Publishing, 1959.

Jacobs, Louis. *Principles of the Jewish Faith.* Northvale, NJ: Jason Aronson Inc., 1988.

———. *The Jewish Religion: A Companion*, Oxford: Oxford University Press, 1995.

Jamieson, Robert, A.R. Fausset, and David Brown, *A Commentary, Critical and Explanatory, on the Old and New Testaments.* New York: 1879.

Jeffrey, D. L. *A Dictionary of Biblical Tradition in English Literature.* Grand Rapids, MI: W.B. Eerdmans, 1992.

Jenni, Ernst, Clause Westermann. *Theological Lexicon of the Old Testament.* Tr. Mark E. Biddle. Peabody, MA: Hendrickson Publishers, 1997.

Jerome, and Robert Hayward. *Saint Jerome's Hebrew Questions on Genesis.* Oxford New York: Clarendon Press; Oxford University Press, 1995.

Jung, Carl G., M.L. von Franz, Joseph L. Henderson, Jolande Jacobi, Aniela Jaffe. *Man and His Symbols.* New York: Doubleday and Company, 1964.

———. *Psychology and Religion* The Terry Lectures. New Haven: Yale UP, 1938 (contained in *Psychology and Religion: West and East Collected Works* Vol. 11.

———. "The Psychology of the Child Archetype" published in *The Archetypes and the Collective Unconscious,* Vol.9, pt. 1, 2nd ed., 1940.

———. "The Psychology of the Child Archetype" in *The Archetypes and the Collective Unconscious,*" published in Vol.9, pt. 1, 2nd ed., (Princeton, NJ: Princeton University Press, 1940.

———. "The Archetypes and the Collective Unconscious" in the *Collected Works of C.G. Jung* Vol. 9, Part I. Princeton: Princeton University Press, 1950

———. *Answer to Job.* Translated by R.F.C. Hull. London: Routledge and Paul, 1954.

———. "Aion: Researches into the Phenomenology of the Self" *The Collective Works of C.G. Jung,* Vol. 9 Part II. Princeton, NJ: Bollingen, 1959.

Kalisch, Marcus Moritz. *A Historical and Critical Commentary on the Old Testament.* London: Longmans, Brown, Green and Dyer, 1858.

Kaplan, Aryeh. *The Living Torah: The Torah and the Haftorahs.* New York: Moznaim, 1981.

Kass, Leon. *The Beginning of Wisdom: Reading Genesis.* New York: Free Press, 2003.

Kasher, Menachem. *Torah Shelemah.* Jerusalem, Hotzat Beit Torah Shlomo,

1994.

Kaufmann, Stephen. *Comprehensive Aramaic Lexicon – Targum Neofiti to the Pentateuch*. Cincinnati: Hebrew Union College, 2005.

Kaufmann, Yechezkel and M Greenberg (tr.). *The Religion of Ancient Israel*. Chicago: University of Chicago Press, 1960.

Keil-Delitzsch. *Commentary on the Old Testament*, Vol.1. Grand Rapids, MI: Eerdmans Publishing Co., 1887.

Keen, Sam. *Hymns to an Unknown God*. New York: Bantam, 1994.

Khan, Hazrat Inayat. *The Message Volumes of Hazrat Inayat Khan* Volume VII. Alameda, CA: Hunter House, 1979, 2nd rev. ed.

Kidner, Derek. *Genesis: An Introduction and Commentary*. Chicago: Inter-varsity Press, 1967.

Kimchi, David (Radak) and H.R. Bresenthal and H. Lebricht (ed.). *The Book of Roots*. Ed. Berlin: Firedlander: 1847.

Kitchen, Kenneth. *On the Reliability of the Old Testament*, Grand Rapids, MI: Eerdmans, 2003.

Klein, A. Daniel. *The Book of Genesis: A Commentary by Shadal* (S. D. Luzzato). Northvale, NJ: Jason Aronson Inc., 1998.

Koehler, L., Baumgartner, W. Richardson, and M., & J. J. Stamm. *The Hebrew and Aramaic Lexicon of the Old Testament*. Volumes 1-4 combined in one electronic edition. (electronic ed.) Leiden; New York: E.J. Brill, 1999, c1994-1996.

Kramer, Samuel Noah, *History Begins at Sumer: Thirty-Nine Firsts in Recorded History*. Philadelphia: University of Pennsylvania Press, 1981.

Kugel, L. James. *The Bible as It Was*. Cambridge, MA: Belnap Press of Harvard University Press, 1997.

———. *How To Read The Bible*. New York: Free Press, 2007.

Lamm, Norman. *Faith and Doubt: Studies in Traditional Jewish Thought*. NY: Ktav, 1986.

———. *The Shema: Spirituality and Law in Judaism*, Philadelphia, PA: JPS,

1998.

Lange, Johann Peter, Tayler Lewis, and A. Gosman. *Genesis, or, the First Book of Moses Together with a General Theological and Homiletical Introduction to the Old Testament.* 5th rev. ed. New York: Charles Scribner, 1884.

Leibowitz, Nehama. *Studies in Bereshit (Genesis): In the Context of Ancient and Modern Jewish Bible Commentary.* 4th rev. ed. Tr. Aryeh Newman. Jerusalem: World Zionist Organization Department for Torah Education and Culture, 1981.

Levenson, Jon D. *Sinai and Zion: An Entry into the Jewish Bible.* San Francisco: Harper and Row Publishers, 1985.

———. *Creation and the Persistence of Evil: The Jewish Drama of Divine Omnipotence.* San Francisco: Harper & Row, 1988.

Levi ben Gershom (Ralbag). *The Wars of the Lord,* Vol. 3. Tr. Seymour Feldman. Philadelphia: Jewish Publication Society, 1984.

Lévinas, Emmanuel. *Israel and the World: Essays in Time of Crisis.* New York: Schocken Books, 1948.

———. *Totality and Infinity.* Pittsburgh: Duquesne University Press, 1969.

———. *Difficult Freedom: Essays on Judaism.* Baltimore: John Hopkins University Press, 1990.

———. *Theory of Intuition in Husserl's Phenomenology:* Second Edition (SPEP). Evanston, IL: Northwestern University Press, 1995.

———. *Is It Righteous To Be?* Stanford, CA: Stanford University Press, 2001.

———. *On Escape: De l'evasion (Cultural Memory in the Present).* Palo Alto, CA: Stanford University Press, 2003.

Lévi-Strauss, Claude. *Structural Anthropology.* New York: Basic Books, 1968.

Levy, B. Barry. *Fixing God's Torah.* Oxford: Oxford University Press, 2001.

Lookshin, Martin. *Rashbam's Commentary on Genesis.* Lewiston, NY: Edwin Mellon Press, 1989.

Luther, Martin. *Lectures on Genesis: Chapters 1-5: Luther's Works.* Tr. J. J.

Pelikan, H. C. Oswald & H. T. Lehmann, Ed. St. Louis: Concordia Publishing House, 1999, c1958.

Maimonides, Moses, *Guide of the Perplexed*. Tr. Michael Friedlander. New York: Pardes Publishing House, 1946.

———.*Guide of the Perplexed*. Tr. Shlomo Pines Chicago: University of Chicago Press, 1963.

———.*Moreh Nebuchim*. Tr. Yosef Kaprach. Jerusalem: Mosaad HaRav Kook, 1977.

Malinowski, Bronislaw. *Magic, Science, and Religion and Other Essays*. Prospect Heights, IL: Waveland Press, 1948.

Moussaieff Masson, Jeffrey. *The Emperor's Embrace: Reflections on Animal Families and Fatherhood*. New York: Pocket Books, 1999.

Moussaieff Masson, Jeffrey and Susan McCarthy. *When Elephants Weep: The Emotional Lives of Animals*. New York: Delta, 1995.

Matt, Daniel. *Zohar, The Book of Enlightenment*. Philadelphia: Paulist Press, 1983.

Matthews, Kenneth A. *Genesis 1-11:26. New American Commentary*. Nashville: TN: Broadman & Holman Publishers, 1996.

Mendenhall, G. E. "Biblical History in Transition," in *The Bible and the Ancient Near East*, Garden City: Doubleday and Company, 1961.

Merton, Thomas. *The New Man*. New York: Farrar, Straus, and Cudahy, 1961.

———. *The New Seeds of Contemplation*. New York: New Directions, 1961.

Meyers, Carol. *Discovering Eve: Ancient Israelite Women in Context*. New York: Oxford University Press, 1988.

Milgrom, Jacob. *Leviticus 1-16 A New Translation with Introduction and Commentary* New York: Doubleday, 1991.

Meyendorff, John. *Byzantine Theology: Historical Trends and Doctrinal Themes*. New York: Fordham UP, 1974.

Neiman, Susan. *Evil in Modern Thought: An Alternative History of* Philosophy. Princeton: Princeton University Press, 2004, 2002.

Neusner, Jacob. *Genesis Rabbah: The Judaic Commentary to the Book of Genesis: A New American Translation*. Atlanta, GA: Scholars Press, 1985.

———. *Genesis and Judaism: The Perspective of Genesis Rabbah: An Analytical Anthology*. Atlanta, GA: Scholars Press, 1985.

———. *Judaism's Story of Creation: Scripture, Halakhah, Aggadah*. Leiden: E. J. Brill, 2000.

———. *The Theology of the Halakhah* . Leiden; New York: Brill, 2001.

Neumann, Erich. The *Origins of Human Consciousness,* Princeton: Bollingen Foundation, Inc, 1954.

———. *The Great Mother*. New York: Princeton-Bollingen Series XLVII, 1991 ed.

———. *Narcissism, Normal Self-Formation and the Primary Relation to the Mother*. New York: The Analytical Psychological Club of New York, 1966.

Noth, Martin. *Pentateuchal Traditions*. Utterup, DK: Scholars Press, 1981.

Ochs, Peter. *The Return to Scripture in Judaism and Christianity: Essays in Postcritical Scriptural Interpretation*, Peter Ochs ed. New York: Paulist Press, 1993.

Origen, and Ronald E. Heine. *Homilies on Genesis and Exodus*. Washington, D.C.: Catholic University of America Press, 1982.

Osborne, Grant R. *The Hermeneutical Spiral: A Comprehensive Guide to Biblical Interpretation*. Downers Grove, IL: InterVarsity Press, 1991.

Panikkar, Raimondo. *Myth, Faith and Hermeneutics*. Philadelphia: Paulist Press, 1980.

Philo, and C. D. Yonge (tr.). *The Works of Philo: Complete and Unabridged*. Peabody, MA: Hendrickson, 1996, 1854.

Philip, Moshe Shlomo Zalman. *Chumash HaRaem* (Rabbanu Eliahu Mizrachi). Petach Tikveh: Hechel Shulchanit, 1995.

Plato. *Timaeus*. Cambridge: Harvard University Press, 1929,

———. *Timaeus and Critias*. New York: Penguin, 1972.

Plaut, W. Gunther. *The Torah: A Modern Commentary*. New York: Union of American Hebrew Congregations, 1981.

Pliny the Elder. *Pliny the Elder's Natural History*. Tr. Trevor Murphy. New York: Oxford University Press, 2004.

Plutarch. *The Parallel Lives by Plutarch* published in Vol. IV. Thomas North New York: Loeb Classics, 1916.

Pope, Alexander and H.F. Cary. *The Poetical Works of Alexander Pope*. London: Routledge, 1859.

Pritchard, James B. The *Ancient Near East: An Anthology of Text and Pictures* (ANET). Princeton: Princeton University Press, 1958.

———. *Ancient Near Eastern Texts Relating to the Old Testament*, second edition. Princeton, 1969.

Rad, G. von. *Genesis*. Tr. J. H. Marks and J. Bowden. London: SCM Press, 1972.

Rashi. *Pentateuch with Rashi's Commentary*. Tr. M. Rosenbaum and A. M. Silbermann. New York: Hebrew Publishing Company, 1934.

Reik, Theodor. *Myth and Guilt: The Crime and Punishment of Mankind*. New York: George Braziller Inc., 1957.

Ricoeur, Paul. *The Symbolism of Evil*. Boston, Beacon, 1967.

———. *The Conflict of Interpretation: Essays in Hermeneutics*. Evanston, IL: Northwestern UP, 1974.

———. *Hermeneutics and the Human Sciences: Essays on Language, Action and Interpretation*. Cambridge: Cambridge University Press, 1989.

Rilke, Rainer Maria and Stephen Mitchell. *Ahead of All Parting: The Selected Poetry and Prose of Rainer Maria Rilke*. New York: Random House, 1995.

Riskin, Shlomo. *The Passover Haggadah*. New York: Ktav, 1983.

Robinson, James. *The Nag Hammadi Library* , Leiden; New York: E.J. Brill, 1996 (4th rev. ed.).

Samuel, Michael. *The Lord Is My Shepherd: The Theology of the Caring God*. Northvale, NJ: Jason Aronson Inc., 1996.

Sarna, Nahum M. *Understanding Genesis.* [1st] ed. New York: Jewish Theological Seminary of America, 1966.

———. *Genesis = [Be-Reshit]: The Traditional Hebrew Text with New JPS Translation.* Philadelphia: Jewish Publication Society, 1989.

Scherman, Nosson, *The Chumash: The Stone Edition* Brooklyn, New York: Mesorah. Publications, 1993.

———. Scherman, Nosson. *Artscroll Yom Kippor Machzor.* Brooklyn: Artscroll, 1986.

Schilling, Harold. *The New Consciousness in Science and Religion.* Philadelphia: Pilgrim Press, 1973,

Scholem, Gershom. *Major Trends in Jewish Mysticism.* New York: Shocken, 1954.

———. *The Mystical Shape of the Godhead.* New York: Shocken, 1991.

Schroeder, Gerald L. *Genesis and the Big Bang: The Discovery of Harmony between Modern Science and the Bible.* New York: Bantam Books, 1990.

———. *The Science of God.* New York: Free Press, 1997.

Shapiro, Marc. *The Limit of Orthodox Theology: Maimonides Thirteen Principles Reappraised.* Portland: Oxford, 2005.

Shea, John. *Stories of God.* Liguori, MO: Liguori Publications, 2007.

Schleiermacher, Friedrich. *On Religion: Speeches To Its Cultured Despisers.* Tr. Richard Crouter. Cambridge: Cambridge University Press, 1996.

———.*Hermeneutics and Criticism: And Other Writings*. Tr. Andrew Bowie. Cambridge: Cambridge University Press, 1999.

Seforno, Ovadiah *Seforno Commentary on the Torah.* Tr. R. Pelcovitz. Brooklyn: ArtScroll Mesora Series 2, 1989.

Sharma, Arvind. *The Philosophy of Religion and Advaita Vedanta: A Comparative Study in Religion and Reason.* University Park, PA: Pennsylvania State University, 1995.

Skinner, J. *A. Critical and Exegetical Commentary on Genesis.* ICC. 2d ed.

Edinburgh: Clark, 1930.

Soloveitchik, Joseph B. *The Emergence of Ethical Man*. Hoboken, NJ: Ktav, 2005.

Speiser, E. A. *Genesis*. 2nd. ed. Garden City, NY: Doubleday, 1964.

Strabo. *Geography of Strabo*. Tr. Horace Leonard Jones. London: William Heinemann 1917.

Swinburne, Richard. *Is There a God?* New York: Oxford University Press, 1996.

Teilhard de Chardin. *Humanity in Progress*. Tr. S. Bartholomew. New York: Harper & Row, 1965.

———. *The Meaning of Human Endeavor*. Tr. S. Bartholomew, New York: Harper & Row, 1965.

Thistleton, Anthony C. *New Horizons in Hermeneutics: The Theory and Practice of Transforming Biblical Reading*. Grand Rapids, MI: Zondervan, 1992

———. *The Two Horizons*, Grand Rapids, MI: Eerdmans, 1980.

Tillich, Paul. *Systematic Theology*, Vol. I, Chicago: University of Chicago, 1955.

———. *Systematic Theology*, Vol. II. Chicago: University of Chicago, 1957.

Trible, Phyllis. *God and the Rhetoric of Sexuality*. Philadelphia: Fortress, 1978.

Tsumura, David Toshio. *Creation and Destruction: A Reappraisal of the Chaoskampf Theory in the Old Testament*. Winona Lake: Eisenbrauns, 2005.

Van der Toorn, Karel, Bob Becking, and Pieter Willem Van Der Horst. *Dictionary of Deities and Demons in the Bible*. Leiden and Boston: Brill, Eerdmans, 1999.

Von Rad, Gerhard. *Genesis: A Commentary*. Philadelphia: Westminster Press. 1972.

Wiesner, Merry E., Julius R. Ruff, and William Bruce Wheeler. *Discovering the Western Past: A Look at the Evidence: Since 1500*. Boston, MA: Houghton Mifflin Company, 2003.

Westermann, Claus. *Genesis: A Commentary*. Tr. John Scullion Minneapolis: Augsburg Publishing House, 1984.

Wenham, Gordon J. *Genesis 1-15*. Dallas: Word Books, 1987.

———. *Genesis 16-50*. Dallas: Word Books, 1994.

White, See Andrew D. *A History of the Warfare of Science with Theology in Christendom*. New York: Prometheus Books, 1993, c. 1908.

Whitehead, A. N. *Process and Reality*. Corrected Ed. New York: Free Press, 1978, c. 1929.

———. *The Adventures of Ideas*. Cambridge: Cambridge University Press, 1938.

Wigoder, Geoffrey, *The Meditation of the Sad Soul: Abraham Hayya*. London: Routledge & Kegan Paul, 1969.

Wolfson, Henry A. *The Philosophy of Spinoza*. Cambridge, MA: Harvard University Press, 1934.

Wyschogrod, Michael. *The Body of Faith*. San Francisco: Harper & Row Publishers, 1983.

Philo, *The Works of Philo: Complete and Unabridged*. Tr. C. D. Yonge Peabody: Hendrickson, 1996, c.1857.

Zlotowitz, Meir, and Nosson Scherman. *Bereishis = Genesis: [Sefer Bereshit] A New Translation with a Commentary Anthologized from Talmudic, Midrashic and Rabbinic Sources*. 2nd; complete in two volumes, ed. Brooklyn: Mesorah Publications, 1988.

Topical Index

A

B

C

I

J

L

M

N

O

P

Q

R

T

V

W

Y

Z

Name Index

White, Lynn, 373-375
Whitehead, Alfred North, 273, 290, 296, 305
Wilber, Ken, 143
Wittgenstein, Ludwig, 202
Wyschogrod, Michael, 291, 454
Zalman, Sheneir, 75, 93, 321, 323-324, 362, 454
Zevin, Yosef R., 44
Zohar, 18, 37, 40-41, 95, 125, 133, 136, 153, 153, 195, 230, 255, 333, 336, 392, 406-407, 432-435, 454

Hebrew Word Studies and Transliteration

Genesis

1:1	בּ	*beth*	*"in" or "with"*	*331*
1:1	ראשׁ	*roʾš*	"head"	75
1:1	בְּרֵאשִׁית	*bêrēʾšît*	"in the beginning"	302
1:1	בָּרָא	*bārāʾ*	"created"	76, 121, 322
1:1	אֱלֹהִים	*ʾĕlōhîm*	"judge" or "magistrate"	78-79
1:2	אֶרֶץ	*ʾéreṣ*	generic expression for "land"	81
1:2	תֹהוּ	*ṯṓhû*	"barren tract of land"	84-85
1:2	רוּחַ	*rûaḥ*	"wind" or "spirit"	87-89
1:2	מְרַחֶפֶת	*mĕrāḥepet*	"swept"	91
1:2	תְהוֹם	*tĕhôm*	"the deep"	87
1:3	אָמַר	*ʾāmar*	"say"	92
1:5	יוֹם	*yōm*	"day," "light," or "measure of time"	101-102
1:11	דֶשֶׁא	*dešeʾ*	"vegetation"	113
1:11	פְּרִי	*pĕrî*	"fruit"	115
1:14	מָאוֹר	*māʾôr*	"luminary"	117
1:14	מוֹעֵד	*môʿēd*	"seasons"	118
1:24	נֶפֶשׁ	*nepeš*	"soul"	122, 125
1:26	צֶלֶם	*ṣélem*	"image"	128
1:26	דְמוּת	*dĕmût*	"likeness"	128, 162
1:26	רָדָה	*raḏā*^{h}	"dominion"	131, 132
1:28	וְכִבְשֻׁהָ	*wəḵiḇšū́hā*	"subdue"	135

1:31	וְהִנֵּה	*wəhinnēʰ*	"behold"	138
1:31	אָדָם	*ādām*	"human being"	133
2:1	צָבָא	*ṣəḇāʾ*	"multitude"	141-142
2:3	שָׁבַת	*šābat*	"rested"	147, 383
2:3	וַיְקַדֵּשׁ	*wayĕqadēš*	"make holy"	146-147
2:3	מְלָאכָה	*məlāʾḵāʰ*	"work"	149-151
2:4	בְּהִבָּרְאָם	*bəhibbāṛʾām*	"made"	154
2:4	בְּיוֹם	*bĕyôm*	"at the time when"	154, 178
2:6	אֵד	*ʻēd*	"stream"	159
2:7	יָצַר	*yāṣar*	"mold"	159, 322
2:7	עָפָר	*ʿāp̄ār*	"pulverized"	160
2:8	גַּן	*gan*	"garden"	165
2:8	מִקֶּדֶם	*mîqqedem*	"in the east"	165
2:12	בְּדלַח	*bĕdōlaḥ*	"bdellium"	173
2:13	גִּיחוֹן	*Gihon*	"burst" "name of a river"	173
2:14	חִדֶּקֶל	*ḥiddéqel*	"Tigris River"	175
2:14	פְּרָת	*pərāṯ*	"Euphrates"	175
2:18	עֵזֶר	*ēzer*	"helper"	185-186
2:19	וַיִּצֶר	*wayyīṣer*	"formed"	188
2:21	תַּרְדֵּמָה	*tardēmā*	"deep sleep"	191
2:21	צֵלָע	*ṣēlā'*	"side" or "rib"	192
2:22	בָּנָה	*bānāh*	"built"	195
2:23	עֶצֶם	*ʻeṣem*	"bone"	196
2:24	דָבַק	*dabaq*	"cleave"	403
3:1	עָרוּם	*ʿarum*	"crafty"	223
3:4	פֶּן	*pen*	"lest"	214
3:5	יָדַע	*yāḏaʿ*	"know"	171
3:7	עָרוֹם	*ʿārôm*	"naked"	223
3:8	מִתְהַלֵּךְ	*mithal□k*	"walking"	231
3:16	עָצֵב	*ʻāṣēḇ*	"pain"	242
3:16	מָשַׁל	*mašl*	"shall rule"	247
3:19	לֶחֶם	*leḥem*	"bread"	251

4:2	אֲדָמָה	*ʾăḏāmā*^{h}	“earth” “clay” or “ground”	160-161
7:23	פָּשַׁט	*pāšáṭ*	“strip”	38-39
38:9	וַיְמָאֵן	*wayəmāʾēn*	“refused”	29
Leviticus				
1:3	דִּבֶּר	*dibber*	“speak”	92
19:19	כִּלְאָיִם	*kil’ayim*	“diverse seeds sown together”	116
Psalms				
73:12	עוֹלָם	*ʿôlām*	“world” or “universe”	388-389
Proverbs				
3:19	רֵאשִׁית	*rē’šît*	“beginning”	75
Isaiah				
34:14	לִילִית	*lîlîṯ*	“screech owl”	404
44:3	יַבָּשָׁה	*yabbāšâ*	“dry land”	82

Greek Terms, Concepts and Transliteration

ἀγάπη	*agápē*	“altruistic love”	72, 295-6
Γένεσις	*genesis*	“Genesis”	56
εἶδος	eidos	*“idea”*	30, 352-3
εἰκών	*eikon*	*“icon”*	352
εισαγεσθαι	*eisagesthai*	“to lead in” or “import”	43
ἐξαγεσθαι	exagesthai	“to interpret out”	43
ἑρμηνεύω	*hermēneuō*	“interpret”	34
ἐποίησεν	*epoiēsen*	“made,” or “created”	316
λόγος	*logos*	“word” or the “reason principle”	94, 142
κόραξ	*korax*	“raven”	188
κτίζω	*ktizō*	“create”	76-77

ὁμοίωσις	*homoiōsis*	"resemblance" or "likeness"	352
πνεῦμα	*pneuma*	"breath"	88, 164
πρόσωπον	*prósōpon*	"face"	305
σύμβολον	*sýmbolon*	"symbol"	189
τετραγράμματον	*Tetragrammaton*	"Tetragrammaton"	172
φρονιμώτατος	*phronimotatos*	"sly"	208
Χάος	*chaos*	"chaos"	82

About the Author:

Michael Leo Samuel writes and lectures at community colleges and leads symposiums on contemporary theological and social issues. He has spent the last twenty-five years as a pulpit rabbi within the Conservative movement. Rabbi Samuel is a graduate of the Lubavitch Rabbinical Seminary (*Yoreh Yoreh, Yadin Yadin*) in Brooklyn and Jerusalem and holds a Doctor of Ministry degree from the San Francisco Theological Seminary. He is the author of *The Lord is My Shepherd:The Theology of the Caring God* (Jason Aronson Inc.,1996).

Made in the USA
Las Vegas, NV
12 March 2022

45550135R00282